D1326276

NUMBER ONE IN THE
*Amerind Foundation*
*New World Studies Series*
Anne I. Woosley
*Series Editor*

EXPLORING THE HOHOKAM

*Hohokam country*

# EXPLORING THE
# ◆HOHOKAM◆

## PREHISTORIC DESERT
## PEOPLES OF THE
## AMERICAN SOUTHWEST

▼▼▼▼▼▼▼▼▼▼▼▼▼▼▼▼▼▼▼▼▼▼▼▼▼▼▼▼▼▼▼▼▼▼▼▼▼▼▼▼▼▼▼▼▼▼▼▼▼▼

*Edited by George J. Gumerman*

▼▼▼▼▼▼▼▼▼▼▼▼▼▼▼▼▼▼▼▼▼▼▼▼▼▼▼▼▼▼▼▼▼▼▼▼▼▼▼▼▼▼▼▼▼▼▼▼▼▼

*An Amerind Foundation Publication*, DRAGOON, ARIZONA
*University of New Mexico Press*, ALBUQUERQUE

Library of Congress Cataloging-in-Publication Data

Exploring the Hohokam : prehistoric desert peoples of the American Southwest / edited by
George J. Gumerman. — 1st ed.
        p.        cm. — (Amerind Foundation New World studies series; no. 1)
    Papers of a seminar held during Feb. 1988 at the Amerind Foundation, Dragoon, Ariz., and
sponsored by the Bureau of Reclamation.
    Includes bibliographical references and index.
    ISBN 0–8263–1228–4
    1. Hohokam culture—Congresses.    2. Sonoran  Desert—Antiquities—Congresses.
3. Southwest, New—Antiquities—Congresses.
I. Gumerman, George J.    II. United States. Bureau of Reclamation.    III. Series.
E99.H68E94   1991
979'.01—dc20                                                                          90–22509
                                                                                          CIP


Design by Susan Gutnik.

# CONTENTS

▼▼▼▼▼▼▼▼▼▼▼▼▼▼▼▼▼▼▼▼▼▼

# LIST OF FIGURES

# LIST OF TABLES

# FOREWORD

▼▼▼▼▼▼▼▼▼▼▼▼▼▼▼▼▼▼▼▼▼▼▼▼▼▼▼

O ver fifty years ago William Shirley Fulton established the Amerind Foundation as an anthropological research facility devoted to the study of the indigenous peoples of the New World. He was particularly interested in the prehistory of the Greater Southwest and in the scholarly community committed to unraveling that past. These interests influenced the direction and goals of the Amerind which, from its early days and as set down in its charter, were threefold: (1) to further the knowledge of native American cultures by initiating scientific research, (2) to promote cooperation among those embarked on similar courses of study, and (3) to disseminate the resultant information for the benefit of all. In reaffirming the ideals of the original charter, the Foundation Board of Directors recently established Amerind New World Studies—a forum where scholars, whatever their institutional affiliation, can come together to consider topical issues in American anthropology.

It is with great pleasure, then, that the Foundation and its staff hosted the Bureau of Reclamation sponsored advanced seminar, "Changing Views on Hohokam Archaeology." In a spirit of mutual cooperation through intellectual exchange, participants addressed problems in Hohokam archaeology, proceeding along several avenues that assessed questions of chronology, social organization, material culture, subsistence, and exchange. These discussions generated a broad perspective of the Hohokam, and by distilling the most recently available information, provided a much stronger understanding of Hohokam prehistory.

The talents and efforts of numerous individuals contributed to the meeting's success. Thomas R. Lincoln of the Bureau of Reclamation was instrumental in selecting the Amerind Foundation as the meeting location and, thereby, critical in launching the Amerind New World Studies series with its first significant seminar. George J. Gumerman, serving as Chair, guided the proceedings and offered much appreciated advice throughout. All participants, by virtue of the quality of their work, provided spirited discussions and ensured the success of this volume. Elizabeth Hadas, director of the University of New Mexico Press, facilitated the cooperative publication venture between Amerind and the Press. The Amerind staff deserves special thanks: to my administrative assistant, Maureen O'Neill, for her assistance in planning and her consistent attention to a myriad of details; to Joe Tapia, Herb Carter, and Gordon Conklin for their restoration labors on the Fulton family home seminar facility; to Linda Conklin, Melissa J. Fulton, and Allan J. McIntyre for many tasks too numerous to list separately; to Alice Easthouse, chef extraordinaire and her assistants, Mary Thomas and Lee Lawson.

The Foundation takes pride in this, the first meeting and publication in the Amerind New World Studies series.

Anne I. Woosley
*Director, Amerind Foundation*

# PREFACE

▼▼▼▼▼▼▼▼▼▼▼▼▼▼▼▼▼▼▼▼▼

There is a desperate need for the re-assessment and dissemination of what is currently thought about the Hohokam. This has resulted from the unprecedented amount of high-quality archaeology that has been undertaken in the last 15 years in the Lower Sonoran life zone of southern Arizona. Perhaps nowhere in the world have so many scholars spent so much time, intellectual effort, and financial resources in such a short period in an attempt to understand the past. The Hohokam tradition is no longer the runt of Southwestern archaeology, but has shown itself to be at least the equal of other major traditions.

Most of the recent work has been the indirect result of the rush by contemporary Americans to work and live in what was once the heartland of the ancient Hohokam. Because of the danger of destruction to Hohokam sites by construction and development projects, the Bureau of Reclamation, the Federal and the Arizona Department of Transportation, and the U.S. Army Corps of Engineers have spent many millions of dollars to fund hundreds of archaeologists in their pursuit of knowlege about the Hohokam. In addition, smaller, but very important projects have been funded by federal and state granting agencies, such as the National Science Foundation and the Arizona State Historic Preservation Office. The latter research has helped to bridge understanding between the larger contract-funded projects that are sometimes constrained by where and what they can investigate.

The largest single construction project, and the one impacting most Hohokam sites, is the Central Arizona Project (CAP), which is designed to distribute water to much of what was once Hohokam country. Because of the size and complexity of the archaeological efforts on the Central Arizona Project, it was selected by the Secretary of the Interior to be reviewed for compliance with federal historic preservation programs. Dr. Bennie Keel directed a team of outside reviewers, consisting of Fred Wendorf of Southern Methodist University, Larry Banks of the U.S. Corps of Engineers, and George Gumerman from Southern Illinois University. The review was, on balance, very favorable toward the many managers, archaeologists, institutions, and firms that have been involved with CAP archaeology. Because a number of large federally funded projects continue to be planned, it is worthwhile to publicize those attributes of CAP that the review team felt contributed to the success of the archaeology program.

- Attitudes of Bureau archaeologists and upper-level managers operating with a spirit of team work
- The generally high quality of the contractors
- Management flexibility at all levels within the Bureau to meet the specialized needs of archaeological investigations
- Commitment to research that is transmitted from the Bureau archaeological staff to contractors and to other Bureau personnel
- Trust established between the various parties involved. This includes the trust between the contracting officer and the archaeological staff, between the State Historic Preservation Officer and the Bureau archaeologists, and between the Bureau archaeologists and the archaeological contractors
- Sustained professional competition between contractors to produce high-quality work
- The participation of scholars in the planning process of the program and the willingness of Bureau personnel to accommodate their participation
- Appropriate levels of funding for all the various archaeological investigations completed to date.

The review team did have a number of suggestions for improving the CAP archaeology program. The team felt most strongly about the need for increased dissemination of scholarly knowledge obtained from the project. One suggestion was that archaeologists submit review articles about their work to peer-reviewed journals. Additionally, there was the obvious need to integrate the information from the many different projects, both within CAP and external to it (no matter who sponsored the work). This would permit information about the Hohokam to be structured by the nature of the archaeology, rather than by the institution or firm doing the work or the agency funding the archaeology. The result of this recommendation was the convocation of the seminar, producing the papers in this volume.

The seminar was structured so that there would be a minimum of outside distraction. As a result, participation was by invitation only and a location conducive to contemplation was chosen—the Amerind Foundation in Dragoon, Arizona. The selection of participants was extraordinarily difficult because of the large number of excellent scholars who have studied the Hohokam in recent years. Furthermore, the number of scholars had to be limited both by the accommodations of the host facility and by group dynamics. Experience has shown that the most effective forum for a seminar-style exchange of information is one limited to 12 or 13 individuals. Participants were selected, in part, by their ability to address broad topics. The topics that needed to be addressed were selected first, and then appropriate scholars were invited to write a paper on the topic. In selecting the individual scholars, no consideration was given to who had received funding from what source or the institutional affiliation or firm. The organizers of the seminar felt that the days of an institutional party line about the Hohokam or allegiance to an institution because of past funding by an agency should be a thing of the past. There are too many good Hohokam scholars to have a seminar constrained by institutional affiliation, scholarly lineages, or the source of funding. The sole criterion for selection was the individual's ability to address the topic.

Participants were asked to prepare a paper on their topic using whatever sources were available to them and to disseminate their paper to all other participants one month prior to the seminar, which was held the week of February 14, 1988. Papers were not read, but a half day's discussion was conducted by the participant on the assigned topic. The final half day of the seminar was devoted to a discussion by Gary Feinman, who provided an overview of the Hohokam from an external perspective. Seminar participants were asked to revise their papers in light of the seminar discussion.

The success of this volume is dependent on hundreds of individuals and institutions, only a few of whom can be singled out. Special praise must go to U.S. Bureau of Reclamation managers. Not only have they consciously adhered to the letter of historic preservation laws, but they have also wholeheartedly supported the spirit of those laws. The Bureau's financial support of the seminar, which led to this publication, is ample evidence of their concern not only for the past in the area they are directly impacting, but for the entire region. It is a rare bureaucrat who has the vision to see beyond the right-of-way they are responsible for and who can understand that no culture can be understood by artificially constraining the intellectual boundaries of study. The late Ward Weakly, the Bureau's first Preservation Officer, did much to foster the generous attitudes towards archaeology in the Bureau of Reclamation, and we therefore dedicate this volume to his memory.

Special thanks also go to the Director of the Amerind Foundation, Anne Woosley, and to her staff who went to great efforts to prepare the Foundation facilities for the seminar, and ensured that the physical and social conditions at the Foundation were highly conducive to the completion of a successful seminar. The formal seminar discussions were decidedly enhanced by the marvelous table, relaxing billiard room, and warm living room that made for less guarded and decidedly more stimulating conversation about the Hohokam.

George J. Gumerman      Thomas R. Lincoln
*Southern Illinois University*      *U.S. Bureau of Reclamation*

# • 1 •

# UNDERSTANDING
# THE HOHOKAM

▼▼▼▼▼▼▼▼▼▼▼▼▼▼▼▼▼▼▼▼▼▼▼▼▼▼▼▼▼▼▼▼▼▼▼▼▼▼▼▼▼▼▼▼

*George J. Gumerman*

## A BRIEF HISTORY
## OF THE HOHOKAM CONCEPT

It is impossible to understand interpretations of Hohokam prehistory
without an understanding of the intellectual development of the Hohokam
concept. Like most North American archaeology, the early archaeology of the
Hohokam was dominated first by a few gifted explorers and then an equally
small number of creative individuals who ordered the spatial and temporal
framework and sketched a Hohokam culture history.

When Frank Hamilton Cushing excavated in the mounds, trash areas,
compounds, and cemeteries of Los Muertos in 1887 and 1888 in what is now
the city of Tempe, he conducted what was probably the first multidisciplinary
program in American archaeology (Cushing 1890; Haury 1945). Cushing's
team included himself as the archaeologist and ethnographer, Adolph Bandelier as the historian, a topographer, a geologist, an anatomist, and a phy-
sician. The analysis of the paleopathologies of the skeletal remains is still the
best work on the subject (Merbs 1985). Cushing's pioneering work was followed by the somewhat less speculative, more controlled work of Jesse Walter

1

Fewkes (1912) at Casa Grande. Fewkes was especially interested in the origins of, and differences among social classes, which paralleled his concerns with the Anasazi, research topics that remain vitally current today. Based on differences in material culture and structural remains, Fewkes distinguished two cultural groups, the Puebloan in the north and what he called the Gila Valley Culture.

Kidder, in his 1924 overview of Southwestern prehistory, remarked on the archaeological differences, especially in ceramics, between the Upper Sonoran and the Lower Sonoran life zones. Despite his recognition of these differences and his insightful views on the prehistory of the Colorado Plateaus, he did not possess sufficient data to grasp the fundamental differences between the prehistoric peoples of the mountains and plateaus, and those of the southern desert.

The definition, extent, and first real understanding of Hohokam culture history were due largely to the efforts of Harold and Winifred Gladwin and their assistant Emil Haury. Gladwin spent five years excavating at Casa Grande and nearby southern Arizona sites beginning in 1927 (Gladwin 1928; Gladwin and Gladwin 1929). The Gladwins' stratigraphic excavations laid the foundation for the Hohokam ceramic sequence and the sketchy beginnings of Hohokam culture history. After founding a private research organization, the Gila Pueblo Archaeological Foundation, the Gladwins began systematic work on the Hohokam. Their team began an extremely intensive and extensive evaluation of what they initially called the red-on-buff culture, after the painted ceramics of the region. Haury's work at the site of Roosevelt 9:6 in the Tonto Basin in 1930 provided information to suggest that even in their developmental stages the Hohokam were distinctive (Haury 1932).

Gladwin's interest in the spatial extent of the Hohokam led him to extensive surveys. He looked for Hohokam ceramics in areas as far away as Texas and the Great Plains. His interest in Hohokam chronology took him to Snaketown, a site with an extremely long occupational sequence (Gladwin et al. 1937). The ideas Gila Pueblo staff generated and tested through survey and excavation in search of answers to cultural-historical questions dominate Hohokam archaeology to this day.

Instead of looking for similarities to prehistoric cultures to the north, the Gila Pueblo team stressed the distinctiveness of the archaeology of the desert region of southern Arizona. They considered the region the homeland of an independent cultural entity, rather than viewing the remains of the southern Arizona desert as derivative of Anasazi culture. As a result, they proposed a new "basic" Southwestern culture, the Hohokam (Gladwin and Gladwin 1929, 1933), a concept that at first had little support from the Southwestern archaeological establishment (Roberts 1935:31). Like many early proponents of new and initially unpopular causes, Harold Gladwin not only championed his theory but tried to weave it into a grand scheme. In addition to considering the Hohokam one of the three major traditions of the Southwest, Gladwin viewed it as the Southwestern mother culture (Gladwin and Gladwin 1934:4). As he reevaluated the position of the Hohokam over the years, especially the data from Snaketown, he took a global view, seeing connections between the Hohokam and other New and Old World cultures, continually revising his ideas about dating and Hohokam origins (Gladwin 1979).

After producing an extraordinary record of archaeological research and publication, Gila Pueblo closed its doors and the rate of Hohokam investigations slowed considerably. While Haury continued to pursue his Hohokam interests, especially at Ventana Cave (Haury 1950), his roles as head of the Department of Anthropology at the University of Arizona and as director of the Arizona State Museum prevented a sustained research effort.

By the early 1950s Charles DiPeso of the Amerind Foundation had begun reevaluating the Hohokam through a series of excavations in southeastern Arizona, and Albert Schroeder did the same thing with data gathered in western Arizona and the Verde Valley region (DiPeso 1953, 1956; Schroeder 1957, 1960). The newly proposed schemes conflicted with one another and with the original formulations about the Hohokam. Because so little work had been done on the Hohokam, there were not enough data to adequately evaluate any of the proposed developmental schemes or the Hohokam chronology. With the state of Hohokam studies in disarray, Haury returned to Snaketown in 1964 and 1965 to attempt to resolve some of the questions surrounding Hohokam culture history (Haury 1976). As a result of the renewed work at Snaketown, Haury changed his ideas about Hohokam origins, but essentially reaffirmed the original chronology.

The state of confusion regarding the nature, origins, and chronology of the Hohokam was at its height when the rapid increase in population in southern Arizona in the 1960s resulted in a frenzy of construction and required that millions of dollars be spent to investigate hundreds of Hohokam sites. The resulting reevaluation of the Hohokam is represented by the papers in this volume.

The Lower Sonoran environment, so attractive to settlers in our air-conditioned era, has had a profound effect on how archaeologists view the Hohokam concept. The absence in the Lower Sonoran desert of trees with annual growth patterns adequate for dating has caused confusion about Hohokam origins and development that persists to this day (Dean, this volume). Dating imprecision has also made understanding of Hohokam external relationships confusing, permitting almost innumerable combinations of models of interactions with northern Mexico, the Anasazi, and Mogollon. In addition, climatic reconstructions are hampered by the absence of suitable tree-ring data, and only recently are perturbations in climate and their effect on the Hohokam being given serious consideration (Graybill 1985; Nials, Gregory, and Graybill 1986; Weaver 1972). Even today, most of these studies are based on proxy data from the Colorado Plateaus and the mountains to the north and west of Hohokam country.

The intense summer heat made the Hohokam country unsuitable for the academic-year schedules of archaeologists, and as a result even those archaeologists who were intellectually attracted to the problems of Hohokam archaeology found it advantageous to have summer field schools in the mountains or plateaus of the Southwest. It is no accident that until large-scale contract operations necessitated placing a priority on scheduling above comfort the major sustained efforts on Hohokam research were done by private research organizations rather than by academic institutions that had to conform to academic schedules.

Even the construction elements of Hohokam sites conspired against their attractiveness to the archaeologist. As has often been pointed out, sites with an absence of surface structural remains are unlikely to be investigated (Upham 1988). The relative scarcity of stone suitable for high-quality masonry and the desirability of open, airy summertime dwellings and work space produced an architectural record with low visibility. Most sites did not have long-lasting masonry construction but were made of more ephemeral materials, which profoundly skewed archaeologists' understanding of the size and nature of many sites. Not only was the Hohokam area largely ignored by most early investigators, but when attention did focus on southern Arizona, data were much more difficult to gather from surface indications than were Mogollon or Anasazi data. Even the relative absence of dramatic settings for sites, such as steep-sided cliffs with overhangs providing protection suitable for large habitations, meant that the Hohokam had difficulty competing for the attention of early archaeologists.

Finally, the obvious direct continuity of the prehistoric Anasazi populations with the modern Pueblos was not duplicated in the Hohokam area, where the relationship between the prehistoric Hohokam and the historic Piman speakers of southern Arizona remains in dispute. Hohokam archaeologists have therefore been largely constrained from exploring relationships between history and prehistory, and from using modern peoples as ethnographic analogs for understanding the past.

As a result of these environmental and historical considerations, Hohokam archaeology was both slow to start and, after the intense activity of the Gila Pueblo Foundation, slow in its development. These trends deeply affected archaeological concepts of the Hohokam. The "type site" model, in which a single site represented an entire period, persisted for the Hohokam until very recently. The names of sites, such as Los Muertos, Roosevelt 9:6, Casa Grande, Ventana Cave, Hodges, University Indian Ruin, Jackrabbit, and especially Snaketown, not only symbolized the Hohokam but almost became them. The division of the Hohokam into a "Desert" and a "River" branch (Haury 1950) only slightly affected the prevailing view of the Hohokam as a monothetic "culture" (Doelle and Wallace, this volume; McGuire, this volume). Until recently, red-on-buff ceramics equaled Hohokam, and there was little recognized internal differentiation except for that caused by differential access to major drainage systems. The distinctive material culture, which during certain periods appeared to be quite uniform, permitted archaeologists to characterize the Hohokam in general terms.

Until the late 1960s, the scarcity of excavated sites resulted in a variety of conflicting models of Hohokam development because the data were insufficient to adequately test the proposed schemes. The small sample of excavated sites hinted at variability in the archaeological record that was ascribed to regional differentiation, differential environmental adaptation, functional variability, differential external contacts, ethnic differences, poor chronological control, archaeologist bias, or various combinations of these factors.

Early Hohokam investigators were often individuals who delighted in grand schemes. They did not like loose ends, but preferred to see a unified theory of Hohokam development. Unlike many Anasazi and Mogollon specialists, they were not content to confine their attention to a small locale, but extrapolated from a few excavations and surveys "explanations" of much of the prehistory of southern Arizona, the Southwest, or even greater areas. The imprecision in dating and the variation in the archaeological record allowed numerous interpretations to coexist. Furthermore, the overshadowing presence of the large, well-reported site of Snaketown engendered Hohokam models emphasizing large sites that controlled surrounding areas of imitative groups in the hinterlands.

The development of grand schemes for "explaining" the Hohokam phenomenon was aided by the nature of archaeological inquiry in the United States until the 1960s. Archaeological projects were dominated by a single individual, trained in a tradition emphasizing the "lone scholar," one who was totally responsible for obtaining funding, directing the intellectual thrust of the project, and supervising excavation, analysis, and interpretation. While the larger projects required numerous archaeologists, they were all under the intellectual and logistical leadership of a single individual. The lone scholar approach fostered and encouraged the grand schemes about the Hohokam, and helped to polarize different interpretations. It solidified the existence of "schools" of thought about the Hohokam and made institutional affiliation an important element in the championing of a specific developmental scheme. Contract archaeology was a major force in changing this situation.

The immigration of large numbers of people into southern Arizona beginning in the late 1960s, and the resulting influx of federally funded projects to accommodate the needs of these new arrivals for transportation, water, water control systems, and energy dramatically changed the nature of Hohokam archaeology and archaeological interpretations. No longer could a single individual control the data or the intellectual direction for an institution's view of large parts of southern Arizona prehistory. Too many scholars were required to fill the needs of contract-oriented studies, and too many institutions and firms were employed to undertake these studies to permit the continuation of a few monolithic schools of thought about the Hohokam.

The initial reaction to the huge increase in financial and intellectual resources brought to bear on the understanding of the Hohokam was confusion (McGuire and Schiffer 1982). Given the numerous models of Hohokam origins, development, and temporal schemes and the few data these were based on, the new wealth of information, often also conflicting and confusing when interpreted, added to the number of developmental schemes, rather than supporting or refuting any existing scheme. It was a case of knowledge breeding confusion; this situation was certainly not unique to Hohokam studies, but common in the history of archaeological inquiry in most areas. With only few data from several excavated sites, pronouncements about cultural development are easy to make—and to refute. As the sample increases, the tendency is to increase the number of models or variations on earlier schemes, which attempt to explain the development of a culture. Competing schemes are nurtured by differences in both the archaeological record and the models, methods, and analysis employed by the archaeologists. The very nature of such factors as variability in artifact production, spatial variability, differential postdepositional characteristics, differences in methods of collection and analysis, and the subjective championing of different models contributes to the development of conflicting models and the difficulty of evaluating any one of them.

The history of Hohokam archaeology, while not unique, is especially dramatic because so little field work and so much talking and writing was the rule for so long. When the increase in field work began, it escalated rapidly to become what is probably the most archaeologically active area in the United States, producing huge amounts of data, and numerous new interpretations and variations on old ones. Analysis and interpretation could not keep pace with publication so that dissemination of information was largely by word of mouth or through underinterpreted publications with limited distribution, which added to the confusion. Despite the increased research on the Hohokam, they remain to this day somewhat neglected in overviews of Southwestern archaeology compared to the Anasazi. In a recent seminar on the Southwest three archaeologists represented the western Anasazi alone, while the Hohokam was represented by a single scholar (Cordell and Gumerman 1989). The discussant dealt only with the Anasazi (Johnson 1989).

Hohokam archaeology is currently in a period of new synthesis and evaluation in which some of the conflicts in interpretation are in the process of being resolved. Much of this clarification is represented by the papers in this volume. The primary source of this better understanding of Hohokam is the result of the rejection of the largely normative perspective on the Hohokam, and the recognition of the Hohokam as a polythetic concept with great temporal and spatial variation. Few scholars operate any longer with the model of the Hohokam as a highly integrated cultural system. In the prevailing view, the term *Hohokam* is simply a label for the phenomena of the archaeological record, i.e., the material culture, its variation, and its relationship to the landscape (Wilcox 1979, 1980). Few contemporary scholars attach any linguistic or ethnic meaning to the archaeological remains. Hohokam as a population is viewed as a "regional system" (Wilcox and Shenk 1977), as a segment of a world system (Whitecotton and Pailes 1986), or by other variations on these themes (McGuire, this volume).

Fortunately, archaeologists today have the opportunity to test polythetic models of the Hohokam because of the greatly increased data base and with data from a much larger area. The data derived from contract archaeology has provided not only evidence of greater temporal variation in the Hohokam developmental scheme than previously suspected (Doyel, this volume) but also documentation for contemporaneous spatial variation on a scale only previously suspected (Doelle and Wallace, this volume; McGuire, this volume). The result of new polythetic models and a greatly increased data base is that generalizations about the Hohokam are difficult to make and are as dated and suspect as stereotypical comments about contemporary ethnic or national groups.

The papers in this volume reflect the increased trend toward caution in Hohokam studies. The grand normative schemes with no loose ends, anchored with few data, and developed with the biases of localized data sets are not apparent in these papers. Confident declarative statements about social hierarchy, the processes of trade in "luxury" items, and the character of Hohokam ethnicity are absent or have been tempered. The lessons taught by the variation in the archaeological record, which have undercut overgeneralizations and grand schemes, are being absorbed.

## A CULTURAL-HISTORICAL OUTLINE

The "flexible" nature of Hohokam chronology has been a major source of disagreement since the Gladwins' development of the concept. Concern with the Hohokam chronology is not, of course, simply an exercise in itself, but bears on questions of origins, cultural development and stability, relationships with external peoples, and the dissolution of the Hohokam pattern. The uncertainty about chronology has aided both the championing of Hohokam developmental schemes and attempts at the destruction of those same schemes. Stratigraphic and ceramic cross correlations have been important in developing the Hohokam sequence, but the independent chronometric techniques of radiocarbon and archaeomagnetic dating currently have the greatest potential for resolving the more difficult chronological problems. While there is still no general consensus on Hohokam chronology, Dean (this volume) has demonstrated a certain consistency in dating much of the Hohokam sequence. This consistency is not the result of consensus through opinion, always suspect in any scientific endeavor, but rather through the steady accumulation of radiocarbon and archaeomagnetic dates.

While Dean (this volume) and Eighmy and McGuire (1989) have firmly fixed some points of the Hohokam sequence, other important periods are poorly represented by either radiocarbon or archaeomagnetic dates. The earliest Hohokam pattern seems established after A.D. 1, roughly concurrent with the two other major Southwestern traditions, the Mogollon and the Anasazi (Fig. 1.1). The end of the archaeologically recognizable Hohokam pattern ends about A.D. 1450 or 1500. Recently, evidence for extensions of the Hohokam sequence on both the beginning and end of the sequence has accumulated. A Red Mountain phase has been proposed for the beginning of the sequence (Cable and Doyel 1987; Doyel, this volume) and the Polvoron phase (Sires 1983, 1985; Crown and Sires 1984) or perhaps Bachi phase (Doyel, this volume) at the end. The proposed beginning and ending phases are more generalized with less formalized attributes, making definition difficult.

The prevailing opinion is that the distinctive Hohokam pattern began sometime after the time of Christ (Fig. 1.1). This period is poorly known because relatively few sites have been identified, and they tend to be small, generalized, and without a formal structure (Doyel, this volume). Hohokam origins have been attributed either to an internal development from an earlier hunting and gathering group or to an immigrant group from Mexico. Evidence that typical indicators of the Hohokam tradition, such as worked shell, stone, and corn agriculture, were in existence during the earlier Archaic period has led most archaeologists to conclude that the Hohokam pattern largely developed out of the Archaic (Huckell 1987). The Pioneer period saw the advanced development of an agricultural way of life based on the domestication of corn, beans, squash, and cotton. Later additions included agave and amaranth and the encouraged growth of cholla cactus, little barley grass, Mexican crucillo, and tobacco (Bohrer 1988; Gasser and Kwiatkowski, this volume). Rabbits, deer, and big-horned sheep were a common source of meat protein throughout the sequence. Cacti fruits, mesquite seeds, and numerous types of weedy annuals were also always dietary staples. Rudimentary canal systems were constructed for field irrigation. Village life was based on clusters of brush structures constructed in shallow, elongated pits. Initially there were two types of structures, indicating social differentiation early in the Pioneer period. A simple but technologically well-constructed ceramic tradition, with plain reddish brown coil-constructed ceramics, shaped and finished by paddle and anvil technique, was developed. Some ceramics were decorated with a red-brown paint. Distinctive Hohokam shell, stone, and figurine complexes also were developed or elaborated during this period.

During the Colonial period, as the name implies, Hohokam (or at least those artifacts that characterize the Hohokam) are found up the tributaries of the Gila-Salt drainage system in more peripheral areas. Irrigation systems were expanded and became more sophisticated, serving populations in larger villages. Increased interaction with Mesoamerica is indicated by the introduction of the platform mound and the ballcourt at some sites (Gregory and

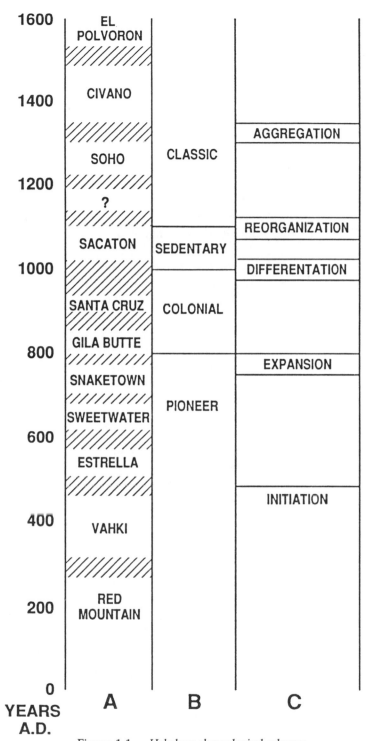

Figure 1.1    *Hohokam chronological schemes.*

Nials 1985; Wilcox and Sternberg 1983). These communal structures probably served as social integrative devices for exchange spheres within the Hohokam system. In addition, there was increased interaction with groups to the north, east, and west. Artifacts became stylistically elaborated, especially "luxury" items. There was a general flamboyance in arts and crafts. Decorated pottery was given a cream-colored wash before the application of reddish painted designs. Houses were often placed in an orderly fashion around a courtyard, and at some sites trash was mounded, rather than scattered throughout the villages, or deposited in pits.

Sedentary period sites are larger than Colonial period sites; some are characterized by more formal platform mounds, larger dwellings, and large plazas. Sites were more differentiated during this period in size, function, and numbers and types of specialized structures, all evidence for a clear site hierarchy. Hohokam material culture and architecture is found as far as east of Flagstaff. Ceramics were made in many more diverse forms, and the working of shell became more elaborate and varied. Copper bells from Mexico were first imported during this period. At the end of the Sedentary period, about A.D. 1150, major organizational change took place throughout the Southwest.

The Classic period is one of major organizational change. There is a contraction of the Hohokam archaeological pattern to the northern edge of the Gila-Salt Basin. Along with pithouses, surface adobe structures become common, some with contiguous rooms. Some room clusters are enclosed by rectangular compound walls. Massive adobe platform mounds are built, and the ballcourt system falls into decline, with few new ones constructed. Common material culture indicators of the Hohokam manifestation, such as carved stone and shell effigy figures and stone palettes and censers, are no longer made. Later in the Classic period, platform mounds function as bases for habitations, and compounds become larger and more numerous. Red ware and polychrome ceramics largely replace those decorated with red designs on a buff background.

The demise of the Hohokam pattern sometime after A.D. 1400–1450 is poorly understood and difficult to explain. The question of the relationship of the Hohokam to the historic Pima and Papago in southern Arizona is a source of controversy (Doyel, this volume). Relationships between the attenuated and less elaborate historic cultures and the Hohokam are difficult to determine, and ethnographic analogs are tenuous. Recent research has hinted at the dissolution of the large Classic period communities to a more dispersed and generalized pattern similar to the Pima and Papago, suggesting a Hohokam to Pima-Papago transition (Doyel, this volume).

## FORCES OF CHANGE

Models that attempt to explain change usually have one to four variables: two are behavioral variables, and two are independent, or at least semi-independent of behavior. The two behaviorally dependent variables are those that view change as being generated from within the society and those that are a result of contacts external to the society. The variables that are more or less independent of behavioral factors are those that view environment as the primary causative factor, and those that emphasize demographic factors. Most models of change consider at least two and sometimes all four of the variables.

The explanations that assign primacy to internal conditions as the cause of change usually view the social and economic conditions within the society as critical, and often unstable factors, which provide positive feedback for change. These explanations are often couched in systemic terms that consider the culture as an integrated system with little interaction from other cultural systems. Explanations that emphasize external contact as the agent of change stress migration or diffusion, and tend to view the cultural system as open and in disequilibrium. Explanations stressing environmental or demographic factors as agents of culture change often view culture as relatively passive, responding to external natural factors.

Explanations for Hohokam origins, change, and demise have considered all of the variables, but the emphasis has been on behavioral factors. The emphasis placed on internal and external forces of change has been not so much a result of scholarly deliberations on the most appropriate models to use, as of more pragmatic considerations of data availability. Since the earliest deliberations, explanations of the cultural evolution of the Hohokam have dwelt on behavioral variables, especially through contact external to southern Arizona (Crown, this volume; McGuire, this volume). Migration, influence, or invasion by people from Mexico (Ferdon 1955; DiPeso 1974) and Salado (Haury 1945) or Sinagua peoples (Schroeder 1947, 1953) from the north have all been used to explain Hohokam culture change. It is difficult to ignore external factors since Mexican traits such as ballcourts, scarlet macaws, shell, copper bells, and platform mounds are present at many of the Hohokam sites. Often this interaction has been interpreted through simple trait listing, but more recently attempts have been made to understand the details of the processes of the interaction (see papers in Mathien and McGuire 1986). Late in the Hohokam sequence, treatment of the dead, certain ceramic types, and above-ground dwellings, some with contiguous rooms, have been attributed to interaction or migration from the north. In these models, which stress change as externally generated, those aspects of the Hohokam that seem to have developed internally are usually viewed as the part of the generalized nondistinctive Archaic life way of the arid west.

Population shifts, often viewed as a major cause of change elsewhere, are not given much consideration in Hohokam studies (with few exceptions, e.g., Fish and Fish, this volume). The major reason for neglecting the role of population shifts in Hohokam culture change seems to be the difficulty of determining clear-cut examples of regional abandonment like those available in Anasazi and Mogollon archaeology, and the difficulty of estimating Hohokam population size. Population figures are enormously difficult to determine from archaeological data for any area, but amount to little more than speculation for the Hohokam. Perishable houses, stability in site location for many generations, and a tendency to live in widely dispersed houses of unknown use-life make any population estimate for the Hohokam dubious. Guesses of population size often differ by two hundred or three hundred percent, and no consensus exists even about population trends (Doyel, this volume; Fish 1989; Fish and Fish, this volume; Teague and Crown 1984). In short, the demographic situation in southern Arizona had enormous influence on Hohokam culture change, but archaeologists have been unable to measure this effect because they have been unable to measure population.

The environment has always been important in explaining the character of the Hohokam, but it has usually been considered static and therefore not a factor in culture change. In fact, the Hohokam have often been defined by the environment because the range of the Hohokam pattern in Arizona is coterminous with the Lower Sonoran environment (Fish and Nabhan, this volume). In its extreme expression, the equation of Hohokam with the Lower Sonoran life zone becomes a tautology, i.e., archaeological remains are sometimes identified as Hohokam simply because they are found in the Lower Sonoran Desert. Spatial variation in the Hohokam environment has been recognized for many years, and has been offered as an explanation for regional cultural variation (Doelle and Wallace, this volume; McGuire, this volume), although others (Masse 1980) feel environmental differences had little effect on Hohokam spatial differences. Only in the last two decades have proxy data from the Colorado Plateaus been used systematically in attempts to retrodict the desert environment of southern Arizona (Weaver 1972). Environmental reconstructions, as explanations for Hohokam culture change, have numerous problems in terms of their projected effects on Hohokam behavior and in the applicability of environmental reconstructions for the plateaus and mountains of the Southwest to the desert of Arizona (Graybill 1985). In addition, these studies tend to treat environmental change more as a series of events than as long-term and perhaps cyclical processes. This view may have resulted in a distorted perspective on Hohokam adaptive responses to the change. Actual environmental events of prehistoric episodic flooding have recently been documented for the Gila-Salt Basin (Doyel, this volume; Nials et al. 1986). These flooding events may have had disastrous effects on Hohokam irrigation systems, a basic feature of Hohokam subsistence and settlement.

Recent funding from contract sources has permitted a great deal of effort to be expended on geomorphological studies in southern Arizona to attempt to relate more realistically the climate of northern Arizona, derived from tree-ring analysis, to the deserts. These attempts at understanding both flooding

events and the processual relationship between the environment of the north
and the southern deserts are reaching a stage where they can be of great help
in understanding Hohokam cultural evolution.

## STASIS AND CHANGE

Hohokam culture did not change at a constant rate but was characterized
by periods of rapid change followed by periods of relative stability. At a recent
conference, it was noted that periods of rapid change and stability seem to
be roughly contemporaneous throughout the Southwest, although the change
was not apparent everywhere. A scheme was developed to chart these processes (Cordell and Gumerman 1989; Fig. 1.1). While the processes of change
seem to have been similar, resulting in organizational shifts that are pan-
Southwestern in scope, the scheme was not meant to suggest that there was
a single adaptive process operating as part of a Southwestwide system, or
that there was a pervasive, all-inclusive interaction network throughout the
Southwest. The scheme was proposed simply because concordances in organizational changes were noted in the major traditions throughout the region; it was offered as a heuristic device. Some correspondence, however,
was noted between periods of major environmental and cultural change on
the Colorado Plateaus (Cordell and Gumerman 1989).

By examining the periods of rapid change, called "hinge points," it may
be possible to provide insights into Hohokam organizational change (Fig.
1.1). The descriptive terms for the hinge points are suggestive of presumed
organizational changes. The use of these terms is not an attempt to impose
yet another developmental scheme on the hapless Hohokam, but is simply
a device to discuss periods of change and stability, to emphasize the irregular
nature of the rate of change, and to indicate the existence of similar processes
throughout much of the Southwest. Any use of the Southwest stage concept
for the Hohokam must address the problem of the imprecision of the dated
sequence, making correspondences with the relatively narrow range of the
hinge points difficult.

The Initiation period is equivalent to the early Pioneer and is characterized
by the development of the basic distinctive Hohokam, Mogollon, and Anasazi
patterns. The difficulty of dating elements of the earliest manifestations of
these traditions (for example, canal irrigation for the Hohokam), as well as
an extended Developmental period, has probably made the Initiation period
hinge point appear longer than it really is.

Numerous authors have noted the similarities in material culture, especially ceramics, for the early part of the Southwestern sequences (Haury 1962;
Martin and Plog 1973; LeBlanc 1982). Most of these authors either use the
noted similarities as a convenient device for discussing the early Southwestern
pattern as a single entity or see them as the result of the common consequence

of early, settled agricultural village life that is generalized with little formalized stylistic elaboration in material culture or structures.

The Expansion period is equivalent to the end of the Pioneer and the beginning of the Colonial period. It corresponds to the areal increase of the Hohokam pattern. The Differentiation period is characterized by more parochial stylistic patterns and the development of more complex organizational systems. For the Hohokam, the era of regionalization appears to have begun with the Colonial period and is not so much a period of rapid change as it is a continuing process. The end of the Sedentary period and the beginning of the Classic is called Reorganization, and is marked by major changes in economic, social, and ideological aspects of the Hohokam. This hinge point and the next one, called Aggregation at the division of the Classic into the Soho and Civano phases, is nearly coterminous throughout the Southwest. The apparent discontinuity in the Hohokam sequence during the Reorganization hinge-point period that is reflected in the chronometric data (Dean, this volume) may be indicative of pan-Southwestern process and events. The hinge point called Aggregation, as the name implies, is characterized by the increasing size of individual sites and corresponding organizational changes. No descriptor was given for the end of the distinctive patterns (probably because it was not as apparent in the Anasazi and Mogollon regions), but the termination of the Hohokam Classic might be designated Dispersion. While some residential stability remained at the large late Classic sites, the settlement pattern generally reverted to a dispersed rancheria form.

It is a dangerous game of speculation to offer explanations for what may or may not be similar organizational responses at approximately the same time across the Southwest; it is especially difficult given the fact that archaeologists now recognize tremendous organizational variation within the Hohokam, Anasazi, and Mogollon traditions. Nevertheless, the similarities and temporal concordances are too great to ignore. Similarities among the three major Southwestern traditions have typically been noted for the Initiation period, a stage that represented a more generalized, less formalized archaeological pattern (LeBlanc 1982; Feinman, this volume; Wilcox 1979). Some models of post–Initiation period prehistory that note organizational similarities between the three major traditions view it as a result of these traditions being tied into a network that was driven by more complexly organized Mesoamerican societies (LeBlanc 1986). A more common view is one that interprets major changes in Southwestern prehistory as a result of varying types and degrees of Mesoamerican interaction without considering Mesoamerica as the font of Southwestern culture change (Feinman, this volume; Mathien and McGuire 1986).

If indeed there is a broad pattern of contemporaneous organizational change throughout the Southwest, research might profitably focus on the cultural evolutionary processes that are conditioned by intensification of agriculture and concomitant population growth. All major traditions in the Southwest began to rely increasingly on agriculture at about the same time. The resulting and apparently similar rates of population increase beginning at this time may tend toward common forms of organizational adaptations. Testing of these kinds of speculations would require better population estimates and a greater understanding of the details of organizational stability and change, their occurrence in some locales and not in others.

## ASPECTS OF CHANGE

To understand the nature of Southwestern cultural evolution better, it is helpful to isolate change in components of the cultural system. Behavioral variables, either internal or external, and demographic or environmental change when reaching threshholds, can cause archaeologically recognizable change in the economy, and the social, political, and ideological aspects of the system.

Change in the Hohokam economic behavior (subsistence, technology, and exchange) has not been a particularly fruitful line of inquiry for understanding major systemic change. Subsistence and technological change have not especially provided insights into Hohokam cultural evolution. Investigations into the complex and often changing network of Hohokam exchange systems have always been a major focus for Hohokam scholars (Crown, this volume). There has, however, with a few exceptions (Doyel 1987a; Teague 1984), been little concern with the purely economic aspects of the large amount of interaction that has been documented. More attention has been given to the social and political importance of exchange (Nelson 1981; Crown, this volume; Mathien and McGuire 1986).

Despite the great efforts expended on trying to reconstruct changes in the Hohokam subsistence base, only hints of changing emphases in domesticated and nondomesticated plants have been noted (Gasser and Kwiatkowski, this volume). Evidence for changes in animal procurement patterns has been even more elusive and has been most abundant for the era of the Archaic to Hohokam transition, as might be expected (Bayham 1982). Because of poor preservation and the difficulty of ensuring comparability in collection and analysis, the small amount of temporal variation noted in food consumption may have been much greater than the present data suggest.

The major domesticates were introduced from Mexico, and almost all were in common use by the end of the Pioneer period (Gasser and Kwiatkowski, this volume). While corn was cultivated during the Archaic (Huckell 1987), the exotic origin of the major food crops is evidence for an external source contributing to the Hohokam subsistence base. Whether these items were the result of adoption by indigenous peoples or the cultural baggage of immigrants is unknown. While the percentage of the diet comprised of locally collected flora and fauna is not known, the richness of the Sonoran desert certainly provided a large percentage of the total subsistence base (Fish and

Nabhan, this volume; Gasser and Kwiatkowski, this volume). Due to the difficulty in dating Hohokam materials and in determining the percentages of local and exotic dietary items, possible changes in subsistence cannot be ascribed to internal or external factors.

While there was a great deal of change in arts, crafts, and in stylistic attributes of material culture, extractive technology did not seem to change much throughout the sequence. Canal systems were used early in the Pioneer period, and although they became larger and more complex, their maximum extent appears to have been reached during the Sedentary period (Neitzel, this volume, Table 5.2; although see Nicholas and Neitzel 1984).

Changes in Hohokam sociopolitical and ideological institutions have traditionally been addressed by investigations of horizontal and vertical relationships. Horizontal relationships exist across space and emphasize sociopolitical, ideological, and economic roles rather than status differences. Examples include interaction between ethnic or other social groups in the form of exchange of subsistence goods, warfare and cooperative alliances, and migration. Vertical relationships are based on status and emphasize interaction involving access to resources, such as labor, information, or goods. Vertical relationships range from those based on equality to those that are highly inequitable in terms of status. Horizontal and vertical relationships are often highly interrelated and distinctions between the two can be difficult to make; however, they provide a way of understanding changing forms of interaction. Contemporary Hohokam scholars have made enormous contributions to understanding both horizontal and vertical relationships using innovative and creative techniques and models. Most of these successful studies have used models that stress the spatial and temporal variation in Hohokam patterns (see especially the papers in Doyel and Plog 1980; Dittert and Dove 1985; this volume).

The nature of horizontal relationships within southern Arizona has become one of the most active and interesting research thrusts in Hohokam archaeology. Although regional variation has been recognized since the distinction between the Desert and Riverine Hohokam was made by Haury (1950), until the 1970s, the Hohokam were considered a single social, economic, and linguistic group. Little consideration was given to interaction within the Lower Sonoran Desert. Even those distinctions by DiPeso (1956) and Schroeder (1957, 1960, 1979), which proposed multiethnic groups in the Lower Sonoran Desert, viewed the Hohokam in a normative way. Horizontal relationship considerations were usually confined to trade and "influence" from areas outside southern Arizona. Recognition of the tremendous internal spatial variation in the Hohokam pattern forced archaeologists to address the nature of the behavior that would account for this variation (Wilcox 1979). Concepts such as core-periphery, interaction spheres, regional systems, world systems, ethnic diversity, local specialization, environmental differences, patterns of peace and conflict, interlocking systems of exchange networks, and nested hierarchies of social networks have all been used in attempts to explain the variation (McGuire, this volume). The situation is in many ways analogous to early attempts at explaining the nature of the midwestern Hopewell pattern in which an overarching pattern of material culture was viewed as indicative of various forms of horizontal and vertical interaction (Caldwell 1958).

The detail of the data now available has permitted a much finer distinction between local areas than desert and riverine or core and periphery. Many of the papers in this volume demonstrate that exchange patterns and social boundaries varied spatially on a local as well as a regional level and at different times. Presumably, these distinctions reflect different and changing economic and social relationships within the Hohokam sphere (Nelson 1981; Doyel 1987a; Teague 1984; Wilcox and Sternberg 1983; and most of the papers in this volume). Local economic specialization seems to occur at least partially independent of environmentally conditioned factors. Land use patterns vary greatly in space and time, not only between riverine locations and the more arid community locations, but within similar environmental communities. These patterns seem to reflect the need for individual community access to various subenvironments (Crown 1987; Gregory and Nials 1985), and different and changing spheres of organizational forms. Episodes of warfare and peace have been used to explain hilltop sites (*trincheras*) and areas of environmentally suitable but unoccupied territory, but there is great disagreement on the role of aggression and peace in explaining Hohokam horizontal relationships (Fish and Fish 1989; Doelle and Wallace, this volume).

These spatial differences have been so frequently noted that they can no longer be dismissed as an accident of sampling, noncomparable data collection, analytical techniques, or as the result of different postdepositional processes. The behavioral correlates that have been proposed to explain these differences are difficult to prove or disprove. As the papers in this volume dealing with horizontal relations indicate, the result is that the existence of the differences is demonstrable, but the behavior associated with material culture differences is often little more than informed speculation. Those reconstructions that emphasize demonstrable local material culture variation, using sophisticated models for exchange, social, and land use patterns, seem most successful. They are based on physical or chemical analyses of materials and the distribution of such public structures as ballcourts, platform mounds, and canal networks. In any case, it is clear that Hohokam horizontal relationships were extremely complicated and fluid. The papers in this volume by Crown, Doelle and Wallace, the Fishes, and McGuire reveal a complex multilevel series of horizontal interactions, few of which are ever in equilibrium. Nested hierarchies of social networks on many scales have been a feature of recent Hohokam research. On the smallest level of horizontal integration is the household, which apparently changed during the Pioneer period (Doyel, this volume). Later in the Pioneer period, increasing scales of integration are indicated at the village level in many sites (Doyel 1987b) by the development of house clusters situated around courtyards. Typically, individual structures are associated with nuclear families and house clusters with extended families. Several courtyard-household groups are village elements often associated with common areas such as trash mounds or cemeteries. Sites, depending on size, can consist of a courtyard group, supra-courtyard groups, and supra-courtyard groups with public structures. Village patterns are often dominated by a plaza, ballcourt, platform mound, or canal. These same structures are also used to delimit intervillage or community patterns covering major parts of drainages. Ballcourts, platform mounds, and sharing of canal networks have been a particularly effective way of defining intersite interaction (for a review see Doyel 1987b; Rice 1987a, 1987b; Fish 1989; Doelle and Wallace, this volume).

Hohokam vertical relationships concerning status differences have been a topic of concern since Cushing excavated Los Muertos in the late 1880s. Archaeological features such as compounds, Great Houses, long canal networks, "prestige" artifacts, occupational specialization, platform mounds, ballcourts, differential burial treatment, hierarchical site relationships, sites with compounds, and differential plant use have all been cited as indications of individual, group, or community status differences. The era is over, however, when the mere existence of exotic goods or public architecture is cited as proof of hierarchical forms of organization, and by inference, the cause of these forms.

The organizational forms that have been posited for the Hohokam include tribal level (Henderson 1987; Martin and Plog 1973; Upham and Rice 1980), segmentary tribes (Rice 1987a), chiefdoms (Grady 1976; Martin and Plog 1973; Wood and McAllister 1980; Rice 1987b), "big man" organizational forms (Wilcox and Shenk 1977), and an urban state (Wood and McAllister 1984). Most of the authors in this volume and others such as Teague (1984), however, eschew categorical levels and instead view Hohokam vertical organization in more general terms, varying along a continuum from egalitarian to some form of hierarchical organization. This approach has encouraged a multilayered systemic view of Hohokam organization and change, one that is less a cultural system changing as a single entity than it is a series of layered systems, each with its own ecology of interactions. Hohokam exchange is viewed not as a unified segment of a larger economic system, but one with two or three layers, one for prestige goods, one for utilitarian objects, and perhaps one for enhancing social networks (Crown, this volume; Doyel 1987a; Nelson 1981). Each of these layers varies through time in intensity, direction, and content, independent of one another.

In this multilayered model of the Hohokam, increased complexity in one layer of the system does not necessarily mean synchronic major systemic change throughout the system. Economic specialization is not necessarily viewed as having to be synchronous with ideological change or social ranking. While Neitzel (this volume) demonstrates the linkages between craft spe-

cialization, labor investment in public projects, the elaboration of ritual activities, and increasing vertical complexity, she does not view them as changing
in unison or as hallmarks of a specific cultural "stage." Furthermore, this
model of layered systems, partially independent of one another, can provide
more reasonable explanations for cultural evolution. The model accommo-
dates internal and external factors for change, as well as environmental and
demographic variables, and each layer may interact differentially with these
variables.

Changes in vertical complexity are apparent in many forms of material
culture and in intra- and intersite relationships, evidenced in most of the
papers in this volume. Especially interesting are innovative attempts at dem-
onstrating changing social complexity based on differential participation in
ideological activities (Fish 1989).

A trend seems to exist from individual participation to group participation,
and finally to increasing exclusivity. Artifacts, such as censers, palettes, and
figurines, which may be indicative of individualistic participation in ritual
activities, are ubiquitous beginning in the Pioneer period. They become increasingly elaborate throughout the sequence until they disappear abruptly
during the Sedentary period. Ballcourts and clay-capped trash mounds, which
served as rudimentary platform mounds, were constructed beginning in the
Colonial period. Ballcourt construction increased rapidly in the Colonial and
Sedentary periods, occurring in concert with the elaboration of ritual paraphernalia described above. Presumably the ballcourt game, with its ritual
component, was a team event also offering opportunities for whole communities to participate as spectators. The increasing number of pre-Classic
ballcourts meant more and more individuals could participate as players or
spectators. As Fish (1989) has noted, the earliest clay-capped mounds at
Snaketown were not segregated from the site. Palisades surrounded some
mounds in the Sedentary period, and in the late Sedentary and early Classic,
adobe or masonry walls delimited compounds. During the Classic period few
ballcourts, structures that permitted public participation, were constructed.
They were replaced by more exclusionary platform mounds and compounds,
where activities were often blocked from view. At the same time there were
major changes in the treatment of the dead and the funerary ceremonies that
accompanied the burial. Doyel (this volume) shows that in the Phoenix Basin
the early Classic period mounds usually did not have structures and were
presumably used for ceremonial dances and perhaps some storage, while in
the later Classic period the mounds were used for dwellings, presumably of
a small, elite group that had consolidated power (Gregory and Nials 1985).
Casa Grande with its "big house" and compounds epitomizes the specialized
dwellings and exclusionary aspect of the architecture. In sum, as population
increased, Hohokam ritual activity shifted from individualistic performances
and large group ritual performances centered around ballcourts, to ceremo-

nies centered on platforms dominated by small groups, and finally to the even more exclusionary dwellings on the platforms.

The authors of the papers in this volume have documented local variation in these trends, indicating that belief systems of the Hohokam were not consistent over the entire range of what archaeologists call the Hohokam. The vertical organization was as diverse and as complex as the horizontal organization, and the relationship between the two forms is very unclear and probably varied considerably throughout the Hohokam sequence.

The causes for the changes in the horizontal relationships reflected by degrees of ritual participation are unknown. Differential access to irrigated lands, or exotic prestige items obtained through exchange, the need to recruit and organize labor, stimulus from external sources, increasing population, and environmental change have all been cited as stimuli for change. Clearly, the increasing exclusivity of ritual behavior is directly related to complexity in economic specialization, trade, and social differentiation. The relationship of the increasingly complex ideological organization to economic activity such as trade and irrigation and social factors such as ethnicity is difficult to determine and is mostly expressed by general anthropological principles, such as those noted by Neitzel (this volume).

## THE FUTURE

The papers in this volume take the current measure of Hohokam archaeology. By any yardstick the state of Hohokam research has to be judged as one of the most creative in method, analysis, and interpretation of any area in North America. The large number of practitioners of diverse methodological and theoretical persuasions and the generous funding from numerous large construction projects have fostered an atmosphere that has resulted in great scholarly achievement. Especially interesting is the fact that an unusually high percentage of studies deal with human behavior and not simply analysis of architecture or artifacts. The study of material culture in most cases is used as a means for understanding behavior, rather than as an end in itself. Despite the progress in understanding Hohokam archaeology in behavioral terms, the word "Hohokam" still largely refers to the physical archaeological record, the material remains, and their relationships to one another and to the natural environment.

What directions will Hohokam archaeology take in the future? There is no doubt that the questions that have consumed Hohokam archaeology since its earliest days will continue to absorb scholars. The models to be tested will become more complex, involving more variables, and will more closely approach the way humans behave as social animals. The chronological dilemma will continue to be of great interest, despite the progress that is indicated by Dean's paper. As chronologies become more refined so, too, do the questions that are being asked, which depend on accurate temporal placement. As the Anasazi example demonstrates, even with perhaps the finest prehistoric chronology in the world, questions about human behavior that depend on accurate dating almost always outpace our dating resolution ability.

The trend will continue toward a greater understanding of Hohokam complexity along a continuous scale, with emphasis on different aspects of behavior, rather than by categories of complexity. There is also a great need to understand the extraordinarily complex and changing horizontal and vertical relationships among the social, economic, and ideological aspects of the Hohokam. In addition, the character of what constitutes "the Hohokam" needs to be more directly addressed. Questions about the meaning of ethnicity, world systems, and interaction spheres need to be investigated. The encouraging note is that most of these concepts are sufficiently ambiguous at present that they do not carry the intellectual baggage that surrounds terms such as "state" or "tribe." The more general terms being used, while frustrating in their imprecision, permit exploration of many forms of behavior that may or may not have Southwestern or even global ethnographic analogs.

One of the most persistently difficult problems of Hohokam research is the question of population estimates. There presently is simply no satisfactory method for deriving even relative population trends for the Hohokam. Because demographic change is one of the major variables affecting culture change, it is essential that methods be developed for estimating Hohokam populations at different times. It can only be hoped that the destruction of Hohokam sites has not already made this enormously difficult task impossible. The difficulty in estimating Hohokam population and reconstructing past environments probably means that most explanations for major culture change will continue to focus on internal or external factors. The recent potential for success in retrodicting parts of the Hohokam environment may, however, indicate that there will be greater emphasis given to environmental factors as agents of change.

While it is the common wisdom in the archaeological profession that more emphasis will have to be placed on the use of extant collections for research purposes, this is especially true for Hohokam studies. A large percentage of certain classes of Hohokam sites have already been destroyed or scientifically excavated. In the 1970s a commercial air traveler flying into Phoenix could see scores of canals in plowed cotton fields. This is no longer the case. There is no reason to presume that the destruction of sites in the name of development or archaeology will slow in the near future. It is therefore gratifying that so much emphasis has been recently placed on curation, for it protects the resource base for the future. High priority for curation must not be left to chance.

The papers in this volume demonstrate that Hohokam studies have entered a new era. The earlier periods of speculation without data are over, and large reports with uninterpreted or underinterpreted data are becoming rare.

Syntheses and interpretations of specific Hohokam topics based on a vast new body of reliable data are the rule, not the exception.

The new explanations for specific aspects of Hohokam culture and the accumulation of data have generated new problems and may signal the next stage of Hohokam studies. The amount of data on the Hohokam is now so great that it threatens to obscure broad patterns and general trends. Different techniques will have to be found to effectively access and manipulate these data, and new multivariate models of Hohokam organization and change that take behavioral, demographic, and environmental variables into account will need to be generated. The topics that are represented by the various chapters of this volume provide insightful but necessarily incomplete views of the Hohokam. An understanding of the Hohokam will always be incomplete if it is based on a single perspective, and at present viewing the Hohokam as a totality produces incoherence. The challenge of Hohokam studies will be a continuous quest to overcome partial views.

## ACKNOWLEDGMENTS

Patty Crown, Dave Doyel, Paul Fish, and Randy McGuire made many useful suggestions and provided assistance on this paper while it was in manuscript form. I am very grateful for their advice, much of which I followed.

## REFERENCES CITED

Bayham, Frank E.
    1982    *A Diachronic Analysis of Prehistoric Animal Exploitation at Ventana Cave.* Unpublished Ph.D. dissertation, Department of Anthropology, Arizona State University, Tempe.
Bohrer, Vorsila L.
    1988    Recently Recognized Cultivated and Encouraged Plants Among the Hohokam. Paper presented at the 53rd Annual Meeting of the Society for American Archaeology, Phoenix.
Cable, John S., and David E. Doyel
    1987    The Archaic to Hohokam Transition: A View from the Pioneer Period. Paper presented at the 1987 Hohokam Symposium: The Archaic-Hohokam Transition, Commemorating the Hundredth Anniversary of the Hemenway Southwestern Archaeological Expedition, Tempe.
Caldwell, Joseph R.
    1958    *Trend and Tradition in the Prehistory of the Eastern United States.* American Anthropological Association Memoir No. 88, vol. 60, no. 6, pt. 2. Menasha.

Cordell, Linda S., and George J. Gumerman
  1989  Cultural Interaction in the Prehistoric Southwest. In *Dynamics of Southwestern Prehistory*, edited by L. Cordell and G. Gumerman, pp. 1–17. Smithsonian Institution Inquiries in Archaeology. Smithsonian Institution Press, Washington, D.C.

Crown, Patricia L.
  1987  Classic Period Hohokam Settlement and Land Use in the Casa Grande Ruins Area, Arizona. *Journal of Field Archaeology* 14:147–160.

Crown, Patricia L., and E. W. Sires
  1984  Hohokam Chronology in the Salt–Gila Archaeological Project Research. In *Hohokam Archaeology Along the Salt–Gila Aqueduct, Central Arizona Project*, vol. 9, edited by L. S. Teague and P. L. Crown, pp. 1973–1986. Arizona State Museum Archaeological Series 150. Tucson.

Cushing, Frank Hamilton
  1890  Preliminary Notes on the Origin, Working Hypothesis and Primary Researches of the Hemenway Southwestern Archaeological Expedition. *Congress International des Americanistes*, pp. 151–194. W. H. Kuhl, Berlin.

DiPeso, Charles C.
  1953  *The Sobaipuri Indians of the Upper San Pedro Valley, Southeastern Arizona.* Amerind Foundation Publications 6. Dragoon, Arizona.
  1956  *The Upper Pima of San Cayetano del Tumacacori: An Archaeo-historical Reconstruction of the Ootam of Pimeria Alta.* Amerind Foundation Publications 7. Dragoon, Arizona.
  1974  *Casas Grandes: A Fallen Trading Center of the Gran Chichimeca.* Vols. 1–3. Northland Press, Flagstaff.

Dittert, Alfred E., Jr., and Donald E. Dove (editors)
  1985  *Proceedings of the 1983 Hohokam Symposium.* Arizona Archaeological Society Occasional Paper 2. Phoenix.

Doyel, David E.
  1987a The Role of Commerce in Hohokam Society. Paper presented at the Advanced Seminar, Cultural Complexity in the Arid Southwest: The Hohokam and Chacoan Regional Systems. School of American Research, Santa Fe.

Doyel, David E. (editor)
  1987b *The Hohokam Village: Site Structure and Organization.* Southwestern and Rocky Mountain Division of the American Association for the Advancement of Science. Reno.

Doyel, David E., and Fred Plog (editors)
  1980  *Current Issues in Hohokam Prehistory: Proceedings of a Symposium.* Anthropological Research Papers 23. Arizona State University, Tempe.

Eighmy, Jeffrey L., and Randall H. McGuire
  1989  Dating the Hohokam Phase Sequence: An Analysis of a Large Set of Archaeomagnetic Dates. *The Journal of Field Archaeology* 16:215–231.

Ferdon, Edwin N., Jr.
  1955  *A Trial Survey of Mexican-Southwestern Architectural Parallels.* School of American Research Monograph 11. Santa Fe.

Fewkes, Jesse Walter
  1912  Casa Grande, Arizona. In *28th Annual Report of the Bureau of Ethnology, 1906–1907*, pp. 25–179. Washington, D.C.

Fish, Paul R.
   1989   The Hohokam: 1000 Years of Prehistory in the Sonoran Desert. In *Dynamics of Southwestern Prehistory*, edited by L. Cordell and G. Gumerman, pp. 19–63. Smithsonian Institution Inquiries in Archaeology. Smithsonian Institution Press, Washington, D.C.

Fish, Paul R., and Suzanne K. Fish
   1989   Hohokam Warfare from a Regional Prespective. In *Cultures in Conflict*, edited by B. Vivian, pp. 118–132. University of Calgary Press. Calgary.

Gladwin, Harold S.
   1928   *Excavations at Casa Grande, Arizona.* Southwest Museum Papers 2. Los Angeles.
   1979   *Mogollon and Hohokam:* A.D. *600–100.* Medallion Papers 50. Privately printed. Santa Barbara.

Gladwin, Winifred, and Harold S. Gladwin
   1929   *The Red-on-buff Culture of the Gila Basin.* Medallion Papers 3. Gila Pueblo, Globe.
   1933   *Some Southwestern Pottery Types: Series III.* Medallion Papers 13. Gila Pueblo, Globe.
   1934   *A Method for Designation of Cultures and Their Variation.* Medallion Papers 15. Gila Pueblo, Globe.

Gladwin, Harold S., Emil W. Haury, E. B. Sayles, and Nora Gladwin
   1937   *Excavations at Snaketown: Material Culture.* Medallion Papers 25. Gila Pueblo, Globe.

Grady, Mark
   1976   *Aboriginal Agrarian Adaptation to the Sonoran Desert: A Regional Synthesis and Research Design.* Unpublished Ph.D. dissertation, Department of Anthropology, University of Arizona, Tucson.

Graybill, Donald A.
   1985   Paleoclimate of the Hohokam Area: Problems and Prospects. In *Proceedings of the 1983 Hohokam Symposium*, edited by A. E. Dittert, Jr. and D. Dove, pp. 308–322. Arizona Archaeological Society Occasional Paper 2. Phoenix.

Gregory, David A., and Fred L. Nials
   1985   Observations Concerning the Distribution of Classic Period Hohokam Platform Mounds. In *Proceedings of the 1983 Hohokam Symposium*, edited by A. E. Dittert, Jr. and D. Dove, pp. 373–389. Arizona Archaeological Society Occasional Paper 2. Phoenix.

Haury, Emil W.
   1932   *Roosevelt 9:6, a Hohokam Site of the Colonial Period.* Medallion Papers 11. Gila Pueblo, Globe.
   1945   *The Excavation of Los Muertos and Neighboring Ruins in the Salt River Valley, Southern Arizona.* Papers of the Peabody Museum of Archaeology and Ethnology 24. Harvard University Press, Cambridge.
   1950   *The Stratigraphy and Archaeology of Ventana Cave, Arizona.* University of Arizona Press, Tucson.
   1962   The Greater American Southwest. In *Courses Toward Urban Life*, edited by R. J. Braidwood and G. R. Willey, pp. 106–131. Viking Fund Publications in Anthropology 32. New York.
   1976   *The Hohokam: Desert Farmers and Craftsmen.* University of Arizona Press, Tucson.

Henderson, T. Kathleen
　　1987　*Structure and Organization at La Ciudad.* Anthropological Field Studies 18. Arizona State University, Tempe.
Huckell, Bruce B.
　　1987　Agriculture and Late Archaic Settlements in the River Valleys of Southeastern Arizona. Paper presented at the Third Hohokam Conference: The Archaic-Pioneer Transition, Tempe.
Johnson, Gregory A.
　　1989　Dynamics of Southwestern Prehistory: Far Outside—Looking In. In *Dynamics of Southwestern Prehistory*, edited by L. Cordell and G. Gumerman, pp. 371–389. Smithsonian Institution Inquiries in Archaeology. Smithsonian Institution Press, Washington, D.C.
Kidder, Alfred V.
　　1924　*An Introduction to the Study of Southwestern Archaeology.* (Reprinted in 1962.) Yale University Press, New Haven.
LeBlanc, Steven A.
　　1982　The Advent of Pottery in the Southwest. In Southwestern Ceramics, a Comparative Review, edited by A. H. Schroeder, pp. 27–51. *The Arizona Archaeologist* 15. The Arizona Archaeological Society, Phoenix.
　　1986　Aspects of Southwestern Prehistory: A.D. 900–1400. In *Ripples in the Chichimec Sea: New Considerations of Southwestern–Mesoamerican Interactions*, edited by F. Mathien and R. McGuire, pp. 105–134. The Center for Archaeological Investigations and Southern Illinois University Press, Carbondale and Edwardsville.
Martin, Paul S., and Fred Plog
　　1973　*The Archaeology of Arizona.* Natural History Press, Doubleday, Garden City.
Masse, W. Bruce
　　1980　*Excavations at Gu Achi.* Western Archaeological Center Publications in Archaeology 12. National Park Service, Tucson.
Mathien, Frances Joan, and Randall H. McGuire (editors)
　　1986　*Ripples in the Chichimec Sea: New Considerations of Southwestern-Mesoamerican Interaction.* The Center for Archaeological Investigations and Southern Illinois University Press, Carbondale and Edwardsville.
McGuire, Randall H., and Michael B. Schiffer
　　1982　*Hohokam and Patayan: Prehistory of Southwestern Arizona.* Academic Press, New York.
Merbs, Charles
　　1985　Paleopathology of the Hohokam. In *Proceedings of the 1983 Hohokam Symposium*, edited by A. E. Dittert, Jr. and D. Dove, pp. 219–230. Arizona Archaeological Society Occasional Paper 2. Phoenix.
Nelson, Richard
　　1981　*The Role of the Pochteca System in Hohokam Exchange.* Ph.D. dissertation, New York University, New York University Microfilms.
Nials, Fred, David Gregory, and Donald Graybill
　　1986　Salt River Streamflow and Hohokam Irrigation Systems. In *The 1982–1984 Excavations at Las Colinas: Environment and Subsistence*, edited by C. Heathington and D. Gregory. Arizona State Museum Archaeological Series 162.
Nicholas, Linda, and Jill Neitzel
　　1984　Canal Irrigation and Socio-political Organization in the Lower Salt River

Valley: A Diachronic Analysis. In *Prehistoric Agricultural Strategies in the Southwest*, edited by S. K. Fish, and P. R. Fish, pp. 161–178. Anthropological Research Papers 30. Arizona State University, Tucson.

Rice, Glen E.
1987a The Organization of the Early Hohokam Village. In *The Hohokam Community of La Ciudad*, edited by G. Rice, pp. 134–147. Office of Cultural Resource Management Report 69. Arizona State University, Tempe.
1987b The Marana Community Complex: A Twelfth Century Hohokam Chiefdom. In *Studies in the Hohokam Community of Marana*, edited by G. Rice, pp. 119–126. Anthropological Field Studies 15. Arizona State University, Tempe.

Roberts, Frank H. H., Jr.
1935 A Survey of Southwestern Archaeology. *American Anthropologist* 37:1–35.

Schroeder, Albert H.
1947 Did the Sinagua of the Verde Valley Settle in the Salt River Valley? *Southwestern Journal of Anthropology* 3:230–246.
1953 The Bearing of Architecture on Developments in the Hohokam Classic Period. *Southwestern Journal of Anthropology* 9:174–194.
1957 The Hakataya Cultural Tradition. *American Antiquity* 23:176–178.
1960 *The Hohokam, Sinagua, and Hakataya*. Society for American Archaeology, Archives of Archaeology No. 5. Menasha.
1979 Prehistory: Hakataya. In *Handbook of North American Indians*, vol. 9, edited by Alfonso Ortiz, pp. 279–311. Smithsonian Institution, Washington, D.C.

Sires, Earl W., Jr.
1983 Archaeological Investigations at Las Fosas (AZ U:15:19): A Classic Period Settlement on the Gila River. In *Hohokam Archaeology Along the Salt-Gila Aqueduct, Central Arizona Project*, vol. 6, edited by L. S. Teague and P. L. Crown, pp. 493–657. Arizona State Museum Archaeological Series 150. Tucson.
1984 Hohokam Architecture and Site Structure. In *Hohokam Archaeology Along the Salt-Gila Aqueduct, Central Arizona Project*, vol. 9, edited by L. S. Teague and P. L. Crown, pp. 115–139. Arizona State Museum Archaeological Series 150. Tucson.

Teague, Lynn S.
1984 The Organization of Hohokam Economy. In *Hohokam Archaeology Along the Salt-Gila Aqueduct, Central Arizona Project*, vol. 9, edited by L. S. Teague and P. L. Crown, pp. 187–250. Arizona State Museum Archaeological Series 150. Tucson.

Teague, Lynn S., and Patricia L. Crown (editors)
1984 *Hohokam Archaeology Along the Salt-Gila Aqueduct, Central Arizona Project*, vol. 9. Arizona State Museum Archaeological Series 150. Tucson.

Upham, Steadman
1988 Archaeological Visibility and the Underclass of Southwestern Prehistory. *American Antiquity* 53:245–261.

Upham, Steadman, and Glen E. Rice
1980 Up the Canal Without a Pattern: Modelling Hohokam Interaction and Exchange. In *Current Issues in Hohokam Prehistory: Proceedings of a Symposium*, edited by D. Doyel and F. Plog, pp. 78–105. Anthropological Research Paper 23. Arizona State University, Tempe.

Weaver, Donald E., Jr.
1972 A Cultural-ecological Model for the Classic Hohokam Period in the Lower Salt River Valley. *The Kiva* 38:43–52.

Whitecotton, Joseph W., and Richard A. Pailes
  1986   New World Precolumbian World Systems. In *Ripples in the Chichimec Sea: New Considerations of Southwestern-Mesoamerican Interaction*, edited by F. J. Mathien and R. H. McGuire, pp. 183–204. The Center for Archaeological Investigations and Southern Illinois University Press, Carbondale and Edwardsville.
Wilcox, David R.
  1979   The Hohokam Regional System. In *An Archaeological Test of Sites in the Gila Butte-Santan Region, South-Central Arizona*, edited by Glen Rice, pp. 77–116. Anthropological Research Papers 18. Arizona State University, Tempe.
  1980   The Current Status of the Hohokam Concept. In *Current Issues in Hohokam Prehistory: Proceedings of a Symposium*, edited by D. Doyel and F. Plog, pp. 236–242. Anthropological Research Papers 23. Arizona State University, Tempe.
Wilcox, David R., and Lynette O. Shenk
  1977   *The Architecture of the Casa Grande and Its Interpretation*. Arizona State Museum Archaeological Series 115. Tucson.
Wilcox, David R., and Charles Sternberg
  1983   *Hohokam Ballcourts and Their Interpretation*. Arizona State Museum Archaeological Series 160. Tucson.
Wood, J. Scott, and Martin E. McAllister
  1980   Foundation and Empire: The Colonization of the Northeastern Hohokam Periphery. In *Current Issues of Hohokam Prehistory*, edited by D. Doyel and F. Plog, 111–127. Anthropological Research Papers 23. Arizona State University, Tempe.
  1984   Second Foundation: Settlement Patterns and Agriculture in the Northeastern Hohokam Periphery, Central Arizona. In *Prehistoric Agricultural Strategies in the Southwest*, edited by S. Fish and P. Fish, pp. 271–289. Anthropological Research Papers 23. Arizona State University, Tempe.

# •2•

# DESERT AS CONTEXT: THE HOHOKAM ENVIRONMENT

*Suzanne K. Fish*

*Gary P. Nabhan*

The northern Sonoran Desert (Fig. 2.1) provided resources and opportunities that figured prominently in Hohokam cultural identity. Broad geographic and biotic similarities contributed to widespread commonalities in lifestyle throughout the Hohokam range and underwrote the distribution of shared material culture by which these prehistoric peoples are recognized. From a complementary perspective, a level of secondary but significant environmental variability can be distinguished within the cultural domain.

The presence of cultivators in southern Arizona is well established for a time prior to emergence of the Hohokam tradition (Huckell 1988; S. Fish et al 1990), if this name is reserved for the first makers of pottery. Their ceramic successors can be regarded as primarily agriculturalists whose subsistence also included a broad range of natural products, many of which were abundant in culturally modified habitats. Groups with predominantly hunting and gathering strategies may have coexisted with the Hohokam in a relationship resembling that between the historic Sand Papago and more agriculturally

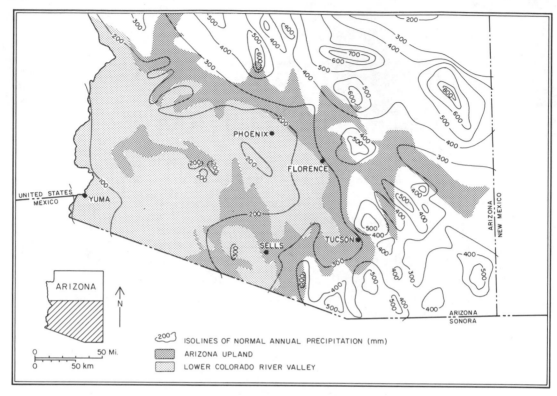

Figure 2.1    *Subdivisions of the Sonoran Desert in Arizona.*

oriented Pimans. Nevertheless, remains of such groups have not been archaeologically identified as Hohokam (e.g., Hayden 1967), although they may
have been linguistically or genetically related.

In the sense that they circumscribe the distribution of unequivocally and
distinctively Hohokam assemblages, two factors can be considered key environmental determinants of Hohokam culture. These are location within the
northeast Sonoran Desert and, with few exceptions, an elevational range
below 3,500 ft (1,065 m). Residence and subsistence activity was concentrated
on the floors and slopes (bajadas) of basins, and frequently extended into
moderate elevations of adjacent desert mountains. Even where larger mountain masses occur, as in the Santa Catalinas, utilization of higher slopes and
valleys was minor when compared with upland habitation and farming by
other Southwestern cultures.

The Hohokam inhabited the Sonoran Desert without extending into its
driest facies to the west and southwest or into the more tropically influenced
ones to the south. To the north and east, boundaries for the Hohokam largely
coincide with those for this desert type. In keeping with their elevational
tendencies, the Hohokam were rarely out of contact with arborescent desert
plants characterizing the Sonoran biome. Such conjunction can be illustrated

by a correlation between the great majority of Hohokam occupations and distributions of two conspicuous elements of this vegetational assemblage, the saguaro and mesquite. The interplay of environmental factors shaping Sonoran Desert biota were also central forces in the patterns of Hohokam adaptation.

## DISTANCE AND DIVERSITY
## IN HOHOKAM BASINS

That portion of the Basin-and-Range Province (Fenneman 1931) settled by the Hohokam consists of parallel northeast-southwest trending basins bordered by relatively low and often discontinuous mountain ranges of limited mass. Intervening basins typically are broader than their mountain borders and are filled with detrital sediments to great depth. Along the flanks of the mountains, rock pediments formed by erosional recession of the mountain front are overlain by a thinner soil mantle, typically less than 2 m in depth. Streams with upland catchments deposit soil as they leave the mountains, creating alluvial fans on the upper bajada or valley slope. Further downslope, outwash materials from individual fans coalesce on the lower bajada. Terraces frequently border floodplains of major axial drainages, which are positioned at the juncture of bajadas from opposing mountain ranges.

The structure of Sonoran Desert basins has implications for Hohokam subsistence patterns as a whole. Localized environmental conditions create a gradient of differentiated habitats along the transect from mountain peak to floodplain. These are duplicated in a generalized progression on both valley slopes. Only in the few cases of higher ranges do mountains on one side of a basin afford substantial resources unavailable on the other side or on the upper reaches of bajadas. Within Hohokam territory, the level of biotic uniformity occasioned by the lower elevation Sonoran Desert biome is intensified by this intravalley redundancy.

Typically, widths of well-defined basins range from 6 to 20 mi (10 to 32 km), and average about 12 mi (19 km). Even the broadest expanses, associated with junctures of major drainages as in the Phoenix area or with an absence of linear mountain chains as in the Santa Cruz Flats, rarely exceed 30 mi (48 km). Since the majority of resources could be acquired on a single slope without necessitating travel across the full valley width, access was not excessive from most points in any basin.

Most hunting and gathering forays from habitations near domestic and agricultural water could be completed within a single day. The six to seven quarts of water needed by active persons at high summer temperatures (Adolph 1947:113) could be reasonably transported, with the weight of gathered products replacing consumed water for the return. The linear conformation of most Hohokam basins permitted practical foraging radii that were essential to routine acquisition of resources from the waterless bajada. Furthermore, while there might be labor-scheduling conflicts during the busiest agricultural periods, permanency of residence for farming did not preclude access to a full array of wild resources in season.

Although the basins of southern Arizona share a structural pattern, geomorphic and topographic attributes significant to hunters, gatherers, and farmers exhibit variability between basins as well as locally within a single basin. In general, the mechanics of outwash transport create coarser soils on upper bajada slopes and finer soils below. However, parent materials differ among basins and among ranges bordering the same basin. Bajada widths influence the details of slope morphology. Degree of dissection affects both the extent of riparian communities and agricultural opportunities. Slope aspect differs with directional trend of each basin, between opposing slopes, and even for individual intravalley locations. Such differences create variety in plant densities and distributions within broader vegetation zones and may be critical elements in differential crop success under conditions of agricultural stress.

Variation among basin cross sections also has consequences for subsistence practices. Degree of slope affects runoff that supports vegetative resources and permits floodwater farming in favorable situations. Valley morphology associated with major axial drainages is an important variable controlling irrigation potential. Successful diversion during any period depends on channel incision and stability. Width of the floodplain, the abruptness of the valley slope at the floodplain margin, and terrace structure determine the extent of irrigable acreage. The angle of the valley slopes as it intersects the floodplain controls not only the lateral extent of canals from the river, but also the force of flow in tributary drainages over which canals must pass.

## HYDROLOGICAL REGIMES

Characteristics of two major divisions of desert watercourses correspond to a division between primary emphases in agricultural orientation among the Hohokam. Perennial rivers fed by watersheds outside the desert provided the basis for subsistence systems centered on large-scale riverine irrigation (Fig. 2.2). Intermittent streams and smaller ephemeral washes supported a range of more restricted irrigation and floodwater cultivation.

The exogenous Gila and Salt rivers heading on the Mogollon Rim to the north and east, carry water from uplands of substantially higher rainfall into the lower desert. The Verde River shares many of the characteristics of the Salt, of which it is a tributary. Watersheds tap upland areas of winter snowfall, with resultant high flow in late winter and early spring. The Salt below the Verde confluence in the upper Phoenix Basin drains 12,900 sq mi (33,400 sq km) and the Gila drains 20,615 sq mi (53,400 sq km) (U.S. Geological Survey

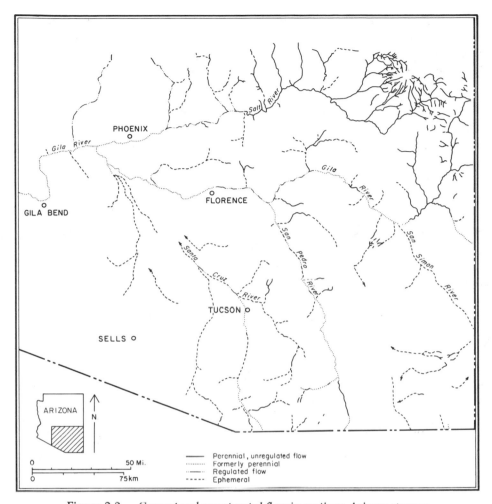

Figure 2.2 *Current and recontructed flow in southern Arizona streams.*

1954). Before modern damming, these rivers provided perennial flow for the
Phoenix Basin and, prehistorically, for areas along much of their joint course
to the Colorado River. Historic travel by flatboat was possible at times between
the confluence of the two rivers and the Colorado (Castetter and Bell 1942:13).

Vast, higher rainfall watersheds resulted in sustained flow and seasonal
periodicity largely independent of precipitation in the desert basins. Flow
peaked by the early spring in the Salt River, with a considerably lesser summer
increase. Early spring and late summer peaks are documented for the upper
and middle Gila. Bimodal streamflow regimes could have supported more
than one crop in a growing season if other conditions permitted. Along the
Salt and Gila, gently sloping terrace and basin floor morphology allowed canal
networks to be extended laterally from the riverbeds, creating wide expanses
of irrigable land.

Intermittent Hohokam rivers and other larger drainages originate in lower, less massive uplands within the Sonoran Desert or along its northern and eastern edge below the Mogollon Rim. Watershed sizes are highly variable. The Santa Cruz River, with the largest, drains 8,524 sq mi (22,100 sq km) at Laveen (U.S. Geological Survey 1954). Rainfall and runoff in the watersheds is lower than in the Mogollon highlands; snowmelt does not figure as significantly or at all in annual supply. Consequently these watercourses, almost all of which ultimately join the Salt and Gila network, carry water only seasonally over parts or all of their courses. Flow in major streams south and west of the Phoenix Basin peaks in conjunction with summer rains rather than in the spring and is not well timed for extensive early crops. Valley slopes rise more steeply from floodplains, restricting the width of irrigated acreage. While canal systems of secondary size could be constructed in some locales as along New River (Doyel 1984) and the Santa Cruz (Bernard-Shaw 1988), groups living along these watercourses placed greater emphasis on alternative farming technologies.

Much of the moisture moving through Sonoran Desert basins flows below the surface in deep valley fill and generally follows gradients of surface water channels. Where this underflow encounters a bedrock obstacle, it is forced toward the surface. Igneous intrusions beneath basin floors are therefore correlates of sustained surface flow in intermittent streams. An example is along the Santa Cruz in the vicinity of Tucson. Water is forced upward near San Xavier, at the end of the Tucson Mountains, and again near the modern town of Red Rock (Smith 1910:176–178). Shallow wells might be filled from high water tables in such areas during drier intervals when surface flow had ceased. Similar geological intrusions created maximal discharge and channel stability for canal headings on the permanently flowing Salt and Gila (Lee 1905; Pewe 1978; Graybill and Nials 1989). Instances occur on the Gila River just above Snaketown and on the Salt in the vicinity of the Tempe Buttes.

Current and reconstructed flow in southern Arizona streams according to Hendrickson and Minckley (1984) is shown in Figure 2.2. During drier seasons, water along segments of intermittent rivers might be sufficient for domestic supply, if not for irrigation. Such stretches would have been continuously preferred for occupation. However, locations of perennial flow varied somewhat over time even in favored locales. Well-developed cienegas have disappeared in recent times after downcutting by major floods and lowering of water tables (Betancourt and Turner 1988; Hastings and Turner 1965; Hendrickson and Minckley 1984; Dobyns 1981). An example of prehistoric incision with similar consequences is well documented near San Xavier on the Santa Cruz (Waters 1988).

In addition to axial drainages, long-term surface water in the Sonoran Desert can be found in the lower canyons of mountains bordering basins and on their pediments. Upland catchments receive more regular precipitation and greater quantities than lower basins. As streams leave the mountains, rocky basements beneath pediment channels maintain flow at or near the surface. Floodplains of drainages along the mountain edge offer potential for dry season water sources in hand-dug wells and impoundments. From larger mountains such as the Catalinas or Bradshaws, persistent or perennial stream-flow may be found on the mountain flanks and may occur locally in channels for some distance onto the upper valley slope. Flanks of even moderate-sized desert ranges also give rise to occasional permanent springs and rock-lined tanks such as those supplying the historic Tohono O'odham (Papago) well villages (Underhill 1939:57).

As drainages with upland sources pass over deep valley fill beyond the pediments water infiltrates porous channels and disappears from the surface. Lesser drainages finger into smaller channels as gradient diminishes on lower bajada alluvial fans. Typically, only a few larger tributaries maintain contin-uous transbajada courses and carry water to the rivers after storms. Where the floodplains of such large tributaries or arroyos are sufficiently wide, sea-sonal floods could be diverted onto fields beside channels.

Numerous ephemeral drainages head on bajadas or on small ranges. Larger channels may join through-going streams crossing the valley slope. Minor ones cut and fill cyclically as they intercept overland runoff following storms, without forming continuous drainage networks. Potential water sources for floodwater farming on alluvial fans include both tributaries originating in the mountains and larger ephemeral drainages heading on the bajadas.

## GEOGRAPHIC PATTERNS OF CLIMATE

With exceptions on the north and east fringes, present annual precipitation in the area inhabited by the Hohokam (Figs. 2.1, 2.3 and Table 2.1) averages less than 15 in (400 mm). The extremes for yearly rainfall within the area vary by a factor of two, with the low end of the range to the west (Sellers et al. 1985). Totals from 7 to 12 in (175 to 300 mm) are widespread, but a few locales such as Gila Bend receive less than 6 in (150 mm). The areas of highest summer temperatures coincide with annual rainfall below 9 in (225 mm) in the vicinity of Phoenix and southwest to Gila Bend. Lower annual precipitation is also correlated with greater variation about the mean. Harsher climatic conditions reduce both wild resources and the potential for farming with local rainfall. These disadvantages were offset along the Salt and Gila by harvestable plants of rich riparian communities and by abundant water for riverine irrigation.

In addition to variation in yearly amounts, seasonal precipitation exhibits geographical patterns. The percentage of total precipitation occurring in the summer months decreases from east to west (Hastings and Turner 1965:14), while evapotranspiration increases. Proportionally lower summer rainfall oc-curs in conjunction with lower total precipitation and high annual coefficients

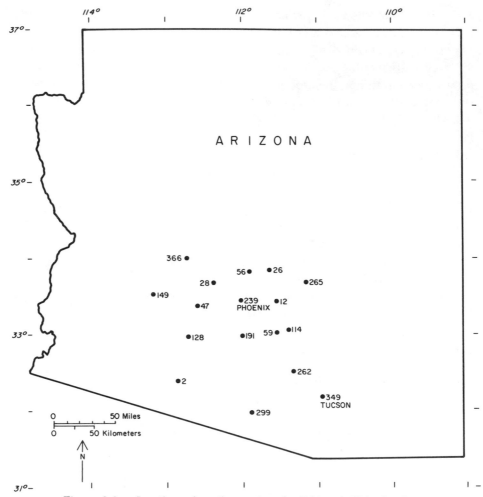

Figure 2.3    *Locations of weather stations furnishing precipitation data.*

of variation to the west, producing maximal summer drought as a limiting factor for vegetation.

A bimodal distribution of rainfall in the Hohokam area contrasts with winter dominance to the west and summer dominance to the east. This balance has been associated both with the greater structural diversity of Sonoran Desert vegetation and with the arborescent character of many of its perennials (Turner and Brown 1982:182), compared to shrub dominance in the Chihuahuan, Great Basin, and Mohave deserts. Distinctively large Sonoran Desert lifeforms include such important economic plants as paloverde, ironwood, and saguaro. Less seasonally balanced rainfall and lower annual amounts correspond with diminished desert arboreals. Higher precipitation in a broad arc to the north, east, and south of the greater Phoenix Basin is correlated with increased density and diversity in these key food species.

Table 2.1 *Precipitation Data for Selected Stations in the Area of Hohokam Occupation*

| Weather Station | Years of Record | Average Annual Precipitation (inches) | Average July–September Precipitation (inches) |
|---|---|---|---|
| 366 Wickenburg | 71 | 11.15 | 4.32 |
| 56 Carefree | 13 | 12.26 | 4.04 |
| 26 Bartlett Dam | 43 | 12.70 | 3.88 |
| 265 Roosevelt | 76 | 15.74 | 4.74 |
| 12 Apache Junction | 13 | 9.53 | 2.80 |
| 28 Beardsley | 28 | 7.36 | 2.61 |
| 239 Phoenix Airport | 34 | 7.50 | 2.44 |
| 191 Maricopa | 51 | 7.47 | 3.20 |
| 59 Casa Grande Ruins | 59 | 8.79 | 3.11 |
| 114 Florence | 69 | 9.93 | 3.52 |
| 262 Red Rock | 44 | 9.72 | 4.21 |
| 349 Tucson Airport | 34 | 11.09 | 5.91 |
| 299 Sells | 26 | 12.26 | 6.66 |
| 2 Ajo | 68 | 8.83 | 4.20 |
| 128 Gila Bend | 77 | 5.82 | 2.14 |
| 47 Buckeye | 80 | 7.43 | 2.65 |
| 149 Harquahala Plains | 24 | 6.17 | 2.42 |

(data compiled from Sellers et al. 1985, table 11)

Winter precipitation originates largely over the Pacific Ocean and is cyclonic or frontal in nature. Broad geographic expanses of rain at relatively gentle rates are common in this season. Sources for most summer moisture are storms developing in the Gulf of Mexico. Thunderstorms of restricted size and rapid delivery are typical, but may be followed by several hours of gentler rain (Turnage and Mallory 1941). In spite of the areally extensive nature of winter frontal systems, summer rainfall is less variable in total amount and exhibits a more seasonally predictable onset (McDonald 1956).

For Hohokam farmers lacking opportunities for riverine irrigation, summer rainfall was a particularly pivotal factor in annual crop production. Summer rainfall is also a significant source of soil moisture for irrigated crops. Higher amounts decrease the need for supplemental water or, conversely, raise the potential for successful harvests with minimal irrigation. Abundance and predictability of summer rains were critical for irrigators along many watercourses other than the Salt and Gila, since high and sustained flows occur as a result of precipitation in these months.

All along the western border of the Hohokam territory, precipitation in the summer months of July, August, and September (Sellers et al. 1985) is less than 4 in (100 mm). This amount also is not exceeded in a more central area about the Phoenix Basin and extending to Wickenburg and Bartlett Dam on the north, beyond Florence on the east, and as far south as Red Rock. In most of the Phoenix Basin, summer rainfall is below 2.5 in (60 mm), increasing to about 3.5 in (90 mm) in the vicinity of Florence. To the south and east, the middle Santa Cruz and San Pedro valleys receive 6 to 7 in (150 to 175 mm) of rain in the summer. These higher quantities extend across the Tucson Basin and to the west beyond Fresnal (6.5 in or 165 mm) on the Tohono O'odham Reservation.

Advantages of predictable onset and quantity were greater for Hohokam cultivators in the areas of higher summer rainfall, since coefficients of seasonal variation generally decrease as precipitation totals increase. In the Tucson area, coefficients of variation (Raymond Turner, 1989 personal communication of unpublished data) for June through August precipitation are near .40. Values increase to near .60 at Florence and Casa Grande, and exceed .70 in the central Phoenix Basin. High values continue north of Phoenix as far as Wickenburg and Bartlett Dam before decreasing. In the vicinity of Sells in recent times, summer storm runoff events of 1 in (25 mm) or more rainfall allow floodwater production. Runoff initiation events of sufficient magnitude failed to occur in some years between 1941 and 1973, suggesting that this cultivation technique would not be successful every year (Nabhan 1983).

Rapid rainfall and runoff during summer cloudbursts, their spotty distribution across the landscape, and most frequent occurrence from afternoon until midnight (Turnage and Mallory 1941) would have allowed Hohokam cultivators little opportunity to reach distant fields for diversion and distribution of water. Manipulations to avoid water loss must be accomplished quickly. For example, nighttime torchlit irrigation by the O'odham reduced wastage of temporary streamflow following summer storms. Overabundances in fields must be dispersed equally rapidly to prevent washouts and damage to growing crops. Protective constructions serve these purposes, but the timely presence of farmers for adjustment would be most critical where summer rainfall was a central factor in annual food production. The benefits of field proximity may have particularly encouraged dispersed patterns of settlement among the Hohokam in areas not served by the Salt and Gila canals.

Local effects in some cases exert substantial influence on the expression of climatic factors. Mountains usually create higher rainfall on the adjacent windward basin and a rain shadow of reduced precipitation on the adjacent leeward basin. Low desert mountains of small mass may have little effect in this regard, while ones of greater bulk and height have a pronounced influence.

On the broad, low, and hottest valley floors, cold temperatures present minimal restriction of growing season. Major expanses with little yearly frost in the Salt and Gila valleys coincide with peak river flow in the early months of the year and extended availability of water. Spring peaks also characterize tributaries originating along the Mogollon Rim. Elsewhere in Hohokam territory, conflict in the scheduling of spring crops would have arisen between the need to plant sufficiently early in the year to benefit from winter rains, and the need to avoid desiccation of maturing crops during the late spring-early summer drought. Since both a greater proportion of annual rainfall and high flow occur in these areas during summer, spring crops would have been limited to particularly favored locales. Situations advantageous to early crops would be found in the best-watered fields at higher elevations on the basin edge, above levels of cold air inversion on the valley floor (S. Fish et al. 1984).

## VEGETATION AND HABITAT COMPLEXITY: FUNCTIONAL VARIATION IN THE SONORAN DESERT

The Sonoran Desert includes almost 120,000 sq mi (310,000 sq km) of desertscrub and enclaves of upland vegetation types within Arizona, Sonora, southeastern California, and Baja California (McGinnies 1981:41). Within the Hohokam range in Arizona (Fig. 2.1), two vegetational subdivisions of the Sonoran Desert biome predominate: the Arizona Upland on the northeast edge, and the western-lying Lower Colorado Valley (Turner and Brown 1982). At the extreme east of the Hohokam range in the San Pedro drainage, the Sonoran Desert interdigitates with depauperate elements of the Chihuahuan Desert to form a "generic desert" of creosote (*Larrea*), mesquite (*Prosopis*), acacias (*Acacia*), and yuccas (*Yucca*), while lacking saguaros (*Carnegiea gigantea*). At slightly higher elevations (above 3,500 ft/1,200 m), semidesert grassland, interior chaparral or madrean, and evergreen woodlands are encountered, all but the latter within 60 mi (100 km) of any place within Hohokam country. Within a 120 mi (200 km) reach can be found Rocky Mountain subalpine conifer forest above 6,000 ft (1,900 m), a vegetation formation that the Hohokam may have drawn upon to obtain the long coniferous vigas at Casa Grande (Wilcox and Shenk 1977) and elsewhere.

Although wetland and riparian areas make up far less than 0.1 percent of the Sonoran Desert lands today, oasis marshes and riparian forests (bosques) contributed disproportionately to habitat complexity and overall diversity of available plant species. This is illustrated by a recent riparian classification (Asplund et al. 1988) of great utility in assessing habitat heterogeneity along watercourses. The resource richness of these zones for human hunting and gathering cannot be underestimated.

Archaeological correlations with habitat heterogeneity frequently suffer from inappropriate comparisons of communities or series with higher order units (biomes, formations) as if they were equivalent entities. When habitat heterogeneity is assessed, as by the proximity of physiognomic vegetation formations (desert, grassland, woodland, forest) along an elevational or latitudinal gradient, comparison of elements within the same level of a classification hierarchy is important for consistency. Within Sonoran Desert thornscrub, at least four mappable communities can be located in Arizona's Lower Colorado Subdivision, and three within the Arizona Upland Subdivision. These communities or series (Lowe and Brown 1982) are the vegetation units with which archaeological variation can and should be correlated. A brief description of each community follows.

The paloverde-cacti mixed scrub series is the Arizona Upland subunit best known on upper bajadas in the Tucson Basin, the "classic" Sonoran Desert landscape. Structurally complex with a diversity of lifeforms, from towering saguaros to a variety of tree legumes, halfshrubs, and herbaceous annuals and root perennials, 90 percent of this series appears on bajadas and sloping plains. It is the best-watered, least desertlike series in the Arizona desertscrub formation. The jojoba-mixed shrub series is often at the Sonoran Desert's upper limits, particularly in the northeastern reaches. Although it physiognomically appears like chaparral, its species do not mix with chaparral species per se. At the northern reaches, a crucifixion thorn (*Canotia holocantha*) co-dominates with creosote at moderate elevations in the Verde, Gila, and Hassayampa valleys, but it mixes with chaparral at slightly higher elevations. Near Safford, this crucifixion thorn-creosote series also mixes with Chihuahuan elements to form generic desertscrub.

At lower elevations, particularly in the west, the creosote-bursage series forms the dominant community in the Lower Colorado Subdivision. Structurally simple, and poorer in perennial species diversity compared to the Arizona Upland, this community can nevertheless be rich in ephemeral annuals that flower, seed, and die after rains. On lowlands subject to flooding and salinization, saltbush (*Atriplex*) dominates with other compact shrubs. The saltbush series extends up the Gila River at least as far as Snaketown. Close to the Lower Colorado River itself, a creosote-big galleta grass (*Hilaria rigida*) series occurs on sandy soils. The most complex series in the Lower Colorado Subdivision is a mixed scrub series that occurs on the granitic and volcanic outlying mountains. Although little-leaf paloverde and saguaros may be rare or absent, other tree legumes, desert lavender (*Hyptis*), tree *Nolinas*, *Agave*, and jojoba may be present. This vegetation series is present near waterholes and ruins in the Tinajas Altas.

Along a gradient of increasing aridity in the Sonoran Desert, ephemerals make up a larger percentage of the total flora, as perennials decrease in diversity. Wildlife densities and diversity also decrease on this gradient (Vander Wall and MacMahan 1984). However, many of the ephemerals produce energy-rich seeds (Felger and Nabhan 1976), which were important food sources, and the shrubs are well endowed with secondary compounds (terpenes, etc.) of medicinal value.

To understand the full complement of environmental variability with which the Hohokam dealt prehistorically, it must be noted that at times they drew upon areas outside the Sonoran Desert proper for their sources of raw materials, foods, and refined products. Guayule (*Parthenium argentatum*) and perhaps even peyote (*Lophophora williamsii*) have been historically and/or pre-historically traded into this region. Ethnographically, chiltepines (*Capsicum annum*), wild beans (*Phaseolus* spp.), and bellotas (*Quercus emoryi*) have been traded in or sought in higher elevations, mostly to the south of Hohokam territory.

Exogenous resources may have been used by the Hohokam occasionally to buffer themselves from seasonal failures in desert plant production. Higher elevation resources within Hohokam territory also may have served this purpose in addition to providing dietary variety. Without animal transport, however, acquisition in bulk of both exogenous and high elevation resources would have been more difficult, probably less regular than in historic times, and likely restricted to high-value items such as materials for medicinal, psychotropic, or ceremonial use. The strength of the primary orientation in Hohokam subsistence toward basin interiors and the low slopes of bordering mountains is attested by the infrequent archaeological recovery of extraneous biotic remains and by low quantities in those instances when they are present (Gasser 1981). In a geographically diversified compilation of 1,963 flotation samples (Miksicek, in preparation), a significant record of resources unobtainable in these settings was present only among remains from the Santa Rita Mountains, at atypically high elevations on the edge of Hohokam territory.

## DISTRIBUTION OF WILD PLANT RESOURCES

Compared to the Chihuahuan Desert and the northern tropics of Mexico, the Sonoran Desert has a higher ratio of food plants to medicinal plants in its flora (Nabhan 1988). Perhaps one ecological explanation for this is that the Sonoran Desert's high percentage of ephemeralized annual plants (many of them winter-blooming) generally lack bitter or toxic secondary compounds to protect them from insect and vertebrate predators. Because they mature and set seed so rapidly, they escape much of the predation with which longer lived plants must contend. In the tropics and the Chihuahuan Desert, plants with terpenes and alkaloids as feeding deterrents make up a higher percentage of their respective floras; even in the Sonoran Desert, such plants are the typical sources of medicine.

Within the Sonoran Desert region north of Mexico, there are more than 250 native plant species that have served as food for Native Americans, according to ethnographic documentation summarized by Hodgson (1982, in press). It is remarkable to many observers that even in the hottest, driest portions of the Sonoran Desert (e.g., Tiburon Island, the Pinacate), edible calories or available food energy was not so much a limiting factor as potable water. Desert ephemerals have extremely high ratios of reproductive to vegetative biomass; in other words, they efficiently translocate much of their productivity into nontoxic, energy-rich seeds (Felger and Nabhan 1976).

Not surprisingly then, the seeds of desert plants are the most frequently documented plant product used as food ethnohistorically. More than 100 species in the northern Sonoran Desert produce edible and harvestable seeds (including grass caryopses or "grains"); more than 50 species produce flesh fruit; and more than 75 species produce leaves, used primarily when immature (Hodgson, in press). Roots, rhizomes, flower stalks, flowers, flower buds, and stem exudes were also used as food by native cultures of the Sonoran Desert in prehistoric and historic times.

Although the ethnographically documented plants of the region constitute an inventory far larger than the number of species found to date within contexts of use in Hohokam sites, such an inventory can be considered as a baseline of potential resources accessible to the Hohokam. Why they may have failed to use plants amply utilized by the O'odham or by Yuman cultures, or vice-versa, constitutes an interesting question with regard to archaeological recovery, and cultural continuity and change. Rea (1981a) has used contrasts of culture-specific foods and tabooed plants to test in a preliminary way hypotheses regarding a Piman (O'odham) versus Yuman continuum with the Hohokam. Most foods attributed to the Hohokam are also eaten by both Piman and Yuman speakers today, and the number of exceptions encountered to date are in no way definitive.

Aside from cultural differences in plant utilization, there is geographic variation in the distribution of potential resources within Hohokam country. Figures 2.4, 2.5, and 2.6 show distributions of saguaro, mesquite, and palo-verde and the more restricted occurrence of agave and yucca at higher elevations. Three trends emerge from overall patterns for major Hohokam resources: (1) the majority of these resource plants are most densely and continuously distributed along riparian corridors; (2) to the southwest and with decreasing rainfall, increasing temperature, and increasing unpredictability of precipitation, the major resource plants become more patchy in distribution and less available overall; and (3) to the northeast, the Mogollon Rim and other uplands most abruptly limit the distribution of these resource plants. Thus greater similarity would be expected between the subsistence of the Hohokam and desert dwellers to the south and west, than with those above the Mogollon Rim.

## MODIFIED LANDSCAPES AND
## THEIR RESOURCES

In the introduction to this chapter, the role of the Hohokam as farmer-gatherers in anthropogenic vegetation was emphasized. In large part, insight regarding this behavior derives from ethnographic studies of plant use by

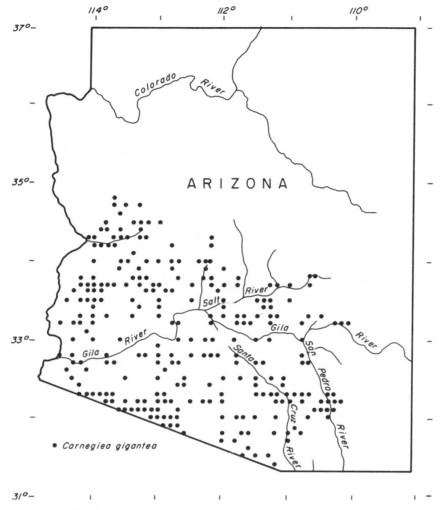

Figure 2.4    *Distribution of saguaro in southern Arizona.*

groups who intensively harvest wild plants (as well as crops) in field, ditch, hedgerow, abandoned field, and dooryard garden microhabitats (Rea 1981b, 1983; Crosswhite 1981; Nabhan et al. 1983). However, none of these plants concentrated in anthropogenic contexts is found exclusively in Native American fields; they are also common where natural disturbance occurs along watercourses or on valley plains.

Current distributions of utilized species are not sufficient indicators of prehistoric availability if the Hohokam capacity is acknowledged for transporting, transplanting, irrigating, burning, or otherwise managing wild plants for their desirable products. While the presence of particular weedy or semi-cultivated species in the archaeobotanical record is not definitive evidence for origin in anthropogenic communities, patterns of quantitative contrast and

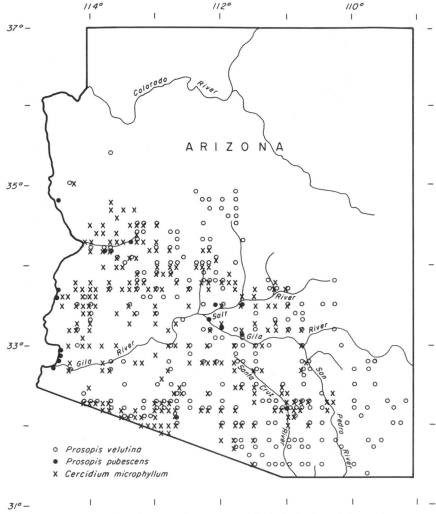

Figure 2.5    *Distributions of mesquite and little-leaf paloverde in southern*
             *Arizona.*

of contextual correspondence have been increasingly identified in recent studies. These provide the basis for reconstructing environmental alterations that may have included both intentional manipulation and unintentional enhancement of species other than cultigens.

The nature and degree of Hohokam modification of natural landscapes would have varied according to local environmental attributes and cultural practice. Agricultural activity was likely a primary factor in the most far-reaching modifications, and would have produced a wide range of effects (Bohrer 1970; Gasser 1982; Fish 1984, 1985; Miksicek 1984, 1988). Runoff farming on floodplains, locationally tied to the environs of drainages, might be expected to create the least divergence from surrounding plant communities

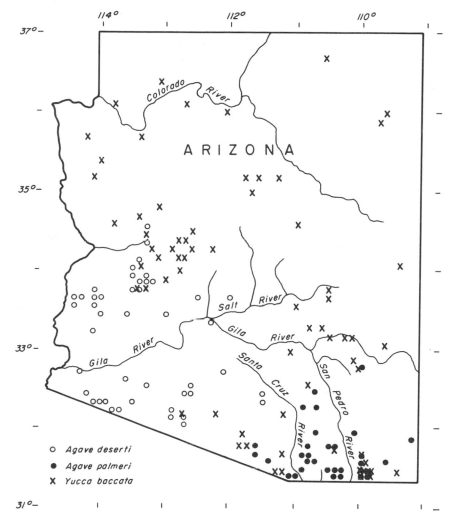

Figure 2.6    *Distributions of agave and yucca in southern Arizona.*

in naturally disturbed riparian habitats. Even in these situations, manipulation through such documented aboriginal practices as selective removal of unwanted species, reseeding and tending of utilized ones, or introduction of nonlocal taxa could have altered distributions toward advantageous ends.

Canals transporting water laterally as well as downstream for miles beyond drainage sources had the greatest potential for creating biotic conditions dissimilar to locally prevailing natural ones. Riverine canals traversed flatter portions of lower basins among xeric saltbush or creosote communities that contrasted with irrigated fields in the absence of both supplemental water and surface disturbance. Surface preparation to increase infiltration, concentration of surface runoff, and diversion of ephemeral drainages in terrace, bajada, or hillslope agricultural complexes also generated contrastive growth conditions, although augmenting moisture less than canal irrigation. Even without management, weedy plants of these latter two agricultural contexts would have differed at least in densities from adjacent uncultivated land. A role for fire in landscape alteration and management has also been suggested (Miksicek 1984; Bohrer 1971).

Pollen assemblages that differ from natural analogs in the distribution of weedy taxa, and suites of similar species in charred remains have been recognized as reflecting anthropogenic plant communities in diverse residential and agricultural provenances (e.g., Fish 1984, 1985, 1987; Bohrer 1984; Miksicek 1987, 1988; Gish 1987). The modified plant communities of prehistoric occupations have been linked to corresponding faunal distributions, particularly for those mainstays of Hohokam cuisine, the lagomorphs (Szuter 1984, 1986). Animal as well as plant resources appear to have been abundantly harvested in fields and settlement margins.

Classification of archaeobotanical remains into the exhaustive dual categories of wild plants and cultigens may provide inadequate insight into an important continuum among species and activities. Active intervention involving a variety of plants beyond those recognized as cultigens is probable in Hohokam agriculture. Proposed species include mesquite (*Prosopis*), cholla (*Opuntia* spp.), hedgehog cacti (*Echinocereus engelmannii*), wolfberry (*Lycium* spp.), hog potato (*Hoffmanseggia densiflora*), amaranth (*Amaranthus palmeri*), chenopods (*Chenopodium berlandieri, C. murale, Monolepis nutalliana, Atriplex wrightii*), little barley (*Hordeum pusillum*), tobacco (*Nicotiana trigonophylla*), and spiderling (*Boerhaavia* spp.).

Numerous combinations of happenstance and design are probably embodied in the array of noncultigens now thought to have been productively enhanced or concentrated in cultural contexts by the Hohokam. Among this group are plants such as mesquite that may have been differentially spared in field clearing, become dense in hedgerows, thrived on canal seepage, or been tended and selectively harvested in adjacent natural settings. Species such as cholla may have been transplanted to dooryard gardens or fields as a "crop," to out-of-the-way spots among habitations and fields, or employed as residential fencing. Chenopods and spiderling are representative of weedy herbaceous plants that may have received focused attention or none at all in fields and in other culturally disturbed habitats.

All species suspected of increasing in abundance in Hohokam-managed fields and vegetation could also be found in quantity in some undisturbed locales. Most exhibit no morphological characters attributable to intervention or domestication. Quantitative or qualitative variance has been examined in a few instances for amaranths (*Amaranthus hybridus*) (Miksicek, in preparation) and little barley (*Hordeum pusillum*) (Bohrer 1984; Adams 1987). However, evidence for even active cultivation as in the case of agave (Fish et al. 1985) may not be reflected in distinctive attributes of associated plant remains.

Replicable quantitative and contextual data and innovative approaches are needed to refine current understanding of this sphere of Hohokam subsistence and environment.

# WATER CONTROL FOR AGRICULTURE

Recent attempts to define the kinds of agricultural systems within arid zones, and to classify those of the Sonoran Desert accordingly (e.g., Vivian 1974; Lawton and Wilke 1979; Nabhan 1979), suffer from either ambiguous use of terms, or from noncomprehensiveness (e.g., Nabhan 1985; Rankin and Katzer, in press). Rankin and Katzer (in press) have progressed furthest in straightening out the current tangle of terms by considering four variables: (1) whether a field receives an augmented water supply over and above the precipitation that falls directly on its surface; (2) whether an area above or within a field has had surface preparation to generate more runoff or conversely to increase infiltration; (3) the geomorphic setting (alluvial fan, swale, floodplain terraces) of field location; and (4) whether a crop has had water diverted to it, or is in the direct path of natural inundation. A fifth variable is alluded to in their discussion but does not fully enter into their classification: the duration of waterflow along a stream course (perennial, intermittent, or ephemeral). In addition, Rankin and Katzer correlate field surface areas with watershed or catchment sizes, and find a positive relationship between these two variables.

## ETHNOGRAPHIC TECHNOLOGY

Because all aspects of productive technology are not preserved archaeologically, ethnographic practices amplify direct evidence for Hohokam cultivation. If a multidimensional matrix of interaction were reconstructed from the five variables in the preceding classification system, an ethnographic or prehistoric example of nearly each combination could be found within the Southwest. Perhaps the only set of variables for which a good ethnographic example is not known in the Sonoran Desert proper is that of dry farming (a nonaugmented water supply) in any of the geomorphic habitats (Nabhan 1979). Although modern farmers in the Avra Valley have been known to harvest a wheat crop by winter dry farming on normally irrigated fields, most ethnographic examples show some effort at augmenting soil moisture by diversion or surface preparation. Cooke and Reeves (1976) contend that historic Papago (Tohono O'odham) did both, by clearing vegetation to increase runoff in watershed catchment areas upstream from fields, then channelizing and diverting this augmented supply onto their annual crops.

Water control features of traditional Sonoran Desert farmers include canals, shallow ditches, rock or brush diversion weirs, rock or brush water spreaders, living cottonwood and willow fencerow silt traps, multicourse cobble terraces, and single-course alignments. The same materials may be used for different functions in different geomorphic locations; mesquite posts with interwoven brush are still used by the Tohono O'odham as diversion weirs from watercourses to fields, water spreaders at the *ak-chin* location just above fields, water spreaders in fields, and baffles just above fields.

With all runoff agricultural systems, the greater the watershed size about a field system, the greater the probability of sufficient soil moisture being provided (Hack 1942). However, social organization for water control must be sophisticated, and even on ephemeral watercourses supplying more than 200 ha of fields, the Tohono O'odham had ditch bosses coordinating irrigation crews much like those of the Pima on the Gila River (Spicer 1943). Thus, there was a gradient in sophistication of water control from ephemeral through intermittent to perennial streams, not a clear-cut separation of system sizes and functions.

## HOHOKAM AGRICULTURAL TECHNOLOGY

Agricultural technology represents a major arena of interaction between the Hohokam and their Sonoran Desert environment. Boundaries encompassing canal networks in the broad valleys of perennial rivers have long been perceived as a cultural watershed, dividing large-scale irrigators from their less fortunate contemporaries. These concepts are embodied in the terms riverine and nonriverine or desert Hohokam, with the implication that social organization as well as productive capacity was linked with the requirements of irrigation.

The dichotomy has become less sharply drawn as ongoing investigations in nonriverine areas have revealed evidence of a previously unrecognized degree of cultural elaboration (e.g., Wilcox and Sternberg 1983; Gregory 1987; Fish et al. 1989; Rice 1987; Wilcox and Ciolek-Torrello, 1988). Similarly, research has confirmed the presence of substantial canals on larger intermittent watercourses (Bernard-Shaw 1988; Kinkade and Fritz 1975; Scantling 1940), and documented cases of multimile systems as on the Santa Cruz (Fish et al. 1989), New River (Doyel 1984), and Queen Creek (Dart 1983).

Technical understanding of Hohokam irrigation has been refined for the large networks of the Salt and Gila. To basic knowledge of the systems (e.g., Woodbury 1960, 1961; Haury 1976; Midvale 1965, 1968; Masse 1981; Herskovits 1981) has been added a new wealth of detail. System outliers from pre-urban maps have been augmented by aerial photographs, documentary study, and correlation with archaeological settlement pattern (e.g., Upham and Rice 1980; Crown 1987; Masse 1987; Howard 1987; Nicholas and Neitzel 1984; Cable and Mitchell 1988).

Two recent analyses (Ackerly et al. 1987; Nials et al. 1989) of overall system capacity in the Phoenix Basin concur in a total for irrigated acreage, downscaled from some previous estimates, to a range between 30,000 and 60,000 acres (12,100 to 24,200 ha). Multiple excavated examples of canal interruption, abandonment, and rebuilding have increased appreciation of the dynamic nature of these systems and cautioned against assumptions for contemporary use of all detectable segments, a point strongly made by Ackerly et al. (1987). Knowledge is rapidly accumulating concerning environmental correlates of canal construction, engineering attributes, and ancillary structures such as headgates, settling ponds, and canal junctures (e.g., Nials and Fish 1988; Ackerly et al. 1987; Masse 1987; Dart 1986). Knowledge of irrigation systems should be dramatically extended by a number of ongoing excavation projects in the Phoenix area.

Appreciation is emerging for the role of nonriverine farming in the total pattern of Hohokam production. Runoff technologies across widely diverse topography, reported formerly in anecdotal fashion, are now being studied as segments of larger subsistence systems and in relation to other aspects of settlement pattern (e.g., Crown 1987; Doyel 1984; Fish et al. 1985; Spoerl and Gumerman 1984; Rankin and Katzer, in press). Fine-grained study of technological detail and systematic recording of component or system extent provide a basis for estimating such parameters as acreage, labor, and yield (Fish et al. 1985; Fish et al. 1989; Crown 1987; Doyel 1984). Recognition of environmental variables affecting cultivation has clarified productive opportunities, limitations, and Hohokam strategies in these areas (e.g., Field 1985; Waters and Field 1986; Fish et al. 1985; Wilson 1985; Rankin and Katzer, in press).

Regional orientations and systematic recording or compilation of settlement reveal integrated subsistence activities spanning environmental diversity. A zonal concept of settlement and landscape organization with sociopolitical implications has been described for inclusive systems in nonriverine regions (Fish et al. 1989; Rice 1987; Doyel 1984) and along the Gila River (Crown 1987). Agricultural technologies, crops, and natural resources varying with environmental gradients, particularly across basin profiles, appear to have functioned as components of broadly based subsistence and settlement units rather than as independent and localized entities. Zonal organization entails an appreciable degree of intrabasin productive differentiation, exchange, and integrative interaction. Such organization appears as central to the cohesion of nonriverine multisite communities, as canal networks are to their riverine counterparts on the Salt and Gila.

It is becoming increasingly clear that the maximum variety of agricultural technologies and settings were utilized in prehistoric times. Reduction during the historic period is likely the result of population loss and rearrangement, alternative economic pursuits, and the absence of farmers in regions and zones of archaeological occupation, particularly upland locales. Adequate analogs are lacking for agricultural complexes on bajadas, hillslopes, and smaller drainages that combine terraces, rock piles, checkdams, and diversions. The greatest density and variety of features has been encountered in areas of higher potential for such rainfall-dependent technologies. Although influenced by intensity of archaeological investigation, distributions tend to correlate with increasing summer and annual precipitation to the north, east, and south of the Phoenix Basin.

At present, chronological trends in subsistence and technology cannot be analyzed against independent sequences of comprehensive, long-term environmental evidence derived within the boundaries of Hohokam territory. Dendrochronologically sensitive timbers are irregularly incorporated in Hohokam dwellings, pollen distributions are strongly shaped by herbaceous types responsive to cultural habitats, and other plant remains in sites have passed through a cultural filter. Trajectories of change initiated by post-contact forces illuminate process dynamics of change (e.g., Hastings and Turner 1965; Dobyns 1981; Rea 1983; Cooke and Reeves 1976), but cannot characterize sequential environmental patterns over archaeological time.

Recent studies spanning substantial intervals represent encouraging exceptions to the paucity of systematic prehistoric data. Settlement patterns in adjacent portions of the riverine environment have been tied to change over time in channel morphology and hydrological characteristics of the Santa Cruz (Waters 1988). In a major contribution, Graybill (1985, Graybill and Nials 1989) has analyzed relevant dendrochronological information from the Salt River watershed and established a link between conditions in these areas and streamflow in the Phoenix Basin. An absolute chronology of streamflow, influencing irrigation and flooding potential, provides a temporal resolution unavailable with other techniques and spans much of Hohokam occupation. Studies of geological evidence for flooding in the Phoenix area concur in the general timing of major events and add detail to local extent (Ely and Baker 1985, 1988).

## ETHNOGRAPHIC ANALOGY AND HOHOKAM ENVIRONMENTAL RELATIONSHIPS

Interactive connections between environmental variables and archaeological remains cannot always be bridged by reference to ethnographic analogy. In cases lacking historic parallels, interpretation must be generated largely from patterning in these two classes of evidence. Divergence between ethnographic and prehistoric expressions is commonly acknowledged for the largest irrigation networks. Recognition of the magnitude and diversity of runoff agriculture and its importance in regional economies has been delayed by a lack of adequate analogs for pertinent methods of cultivation and associated features. Conversely, the opportunity to actively learn from ethnographic practice is far from exhausted as indicated by a number of recent studies (e.g., Greenhouse et al. 1981; Doelle 1976; Nabhan et al. 1983; Doolittle

1987; Rea 1983; Felger and Moser 1985). Many earlier historic documents also await research.

Hohokam use of agave illustrates the need for interpretive elaboration beyond immediate analogy. Many records for the O'odham describe acquisition through the harvesting of wild stands. This mode was commonly assumed to account for Hohokam remains, although agave had been recovered in Hohokam roasting pits at a distance from natural populations (Haury 1945:39; Fewkes 1912; Hayden 1957:103) and is widely cultivated in Mexico. Culturally affected distributions and suggestions concerning cultivation were advanced by Gentry (1972, 1982), Ford (1981), Minnis and Plog (1976), and Crosswhite (1981). Distributions of plant parts supporting an inference of cultivation, and agricultural features in conjunction with agave remains were subsequently noted (Miksicek 1984; Gasser and Miksicek 1985; P. Fish et al. 1984). Conclusive evidence for production rather than gathering was established by the replicable association between agricultural features and plant remains, processing facilities, and appropriate artifactual assemblages (Fish et al. 1985). The identity of a cultivated species, *Agave murpheyi*, and possibly additional ones, has been greatly strengthened by discovery of relict populations among agricultural features in the Tonto and New River basins (G. R. Delamater, 1989, personal communication).

A second example of the need for caution in resorting to literal analogy is illustrated by the relationship of Tohono O'odham settlement to potable water. In the post–1850 period of most extensive recording, annual movement between two settlements was a dominant pattern. Residence at villages with *ak-chin* fields near valley bottoms could be sustained only for the duration of potable water in reservoirs following summer rains. Water was also a limiting factor on group size at settlements; Underhill (1939:58–59) notes that development of sustained water sources decreased annual movement. At the time of ethnographic observation and for many years previously, the Tohono O'odham had possessed cattle and horses. A population of approximately 5,000 persons was estimated to own 20,000 cattle (Underhill 1939:29), also requiring water. Comparison of consumption for cattle and people in summer (Adolph 1947; McKee and Wolf 1963; Tom Wegner, 1989 personal communication) reveals that total water requirements were multiplied by a factor of 45 or more in order to support both cattle and people. Thus, the relationship between O'odham settlement and water may diverge significantly from that of the Hohokam in similar environments, with concomitant differences in strategies for agriculture and wild resource procurement.

## HOHOKAM ENVIRONMENT IN SUMMARY

The Sonoran Desert occupied by the Hohokam is one of the truly rich areas for the gatherer in North America in terms of multiseason abundance, diversity, and storability of plant foods. Bimodal rainfall in southern Arizona supports a distinctive array of productive arboreal and succulent perennials in addition to a wide variety of seedy annuals. Linear valleys create elevational diversity within transverse distances. Most resources could have been acquired on a routine basis from settlements near long-term water at river or mountain edge. Diminished desert arboreals in drier central and western regions are countered in the Phoenix Basin and further downstream along the Gila by concentrated resources in riparian borders of perennial rivers.

The Hohokam created further diversity in the anthropogenic plant communities surrounding their settlements. The degree of management toward desired configurations of wild plants is currently under investigation. However, it appears that the culturally modified landscape furnished a significant increment of gathered species as well as small game.

Two major divisions in Hohokam agricultural orientation have long been recognized. Irrigators from perennial rivers had access to a more extended regime of agricultural water than did farmers with irrigated and nonirrigated fields dependent on seasonal rainfall. Topographic and streamflow prerequisites for large-scale riverine irrigation coincided with lower precipitation along desert reaches of the Salt and Gila. In surrounding areas to the north, south, and east, higher summer and annual rainfall created a distinct advantage for alternative technologies that also supported a Hohokam lifestyle. Documentation of the variety and productivity of agricultural complexes away from the major rivers has increased rapidly in recent years. These modes of cultivation can now be seen as parts of larger subsistence systems, integrating production across diverse environments.

## ACKNOWLEDGMENTS

We gratefully acknowledge Raymond M. Turner of the United States Geological Survey for shared data and insights on the Sonoran Desert.

## REFERENCES CITED

Ackerly, Neal, Jerry B. Howard, and Randall H. McGuire
    1987    *La Ciudad Canals: A Study of Hohokam Irrigation Systems at the Community Level*. Arizona State University Anthropological Field Studies 17.
Adams, Karen
    1987    Little Barley (*Hordeum pusillum* Nutt.) as a Possible New Wild Domesticate. In *Specialized Studies in the Economy, Environment, and Culture of La Ciudad,*

edited by J. Kisselburg, Glen Rice, and B. Shears, pp. 203–238. Arizona State University Anthropological Field Studies 20.

Asplund, K., F. Baucom, W. Bayham, T. Cordery, D. Haywood, W. Hinter, A. Laurenzi, K. Reichhardt, and R. Szaro
1988    *Riparian Classification for Arizona.* Arizona Riparian Council, Riparian Classification Inventory Committee, Phoenix.

Adolph, E. F.
1947    *Physiology of Man in the Desert.* Interscience Publishers, Inc., New York.

Bernard-Shaw, Mary
1988    Hohokam Canal Systems and Late Archaic Wells: The Evidence from the Los Morteros Site. In *Recent Research on Tucson Basin Prehistory: Proceedings of the Second Tucson Basin Conference,* edited by W. Doelle and P. Fish, pp. 153–174. Institute for American Research Anthropological Papers 10.

Betancourt, Julio and Raymond Turner
1988    Historic Arroyo-Cutting and Subsequent Channel Changes at the Congress Street Crossing, Santa Cruz River, Tucson, Arizona. *Arid Lands: Today and Tomorrow,* edited by E. Whitehead, C. Hutchinson, B. Timmerman, and Robert Varady, pp. 1353–1372. Westview Press, Boulder.

Bohrer, Vorsila L.
1970    Ethnobotanical Aspects of Snaketown, A Hohokam Village in Southern Arizona. *American Antiquity* 35:413–430.
1971    Paleoecology of Snaketown. *The Kiva* 36:11–19.
1984    Domesticated and Wild Crops in the CAEP Study Area. In *Prehistoric Cultural Development in Central Arizona: Archaeology of the Upper New River Region,* edited by P. Spoerl and G. Gumerman, pp. 183–259. Southern Illinois University Center for Anthropological Investigations Occasional Paper 5.

Cable, John, and Douglas Mitchell
1988    La Lomita Pequeña in Regional Perspective. In *Excavations at La Lomita Pequeña: A Santa Cruz/Sacaton Phase Hamlet in the Salt River Valley,* edited by Douglas Mitchell, pp. 395–446. Soil Systems Publications in Archaeology 10.

Castetter, Edward F., and Willis H. Bell
1942    *Pima and Papago Indian Agriculture.* University of New Mexico Inter American Studies 1.

Cooke, Ronald U., and Richard W. Reeves
1976    *Arroyos and Environmental Change.* Oxford Research Studies in Geography. Clarendon Press, Oxford.

Crosswhite, Frank
1981    Desert Plants, Habitat and Agriculture in Relation to the Major Pattern of Cultural Differentiation in the O'odham People of Southern Arizona. *Desert Plants* 3:47–76.

Crown, Patricia
1987    Classic Period Hohokam Settlement and Land Use in the Casa Grande Ruins Area, Arizona. *Journal of Field Archaeology* 14:147–162.

Dart, Allen
1983    Prehistoric Agricultural and Water Control Systems along the Salt-Gila Aqueduct. In *Hohokam Archaeology along the Salt-Gila Aqueduct, Central Arizona Project,* vol. 3, Specialized Activity Sites, edited by L. Teague and P. Crown, pp. 345–573. Arizona State Museum Archaeological Series 150.

1986      Sediment Accumulation along Hohokam Canals. *The Kiva* 51:63–84.
Dobyns, Henry
1981      *From Fire to Flood: Historic Human Destruction of Sonoran Desert Riverine Oases.*
          Ballena Press, Socorro.
Doelle, William
1976      *Desert Resources and Hohokam Subsistence: The Conoco Florence Project.* Arizona
          State Museum Archaeological Series 103.
Doolittle, William
1987      *Pre-Hispanic Occupance in the Valley of Sonora, Mexico: Archaeological Confir-
          mation of Early Spanish Reports.* Anthropological Papers of the University of
          Arizona 48.
Doyel, David
1984      Sedentary Period Hohokam Paleo-Economy in the New River Drainage,
          Central Arizona. In *Prehistoric Agricultural Strategies in the Southwest,* edited
          by S. Fish and P. Fish, pp. 35–52. Arizona State University Anthropological
          Research Papers 33.
Ely, Lisa, and Victor Baker
1985      Reconstructing Paleoflood Hydrology with Slackwater Deposits: Verde River,
          Arizona. *Physical Geography* 6:103–126.
Ely, Lisa, J. E. O'Connor, V. R. Baker
1988      Paleoflood Hydrology of the Salt and Verde Rivers. In *Friends of the Pleis-
          tocene, Rocky Mountain Cell, Fall Fieldtrip Guidebook,* assembled by L. An-
          derson and L. Piety. Arizona State University, Tempe.
Felger, Richard and Mary Moser
1985      *People of the Desert and Sea: Ethnobotany of the Seri Indians.* University of
          Arizona Press, Tucson.
Felger, Richard and Gary Nabhan
1976      Deceptive Barrenness. *Ceres/FAO Journal* 9:34–39.
Fenneman, Nevin
1931      *Physiography of the Western United States.* McGraw-Hill, New York.
Fewkes, Jesse Walter
1912      Casa Grande, Arizona. *28th Annual Report of the Bureau of Ethnology, 1906–
          1907.* Washington, D.C.
Field, John
1985      *Depositional Facies and Hohokam Settlement Patterns on Holocene Alluvial Fans,
          Northern Tucson Basin.* M.S. thesis, Department of Geosciences, University
          of Arizona, Tucson.
Fish, Suzanne K.
1984      The Modified Environment of the Salt-Gila Aqueduct Project Sites: A Paly-
          nological Perspective. In *Hohokam Archaeology along the Salt-Gila Aqueduct,
          Central Arizona Project,* vol. 7: Environment and Subsistence, edited by L.
          Teague and P. Crown, pp. 39–52. Arizona State Museum Archaeological
          Series 150.
1985      Prehistoric Disturbance Floras of the Lower Sonoran Desert and Their
          Implications. In *Late Quaternary Vegetation and Climates of the American South-
          west,* edited by B. Jacobs, P. Fall, and O. Davis, pp. 77–88. American
          Association of Stratigraphic Palynologists Contribution 16.
1987      Marana Sites Pollen Analysis. In *Studies in the Hohokam Community of Mar-
          ana,* edited by Glen Rice, pp. 161–170. Arizona State University Anthro-
          pological Field Studies 15.

Fish, Suzanne K., Paul R. Fish, and Christian Downum
1984    Hohokam Terraces and Agricultural Production in the Tucson Basin. In *Prehistoric Agriculture Strategies in the Southwest*, edited by S. K. Fish and P. R. Fish, pp. 55–71. Arizona State University Anthropological Research Papers 33.
Fish, Suzanne K., Paul R. Fish, and John Madsen
1985    A Preliminary Analysis of Hohokam Settlement and Agriculture in the Northern Tucson Basin. In *Proceedings of the 1983 Hohokam Symposium*, edited by A. E. Dittert and D. E. Dove, pp. 75–100. Arizona Archaeological Society Occasional Paper 2.
1989    Classic Period Hohokam Community Integration in the Tucson Basin. In *The Sociopolitical Structure of Prehistoric Southwestern Societies*, edited by S. Upham, K. Lightfoot, and R. Jewett, pp. 237–268. Westview Press, Boulder.
1990    Sedentism and Settlement Mobility Prior to A.D. 1000 in the Tucson Basin. In *Proceedings of the Southwest Symposium*, edited by Paul Minnis and Charles Redman. Westview Press, Denver.
Fish, Suzanne K., Paul R. Fish, Charles Miksicek, and John Madsen
1985    Prehistoric Agave Cultivation in Southern Arizona. *Desert Plants* 7:107–112.
Ford, Richard I.
1981    Gardening and Farming before A.D. 1000: Patterns of Prehistoric Cultivation North of Mexico. *Journal of Ethnobiology* 1:6–27.
Gasser, Robert
1981    The Plant Remains from the Escalante Ruin Group. In *Late Hohokam Prehistory in Southern Arizona*, by David E. Doyel. Gila Press Contributions to Archaeology 2.
1982    Hohokam Use of Desert Food Plants. *Desert Plants* 2:216–235.
Gasser, Robert and Charles Miksicek
1985    The Specialists: A Reappraisal of Hohokam Exchange and the Archaeobotanical Record. In *Proceedings of the 1983 Hohokam Symposium*, edited by A. E. Dittert and D. E. Dove, pp. 483–498. Arizona Archaeological Society Occasional Paper 2.
Gentry, Howard S.
1972    *The Agave Family in Sonora*. U.S. Department of Agriculture Handbook 399.
1982    *Agaves of Continental North America*. University of Arizona Press, Tucson.
Gish, Jannifer
1987    Structured Diversity on the Resource Base of a Hohokam Village: The Pollen Evidence from La Ciudad. In *La Ciudad: Specialized Studies in Economy, Environment, and Culture of La Ciudad*, edited by V. Kisselburg, G. Rice, and B. Shears, pp. 1–67. Arizona State University Anthropological Field Studies 20.
Graybill, Donald A.
1985    Paleoclimate of the Hohokam Area: Problems and Prospects. In *Proceedings of the 1983 Hohokam Symposium*, edited by A. Dittert and D. Dove, pp. 29–44. Arizona Archaeological Society Occasional Paper 2.
Graybill, Donald A., and Fred L. Nials
1989    Aspects of Climate, Streamflow, and Geomorphology Affecting Irrigation Systems in the Salt River Valley. In *The 1982–1984 Excavations at Las Colinas: Environment and Subsistence*, edited by C. A. Heathington and D. A. Gregory, pp. 39–58. Arizona State Museum Archaeological Series 162.

Greenhouse, Ruth, R. Gasser, and J. Gish
    1981        Cholla Bud Roasting Pits: An Ethnoarchaeological Example. *The Kiva* 46:227–
                242.
Gregory, David
    1987        The Morphology of Platform Mounds and the Structure of Classic Period
                Hohokam Sites. In *The Hohokam Village: Site Structure and Organization,*
                edited by David Doyel, pp. 183–210. Southwestern and Rocky Mountain
                Division of the American Association for the Advancement of Science,
                Glenwood.
Hack, John T.
    1942        *The Changing Physical Environment of the Hopi Indians of Arizona, Reports of
                the Awatovi Expedition I.* Papers of the Peabody Museum of American Ar-
                chaeology and Ethnology 35.
Hastings, James R., and Raymond M. Turner
    1965        *The Changing Mile: An Ecological Study of Vegetation Change with Time in the
                Lower Mile of an Arid and Semiarid Region.* University of Arizona Press,
                Tucson.
Haury, Emil
    1945        *The Excavation of Los Muertos and Neighboring Ruins in the Salt River Valley,
                Southern Arizona.* Papers of the Peabody Museum of American Archaeology
                and Ethnology 24.
    1976        *The Hohokam: Desert Farmers and Craftsmen.* University of Arizona Press,
                Tucson.
Hayden, Julian
    1957        *Excavations, 1940, at University Indian Ruin.* Southwestern Monuments As-
                sociation Technical Series 5.
    1967        A Summary Prehistory and History of the Sierra Pinacate, Sonora, Mexico.
                *American Antiquity* 41:274–289.
Hendrickson, Dean A., and W. L. Minckley
    1984        Cienegas: Vanishing Climax Communities of the American Southwest.
                *Desert Plants* 6:131–175.
Herskovitz, Robert M.
    1981        AZ U:9:46—A Dual Component Hohokam Site in Tempe, Arizona. *The Kiva*
                47:1–98.
Hodgson, Wendy C.
    1982        *Edible Native and Naturalized Plants of the Sonoran Desert North of Mexico.*
                M.S. thesis, Arizona State University, Tempe. University Microfilms, Ann
                Arbor.
    In Press    *Some of My Best Friends Are Edible Plants: Food Plants of the Sonoran Desert.*
                University of Arizona Press, Tucson.
Howard, Jerry B.
    1987        The Lehi Canal System: Organization of Classic Period Community. In *The
                Hohokam Village: Site Structure and Organization,* edited by David Doyel, pp.
                211–222. Southwestern and Rocky Mountain Division of the American
                Association for the Advancement of Science, Glenwood Springs, Colorado.
Huckell, Bruce
    1988        Late Archaic Archaeology of the Tucson Basin: A Status Report. In *Recent
                Research on Tucson Basin Prehistory: Proceedings of the Second Tucson Basin*

     *Conference,* edited by William Doelle and Paul Fish, pp. 57–80. Institute for
     American Research Anthropological Paper 10.
Kinkade, Gay M., and Gordon Fritz
  1975    *The Tucson Sewage Project: Studies of Two Archaeological Sites in the Tucson
       Basin.* Arizona State Museum Archaeological Series 64.
Lawton, H., and P. Wilke
  1979    Ancient Agricultural Systems in Dry Regions. In *Agriculture in Semi-Arid
       Environments,* edited by A. Hill, G. Cannell, and H. Lawton. Springer-
       Verlag, New York.
Lee, Willis T.
  1905    *Underground Waters of the Salt River Valley, Arizona.* U.S. Geological Survey
       Professional Paper 252.
Lowe, Charles, and David Brown
  1982    Introduction. *Desert Plants* 4:17–24.
McDonald, James E.
  1956    *Variability of Precipitation in an Arid Region: A Survey of Characteristics for
       Arizona.* University of Arizona Institute of Atmospheric Physics Technical
       Report 1.
McGinnies, William
  1981    *Discovering the Desert: Legacy of the Carnegie Desert Botanical Laboratory.* Uni-
       versity of Arizona Press, Tucson.
McKee, Jack E., and H. Wolf
  1963    *Water Quality Criteria.* U.S. Department of Health, Education, and Welfare,
       Division of Water Supply and Pollution Control, Sacramento.
Masse, W. Bruce
  1981    Prehistoric Irrigation Systems in the Salt River Valley, Arizona. *Science*
       214:408–415.
  1987    *Archaeological Investigations of Portions of the Las Acequias–Los Muertos Irri-
       gation System.* Arizona State Museum Archaeological Series 176.
Midvale, Frank
  1965    Prehistoric Irrigation of the Casa Grande Ruins Area. *The Kiva* 30:82–86.
  1968    Prehistoric Irrigation in the Salt River Valley, Arizona. *The Kiva* 34:28–34.
Miksicek, Charles
  1984    Historic Desertification, Prehistoric Vegetation Change, and Hohokam
       Subsistence in the Salt-Gila Basin. In *Hohokam Archaeology along the Salt Gila
       Aqueduct, Central Arizona Project,* vol. 7: Environment and Subsistence, ed-
       ited by L. Teague and P. Crown, pp. 53–80. Arizona State Museum Ar-
       chaeological Series 150.
  1987    Late Sedentary–Early Classic Period Hohokam Agriculture: Plant Remains
       from the Marana Community Complex. In *Studies in the Hohokam Community
       of Marana,* edited by Glen Rice, pp. 197–216. Arizona State University
       Anthropological Field Studies 15.
  1988    Rethinking Hohokam Paleoethnobotanical Assemblages: A Progress Report
       for the Tucson Basin. In *Recent Research on Tucson Basin Prehistory: Proceedings
       of the Second Tucson Basin Conference,* edited by William Doelle and Paul
       Fish, pp. 47–56. Institute for American Research Anthropological Papers
       10.
In Prep.  *Plant Remains from the Land of the Stone Hoe: A Century of Hohokam Archaeo-
       botany.* Ph.D. dissertation. Office of Arid Land Studies, University of Ari-
       zona, Tucson.

Minnis, Paul, and Stephen Plog
   1976      A Study of the Site Specific Distribution of *Agave parryi* in East-Central
             Arizona. *The Kiva* 41:299–308.
Nabhan, Gary P.
   1979      The Ecology of Floodwater Farming in Southwestern North America. *Agro-
             Ecosystems* 5:245–255.
   1983      *Papago Fields: Arid Lands Ethnobotany and Agricultural Ecology.* Ph.D. disser-
             tation. Office of Arid Land Studies, University of Arizona, Tucson.
   1986      Ak-chin "Arroyo Mouth" and the Environmental Setting of the Papago
             Indian Fields in the Sonoran Desert. *Applied Geography* 6:61–75.
   1988      Ethnobotany of the Biosphere Reserves of the U.S./Mexico Borderlands:
             Preliminary Assessment of Trends. Paper presented at the First Conference
             on the El Cielo Biosphere Reserve, Ciudad Victoria, Tamaulipas.
Nabhan, Gary P., A. M. Rea, K. L. Reichhardt, E. Mellink, and C. F. Hutchinson
   1983      Papago Influences on Habitat and Biotic Diversity: Quitovac Oasis Eth-
             noecology. *Journal of Ethnobiology* 2:124–143.
Nials, Fred and Suzanne Fish
   1988      Canals and Related Features. *The 1982–1984 Excavations at Las Colinas: The
             Site and Its Features,* by D. Gregory, W. Deaver, S. Fish, R. Gardiner, R.
             Layhe, F. Nials, and L. Teague, pp. 275–306. Arizona State Museum Ar-
             chaeological Series 162.
Nials, Fred, David Gregory, and Donald Graybill
   1989      Salt River Streamflow and Hohokam Irrigation Systems. In *The 1982–1984
             Excavations at Las Colinas: Environment and Subsistence,* edited by C. Heath-
             ington and D. Gregory, pp. 59–78. Arizona State Museum Archaeological
             Series 162.
Nicholas, Linda, and Jill Neitzel
   1984      Canal Irrigation and Sociopolitical Organization in the Lower Salt River
             Valley: A Diachronic Analysis. In *Prehistoric Agricultural Strategies in the
             Southwest,* edited by S. Fish and P. Fish, pp. 161–178. Arizona State Uni-
             versity Anthropological Research Papers 33.
Pewe, Troy L.
   1978      Terraces of the Lower Salt River Valley in Relation to the Late Cenozoic
             History of the Phoenix Basin, Arizona. In *Guidebook to the Geology of Central
             Arizona,* edited by D. M. Burt and T. Pewe, pp. 1–46. State of Arizona
             Bureau of Geology and Mineral Technology Special Paper 23.
Rankin, A. and K. Katzer
   In Press *Agricultural Systems in the ACS Waddell Project Area.* Archaeological Con-
             sulting System Archaeological Report.
Rea, Amadeo
   1981a     Resource Utilization and Food Taboos of Sonoran Desert Peoples. *Journal
             of Ethnobiology* 1:69–83.
   1981b     The Ecology of Pima Fields. *Environment Southwest* 484:8–15.
   1983      *Once a River: Bird Life and Habitat Changes on the Middle Gila.* University of
             Arizona Press, Tucson.
Rice, Glen
   1987      The Marana Community Complex: A Twelfth Century Hohokam Chief-
             dom. In *Studies in the Hohokam Community of Marana,* edited by Glen Rice,
             pp. 249–254. Arizona State University Anthropological Field Studies 15.

Scantling, F. H.
1940    *Excavations at the Jackrabbit Ruin, Papago Indian Reservation, Arizona.* M.A. thesis, Department of Anthropology, University of Arizona, Tucson.
Sellers, William D., Richard H. Hill, and Margaret Sanderson-Rae
1985    *Arizona Climate: The First Hundred Years.* University of Arizona Press, Tucson.
Sheridan, Thomas, and Gary P. Nabhan
1978    Living with a River: Traditional Farmers of the Rio San Miguel. *The Journal of Arizona History* 19:1–17.
Smith, G. E. P.
1910    *Groundwater Supply and Irrigation in the Rillito Valley.* University of Arizona Agricultural Experiment Station Bulletin 64.
Spicer R. B.
1943    An Outline of Papago Society in the Baboquivari District. Unpublished manuscript, Arizona State Museum Library, University of Arizona, Tucson.
Spoerl, Patricia, and George Gumerman
1984    *Prehistoric Cultural Development in Central Arizona Archaeology: Archaeology of the Upper New River Region.* Southern Illinois University Center for Archaeological Investigations Occasional Paper 5.
Szuter, Christine
1984    Faunal Exploitation and the Reliance on Small Animals among the Hohokam. In *Hohokam Archaeology along the Salt Gila Aqueduct, Central Arizona Project,* vol. 7: Environment and Subsistence, edited by Lynn Teague and P. Crown, pp. 139–170. Arizona State Museum Archaeological Series 150.
1986    Lagomorph and Artiodactyl Exploitation among the Inhabitants of the West Branch Site. In *Archaeological Investigations at the West Branch Site: Early and Middle Rincon Occupation in the Southern Tucson Basin,* edited by F. Huntington, pp. 273–288. Institute for American Research Anthropological Paper 3.
Turnage, W. V., and T. D. Mallory
1941    *An Analysis of Rainfall in the Sonoran Desert and Adjacent Territory.* Carnegie Institution of Washington Publication 519.
Turner, Raymond, and David E. Brown
1982    Sonoran Desertscrub. *Desert Plants* 1982:181–222.
Underhill, Ruth M.
1939    *Social Organization of the Papago Indians.* Columbia University Press, New York.
U.S. Geological Survey
1954    *Compilation of Records of Surface Waters of the United States through September 1950,* Part 9, Colorado River Basin. U.S. Geological Survey Water Supply Paper 1926.
Upham, Steadman, and Glen Rice
1980    Up the Canal without a Pattern: Modelling Hohokam Interaction and Exchange. In *Current Issues in Hohokam Prehistory: Proceedings of a Symposium,* edited by D. Doyel and F. Plog, pp. 78–105. Arizona State University Anthropological Research Papers 23.
Vander Wall, S. B., and J. A. MacMahan
1984    Avian Distribution Patterns along a Sonoran Desert Bajada. *Journal of Arid Environments* 7:59–74.

Vivian, R. Gwinn
    1974        Conservation and Diversion: Water-Control Systems in the Anasazi South-
                west. In *Irrigation's Impact on Society,* edited by T. E. Downing and M.
                Gibson, pp. 95–112. University of Arizona Anthropological Papers 25.
Waters, Michael
    1988        The Impact of Fluvial Processes and Landscape Evolution on Archaeolog-
                ical Sites and Settlement Patterns along the San Xavier Reach of the Santa
                Cruz River, Arizona. *Geoarchaeology* 3:205–219.
Waters, Michael, and John Field
    1986        Geomorphic Analysis of Hohokam Settlement Patterns on Alluvial Fans
                along the Western Flank of the Tortolita Mountains, Arizona. *Geoarchaeology*
                1:29–35.
Wilcox, David, and Richard Ciolek-Torello
    1988        *Hohokam Settlement along the Slopes of the Picacho Mountains, Synthesis and
                Conclusions, Tucson Aqueduct Project.* Museum of Northern Arizona Research
                Papers 35.
Wilcox, David, and Lynette Shenk
    1981        *The Architecture of the Casa Grande and Its Interpretation.* Arizona State Mu-
                seum Archaeological Series 115.
Wilcox, David, and Charles Sternberg
    1983        *Hohokam Ballcourts and Their Interpretation.* Arizona State Museum Archae-
                ological Series 160.
Wilson, John P.
    1985        Early Piman Agriculture: A New Look. In *Southwestern Culture History:
                Collected Papers in Honor of Albert H. Schroeder,* edited by Charles H. Lange,
                pp. 129–138. The Archaeological Society of New Mexico 10.
Woodbury, Richard B.
    1960        The Hohokam Canals at Pueblo Grande, Arizona. *American Antiquity* 26:267–
                270.
    1961        A Reappraisal of Hohokam Irrigation. *American Anthropologist* 63:550–560.

# •3•

# THOUGHTS ON HOHOKAM CHRONOLOGY

▼▼▼▼▼▼▼▼▼▼▼▼▼▼▼▼▼▼▼▼▼▼▼▼▼▼▼▼▼▼▼▼▼▼▼▼▼▼▼▼▼▼▼▼▼▼▼▼▼▼▼▼▼▼▼▼▼▼▼▼▼

## Jeffrey S. Dean

## INTRODUCTION

More than half a century ago, accumulating physical evidence compelled the recognition of significant differences between the archaeological remains of the Sonoran Desert and those of the northern Southwest. Ever since this recognition was formalized by the assignment of the name Hohokam to the former, chronology has been an overriding concern of desert archaeology. The result has been a plethora of chronological schemes with nearly a dozen different chronologies currently vying for acceptance. Haury (1937, 1976) has been the chief proponent of the "long count" chronologies, which place the beginning of the Hohokam tradition in the last few centuries B.C. "Short count" chronologies, which place the beginning of the sequence well within the first millennium A.D., have been proposed by Gladwin (1942, 1948), Bullard (1962), and Plog (1980) and currently are championed by Schiffer (1982a, 1987:315) and others. Recently, Cable and Doyel (1987), Wilcox and Shenk (1977), and Wilcox and Sternberg (1983:223) have offered formulations intermediate between the two extremes.

Despite the general lack of consensus, a few points of agreement have emerged from 50 years of chronological debate. Few deny that the order of the Hohokam phases is correct, and a fair degree of concord exists with regard to the dating of the Colonial-Sedentary and Sedentary-Classic transitions. There is, however, little accord regarding the beginning and termination dates of the Hohokam expression, and there is considerable disagreement over the dating of the phases themselves, especially those of the Pioneer and Colonial periods. Given these circumstances, it can be seen that a rather uncertain foundation underlies any effort to evaluate the Hohokam chronology.

Three different types of chronological placement have proved relevant to Hohokam archaeology. Stratigraphic and contextual analyses establish the integrity and order of the phases. Ceramic cross correlation provides chronological estimates for Hohokam materials associated with exogenous pottery types dated by independent chronometric techniques, primarily dendrochronology. Independent dates (Dean 1978) provide more refined calendric estimates for the Hohokam sequence. Although a wide array of independent dating techniques is available, only radiocarbon and archaeomagnetic dating have contributed directly to the development of the Hohokam chronology.

Following a brief consideration of the nature of the Hohokam chronology problem, the contributions of each of the above chronometric approaches are individually assessed. Stratigraphic-contextual issues receive little attention because they have remained relatively unchanged for decades. Ceramic cross dating and seriation are considered to the extent that new information helps elucidate the problem. The bulk of these analyses, however, is focused on aspects of independent chronometry, particularly archaeomagnetic and radiocarbon dating, that impinge on Hohokam chronology building. This facet of the study involves theoretical and methodological considerations and the evaluation of a large number of dates. The results of these analyses are used to evaluate the chronology of Hohokam origins, development, and demise.

## STRATIGRAPHIC AND CONTEXTUAL ANALYSES

There seems to be a general consensus that these fundamental archaeological procedures establish beyond reasonable doubt both the validity and sequence of the Hohokam phases. The existence of single-component deposits containing "pure" assemblages of individual pottery types verifies the discreteness of both the ceramic types and the phases of which they are diagnostic. The superposition at Snaketown and other sites of single-phase deposits confirms the original ordering of phases (Gladwin et al. 1937). The less definitive metrical and natural stratigraphy of dissected trash mounds (Gladwin 1942, 1948; Plog 1980) in general supports the conclusions drawn from the relationships among discrete deposits (Cable and Doyel 1987; Eighmy and

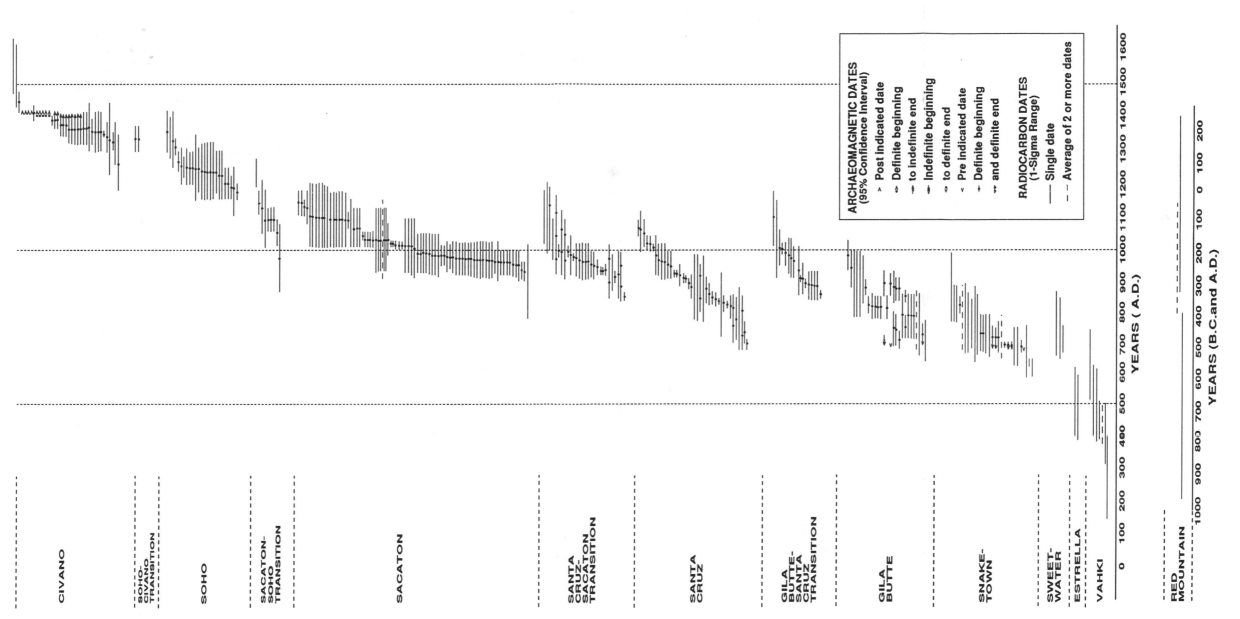

Figure 3.1    *Archaeomagnetic and radiocarbon dates from Phoenix Basin Hohokam sites.*

Doyel 1987; Wallace and Craig 1986). While contextual and stratigraphic relationships affirm that the phases represent genuine analytical units that have
been arranged in the correct order, they reveal nothing of the absolute chronological placement of these units.

## CERAMIC CROSS DATING AND SERIATION

Prior to the advent of radiocarbon and archaeomagnetic chronometry,
ceramic dating formed the backbone of Hohokam chronology. The initial use
of ceramics for this purpose rested on the presence in Hohokam contexts of
exogenous pottery that had been dendrochronologically dated in other areas.
The application of these dates to associated Hohokam materials provided the
first calendric estimates for the Hohokam tradition. Recently, seriation has
been used to "date" design style variations that can then be used to place
associated materials in time (Ciolek-Torrello 1988:54–57).

### CERAMIC CROSS DATING

The key to extracting useful chronological information from ceramic cross
dating is the evaluation of the associations between dated pottery types and
Hohokam materials. Such associations consist of (1) the occurrence of "foreign" ceramics in Hohokam contexts, (2) Hohokam ceramic intrusions into
distant sites, and (3) the co-occurrence of Hohokam and dated foreign pottery
in sites representing a third ceramic tradition. A second consideration is the
nature of the chronological information carried by dendrochronologically dated
pottery types. The validity of this information depends, of course, on the
associations between the pottery and the dated wood or charcoal samples
(Breternitz 1966; Dean 1978). The exogenous types utilized in this analysis
have been securely dated on the Colorado Plateau.

Two approaches to ceramic cross dating are possible. Schiffer (1982a:308–
311, 1987:315–317) describes one of these in his critique of attempts to correlate
Hohokam phases with Anasazi, Mogollon, or Sinagua phases that include
pottery types found as intrusives in Hohokam contexts. He accurately characterizes the poor resolution of this technique by noting the wide range of
overlap possible in the matching of phases that may each be up to 200 years
in duration. This drawback is compounded by the fact that many Anasazi
pottery types are associated with more than one phase.

The second approach, which is adopted here, employs the chronological
information inherent in the pottery itself rather than in the phase associations
of particular types. While a type such as Black Mesa Black-on-white occurs
in phases that span 300 years (A.D. 850 to 1150), the type itself was manufactured over a much shorter interval, approximately A.D. 1000 to 1125. Furthermore, constellations of Anasazi pottery types can considerably reduce the

time span involved. For example, the co-occurrence of Kana'a and Black Mesa Black-on-white specifies a brief span of a couple of decades around A.D. 1000. This approach substantially increases the accuracy and resolution of the dates that can be assigned to Hohokam materials associated with the dated pottery.

As pointed out by Doyel (this volume), more than 4,500 exogenous ceramic items have been recovered from Hohokam contexts. Unfortunately, the vast majority of these objects have no temporal value because they cannot be accurately typed, they represent extremely long-lived types, or they represent undated types. Excluding these temporally insensitive examples produces a meager suite of relevant data. Examples of Hohokam intrusives into distant sites that can be dated by dendrochronology or ceramics are surprisingly rare. Even less common are instances in which Hohokam and dated intrusives occur together in contexts representing other ceramic traditions. Crown (1984) summarizes these aspects of Hohokam ceramic associations, and there is no need to present these data again.

Beginning at the late end of the sequence, the presence of Gila and Tonto Polychromes places the Civano phase after A.D. 1300. This placement is supported by the occurrence of Jeddito Black-on-yellow in Civano contexts at Las Colinas and elsewhere. Salado polychromes excepted, Civano phase pottery is rarely found in non-Hohokam contexts.

Intrusive ceramics are not abundant in Soho phase proveniences. Those that do occur are primarily Pueblo III Cibola White Ware types (principally Roosevelt and Tularosa Black-on-white) that date to the A.D. 1150–1300 interval. Soho phase ceramics rarely appear in sites north of the desert and cannot be dated as intrusives into Anasazi or Mogollon contexts. An exception to this generalization is the occurrence of Casa Grande Red-on-buff with Tularosa Black-on-white in sites near Bylas in the middle Gila drainage (Johnson and Wasley 1966), a relationship that is consistent with the northern types found in Soho contexts.

A strong association between the Sacaton phase and Pueblo II Anasazi ceramics has been acknowledged since the original work at Snaketown (Gladwin et al. 1937:215). By and large, this relationship works in both directions; Anasazi and Mogollon pottery of this period occurs in Sacaton deposits, and Sacaton Red-on-buff is found in northern sites of equivalent age. The datable foreign types most frequently associated with Sacaton Red-on-buff fall into the Tusayan White Ware (Kana'a, Black Mesa, Sosi, and Flagstaff Black-on-white), Cibola White Ware (Red Mesa, Snowflake, and Reserve Black-on-white), Little Colorado White Ware (Holbrook and Walnut Black-on-white), and Mogollon Brown Ware (Three Circle Red-on-white and Mimbres Classic Black-on-white) pottery series. These relationships firmly anchor the Sacaton phase in the eleventh and twelfth centuries. Refinement of this general placement is indicated by the combinations in which the types occur. The association of Santa Cruz and Sacaton Red-on-buff together and Sacaton Red-on-buff alone with mixed Kana'a and Black Mesa Black-on-white and Red Mesa

Black-on-white assemblages places the Santa Cruz–Sacaton transition shortly before A.D. 1000. At the other end of the scale, association of Sacaton Red-on-buff with Snowflake, Flagstaff, and Walnut Black-on-white and Wingate Black-on-red and Polychrome coupled with the absence of full Pueblo III types, such as Tusayan and Kayenta Black-on-white and St. Johns Polychrome, date the termination of the Sacaton phase to about 1150.

As noted above, ceramic cross dating places the Santa Cruz–Sacaton transition in the late 900s. Fairly strong internal and external relationships of Santa Cruz Red-on-buff with Kana'a, Kiatuthlanna, and Red Mesa Black-on-white and Three-Circle Red-on-white is consistent with the evidence for the end of the Santa Cruz phase. Kana'a Black-on-white was produced between A.D. 850 and 1000, Red Mesa between A.D. 850 and 1025, Kiatuthlanna in the ninth century, and Three Circle Red-on-white in the 800s and 900s. The association of White Mound Black-on-white with Santa Cruz Red-on-buff at Snaketown pushes the beginning date of the Santa Cruz phase into the early 800s, but the presence of only a few sherds of Mogollon Red-on-brown and the virtual absence of Basketmaker III pottery indicate that it did not go much earlier. Thus, ceramic cross dating suggests that the Santa Cruz phase extended from the early ninth century into the late tenth century.

Gila Butte Red-on-buff exhibits a fairly strong association with White Mound Black-on-white in Hohokam and other contexts. In addition, both these types occur together with Lino Gray and Lino Black-on-gray in the Vosburg District of central Arizona (Morris 1969b, 1970). The lack of an association between Gila Butte Red-on-buff and unpainted Basketmaker III pottery alone suggests that the Gila Butte phase did not begin before 600. Thus, ceramics indicate the Gila Butte phase to date between 600 and 850.

Since Basketmaker III represents the beginning of the Anasazi ceramic tradition, Anasazi pottery should not and does not occur in Hohokam contexts that predate the Gila Butte phase. Pioneer period contexts contain Mogollon pottery, but this material is poorly dated. As a result, ceramic cross correlation serves only to place the end of the Pioneer period prior to 600.

Lest the ceramic dating picture appear too rosy, a couple of exceptions to the patterns outlined above must be noted. The apparent association of Sacaton Red-on-buff with White Mound Black-on-white at Tule Tubs Cave probably is due to admixture, for Salado polychromes occur in the same deposits (Gifford 1980:120, table 12). The most conspicuous inconsistency is the presence of an unidentifiable, but not early, painted Hohokam sherd in the Bluff site (Haury 1976:330, Haury and Sayles 1947:57), which is tree-ring dated to the early fourth century. The possibility that the Hohokam pottery is associated with a later occupation of the site (Wilcox and Shenk 1977:179) coupled with the anomalous character of this occurrence relative to other instances of Hohokam-Mogollon ceramic association indicate that this case alone cannot support the early placement of Hohokam painted pottery.

In conclusion, ceramic correlation reveals the gross outlines of Hohokam chronology. The absence of datable pottery precludes the ceramic dating of the Pioneer phases. However, the facts that the Colonial period opens with the earliest Anasazi pottery types and that subsequent Hohokam phases display the known progression of Anasazi types indicate that the Pioneer period predates the advent of western Anasazi ceramics in the late 500s. Therefore, the Pioneer period probably ended around 600, although, given the mixture of exogenous types present during the Colonial period and the probability of some lag between the inception of Anasazi pottery and its spread into the desert, the Pioneer period could have persisted as late as 700.

Accepting a 600–700 date for the Pioneer-Colonial transition, ceramic associations allow approximate time ranges to be assigned to the subsequent phases. The Gila Butte phase lasts to approximately 825. The Santa Cruz phase extends from about 825 to 975. The Sacaton phase falls in the interval between 975 and 1150. The Soho phase dates between 1150 and 1300. The Civano phase postdates 1300. Ceramics, or the absence thereof, place the terminal date of the Hohokam sequence sometime after 1450.

## CERAMIC SERIATION

Several attempts have been made to refine Hohokam ceramic dating through the use of seriation. Henderson (1987a, 1987b:47–100) regressed ceramic design attributes against mean radiocarbon and archaeomagnetic dates from carefully selected provenience units at La Ciudad to construct an intrasite chronology for investigating the dynamics of household and community establishment, growth, and decline. Ciolek-Torrello (1988:54–120) used factor analyses of the percentages of plain ware and painted pottery types in structures to identify phase-specific assemblages that could be assigned calendar dates on the basis of associated archaeomagnetic and radiocarbon determinations. Wallace and Craig (1986) seriated painted design elements on Sedentary and Classic period pottery in the Tucson Basin. Ceramic typology and contextual relationships established the chronological trajectory, and mean radiocarbon and archaeomagnetic dates provided the chronometric control. Although high resolution has been claimed for some of these seriations, none possesses sufficient calendric resolution to discriminate adjacent phases (Ciolek-Torrello 1988:57). While seriation is a technique of great potential, it has as yet been too narrowly applied to clarify the Hohokam chronology.

## INDEPENDENT DATING

Hohokam archaeology has always suffered from the lack of high resolution temporal control. As a result, students of desert prehistory responded with alacrity to the promise of universally applicable techniques of independent dating. Radiocarbon dating, which appeared shortly after World War II, was followed in the late 1950s by archaeomagnetic dating, which seemed to offer a degree of resolution greater than that of C-14. Both techniques were widely applied in a concerted effort to resolve Hohokam chronological problems. Other independent dating methods also were tried but proved to be inadequate and soon were deemphasized in favor of C-14 and archaeomagnetic dating.

Due to a number of factors, independent dating did not fulfill archaeologists' hopes by immediately solving the chronological problem. This unsatisfactory outcome triggered a burst of criticism that, as might be expected, was directed primarily at the archaeological, rather than chronometric, aspects of the problem. Most archaeologists believed that independent chronometry would produce a refined Hohokam chronology if they could develop sampling and analytical procedures worthy of the dating techniques. This attitude stimulated a number of attempts to refine, clarify, reevaluate, and reinterpret the existing corpus of dates. The failure of these efforts to produce an acceptable chronology led directly to the heavy emphasis on independent dating that has characterized subsequent Hohokam research. Chronology building has been an important component of nearly every project since Snaketown II, and no project is deemed satisfactory without a large budget for independent dates. As numerous recent discussions attest (Cable and Doyel 1987; Eighmy and Doyel 1987; Plog 1980; Schiffer 1982a, 1986, 1987:305–321; Wilcox 1979:88–93; Wilcox and Shenk 1977:176–180; Wilcox and Sternberg 1983:222–225), this investment in chronometry has produced surprisingly little in the way of consensus.

## APPROACHES TO THE PROBLEMS

Independent dates have been applied in three different ways in Hohokam archaeology: (1) the direct dating of individual provenience units, (2) the analysis of particularly informative cases, and (3) the analysis of dates independent of feature and site provenience.

### Direct Dating

The use of independent dates for the temporal placement of individual features and sites underlies the contribution of dendrochronology to Anasazi and Mogollon chronology. Although the most productive approach, direct dating is effective only when large numbers of high-quality dates are available. Unfortunately, the low precision and resolving power of the chronometric techniques applicable in the desert coupled with the comparatively low number of dates vitiates this procedure as far as Hohokam chronology is concerned. As yet, it simply is not possible to date enough individual provenience units finely enough to synthesize a general chronology from a sequence of dated features. Consequently, this approach is pursued no further here.

## The "Strong Case" Approach

Lacking a comprehensive sequence of well-dated provenience units, archaeologists have resorted to the strong case approach to Hohokam chronology building (Schiffer 1986). This approach seeks to minimize dating anomalies by carefully screening all pertinent archaeological and chronometric data to select analytical situations that can be expected to yield high-quality dating information.

The objectives of this approach are realized first through the careful control of the contexts from which datable samples are taken. The focus is on short-lived, single-component sites or, preferably, individual structures or features that exhibit characteristics diagnostic of brief use spans. Strong cases are further characterized by careful selection of the dated samples in order to maximize the relevance of the dates by controlling the attributes of the sample itself and its relationship to the feature to be dated. Finally, strong cases involve enough dates to allow the recognition and elimination of anomalous dates and the assessment of the accuracy and precision of the placement (Dean 1978).

Despite the conceptual rigor of this approach, it has contributed less toward the solution of the problem than might have been expected. There are surprisingly few cases strong enough to accomplish the desired ends. Schiffer (1986) was able to document only two such instances. House 2:9E at Snaketown produced Sweetwater phase de facto refuse and four radiocarbon dates from wood and annual plants that ostensibly place the structure in the eighth century. House 1:15E at Snaketown, a Snaketown phase structure, produced one radiocarbon date each from wood and maize that also place the house in the eighth century. Even granting the possible existence of additional strong cases, there are far too few of them to support a Hohokam chronology.

A second weakness of this approach lies in the fact that the low resolution of the dates often prohibits the differentiation of the dated units. Despite the strength of Schiffer's two cases, overlap in the one-sigma ranges of the dates does not permit the two houses to be temporally segregated from one another.

A final, and perhaps fatal, flaw of the strong case approach is that the nature of the available dates makes it virtually impossible to determine whether one has a strong case or a weak case even when all other factors are carefully controlled. As was indicated above, the dates do not allow Schiffer's two strong cases to be chronometrically distinguished from one another. Even worse (as developed below), the dates from the Sweetwater phase House 2:9E fall squarely within the range of the aggregated Snaketown phase radiocarbon and archaeomagnetic dates. This situation can be taken to indicate that the two phases overlap, that they are so brief and close in time that radiocarbon dates cannot separate them, or that the dating of one or both houses is erroneous despite the apparent strength of the contexts.

At first blush, the comparatively tight clustering of the dates from House 2:9E would seem to render the third option untenable. Other strong contextual cases, however, demonstrate the possible validity of this option. The Arizona State Museum, as part of the Tucson Aqueduct Project, recently excavated the single component Hawk's Nest site (AZ AA:12:484), which was briefly occupied during the late Snaketown phase (Czaplicki and Ravesloot 1989). Cognizant of the potential of this site for elucidating the Hohokam chronology, the excavators ran a series of ten accelerator dates on carefully controlled maize samples and acquired five archaeomagnetic determinations (Ravesloot et al. 1989). Despite the manifest integrity of the dating situation, calibrated radiocarbon and archaeomagnetic dates ranges across three centuries (A.D. 604–914) with confidence intervals that spanned twice that range (A.D. 430–1147). An even more extreme example is provided by a Tanque Verde phase pithouse with a fair amount of diagnostic de facto refuse at the San Xavier Bridge site (Ravesloot 1987). This structure (Feature 83) yielded three radiocarbon and two archaeomagnetic dates whose one-sigma bands range from 507 B.C. to A.D. 1410. If behavioral, natural, or chronometric processes can produce a 1,917-year spread of dates from one structure, they probably also could create a spurious cluster of dates from another (i.e., House 2:9E at Snaketown). These cases indicate that without a large number of comparable strong instances, it simply is not possible to be confident of the array of C-14 and archaeomagnetic dates from a single provenience unit.

### Aggregated Dating

Given the inapplicability of direct dating and the lack of enough strong cases to resolve the issue, the only alternative is to determine whether any useful chronological information can be extracted from the entire array of independent dates from assignable Hohokam contexts. Basically, this technique consists of assembling all available dates that can be assigned to minimally relevant units, usually phases, and seeing if any meaningful patterns can be abstracted from the array. This was a fairly simple undertaking when Schiffer (1982a) evaluated 79 radiocarbon dates. A considerably more daunting task awaits anyone with the temerity to address the more than 600 independent dates now available. Nevertheless, this approach is attempted here.

# YET ANOTHER ANALYSIS OF HOHOKAM RADIOCARBON AND ARCHAEOMAGNETIC DATES

The only justification for rehashing the Hohokam archaeomagnetic and radiocarbon dates once more is that a perspective shaped by the lack of a vested interest in Hohokam archaeology might lead to fresh insights that shed some light on the problem. The goal of this review is to use independent dates to anchor the beginning and ending of the Hohokam continuum in absolute time and to provide the best dates possible for the internal divisions (phases) of the sequence. Several analytical steps are involved in this effort: (1) certain minimal assumptions about the data are outlined; (2) the raw archaeomagnetic and radiocarbon data are presented and characterized; (3) anomalous dates are identified and deleted; (4) several data manipulations intended to enhance the applicability of the dates to the Hohokam sequence are performed; and (5) the resulting data are used to construct a provisional Hohokam chronology suitable for testing.

## PROCEDURAL CONSIDERATIONS

This examination of the Hohokam independent dates takes several things as given. The stratigraphically established phase sequence is assumed to be correct. Although alternatives to this assumption have been offered (Plog 1980), the basic validity of the sequence is so widely accepted that it requires no further justification here. Ceramic cross dating is considered to have provided generally acceptable, albeit gross, placement of the Sedentary and Classic portions of the sequence. Unless there is strong archaeological or chronometric evidence to the contrary, all dates are assumed to be correct. The problem then becomes one of identifying and eliminating anomalous dates (Dean 1978:228–229). Unless compelling evidence to the contrary can be adduced, the original excavators' provenience designations and phase assignments are accepted. If the excavators' assessments are not available, second-hand phase ascriptions are used. In some cases, other evaluations of the relevance of dates, such as those of Cable and Doyel (1987), Eighmy and Doyel (1987), Eighmy and McGuire (1988), Schiffer (1982a, 1982b), and Schiffer and Staski (1982) are utilized.

Radiocarbon age determinations are presented (Table 3.1) in the standard format of radiocarbon years B.P. (before present, present defined as A.D. 1950) plus-or-minus one standard deviation (sigma). When available, dates corrected for counting time and fractionation are used rather than the uncorrected alternatives. Radiocarbon "dates" are produced by calibrating the age determinations against the scale of absolute time provided by North American bristlecone pine and European oak tree-ring chronologies. Several standards for calibrating radiocarbon age determinations have been advanced in the last 20 years (Damon et al. 1974; Klein et al. 1982; Pearson and Stuiver 1986; Stuiver and Becker 1986; Stuiver 1982; Stuiver and Pearson 1986; Suess 1967, 1970). Changes in calibration procedure have had some interesting consequences for Hohokam chronology. Early calibrations (Damon et al. 1974; Klein et al. 1982) seemed to have created more problems than they solved by transforming fairly straightforward age determinations into sets of alternative dates that compounded the already low resolution of the former. It was a pleasant surprise to discover that the latest calibrations (Pearson and Stuiver 1986; Stuiver and Becker 1986) actually tighten the dating in some cases, thus

rendering temporal placement simpler rather than more difficult. All the radiocarbon dates presented in Table 3.1 and Figures 3.1 and 3.2 were calculated
by computer program CALIB (Stuiver and Reimer 1987) provided by the
Quaternary Isotope Laboratory at the University of Washington, which is
based on the European oak calibration of Stuiver and Becker (1986).

Archaeomagnetic dates have been calculated in a number of ways and
presented in a variety of formats. It is generally agreed that dates derived
early in the development of the technique are outmoded and should not be
used; however, a few such dates are given here when nothing else is available.
A number of Dubois' dates have been corrected by Eighmy and Doyel (1987),
and their dates are used here. Several of the dates listed here were derived
using Sternberg's (1982) revision of Dubois' Southwestern VGP curve. Recently, Eighmy (Eighmy et al. 1985, 1987) revised the curve again, and many
of the dates are based on his VGP. The Arizona State Museum archaeomagnetic dating program often listed dates derived from both Sternberg's and
Eighmy's reference curves. Whenever such alternatives are given, dates based
on the latter are presented here. A massive reanalysis of Hohokam archaeomagnetic dates by Eighmy and McGuire (1988) is based on a version of the
Eighmy VGP from which all Hohokam reference dates have been removed.
The recalculated dates that resulted from this study provide the firmest chronometric basis yet achieved for developing an absolute Hohokam chronology.

Table 3.1 includes all the revised archaeomagnetic dates listed by Eighmy
and McGuire and many additional dates that they omitted due to problems
with the VGP curve, the pole positions of the samples, or the phase ascriptions
of the dates. The additional dates are included to maximize the amount of
chronological information. On the assumption that newer work is more applicable, the most recently calculated archaeomagnetic date is used. Thus,
Eighmy and Doyel's (1987) revisions take priority over Dubois' original determinations, and Eighmy and McGuire's dates take precedence over all earlier versions of the same dates. Although I have uniformly used Eighmy and
McGuire's dates, I have not always adhered to their phase ascriptions. Rather,
phase assignments given in the published site reports are sometimes used
because many of these ascriptions represent more recent analyses of the
contexts of the dated samples than those given by Eighmy and McGuire. In
conformance with current practice, the dates listed in Table 3.1 are those
representing the 95 percent confidence level rather than the 63 percent interval
or subjective "best fit" determinations.

The chronometric data on which this analysis is based are presented in
several sequential formats. Each step in this procedure is the product of a
winnowing process designed to enhance and clarify the information provided
in the preceding step. The raw data on which the analysis is based are the
radiocarbon and archaeomagnetic determinations that were available as of
the spring of 1988. This arbitrary cutoff point was selected in the realization
that any attempt to keep up with the continuing flow of newly derived dates

would result in no foreseeable end to the analysis. Table 3.1 lists 622 dates, 219 radiocarbon and 403 archaeomagnetic. The listing is divided into two groups representing, respectively, the Phoenix and Tucson Basins. Each group is broken down into its constituent phases and interphase transitional periods arranged from early to late.

The dates for each phase were plotted using the one-sigma interval for the radiocarbon dates and the 95 percent confidence interval for the archaeomagnetic dates. Each phase and phase-transition grouping was then inspected for dates that could be eliminated. Several objective rejection standards were employed. A general criterion was established by the fact that dates with confidence interval ranges greater than 250 years lacked the resolving power to discriminate phase intervals that, in terms of the conventional wisdom at least, did not exceed two centuries. Therefore, all dates with a range exceeding 250 years were automatically deleted from the analysis.

Once dates with confidence interval ranges of 250 years or more had been eliminated, other rejection criteria designed to identify anomalous dates came into play. Multiple dates from individual structures and sites were examined for archaeological or chronometric indications of potential anomalies. Gaps in the ranges of dates from a single structure required either the elimination of all the dates or the objective identification of anomalous dates. The latter was accomplished in one of three ways. First, dates that fell outside the range of a cluster of dates from a particular provenience unit were deleted. Second, archaeological relationships sometimes indicated which one of a pair of conflicting dates from a single structure was anomalous. For example, a radiocarbon date that was considerably earlier than an archaeomagnetic date could be rejected as probably representing old wood. Conversely, a fill context radiocarbon date from a structure with an earlier archaeomagnetic date could sometimes be assigned to post abandonment trash deposition rather than construction. Finally, dates that fell outside the cluster of dates from the phase to which the structure was assigned could be deleted as anomalous.

Identification of anomalous archaeomagnetic dates is complicated by the necessity to deal with multiple as well as single placements for individual samples. Choosing the alternative that conforms to the accepted date of the associated phase is not acceptable because the phase assignment enters into the determination of the date. In this way, the dates lose the "independence" that is their chief contribution to archaeological chronology building. However, "outliers" from the cluster of archaeomagnetic and radiocarbon dates from single-phase contexts often identify anomalous alternative archaeomagnetic placements that can be deleted. In addition, single placement archaeomagnetic dates often specify which alternative of a multiple placement date is anomalous. For example, if the array of dates representing a single phase includes some that fall at, say, 1000–1050 and some that have alternative placements at 1000–1050 and 1250–1350, the earlier alternative of the latter group is selected. The opposite distribution—that is, multiple dates at 1000–

1050 and 1250–1350 and single placements at 1250–1375—would result in the selection of the later alternative. Choices sometimes can be based on the clustering of dates from other phases. For example, if a phase produced alternative placements at 950–1000 and 1300–1400, the knowledge that a stratigraphically earlier phase produced a strong cluster in the 900–1000 range is sufficient to select the later placement for the former phase.

Elimination of anomalous dates through the systematic application of the above criteria left a residue of 443 usable dates. Those dates that come from assignable phase and interphase contexts are graphed in Figures 3.1 and 3.2. Given the statistical nature of radiocarbon and archaeomagnetic determinations and a large enough sample per classificatory unit, the distribution of dates per unit should approach normality. Therefore, the plotted dates from each phase should assume an S shape with flattened "tails" at either end of a steeply sloped segment denoting the clustering of dates around the middle of the phase. In most cases, the expected quasinormal distributions are evident in the graphs (Figs. 3.1 and 3.2).

The resolution of the dates can be enhanced by collapsing the data into more inclusive categories. Figure 3.3 illustrates the confidence interval span for each phase. Ideally, the actual date of a phase should fall within the corresponding confidence interval range. Unfortunately, the amount of overlap among these ranges makes it impossible to discriminate individual phases. The potential resolution of the dates can be enhanced by focusing on the midpoints of the archaeomagnetic dates and on the means of the calibrated radiocarbon dates (Table 3.2). The ranges of phase midpoint dates (Fig. 3.4) are considerably tighter than the confidence interval spans (Fig. 3.3), but the total array still exhibits too much overlap to be useful. Plotting the midpoint means and standard deviation ranges (Fig. 3.5) substantially increases resolution at the expense of further reduction of the data.

## GENERAL CHARACTERISTICS

Perhaps the most obvious attribute of the independent dates is their failure to delineate unambiguous temporal boundaries for the individual phases. This result is not due to a lack of date clustering within phases and the transitional intervals between phases. When many dates are available, they assume normal or near-normal distributions within these periods. This result suggests that the taxonomic units are genuine, that the majority of the dates are correctly assigned, and that the samples of dates from the units are adequate. Under these circumstances, the central tendencies of the dates should reflect the chronological placement of the units to which they are assigned. Thus, the lack of chronological definition stems not from the distribution of dates within the taxonomic units, but rather from significant overlap in the ranges of dates from adjacent taxonomic units. This overlap prohibits the clear

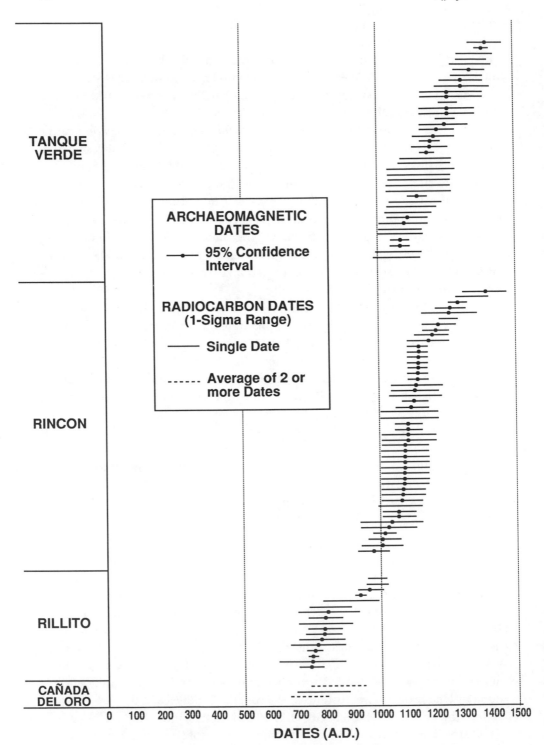

Figure 3.2    *Archaeomagnetic and radiocarbon dates from Tucson Basin Hohokam sites.*

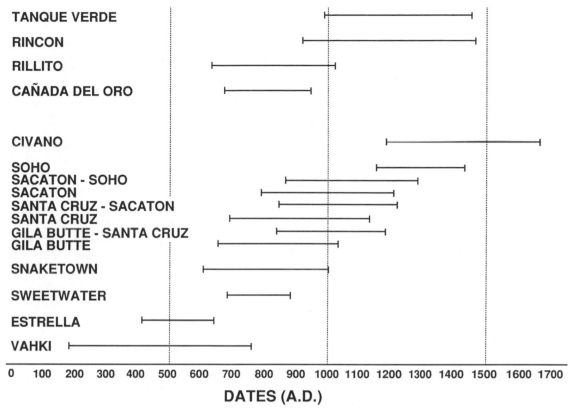

Figure 3.3    *Confidence interval ranges for independent dates from Ho-*
              *hokam phases.*

chronological separation of one unit from another. The data reduction steps
outlined above do not enhance resolution enough to eliminate this problem.

The degree of interphase overlap in the independent dates evident in
Figures 3.1–3.5 can be attributed to several factors operating individually or
in combination. First, the available chronometric techniques lack the resolving
power to discriminate intervals of less than about 100 years. Thus, the dates
are not capable of differentiating adjacent phases, especially short-lived ones.
Second, problems in the assignment of dates to phases could blur the separation between units. Hohokam ceramic distinctions are notoriously min-
uscule, and differences among investigators in the typing of sherds could
very well produce conflicting phase designations. Third, the intraphase position of the dates could exacerbate this problem. Dates from the late end of
one phase could not be chronometrically discriminated from those from the
early end of the following phase. This problem can become particularly acute
when only one or two sites contribute the majority of the dates from adjacent
phases.

Despite these problems of discrimination, the data exhibit some inform-

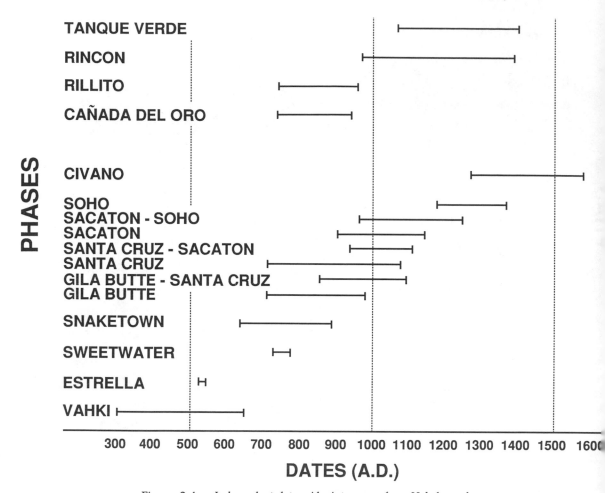

Figure 3.4    *Independent date midpoint ranges from Hohokam phases.*

ative regularities, no matter how they are plotted (Figs. 3.1–3.5). Perhaps the most striking, and certainly the most gratifying, attribute of the total array of dates is that, with one exception, the trend from early to late conforms to the established phase sequences for both the Phoenix and Tucson basins. By and large, both the means and probability ranges of the dates grow progressively later from the Red Mountain through Civano phases and the Cañada del Oro through Tanque Verde phases. Only two possible dating reversals are evident: between the Sweetwater and Snaketown phases and between the Gila Butte–Santa Cruz transitional interval and the Santa Cruz phase. Furthermore, the temporal placements indicated by the independent dates are generally consistent with those suggested by the ceramic data.

Taken as a group, the independent chronometric dates have several broad implications for Hohokam chronology. With the exception of a couple of ambiguous cases, the clustering and overall trend of the dates (Figs. 3.1–3.5)

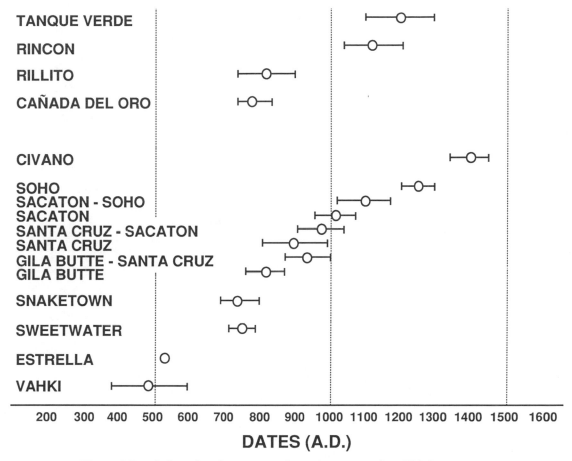

Figure 3.5    *Independent date means and one-sigma ranges from Hohokam phases.*

support the validity of the established Phoenix and Tucson basin phases as temporally distinct taxonomic units. In addition, they affirm the general authenticity of the traditional phase sequence as worked out originally at Snaketown and elaborated elsewhere. These results are encouraging in that they establish the potential of the available dating techniques for elucidating the Hohokam chronology; however, they do not advance the cause of a refined Hohokam chronology much beyond what was already known. Further development of the chronological parameters of the Hohokam sequence must be accomplished through the detailed consideration of the distribution of dates within the individual phases.

## RED MOUNTAIN PHASE

Recently, Cable and Doyel (1987; Doyel, this volume) have proposed the addition of a Red Mountain phase to the beginning of the Hohokam sequence.

Table 3.2  *Summary Chronometric Data for Hohokam Phases*

| | ALL DATES | | | | | RADIOCARBON DATES | | | ARCHAEOMAGNETIC DATE MIDPOINTS | | |
|---|---|---|---|---|---|---|---|---|---|---|---|
| | N | Confidence Interval Range | Range | Midpoints $\bar{x} \pm 1s$ | 1s Range | N | Mean Age $\pm 1s$ | Calibrated 1s Range | N | $\bar{x} \pm 1s$ | 1s Range |
| **TUCSON BASIN** | | | | | | | | | | | |
| Tanque Verde | 40 | 982–1450 | 1065–1388 | 1198 ± 95 | 1103–1293 | 21 | 845 ± 14 | 1163–1219 | 19 | 1214 ± 93 | 1121–1307 |
| Rincon | 48 | 910–1460 | 968–1330 | 1123 ± 82 | 1041–1205 | 8 | 868 ± 21 | 1134–1212 | 40 | 1116 ± 80 | 1036–1196 |
| Rillito | 17 | 620–1019 | 738–957 | 820 ± 80 | 740–900 | 5 | 1144 ± 25 | 783–976 | 12 | 795 ± 70 | 725–865 |
| Cañada del Oro | 3 | 671–937 | 735–937 | 784 ± 50 | 734–834 | 5 | 1235 ± 32 | 692–854 | 0 | | |
| **PHOENIX BASIN** | | | | | | | | | | | |
| Civano | 37 | 1180–1656 | 1265–1571 | 1393 ± 53 | 1340–1446 | 4 | 403 ± 34 | 1439–1488 | 33 | 1384 ± 36 | 1348–1420 |
| Soho | 25 | 1150–1425 | 1175–1362 | 1249 ± 46 | 1203–1295 | 2 | 711 ± 51 | 1261–1285 | 23 | 1245 ± 44 | 1201–1289 |
| Sacaton-Soho | 9 | 860–1278 | 965–1236 | 1096 ± 73 | 1023–1169 | 1 | | | 8 | 1078 ± 54 | 1024–1132 |
| Sacaton | 81 | 782–1200 | 900–1138 | 1016 ± 56 | 960–1072 | 5 | 989 ± 35 | 997–1148 | 77 | 1015 ± 54 | 961–1069 |
| Santa Cruz-Sacaton | 28 | 840–1210 | 938–1104 | 977 ± 65 | 912–1042 | 3 | 997 ± 40 | 993–1147 | 26 | 964 ± 64 | 900–1028 |
| Santa Cruz | 38 | 690–1125 | 708–1075 | 901 ± 89 | 812–990 | 5 | 1157 ± 28 | 780–942 | 33 | 907 ± 92 | 815–999 |
| Gila Butte–Santa Cruz | 17 | 835–1175 | 850–1088 | 937 ± 65 | 872–1002 | 1 | | | 16 | 932 ± 63 | 869–995 |
| Gila Butte | 27 | 644–1025 | 708–975 | 821 ± 58 | 763–879 | 8 | 1186 ± 25 | 777–888 | 20 | 819 ± 53 | 766–872 |
| Snaketown | 28 | 606–991 | 635–883 | 743 ± 54 | 689–797 | 24 | 1270 ± 12 | 686–772 | 11 | 730 ± 36 | 694–766 |
| Sweetwater | 3 | 683–875 | 727–776 | 756 ± 26 | 730–782 | 3 | 1271 ± 15 | 685–772 | 0 | | |
| Estrella | 2 | 413–631 | 525–534 | 530 ± 6 | 524–536 | 2 | 1525 ± 64 | 429–635 | 0 | | |
| Vahki | 7 | 174–758 | 302–649 | 486 ± 106 | 380–592 | 8 | 1586 ± 26 | 423–534 | 0 | | |
| Red Mountain | 2 | 968 B.C.–A.D. 212 | | | | 2 | 2169 ± 131 | 390–48 B.C. | 0 | | |

Stratigraphic relationships at Pueblo Patricio and material at the Red Mountain site (Morris 1969a) provide the empirical basis for this unit. Only two dates are associated with this phase (Table 3.1, Fig. 3.1), both C-14 dates from carefully selected samples in a single pithouse at Pueblo Patricio. Although neither date satisfies the 250-year criterion, they are used here because there are no others and because of the unidirectional nature of the dating situation. Unfortunately, these dates are widely separated, and their one-sigma ranges do not overlap. Given this spread, no objective means exists for determining which, if either, date actually applies to Feature 1 at Pueblo Patricio and to the Red Mountain phase. Taking a "conservative" approach (i.e., one that produces the most recent placement), Cable and Doyel (1987) consider the later date to most closely approximate the true age of the house and the phase. About the most that can be inferred from the meager evidence, however, is that one manifestation of the Red Mountain phase predates A.D. 200, but the phase itself could persist later. The temporal placement of the Red Mountain phase will be clarified only when future excavations produce additional data bearing on its validity, content, and dating.

## VAHKI PHASE

Despite the universally acknowledged importance of dating the inception of the Hohokam sequence, only twelve C-14 dates can be assigned to Vahki phase contexts (Table 3.1). Four of these are eliminated from consideration; three violate the 250-year rule, and one is obviously anomalous relative to the group as a whole. Averaging two dates from Feature 89 at Pueblo Patricio reduces the plotted sample to seven C-14 dates, which represent eight individual determinations. The seven dates exhibit the expected S-shaped curve (Fig. 3.1) with one-sigma ranges extending from A.D. 174 to 758 (Fig. 3.3). Date midpoints range from A.D. 302 to 649 (Table 3.2, Fig. 3.4), with the mean at A.D. 486 ± 106 (380–592).

It is noteworthy that all recently derived Vahki C-14 dates predate 500, and that all the post-500 dates come from the first group of C-14 determinations ever run on Hohokam materials. Perhaps the radiocarbon dating technology of the 1950s preserved the internal chronological relationships of the samples while at the same time inaccurately dating the group as a whole. If possible, duplicates of these samples should be analyzed to determine how modern radiocarbon methods would affect the clustering and placement of the dates. Failing that, we can only speculate that the apparent disparity between dates derived in the 1950s and those run recently may be due to changes in radiocarbon technology and that the more recently derived determinations more accurately place the phase prior to 500. In any case, the available dates indicate that the Vahki phase may have begun as early as 200 and lasted as late as the 600s and that it probably dates between 300 and 500.

Only one of the five radiocarbon dates assigned to the Vahki-Estrella transition (Table 3.1) meets the standards for retention. This date specifies nothing about the transition between these two phases.

## ESTRELLA PHASE

Only three C-14 dates from Snaketown are assigned to the Estrella phase (Table 3.1). One of these nearly falls outside the range of the other two and is rejected as anomalous. The two remaining determinations (Fig. 3.1) have calibrated one-sigma bands spanning the 413–641 interval, a 525–534 midpoint range, and a mean midpoint of 530 ± 6 (524–536). Averaging the dates produces an intercept of 540 ± 5 (535–545). All these measures fall entirely within the ranges of corresponding measures of their Vahki phase counterparts (Figs. 3.3–3.5). This overlap probably is a function of the low number of Estrella dates, but may also indicate that both phases are too brief to be discriminated with radiocarbon dates. The possibility that there is no temporal difference between the two phases can be rejected on the basis of stratigraphic relationships at Snaketown and elsewhere. In conclusion, the weak chronometric data suggest only that the Estrella phase is of short duration and falls in the sixth century. Many more high-quality dates are necessary to elucidate this situation.

Only one of the three dates assigned to the Estrella-Sweetwater transition (Table 3.1) survives the 250-year rejection criterion. This date, which has a one-sigma range of 538–645 and an intercept of 600, is consistent with the indication that the Estrella phase dates to the sixth century. While the Estrella-Sweetwater boundary may fall around 600, additional chronometric work is required to satisfactorily evaluate this possibility.

## SWEETWATER PHASE

Two of the six radiocarbon dates (Table 3.1) assigned to the Sweetwater phase fail the 250-year test, and a third does not overlap the others. The three remaining dates, all of which come from wood and maize charcoal on the floor of House 2:9E at Snaketown, have a one-sigma range of 683 to 875, midpoints ranging from 727 to 776, and a mean midpoint of 756 ± 26 (730–782). Averaging the three determinations produced a one-sigma interval of 685–772 with intercepts at 692, 699, 712, 748, and 766. The tight cluster formed by these dates clearly is anomalous compared to the dates from the other Hohokam phases (Figs. 3.1, 3.3–3.5). In fact, the Sweetwater determinations fall entirely within the range of Snaketown phase dates. Thus, the Sweetwater dates appear to be too late in terms of both the overall trend of phase dates and their relationship to the dates of adjacent phases.

Several explanations for the apparently aberrant position of the Sweetwater dates are possible, all of which have important implications for the validity of the phase. If the structure itself dates to the middle of the eighth century, the de facto Sweetwater refuse on the floor must be attributed to overlap between the Sweetwater and Snaketown phases or to the spurious association of Sweetwater vessels with a later structure. Alternatively, the dates could represent later charcoal introduced into a genuine Sweetwater structure. General stratigraphic considerations and contextual relationships, respectively, argue against the first two possibilities. The last option, however, is supported by the fact that a Gila Butte phase pit intrudes into House 2:9E (Haury 1976:67). Whatever the true situation with House 2:9E, it is clear that many more well-controlled dates from other contexts will be necessary to affirm the chronological validity of the Sweetwater phase and to place it accurately in time.

Because of the tight clustering of four dates (the three used here plus one that violated the 250-year criterion), the good provenience control on the samples, and the de facto Sweetwater refuse on the floor, Schiffer (1986) used House 2:9E as one of the strong cases underlying his upward revision of the Hohokam chronology. If, as seems probable from contextual and stratigraphic relationships at Snaketown and elsewhere, the Sweetwater phase is a genuine taxonomic unit separating the Estrella and Snaketown phases and if House 2:9E is a genuine Sweetwater structure, the independent chronometric evidence (Figs. 3.3–3.5) shows the dates from this house to be aberrant. Because of this anomaly, these dates alone cannot support an upward adjustment of the Hohokam chronology. Apart from this situation's bearing on Hohokam chronology, it clearly illustrates the pitfalls of chronometric analysis. What, by all objective archaeological and chronometric criteria, appears to be an exceptionally strong case turns out to be highly equivocal.

In conclusion, the Sweetwater phase cannot, at present, be directly dated. The general dating trend (Fig. 3.5) suggests that the phase should center in the 600s, but this placement remains an extremely tentative hypothesis that must be tested through the acquisition of additional dates from Sweetwater contexts.

Only two dates, both from Snaketown, are ascribed to the interval between the Sweetwater and Snaketown phases (Table 3.1). Because both lie within the range of the Santa Cruz phase dates, they contribute nothing to these analyses.

## SNAKETOWN PHASE

Fifty-seven dates (46 radiocarbon and 11 archaeomagnetic) have been assigned to Snaketown phase contexts (Table 3.1). Eleven dates are rejected because they span more than 250 years, seven lie beyond the range of other dates from the phase, and four fall outside the range of other dates from the same contexts. Averaging reduces the number of plotted radiocarbon dates by seven. Six dates of seven from Feature 882 at La Ciudad are combined, as are two of three dates from Feature 1751 at La Ciudad and two dates from House 1:15E at Snaketown. These operations produce a total of 11 archaeomagnetic and 17 C-14 dates (Figure 3.1), which represent 35 individual determinations. The confidence intervals of these dates span the 606–991 interval, the midpoints range from 635 to 883, and the mean midpoint falls at 743 ± 54 (689–797).

There are no substantial differences in the radiocarbon and archaeomagnetic dates from the phase (Table 3.2). The archaeomagnetic date midpoints exhibit a narrow confidence interval range (694–766) that falls entirely within the corresponding range (677–769) of the averaged radiocarbon dates. The earlier (pre-690–735) of Eighmy and McGuire's (1988:45, table 5) alternative residual date ranges for this phase also falls within this span. Their later alternative (835–940) can be objectively rejected because it lies outside the distribution of other dates from Snaketown phase contexts.

The preponderance of the evidence favors placing the Snaketown phase between A.D. 650 and 900 with the most probable range lying within the eighth century.

Only four dates can be assigned to the Snaketown–Gila Butte transitional interval (Table 3.1), one of which falls outside the cluster representing this unit. The remaining three fall within the range of the Snaketown phase dates and contribute nothing to dating the break between the two taxonomic units.

## GILA BUTTE PHASE

Thirty-eight dates (14 radiocarbon and 24 archaeomagnetic) are available for the Gila Butte phase (Table 3.1). Ten of these are deleted: violation of the 250-year criterion (one date), falling outside the phase cluster (two), falling outside a cluster of dates from a single provenience unit (one), lack of objective criteria for choosing between alternative archaeomagnetic placements (four), and equivocal phase assignments (two). Averaging two radiocarbon dates from the fill of Pit 6:9E at Snaketown reduces the total by an additional date. These operations produce a corpus of 27 dates (Fig. 3.1), which represents 28 individual samples. The confidence interval range of these dates encompasses the 644–1025 interval (Fig. 3.3), the date midpoints range from 708 to 975; and the mean midpoint is 821 ± 58 (763–879).

There are no appreciable differences between the archaeomagnetic and radiocarbon dates from Gila Butte phase contexts (Table 3.2). The confidence interval range of archaeomagnetic date midpoints (766–872) overlaps the one-sigma range of the averaged radiocarbon dates (777–888). The earlier (710–800) of Eighmy and McGuire's (1988:45, table 5) two residual date ranges for this phase overlaps the C-14 date range (777–888), while the later (830–865) is totally encompassed by the radiocarbon date range. Thus, neither of their alternative placements can be rejected on the basis of the present study.

Taken together, the independent dates indicate that the Gila Butte phase falls between 700 and 1000 and that it most likely extends from the late eighth century to between 850 and 900. This placement falls toward the late end of the maximum possible date range indicated by associations with exogenous ceramics (circa 600 to the early 800s).

## GILA BUTTE–SANTA CRUZ TRANSITION

Of 25 dates (4 C-14 and 21 archaeomagnetic) attributed to this interval (Table 3.1), 3 are deleted on the basis of the 250-year criterion, and 5 are eliminated due to dating inconsistencies within individual provenience units. The 17 remaining dates have a confidence interval range of 835 to 1175, a midpoint range of 850–1088, and a mean midpoint of 937 ± 65 (872–1002). The distribution of these transitional dates is later than the dates for the subsequent Santa Cruz phase. Reasons for this apparent reversal, the only one other than the Sweetwater phase disparity, are difficult to specify. Enough acceptable dates are available from both Gila Butte–Santa Cruz (17) and Santa Cruz (38) contexts to minimize the effects of sampling deficiencies. Inconsistencies in the assignment of dates to these taxonomic units are the most probable cause; however, the inability of low-resolution chronometric techniques to differentiate adjacent periods of such short duration cannot be ruled out. Whatever the cause of the reversal, it is apparent that the dates assigned to this unit cannot be used to place the Gila Butte–Santa Cruz boundary.

## SANTA CRUZ PHASE

Eight C-14 and 34 archaeomagnetic dates are assigned to the Santa Cruz phase (Table 3.1). Four of these dates are eliminated on the basis of the 250-year standard (one date), failure to overlap the phase cluster (one), and excavators' decisions (two). The remaining 38 dates exhibit a version of the S-shaped distribution (Fig. 3.1), which specifies two date clusters, one in the ninth century and one in the tenth century. The later cluster is dominated by samples from La Ciudad and could very well reflect the temporal placement of dated proveniences at a single site. The earlier cluster, which has only one sample from La Ciudad, represents a number of sites. This distribution indicates that the phase brackets 900. The confidence interval range for the Santa Cruz phase dates extends from 690 to 1125, the midpoints span the 708–1075 interval, and the mean midpoint is 901 ± 89 (812–990).

Although the radiocarbon dates are generally earlier than the archaeomagnetic dates, the one-sigma range of their midpoints, 780–942 and 815–999 respectively, overlap. There are so few C-14 dates that this minor inconsistency could easily be due to chance. Eighmy and McGuire (1988:45, table 5) list two possible residual date ranges for this phase, 690–730 and 900–1000. The former falls well outside the date range indicated by this analysis and can be provisionally rejected. Their later alternative is compatible with the range given here.

The independent chronometric data indicate that the Santa Cruz phase falls somewhere in the interval between 700 and 1100. The internal patterning of the dates and relationships to those from adjacent phases suggest that the phase probably falls between 850 and 975, a placement that is consistent with the dating based on associations with exogenous ceramics.

## SANTA CRUZ–SACATON TRANSITION

Thirty-six dates (26 archaeomagnetic and 10 radiocarbon) have been ascribed to this interval. Seven of these are eliminated on the basis of the 250-year criterion (two dates), failure to overlap the distribution of phase dates (three), or excavators' decisions (two). Averaging two dates from roof posts in Area 1 at Gu Achi reduces the count to 28 plotted dates (Fig. 3.1) that represent 29 samples. Many of the archaeomagnetic determinations from this period have two or even three alternative placements. Selection of alternatives was based on excavators' decisions or on the criteria discussed in a previous section of this report. The accepted dates form a broad S-shaped curve centered in the latter half of the tenth century. The confidence intervals of the date midpoints range from 840 to 1210, and the midpoints range from 938 to 1104 with the mean midpoint falling at 977 ± 65 (912–1042). These figures are compatible with placing this phase boundary in the late 900s; however, a broad range of possible dates on either side of this placement is indicated.

## SACATON PHASE

The Sacaton phase has more dates (107) than any other. All but 11 of these are archaeomagnetic determinations. Sixty-four of the dates are from Las Colinas, while the rest represent a number of other sites (Table 3.1). Twenty-five dates are omitted from consideration due to their exceeding 250 years in span (19 dates), falling outside the range of the phase dates (3), conflicts within provenience units (2), or lack of objective criteria for selecting alternative archaeomagnetic placements (1). Averaging collapses two radiocarbon determinations from House 1:10F at Snaketown into a single date. The resulting array of 81 dates represents 82 individual determinations and approximates a straight line rather than the expected S-shaped curve (Fig. 3.1). This distribution reflects tight clustering that is a function of the large sample of dates, the relative ease of assigning materials to this phase, the large number of dates from a single site (Las Colinas), the brief time range of the sites assigned to the phase, the short duration of the phase, or a combination of any or all of these factors. The confidence interval range of dates from the Sacaton phase encompasses the 782–1200 period, the date midpoints range from 900–1138, and the mean midpoint is 1016 ± 56 (960–1072).

Four clusters are apparent in the distribution of dates (Fig. 3.1). These clusters are centered, respectively, in the last half of the tenth century (35 dates), the first half of the eleventh century (21 dates), around 1060 (3 dates), and between 1085 and 1100 (14 dates). These clusters may be due to chance or systematic biases in the dating systems. Alternatively, they may represent genuine use episodes during the Sacaton phase. If so, three of the clusters result in large part from activities at Las Colinas. Approximately half the dates from the earliest and latest clusters, 17 of 35 and 8 of 14 dates respectively, come from this site, as do two of the three dates from the third cluster. Only 3 of 21 dates in the second cluster, centered in the first half of the eleventh century, come from Las Colinas; therefore, this cluster primarily represents Sacaton phase events at other sites. Whatever the exact significance of the apparent clustering, the tight concentration of dates suggests that the contexts that produced them were occupied over a fairly brief span of time, perhaps not much more than a century.

The earlier (920–1025) of Eighmy and McGuire's (1988:45, table 5) two residual date ranges for the phase overlaps with the one-sigma range (997–1148) of the five C-14 dates. Their later alternative (1150–1375) falls outside this range and can be provisionally rejected.

The distribution of the dates places the Sacaton phase between 800 and 1200. The internal patterning of the dates coupled with the dates from adjacent phases indicates that the Sacaton phase most likely dates from the last half of the tenth century to the first half of the twelfth century. This interval falls well within the maximum time span indicated by ceramic cross correlations. Terminating the phase at 1150 creates an apparent gap between Sacaton and the subsequent Soho phase, which is felt to begin around 1200. This apparent break could simply be an artifact of a lack of dated material from the relevant time period, or it may reflect a real condition of the archaeological record.

## SACATON-SOHO TRANSITION

The Sacaton-Soho boundary, which marks the change from the Sedentary to the Classic period, has long been recognized as a major watershed in Hohokam prehistory. A transitional unit, the Santan phase, once was inserted in this interval but subsequently was deleted. Recently, sentiment in favor of reinstating the Santan phase has developed. The dates considered here are those that have been assigned to the Santan phase or to the Sacaton-Soho transitional interval.

Only 18 dates are assigned to the period (Table 3.1), and half are deleted due to excessive length (four samples), failure to overlap the period cluster (four), or the lack of an objective means of choosing between alternative archaeomagnetic placements (one). The remaining eight archaeomagnetic and one radiocarbon determinations form the expected S-shaped distribution (Fig. 3.1). The confidence intervals span the 860–1278 interval, the midpoints range from 965 to 1236 with the mean midpoint at 1096 ± 73 (1023–1169). These figures reflect the fact that six of the dates cluster fairly tightly, their midpoints falling between 1088 and 1138.

Although far from conclusive, these few determinations are consistent with a termination date of around 1150 for the Sacaton phase. Significantly, the transition period dates as a group cluster well before the beginning of the Soho phase date cluster. This fact strengthens the possibility that a chronological gap separates the Sacaton and the Soho phases. The chronometric data offer considerable support for reinstating the Santan phase or at least the formal recognition of a transitional unit between the two phases. An important question that cannot at present be answered is why the intensive sampling of Hohokam sites during the last 20 years has failed to produce chronometric samples that fall into the 1150–1200 interval. Theoretically, the assignment of samples to the various taxonomic units should have no bearing on where the dates fall. Unless there really is some sort of gap between the Sacaton and Soho phases, a representative sample of Hohokam proveniences should have produced a more continuous distribution of dates. The only other possibility is that this apparent gap is an artifact of some sort of systematic bias in the chronometric systems that produced the dates. Intensive, carefully focused research is needed to determine whether the break is due to prehistoric human behavior, archaeological practice, or chronometric method.

## SOHO PHASE

A total of 43 dates is available for the Soho phase (Table 3.1). Eighteen of these are deleted due to violations of the 250-year criterion (16 samples), excavators' decision (1), and the absence of a clear means of choosing between alternative archaeomagnetic placements (1). The remaining 23 archaeomagnetic and 2 C-14 determinations exhibit an S-shaped distribution (Fig. 3.1). Confidence intervals range from 1150 to 1425, date midpoints span the 1175–1362 interval, and the mean midpoint falls at 1249 ± 46 (1203–1295). The majority of the dates fall between 1200 and 1300 with a substantial tail extending into the 1300s.

With its narrow confidence interval span and tight cluster of dates, the Soho phase is one of the most securely dated units in the Hohokam sequence. The evidence is strong that it began around 1200 and extended into the first half of the fourteenth century. This placement falls toward the late end of the distribution suggested by ceramic cross correlation and extends somewhat beyond the fairly sharp ceramic boundary that separates the Soho and Civano phases at 1300. Eighmy and McGuire's (1988:45, table 5) residual date range of 1150 to 1325 is similar to that determined here, although the former extends somewhat farther back in time than the latter.

Only six dates are assigned to the Soho-Civano transition period, and four of these are rejected on the basis of confidence interval spans in excess of 250 years (Table 3.1). The two surviving dates center near 1340, which is consistent with the internal chronometric evidence that places the end of the Soho phase shortly after 1300.

## CIVANO PHASE

Forty-six dates are assigned to the Civano phase (Table 3.1). Of the seven dates eliminated due to their failure to overlap the phase distribution, three predate 1025, one predates 1212, and two are postbomb radiocarbon determinations. Two additional dates were rejected on the basis of the 250-year standard. The remaining four C-14 and 33 archaeomagnetic dates form a rather odd distribution with two prominent tails joined by a long, nearly vertical segment (Fig. 3.1). This aberrant configuration is due to the fact that the upper terminus for most of the archaeomagnetic dates is given as "post 1425." The plotting convention used for these dates (Fig. 3.1) imparts the uncharacteristic shape to the curve. The indeterminate nature of the archaeomagnetic determinations also affects the statistics presented in Table 3.2 and Figures 3.3–3.5, which are highly skewed to the left. That is, the late portion of the date distribution for this phase is significantly underrepresented; therefore, the phase undoubtedly lasted longer than the period indicated by the spans and means. The skewed confidence bands range from 1180 to 1656, the midpoints span the 1265–1571 interval, and the mean midpoint falls at 1393 ± 53 (1340–1446). The dates cluster strongly between 1350 and 1450.

The distribution of Civano phase dates fairly clearly places this unit between 1300 and 1550 with a high probability that it extends from the early 1300s to nearly 1500. This placement is consistent with Eighmy and McGuire's (1988:45, table 5) residual date range of 1375 to 1450 for the phase. The indeterminate later limits of many of the archaeomagnetic dates suggest that the phase could have lasted somewhat longer than indicated by the illustrated distributions and may have persisted until 1500. This placement fits quite well with the dating based on ceramic cross correlations.

## EL POLVORON PHASE

Only one of the five El Polvoron phase dates is acceptable; therefore, independent chronometry contributes nothing to the dating of this as yet rather provisional unit.

## CAÑADA DEL ORO PHASE

All seven dates for this phase (Table 3.1) are radiocarbon determinations from the Dakota Wash site. Two dates are deleted due to conflicts with the overall phase dating or with dates from the same provenience unit. The number of plotted dates (Fig. 3.2) is reduced by an additional two due to the averaging of pairs of dates from two pithouses, Features 10 and 48. The three remaining dates, which represent five dated samples, center in the late eighth century. These few dates, however, provide only a weak indication of the chronological position of the phase as a whole. It appears to have lasted into the 800s and to overlap the ensuing Rillito phase. Much more chronometric research is needed to isolate the true temporal parameters of this unit.

## RILLITO PHASE

Twenty-three dates are assigned to the Rillito phase (Table 3.1). Removal of five dates for violating the 250-year rule and one date for failure to overlap the phase cluster leaves 17 acceptable dates, 5 C-14 and 12 archaeomagnetic. Ten of the 17 dates come from one site, Waterworld. The dates form a rather odd curve (Fig. 3.2) characterized by what appear to be two clusters separated by nearly a century. The larger cluster is centered in the eighth century and the smaller, comprising only four dates, in the tenth. This bimodal distribution does not appear to be due primarily to differences in site occupation spans because dates from Water World occur in both clusters and several sites contribute dates to the earlier group. The later cluster, however, may result from erroneous assignment of the samples because it clearly overlaps the dates from the Rincon phase (Fig. 3.2). If these late dates are assigned to the later phase, a substantial gap must exist between the Rillito and Rincon phase. Alternatively, the apparent gap between the clusters may be a result of sampling deficiencies within the Rillito phase itself.

The confidence intervals of the Rillito phase dates range from 620 to 1019, the midpoints span the 738–957 interval, and the mean midpoint falls at 820 ± 80 (740–900). The patterning of dates indicates that this phase falls somewhere between 600 and 1000. A more likely range is 700 to 1000. If the late, isolated cluster of four dates can be attributed to sampling or assignment error, a much tighter span of around 700 to 900 is specified. Eighmy and McGuire's (1988:45, table 5) residual date range of 710–790 falls at the early end of this interval. Additional dates from unambiguous contexts are needed to resolve the chronological problems that afflict this phase, which on the basis of present evidence appears to totally encompass the Cañada del Oro phase and to possibly overlap the Rincon phase.

## RINCON PHASE

Seventy-four dates are available for this unit (Table 3.1). Of these, 26 are deleted on the basis of exceeding the 250-year limit (16 dates), conflicts with the general phase cluster (4), conflicts with dates from the same provenience (5), and the lack of objective criteria for choosing between alternative archaeomagnetic determinations (1). The resulting sample of 48 acceptable dates includes 8 radiocarbon and 40 archaeomagnetic determinations (Fig. 3.2).

These dates exhibit the expected S-shaped curve, although the upper tail is exaggerated. Two major clusters, with midpoints centered in the late eleventh and middle twelfth centuries are evident. This clustering does not appear to be due to individual site occupations; therefore, it may represent activity throughout the Tucson Basin. A major attribute of the overall distribution is the significant overlap with the date range for the following Tanque Verde phase. At this juncture, it is not possible to determine whether this overlap is a result of sampling problems, chronometric bias, or actual contemporaneity of Rincon and Tanque Verde occupations.

Rincon phase confidence intervals exhibit a wide range (910–1460), the midpoints range from 968–1380, and the mean midpoint falls at 1123 ± 82 (1041–1205). The one-sigma midpoint range brackets Eighmy and McGuire's (1988:45, table 5) residual date range for this phase of 1000 to 1175. On the basis of these data, it can be said that this phase falls somewhere in the 950–1400 interval, most likely between 1050 and 1200. Much more chronometric work, including the analysis of additional samples from tightly controlled proveniences, is necessary to confirm or tighten the broad temporal range indicated by the available data and to illuminate the ambiguous nature of the juncture between the Rillito and Rincon phases and the possible overlap between the Rincon and Tanque Verde phases.

## TANQUE VERDE PHASE

Fifty-six dates are attributed to this phase (Table 3.1). Sixteen are deleted due to violation of the 250-year standard (eight dates) or failure to overlap with the general phase clustering (eight). Many of the latter are wildly improbable C-14 dates from the Tanque Verde phase San Xavier Bridge site, which range from 507–382 B.C. to A.D. 1440–1953. Data reduction produces 40 acceptable dates divided nearly equally between archaeomagnetic (19) and radiocarbon (21) determinations. Once again, the radiocarbon and archaeomagnetic confidence intervals cover similar time spans, although in this instance the former (1163–1219) lies entirely within the latter (1121–1307). The radiocarbon date range (1163–1219) allows the later (1150–1350) of Eighmy and McGuire's (1988:45, table 5) alternative residual date ranges to be accepted in favor of the earlier one (925–1125). The dates do not form the expected S-shaped curve; rather, they tend to fall along a straight line (Fig. 3.2). The confidence intervals of Tanque Verde phase dates span the interval 982–1450, the midpoints range from 1065–1388, and the mean midpoint falls at 1198 ± 95 (1103–1293). As noted above, the Tanque Verde dates overlap substantially with those from Rincon phase contexts.

The combined chronometric data place the Tanque Verde phase somewhere in the 1050–1400 period, most likely between 1150 and 1300. Like all

Table 3.3    *Independent Dating of Hohokam Phases*

| PHASE | DATING | | |
|---|---|---|---|
| | *Maximum Range* | *Interphase Boundary* | *Probable Range* |
| Tanque Verde | 1050 to 1400 | | 1150 to 1300 |
| Rincon | 950 to 1400 | | 1050 to 1200 |
| Rillito | 600 to 1000 | | 700 to 1000 |
| Cañada del Oro | 700 to 800–850 | | 700 to 800–850 |
| Civano | 1300 to 1550 | 1340 | 1300–1350 to c. 1500 |
| Soho | 1200 to 1350 | 1150 | 1200 to 1300–1350 |
| Sacaton | 800 to 1200 | 950–1000 | 950–1000 to 1100–1150 |
| Santa Cruz | 700 to 1100 | ? | 850–900 to 950–1000 |
| Gila Butte | 700 to 1000 | ? | c. 775 to 850–900 |
| Snaketown | 650 to 900 | ? | 700s |
| Sweetwater | — | 600? | 600s |
| Estrella | — | ? | 500s |
| Vahki | 200 to 600 | ? | c. 300 to 500 |
| Red Mountain | — | | ? to c. 300 |

the Tucson Basin phases, there is considerable ambiguity about this placement that can be remedied only through the acquisition of many more dates from well-controlled proveniences.

## THE END OF THE HOHOKAM

Independent chronometry as yet provides little information on the termination date of the archaeologically recognizable Hohokam tradition. This situation is due in part to the fact that both the radiocarbon and archaeomagnetic dating systems are approaching the upper limits of their temporal sensitivity. Equally significant is the difficulty in identifying contexts and materials that represent the protohistoric period. Traditionally, an end date of A.D. 1450 to 1500 is based on the ceramics associated with Civano phase sites. This date seems to be the best estimate that can be made at present. Intensive, directed research is badly needed to bridge the informational void between the demise of the Hohokam and the advent of Europeans in what was to become southern Arizona.

## SUMMARY, COMPARISONS, AND CONCLUSIONS

The above analyses allow the construction of yet another chronology for the Hohokam archaeological sequence. The Phoenix and Tucson basin chronologies presented here (Table 3.3, Fig. 3.6) are hypotheses designed to be further tested against independent chronometric and archaeological data.

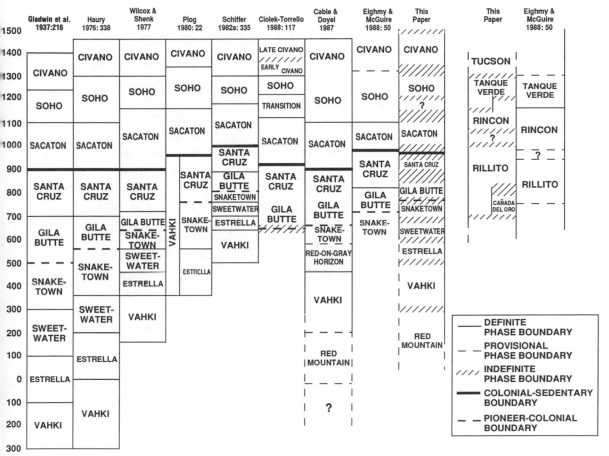

Figure 3.6    *Hohokam phase chronology based on independent chronometry.*

They represent a comprehensive analysis of the independent dates available
as of the spring of 1988. Data issued since then may require one or both of
these schemes to be modified; however, in order to achieve analytical closure,
these data are not considered here. Future research will dictate additional
revisions that will transform this formulation into a new, more accurate chronology. This process of formulation, testing, reformulation, and retesting will
continue until attainment of the absolute limits of the available chronometric
techniques' resolving power results in no further improvement. Once that
point has been reached, only improvement in the chronometric techniques
or the application of different, higher resolution dating methods will produce
a more accurate chronology for the Hohokam cultural sequence.

A firm date for the beginning of the Hohokam sequence has proved to be
just as elusive as ever. Dates from Hohokam contexts, primarily those from
so-called Red Mountain phase proveniences, indicate only that the inception
of Hohokam may predate A.D. 200 by an unknown number of years. Accum-

ulating evidence that terminal Archaic remains in the deserts and elsewhere date to the first three centuries A.D. suggests that the Hohokam tradition did not begin much before 200. On the other hand, the possibility that early Hohokam and late Archaic occupations overlapped in time proscribes the use of San Pedro Cochise dates to place a lower limit on Hohokam. Resolution of this issue depends on the accomplishment of two things. First, archaeological remains that can be unambiguously assigned to the inception of the Hohokam tradition must be identified and analyzed. Second, a large number of high-quality dates must be derived from samples associated with these remains. The identification of the Red Mountain phase as a candidate for the initial unit in the Hohokam sequence is a step toward these goals, but additional, focused research is necessary to confirm its status and to determine its chronological position.

Leaving aside the unresolved problem of origins, the available chronometric data allow the temporal boundaries of most of the Hohokam phases to be estimated with a fair degree of accuracy but, given the nature of the dates, a relatively low level of precision (Table 3.3, Fig. 3.6). These limits are indicated on Figure 3.6 as hatched bands rather than solid lines to reflect this situation. This convention should not be taken to indicate that the phases are not sharply bounded; rather, it is intended to signify the inability of radiocarbon and archaeomagnetic determinations to discriminate narrow intervals of time. In point of fact, the available dates cannot specify whether the phases are totally discrete or overlap to any extent. It does seem probable, however, that the boundaries between adjacent phases lie somewhere within the bands that separate the units.

Detailed discussions of the dating of individual phases are presented above, and there is no need to repeat them here. Rather, a few salient features of the sequence are reemphasized. The placement of the Estrella and Snaketown phases is based primarily on the clustering rather than the range of radiocarbon dates. These clusters show the phases to center in the sixth and eighth centuries, respectively, but indicate little about the boundaries of these two units. The Sweetwater phase is placed entirely by interpolation relative to the overall phase chronology, because the dates for this unit are anomalous. The significance of the gap in the date sequence between the Sacaton and Soho phases is unclear. As noted above, it is difficult to ascribe this break to sampling unless the spate of archaeological work during the last 20 years has systematically bypassed remains dating to this interval. Alternatively, it could be an artifact of an as yet undetected bias in one or both of the dating techniques. Finally, it may reflect the need to resurrect the Santan phase, to adjust the criteria or dating of the Sacaton and Soho phases, or to insert a new temporal-cultural unit between these two phases. All the chronological uncertainties mentioned here are valid and important topics for further, directed research in Hohokam archaeology.

The Tucson Basin chronometric data present a far less coherent picture than do those from Phoenix Basin contexts. There is a much greater degree of chronological overlap apparent in the former. The Cañada del Oro phase, for example, seems to fall almost entirely within the span of the Rillito phase. Similarly, a considerable degree of overlap is evident between the Rincon and Tanque Verde phases. In contrast to these temporal coincidences is a gap between the Rillito and Rincon phases which spans the 1000–1050 interval. The reasons for these apparent irregularities are not obvious. Small sample size could be responsible for the Cañada del Oro–Rillito congruence but does not seem a likely cause for the Rincon–Tanque Verde overlap or the gap between the Rillito and Rincon date distributions. A nonrepresentative sample of the Tucson Basin archaeological universe could be responsible for the dating problems. Alternatively, the developmental status of Tucson Basin ceramic typology, which makes diagnostic ceramic types difficult to segregate, could have led to inconsistencies in the assignment of dates to phases. Either sampling or assignment problems could be due to the relative recency of sustained archaeological research in the Tucson Basin. Thus, the apparent differences in resolution between the Tucson and Phoenix basin chronologies may reflect nothing more than the greater amount of research that has been done in the latter area. Many of the disparities in the quality of the two sequences undoubtedly will disappear as additional research in the Tucson Basin produces more dates, sharper distinctions between phases, and more refined criteria for assigning datable samples to phases.

Taken at face value, the Phoenix and Tucson basin chronologies present some interesting similarities and differences. The Cañada del Oro phase corresponds fairly well with its northern counterpart, the Gila Butte phase. There are, however, too few Cañada del Oro dates to establish a firm relationship with the Phoenix Basin sequence. The Rillito phase appears to be coeval with three northern units: the Snaketown phase, the Gila Butte phase, and Rillito's supposed equivalent, the Santa Cruz phase. The overlap with the Snaketown phase could result from the misassignment of Cañada del Oro samples to the Rillito phase or simply from random variations in the age determinations. If the beginning of the Rillito phase is moved up to the end of Cañada del Oro (800–850), the former still overlaps both the Gila Butte and Santa Cruz phases. At present, the independent dates offer no basis for determining whether the Rillito phase really lasted that long or other factors are responsible for its apparent longevity compared to the Phoenix Basin series.

By and large, the Rincon phase seems to be coeval with its northern equivalent, the Sacaton phase, especially if the former is terminated at the early end of the Tanque Verde phase range (about 1150). Because the Rincon–Tanque Verde overlap period coincides with the Sacaton-Soho gap in the Phoenix Basin sequence, it is tempting to infer that the overlap period represents the Late Rincon phase recently inserted into the Tucson sequence. Unfortunately, the dates that fall in the overlap period are attributed to contexts ranging from early Rincon to late Tanque Verde, and dates that are assigned to the Late Rincon phase are distributed throughout the general Rincon phase span. The chronometric data, therefore, suggest that the Late Rincon phase is not a valid cultural or temporal unit. The Tanque Verde phase correlates quite well with its northern counterpart, the Soho phase. The absence of dates prohibits an evaluation of the relationship of the Tucson phase to the Civano phase.

The intraphase patterning of dates has some intriguing implications for relationships between the Phoenix and Tucson basins. While the time ranges of equivalent phases in both sequences tend to overlap, they do not always coincide. Thus, while these paired units may be materially correlative, they may not be isochronous. The apparent lags and overlaps, if they are real, may provide important clues to the nature of interaction between the two centers of Hohokam development. Each sequence exhibits a gap that is coeval with a period represented by a large number of dates in the other sequence: the 1000–1050 break in the Tucson series corresponds with the Sacaton phase, while the 1150–1200 gap in the Phoenix sequence corresponds to the Rincon–Tanque Verde overlap period. If the date distributions are at all representative, these relationships between the local chronologies may reflect reciprocal interaction between northern and southern Hohokam populations.

Several interesting features emerge from a comparison of the chronology developed here with a few of the other Hohokam chronologies that have been advanced (Fig. 3.6). Little change is evident in the terminal date of the Hohokam sequence, which ranges from 1400 in Gladwin et al. (1937) to circa 1500 here. If the latter figure reflects the inclusion of materials representing a post-Civano expression (the El Polvoron phase or an equivalant unit), the terminal dates would be virtually identical. Another limit that has changed remarkably little is the boundary between the Colonial and Sedentary periods as marked by the beginning of the Sacaton phase. Since 1937, the dating of the lower Sacaton boundary has fluctuated by only 100 years, a trivial amount when measured against the total length of the series. The stability of this placement reflects the accuracy with which the Pueblo II ceramics associated with this phase have been dated since 1937. Differences in the dating of Sedentary and Classic period phases between the relatively stable upper and lower limits reflect changes in archaeologists' conceptions of the units, refinements in the dating of Anasazi and Mogollon ceramics, and the influence of independent chronometry.

Perhaps the most important post-Colonial difference between the construct presented here and earlier chronologies is the apparent gap in the former between the Sacaton and Soho phases. As noted previously, this break could reflect any one of several things: a genuine gap in the sample of Hohokam archaeological sites, a consistent bias in the dating techniques, or the existence of a transitional period between Sacaton and Soho that deserves the recognition conferred by a phase name, either Santan or something else. Further research is necessary to elucidate the nature of this apparent break in the Phoenix Basin sequence. A similar but earlier gap in the Tucson Basin sequence also deserves attention.

In contrast to the relative chronological stability of the Sedentary and Classic periods, major alterations have been suggested for the earlier portion of the Hohokam chronology. The inferred beginning date of the sequence has been raised from its initial placement at 300 B.C. to as late as A.D. 500. Since reaching this extreme in Schiffer's (1982a) chronology, the lower limit has gone back down a bit, partly due to the proposed addition of a new phase (Red Mountain) at the beginning of the sequence. The recent reversion, however, has not totally offset the upward adjustments made since 1976, and the Hohokam sequence, even with the addition of the Red Mountain phase, seems to fall entirely within the A.D. period.

The upward revision of the initial date has caused considerable compression of the Pioneer and Colonial period phases against the comparatively inflexible upper limit set by the beginning of the Sacaton phase. Thus, the pre-Sedentary phases appear to be considerably shorter than originally hypothesized; many may have lasted no longer than a century. The shortening of the Colonial period is a result of two factors. First, during the last 20 years, the dates of pre-Pueblo II Anasazi pottery types have been revised upward, which requires concomitant adjustments in the ceramic cross dating of Hohokam contexts. Second, independent chronometry, as summarized above, has made upward revision necessary.

A major difference between the chronology suggested here and nearly all others is the late placement of the Snaketown phase (circa 700 to 775) in the former. Except for Schiffer's (1982a) formulation, all other Hohokam chronologies place the greater part of the Snaketown phase prior to 700. Even the ceramic evidence suggests that this phase should be somewhat earlier. Ceramics were in production in the western Anasazi area by 600, yet sherds of the relevant types rarely occur in Snaketown phase contexts. If this phase really dates to the eighth century, the paucity of Basketmaker III trade pottery can be attributed only to the absence of trade relations between the Anasazi and other eighth century populations of the region. The chronometric evidence for the placement of the Snaketown phase, however, is strong, and until equally strong contradictory data are forthcoming, there is no alternative to accepting the indications of the available information.

This review of Hohokam chronometry identifies several lines of research necessary to progress toward the ultimate achievable Hohokam chronology. First, more work on the proposed Red Mountain phase is needed to confirm the reality of this construct, define its content, and establish its temporal limits. Such research will illuminate both the nature and the timing of the inception of the Hohokam cultural tradition. Second, the Vahki, Estrella, and Sweetwater phases are seriously underrepresented in terms of the number of dates. Because of the apparent brevity of these units, large numbers of dates are necessary to establish discrete central tendencies for each of these phases; therefore, the number of chronometric samples from these contexts should be augmented. Third, an apparent dating anomaly may be symptomatic of more fundamental problems regarding the Sweetwater phase. Minimally, some attempt should be made to determine whether the dating of House 2:9E at Snaketown is truly anomalous or actually represents the placement of Sweetwater materials. If the latter, major revisions in the Hohokam phase sequence will be necessary. In either case, additional dates from good Sweetwater contexts are vital to resolving this issue. Fourth, despite the number of dates (28), there is evidence that the Snaketown phase is dated too late. A directed attempt to acquire additional dates from unambiguous Snaketown phase contexts is the obvious approach to resolving this problem.

Fifth, the anomalous position of the date cluster representing the Gila Butte–Santa Cruz transitional interval reveals a problem in the definition of this taxonomic unit or in the assignment of materials to it. The criteria by which these assignments were made should be examined, and a concentrated effort to acquire additional dates for this period may be warranted. Sixth, the dating of the Sacaton phase remains a perennial problem. Ceramics seem to indicate that the Sacaton occupation at Snaketown may have ended in the late eleventh century, but the independent dates indicate that it persisted elsewhere into the early 1100s. Despite the number of dates already available for this phase, its pivotal role in the sequence would seem ample reason to acquire many additional dates from solid contexts, particularly those representing the late end of the phase. Seventh, the apparent chronological gap between the Sacaton and Soho phases is a prime candidate for intensive investigation. Initially, the possibility that the gap reflects some sort of regular bias inherent in the chronometric systems must be either confirmed or rejected. Such an evaluation will require the cooperation of archaeologists and chronometricians in a reconsideration of the existing dates and the collection and analysis of new material pertinent to the problem. If the gap is due to chronometric factors, adjustments in dating standards and techniques should eliminate the problem. If the gap proves to truly reflect the archaeological situation, a concerted effort to identify and recover materials falling within the gap will be necessary to illuminate the transition from the Sedentary to the Classic. Eighth, more research is needed to characterize and date the end of the Hohokam tradition. The existence and temporal placement of post-Civano Hohokam expressions can be documented only through the excavation and analysis of sites with the archaeological traits diagnostic of this period. Such research should, of course, include the collection and analysis of many chronometric samples. These analyses may be seriously impeded, however, by the fact that radiocarbon and archaeomagnetic dating are reaching the upper limits of their sensitivity. Dating the upper end of the Hohokam sequence may, therefore, require intensive chronometric research to attune the dating systems to the time range involved.

Finally, the muddled chronological picture in the Tucson Basin must be resolved through the collection and analysis of many additional datable samples from well-controlled contexts that represent the individual phases. Given the poor resolution of the available dates, this effort probably should involve the development and application of unambiguous archaeological criteria for defining the phases and assigning datable materials to them. Only in this way will the apparent overlaps and gaps in the Tucson Basin sequence be eliminated or explained.

Effective implementation of the chronometric research suggested above will require some changes in the ways in which Hohokam archaeology has been conducted. Modern Hohokam archaeology is characterized by a high degree of interaction among its practitioners (Gumerman, this volume); however, even greater coordination and cooperation may be necessary to resolve the chronological difficulties that exist. A useful initial step would be general agreement on what the important chronological problems are and their rank relative to the major issues of Hohokam prehistory. Secondarily, clarity would be immediately enhanced if agreement could be reached on which of the many available independent dates are anomalous and can be permanently eliminated from further consideration. Accord of this type would almost automatically indicate the research necessary to elucidate the chronological issues in Hohokam archaeology. Given the ways in which modern archaeological research is done, it is unlikely that direct, problem-oriented attacks on all these problems could be implemented. Nevertheless, agreement on the general issues would sensitize scholars to situations likely to provide data pertinent to answering key chronological questions. Thus sensitized, archaeologists would be more likely to recognize and exploit such situations when they arise in the context of research directed primarily toward other objectives.

Greater cooperation between archaeologists and chronometricians could advance the cause of Hohokam chronology. One of the perennial problems of radiocarbon and, to a lesser extent, archaeomagnetic dating is the production of dates that are wildly out of line with the archaeological placement of the site or with other dates from the same context. Prior consultation between archaeologists and chronometricians could substantially reduce this problem. The more known about the samples, how they were collected, and their archaeological significance, the better the control over the analytical process. In certain situations, it might be productive to bring chronometricians into the field to advise on or even participate in the selection and collection of samples. Increased communication between archaeologists and chronometricians certainly would benefit the evaluation of the dates. The former control vital information on the contexts of the samples, while the latter are familiar with the circumstances under which the dates were derived, with any problems that arose in the process, and with the nature of the dates. Integrating both types of evidence often helps identify and explain anomalous dates.

Sponsors of major contract projects could contribute to the suggested effort by affording archaeologists the flexibility to exploit situations that exhibit potential for clarifying chronological issues. Provisions could be made to expend extra time and care in the excavation of especially promising contexts and in the documentation and collection of chronometric samples from them. Provision also should be made for processing large numbers of samples from these contexts and for augmented analyses involving procedures such as extended counting times, high-precision counting, and accelerator processing in radiocarbon dating and the use of large numbers of subsamples in archaeomagnetic dating. Finally, mechanisms should be created to foster cooperative chronometric research among different projects focused on different areas and funded by different sponsors. Undoubtedly, such a program would require additional funding and a certain amount of coordination among sponsoring agencies. Nevertheless, the increased control of Hohokam chronology and the better understanding of the prehistory of southern Arizona that would result would well repay the added effort and expense. In the long run, an integrated, highly focused attack such as this would be the most efficient and productive way to resolve the chronological problems that afflict Hohokam archaeology. Until these problems are eliminated or diminished, many of the important questions of Hohokam prehistory will remain unanswerable.

Table 3.1 Archaeomagnetic and Radiocarbon Dates from Hohokam Contexts

| Date No. | Lab No. | E&M No. | Site | Provenience | Nature of Sample | Assoc | Bias | C-14 Age | Dates | Refs | Remarks |
|---|---|---|---|---|---|---|---|---|---|---|---|
| | | | | | | | | | | | |
| UNDIFFERENTIATED PIONEER PERIOD | | | | | | | | | | | |
| 1 | A1072 | — | SNAKETOWN U:13:1 | CREMATORIUM 1:8E | CHCL FUEL? | PRIM? | – | 1540 ± 70 | 426–599 | 25, 38 | SAME PROV. AS 2 |
| 2 | A689 | — | SNAKETOWN U:13:1 | CREMATORIUM 1:8E | MESQ LOGS FUEL? | PRIM? | – | 1030 ± 120 | 890–1154 | 25, 38 | SAME PROV. AS 1 |
| 1-2 | — | — | SNAKETOWN U:13:1 | CREMATORIUM 1:8E | FUEL? | PRIM? | – | 1410 ± 60 | 581–662 | 25, 38 | AVE. OF 1 AND 2 |
| RED MOUNTAIN PHASE | | | | | | | | | | | |
| 3 | B10768 | — | PUEBLO PATRICIO T:12:9 | F1 (PH) FLOOR | ROOF BEAM | PRIM | – OR 0 | 2540 ± 230 | 968BC–390BC | 6 | SAME PH AS 4 |
| 4 | B7677 | — | PUEBLO PATRICIO T:12:9 | F1 (PH) POSTHOLE 1-20 | STRUCT ELEM | PRIM | – OR 0 | 1990 ± 160 | 336BC–AD212 | 6 | SAME PH AS 3 |
| VAHKI PHASE | | | | | | | | | | | |
| 5 | GX329 | — | SNAKETOWN U:13:1 | TRASHFILLED WELL | ? | SEC | + | 2375 ± 110 | 760BC–380BC | 25, 38 | R (1) |
| 6 | A873 | — | SNAKETOWN U:13:1 | ROASTING PIT 1:11I | FUEL? | PRIM | – | 1890 ± 220 | 169BC–AD360 | 25, 38 | R (1) |
| 7 | A816 | — | SNAKETOWN U:13:1 | TRASH BENEATH S.C. PH 1 & 2:66 | FINE CHCL | ? | ? | 1710 ± 110 | 174–430 | 25, 38 | SAME PROV. AS 8 |
| 8 | A815 | — | SNAKETOWN U:13:1 | TRASH BENEATH S.C. PH 1 & 2:66 | FINE CHCL | ? | ? | 1150 ± 200 | 660–1148 | 25, 38 | SAME PROV. AS 7. R (1) |
| 9 | B7678 | — | PUEBLO PATRICIO T:12:9 | F 57 (PH) FLOOR | CHCL | PRIM | – | 1630 ± 60 | 344–531 | 6 | |
| 10 | B7679 | — | PUEBLO PATRICIO T:12:9 | F 89 (PH) POSTHOLE L | ROOF POST | PRIM | – OR 0 | 1600 ± 60 | 392–538 | 6 | SAME PH AS 11 |
| 11 | B10769 | — | PUEBLO PATRICIO T:12:9 | F 89 (PH) POSTHOLES | MIXED STRUCT ELEMS | PRIM | – OR 0 | 1580 ± 100 | 358–595 | 6 | SAME PH AS 10 |

Table 3.1   continued

| Date No. | Lab No. | E&M No. | Site | Provenience | Nature of Sample | Assoc | Bias | C-14 Age | Dates | Refs | Remarks |
|---|---|---|---|---|---|---|---|---|---|---|---|
| 10–11 | | — | PUEBLO PATRICIO T:12:9 | F 89 (PH) | MIXED STRUCT ELEMS | PRIM | – OR 0 | 1595 ± 51 | 407–537 | | AVE. OF 10 AND 11 |
| 12 | ? | — | DAIRY SITE AA:12:285 | F20 | MAIZE | D.F. REFUSE | 0 OR + | 1580 ± 46 | 414–539 | 17 | |
| 13 | M1838 | — | T:16:19 (ASU) | PIT HOUSE | ROOF BEAM | PRIM | – OR 0 | 1520 ± 120 | 410–640 | 38 | |
| 14 | M1837 | — | T:16:19 (ASU) | HOUSE | POST | PRIM | – OR 0 | 1500 ± 120 | 420–650 | 38 | |
| 15 | M1842 | — | T:16:19 (ASU) | PIT FILL | ? | SEC | 0 OR + | 1300 ± 120 | 640–870 | 38 | R (3) |
| 16 | M1836 | — | RED MOUNTAIN U:10:2 (ASU) | BASE OF DEPOSIT | CHARRED LOGS | ? | ? | 1410 ± 120 | 540–758 | 38 | |

VAHKI-ESTRELLA TRANSITION

| Date No. | Lab No. | E&M No. | Site | Provenience | Nature of Sample | Assoc | Bias | C-14 Age | Dates | Refs | Remarks |
|---|---|---|---|---|---|---|---|---|---|---|---|
| 17 | A88BIS | — | MATTY WASH MARKER BED | STRATUM ABOVE VAHKI-ESTRELLA PH | DETRITAL CHCL | STRAT | + | 2010 ± 150 | 200BC–AD130 | 30, 38 | R (3) |
| 18 | A771 | — | SNAKETOWN U:13:1 | PIT BENEATH HSE 12:11F | FINE CHCL | SEC | + | 1810 ± 300 | 169BC–AD540 | 25, 38 | R(1) |
| 19 | A743 | — | SNAKETOWN U:13:1 | PIT 42:11F TEST 1 | FINE CHCL | SEC | + | 1640 ± 250 | 80–640 | 25, 38 | SAME PIT AS 20. R (1) |
| 20 | A818 | — | SNAKETOWN U:13:1 | PIT 42:11F TEST 2, LEVEL 8 | FINE CHCL | SEC | + | 1400 ± 120 | 540–764 | 25, 38 | SAME PIT AS 19 |
| 21 | A788 | — | SNAKETOWN U:13:1 | HOUSE 1:7H | MAIZE | D.F. REFUSE | 0 OR + | 900 ± 120 | 1000–1260 | 25, 38 | R (3) |

ESTRELLA PHASE

| Date No. | Lab No. | E&M No. | Site | Provenience | Nature of Sample | Assoc | Bias | C-14 Age | Dates | Refs | Remarks |
|---|---|---|---|---|---|---|---|---|---|---|---|
| 22 | A814 | — | SNAKETOWN U:13:1 | PIT 42:11F TEST 3, LEVEL 7–8 | FINE CHCL | SEC | + | 1540 ± 90 | 413–637 | 25, 38 | |
| 23 | A742 | — | SNAKETOWN U:13:1 | TEST 4:10G TRASH | FINE CHCL | ? | ? | 1510 ± 90 | 427–641 | 25, 38 | |
| 24 | A786 | — | SNAKETOWN U:13:1 | PIT BENEATH HSE 1:5G, L3 | FINE CHCL | SEC? | + | 1350 ± 80 | 613–767 | 25, 38 | R (3) |

| No. | Sample | | Provenience | Feature | Material | Context | Date | Range | Refs | Notes |
|---|---|---|---|---|---|---|---|---|---|---|
| | | | | | ESTRELLA-SWEETWATER TRANSITION | | | | | |
| 25 | B7683 | — | PUEBLO PATRICIO T:12:9 | F 162 (PH) WALL GROOVES & POSTHOLES | CHCL IN TRASH | PRIM | − OR 0 1460 ± 70 | 538–645 | 6 | |
| 26 | A735 | — | SNAKETOWN U:13:1 | MOUND 40:11F TIER 2, LEVEL 9 | TRASH | ? | ? 1240 ± 110 | 660–939 | 25, 38 | R (1) |
| 27 | M1840 | — | T:16:19 (ASU) | TEST TRENCH 2 COOKING PIT? | FUEL? | PRIM? | − OR 0 1180 ± 110 | 686–980 | 38 | R (1) |
| | | | | SWEETWATER PHASE | | | | | | |
| 28 | GX328 | — | SNAKETOWN U:13:1 | PIT 14:11F TIER 2, LEVEL 1 | PIT FILL | SEC | + 1580 ± 105 | 355–596 | 25, 38 | R (3) |
| 29 | A3888 | — | SNAKETOWN U:13:1 | HOUSE 2:9E (PH) FLOOR | MAIZE | D.F. REFUSE | 0 OR + 1274 ± 16 | 683–771 | 5 | SAME PROV. AS 30–32 |
| 30 | SI189 | — | SNAKETOWN U:13:1 | HOUSE 2:9E (PH) FLOOR | STRUCT ELEM | PRIM | − OR 0 1260 ± 70 | 668–863 | 25, 38 | SAME PROV. AS 29, 31–32 |
| 31 | SI188 | — | SNAKETOWN U:13:1 | HOUSE 2:9E (PH) FLOOR | MAIZE | D.F. REFUSE | 0 OR + 1240 ± 70 | 676–875 | 25, 38 | SAME PROV. AS 29, 30–32 |
| 32 | A599 | — | SNAKETOWN U:13:1 | HOUSE 2:9E (PH) FLOOR | MAIZE | D.F. REFUSE | 0 OR + 1170 ± 120 | 686–990 | 25, 38 | SAME PROV. AS 29–31. R (1) |
| 29, 31, 32 | | | SNAKETOWN U:13:1 | HOUSE 2:9E (PH) FLOOR | MAIZE | D.F. REFUSE | 0 OR + 1271 ± 16 | 685–772 | 25, 38 | AVE. OF 29, 31, 32 MAIZE FROM HSE 2:9E |
| 29–32 | | | SNAKETOWN U:13:1 | HOUSE 2:9E (PH) FLOOR | MIXED | MIXED | − OR 0 1270 ± 15 | 685–772 | 25, 38 | AVE. OF 29–32 |
| 33 | M1839 | — | T:16:19 (ASU) | HOUSE 3 ASH LENS ON FLOOR | ? | ? | ? 1180 ± 120 | 680–990 | 38 | R (1) |
| | | | | SWEETWATER-SNAKETOWN TRANSITION | | | | | | |
| 34 | SI187 | — | SNAKETOWN U:13:1 | STRAT TEST 1:10D LEVEL 6 | CHCL IN TRASH | ? | ? 1130 ± 70 | 779–987 | 25, 38 | STRATIGRAPHICALLY BELOW 35 |
| 35 | A596 | — | SNAKETOWN U:13:1 | STRAT TEST 1:10D LEVEL 4 | CHCL IN TRASH | ? | ? 1050 ± 100 | 890–1148 | 25, 38 | STRATIGRAPHICALLY ABOVE 34 |
| | | | | SNAKETOWN PHASE | | | | | | |
| 36 | B10774 | — | PUEBLO PATRICIO T:12:14 | BLOCK 24E F154 (PH), FLOOR | CHCL | ? | ? 1630 ± 460 | 161BC–AD874 | 6, 39 | R (1) |

Table 3.1 *continued*

| Date No. | Lab No. | E&M No. | Site | Provenience | Nature of Sample | Assoc | Bias | C-14 Age | Dates | Refs | Remarks |
|---|---|---|---|---|---|---|---|---|---|---|---|
| 37 | B10773 | — | PUEBLO PATRICIO T:12:14 | BLOCK 24E F141 (PH), FLOOR | CHCL | ? | ? | 1630 ± 90 | 261–537 | 6, 39 | R (1) |
| 38 | B6059 | — | PUEBLO PATRICIO T:12:14 | BLOCK 1&2, F10 FLOOR | CHCL | ? | ? | 1630 ± 60 | 344–531 | 6, 39 | R (1) |
| 39 | B10772 | — | PUEBLO PATRICIO T:12:14 | BLOCK 24E F130, PIT | PIT FILL | SEC | + | 1500 ± 60 | 434–638 | 6, 39 | R (3) |
| 40 | B10771 | — | PUEBLO PATRICIO T:12:14 | BLOCK 24E F120 (PH) | CHCL | ? | ? | 1410 ± 220 | 410–863 | 6, 39 | R (1) |
| 41 | B7682 | — | PUEBLO PATRICIO T:12:14 | BLOCK 24E F113 (PH), FLOOR | CHCL | ? | ? | 1340 ± 70 | 641–768 | 6, 39 | |
| 42 | B8229 | — | LA CIUDAD T:12:37 (ASU) | F882 (PH) FILL | WOOD | SEC | ? | 1390 ± 110 | 560–764 | 28 | SAME PH AS 43–49 |
| 43 | AA968 | — | LA CIUDAD T:12:37 (ASU) | F882 (PH) FILL | SMALL BRANCH | SEC | – OR 0 | 1390 ± 100 | 560–759 | 28 | SAME PH AS 42, 44–49 |
| 44 | B8228 | — | LA CIUDAD T:12:37 (ASU) | F882 (PH) FILL | ? | SEC | ? | 1290 ± 80 | 652–801 | 28 | SAME PH AS 42, 43, 45–49 |
| 45 | B8230 | — | LA CIUDAD T:12:37 (ASU) | F882 (PH) FILL | SMALL TWIG | SEC | 0 OR + | 1260 ± 90 | 660–875 | 28 | SAME PH AS 42–44, 46–49 |
| 46 | B8239 | — | LA CIUDAD T:12:37 (ASU) | F882 (PH) FILL | LARGE LIMB | SEC | – | 1160 ± 130 | 686–1000 | 28 | SAME PH AS 42–45, 47–49 |
| 47 | AA964 | — | LA CIUDAD T:12:37 (ASU) | F882 (PH) FILL | SMALL BRANCH | SEC | – OR 0 | 1160 ± 80 | 773–982 | 28 | SAME PH AS 42–46, 48, 49 |
| 48 | AA965 | — | LA CIUDAD T:12:37 (ASU) | F882 (PH) FILL | SMALL TWIG | SEC | 0 OR + | 980 ± 80 | 984–1157 | 28 | SAME PH AS 42–47, 49. R (2) |
| 42–47 | | — | LA CIUDAD T:12:37 (ASU) | F882 (PH) FILL | MIXED | | 0 OR + | 1270 ± 38 | 675–797 | | AVE. OF 42–47 |
| 49 | (C)129 | (SK11) | LA CIUDAD T:12:37 (ASU) | F882 (PH) FILL | HEARTH | PRIM | 0 | — | PRE 700 | 22 | |
| 50 | AA959 | — | LA CIUDAD T:12:37 (ASU) | F1751 (PH) FILL | SMALL TWIG | SEC | 0 OR + | 1260 ± 90 | 660–875 | 28 | SAME PH AS 51, 52 |

| No. | Lab No. | | Site | Feature | Material | Prim/Sec | Correction | Date | Range | | Notes |
|---|---|---|---|---|---|---|---|---|---|---|---|
| 51 | AA967 | — | LA CIUDAD T:12:37 (ASU) | F1751 (PH) FILL | SMALL BRANCH | SEC | - OR 0 | 1180 ± 80 | 694–978 | 28 | SAME PH AS 50, 52 |
| 52 | AA963 | — | LA CIUDAD T:12:37 (ASU) | F1751 (PH) FILL | GRASS STEM | SEC | 0 OR + | 990 ± 80 | 982–1155 | 28 | SAME PH AS 50, 51. R (2) |
| 50–51 | | — | LA CIUDAD T:12:37 (ASU) | F1751 (PH) FILL | MIXED | SEC | - TO 0 | 1215 ± 60 | 690–888 | | AVE. OF 50, 51 |
| 53 | AA960 | — | LA CIUDAD T:12:37 (ASU) | F887 (PH) FILL | SMALL TWIG | SEC | 0 OR + | 1260 ± 70 | 668–863 | 28 | SAME PH AS 54 |
| 54 | AA966 | — | LA CIUDAD T:12:37 (ASU) | F887 (PH) FILL | SMALL BRANCH | SEC | - OR 0 | 1020 ± 80 | 904–1149 | 28 | SAME PH AS 53. R (2) |
| 55 | (C)116 | (SK8) | LA CIUDAD T:12:37 (ASU) | F887 (PH) FILL | HEARTH | PRIM | 0 | — | PRE 700–760* / 860–1000 | 22 | *A |
| 56 | AA961 | — | LA CIUDAD T:12:37 (ASU) | F512 (PH) FILL | SMALL TWIG | SEC | 0 OR + | 1250 ± 70 | 672–869 | 28 | SAME PH AS 57, 58 |
| 57 | AA962 | — | LA CIUDAD T:12:37 (ASU) | F512 (PH) FILL | SMALL BRANCH | SEC | - OR 0 | 1120 ± 80 | 779–996 | 28 | SAME PH AS 56, 58 |
| 58 | AA956 | — | LA CIUDAD T:12:37 (ASU) | F512 (PH) FILL | SMALL BRANCH | SEC | - OR 0 | 650 ± 60 | 1279–1391 | 28 | SAME PH AS 56, 57. R (2) |
| 56–57 | | — | LA CIUDAD T:12:37 (ASU) | F512 (PH) FILL | MIXED | SEC | - TO + | 1194 ± 53 | 680–980 | 28 | AVE. OF 56 AND 57. R (1) |
| 59 | B10954 | — | LA CIUDAD T:12:37 (ASU) | F1624 (PH) FILL | ? | SEC | ? | 1240 ± 70 | 676–875 | 28 | |
| 60 | 127 | (SK9) | LA CIUDAD T:12:37 (ASU) | F411 (PH) FILL | BURNED AREA | PRIM | 0 OR + | — | PRE 700–725 | 22 | SAME PH AS 61–63 |
| 61 | B8231 | — | LA CIUDAD T:12:37 (ASU) | F411 (PH) FILL | SMALL TWIG | SEC | 0 OR + | 1140 ± 90 | 775–991 | 28 | SAME PH AS 60, 62, 63 |
| 62 | AA957 | — | LA CIUDAD T:12:37 (ASU) | F1411 (PH) FILL | MAIZE KERNELS | SEC | + | 960 ± 80 | 994–1186 | 28 | SAME PH AS 60, 61, 63 |
| 63 | AA955 | — | LA CIUDAD T:12:37 (ASU) | F1411 (PH) FILL | MAIZE KERNELS | SEC | + | 780 ± 80 | 1165–1281 | 28 | SAME PH AS 60–62 |
| 62–63 | | — | LA CIUDAD T:12:37 (ASU) | F1411 (PH) FILL | MAIZE KERNELS | SEC | + | 870 ± 57 | 1040–1224 | | AVE. OF 62, 63. R (3) |
| 64 | (C)157 | (SK12) | LA CIUDAD T:12:37 (ASU) | F1780 (PH) FILL | HEARTH | PRIM | 0 | — | PRE 700–765* / 865–940 | 22 | *A |

Table 3.1 *continued*

| Date No. | Lab No. | E&M No. | Site | Provenience | Nature of Sample | Assoc | Bias | C-14 Age | Dates | Refs | Remarks |
|---|---|---|---|---|---|---|---|---|---|---|---|
| 65 | (C)128 | (SK10) | LA CIUDAD T:12:37 (ASU) | F538 (HORNO) | HORNO | PRIM | 0 | — | 700–725* 880–890 | 22 | *A |
| 66 | ? | — | DAIRY SITE AA:12:285 | F5 (PH) FILL | MAIZE | D.F. REFUSE | 0 OR + | 1339 ± 99 | 607–770 | 17 | |
| 67 | ? | — | DAIRY SITE AA:12:285 | F21 (PH) FILL | MAIZE | D.F. REFUSE | 0 OR + | 1393 ± 45 | 606–664 | 17 | |
| 68 | B16301 | — | LAS CANOPAS | HOUSE 1, FLOOR, ADJ. TO POSTHOLE C | OUTER 1/3 OF STR. EL | PRIM | – OR 0 | 1370 ± 50 | 639–675 | 5 | SAME PH AS 69 |
| 69 | B16302 | — | LAS CANOPAS | HOUSE 1, FLOOR, FILL OF POSTHOLE A | OUTER 1/3 ROOF POST | PRIM | – OR 0 | 1050 ± 130 | 782–1153 | 5 | SAME PH AS 68 |
| 70 | ? | — | LAS CANOPAS KITCHELL LOCUS | UNIT 56 (TRASH PIT) LOWER LAYER | FILL CHCL | SEC | + | 1230 ± 80 | 676–890 | 5 | SAME PIT AS 71 |
| 71 | ? | — | LAS CANOPAS KITCHELL LOCUS | UNIT 56 (TRASH PIT) UPPER LAYER | FILL CHCL | SEC | + | 1790 ± 110 | 80–384 | 5 | SAME PIT AS 70. R (3) |
| 72 | A734 | — | SNAKETOWN U:13:1 | HOUSE 1:15E FLOOR OR FILL | CHCL | ? | ? | 1340 ± 100 | 606–770 | 25, 38 | SAME PROV. AS 73 |
| 73 | A2470 | — | SNAKETOWN U:13:1 | HOUSE 1:15E FLOOR OR FILL | MAIZE | D.F. REFUSE OR SEC | 0 OR + | 1246 ± 82 | 669–886 | 5 | SAME PROV. AS 72 |
| 72–73 | — | — | SNAKETOWN U:13:1 | HOUSE 1:15E FLOOR OR FILL | MIXED | SEC? | 0 OR + | 1283 ± 63 | 661–799 | | AVE. OF 72, 73 |
| 74 | A731 | — | SNAKETOWN U:13:1 | MOUND 40:11F TIER 1, LEVEL 6 | CHCL IN TRASH | ? | ? | 1240 ± 160 | 640–980 | 25, 38 | R (1) |
| 75 | (D)52 | — | SNAKETOWN U:13:1 | HOUSE 19:10G | HEARTH | PRIM | 0 | — | PRE 700–725* 850–930 | 13, 24 | *A |
| 76 | M1720 | — | DRAG STRIP SITE U:5:21 (ASU) | PIT FILL | CHCL | ? | ? | 1260 ± 110 | 650–890 | 38 | |
| 77 | M1841 | — | U:9:25 (ASU) | HEARTH | FUEL? | PRIM? | – | 1180 ± 120 | 680–990 | 38 | R (1) |
| 78 | AA2274 | — | HAWK'S NEST AA:12:484 | F40 (ROASTING PIT) FILL | MAIZE | D.F. REFUSE OR SEC | 0 OR + | 1448 ± 151 | 430–680 | 35 | R (1) |

| No. | Sample | (SK) | Site | Feature | Material | Context | Measurement | Date Range | | Notes |
|---|---|---|---|---|---|---|---|---|---|---|
| 79 | AA2207 | — | HAWK'S NEST AA:12:484 | F25 (ROASTING PIT) FILL | MAIZE | D.F. REFUSE OR SEC | 0 OR + 1382 ± 36 | 639–665 | 35 | |
| 80 | AA2273 | — | HAWK'S NEST AA:12:484 | F34 (ROASTING PIT) FILL | MAIZE | D.F. REFUSE OR SEC | 0 OR + 1371 ± 146 | 540–798 | 35 | R (1) |
| 81 | AA2208 | — | HAWK'S NEST AA:12:484 | F27 (EXTRAMURAL PIT) FILL | MAIZE | SEC | + 1341 ± 61 | 642–765 | 35 | |
| 82 | AA2209 | — | HAWK'S NEST AA:12:484 | F22 (ROASTING PIT) FILL | MAIZE | D.F. REFUSE OR SEC | 0 OR + 1269 ± 56 | 669–800 | 35 | |
| 83 | AA2271 | — | HAWK'S NEST AA:12:484 | F7 (PH) HEARTH | MAIZE | D.F. REFUSE OR SEC | 0 OR + 1127 ± 175 | 680–1174 | 35 | R (1) |
| 84 | AA2272 | — | HAWK'S NEST AA:12:484 | F3 (ROASTING PIT) FILL | MAIZE | D.F. REFUSE OR SEC | 0 OR + 1177 ± 145 | 670–1000 | 35 | R (1) SAME PH AS 86. *A |
| 85 | (C)7 | — | HAWK'S NEST AA:12:484 | F13 (PH) | HEARTH | PRIM | 0 | — | 680–720* 845–1000 | 34 | |
| 86 | (C)2 | (SK5) | HAWK'S NEST AA:12:484 | F13 (PH) | HEARTH | PRIM | 0 | — | 680–780* 925–1000 | 34 | SAME PH AS 85. *A |
| 87 | (C)4 | (SK 7) | HAWK'S NEST AA:12:484 | F1 (ROASTING PIT) | ROASTING PIT | PRIM | 0 | — | 680–795* 840–1025 | 34 | *A |
| 88 | (C)5 | — | HAWK'S NEST AA:12:484 | F7 (PH) PIT | ? | ? | ? | 680–805* 825–1025 1225–1450 | 34 | *A |
| 89 | AA2206 | — | HAWK'S NEST AA:12:484 | F5 (PH) FLOOR | MAIZE | D.F. REFUSE OR SEC | 0 OR + 1233 ± 36 | 691–859 | 35 | |
| 90 | AA2211 | — | HAWK'S NEST AA:12:484 | F15 (PH) SUBFLOOR PIT, FILL | MAIZE | D.F. REFUSE OR SEC | 0 OR + 1205 ± 35 | 773–585 | 35 | |
| 91 | AA2210 | — | HAWK'S NEST AA:12:484 | F41 (ROASTING PIT) FILL | MAIZE | D.F. REFUSE OR SEC | 0 OR + 1191 ± 36 | 775–889 | 35 | |
| 92 | (C)3 | (SK 6) | HAWK'S NEST AA:12:484 | F4 (ROASTING PIT) | PIT WALL | PRIM | 0 | — | 805–850 | 34 | |
| | | | | SNAKETOWN–GILA BUTTE TRANSITION | | | | | | |
| 93 | A741-1 | — | SNAKETOWN U:13:1 | PIT 33:11F LEVEL 3 | FILL CHCL | SEC | 0 OR + 1430 ± 110 | 540–670 | 25, 38 | |
| 94 | B7681 | — | PUEBLO PATRICIO T:12:9 | BLOCK 24E F97 (PH) FLOOR | CHCL | ? | ? 1280 ± 70 | 660–845 | 6 | R (3) |

---

Table 3.1  continued

| Date No. | Lab No. | E&M No. | Site | Provenience | Nature of Sample | Assoc | Bias | C-14 Age | Dates | Refs | Remarks |
|---|---|---|---|---|---|---|---|---|---|---|---|
| 95 | (C)98 | — | LA CIUDAD T:12:37 (ASU) | F1271 (PH) | HEARTH | PRIM | 0 | — | 700–780*<br>840–1050<br>1125–POST 1425 | 22 | *A |
| 96 | (C)53 | (GB25) | LA CIUDAD T:12:37 (ASU) | F1188 (HORNO) | HORNO | PRIM | 0 | — | 780–790<br>840–860 | 22 | |
| GILA BUTTE PHASE | | | | | | | | | | | |
| 97 | B14879 | — | PICACHO PASS SITE NA 18030 | F15 | ? | ? | ? | 1420 ± 60 | 576–658 | 3 | R (3) |
| 98 | B14878 | — | PICACHO PASS SITE NA 18030 | F18 (LARGE PH) | ? | ? | ? | 1390 ± 70 | 599–674 | 3 | SAME PH AS 99. |
| 99 | (C)7 | (GB10) | PICACHO PASS SITE NA 18030 | F18 (LARGE PH) | HEARTH | PRIM | 0 | — | 780–850 | 21 | R (2) |
| 100 | (C)3 | (GB7) | PICACHO PASS SITE NA 18030 | F1 (FORMAL PIT STRUCT) | HEARTH | PRIM | 0 | — | 680–740*<br>835–915* | 21 | SAME PH AS 98 |
| 101 | (C)2 | (GB6) | PICACHO PASS SITE NA 18030 | F14 (FORMAL PIT STRUCT) | HEARTH | PRIM | 0 | — | 775–860 | 21 | *A |
| 102 | (C)5 | (GB8) | PICACHO PASS SITE NA 18030 | F23 (LARGE PH) | HEARTH | PRIM | 0 | — | 780–850 | 21 | SAME PH AS 103 |
| 103 | B14877 | — | PICACHO PASS SITE NA 18030 | F23 (LARGE PH) | ? | ? | ? | 1120 ± 60 | 782–987 | 1 | SAME PH AS 102 |
| 104 | B13190 | — | PICACHO PASS SITE NA 18030 | F13 | CHCL | PRIM | – OR 0 | 1130 ± 60 | 781–984 | 1 | |
| 105 | (C)8 | (GB11) | PICACHO PASS SITE NA 18030 | F34 (LARGE PH) | HEARTH | PRIM | 0 | — | 925–1025 | 21 | |
| 106 | A601 | — | SNAKETOWN U:13:1 | PIT 6:9E FILL | CHCL | SEC | + | 1370 ± 130 | 560–770 | 25, 38 | SAME PIT AS 107 |
| 107 | SI190 | — | SNAKETOWN U:13:1 | PIT 6:9E FILL | CHCL | SEC | + | 1200 ± 70 | 691–940 | 25, 38 | SAME PIT AS 106 |

Jeffrey S. Dean

| No. | Cat. No. | GB No. | Site | Provenience | CHCL | SEC | + | Date | Calibrated | n | Notes |
|---|---|---|---|---|---|---|---|---|---|---|---|
| 106–107 | — | — | SNAKETOWN U:13:1 | PIT 6:9E FILL | FUEL | PRIM | + | 1238 ± 62 | 681–871 |  | AVE. OF 106 AND 107 |
| 108 | A817 | — | SNAKETOWN U:13:1 | MOUND 38 HEARTH UNDER CREMATORY FLOOR | HEARTH | PRIM | – | 1310 ± 180 | 560–939 | 25, 38 | R (1) |
| 109 | (D)56 | — | SNAKETOWN U:13:1 | HEARTH BELOW CREMATORY FLOOR | HEARTH | PRIM | 0 | — | PRE 700–725*; 850–930* | 13, 24 | *A |
| 110 | (D)32 | — | SNAKETOWN U:13:1 | HOUSE 8:9F | BURNED ROOF ELS | PRIM | 0 | — | PRE 700*; 850–925* | 13, 24 | *A |
| 111 | B1379 | — | BRADY WASH SITE NA 18003, LOC C | F33 (PIT STR) FILL | CHCL | ? | – | 1320 ± 70 | 644–773 | 2 |  |
| 112 | ? | — | LAS CANOPAS KITCHELL LOCUS | QUAD 42 PH FLOOR | ? | ? | ? | 1270 ± 80 | 660–863 | 5 |  |
| 113 | (C)16 | GB17 | T:12:42 | ? | ? | ? | ? | — | 690–725; 900–1000 | 14 | R (4) |
| 114 | (C)18 | GB19 | T:12:42 | ? | ? | ? | ? | — | 690–730; 860–1000 | 14 | R(4) |
| 115 | (C)19 | GB20 | T:12:42 | ? | ? | ? | ? | — | 690–740; 855–940 | 14 | R (4) |
| 116 | (C)3 | GB14 | T:12:43 | ? | ? | ? | ? | — | 690–780; 855–1000 | 14 | R (4) |
| 117 | (C)7 | GB15 | T:12:43 | ? | ? | ? | ? | — | 690–790; 835–915 | 14 |  |
| 118 | AA:1:66-17 | GB4 | AA:1:66 | ? | ? | ? | ? | — | 690–800; 830–930 | 14 |  |
| 119 | (C)16 | GB3 | AA:1:66 | ? | ? | ? | ? | — | 715–860 | 14 |  |
| 120 | (C)7 | GB2 | AA:1:66 | ? | ? | ? | ? | — | 715–860 | 14 |  |
| 121 | (C)3 | — | LA CIUDAD T:12:37 | F398 HORNO | HORNO | PRIM | 0 | — | PRE 700–765*; 925–POST 1425 | 22 | SAME HORNO AS 122. *A |
| 122 | (C)2 | GB22 | LA CIUDAD T:12:37 | F398 HORNO | HORNO | PRIM | 0 | — | 715–860 | 14, 22 | SAME HORNO AS 121 |
| 123 | (C)76 | — | LA CIUDAD T:12:37 | F732 PH REMNANT | HEARTH | PRIM | 0 | — | PRE 700–780; 850–900* | 22 | *B |

Table 3.1  *continued*

| Date No. | Lab No. | E&M No. | Site | Provenience | Nature of Sample | Assoc | Bias | C-14 Age | Dates | Refs | Remarks |
|---|---|---|---|---|---|---|---|---|---|---|---|
| 124 | (C)34 | (GB24) | LA CIUDAD T:12:37 | F239 PH REMNANT | HEARTH | PRIM | 0 | — | 700–725 880–990* | 22 | *B |
| 125 | (C)99 | GB29 | LA CIUDAD T:12:37 | F943 (HORNO) | (HORNO) | PRIM | 0 | — | 715–790 | 14, 22 | SAME HORNO AS 126 |
| 126 | B10943 | — | LA CIUDAD T:12:37 | F943 (HORNO) | MESQ. CHCL FUEL? | PRIM | - | $1040 \pm 60$ | 830–865 | 28 | SAME HORNO AS 125. |
| 127 | (C)143 | GB31 | LA CIUDAD T:12:37 | F598 (PH) | BURNED AREA | SEC? | + | — | 904–1023 | 14, 22 | R (3) |
| 128 | B10941 | — | LA CIUDAD T:12:37 (ASU) | F374 (HORNO) FILL | MESQ. CHCL FUEL? | PRIM? | - | $1160 \pm 75$ | 774–981 | 28 | SAME HORNO AS 129 |
| 129 | (C)110 | GB30 | LA CIUDAD T:12:37 (ASU) | F374 (HORNO) FILL | HORNO | PRIM | 0 | — | 795–845 | 14, 22 | SAME HORNO AS 128 |
| 130 | (C)150 | GB32 | LA CIUDAD T:12:37 (ASU) | F1660 (PH) | HEARTH | PRIM | 0 | — | 775–850 | 14, 22 | |
| 131 | (C)89 | GB28 | LA CIUDAD T:12:37 (ASU) | F766 (PH) | HEARTH | PRIM | 0 | — | 780–850 | 14, 22 | |
| 132 | B10938 | — | LA CIUDAD T:12:37 (ASU) | F13 (HORNO) FILL | ROOT FUEL? | PRIM? | - | $1120 \pm 65$ | 781–989 | 28 | |
| 133 | ? | — | DAIRY SITE AA:12:285 | F23 (HEARTH) FILL | MAIZE | D.F. REFUSE OR SEC | 0 OR + | $1136 \pm 91$ | 776–994 | 17 | R (6) |
| 134 | ? | — | DAIRY SITE AA:12:285 | F33 (PH) FILL | MAIZE | D.F. REFUSE OR SEC | 0 OR + | $1067 \pm 49$ | 898–1016 | 17 | R (6) |
| | | | | | GILA BUTTE–SANTA CRUZ TRANSITION | | | | | | |
| 135 | (A)SD002 | — | SIPHON DRAW U:10:6 | STR 24 (PH) | HEARTH | PRIM | 0 | — | 620–960 | 7 | R (1) |
| 136 | (A)SD003 | SC12 | SIPHON DRAW U:10:6 | STR 22 (PH) | HEARTH | PRIM | 0 | — | 715–855 | 7, 14 | SAME PH AS 137, 138. R (2) |
| 137 | A3522 | — | SIPHON DRAW U:10:6 | STR 22 (PH) | STRUCT ELEMS | PRIM | - OR 0 | $480 \pm 50$ | 1411–1442 | 8 | SAME PH AS 136, 138. R (2) |

| No. | | | Site | Feature | STRUCT ELEMS | | – OR 0 POST BOMB | | Date | | |
|---|---|---|---|---|---|---|---|---|---|---|---|
| 138 | A3523 | — | SIPHON DRAW U:10:6 | STR 22 (PH) | — | PRIM | | | — | 8 | SAME PH AS 136, 137. R (2, 3) |
| 139 | (C)1 | GB5 | PICACHO PASS SITE NA 18030 | F12 (SMALL PH) | HEARTH | PRIM | 0 | — | 680–705 / 715–870 | 14, 21 | SAME PH AS 140. R (2) |
| 140 | B13802 | — | PICACHO PASS SITE NA 18030 | F12 (SMALL PH) | STRUCT ELEM | PRIM | – OR 0 | 1030 ± 60 | 978–1026 | 3 | SAME PH AS 139. R (2) |
| 141 | (C)4 | — | PICACHO PASS SITE NA 18030 | F11 (CREMATION PIT) | PIT | PRIM | 0 | — | 680–1000 | 21 | R (1) |
| 142 | (C)6 | (GB9) | PICACHO PASS SITE NA 18030 | F21 (FORMAL PIT STRUCT) | HEARTH | PRIM | 0 | — | 840–860 | 21 | |
| 143 | (C)5 | SC17 | LA CIUDAD T:12:37 (ASU) | F74 (PH) | HEARTH | PRIM | 0 | — | 690–725 / 900–1025* | 14, 22 | *A |
| 144 | (C)145 | SC45 | LA CIUDAD T:12:37 (ASU) | F1222 (PH) | HEARTH | PRIM | 0 | — | 690–730 / 900–1000* | 14, 22 | *A |
| 145 | (C)55 | GB26 | LA CIUDAD T:12:37 (ASU) | F597 (PH) | HEARTH | PRIM | 0 | — | 690–735 / 840–915* | 14, 22 | *A |
| 146 | (C)81 | GB27 | LA CIUDAD T:12:37 (ASU) | F597 (PH) | HEARTH | PRIM | 0 | — | 690–735 / 845–1000* | 14, 22 | *A |
| 147 | (C)155 | SC47 | LA CIUDAD T:12:37 (ASU) | F1A (HORNO) | HORNO | PRIM | 0 | — | 690–745 / 840–915* | 14, 22 | *A |
| 148 | (C)100 | SC39 | LA CIUDAD T:12:37 (ASU) | F1282 (PH) | HEARTH | PRIM | 0 | — | 690–1000 | 14, 22 | R (1) |
| 149 | (C)90 | — | LA CIUDAD T:12:37 (ASU) | F47 (PH) | HEARTH | PRIM | 0 | — | PRE 700 / 940–1050* / 1375–POST 1425 | 22 | *B |
| 150 | (C)70 | (SC36) | LA CIUDAD T:12:37 (ASU) | F607 (PH) | HEARTH | PRIM | 0 | — | PRE 700 / 940–1015* | 14, 22 | *B |
| 151 | (C)77 | — | LA CIUDAD T:12:37 (ASU) | F1266 (PH) | HEARTH | PRIM | 0 | — | 700–785 / 855–950* | 2 | *B |
| 152 | (C)109 | (GBSC6) | LA CIUDAD T:12:37 (ASU) | F733 (PH) | HEARTH | PRIM | 0 | — | PRE 700–760 / 875–900* | 14, 22 | *B |
| 153 | (C)138 | — | LA CIUDAD T:12:37 (ASU) | F901 (HORNO) | HORNO | PRIM | 0 | — | 855–865 / 895–910* | 22 | *B |

Table 3.1  *continued*

| Date No. | Lab No. | E&M No. | Site | Provenience | Nature of Sample | Assoc | Bias | C-14 Age | Dates | Refs | Remarks |
|---|---|---|---|---|---|---|---|---|---|---|---|
| 154 | (C)136 | GBSC7 | LA CIUDAD T:12:37 (ASU) | F1101 (PH) | HEARTH | PRIM | 0 | — | 915–1025 | 14, 22 | |
| 155 | (C)52 | — | LA CIUDAD T:12:37 (ASU) | F1307 (HORNO) | HORNO | PRIM | 0 | — | 975–1010* | 22 | *B |
| 156 | (C)19 | GB23 | LA CIUDAD T:12:37 (ASU) | F310 (PH) | HEARTH | PRIM | 0 | — | 1200–1275; 1000–1175 | 14, 22 | |
| 157 | (C)9 | GBSC3 | T:16:85 | ? | ? | ? | ? | — | 690–745; 835–915 | 14 | |
| 158 | (C)7 | GBSC2 | T:16:85 | ? | ? | ? | ? | — | 690–790; 835–915 | 14 | |
| 159 | A1345 | — | TA-E-WUN V:9:13 | F1, UNIT 10, BELOW S.C. SURFACE | PIT CHCL | SEC | + | 1020 ± 80 | 904–1149 | 4 | |
| | | | | | SANTA CRUZ PHASE | | | | | | |
| 160 | (A)FT014 | — | FROGTOWN U:15:61 | STR 24 (PH) | HEARTH | PRIM | 0 | — | 620–720 | 7 | |
| 161 | (A)FT013 | — | FROGTOWN U:15:61 | STR 3 (PH) | HEARTH | PRIM | 0 | — | 890–960 | 7 | |
| 162 | (A)FT001 | SC13 | FROGTOWN U:15:61 | F76 (HORNO) | HORNO | PRIM | 0 | — | 620–800; 810–960 | 7, 14 | |
| 163 | (A)FT002 | SC14 | FROGTOWN U:15:61 | F72 (HORNO) | HORNO | PRIM | 0 | — | 690–725 | 7, 14 | |
| 164 | (A)FT007 | SC16 | FROGTOWN U:15:61 | STR 44 (PH) | HEARTH | PRIM | 0 | — | 690–865; 700–750 | 7, 14 | |
| 165 | (A)FT005 | (SC15) | FROGTOWN U:15:61 | S0 18, FLOOR | PLASTER FLOOR | PRIM | 0 | — | 910–940 | 7 | |
| 166 | (A)SD001 | — | SIPHON DRAW U:10:6 | STR 8 (PH) | HEARTH | PRIM | 0 | — | 790–860; 640–940 | 7 | R (1) |
| 167 | (A)SD004 | — | SIPHON DRAW U:10:6 | STR 23 (PH) | HEARTH | PRIM | 0 | — | 810–860 | 7 | |

| | | | | | STRUCT ELEMS? | | | | | | R (3) |
|---|---|---|---|---|---|---|---|---|---|---|---|
| 168 | B14874 | — | PICACHO PASS SITE NA 18030 | F37 (FORMAL PIT STRUCT) | STRUCT ELEMS? | PRIM | – | 1220 ± 60 | 689–887 | 3 | |
| 169 | B14876 | — | PICACHO PASS SITE NA 18030 | F30 (OTHER STRUCT) | STRUCT ELEMS? | PRIM | – | 1190 ± 60 | 733–940 | 3 | |
| 170 | B13801 | — | PICACHO PASS SITE NA 18030 | F11 (PRIMARY CREMATION) | FUEL? | PRIM | – | 1110 ± 60 | 783–992 | 3 | |
| 171 | B13188 | — | PICACHO PASS SITE NA 18030 | F6 (FORMAL PIT STRUCT) | STRUCT ELEMS? | PRIM | – | 869 ± 60 | 1039–1226 | 3 | |
| 172 | (C)9 | LTSC1 | U:9:66 | ? | ? | ? | ? | — | 690–720 / 920–940* | 14 | *A |
| 173 | (C)1 | SC5 | T:8:17 | | ? | ? | ? | — | 690–740 | 14 | *A |
| 174 | (C)2 | SC6 | T:8:17 | | ? | ? | ? | — | 840–925* | 14 | *A |
| 175 | (C)5 | SC9 | T:8:17 | | ? | ? | ? | — | 690–790 / 915–1000* | 14 | *A |
| 176 | (C)4 | SC8 | T:8:17 | | ? | ? | ? | — | 690–810 / 825–870* | 14 | *A |
| 177 | (C)3 | SC7 | T:8:17 | | ? | ? | ? | — | 715–865 | 14 | |
| 178 | (C)62 | SC48 | LA CIUDAD T:12:37 (ASU) | F1021 | ? | ? | ? | — | 830–875 / 690–730 | 14, 22 | *A |
| 179 | (C)102 | SC40 | LA CIUDAD T:12:37 (ASU) | F157 (PH) | HEARTH | PRIM | 0 | — | 900–925* / 700–720 | 14, 22 | *A |
| 180 | (C)21 | SC20 | LA CIUDAD T:12:37 (ASU) | F73 (PH) | HEARTH | PRIM | 0 | — | 910–1025* | 14, 22 | |
| 181 | B10950 | — | LA CIUDAD T:12:37 (ASU) | F65 (TRASH FILLED PIT) | FILL CHCL | SEC | 0 | 1120 ± 70 | 710–780 | 28 | |
| 182 | (C)103 | (SC41) | LA CIUDAD T:12:37 (ASU) | F160 (PH) | HEARTH | PRIM | 0 | — | 781–992 | 22 | *B |
| 183 | (C)94 | SC38 | LA CIUDAD T:12:37 (ASU) | F1060 (PH) | HEARTH | PRIM | 0 | — | 855–870 / 885–920* | 14, 22 | |
| 184 | (C)31 | SC26 | LA CIUDAD T:12:37 (ASU) | F37 (PH) | HEARTH | PRIM | 0 | — | 910–1000 | 14, 22 | |
| 185 | (C)49 | SC31 | LA CIUDAD T:12:37 (ASU) | F1119 (PH) | HEARTH | PRIM | 0 | — | 910–1025 / 925–1050 | 14, 22 | |

Table 3.1   *continued*

| Date No. | Lab No. | E&M No. | Site | Provenience | Nature of Sample | Assoc | Bias | C-14 Age | Dates | Refs | Remarks |
|---|---|---|---|---|---|---|---|---|---|---|---|
| 186 | (C)47 | (SC30) | LA CIUDAD T:12:37 (ASU) | F1005 (PH) | HEARTH | PRIM | 0 | — | 1000–1025* 1150–1325 | 22 | *B |
| 187 | (C)27 | SC22 | LA CIUDAD T:12:37 (ASU) | F36 (PH) | HEARTH | PRIM | 0 | — | 1000–1050 | 14, 22 | |
| 188 | (C)18 | SC18 | LA CIUDAD T:12:37 (ASU) | F331 (PH) | HEARTH | PRIM | 0 | — | 1000–1125 | 14, 22 | SAME PH AS 189 |
| 189 | B10934 | — | LA CIUDAD T:12:37 (ASU) | F331 (PH) FILL | PALO VERDE CHCL | SEC? | + | 750 ± 60 | 1222–1282 | 28 | SAME PH AS 188. R (5) |
| 190 | B10945 | — | LA CIUDAD T:12:37 (ASU) | F1105 (PH) FILL | PALO VERDE CHCL | SEC? | + | 925 ± 60 | 1021–1191 | 28 | SAME PH AS 191. R (5) |
| 191 | (C)68 | (SC35) | LA CIUDAD T:12:37 (ASU) | F1105 (PH) | HEARTH | PRIM | 0 | — | 1015–1100 | 22 | SAME PH AS 190 |
| 192 | (C)30 | (SC25) | LA CIUDAD T:12:37 (ASU) | F696 (PH) | HEARTH | PRIM | 0 | — | 1010–1050 | 22 | |
| 193 | (C)20 | (SC19) | LA CIUDAD T:12:37 (ASU) | F663 (PH) | HEARTH | PRIM | 0 | — | 1050–1100 | 22 | |
| 194 | (D)57 | — | SNAKETOWN U:13:1 | HOUSE 2:9B | HEARTH | PRIM | 0 | — | PRE 700 850–925* | 13, 24 | *C (13) |
| 195 | (D)38 | — | SNAKETOWN U:13:1 | HOUSE 7:10G | HEARTH | PRIM | 0 | — | 700–780 830–900* | 13, 24 | *A |
| 196 | (D)912 | — | SUPERSTITION FREEWAY U:9:46 | HOUSE 4 | HEARTH | PRIM | 0 | — | PRE 700–725 900–935* | 13, 29 | *C (13) |
| 197 | (C)2 | SC10 | T:16:83 (ASM) | ? | ? | ? | ? | — | 720–855 | 14 | |
| 198 | (C)3 | SC11 | T:16:83 (ASM) | ? | ? | ? | ? | — | 815–835 | 14 | |
| 199 | B14873 | — | McCLELLAN WASH SITE NA 18031 | F11 (PH) | STRUCT ELEM? | PRIM | - | 1130 ± 70 | 779–987 | 3 | |
| 200 | (C)8 | (SC1) | BRADY WASH SITE NA 18003 | LOCUS E, F 5K (PIT STRUCTURE) | FIRE-PIT | PRIM | 0 | — | 835–850 | 20 | |
| 201 | (C)1 | SC2 | T:4:12 (ASM) | ? | ? | ? | ? | — | 920–1025 | 14 | |

SANTA CRUZ–SACATON TRANSITION

| No. | Sample | Lab | Site | Provenience | Context | Assoc | ± | Date | Range | Phase | Comment |
|---|---|---|---|---|---|---|---|---|---|---|---|
| 202 | B14875 | — | PICACHO PASS SITE NA 18030 | F16 (PH) | STRUCT ELEM? | PRIM | - | 1690 ± 60 | 257–415 | 21 | R (5) |
| 203 | B13189 | — | PICACHO PASS SITE NA 18030 | F7 (RAMADA) | STRUCT ELEM? | PRIM | - | 1340 ± 90 | 614–772 | 21 | R (3) |
| 204 | G2 | — | GU ACHI | AREA 1, RAMADA, HEARTH FILL | FUEL | PRIM | - | 1400 ± 125 | 540–766 | 38 | SAME STR AS 205, 206. |
| 205 | G1 | — | GU ACHI | AREA 1, RAMADA | ROOF POST | PRIM | - | 1165 ± 130 | 680–1000 | 38 | SAME STR AS 204, 206. SAME POST AS 206? |
| 206 | A1819 | — | GU ACHI | AREA 1, RAMADA | ROOF POST | PRIM | - | 970 ± 70 | 993–1157 | 38 | SAME STR AS 204, 205. SAME POST AS 205? |
| 205–206 | | — | GU ACHI | AREA 1, RAMADA | ROOF POST | PRIM | - | 1014 ± 62 | 981–1148 | | AVE. OF 205 AND 206 |
| 207 | G3 | — | GU ACHI | AREA 2, UPPER SURF HEARTH FILL | FUEL | PRIM | - | 1190 ± 130 | 670–990 | 38 | R (1) |
| 208 | B13180 | — | BRADY WASH SITE NA 18003 | LOCUS N, F 3 (P T STR) FILL | FILL | SEC | + | 1260 ± 60 | 672–855 | 2 | R (3) |
| 209 | (A)PI002 | — | BRADY WASH SITE NA 18003 | LOCUS H, F1 (PH) | CHCL | PRIM | 0 | — | 910–1100 | 14, 20 | |
| 210 | (C)65 | (SAC 38) | LA CIUDAD T:12:37 (ASU) | F688 (PH) | HEARTH | PRIM | 0 | — | PRE 700 | 22 | SAME PH AS 211. |
| 211 | (C)64 | (SAC 37) | LA CIUDAD T:12:37 (ASU) | F688 (PH) | HEARTH | PRIM | 0 | — | PRE 700–755 / 805–885 / 925–975* | 22 | R (5) / *B |
| 212 | (C)154 | — | LA CIUDAD T:12:37 (ASU) | F1139 (PH) | HEARTH | PRIM | 0 | — | 700–760 / 870–885 / 920–955* | 22 | *B |
| 213 | B10933 | — | LA CIUDAD T:12:37 (ASU) | F109 (PH) FILL | ? | ? | ? | 1100 ± 65 | 875–997 | 28 | SAME PH AS 214, 215 |
| 214 | (C)14 | SAC 33 | LA CIUDAD T:12:37 (ASU) | F109 (PH) | HEARTH | PRIM | 0 | — | 925–1050* / 1150–1400 | 14, 22 | SAME PH AS 213, 215. *A |
| 215 | (C)16 | SAC 34 | LA CIUDAD T:12:37 (ASU) | F109 (PH) | HEARTH | PRIM | 0 | — | 925–1125* / 1150–1325 | 14, 22 | SAME PH AS 213, 214. *A |

Table 3.1 *continued*

| Date No. | Lab No. | E&M No. | Site | Provenience | Nature of Sample | Assoc | Bias | C-14 Age | Dates | Refs | Remarks |
|---|---|---|---|---|---|---|---|---|---|---|---|
| 216 | (C)141 | SAC 46 | LA CIUDAD T:12:37 (ASU) | F1360 (PH) | SUBFLOOR PIT | ? | ? | — | 920–1025* 1150–1200 | 14, 22 | *A |
| 217 | (C)72 | SAC 15 | LA CIUDAD T:12:37 (ASU) | F900 (PH) | HEARTH | PRIM | 0 | — | 925–1175* 1225–1325 | 14, 22 | SAME PH AS 218. *A |
| 218 | (C)74 | SAC 16 | LA CIUDAD T:12:37 (ASU) | F900 (PH) | HEARTH | PRIM | 0 | — | 1000–1200* 1250–1300 | 14, 22 | SAME PH AS 217. *A |
| 219 | (C)93 | — | LA CIUDAD T:12:37 (ASU) | F802 (PH) | HEARTH | PRIM | 0 | — | 950–1000 | 22 | |
| 220 | (C)92 | — | LA CIUDAD T:12:37 (ASU) | F132 (PH) | HEARTH | PRIM | 0 | — | 975–1015* 1250–POST 1425 | 22 | *B |
| 221 | B10939 | — | LA CIUDAD T:12:37 (ASU) | F1000 (PH) FILL | ? | ? | ? | $930 \pm 60$ | 1020–1189 | 28 | SAME PH AS 222 |
| 222 | (C)48 | — | LA CIUDAD T:12:37 (ASU) | F1000 (PH) | HEARTH | PRIM | 0 | — | 1000–POST 1425 | 22 | SAME PH AS 221. R (1) |
| 223 | (C)41 | — | LA CIUDAD T:12:37 (ASU) | F675 (PH) | HEARTH | PRIM | 0 | — | 1010–1075 | 22 | |
| 224 | (D)911 | — | SUPERSTITION FREEWAY U:9:46 | HOUSE 2 | HEARTH | PRIM | 0 | — | PRE 700–725 900–935* | 13, 29 | *C (13) |
| 225 | (D)910 | — | SUPERSTITION FREEWAY U:9:46 | HOUSE 3 | HEARTH | PRIM | 0 | — | 925–950 | 13, 29 | |
| 226 | (D)913 | — | SUPERSTITION FREEWAY U:9:46 | HOUSE 1 | HEARTH | PRIM | 0 | — | 925–950 | 13, 29 | |
| 227 | (C)36 | SCSAC 10 | T:12:37 (ASM) | ? | ? | ? | ? | — | 840–870 | 14 | |
| 228 | (C)6 | SCSAC 5 | U:9:66 | ? | ? | ? | ? | — | 840–1000 | 14 | |
| 229 | (C)19 | SCSAC 7 | U:9:66 | ? | ? | ? | ? | — | 850–1000 | 14 | |
| 230 | (C)26 | SCSAC8 | U:9:66 | ? | ? | ? | ? | — | 910–1000 | 14 | |
| 231 | (C)17 | SCSAC 6 | U:9:66 | ? | ? | ? | ? | — | 915–1025 1150–1175 | 14 | |

| No. | | | Site | | | | | | Date Range | | |
|---|---|---|---|---|---|---|---|---|---|---|---|
| 232 | (C)21 | SCSAC4 | AA:1:66 | ? | ? | ? | ? | — | 850–1025 | 14 | |
| 233 | (C)14 | SCSAC 3 | AA:1:66 | ? | ? | ? | ? | — | 910–1025 | 14 | |
| 234 | (C)4 | SCSAC 11 | T:12:43 | ? | ? | ? | ? | — | 1150–1250 | 14 | |
| 235 | (C) 5 | SCSAC 12 | T:12:43 | ? | ? | ? | ? | — | 910–1025 | 14 | |
| 236 | (A)FT012 | SCSAC 13 | FROGTOWN U:15:61 | STR 39 (PH) | HEARTH | PRIM | 0 | — | 920–1000 | 7, 14 | |
| 237 | RL597 | — | T:8:31 (ASU) | COMP B, F12 (PH) POSTHOLE | STRUCT ELEM | PRIM | — | 940 ± 100 | 990–1210 | 36 | |
| 238 | (A)LC166 | LCI 55 | LAS COLINAS T:12:10 | ? | ? | ? | ? | — | 900–1000 | 14 | |
| 239 | (A)LC104 | LCI 41 | LAS COLINAS T:12:10 | ? | ? | ? | ? | — | 905–1025 | 14 | |
| 240 | (A)LC014 | LCI 8 | LAS COLINAS T:12:10 | ? | ? | ? | ? | — | 910–1000 | 14 | |
| 241 | (A)LC054 | LCI 24 | LAS COLINAS T:12:10 | ? | ? | ? | ? | — | 910–1025 | 14 | |
| 242 | (A)LC081 | LCI 37 | LAS COLINAS T:12:10 | ? | ? | ? | ? | — | 910–1025 | 14 | |
| 243 | (A)LC043 | LCI 21 | LAS COLINAS T:12:10 | ? | ? | ? | ? | — | 910–1025* / 1150–1200 | 14 | *A |
| 244 | (A)LC152 | LCI 52 | LAS COLINAS T:12:10 | ? | ? | ? | ? | — | 910–1025* / 1375–1450 | 14 | *A |
| 245 | (A)LC051 | LCI 23 | LAS COLINAS T:12:10 | ? | ? | ? | ? | — | 910–1050* / 1150–1450 | 14 | *A |
| 246 | (A)LC169 | LCI 56 | LAS COLINAS T:12:10 | ? | ? | ? | ? | — | 920–1000 | 14 | |
| 247 | (A)LC176 | LCI 57 | LAS COLINAS T:12:10 | ? | ? | ? | ? | — | 920–1000 | 14 | |
| 248 | (A)LC002 | LCI 1 | LAS COLINAS T:12:10 | ? | ? | ? | ? | — | 920–1025 | 14 | |
| 249 | (A)LC105 | LCI 42 | LAS COLINAS T:12:10 | ? | ? | ? | ? | — | 920–1025* / 1150–1250 | 14 | *A |

Table 3.1  *continued*

| Date No. | Lab No. | E&M No. | Site | Provenience | Nature of Sample | Assoc | Bias | C-14 Age | Dates | Refs | Remarks |
|---|---|---|---|---|---|---|---|---|---|---|---|
| 250 | (A)LC018 | LCI 12 | LAS COLINAS T:12:10 | ? | ? | ? | ? | — | 920–1050* / 1150–1450 | 14 | *A |
| 251 | (A)LC056 | LCI 26 | LAS COLINAS T:12:10 | ? | ? | ? | ? | — | 920–1125* / 1150–1450 | 14 | *A |
| 252 | (A)LC017 | LCI 11 | LAS COLINAS T:12:10 | ? | ? | ? | ? | — | 920–1350 | 14 | R (1) |
| 253 | (A)LC019 | LCI 13 | LAS COLINAS T:12:10 | ? | ? | ? | ? | — | 920–1350 | 14 | R (1) |
| 254 | (A)LC075 | LCI 34 | LAS COLINAS T:12:10 | ? | ? | ? | ? | — | 925–1000* / 1150–1200 | 14 | *A |
| 255 | (A)LC013 | LCI 7 | LAS COLINAS T:12:10 | ? | ? | ? | ? | — | 925–1050* / 1150–1375 | 14 | *A |
| 256 | (A)LC064 | LCI 30 | LAS COLINAS T:12:10 | ? | ? | ? | ? | — | 925–1050* / 1150–1375 | 14 | *A |
| 257 | (A)LC154 | LCI 53 | LAS COLINAS T:12:10 | ? | ? | ? | ? | — | 925–1050* / 1150–1425 | 14 | *A |
| 258 | (A)LC006 | LCI 2 | LAS COLINAS T:12:10 | ? | ? | ? | ? | — | 925–1100* / 1150–1400 | 14 | *A |
| 259 | (A)LC012 | LCI 6 | LAS COLINAS T:12:10 | ? | ? | ? | ? | — | 925–1200 / 1225–1375 | 14 | R (1) |
| 260 | (A)LC025 | LCI 17 | LAS COLINAS T:12:10 | ? | ? | ? | ? | — | 925–1300 | 14 | R (1) |
| 261 | (A)LC021 | LCI 15 | LAS COLINAS T:12:10 | ? | ? | ? | ? | — | 925–1350 | 14 | R (1) |
| 262 | (A)LC084 | LCI 38 | LAS COLINAS T:12:10 | ? | ? | ? | ? | — | 925–1350 | 14 | R (1) |
| 263 | (A)LC065 | LCI 31 | LAS COLINAS T:12:10 | ? | ? | ? | ? | — | 925–1375 | 14 | R (1) |
| 264 | (A)LC101 | LCI 40 | LAS COLINAS T:12:10 | ? | ? | ? | ? | — | 1000–1050* / 1150–1300 | 14 | *A |

| No. | Code | LCI | Site | | | | Dates | | |
|---|---|---|---|---|---|---|---|---|---|
| 265 | (A)LC126 | LCI 46 | LAS COLINAS T:12:10 | ? | ? | — | 1000–1050* / 1150–1350 | 14 | *A |
| 266 | (A)LC124 | LCI 44 | LAS COLINAS T:12:10 | ? | ? | — | 1000–1125* / 1150–1325 | 14 | *A |
| 267 | (A)LC098 | LCI 39 | LAS COLINAS T:12:10 | ? | ? | — | 1000–1125* / 1150–1350 | 14 | *A |
| 268 | (A)LC008 | LCI 4 | LAS COLINAS T:12:10 | ? | ? | — | 1000–1175 | 14 | |
| 269 | (A)LC011 | LCI 5 | LAS COLINAS T:12:10 | ? | ? | — | 1000–1175 | 14 | |
| 270 | (A)LC016 | LCI 10 | LAS COLINAS T:12:10 | ? | ? | — | 1000–1175 | 14 | |
| 271 | (A)LC020 | LCI 14 | LAS COLINAS T:12:10 | ? | ? | — | 1000–1175* / 1250–1300 | 14 | *A |
| 272 | (A)LC135 | LCI 49 | LAS COLINAS T:12:10 | ? | ? | — | 1000–1200 | 14 | |
| 273 | (A)LC136 | LCI 50 | LAS COLINAS T:12:10 | ? | ? | — | 1000–1200 | 14 | |
| 274 | (A)LC040 | LCI 20 | LAS COLINAS T:12:10 | ? | ? | — | 1000–1200* / 1225–1300 | 14 | *A |
| 275 | (A)LC056 | LCI 22 | LAS COLINAS T:12:10 | ? | ? | — | 1000–1200* / 1225–1325 | 14 | *A |
| 276 | (A)LC073 | LCI 32 | LAS COLINAS T:12:10 | ? | ? | — | 1000–1350 | 14 | R (1) |
| 277 | (A)LC079 | LCI 36 | LAS COLINAS T:12:10 | ? | ? | — | 1000–1350 | 14 | R (1) |
| 278 | (A)LC057 | LCI 27 | LAS COLINAS T:12:10 | ? | ? | — | 1000–1375 | 14 | R (1) |
| 279 | (A)LC015 | LCI 9 | LAS COLINAS T:12:10 | ? | ? | — | 1100–1175 | 14 | |
| 280 | (A)LC038 | LCI 19 | LAS COLINAS T:12:10 | ? | ? | — | 1100–1175 | 14 | |

MIDDLE SACATON PHASE

| No. | Code | LCI | Site | | | | | | | Dates | | |
|---|---|---|---|---|---|---|---|---|---|---|---|---|
| 281 | (C)1 | MDSAC 1 | U:9:66 | ? | ? | ? | ? | ? | — | 910–1025* / 1150–1200 | 14 | *A |

Table 3.1 *continued*

| Date No. | Lab No. | E&M No. | Site | Provenience | Nature of Sample | Assoc | Bias | C-14 Age | Dates | Refs | Remarks |
|---|---|---|---|---|---|---|---|---|---|---|---|
| 282 | (C)11 | MDSAC 3 | U:9:66 | ? | ? | ? | ? | — | 915–1025 | 14 | |
| 283 | (C)2 | MDSAC 2 | U:9:66 | ? | ? | ? | ? | — | 915–1025* | | |
| 284 | (C)25 | MDSAC 6 | U:9:66 | ? | ? | ? | ? | — | 1150–1200 | 14 | *A |
| | | | | | | | | | 925–1125* | | |
| 285 | (C)15 | MDSAC 5 | U:9:66 | ? | ? | ? | ? | — | 1150–1350 | 14 | *A |
| | | | | | | | | | 925–1125* | | |
| 286 | (C)12 | MDSAC 7 | U:9:66 | ? | ? | ? | ? | — | 1150–1375 | 14 | *A |
| | | | | | | | | | 925–1200 | | |
| | | | | | | | | | 1225–1350 | 14 | R (1) |
| **SACATON PHASE** | | | | | | | | | | | |
| 287 | (A)FT008 | — | FROGTOWN U:15:61 | STR 1 (PH) UPPER FLOOR | HEARTH | PRIM | 0 | — | 620–700 | | SAME PH AS 288. |
| | | | | | | | | | 900–960* | 7 | *A |
| 288 | (A)FT009 | SAC 15 | FROGTOWN U:15:61 | STR 1 (PH) LOWER FLOOR | HEARTH | PRIM | 0 | — | 920–1100* | | SAME PH AS 287. |
| | | | | | | | | | 1150–1450 | 7, 14 | *A |
| 289 | (A)FT010 | — | FROGTOWN U:15:61 | STR 9 (PH) EARLY HEARTH | HEARTH | PRIM | 0 | — | 620–720 | | SAME PH AS 290. |
| | | | | | | | | | 910–960* | 7 | *A |
| 290 | (A)FT004 | SAC 13 | FROGTOWN U:15:61 | STR 9 (PH) LATE HEARTH | HEARTH | PRIM | 0 | — | 925–1100* | | SAME PH AS 289. |
| | | | | | | | | | 1150–1200 | 7, 14 | *A |
| 291 | (A)FT003 | — | FROGTOWN U:15:61 | STR 29 (PH) | HEARTH | PRIM | 0 | — | 620–720 | 7 | R (3) |
| 292 | (A)FT006 | SAC 14 | FROGTOWN U:15:61 | STR 23 (PH) | HEARTH | PRIM | 0 | — | 910–1025* | | |
| | | | | | | | | | 1125–1250 | 7, 14 | *A |
| 293 | (A)FT015 | SAC 16 | FROGTOWN U:15:61 | STR 53 (PH) | HEARTH | PRIIM | 0 | — | 1000–1325 | 7, 14 | R (1) |
| 294 | B10937 | — | LA CIUDAD T:12:37 (ASU) | F 129 (PH) FILL | FILL CHCL | ? | ? | 1270 ± 80 | 660–863 | 28 | SAME PH AS 295, 296. R (2) |
| 295 | B10936 | — | LA CIUDAD T:12:37 (ASU) | F 129 (PH) FILL | FILL CHCL | ? | ? | 960 ± 65 | 998–1158 | 22 | SAME PH AS 294, 296 |

| No. | Lab No. | | Site | Provenience | Material | Context | | C14 Date | Date Range | | Notes |
|---|---|---|---|---|---|---|---|---|---|---|---|
| 296 | (C)63 | SAC 36 | LA CIUDAD T:12:37 (ASU) | F 129 A (PH) | HEARTH | PRIM | 0 | — | 1020–1050 | 22 | SAME PH AS 294, 295 |
| 297 | (C)115 | SAC 41 | LA CIUDAD T:12:37 (ASU) | F 1768 (PH) | HEARTH | PRIM | 0 | — | 950–1015*<br>1175–1275 | 22 | SAME PH AS 298.<br>*B |
| 298 | B10935 | — | LA CIUDAD T:12:37 (ASU) | F 1768 (PH) FILL | MESQ CHCL | ? | ? | 860 ± 65 | 1041–1257 | 28 | SAME PH AS 297.<br>R (2) |
| 299 | B10935 | — | LA CIUDAD T:12:37 (ASU) | F 689 (PH) FILL | MESQ CHCL | ? | ? | 930 ± 65 | 1004–1191 | 28 | |
| 300 | (A)PI013 | (SAC 1) | BRADY WASH SITE NA 18003 | LOCUS H, F 12 (PH) | HEARTH | PRIM | 0 | — | 820–930<br>850–1070<br>1210–1450 | 20 | R (4) |
| 301 | (A)PI020 | (SAC 2) | BRADY WASH SITE NA 18003 | LOCUS H, F 21 (PH) | HEARTH | PRIM | 0 | — | 970–1070*<br>1090–1330 | 20 | *A |
| 302 | (A)PI026 | (SCSAC2) | BRADY WASH SITE NA 18003 | LOCUS C, F 33-A (PIT STR) | HEARTH | PRIM | 0 | — | 1060–1110 | 20 | |
| 303 | RL397 | — | WESTWING SITE T:2:27 (ASU) | F 5 (PIT) FILL | CHCL | SEC | + | 1090 ± 90 | 782–1019 | 38, 42 | |
| 304 | A604 | — | SNAKETOWN U:13:1 | HOUSE 1:10F | ? | ? | ? | 1050 ± 100 | 890–1148 | 25, 38 | SAME HOUSE AS 305 |
| 305 | A603 | — | SNAKETOWN U:13:1 | HOUSE 1:10 F | ? | ? | ? | 1010 ± 100 | 901–1155 | 25, 38 | SAME HOUSE AS 304 |
| 304, 305 | | — | SNAKETOWN U:13:1 | HOUSE 1:10F | MIXED | ? | ? | 1030 ± 71 | 904–1146 | | AVE. OF 304 AND 305 |
| 306 | (D)48 | — | SNAKETOWN U:13:1 | HOUSE 9:5G | HEARTH | PRIM | 0 | — | 940–1010*<br>POST 1475 | 13, 24 | *C (13) |
| 307 | (D)44 | — | SNAKETOWN U:13:1 | HOUSE 5:5F | HEARTH | PRIM | 0 | — | 1000–1025*<br>1200–1325 | 13, 24 | *C (13) |
| 308 | (D)42 | — | SNAKETOWN U:13:1 | HOUSE 4:111 | HEARTH | PRIM | 0 | — | 1000–1025*<br>1200–1325 | 13, 24 | *C (13) |
| 309 | (D)41 | — | SNAKETOWN U:13:1 | HOUSE 1:5F | HEARTH | PRIM | 0 | — | 1010–1025*<br>1250–1325 | 13, 24 | *C (13) |
| 310 | (D)43 | — | SNAKETOWN U:13:1 | HOUSE 3:111 | HEARTH | PRIM | 0 | — | 1010–1025*<br>1200–1315 | 13, 24 | *C (13) |

Table 3.1  *continued*

| Date No. | Lab No. | E&M No. | Site | Provenience | Nature of Sample | Assoc | Bias | C-14 Age | Dates | Refs | Remarks |
|---|---|---|---|---|---|---|---|---|---|---|---|
| 311 | M324 | — | SNAKETOWN U:13:1 | HOUSE 8:6G FLOOR | TEXTILES IN JAR | D.F. REFUSE | 0 | 700 ± 250 | 1030–1440 | 25, 38 | R (1) |
| 312 | A598 | — | SNAKETOWN U:13:1 | CREMATORIUM 1:10D | CHCL FUEL | PRIM | — | 220 ± 110 | 1521–1955 | 25, 38 | R (3) |
| 313 | (C) 1 | SAC 8 | T:12:37 (ASM) | ? | ? | ? | ? | — | 915–1000 | 14 | |
| 314 | (A)LC063 | SAC 23 | LAS COLINAS T:12:10 | ? | ? | ? | ? | — | 920–1000 | 14 | |
| 315 | (A)LC095 | SAC29 | LAS COLINAS T:12:10 | ? | ? | ? | ? | — | 920–1000 | 14 | |
| 316 | (A)LC076 | SAC 24 | LAS COLINAS T:12:10 | ? | ? | ? | ? | — | 920–1000 | 14 | R (1) |
| 317 | (A)LC080 | SAC 25 | LAS COLINAS T:12:10 | ? | ? | ? | ? | — | 920–1325 / 920–1375 | 14 | R (1) |
| 318 | (A)LC096 | SAC 30 | LAS COLINAS T:12:10 | ? | ? | ? | ? | — | 925–1050* / 1150–1375 | 14 | *A |
| 319 | (A)LC037 | SAC 19 | LAS COLINAS T:12:10 | ? | ? | ? | ? | — | 930–1025 | 14 | |
| 320 | (A)LC027 | SAC 17 | LAS COLINAS T:12:10 | ? | ? | ? | ? | — | 1000–1025* / 1150–1350 | 14 | *A |
| 321 | (A)LC097 | SAC31 | LAS COLINAS T:12:10 | ? | ? | ? | ? | — | 1000–1175 | 14 | |
| 322 | (A)LC089 | SAC 27 | LAS COLINAS T:12:10 | ? | ? | ? | ? | — | 1000–1200* / 1225–1325 | 14 | *A |
| 323 | (A)LC060 | SAC 22 | LAS COLINAS T:12:10 | ? | ? | ? | ? | — | 1100–1150 | 14 | |
| 324 | (?)947 | — | MIAMI WASH V:9:56 | PITHOUSE 1 F 1 (PH) | HEARTH FILL | PRIM | 0 | — | 950–1010* / 1350–1425 | 11, 13, 37 | *C (13) |
| 325 | RL595 | — | T:8:38 (ASU) | BURNED FILL | CHCL | SEC? | ? | 940 ± 140 | 980–1256 | 36 | R (1) |

| # | Code | Sub-code | Site | Provenience | Material | | | C14 date | Calibrated range | ± | Ref |
|---|---|---|---|---|---|---|---|---|---|---|---|
| 326 | RL596 | — | T:8:38 (ASU) | F 2 (TRASH MOUND) 28 CM BELOW SURF | CHCL | ? | ? | 820 ± 100 | 1043–1280 | 36 | R (3) |
| 327 | (C)1 | SAC 9 | T:16:16 | ? | ? | ? | ? | — | 1000–1050* / 1150–1300 | 14 | *A |
| 328 | (C)3 | SAC 11 | T:16:16 | ? | ? | ? | ? | — | 1000–1175* / 1225–1325 | 14 | *A |
| 329 | AM001 | — | ADOBE DAM SITE NA 15909 | PITHOUSE | HEARTH | PRIM | 0 | — | 1050–1300 | 37 | R (1) |
| | | | | LATE SACATON PHASE | | | | | | | |
| 330 | (C)8 | LTSAC 2 | U:9:66 | ? | ? | ? | ? | — | 910–1100* / 1150–1325 | 14 | *A |
| 331 | (C)5 | LTSAC1 | U:9:66 | ? | ? | ? | ? | — | 920–1125* / 1150–1400 | 14 | *A |
| 332 | (C)27 | LTSAC 6 | U:9:66 | ? | ? | ? | ? | — | 925–1050* / 1150–1400 | 14 | *A |
| 333 | (C)20 | LTSAC 5 | U:9:66 | ? | ? | ? | ? | — | 1000–1325 | 14 | R (1) |
| 334 | (A)LC061 | LCII 6 | LAS COLINAS T:12:10 | ? | ? | ? | ? | — | 900–1025 | 14 | |
| 335 | (A)LC102 | LCII 7 | LAS COLINAS T:12:10 | ? | ? | ? | ? | — | 920–1025* / 1150–1275 | 14 | *A |
| 336 | (A)LC110 | LCII 8 | LAS COLINAS T:12:10 | ? | ? | ? | ? | — | 920–1025* / 1300–1400 | 14 | *A |
| 337 | (A)LC010 | LCII 1 | LAS COLINAS T:12:10 | ? | ? | ? | ? | — | 925–1025* / 1150–1275 | 14 | *A |
| 338 | (A)LC127 | LCII 9 | LAS COLINAS T:12:10 | ? | ? | ? | ? | — | 925–1050* / 1150–1375 | 14 | *A |
| 339 | (A)LC162 | LCII 12 | LAS COLINAS T:12:10 | ? | ? | ? | ? | — | 925–1125* / 1150–1325 | 14 | *A |
| 340 | (A)LC048 | LCII 5 | LAS COLINAS T:12:10 | ? | ? | ? | ? | — | 925–1350 | 14 | R (1) |
| 341 | (A)LC131 | LCII 11 | LAS COLINAS T:12:10 | ? | ? | ? | ? | — | 1000–1050* / 1075–1175 | 14 | *A |

Table 3.1  *continued*

| Date No. | Lab No. | E&M No. | Site | Provenience | Nature of Sample | Assoc | Bias | C-14 Age | Dates | Refs | Remarks |
|---|---|---|---|---|---|---|---|---|---|---|---|
| 342 | (A)LC029 | LCII 4 | LAS COLINAS T:12:10 | ? | ? | ? | ? | — | 1000–1125* / 1150–1200 | 14 | *A |
| 343 | (A)LC028 | LCII 3 | LAS COLINAS T:12:10 | ? | ? | ? | ? | — | 1075–1175 | 14 | |
| 344 | (A)LC023 | LCII 2 | LAS COLINAS T:12:10 | ? | ? | ? | ? | — | 1000–1200 | 14 | |
| | | | | | SACATON-SOHO TRANSITION | | | | | | |
| 345 | (A)SG008 | — | GOPHERETTE SITE U:15:87 | STR 3 (PH) | HEARTH | PRIM | 0 | — | 620–700 / 900–960 | 7 | R (3) |
| 346 | (A)SG009 | — | GOPHERETTE SITE U:15:87 | STR 1 (PH) | HEARTH | PRIM | 0 | — | 620–710 / 900–960 | 7 | R (3) |
| 347 | (A)SG003 | — | JONES RUIN U:15:48 | LOCUS A, STR 4 (PH) | HEARTH | PRIM | 0 | — | 700–1450 | 7 | R (1) |
| 348 | (A)SG002 | — | JONES RUIN U:15:48 | F 120 (EXTRAMURAL HEARTH) | HEARTH | PRIM | 0 | — | 1040–1210 | 7 | |
| 349 | (A)PI023 | (SASOH 3) | BRADY WASH SITE NA 18001, LOCUS D | F 34 (PH) | FLOOR | PRIM | 0 | — | 820–920 / 860–1070* / 1140–1450 | 20 | SAME PH AS 350. *B |
| 350 | (A)PI024 | (SASOH 4) | BRADY WASH SITE NA 18003, LOCUS D | F 34 (PH) | HEARTH | PRIM | 0 | — | 970–1090 / 1080–1350 | 20 | SAME PH AS 349. R (1) |
| 351 | (A)PI001 | (SASOH 1) | BRADY WASH SITE NA 18003, LOCUS D | F 14 (PH) | ? | ? | ? | — | 1000–1090 | 20 | |
| 352 | (A)PI003 | — | BRADY WASH SITE NA 18003, LOCUS D | F 24 (PH) | ? | ? | ? | — | 1000–1180 | 20 | |
| 353 | B13178 | — | BRADY WASH SITE NA 18003, LOCUS D | F 33 (SURFACE ADOBE) | ? | ? | ? | 650 ± 50 | 1280–1390 | 2 | SAME PH AS 355. |
| 354 | (C)12 | SASOH 6 | McCLELLAN WASH SITE NA 18031 | F 31 (PH) | HEARTH | PRIM | 0 | — | 910–1100 / 1150–1450 | 14, 21 | R (1) |

| No. | | | Site / Provenience | Feature | | | | | Date Range | | Refs | Notes |
|---|---|---|---|---|---|---|---|---|---|---|---|---|
| 355 | B14872 | — | McCLELLAN WASH SITE NA 18031 | F 31 (PH) | STRUCT ELEMS | PRIM | — | 790 ± 60 | 1193–1278 | | 3 | SAME PH AS 354 |
| 356 | (C)8 | SASOH 5 | McCLELLAN WASH SITE NA 18031 | F 26 (PH) | HEARTH | PRIM | 0 | — | 925–1350 | | 14, 21 | SAME PH AS 357. R (1) |
| 357 | B13185 | — | McCLELLAN WASH SITE NA 18031 | F 26 (PH) | STRUCT ELEMS | PRIM | — | 310 ± 90 | 1450–1659 | | 3 | SAME PH AS 356. R (3) |
| 358 | (C)15 | SASOH 8 | T:12:37 (ASM) | ? | ? | ? | ? | — | 1050–1125 | | 14 | |
| 359 | (C)14 | SASOH 7 | T:12:37 (ASM) | ? | ? | ? | ? | — | 1000–1200 | | | |
| 360 | (A)LC085 | SASOH 11 | LAS COLINAS T:12:10 | ? | ? | ? | ? | — | 1225–1325 | | 14 | R (4) |
| 361 | (A)LC160 | SASOH 13 | LAS COLINAS T:12:10 | ? | ? | ? | ? | — | 1050–1125 | | 14 | |
| 362 | (A)LC091 | SASOH 12 | LAS COLINAS T:12:10 | ? | ? | ? | ? | — | 1050–1175 | 1100–1175 | 14 | |
| **EARLY SOHO PHASE** | | | | | | | | | | | | |
| 363 | (A)PI012 | SOH 2 | BRADY WASH SITE NA 18003, LOCUS B | F 12 (PH) | ? | ? | ? | — | 1000–1325 | | 14, 20 | R (1) |
| 364 | (A)PI010 | SOH 1 | BRADY WASH SITE NA 18003, LOCUS B | F 6 (PH) | ? | ? | ? | — | 1000–1325 | | 14, 20 | R (1) |
| 365 | ? | — | LAS COLINAS T:12:10 | F 100 (PIT ROOM) | ? | ? | ? | — | 1015–1300 | | 13, 19, 37 | R (1) |
| 366 | ? | — | LAS COLINAS T:12:10 | F 125 (PIT ROOM) | ? | ? | ? | — | 1015–1300 | | 13, 19, 37 | R (1) |
| **SOHO PHASE** | | | | | | | | | | | | |
| 367 | (C)13 | SOH 13 | T:12:37 (ASM) | ? | ? | ? | ? | — | 915–1025 | 1150–1200* | | *A |
| 368 | (C)11 | SOH 12 | T:12:37 (ASM) | ? | ? | ? | ? | — | 915–1025 | 1150–1300* | 14 | *A |
| 369 | (C)2 | SOH 9 | T:12:37 (ASM) | ? | ? | ? | ? | — | 925–1325 | | 14 | |
| 370 | (C)18 | SOH 14 | T:12:37 (ASM) | ? | ? | ? | ? | — | 1000–1050 | 1150–1325* | 14 | *A |

Table 3.1 *continued*

| Date No. | Lab No. | E&M No. | Site | Provenience | Nature of Sample | Assoc | Bias | C-14 Age | Dates | Refs | Remarks |
|---|---|---|---|---|---|---|---|---|---|---|---|
| 371 | (C)7 | SOH 10 | T:12:37 (ASM) | ? | ? | ? | ? | — | 1000–1125 / 1150–1325* | 14 | *A |
| 372 | (A)GB002 | SOH 23 | ? | | ? | ? | ? | — | 915–1025 / 1150–1250* | 14 | *A |
| 373 | (A)GB001 | SOH 22 | ? | ? | ? | ? | ? | — | 1000–1325 | 14 | R (1) |
| 374 | (A)PI015 | SOH 3 | BRADY WASH SITE NA 18003, LOCUS B | F 7-2 (PH) | ? | ? | ? | — | 920–1100 / 1150–1275 | 14, 20 | R (4) |
| 375 | (A)LC142 | SOH 20 | LAS COLINAS T:12:10 | ? | ? | ? | ? | — | 920–1025 / 1150–1225* | 14 | *A |
| 376 | (A)LC113 | SOH 16 | LAS COLINAS T:12:10 | | ? | ? | ? | — | 920–1050 / 1150–1325* | 14 | *A |
| 377 | (A)LC139 | SOH 21 | LAS COLINAS T:12:10 | ? | ? | ? | ? | — | 925–1050 / 1150–1400 | 14 | R (1) |
| 378 | (A)LC072 | SOH 19 | LAS COLINAS T:12:10 | ? | ? | ? | ? | — | 1000–1125 / 1150–1300* | 14 | *A |
| 379 | ? | — | LAS COLINAS T:12:10 | F 76 (POST REIN-FORCED ADOBE ROOM) | ? | ? | ? | — | 1015–1300 | 13, 19, 37 | R (1) |
| 380 | ? | — | LAS COLINAS T:12:10 | F 80 (POST REIN-FORCED ADOBE ROOM) | ? | ? | ? | — | 1150–1250 | 13, 19, 37 | |
| 381 | (C)3 | SOH 8 | McCLELLAN WASH SITE NA 18031 | F 13 (SEMISUBTERR. ADOBE WALLED ST.) | HEARTH | PRIM | 0 | — | 920–1025 / 1150–1450 | 14, 21 | R(1) |
| 382 | (C)2 | SOH 7 | McCLELLAN WASH SITE NA 18031 | F 7 (SEMISUBTER. ADOBE WALLED ST.) | HEARTH | PRIM | 0 | — | 920–1125 / 1150–1325* | 14, 21 | *A |
| 383 | (C)7 | — | McCLELLAN WASH SITE NA 18031 | F 6 (SEMISUBTERR. ADOBE WALLED ST.) | HEARTH | PRIM | 0 | — | 925–1350 | 21 | SAME STR AS 384. |
| 384 | B13184 | — | McCLELLAN WASH SITE NA 18031 | F 6 (SEMISUBTERR. ADOBE WALLED ST.) | STRUCT ELEMS | PRIM | - | 740 ± 60 | 1227–1283 | 3 | SAME STR AS 383 / R (1) |
| 385 | (C)25 | (CIV 14) | BRADY WASH SITE NA 18003, LOCUS E | F 12A (ADOBE STRUCT) | HEARTH | PRIM | 0 | — | 925–1025 / 1175–1425 | 20 | R (1) |

| No. | Code 1 | Code 2 | Site | Feature | Context | | | | Date 1 | Date 2 | Ref | Note |
|---|---|---|---|---|---|---|---|---|---|---|---|---|
| 386 | (C)5 | (CIV 12) | BRADY WASH SITE NA 18003, LOCUS E | F 3A (ADOBE STRUCT) | HEARTH | PRIM | 0 | — | 925–1025 | 1150–1325* | 20 | *A |
| 387 | (C)4 | (LCIV 3) | BRADY WASH SITE NA 18003, LOCUS C | F 83-A (ADOBE ST.) | HEARTH | PRIM | 0 | — | 925–1025 | 1250–1425* | 20 | *A |
| 388 | (C)2 | (LCIV 1) | BRADY WASH SITE NA 18003, LOCUS C | F 82-A (ADOBE ST.) | HEARTH | PRIM | 0 | — | 925–1025 | 1300–1425* | 20 | *A |
| 389 | (A)PI005 | (SASOH 2) | BRADY WASH SITE NA 18003, LOCUS C | F 3 (ADOBE STR.) | FIREPIT | PRIM | 0 | — | 1000–1280 | | 1 | R (1) |
| 390 | (A)PI006 | — | BRADY WASH SITE NA 18003, LOCUS D | F 32 (HORNO) | HORNO | PRIM | 0 | — | 940–1070 | 1170–1300* | 1 | *A |
| 391 | ? | — | ESCALANTE RUIN U:15:3 | PLAZA 1 | FLOOR | PRIM | 0 | — | 950–1010 | | 12, 13, 37 | R (4)  SAME PROV AS 392. |
| 392 | ? | — | ESCALANTE RUIN U:15:3 | PLAZA 1 | HEARTH | PRIM | 0 | — | 1000–1015 | 1200–1300* | 12, 13, 37 | *C (13)  SAME PROV AS 391. |
| 393 | ? | — | ESCALANTE GROUP U:15:32 | ROOM 2 | HEARTH | PRIM | 0 | — | 1000–1015 | 1200–1300* | 12, 13, 37 | *C (13) |
| 394 | ? | — | ESCALANTE GROUP U:15:32 | ROOM 6 | HEARTH | PRIM | 0 | — | 1000–1320 | | 12, 13, 37 | R (1) |
| 395 | ? | — | ESCALANTE GROUP U:15:32 | ROOM 3 | HEARTH | PRIM | 0 | — | 1010–1025 | 1200–1310* | 12, 13, 37 | *C (13) |
| 396 | ? | — | ESCALANTE GROUP U:15:32 | ROOM 5 | HEARTH | PRIM | 0 | — | 1125–1250 | | 12, 13, 37 | |
| 397 | ? | — | ESCALANTE GROUP U:15:32 | ROOM 4 | HEARTH | PRIM | 0 | — | 1240–1300 | | 12, 13, 37 | |
| 398 | ? | — | ESCALANTE GROUP U:15:22 | ROOM 2 | HEARTH | PRIM | 0 | — | 1010–1025 | 1175–1315* | 12, 13, 37 | *C (13) |
| 399 | ? | — | ESCALANTE GROUP U:15:22 | ROOM 6 | HEARTH | PRIM | 0 | — | 1010–1060 | 1200–1315* | 12, 13, 37 | *C (13) |
| 400 | ? | — | ESCALANTE GROUP U:15:27 | ROOM 7 | HEARTH | PRIM | 0 | — | 1015–1275 | | 12, 13, 37 | *C (13) |
| 401 | (D)909 | — | SUPERSTITION FREEWAY U:9:46 | HOUSE 6 | HEARTH | PRIM | 0 | — | 1015–1310 | | 13, 29 | R (1) |

Table 3.1 *continued*

| Date No. | Lab No. | E&M No. | Site | Provenience | Nature of Sample | Assoc | Bias | C-14 Age | Dates | Refs | Remarks |
|---|---|---|---|---|---|---|---|---|---|---|---|
| 402 | (D)908 | — | SUPERSTITION FREEWAY U:9:46 | HOUSE 5 | HEARTH | PRIM | 0 | — | 1075–1275 | 13, 29 | R (1) |
| 403 | B13187 | — | NA 18037 | CHCL ON FLOOR | STRUCT ELEM | PRIM | - | 630 ± 100 | 1280–1410 | 3 | |
| LATE SOHO PHASE | | | | | | | | | | | |
| 404 | (A)PI018 | LTSOH 1 | BRADY WASH SITE NA 18003, LOCUS B | F 15-1 (PH) | ? | ? | ? | — | 925–1050 1150–1350* | 14, 20 | *A |
| 405 | (A)PI017 | SOH 5 | BRADY WASH SITE NA 18003, LOCUS B | F 8 (PH) | ? | ? | ? | — | 1000–1050 1290–1340* | 14, 20 | *A |
| SOHO-CIVANO TRANSITION | | | | | | | | | | | |
| 406 | (C)17 | CIV 3 | BRADY WASH SITE NA 18003, LOCUS E | F 236 (ADOBE STR) | HEARTH | PRIM | 0 | — | 1300–1375 | 14, 20 | |
| 407 | (C)6 | SOH 5 | BRADY WASH SITE NA 18003, LOCUS I | F 4 (ADOBE STR) | HEARTH | PRIM | 0 | — | 925–1050 1150–1375 | 14, 20 | R (1) |
| 408 | (C)7 | CIV 4 | BRADY WASH SITE NA 18003, LOCUS I | F 25 (ADOBE STR) | HEARTH | PRIM | 0 | — | 925–1425 | 14, 20 | R (1) |
| 409 | (C)1 | SOH 6 | McCLELLAN WASH SITE NA 18031 | F 12 (SMALL SEMISUBTERR. ADOBE WALLED STR) | HEARTH | PRIM | 0 | — | 925–1025 1150–1425 | 14, 21 | R (1) |
| 410 | (C)14 | — | BRADY WASH SITE NA 18003, LOCUS S | F 5 (ADOBE ROOM) | HEARTH | PRIM | 0 | — | 925–1100 1175–1425 | 21 | R (1) |
| 411 | (C)12 | — | BRADY WASH SITE NA 18003, LOCUS D | F 35 (SEMISUBTERR. ADOBE) | ? | ? | ? | — | 1300–1375 | 21 | |
| EARLY CIVANO PHASE | | | | | | | | | | | |
| 412 | ? | — | LAS COLINAS T:12:10 | F 34 (PH) | HEARTH B | PRIM | 0 | — | 940–1000 1400–POST 1425* | 13, 19, 37 | SAME PH AS 413. *C (13) |

| No. | Code A | Code B | Site | Feature | HEARTH | PRIM | | C14 | Dates | Refs | SAME PH AS 412. |
|---|---|---|---|---|---|---|---|---|---|---|---|
| 413 | ? | — | LAS COLINAS T:12:10 | F 34 (PH) | A | PRIM | 0 | — | 950–1010 / 1325–POST 1425* | 13, 19, 37 | *C (13) |
| 414 | ? | — | LAS COLINAS T:12:10 | F 40 (PH) | ? | ? | ? | — | 940–1000 / 1400–POST 1425* | 13, 19, 37 | *C (13) |
| 415 | ? | — | LAS COLINAS T:12:10 | F 39 (PH) | ? | ? | ? | — | 950–1015 / 1325–1425* | 13, 19, 37 | *C (13) |
| 416 | ? | — | LAS COLINAS T:12:10 | F 26 (PH) | ? | ? | ? | — | 1297–1393 | 13, 19, 37 | |
| | | | | | | | | | **CIVANO PHASE** | | |
| 417 | (C)15 | (LCIV 7) | BRADY WASH SITE NA 18003, LOCUS E | F 24 A (ADOBE STR) | HEARTH | PRIM | 0 | — | 680–735 / 900–1025 | 20 | R (3) |
| 418 | (A)PI022 | (LCIV 12) | BRADY WASH SITE NA 18003, LOCUS I | F 9 (ADOBE STR) | FIREPIT | PRIM | 0 | — | 695–720 / 925–1025 | 20 | R (3) |
| 419 | B13180 | — | BRADY WASH SITE NA 18003, LOCUS I | F 18 | ? | ? | ? | 910 ± 70 | 1022–1212 / 880–1070 | 2 | R (3) |
| 420 | (A)PI007 | — | BRADY WASH SITE NA 18003, LOCUS C | F 26-B (ADOBE STR) | HEARTH | PRIM | 0 | — | 1400–1450* / 900–1000 | 20 | *A |
| 421 | (D)50 | — | UU:13:22 | ROOM 8 | HEARTH | PRIM | 0 | — | 1400–POST 1425* | 13, 24 | *C (13) |
| 422 | (D)49 | — | UU:13:22 | ROOM 10 | HEARTH | PRIM | 0 | — | 910–940 / POST 1425* | 13, 24 | *C (13) |
| 423 | (D)53 | — | UU:13:22 | ROOM 7 | HEARTH | PRIM | 0 | — | 940–1000 / 1400–POST 1425* | 13, 24 | *C (13) |
| 424 | (D)51 | — | UU:13:22 | ROOM 4 | HEARTH | PRIM | 0 | — | 950–1015 / 1350–POST 1425* | 13, 24 | *C (13) |
| 425 | ? | — | ESCALANTE RUIN U:15:3 | ROOM 16 | FLOOR | PRIM | 0 | — | 910–940 / POST 1425* | 12, 13, 37 | *C (13) |
| 426 | ? | — | ESCALANTE RUIN U:15:3 | ROOM 2 | FLOOR | PRIM | 0 | — | 930–1000 / POST 1425* | 12, 13, 37 | *C (13) |
| 427 | ? | — | ESCALANTE RUIN U:15:3 | ROOM 4 | HEARTH | PRIM | 0 | — | 940–1000 / 1400–POST 1425* | 12. 13, 37 | *C (13) |

Table 3.1    *continued*

| Date No. | Lab No. | E&M No. | Site | Provenience | Nature of Sample | Assoc | Bias | C-14 Age | Dates | Refs | Remarks |
|---|---|---|---|---|---|---|---|---|---|---|---|
| 428 | ? | — | ESCALANTE RUIN U:15:3 | ROOM 17 | WALL | PRIM | 0 | — | 950–1015 / 1350–POST 1425* | 12, 13, 37 | *C (13) |
| 429 | ? | — | ESCALANTE RUIN U:15:3 | ROOM 22 | HEARTH | PRIM | 0 | — | 975–1010 / 1325–POST 1425* | 12, 13, 17 | *C (13) |
| 430 | ? | — | ESCALANTE RUIN U:15:3 | ROOM 1 | HEARTH | PRIM | 0 | — | 1308–1352 | 12, 13, 37 | |
| 431 | ? | — | ESCALANTE RUIN U:15:3 | ROOM 5 | HEARTH | PRIM | 0 | — | 1346–1364 | 12, 13, 37 | |
| 432 | ? | — | ESCALANTE GROUP U:15:27 | ROOM 2 | HEARTH | PRIM | 0 | — | 950–1015 / 1350–POST 1425* | 12, 13, 37 | *C (13) |
| 433 | (C)13 | (LCIV 6) | BRADY WASH SITE NA 18003, LOCUS S | F 11 (ADOBE ROOM) | HEARTH | PRIM | 0 | — | 925–1025 | 20 | R (3) |
| 434 | (C)11 | (CIV 5) | BRADY WASH SITE NA 18003, LOCUS S | F 23 (ADOBE ROOM) | HEARTH | PRIM | 0 | — | 925–1025 / 1300–1425* | 20 | *A |
| 435 | (C)12 | — | BRADY WASH SITE NA 18003, LOCUS S | F 6 (ADOBE ROOM) | HEARTH | PRIM | 0 | — | 925–1100 / 1150–1425 | 20 | R (1) |
| 436 | B13182 | — | BRADY WASH SITE NA 18003, LOCUS S | F 2 (POST REINFORCED ADOBE HOUSE) | FILL CHCL | ? | ? | 300 ± 70 | 1486–1656 | 2 | |
| 437 | ? | — | CASA GRANDE | COMPOUND A STRUCTURE 5 | HEARTH | PRIM | 0 | — | 950–1015 / 1375–POST 1425* | 12, 37, 43 | *C (13) |
| 438 | (A)PI008 | — | BRADY WASH SITE NA 18003, LOCUS H | F 9 (HORNO) | HORNO | PRIM | 0 | — | 970–1070 / 1180–1350* | 20 | *A |
| 439 | ? | — | LAS COLINAS T:12:10 | F 114 (PH) | ? | ? | ? | — | 975–1010 / 1325–POST 1425* | 13, 19, 37 | *C (13) |
| 440 | ? | — | LAS COLINAS T:12:10 | F 41 (PH) | HEARTH | PRIM | 0 | — | 1383–1417 | 19 | |

| No. | Lab No. | Code | Site | Provenience | Material | PRIM OR SEC | – TO + | Date | Ref | Notes |
|---|---|---|---|---|---|---|---|---|---|---|
| 441 | A3527 | — | LAS FOSAS U:15:19 | STR 12 FLOOR, ASH LENS | CHCL | | – TO + 680 ± 110 | 1257–1395 | 8 | SAME STR AS 442 |
| 442 | A3528 | — | LAS FOSAS U:15:19 | STR 12 FLOOR, ASH LENS | AGAVE | D.F. REFUSE OR SEC | 0 OR + 370 ± 60 | 1441–1635 | 8 | SAME STR AS 441 |
| 443 | A3526 | — | LAS FOSAS U:15:19 | STR 11 FLOOR | COTTON SEEDS | D.F. REFUSE OR SEC | 0 430 ± 60 | 1425–1488 | 8 | SAME STR AS 444, 445 |
| 444 | A3525 | — | LAS FOSAS U:15:19 | STR 11 | REED ROOF MATERIAL | PRIM | 0 POST BOMB | — | 8 | SAME STR AS 443, 445. R(3) |
| 445 | A3524 | — | LAS FOSAS U:15:19 | STR 11 | ROOF BEAMS | PRIM | 0 POST BOMB | — | 8 | SAME STR AS 443, 444. R(3) |
| | | | | | | **LATE CIVANO PHASE** | | | | |
| 446 | (C)10 | (LCIV 5) | BRADY WASH SITE NA 18003, LOCUS E | F 11 A (ADOBE STR) | HEARTH | PRIM | 0 — | 700–720 925–1025 | 20 | R (3) |
| 447 | (C)23 | (LCIV 10) | BRADY WASH SITE NA 18003, LOCUS E | F 14 A (PH) | HEARTH | PRIM | 0 — | 925–1025 1300–1425* | 20 | *A |
| 448 | (C)3 | (LCIV 2) | BRADY WASH SITE NA 18003, LOCUS E | F 60 A (PH) | HEARTH | PRIM | 0 — | 925–1025 1300–1425* | 20 | *A |
| 449 | (C)19 | (LCIV 9) | BRADY WASH SITE NA 18003, LOCUS E | F 89 A (PH) | HEARTH | PRIM | 0 — | 925–1025 1325–1400* | 20 | *A |
| 450 | (C)16 | (LCIV 8) | BRADY WASH SITE NA 18003, LOCUS E | F 57 A (PH) | HEARTH | PRIM | 0 — | 925–1025 1325–1425* | 20 | *A |
| 451 | (C)9 | (LCIV 4) | BRADY WASH SITE NA 18003, LOCUS E | F 58 A (ADOBE STR) | HEARTH | PRIM | 0 — | 925–1025 1375–1425* | 20 | *A |
| 452 | (A)PI021 | (LCIV 11) | BRADY WASH SITE NA 18003, LOCUS C | F 51-B (PH) | HEARTH | PRIM | 0 — | 820–1070 1230–1450* | 20 | *A |
| 453 | (A)PI029 | (LCIV 13) | BRADY WASH SITE NA 18003, LOCUS C | F 45-B (PH) | HEARTH | PRIM | 0 — | 880–1070 1180–1450 | 20 | R (1) |
| 454 | (A)PI031 | (LCIV 14) | BRADY WASH SITE NA 18003, LOCUS C | F 44-C (PH) | HEARTH | PRIM | 0 — | 910–1070 1300–1450* | 20 | *A |
| 455 | ? | — | LAS COLINAS T:12:10 | F 74 (PH) | ? | ? | ? — | 925–950 POST 1425* | 13, 19 | *C (13) |

Table 3.1   *continued*

| Date No. | Lab No. | E&M No. | Site | Provenience | Nature of Sample | Assoc | Bias | C-14 Age | Dates | Refs | Remarks |
|---|---|---|---|---|---|---|---|---|---|---|---|
| 456 | ? | — | LAS COLINAS T:12:10 | F 35 (PH) | HEARTH B | PRIM | 0 | — | 950–1010 / 1325–POST 1425* | 13, 19 | SAME PH AS 456. *C (13) |
| 457 | ? | — | LAS COLINAS T:12:10 | F 35 (PH) | HEARTH A | PRIM | 0 | — | 950–1015 / 1325–1425* | 13, 19 | SAME PH AS 455. *C (13) |
| | | | | | EL POLVORON PHASE | | | | | | |
| 458 | (A)PV001 | (EP 6) | EL POLVORON U:15:59 | STR 5 (PH) | HEARTH | PRIM | 0 | — | 700–900 / 1060–1450 | 7 | R (1) |
| 459 | (A)PV002 | (EP 7) | EL POLVORON U:15:59 | STR 4 (PH) | HEARTH | PRIM | 0 | — | 700–1060 | 7 | SAME PH AS 460, 461. R (1) |
| 460 | A3529 | — | EL POLVORON U:15:59 | STR 4 (PH) | STRUCT ELEM | PRIM | – | 390 ± 70 | 1434–1629 | 8 | SAME PH AS 459, 461. R (2) |
| 461 | A3530 | — | EL POLVORON U:15:59 | STR 4 (PH) | STRUCT ELEM | PRIM | – | POST BOMB | — | 8 | SAME PH AS 459, 460. R (2) |
| 462 | (A)PV003 | (EP 8) | EL POLVORON U:15:59 | STR 6 (PH) | HEARTH | PRIM | 0 | — | 930–1070 / 1340–1450* | 7 | *A |
| | | | | | CAÑADA DEL ORO PHASE | | | | | | |
| 463 | B12552 | — | DAKOTA WASH SITE AA:16:49 | F 4 (PH) FLOOR OR ROOF LEVEL | CHCL | PRIM | – | 1390 ± 50 | 605–666 | 40 | R (3) |
| 464 | B14158 | — | DAKOTA WASH SITE AA:16:49 | F 10 (PH) ROOF SUPP POST | OUTER RINGS (PROSOPIS) | PRIM | – OR 0 | 1330 ± 70 | 642–770 | 40 | SAME PH AS 465 |
| 465 | B12555 | — | DAKOTA WASH SITE AA:16:49 | F 10 (PH) ROOF SUPP POST | OUTER RINGS (PROSOPIS) | PRIM | – OR 0 | 1210 ± 70 | 689–937 | 40 | SAME PH AS 464 |
| 464–465 | — | — | DAKOTA WASH SITE AA:16:49 | F 10 (PH) ROOF SUPP POST | OUTER RINGS (PROSOPIS) | PRIM | – OR 0 | 1270 ± 50 | 671–799 | 40 | AVE. OF 464 AND 465 |
| 466 | B14159 | — | DAKOTA WASH SITE AA:16:49 | F 11 (PH) "BEAMS" | CHCL | PRIM | – | 1230 ± 60 | 686–877 | 40 | SAME PH AS 467 |

| No. | Sample | | Site | Provenience | CHCL | Context | | Date | Calibrated | | Notes |
|---|---|---|---|---|---|---|---|---|---|---|---|
| 467 | B12556 | — | DAKOTA WASH SITE AA:16:49 | F 11 (PH) "BEAMS" | | PRIM | – | 1010 ± 50 | 984–1146 | 40 | SAME PH AS 466. R (2) |
| 468 | B14157 | — | DAKOTA WASH SITE AA:16:49 | F 48 (PH) BOWL ON FLOOR | MAIZE | DE FACTO | 0 | 1220 ± 80 | 681–937 | 40 | SAME PH AS 469 |
| 469 | B12551 | — | DAKOTA WASH SITE AA:16:49 | F 48 (PH) BOWL ON FLOOR | MAIZE | DE FACTO | 0 | 1170 ± 80 | 733–980 | 40 | SAME PH AS 468 |
| 468–469 | — | — | DAKOTA WASH SITE AA:16:49 | F 48 (PH) BOWL ON FLOOR | MAIZE | DE FACTO | 0 | 1195 ± 57 | 731–937 | 40 | AVE. OF 468 AND 469 |
| | | | | | | | | | RILLITO PHASE | | |
| 470 | UA026 | — | HODGES RUIN AA:12:18 | F 13 (PH) | HEARTH | PRIM | 0 | — | 610–860 | 41 | R (1) |
| 471 | UA025 | — | HODGES RUIN AA:12:18 | F 17 (PH) | HEARTH | PRIM | 0 | — | 620–780* / 800–860 | 41 | *A |
| 472 | UA027 | — | HODGES RUIN AA:12:18 | F 14 (PH) | HEARTH | PRIM | 0 | — | 660–770* / 730–860* | 41 | *A |
| 473 | (C)17 | — | WATER WORLD AA:16:94 | F 79 (HEARTH) | BURNED FLOOR | PRIM | 0 | — | 680–815 / 830–1025 | 9 | R (1) |
| 474 | (C)5 | — | WATER WORLD AA:16:94 | F 76 (HEARTH) | HEARTH | PRIM | 0 | — | 680–950 | 9 | R (1) |
| 475 | (C)7 | — | WATER WORLD AA:16:94 | F 55 (PH) | HEARTH | PRIM | 0 | — | 680–950 | 9 | R (1) |
| 476 | (C)10 | — | WATER WORLD AA:16:94 | F 27 (PH) | HEARTH | PRIM | 0 | — | 680–1000 | 9 | SAME PH AS 477. R (1) |
| 477 | AA2885 | — | WATER WORLD AA:16:94 | F 27 (PH), FLOOR FILL FLOTATION SAMPLE | MAIZE CUPULE | SEC | 0 OR + | 1214 ± 57 | 691–888 | 9 | SAME PH AS 476 |
| 478 | (C)12 | RILL 9 | WATER WORLD AA:16:94 | F 7 (PH) | HEARTH | PRIM | 0 | — | 690–730 / 900–940* | 9, 14 | *A |
| 479 | (C)11 | RILL 8 | WATER WORLD AA:16:94 | F 29 (PH) | HEARTH | PRIM | 0 | — | 690–785 | 9, 14 | |
| 480 | (C)3 | RILL 5 | WATER WORLD AA:16:94 | F 19 (PH) | HEARTH | PRIM | 0 | — | 690–790* / 840–860* | 9, 14 | *A |

Table 3.1  *continued*

| Date No. | Lab No. | E&M No. | Site | Provenience | Nature of Sample | Assoc | Bias | C-14 Age | Dates | Refs | Remarks |
|---|---|---|---|---|---|---|---|---|---|---|---|
| 481 | (C)8 | RILL 7 | WATER WORLD AA:16:94 | F 53 (PH) | HEARTH | PRIM | 0 | — | 690–795* / 830–915* | 9, 14 | SAME PH AS 482. *A |
| 482 | AA2886 | — | WATER WORLD AA:16:94 | F 27 (PH) FILL FLOTATION SAMPLE | MAIZE CUPULE | SEC | + | 1205 ± 48 | 730–888 | 9 | |
| 483 | (C)4 | RILL 6 | WATER WORLD AA:16:94 | F 20 (PH) | HEARTH | PRIM | 0 | — | 700–725 / 905–1000* | 9, 14 | SAME PH AS 481 *A |
| 484 | (C)13 | RILL 10 | WATER WORLD AA:16:94 | F 36 (PH) | BURNED FLOOR | PRIM | 0 | — | 720–780 | 9, 14 | |
| 485 | (C)14 | RILL 11 | WATER WORLD AA:16:94 | F 35 (PH) | PIT | PRIM | 0 | — | 725–850 | 9, 14 | |
| 486 | B9237 | — | WATER WORLD AA:16:94 | F 9 (ROASTING PIT) LOWER FILL | PROSOPIS CHCL, FUEL | PRIM | - | 1130 ± 60 | 781–984 | 9 | |
| 487 | B9257 | — | WATER WORLD AA:16:94 | F 4 (ROASTING PIT) LOWER FILL | PROSOPIS CHCL, FUEL | PRIM | - | 1020 ± 60 | 980–1146 | 9 | R (3) |
| 488 | (C)11 | RILL 3 | FASTIMES AA:12:384 | ? | HEARTH | PRIM | 0 | — | 715–855 | 14, 33 | |
| 489 | (C)15 | RILL 4 | FASTIMES AA:12:384 | ? | HEARTH | PRIM | 0 | — | 725–760 | 14, 33 | |
| 490 | (C)10 | RILL 2 | FASTIMES AA:12:384 | ? | HEARTH | PRIM | 0 | — | 725–855 | 14, 33 | |
| 491 | A3559 | — | EE:2:76 (ROSEMONT) | F 8 (PH), FLOOR 1, WALL POST | CHCL | PRIM | – OR 0 | 1070 ± 70 | 891–1019 | 16, 40 | |
| 492 | A3562 | — | EE:2:105 (ROSEMONT) | F 71200 (PH), FLOOR STRUCT. MEMBER | CHCL | PRIM | - | 1070 ± 50 | 897–1016 | 16, 40 | |
| EARLY RINCON PHASE | | | | | | | | | | | |
| 493 | (A)MR008 | — | WEST BRANCH SITE AA:16:3 | F 1007 (PH) | HEARTH | PRIM | 0 | — | 810–1450 | 41 | R (1) |

| No. | Lab No. | Lab No. 2 | Site | Feature | Material | Prim/Sec | Sign | Date ± | Range | Index | Notes |
|---|---|---|---|---|---|---|---|---|---|---|---|
| 494 | (A)MR025 | ERRIN 2 | WEST BRANCH SITE AA:16:3 | F 1178 (PH) | HEARTH | PRIM | 0 | — | 910–1025* 1150–1250 | 14, 41 | *A |
| 495 | (A)MR005 | ERRIN 1 | WEST BRANCH SITE AA:16:3 | F 1000C (PH) | HEARTH | PRIM | 0 | — | 925–1125* 1150–1300 | 14, 41 | *A |
| 496 | B7169 | — | VALENCIA ROAD SITE BB:13:15 | F 17 (PH) FLOOR, VESSEL | ROOT | PRIM OR SEC | + | 1000 ± 50 | 987–1148 | 40 | |
| 497 | B7190 | — | VALENCIA ROAD SITE BB:13:15 | F 40 (PH) ROOF SUPP POST | PROSOPIS OUTER RINGS | PRIM | – OR 0 | 880 ± 50 | 1039–1217 | 40 | |
| 498 | (C)1 | — | VALENCIA ROAD SITE BB:13:15 | F 64 (PH) | HEARTH | PRIM | 0 | — | 950–1050* 1195–1425 | 41 | *A |
| 499 | (A)AR009 | MIDRIN 20 | EE:2:129 (ROSEMONT) | F 2 (PH) | HEARTH | PRIM | 0 | — | 925–1425 | 14, 41 | R (1) |

MIDDLE RINCON PHASE

| No. | Lab No. | Lab No. 2 | Site | Feature | Material | Prim/Sec | Sign | Date ± | Range | Index | Notes |
|---|---|---|---|---|---|---|---|---|---|---|---|
| 500 | (A)AR004 | — | EE:2:105 (ROSEMONT) | F 81 (PH) | HEARTH | PRIM | 0 | — | 820–1450 | 15, 41 | R (1) |
| 501 | A3560 | — | EE:2:76 (ROSEMONT) | F 8 (PH), FLOOR ROOF SUPP POST | OUTER RINGS JUNIPER | PRIM | 0 | 1360 ± 60 | 640–685 | 16 | SAME PH AS 502. R (3) |
| 502 | A3891 | — | EE:2:76 (ROSEMONT) | F 8 (PH), FLOOR ROOF SUPP POST | OUTER RINGS JUNIPER | PRIM | 0 | 1250 ± 60 | 676–863 | 16 | SAME PH AS 501. R (3) |
| 503 | B10054 | — | WEST BRANCH SITE AA:16:3 | F 1008 (PH) ROOF SUPP POST | PROSOPIS OUTER RINGS | PRIM | – OR 0 | 1200 ± 70 | 691–940 | 40 | SAME PH AS 504. R (2) |
| 504 | (A)MR026 | — | WEST BRANCH SITE AA:16:3 | F 1008 (PH) | HEARTH | PRIM | 0 | — | 1000–1270 | 41 | SAME PH AS 503. R (2) |
| 505 | B10053 | — | WEST BRANCH SITE AA:16:3 | F 1006 (PH) ROOF SUPP POST | PROSOPIS OUTER RINGS | PRIM | – OR 0 | 1210 ± 50 | 694–887 | 40 | SAME PH AS 506. R (2) |
| 506 | (A)MR011 | — | WEST BRANCH SITE AA:16:3 | F 1006 (PH) | HEARTH | PRIM | 0 | — | 1300–1460 | 41 | SAME PH AS 505 |
| 507 | B10055 | — | WEST BRANCH SITE AA:16:3 | F 1199 (PH) ROOF SUPP POST | PROSOPIS OUTER RINGS | PRIM | – OR 0 | 880 ± 60 | 1035–1221 | 40 | SAME PH AS 508 |
| 508 | (A)MR018 | — | WEST BRANCH SITE AA:16:3 | F 1199 (PH) | HEARTH | PRIM | 0 | — | 1000–1160* 1180–1350 | 41 | *A |

Table 3.1 *continued*

| Date No. | Lab No. | E&M No. | Site | Provenience | Nature of Sample | Assoc | Bias | C-14 Age | Dates | Refs | Remarks |
|---|---|---|---|---|---|---|---|---|---|---|---|
| 509 | (A)MR023 | MIDRIN 8 | WEST BRANCH SITE AA:16:3 | F 1009 (PH) | HEARTH 2 | PRIM | 0 | — | 1000–1175 | 14, 41 | SAME PH AS 510 |
| 510 | (A)MR020 | MIDRIN 6 | WEST BRANCH SITE AA:16:3 | F 1009 (PH) | HEARTH 3 | PRIM | 0 | — | 1000–1350 | 14, 41 | SAME PH AS 509. R (1) |
| 511 | (A)MR022 | MIDRIN 7 | WEST BRANCH SITE AA:16:3 | F 2029 (PH) | HEARTH | PRIM | 0 | — | 1000–1175 | 14, 41 | |
| 512 | (A)MR027 | — | WEST BRANCH SITE AA:16:3 | F 2003 (PH) | HEARTH | PRIM | 0 | — | 1000–1150 | 41 | |
| 513 | (A)MR016 | — | WEST BRANCH SITE AA:16:3 | F 2015 (PH) | HEARTH | PRIM | 0 | — | 1000–1160 | 41 | |
| 514 | (A)MR013 | MIDRIN 3 | WEST BRANCH SITE AA:16:3 | F 1035 (PH) | HEARTH | PRIM | 0 | — | 1075–1175 | 14, 41 | |
| 515 | (A)MR017 | MIDRIN 5 | WEST BRANCH SITE AA:16:3 | F 1002 (PH) | HEARTH | PRIM | 0 | — | 1100–1175 | 14, 41 | |
| 516 | (A)MR006 | MIDRIN 1 | WEST BRANCH SITE AA:16:3 | F 1003 (PH) | HEARTH | PRIM | 0 | — | 1100–1175 | 14, 41 | |
| 517 | (A)MR015 | MIDRIN 4 | WEST BRANCH SITE AA:16:3 | F 1004 (PH) | HEARTH | PRIM | 0 | — | 1100–1175 | 14, 41 | |
| 518 | (A)MR009 | MIDRIN 2 | WEST BRANCH SITE AA:16:3 | F 1014 (PH) | HEARTH | PRIM | 0 | — | 1100–1175 | 14, 41 | |
| 519 | (A)MR024 | MIDRIN 9 | WEST BRANCH SITE AA:16:3 | F 1066 (PH) | HEARTH | PRIM | 0 | — | 1100–1175 | 14, 41 | |
| 520 | (A)AR002 | — | EE:2:77 (ROSEMONT) | F 1 (PH) | HEARTH | PRIM | 0 | — | 700–1340 920–1025 | 15, 41 | R (1) |
| 521 | (A)UA003 | MIDRIN 14 | ? | ? | ? | ? | ? | — | 1150–1275* | 14 | *A |
| 522 | (C)1 | — | BB:9:143 | F 13 (PH) | HEARTH | PRIM | 0 | — | 925–1075* 1100–1425 | 41 | *A |

| No. | Code | Feature | Site / BB Ref | Provenience | Material | Type | | | Date | Lab No. | Notes |
|---|---|---|---|---|---|---|---|---|---|---|---|
| 523 | (C)4 | MIDRIN 12? | BB:9:143 | F 310 (PH) | HEARTH | PRIM | 0 | — | 1000–1125 / 1150–1350* | 14, 41 | *A |
| 524 | (C)3 | MIDRIN 11 | BB:9:143 | F 4 (PH) | HEARTH | PR M | 0 | — | 1000–1350 | 14, 41 | R (1) |
| 525 | (C)2 | MIDRIN 10 | BB:9:143 | F 71 (PH) | HEARTH | PRIM | 0 | — | 1100–1175 | 14, 41 | |
| 526 | (A)NS002 | LTRIN 2 | VALENCIA ROAD SITE BB:13:74 | F 4 | HEARTH | PRIM | 0 | — | 925–1200 | 14, 41 | R (1) |
| 527 | (A)NS004 | LTRIN 3 | VALENCIA ROAD SITE BB:13:74 | F 8 (PH) | HEARTH | PRIM | 0 | — | 1000–1175 | 14, 41 | |
| 528 | (A)NS005 | RIN 2 | VALENCIA ROAD SITE BB:13:74 | F 9 (PH) | HEARTH | PFIM | 0 | — | 1000–1175 | 14, 41 | |
| 529 | (A)NA003 | RIN 1 | VALENCIA ROAD SITE BB:13:74 | F 2 (PH) | HEARTH | PRIM | 0 | — | 1000–1325 | 14, 41 | R (1) |
| 530 | (A)NS001 | LTRIN 1 | VALENCIA ROAD SITE BB:13:74 | F 3 (PH) | HEARTH | PRIM | 0 | — | 1050–1150 | 14, 41 | |
| 531 | (C)6 | LTRIN 6 | VALENCIA ROAD SITE BB:13:15 | F 46 (PH) | HEARTH | PRIM | 0 | — | 925–1350 | 14, 41 | SAME PH AS 532. R (1) |
| 532 | B7171 | — | VALENCIA ROAD SITE BB:13:15 | F 46 (PH) ROOF SUPP POST | PROSOPIS OUTER RINGS | PRIM | – OR 0 | 680 ± 60 | 1276–1387 | 40 | SAME PH AS 531 |
| 533 | (C)2 | MIDRIN 16 | TANQUE VERDE WASH BB:13:68 | F 9 (PH) | HEARTH | PRIM | 0 | — | 925–1350 | 14, 41 | R (1) |
| 534 | (C)1 | MIDRIN 15 | TANQUE VERDE WASH BB:13:68 | F 8 (PH) | HEARTH | PRIM | 0 | — | 1000–1050* | 14, 41 | |
| 535 | (C)4 | MIDRIN 17 | TANQUE VERDE WASH BB:13:68 | F 16 (PH) | HEARTH | PRIM | 0 | — | 1050–1175* / 1000–1125* | 14, 41 | *A |
| 536 | (C)7 | (MIDRIN 19) | TANQUE VERDE WASH BB:13:68 | F 10 (PH) | HEARTH | PRIM | 0 | — | 1150–1325 / 1050–1150 | 41 | *A |
| 537 | (C)6 | MIDRIN 18 | TANQUE VERDE WASH BB:13:68 | F 18 (PH) | HEARTH | PRIM | 0 | — | 1100–1175 | 14, 41 | |
| 538 | (C)5 | — | TANQUE VERDE WASH BB:13:68 | F 25 (PH) | HEARTH | PRIM | 0 | — | 1050–1325 | 41 | R (1) |

Table 3.1   *continued*

| Date No. | Lab No. | E&M No. | Site | Provenience | Nature of Sample | Assoc | Bias | C-14 Age | Dates | Refs | Remarks |
|---|---|---|---|---|---|---|---|---|---|---|---|
| 539 | (A)UP001 | LTRIN 4 | OBSERVATORY SITE BB:9:101 | F 2 (PH) | HEARTH | PRIM | 0 | — | 1000–1125* 1150–1350 | 14, 41 | *A |
| 540 | (A)AR007 | MIDRIN 13 | EE:2:109 (ROSEMONT) | F 2 (PH) | HEARTH | PRIM | 0 | — | 1000–1175 | 14, 15, 41 | |
| | | | | | **RINCON PHASE** | | | | | | |
| 541 | (A)LM003 | RIN 3 | LOS MORTEROS AA:12:57 | ? | ? | ? | ? | — | 920–1150 | 14 | |
| 542 | (A)LM009 | RIN 4 | LOS MORTEROS AA:12:57 | ? | ? | ? | ? | — | 925–1350 | 14 | R (1) |
| 543 | (A)LM011 | RIN 6 | LOS MORTEROS AA:12:57 | ? | ? | ? | ? | — | 925–1350 | 14 | R (1) |
| 544 | (A)LM016 | RIN 10 | LOS MORTEROS AA:12:57 | ? | ? | ? | ? | — | 975–1050* 1150–1350 | 14 | *A |
| 545 | (A)LM013 | RIN 7 | LOS MORTEROS AA:12:57 | ? | ? | ? | ? | — | 1000–1175 | 14 | |
| 546 | (A)LM014 | RIN 8 | LOS MORTEROS AA:12:57 | ? | ? | ? | ? | — | 1000–1175* 1225–1325 | 14 | *A |
| 547 | (A)LM015 | RIN 9 | LOS MORTEROS AA:12:57 | ? | ? | ? | ? | — | 1000–1200* 1225–1325 | 14 | *A |
| 548 | (A)LM017 | RIN 11 | LOS MORTEROS AA:12:57 | ? | ? | ? | ? | — | 1000–1325 | 14 | R (1) |
| 549 | (A)LM010 | RIN 5 | LOS MORTEROS AA:12:57 | ? | ? | ? | ? | — | 1000–1325 | 14 | R (1) |
| | | | | | **LATE RINCON PHASE** | | | | | | |
| 550 | ? | — | MUCHAS CASAS AA:12:2 | LOCUS F, F129 (PH) SUPERSTRUCTURE | CONST ELEM | PRIM | – | 1120 ± 70 | 781–992 | 26 | R (3) |

| | | | | | | | | | | | |
|---|---|---|---|---|---|---|---|---|---|---|---|
| 551 | ? | ? | MUCHAS CASAS AA:12:2 | LOCUS D, F 321 (ADOBE-LINED PH) | HEARTH | PRIM | 0 | — | 855–1025; 1300–1450 | 27 | R (4) |
| 552 | ? | — | MUCHAS CASAS AA:12:2 | LOCUS D, F 87 (ADOBE LINES PH), SUPERSTRUCT. | CONST ELEM | PRIM | – | 1100 ± 60 | 785–996 | 26 | SAME PH AS 553. R (2) |
| 553 | ? | ? | MUCHAS CASAS AA:12:2 | LOCUS D, F 87 (ADOBE-LINED PH) | HEARTH | PRIM | 0 | — | 925–1450 | 27 | SAME PH AS 552. R (2) |
| 554 | ? | — | MUCHAS CASAS AA:12:2 | LOCUS E, F 410 (PH) SUPERSTRUCTURE | CONST ELEM | PRIM | – | 1060 ± 80 | 891–1023 | 26 | R (3) |
| 555 | ? | — | MUCHAS CASAS AA:12:2 | LOCUS E, F 128 (STORAGE PH), SUPERSTR. | CONST ELEM | PRIM | – | 920 ± 80 | 1003–1212 | 26 | R (1) |
| 556 | (A)UA031 | LTRIN 5 | WEST BRANCH SITE BB:13:15 | ? | ? | ? | ? | — | 925–1350 | 14 | |
| 557 | (C)8 | LTRIN? | ? | F 1 (PH) | HEARTH | PRIM | 0 | — | 1000–1200 | 14, 41 | |
| 558 | ? | — | RANCHO BAJO AA:12:1 | F 31 (PH) SUPERSTRUCTURE | CONST ELEM | PRIM | – | 940 ± 90 | 997–1209 | 26 | |
| 559 | ? | — | RANCHO BAJO AA:12:1 | F 29 (STORAGE PH) SUPERSTRUCTURE | CONST ELEM | PRIM | – | 770 ± 60 | 1214–1280 | 26 | |
| 560 | (D)106 | — | PUNTA DE AGUA BB:13:50 | UNIT 2, HOUSE 10 (PH) | HEARTH | PRIM | 0 | — | 1010–1025 | 13, 18 | |
| 561 | (D)102 | — | PUNTA DE AGUA BB:13:50 | UNIT 2, HOUSE 23 (PH) | HEARTH | PRIM | 0 | — | 1250–1315* | 13, 18 | *A |
| 562 | (D)101 | — | PUNTA DE AGUA BB:13:50 | UNIT 2, HOUSE 14 (PH) | HEARTH | PRIM | 0 | — | 1010–1050 | 13, 18 | |
| 563 | (D)105 | — | PUNTA DE AGUA BB:13:50 | UNIT 2, HOUSE 22 (PH) | HEARTH | PRIM | 0 | — | 1200–1310*; 1100–1250 | 13, 18 | *A |
| 564 | (D)103 | — | PUNTA DE AGUA BB:13:50 | UNIT 1, HOUSE 2 (PH) | HEARTH | PRIM | 0 | — | 1150–1250; 1125–1250 | 13, 18 | |
| 565 | A3561 | — | EE:2:106 (ROSEMONT) | F2 (PH), ROOF OR WALL MEMBER ON FLOOR | CONST ELEM | PRIM | – | 870 ± 50 | 1042–1221 | 16 | |
| 566 | (A)FL005 | LTRIN 8 | ? | ? | ? | ? | ? | — | 1050–1175 | 14 | |

Jeffrey S. Dean

Table 3.1   continued

| Date No. | Lab No. | E&M No. | Site | Provenience | Nature of Sample | Assoc | Bias | C-14 Age | Dates | Refs | Remarks |
|---|---|---|---|---|---|---|---|---|---|---|---|
| EARLY TANQUE VERDE PHASE | | | | | | | | | | | |
| 567 | (A)LM004 | ERTV 1 | LOS MORTEROS AA:12:57 | ? | ? | ? | ? | — | 915–1025 1150–1450 | 14 | R (1) |
| 568 | (A)UA005 | ERTV 2 | ? | ? | ? | ? | ? | — | 915–1125 1150–1350* | 14 | *A |
| TANQUE VERDE PHASE | | | | | | | | | | | |
| 569 | B14542 | — | SAN XAVIER BRIDGE SITE BB:17:14 | F 83 (PH) ROOF SUPP POST | STRUCT ELEM | PRIM | - | 2340 ± 80 | 507BC–382BC | 32 | SAME PH AS 570–573. R (3) |
| 570 | B14543 | — | SAN XAVIER BRIDGE SITE BB:17:14 | F 83 (PH) ROOF SUPP POST | STRUCT ELEM | PRIM | - | 2300 ± 60 | 405BC–262BC | 32 | SAME PH AS 569, 571–573. R (3) |
| 571 | (C)24 | TV 11 | SAN XAVIER BRIDGE SITE BB:17:14 | F 83 (PH) F 100 (HEARTH) | HEARTH | PRIM | 0 | — | 910–1025 1150–1200* | 14, 23, 31 | SAME PH AS 569, 570, 572, 573. *A |
| 572 | (C)23 | TV 10 | SAN XAVIER BRIDGE SITE BB:17:14 | F 83 (PH) F 99 (HEARTH) | HEARTH | PRIM | 0 | — | 920–1375 | 14, 23, 31 | SAME PH AS 569–571, 573. R (1) |
| 573 | B13710 | — | SAN XAVIER BRIDGE SITE BB:17:14 | F 83 (PH) | CHCL | SEC? | + | 650 ± 125 | 1260–1410 | 32 | SAME PH AS 569–572 |
| 574 | B14534 | — | SAN XAVIER BRIDGE SITE BB:17:14 | F 35 (STR) ROOF FALL | STRUCT ELEM | PRIM | - | 1880 ± 160 | 91 BC–AD 337 | 32 | SAME STR AS 575. R (3) |
| 575 | (C)16 | (TV 5) | SAN XAVIER BRIDGE SITE BB:17:14 | F 35 (STR) F 54 (HEARTH) | HEARTH | PRIM | 0 | — | 1350–1400 | 23, 31 | SAME STR AS 574 |
| 576 | B14538 | — | SAN XAVIER BRIDGE SITE BB:17:14 | F 68 (PIT) FILL | CHCL | SEC | + | 1660 ± 100 | 255–533 | 32 | R (3) |
| 577 | B13705 | — | SAN XAVIER BRIDGE SITE BB:17:14 | F 57 (HEARTH) FILL | FUEL | PRIM | - | 1310 ± 75 | 645–796 | 32 | R (3) |
| 578 | B13708 | — | SAN XAVIER BRIDGE SITE BB:17:14 | EXTRAMURAL POST | POST | PRIM | - | 1085 ± 140 | 776–1148 | 32 | R (1) |

| No. | Lab No. | TV | Site | Provenience | Material | Context | Sign | Date | Calibrated | Refs | Notes |
|---|---|---|---|---|---|---|---|---|---|---|---|
| 579 | (C)19 | TV 8 | SAN XAVIER BRIDGE SITE BB:17:14 | F 32 (ROASTING PIT) | PIT | PRIM | 0 | — | 915–1025 / 1150–1225* | 14, 23, 31 | *A |
| 580 | (C)22 | TV 9 | SAN XAVIER BRIDGE SITE BB:17:14 | F 76 (STR) F 77 (HEARTH) | HEARTH | PRIM | 0 | — | 925–1050 / 1150–1375* | 14, 23, 31 | *A |
| 581 | B13704 | — | SAN XAVIER BRIDGE SITE BB:17:14 | LOOSE LOG IN TRASH | CHCL | SEC | – | 930 ± 60 | 1020–1189 | 32 | |
| 582 | B14540 | — | SAN XAVIER BRIDGE SITE BB:17:14 | F 86 (CREMATION) | FUEL | PRIM | – | 880 ± 85 | 1025–1257 | 32 | SAME FEAT AS 583 |
| 583 | B13709 | — | SAN XAVIER BRIDGE SITE BB:17:14 | F 86 (CREMATION) | FUEL | PRIM | – | 300 ± 115 | 1440–1953 | 32 | SAME FEAT AS 582. R (1) |
| 584 | B14533 | — | SAN XAVIER BRIDGE SITE BB:17:14 | F 40 (HEARTH) FILL | FUEL | PRIM | – | 840 ± 70 | 1068–1261 | 32 | |
| 585 | B13698 | — | SAN XAVIER BRIDGE SITE BB:17:14 | OCCUPATION SURFACE | CHCL | SEC | + | 770 ± 75 | 1209–1281 | 32 | |
| 586 | B13699 | — | SAN XAVIER BRIDGE SITE BB:17:14 | F 50 (ROASTING PIT), FILL | FUEL | PRIM | – | 740 ± 85 | 1216–1285 | 32 | |
| 587 | B13703 | — | SAN XAVIER BRIDGE SITE BB:17:14 | F 29 (CREMATORIUM), FILL | FUEL | PRIM | – | 660 ± 80 | 1286–1393 | 32 | |
| 588 | (C)17 | TV 6 | SAN XAVIER BRIDGE SITE BB:17:14 | F 32 (ROASTING PIT) | PIT | PRIM | 0 | — | 1325–1450 | 14, 23, 31 | |
| 589 | B13700 | — | SAN XAVIER BRIDGE SITE BB:17:14 | F 55 (ROASTING PIT), FILL | FUEL | PRIM | – | 420 ± 75 | 1423–1616 | 32 | |
| 590 | ? | — | MUCHAS CASAS AA:12:2 | LOCUS D, F 90 (ADOBE ROOM), SUPERSTRUCT. | STRUCT ELEM | PRIM | – | 1670 ± 100 | 240–530 | 26 | R (3) |
| 591 | ? | — | MUCHAS CASAS AA:12:2 | LOCUS E, F 423 (ADOBE LINED PH), SUPERSTRUCT. | STRUCT ELEM | PRIM | – | 1180 ± 80 | 694–978 | 26 | R (3) |
| 592 | ? | — | MUCHAS CASAS AA:12:2 | LOCUS E, F 456 (ADOBE ROOM), SUPERSTRUCT. | STRUCT ELEM | PRIM | – | 1010 ± 60 | 982–1148 | 26 | R (3) |
| 593 | ? | — | MUCHAS CASAS AA:12:2 | LOCUS A, F 214 (PH) SUPERSTRUCTURE | STRUCT ELEM | PRIM | – | 990 ± 60 | 988–1151 | 26 | |

Table 3.1 *continued*

| Date No. | Lab No. | E&M No. | Site | Provenience | Nature of Sample | Assoc | Bias | C-14 Age | Dates | Refs | Remarks |
|---|---|---|---|---|---|---|---|---|---|---|---|
| 594 | ? | — | MUCHAS CASAS AA:12:2 | LOCUS E, F 430 (ADOBE ROOM), SUPERSTRUCT. | STRUCT ELEM | PRIM | - | 970 ± 60 | 996–1155 | 26 | |
| 595 | ? | ? | MUCHAS CASAS AA:12:2 | LOCUS E, F 435 (ADOBE ROOM) | HEARTH | PRIM | 0 | — | 925–1025 1200–1400* | 27 | *A |
| 596 | ? | ? | MUCHAS CASAS AA:12:2 | LOCUS E F 121 (PH) | HEARTH | PRIM | 0 | — | 925–1075 1150–1350* | 27 | *A |
| 597 | ? | — | MUCHAS CASAS AA:12:2 | LOCUS E, F 425 (ADOBE ROOM), SUPERSTRUCT. | STRUCT ELEM | PRIM | - | 960 ± 60 | 999–1157 | 26 | |
| 598 | ? | — | MUCHAS CASAS AA:12:2 | LOCUS E, F 114 (PH) SUPERSTRUCTURE | STRUCT ELEM | PRIM | - | 880 ± 80 | 1027–1256 | 26 | |
| 599 | ? | — | MUCHAS CASAS AA:12:2 | LOCUS E, F 431 (ADOBE LINED PH), SUPERSTRUCT. | STRUCT ELEM | PRIM | - | 870 ± 80 | 1032–1258 | 26 | |
| 600 | ? | — | MUCHAS CASAS AA:12:2 | LOCUS E, F 438 (ADOBE ROOM), SUPERSTRUCT. | STRUCT ELEM | PRIM | - | 870 ± 80 | 1032–1258 | 26 | |
| 601 | ? | ? | MUCHAS CASAS AA:12:2 | LOCUS A F 219 (PH) | HEARTH | PRIM | 0 | — | 1000–1325 | 27 | R (1) |
| 602 | ? | ? | MUCHAS CASAS AA:12:2 | LOCUS H F 496 (PH) | HEARTH | PRIM | 0 | — | 1000–1325 | 27 | R (1) |
| 603 | ? | — | MUCHAS CASAS AA:12:2 | LOCUS E, F 421 (STORAGE PH), SUPERSTRUCT. | STRUCT ELEM | PRIM | - | 870 ± 60 | 1039–1225 | 26 | |
| 604 | ? | ? | MUCHAS CASAS AA:12:2 | LOCUS A F 226 (PH) | HEARTH | PRIM | 0 | — | 1025–1075 1125–1275* | 27 | *A |
| 605 | ? | ? | MUCHAS CASAS AA:12:2 | LOCUS A F 236 (PH) | HEARTH | PRIM | 0 | — | 1225–1375 | 27 | |
| 606 | ? | — | MUCHAS CASAS AA:12:2 | LOCUS A, F 212 (PH) SUPERSTRUCTURE | STRUCT ELEM | PRIM | - | 850 ± 60 | 1068–1258 | 26 | |

| | | | | | | | | | | |
|---|---|---|---|---|---|---|---|---|---|---|
| 607 | (A)UA002 | ERTV 1 | BB:9:120 | F 4 (PH) | HEARTH | PRIM | 0 | — | 925–1125 / 1150–1375* | 14, 41 | *A |
| 608 | ? | — | LOS MORTEROS AA:12:57 | F 109 (PH) | HEARTH | PRIM | 0 | — | 1040–1110 | 10 | |
| 609 | (A)LM007 | TV 4 | LOS MORTEROS AA:12:57 | ? | ? | ? | ? | — | 1000–1175 | 14 | |
| 610 | (A)LM001 | TV 1 | LOS MORTEROS AA:12:57 | ? | ? | ? | ? | — | 1025–1175 | 14 | |
| 611 | ? | — | LOS MORTEROS AA:12:57 | F 137 (PH) | HEARTH | PRIM | 0 | — | 1040–1110 | 10 | SAME PH AS 612 |
| 612 | A2746 | — | LOS MORTEROS AA:12:57 | F 137 (PH) ROOF SUPP POST | OUTER RINGS | PRIM | — | 600 ± 80 | 1282–1415 | 10 | SAME PH AS 611 |
| 613 | (A)LM006 | TV 3 | LOS MORTEROS AA:12:57 | ? | ? | ? | ? | — | 1100–1175 | 14 | |
| 614 | (A)LM002 | TV 2 | LOS MORTEROS AA:12:57 | ? | ? | ? | ? | — | 1150–1275 | 14 | |
| 615 | ? | — | PUNTA DE AGUA BB:13:50 | UNIT 2, HOUSE 18 (PH) | HEARTH | PRIM | 0 | — | 1010–1310 | 13, 18, 41 | R (1) |
| 616 | ? | — | RANCHO DERRIO AA:12:3 | F 21 (STORAGE PH) SUPERSTRUCTURE | STRUCT ELEM | PRIM | — | 910 ± 50 | 1027–1205 | 26 | |
| 617 | ? | — | RANCHO DERRIO AA:12:3 | F 20 (TRASH FILLED PIT), FILL | CHCL | SEC | + | 860 ± 100 | 1030–1275 | 26 | |
| 618 | ? | — | RANCHO DERRIO AA:12:3 | F 17 (HORNO) | HORNO | PRIM | 0 | — | 1150–1325 | 27 | |
| 619 | ? | — | WHIPTAIL RUIN BB:10:3 | ? | ? | ? | ? | — | 1125–1250 | 13 | |
| 620 | (A)PC001 | — | AA:16:44 | PH | HEARTH | PRIM | 0 | — | 950–1360 | 41 | R (1) |
| 621 | B12554 | — | DAKOTA WASH SITE AA:16:49 | F 5 (PRIMARY CREMATION) | FUEL | PRIM | — | 700 ± 50 | 1264–1377 | 40 | |
| 622 | B12553 | — | DAKOTA WASH SITE AA:16:49 | F 7 (PRIMARY CREMATION) | FUEL | PRIM | — | 690 ± 50 | 1276–1382 | 40 | |

| | |
|---|---|
| Date No: | Dates arranged by phase assignment and numbered sequentially |
| Lab No: | Sample number assigned by analytical laboratory |

Radiocarbon Samples     Archaeomagnetic Samples

- A: University of Arizona     (A) Arizona State Museum
- AA: University of Arizona Accelerator     (C) Colorado State University
- B: Beta Analytic     (D) Robert L. DuBois
- G, GX: Geochron Laboratories
- M: University of Michigan
- RL: Radiocarbon, Ltd.
- Si: Smithsonian Institution

**E. & M. No:** Sample number in Eighmy and McGuire 1988. Applies only to archaeomagnetic dates. Parentheses indicate archaeomagnetic determinations rejected by Eighmy and McGuire.

**Site:** Name and survey number of site that produced the sample. Survey numbers in Arizona State Museum system unless otherwise indicated

- ASU: Arizona State University
- NA: Museum of Northern Arizona

**Provenience:** Sample locus within the site

- F: Feature
- Comp: Component
- PH: Pithouse
- Str: Structure

**Nature of Sample:** Chcl: Charcoal

- Const: Construction
- El., Elem.: Element
- Mesq: Mesquite
- Str., Struct.: Structural

**Assoc:** Nature of association between dated sample and feature to which the date is to be applied.

- D.F.: De facto; material left in position on floor
- Prim: Primary; dated material is an integral part of feature to be dated
- Sec: Secondary; dated material is not an integral part of feature to be dated
- Strat: Relationship between sample and feature is stratigraphic

**Bias:** Probable bias of date relative to actual date of feature

- –: Date likely to be earlier than feature
- 0: Date likely to be same as feature
- +: Date likely to be later than feature

**C-14 Age:** Radiocarbon determination in years before present (A.D. 1950) ± one standard deviation

**Dates:** Calendar dates of radiocarbon and archaeomagnetic samples. All dates A.D. unless otherwise indicated. All C-14 dates are calibrated using University of Washington Quaternary Isotope Laboratory Program CALIB (Stuiver and Reimer 1987) and are given as one-sigma ranges. All alternative archaeomagnetic placements are given in 95% confidence interval form. Alternative archaeomagnetic date selected is indicated by an asterisk (*); nature of selection given in Remarks column.

Refs: Source or sources of the dates.

1. Anonymous 1988a
2. Anonymous 1988b
3. Anonymous 1987
4. Berry and Marmaduke 1982, Appendix 6
5. Cable and Doyel 1986
6. Cable and Doyel 1987:28–29, Table 1
7. Crown and Sires 1984:75, Figure II.1.1
8. Crown and Sires 1984:78, Table II.1.1
9. Czaplicki and Ravesloot, eds., in press
10. Downum 1986
11. Doyel 1978
12. Doyel 1981
13. Eighmy and Doyel 1987
14. Eighmy and McGuire 1988, Appendix C
15. Ferg 1984:727, Table 10.1
16. Ferg 1984:729, Table 10.2
17. Paul Fish, personal communication
18. Greenleaf 1975:21, Table 2.1
19. Hammack and Hammack 1981:36–37, Table 1
20. Hathaway 1988
21. Hathaway 1987a
22. Hathaway 1987b:179–181, Table 3, 4
23. Hathaway 1987c
24. Haury 1976:331, Table 16.5
25. Haury 1976:334, Figure 16.7
26. Henderson 1987c:54, Table 4.1
27. Henderson 1987c:55, Table 4.2
28. Henderson 1987b:50, Table 4.1
29. Herskovits 1981
30. Huckell 1983
31. Ravesloot 1987:65–66, Table 5.3
32. Ravesloot 1987:67, Table 5.4
33. Ravesloot and Czaplicki 1988:25, Table 2.4
34. Ravesloot et al. 1989:132, Table 10.3
35. Ravesloot et al. 1989:133, Table 10.4
36. Rodgers 1977
37. Schiffer 1982b
38. Schiffer and Staski 1982
39. Vokes 1987
40. Wallace and Craig 1986, Table 1
41. Wallace and Craig 1986, Table 2
42. Weaver 1974:50
43. Wilcox 1977:42

Remarks: Pertinent additional information on the samples or their context, on the dates themselves, on the selection of alternative archaeomagnetic placements, and on the reasons for rejecting particular dates.

*A = Archaeomagnetic placement selected by author on basis of one or more of the criteria discussed in the text.
*B = Archaeomagnetic placement selected by excavator.
*C = Archaeomagnetic placement selected by third party indicated by reference number.
R = Date rejected for one or more of the following reasons:

R (1) = Exceeds 250-year confidence interval limit
R (2) = Inconsistencies among dates within individual provenience units
R (3) = Falls outside the cluster of dates from the phase
R (4) = Lack of objective criteria for choosing alternative archaeomagnetic placements
R (5) = Rejected by excavator
R (6) = Equivocal phase assignment

# REFERENCES CITED

Anonymous
  1987      Radiocarbon Analyses, Appendix B. In *Hohokam Settlement Along the Slopes
            of the Picacho Mountains: The Picacho Area Sites*, vol. 3, edited by Richard
            Ciolek-Torrello, pp. 447–448. Museum of Northern Arizona Research Paper
            35.
  1988a     Archaeomagnetic Data Sheets from Arizona State Museum with Paleopole
            Plots by Archaeomagnetic Laboratory, Colorado State University: Season
            1, January–May 1984, Appendix A. In *Hohokam Settlement Along the Slopes
            of the Picacho Mountains: The Brady Wash Sites*, vol. 2, pt. 2, edited by Richard
            Ciolek-Torrello, Martha M. Callahan, and David H. Greenwald, pp. 813–
            862. Museum of Northern Arizona Research Paper 35.
  1988b     Radiocarbon Analyses, Appendix C. In *Hohokam Settlement Along the Slopes
            of the Picacho Mountains: The Brady Wash Sites*, vol. 2, pt. 2, edited by Richard
            Ciolek-Torrello, Martha M. Callahan, and David H. Greenwood, pp. 883–
            885. Museum of Northern Arizona Research Paper 35.
Berry, Claudia F., and William S. Marmaduke
  1982      *The Middle Gila Basin: An Archaeological and Historical Overview.* Northland
            Research, Inc., Flagstaff.
Breternitz, David A.
  1966      *An Appraisal of Tree-Ring Dated Pottery in the Southwest.* Anthropological
            Papers of the University of Arizona 10. The University of Arizona Press,
            Tucson.
Bullard, William R., Jr.
  1962      *The Cerro Colorado Site and Pithouse Architecture in the Southwestern United
            States Prior to A.D. 900.* Papers of the Peabody Museum of American Ar-
            chaeology and Ethnology, Harvard University 44 (2).
Cable, John S., and David E. Doyel
  1986      The 1986 Archaeological Investigations at Las Canopas, Phoenix, Arizona.
            Manuscript on file at Pueblo Grande Museum, Phoenix.
  1987      Pioneer Period Village Structure and Settlement Pattern in the Phoenix
            Basin. In *The Hohokam Village: Site Structure and Organization*, edited by
            David E. Doyel, pp. 21–70. AAAS Publication 87-15. Southwestern and
            Rocky Mountain Division of the American Association for the Advance-
            ment of Science.
Ciolek-Torrello, Richard
  1988      Chronology. In *Hohokam Settlement Along the Slopes of the Picacho Mountains:
            Synthesis and Conclusions*, vol. 6, edited by Richard Ciolek-Torrello and
            David R. Wilcox, pp. 42–120. Museum of Northern Arizona Research Paper
            35.
Crown, Patricia L.
  1984      Ceramic Vessel Exchange in Southern Arizona. In *Hohokam Archaeology
            Along the Salt Gila Aqueduct, Central Arizona Project*, vol. 9, Synthesis and
            Conclusions, edited by Lynn S. Teague and Patricia L. Crown, pp. 251–
            303. Arizona State Museum Archaeological Series 150. University of Ari-
            zona, Tucson.
Crown, Patricia L., and Earl W. Sires, Jr.
  1984      The Hohokam Chronology and Salt-Gila Aqueduct Project Research. In

*Hohokam Archaeology Along the Salt Gila Aqueduct, Central Arizona Project*, vol. 9, Synthesis and Conclusions, edited by Lynn S. Teague and Patricia L. Crown, pp. 73–85. Arizona State Museum Archaeological Series 150. University of Arizona, Tucson.

Czaplicki, Jon S., and John C. Ravesloot (editors)
1989  *Hohokam Archaeology Along Phase B of the Tucson Aqueduct, Central Arizona Project*, vol. 4: Small Sites and Specialized Reports. Arizona State Museum Archaeological Series 178. University of Arizona, Tucson.
In Press  *Hohokam Archaeology Along Phase B of the Tucson Aqueduct, Central Arizona Project*, vol. 3: Excavations at Water World (AZ AA:16:94). Arizona State Museum Archaeological Series 178. University of Arizona, Tucson.

Damon, P. E., C. W. Ferguson, A. Long, and E. I. Wallick
1974  Dendrochronological Calibration of the Radiocarbon Time Scale. *American Antiquity* 39:350–366.

Dean, Jeffrey S.
1978  Independent Dating in Archaeological Analysis. In *Advances in Archaeological Method and Theory*, vol. 1, edited by Michael B. Schiffer, pp. 223–255. Academic Press, New York.

Downum, Christian E.
1986  The Occupation of Hill Space in the Tucson Basin: Evidence from Linda Vista Hill. *The Kiva* 51:219–232.

Doyel, David E.
1978  *The Miami Wash Project: Hohokam and Salado in the Globe-Miami Area, Central Arizona*. Contributions to Highway Salvage Archaeology in Arizona 52. Arizona State Museum, Tucson.
1981  *Late Hohokam Prehistory in Southern Arizona*. Contributions to Archaeology 2. Gila Press, Scottsdale.

Eighmy, Jeffrey L., and David E. Doyel
1987  A Reanalysis of First Reported Archaeomagnetic Dates for the Hohokam Area, Southern Arizona. *Journal of Field Archaeology* 14:331–342.

Eighmy, Jeffrey L., J. Holly Hathaway, and Sharilee Counce
1987  *Independently Dated Virtual Geomagnetic Poles: The CSU Archaeomagnetic Data Base*. Technical Series 1. Archaeomagnetic Laboratory, Department of Anthropology, Colorado State University, Fort Collins.

Eighmy, Jeffrey L., J. Holly Hathaway, and Allen E. Kane
1985  Archaeomagnetic Secular Variation in the American Southwest Between A.D. 700 and 900: Final Results from the Dolores Archaeological Program. Manuscript on file at the Archaeomagnetic Laboratory, Department of Anthropology, Colorado State University, Fort Collins.

Eighmy, Jeffrey L., and Randall H. McGuire
1988  *Archaeomagnetic Dates and the Hohokam Phase Sequence*. Technical Series 3. Archaeomagnetic Laboratory, Department of Anthropology, Colorado State University, Fort Collins.

Ferg, Alan
1984  Discussion. In *Hohokam Habitation Sites in the Northern Santa Rita Mountains*, vol. 2, pt. 2, by Alan Ferg, Kenneth C. Rozen, William L. Deaver, Martyn D. Tagg, David A. Phillips, and David A. Gregory, pp. 725–822. Arizona State Museum Archaeological Series 147. University of Arizona, Tucson.

Gifford, James C.
  1980    *Archaeological Explorations in Caves of the Point of Pines Region, Arizona.* An-
          thropological Papers of the University of Arizona 36. The University of
          Arizona Press, Tucson.
Gladwin, Harold S.
  1942    *Excavations at Snaketown III: Revisions.* Medallion Papers 30. Gila Pueblo,
          Globe.
  1948    *Excavations at Snaketown IV: Reviews and Conclusions.* Medallion Papers 38.
          Gila Pueblo, Globe.
Gladwin, Harold S., Emil W. Haury, E. B. Sayles, and Nora Gladwin
  1937    *Excavations at Snaketown: Material Culture.* Medallion Papers 25. Gila Pueblo,
          Globe.
Greenleaf, J. Cameron
  1975    *Excavations at Punta de Agua in the Santa Cruz River Basin, Southeastern Ari-
          zona.* Anthropological Papers of the University of Arizona 26. The Uni-
          versity of Arizona Press, Tucson.
Hammack, Laurens C., and Nancy S. Hammack
  1981    Architecture. In *The 1968 Excavations at Mound 8, Las Colinas Ruins Group,
          Phoenix, Arizona,* edited and assembled by Laurens C. Hammack and Alan
          P. Sullivan, pp. 15–86. Arizona State Museum Archaeological Series 154.
          University of Arizona, Tucson.
Hathaway, J. Holly
  1987a   Archaeomagnetic Report for the Picacho Sites, Appendix A. In *Hohokam
          Settlement Along the Slopes of the Picacho Mountains: The Picacho Area Sites,*
          vol. 3, edited by Richard Ciolek-Torrello, pp. 425–446. Museum of North-
          ern Arizona Research Paper 35.
  1987b   Archaeomagnetic Report for the La Ciudad Site, Appendix B. In *Structure
          and Organization at La Ciudad,* by T. Kathleen Henderson, pp. 161–198.
          Anthropological Field Studies 18. Office of Cultural Resource Management,
          Department of Anthropology, Arizona State University, Tempe.
  1987c   Archaeomagnetic Report for AZ BB:13:14(ASM), Appendix C. In *The Ar-
          chaeology of the San Xavier Bridge Site (AZ BB:13:14) Tucson Basin, Southern
          Arizona,* edited by John C. Ravesloot, pp. 379–386. Arizona State Museum
          Archaeological Series 171. University of Arizona, Tucson.
  1988    Synthesis of Archaeomagnetic Dates from the Brady Wash Sites: Season
          2, September 1984–January 1985, Appendix B. In *Hohokam Settlement Along
          the Slopes of the Picacho Mountains: The Brady Wash Sites,* vol. 2, pt. 2, edited
          by Richard Ciolek-Torrello, Martha M. Callahan, and David H. Greenwald,
          pp. 863–882. Museum of Northern Arizona Research Paper 35.
Haury, Emil W.
  1937    Pottery Types at Snaketown. In *Excavations at Snaketown: Material Culture,*
          by Harold S. Gladwin, Emil W. Haury, E. B. Sayles, and Nora Gladwin,
          pp. 169–229. Medallion Papers 25. Gila Pueblo, Globe.
  1976    *The Hohokam: Desert Farmers and Craftsmen.* The University of Arizona Press,
          Tucson.
Haury, Emil W., and E. B. Sayles
  1947    An Early Pit House Village of the Mogollon Culture, Forestdale Valley,
          Arizona. *University of Arizona Bulletin* 18 (4). *Social Science Bulletin* 16.

Henderson, T. Kathleen
  1987a    The Growth of a Hohokam Community. In *The Hohokam Village: Site Struc-
           ture and Organization*, edited by David E. Doyel, pp. 97–125. AAAS Pub-
           lication 87-15. Southwestern and Rocky Mountain Division of the American
           Association for the Advancement of Science.
  1987b    *Structure and Organization at La Ciudad*. Anthropological Field Studies 18.
           Office of Cultural Resource Management, Department of Anthropology,
           Arizona State University, Tempe.
  1987c    Ceramics, Dates, and the Growth of the Marana Community. In *Studies of
           the Hohokam Community of Marana*, edited by Glen Rice, pp. 49–78. An-
           thropological Field Studies 15. Office of Cultural Resource Management,
           Department of Anthropology, Arizona State University, Tempe.
Herskovits, Robert M.
  1981     Arizona U:9:46: A Dual Component Hohokam Site in Tempe, Arizona. *The
           Kiva* 47:1–82.
Huckell, Bruce B.
  1983     Additional Chronological Data on Cienega Valley, Arizona, Appendix C.
           In *Cultural and Environmental History of Cienega Valley, Southeastern Arizona*,
           by Frank W. Eddy and Maurice E. Cooley, pp. 57–58. Anthropological
           Papers of the University of Arizona 43. The University of Arizona Press,
           Tucson.
Johnson, Alfred E., and William W. Wasley
  1966     Archaeological Excavations near Bylas, Arizona. *The Kiva* 31:205–253.
Klein, Jeffrey, J. C. Lerman, P. E. Damon, and E. K. Ralph
  1982     Calibration of Radiocarbon Dates: Tables Based on the Consensus Data of
           the Workshop on Calibrating the Radiocarbon Time Scale. *Radiocarbon* 24:103–
           150.
Morris, Donald H.
  1969a    Red Mountain: An Early Pioneer Period Hohokam Site in the Salt River
           Valley of Central Arizona. *American Antiquity* 34:40–53.
  1969b    A 9th Century Salado(?) Kiva at Walnut Creek, Arizona. *Plateau* 42:1–10.
  1970     Walnut Creek Village: A Ninth-Century Hohokam-Anasazi Settlement in
           the Mountains of Central Arizona. *American Antiquity* 35:49–61.
Pearson, Gordon W., and Minze Stuiver
  1986     High-Precision Calibration of the Radiocarbon Time Scale, 500–2500 B.C.
           *Radiocarbon* 28:839–862.
Plog, Fred
  1980     Explaining Culture Change in the Hohokam Preclassic. In *Current Issues
           in Hohokam Prehistory: Proceedings of a Symposium*, edited by David Doyel
           and Fred Plog, pp. 4–22. Arizona State University Anthropological Re-
           search Papers 23.
Ravesloot, John C.
  1987     Chronological Relationships of Features. In *The Archaeology of the San Xavier
           Bridge Site (AZ BB:13:14) Tucson Basin, Southern Arizona*, edited by John C.
           Ravesloot, pp. 61–69. Arizona State Museum Archaeological Series 171.
           University of Arizona, Tucson.
Ravesloot, John C., and Jon S. Czaplicki
  1988     Dating and Site Development. In *Hohokam Archaeology Along Phase B of the*

*Tucson Aqueduct, Central Arizona Project*, vol. 2, Excavations at Fastimes (AZ AA:12:384), A Rillito Phase Site in the Avra Valley, edited by Jon S. Czaplicki and John C. Ravesloot, pp. 17–35. Arizona State Museum Archaeological Series 178. University of Arizona, Tucson.

Ravesloot, John C., Jon S. Czaplicki, and Ronald Gardiner
1989    Interpretation and Chronology. In *Hohokam Archaeology Along Phase B of the Tucson Aqueduct, Central Arizona Project*, vol. 4, Small Sites and Specialized Reports, edited by Jon S. Czaplicki and John C. Ravesloot, pp. 127–136. Arizona State Museum Archaeological Series 178. University of Arizona, Tucson.

Rodgers, James B.
1977    *Archaeological Investigation of the Granite Reef Aqueduct, Cave Creek Archaeological District, Arizona*. Arizona State University Anthropological Research Papers 12.

Schiffer, Michael B.
1982a   Hohokam Chronology: An Essay on History and Method. In *Hohokam and Patayan: Prehistory of Southwestern Arizona*, edited by Randall H. McGuire and Michael B. Schiffer, pp. 299–344. Academic Press, New York.
1982b   Appendix E: Archaeomagnetic Dates Pertaining to the Hohokam Occupation of Southern Arizona. In *Hohokam and Patayan: Prehistory of Southwestern Arizona*, edited by Randall H. McGuire and Michael B. Schiffer, pp. 529–532. Academic Press, New York.
1986    Radiocarbon Dating and the "Old Wood" Problem: The Case of the Hohokam Chronology. *Journal of Archaeological Science* 13:13–30.
1987    *Formation Processes of the Archaeological Record*. University of New Mexico Press, Albuquerque.

Schiffer, Michael B., and Edward Staski
1982    Appendix D: Radiocarbon Dates from Southern Arizona Pertaining to the Post-Archaic Prehistory. In *Hohokam and Patayan: Prehistory of Southern Arizona*, edited by Randall H. McGuire and Michael B. Schiffer, pp. 521–528. Academic Press, New York.

Sternberg, Robert Saul
1982    *Archaeomagnetic Secular Variation of Direction and Paleointensity in the American Southwest*. Ph.D. dissertation, Department of Geosciences, The University of Arizona, Tucson. University Microfilms, Ann Arbor.

Stuiver, Minze
1982    A High-Precision Calibration of the AD Radiocarbon Time Scale. *Radiocarbon* 24:1–26.

Stuiver, Minze, and Bernd Becker
1986    High-Precision Decadal Calibration of the Radiocarbon Time Scale, A.D. 1950–2500 B.C. *Radiocarbon* 28:863–910.

Stuiver, Minze, and Gordon W. Pearson
1986    High-Precision Calibration of the Radiocarbon Time Scale, A.D. 1950–500 B.C. *Radiocarbon* 28:805–838.

Stuiver, Minze, and P. J. Reimer
1987    *CALIB: Radiocarbon Calibration Program, 1987*. Quaternary Isotope Laboratory, University of Washington, Seattle.

Suess, H. E.
1967    Bristlecone Pine Calibration of the Radiocarbon Time Scale from 4100 B.C.

to 1500 B.C. In *Radioactive Dating and Methods of Low-Level Counting*, pp. 143–150. International Atomic Energy Agency, Vienna.

1970 Bristlecone-Pine Calibration of the Radiocarbon Time-Scale 5200 B.C. to the Present. In *Radiocarbon Variations and Absolute Chronology: Proceedings of the Twelfth Nobel Symposium*, edited by Ingrid U. Olsson, pp. 303–309. Almquist and Wiksell, Stockholm.

Vokes, Arthur W.
1987 A Review of the Chronological Placement of the Late Pioneer and Colonial Periods of the Hohokam. Manuscript on file at the Laboratory of Tree-Ring Research, The University of Arizona, Tucson.

Wallace, Henry D., and Douglas B. Craig
1986 The Tucson Basin Hohokam: Chronological Considerations. Paper presented at the Tucson Basin Conference, Tucson, November 14, 1986.

Weaver, Donald E., Jr.
1974 *Archaeological Investigations at the Westwing Site, AZ T:7:27(ASU), Agua Fria River Valley, Arizona*. Arizona State University Anthropological Research Papers 7.

Wilcox, David R.
1977 *Archaeomagnetic Dating in Compounds A and B, Casa Grande Ruins National Monument*. Contributions to Archaeology 1. Gila Press.
1979 The Hohokam Regional System. In *An Archaeological Test of Sites in the Gila Butte–Santan Region, South-Central Arizona*, by Glen Rice, David R. Wilcox, Kevin Rafferty, and James Schoenwetter, pp. 77–116. Arizona State University Anthropological Research Papers 18.

Wilcox, David R., and Lynette O. Shenk
1977 *The Architecture of the Casa Grande and Its Interpretation*. Arizona State Museum Archaeological Series 115. University of Arizona, Tucson.

Wilcox, David R., and Charles Sternberg
1983 *Hohokam Ballcourts and Their Interpretation*. Arizona State Museum Archaeological Research Series 160. University of Arizona, Tucson.

# •4•

# HOHOKAM
# POLITICAL AND
# SOCIAL ORGANIZATION

▼▼▼▼▼▼▼▼▼▼▼▼▼▼▼▼▼▼▼▼▼▼▼▼▼▼▼▼▼▼▼▼▼▼▼▼▼▼▼▼▼▼▼▼▼▼▼▼▼▼▼▼▼

*Paul R. Fish*
*Suzanne K. Fish*

## INTRODUCTION

Hohokam social organization has been traditionally viewed from a political perspective. A perception of political complexity was common among early workers, as with Cushing (1890) at Los Muertos. The scale of remains still evident during the early period of Anglo settlement along the Salt and Gila rivers was at the root of this perception. Public architecture, extent of residential remains, and the impressive canal systems caught the attention of the public as well as archaeologists and led to the recording of distributions that still form the basis of regional data. Pima myths featuring former paramount leaders and conflict of historic scale within and among polities provided an interpretive framework reinforcing complexity (Russell 1975:226–229; Cushing 1890:153–154; Fewkes 1912).

In the following period of professional investigation, the strong influence of ethnographic analogs on Southwestern archaeology led to an emphasis of egalitarian aspects through reference to Pima and Papago organization. Persistent exception to the constraints of Piman analogies have invoked overlays of Mesoamerican forms of social structure or universal evolutionary classifications. Despite increasing technical sophistication and a rapidly growing data base, the most basic consensus has not been reached among Hohokam archaeologists regarding egalitarian versus complex models.

Aside from the much discussed issue of complexity, Hohokam social organization has acquired a political flavor through default. Organizational principles in the Puebloan Southwest are strongly associated with kinship systems that permeate and control social behavior. Some degree of continuity in those principles since prehistoric times can be demonstrated through architectural and artifactual correlates. For ethnographic peoples throughout the southern deserts of the Greater Southwest, kinship principles and structures seem to have lesser influence on the organization of social interaction.

## ETHNOGRAPHIC ANALOGY

The ethnographic record of the Pima and Papago influences directly and indirectly the ways in which Hohokam social organization is interpreted. Problems of analogy are compounded by the late date of recording. Reliable records with any detail for the Hohokam area date to the end of the seventeenth century. By this time, post-Columbian disruptions had affected regional populations for many years (e.g., Ezell 1983; Dobyns 1963, 1981). Major references are no earlier than the turn of the century (Castetter and Bell 1942; Russell 1975; Underhill 1939); historical accounts and recollections extend the record back only to the 1850s when most Pimans were participating in a cash economy.

Even in the earliest Spanish accounts, there are no observations of inhabitants in much of the area formerly occupied by the Hohokam. It is unclear to what extent contact-related factors such as disease might be involved. Many areas of dense earlier population are virtually abandoned and aggregated settlements are modest throughout all of the historic period.

Raiding, mainly by Apaches, constrained locations of settlements and created a constant preoccupation with warfare. This pattern of conflict seems directly tied to historic variables. Horses allowed rapid movement for attack and a means to transport booty. Livestock was often the target of raiding. Firearms and metal weapons heightened the severity of confrontations. A growing Spanish population in northwest Mexico provided a ready market for slaves and animals. Earliest mention of the Sobaipuri suggests that large-scale conflict reflecting these changes had been initiated by Kino's time (Bolton 1936:262–263).

Historic economic changes were dramatic. Old World winter crops added alternatives in the seasonal scheduling of agriculture. The widespread adoption of domestic animals by the end of the seventeenth century (Dobyns 1981:79; Underhill 1939) had even greater consequences. Draft animals were used for plowing and canal construction during the 1800s. Animals greatly increased potable water requirements, undoubtedly contributing to the bi-seasonal Papago settlement model described by Underhill (1939). For example, Underhill (1939:29) notes an average of 10 head of cattle per family and a Papago reservation total of 20,000 for this kind of animal.

While Pimans may represent continuity in many aspects of Hohokam culture, ethnographic analogy and even the earliest Spanish accounts furnish few insights into the most intriguing realms of social organization. There are minimal clues to the social contexts of mounds, ballcourts, and compounds. No sumptuary patterns in exotic and elaborate items, ritual paraphernalia, nor any iconography of status and power can be found in the historic record.

## ARCHAEOLOGICAL FACTORS
## INFLUENCING STUDY OF
## HOHOKAM ORGANIZATION

Because Piman analogy is inadequate for modeling Hohokam organization, formulation of appropriate hypotheses (as well as their evaluation) rests more directly on the archaeological record (Haury 1956:10; Cordell 1989:45). The nature of Hohokam archaeological data has some specific implications for the investigation of social organization. These result from the nature of the remains themselves and from the manner in which the data have been acquired.

More than for other major Southwestern archaeological cultures, areas of greatest Hohokam population density and cultural elaboration have coincided with modern cities and agriculture. The main outlines of canals and the location of many of the large sites have been documented by pre-urban mapping (Midvale 1968; Patrick 1903; Turney 1929). However, many larger sites and all but perhaps 10 percent of the former canals (Woodbury 1960; Wilcox 1987a) had already been obliterated when Gila Pueblo investigations began shaping the concept of a Red-on-buff Culture. While many imaginative attempts are being made to comprehensively reconstruct settlement pattern in the central Hohokam area (Gregory and Nials 1985; Nicholas and Neitzel 1984; Wilcox and Sternberg 1983; Wilcox 1987a; Howard 1987), the opportunity for study in a manner still possible at Chaco Canyon, Mesa Verde, and Casas Grandes is gone. The patterning of smaller settlements, dispersed activities, and overall arrangements of large sites are essentially lost under urban sprawl and cotton fields.

Unlike other Southwestern traditions, the basic sequence and evolutionary scheme for the Hohokam was constructed by intensive excavation at a single, long-term site rather than by integrating studies at multiple sites. Emil Haury's (1976) detailed work at the large and elaborate site of Snaketown was

completed by restudy in the 1960s and has not been repeated in other parts
of the region. This investigative emphasis within the Phoenix Basin has promoted a model of Hohokam culture as emanating from a strong central source,
surrounded by less well developed, imitative, and colonial spheres. Directly
related is an assumption of political centrality. The core-periphery contrast
and perceptions of asymmetrical relationships are undoubtedly magnified by
a lack of thoroughly excavated large sites outside the Salt and Gila heartland.

In order to derive units of social organization from the archaeological data,
it must be possible to discriminate contrastive subsets among comprehensive
and quantitative distributions. This holds for defining horizontal differentiation, as among groups with different productive specialization, as well as for
defining vertical differentiation based on sumptuary patterns. Because distributions of any element are likely to be fragmentary and because systematic
quantitative reporting has been neglected, infrequent contrasts between features, sites and subareas are often based on presence and absence of qualitative traits. The quantities and proveniences of particular items may be
buried or neglected in the literature in favor of more detailed discussion of
typical examples. Insufficiencies in distributional data are significant at a number of scales.

Inherent problems stem from the physical nature of Hohokam remains.
Particularly away from the more densely packed core, the dispersed nature
and areal extent of sociopolitically related sites inhibits detection of organizational structure in settlement pattern. Both in the core area and elsewhere,
large-scale organizational studies have necessarily focused on bigger sites and
the obtrusive features of communal integration. Much less is known about
the structural relationships of small and dispersed rancheria occupations that
may account for equally large proportions of the population.

Even in the largest sites, many of the inhabitants lived in dispersed and
nongeometric arrangements of structures. It would be difficult and prohibi-
tively expensive to routinely acquire total site plans of such weakly nucleated
and extensive settlements. In key urban areas, only fragments of large sites
are preserved. Continuous occupation of many prominent sites over hundreds of years further complicates recovery of diachronic patterns. The efficiency of obtaining intrasite arrangements from surface survey is greatly reduced
by the inability to detect most structural remains without excavation.

Definition of social units at all scales has overwhelmingly emphasized
distributions of architectural rather than artifactual remains. Floor assemblages are not present in many cases, a circumstance probably most pronounced for the large sites with continuous occupation, where the greatest
social differentiation might be anticipated. Few researchers have yet attempted to overcome the sparsity of floor assemblages by resorting to spatial
patterns in secondarily deposited artifacts across a site as a whole (for exceptions, see Rice 1987a, 1987b; Elson 1986; Huntington 1986). Many reports
fail to specify quantitative contents by individual proveniences, discouraging

contrastive comparisons. As a consequence, there are limited numbers of insightful studies on such topics as mortuary inclusions as a means of detecting social differences (some important examples include Anderson 1986; Nelson 1981; McGuire 1987).

# DEMOGRAPHY

Demographic parameters are poorly understood for the Hohokam. While neither population size nor its distribution is a direct predictor of social organization, these attributes may have important implications for the operation of social systems. The scale of population, including absolute densities at levels above individual sites and even within most of the large ones, is inadequately documented. Variability in these aspects within the Hohokam spatial and temporal continuum is even more speculative.

The loosely aggregated nature of large as well as small Hohokam sites illustrates a different interrelationship between population and integrative structure than for other parts of the Southwest, including Puebloan manifestations to the north and Casas Grandes to the south. For example, Los Muertos is one of the largest sites in the Salt River Valley and one of the few for which structure totals can be closely approximated. Plog (Martin and Plog 1973:314) estimates 500 rooms and Wilcox (1987b) suggests a maximum population of only 700 people within an area of approximately 2 sq km containing concentrated adobe structures. Social structures or institutions evolving in a milieu of intensified interactions under strong aggregation are not appropriate models for the southern deserts. To assess the framework of Hohokam social organization, it is necessary to consider total population distributions across broad areas, including the proportions of population in sites of different size and the significance of dispersed settlement in which major sites are embedded.

## POPULATION SIZE

### Problems in Estimation

Population estimates are imprecise at any level and for any period. A formula for translating site extent to numbers of persons does not exist. Lack of surface indications and continuous overlays of sequential components have led to totally unpredictable excavation results at large sites, even after multistage testing. For example, such confusing situations recently caused experienced Hohokam archaeologists to target inappropriate chronological periods in research designs for the Phoenix area. At Las Colinas, an anticipated scale of Classic occupation could not be located (Gregory 1982); rather, major Sacaton remains were found. At La Ciudad, Pioneer, Sedentary, and primarily

Colonial settlements were revealed where an exclusively Sedentary occupation was expected (Rice 1982).

For large, excavated sites, population estimates are not a matter of informed consensus because of the inability to control critical variables. Snaketown is a good example; approximately 50 percent of the central area of concentrated structures and 15 percent of the total site area has been excavated (Wilcox et al. 1981). Haury (1976:75–77) inferred a total of 7,000 houses at this site. He estimated a maximum (Sacaton) population of 2,000 based on his estimate of a 25-year use-life for pithouses. Wilcox and others (1981:185–197) considered differential distributions of houses in various precincts at Snaketown and reduced the total number of potential structures from 7,000 to 1,000. Invoking a variable use-life from 25 to 100 years depending on intrasite location, Wilcox arrived at a population estimate between 600 and 1,000 during the Sacaton phase, later revised downward to less than 500 (Wilcox and Sternberg 1983). Reviewing the pivotal and unresolved issue of pithouse use-life, Plog (1980:14) concluded that it was impossible to produce meaningful population estimates for even the best excavated samples.

## Population and Subsistence Potential

The Sonoran Desert is one of the major food-rich areas for a gathering economy in North America. Food is not only predictable, storable, and abundant, but harvest times for staples are spread over much of the year. Basin-and-Range topography results in elevationally diverse resources over short lineal transects. This pattern is repeated to such an extent that most groups could have comparable access to natural resources within less than a day's walk. Furthermore, a large-scale and intensive agricultural system was used to grow the greatest diversity of cultivated crops north of Mesoamerica (Nabhan 1985; Ford 1981). Wild and cultivated food sources could combine to support regionally large and dense populations.

The abundance of Hohokam riverine agriculture must have been impressive by any standard. The mid-nineteenth-century Gila River Pima, who produced a wheat surplus of up to 1,000,000 lbs per year with technologically similar irrigation (Browne 1869:110; Russell 1975:90), provide a glimpse of the potential productivity of former systems. The Pima surplus was obtained from 5,450 ha watered by eight canals averaging about 9 km each (Southworth 1915, 1919). If an ethnographically large allowance of two irrigated hectares per family (for example, see Kowalewski 1980:153–154; Kirkby 1973:90, 127; Castetter and Bell 1942:54) is assumed, nearly 14,000 persons could have been supported from these systems alone. Even conservative estimates of irrigated land in the Phoenix Basin exceed the historic Pima acreage by several magnitudes. For example, Nials, Gregory, and Graybill (1989) estimate that sufficient water was available in the Salt River to adequately irrigate 17,200 to 25,800 ha.

## Labor Requirements and Population

Canal construction and maintenance requirements were substantial in the Phoenix Basin and perhaps in a limited number of other locations. Over 500 km of main canals representing a variety of time periods have been documented along the Salt River (Masse 1981:408; Midvale 1968; Nicholas and Feinman 1989). On the basis of Classic period site distribution, at least 300 km appear to have been in operation in a contemporaneous network. Extending volume estimates applied by David Gregory (personal communication, see also Masse 1981:408, 411; 1987:101–106; Ackerly et al. 1987:111) to the Las Colinas network, a minimum of 900,000 cu m of earth was moved in the cumulative construction of the total 300 km Classic system. If one person could move one cubic meter of earth per day (World Health Organization estimate is that one person can move one cubic meter a distance of 100 meters per day, using metal shovels and baskets), nearly 3,500 man-years of effort would have been necessary to construct trunklines of the canal systems. In other words, if 100 men gave one month of service annually, it would have taken nearly 420 years to build the network of main canals alone.

Much labor would have been necessary in addition to the construction of primary canals. Intake structures, secondary and tertiary distribution systems, preparation of fields for planting, and repair following floods must have created a persistent demand. Haury (1976:149) published a photograph of 50 Pima men with 21 two-horse wagons repairing a canal intake on the Gila River just before the turn of the century. Haury (1976:150) also documents at least 10 rebuildings of the Snaketown canal and others have presented similar reconstructions along the Salt River (e.g., Ackerly et al. 1987:49–74; Masse 1981:409).

Even the construction of delivery facilities to fields required much effort. Using aerial photographs, Masse (1976:40, 1981:411–413) estimated over 40 secondary distribution or lateral canals per square mile for an apparently contemporaneous system near Tempe. As a proxy for labor investment in yet finer distribution systems, over 23 man-years of effort were estimated to construct intrafield features for direct water delivery on crops in a 20-acre irrigated field in the Verde Valley (Fish and Fish 1984:156).

## POPULATION DISTRIBUTIONS

The relationship between population distribution and labor demand has been considered most significant for social organization in those instances where labor expenditure was most concentrated in time and space. Coordinated, cooperative undertakings must have tapped large numbers of workers. Implications are different if manpower for tangible communal efforts such as canals, mounds, and ballcourts was generated very locally or involved larger areas. One approach to the answer lies in plausibly accounting for construction efforts using variable population catchments.

Over the course of Hohokam studies, archaeologists have looked at the same results of communal effort and concluded that: (1) voluntary, consensual agreements among equals were consistent with the moderate demands of construction; and (2) demands were of a magnitude to precipitate or demonstrate social inequality and complexity. Perhaps the acquisition of data for more precise estimates of labor expenditure and population magnitudes will promote eventual convergence of opinions.

Regional demographic variability is obvious within the boundaries of Hohokam culture. Recent comprehensive survey in the Tucson area (S. Fish et al. 1985, 1989; Doelle et al. 1985) offers one clear illustration of less dense packing than along perennial rivers in the heartland. At the same time, it is becoming clear that lower population densities do not correlate with an absence of remains usually regarded as expressions of elaborated social organization. For instance, numbers of identified platform mounds and ballcourts have multiplied rapidly with the pace of research in noncore regions. It would therefore appear that regional population size and distribution may vary within some appreciable range and still support a common organizational stance. Threshold population numbers for structurally similar social units may simply be dispersed over wider territories in nonriverine settings.

Models of social differentiation and integration have tended to neglect dispersed segments of Hohokam population. Even the relative magnitude of these segments is little understood in currently urbanized and cultivated areas on the Salt and Gila rivers, where regional demographic reconstructions rely heavily on older mappings of canal systems and larger settlements. In other regions, prime riverine occupations are also obscured by modern land use. Degrees of redundancy due to seasonal occupations are unknown between more dispersed loci and aggregated nodes. Upland populations of desert basins in all regions have received comparatively abbreviated study. Recognition of the existence in such settings of substantial and permanent settlements, including ones with public architecture, is emerging with expanded investigation (e.g., S. Fish et al. 1989; Ciolek-Torrello et al. 1988; Rice 1989).

It is apparent that many Hohokam in both core and peripheral areas were rural and not inhabitants of platform mound or ballcourt villages. Contact period population distributions among Yaqui in southern Sonora may provide a useful analog for the Hohokam. In the early seventeenth century, Perez de Ribas (1968:101) reported 80 rancherias averaging somewhat less than 250 individuals each and 8 more nucleated towns numbering about 1,000 inhabitants for a total population of 30,000 in a territory of 900 sq mi, an area roughly comparable to that of the Phoenix Basin. Arguments can be made that already the higher numbers at the 8 more nucleated settlements were a contact-period phenomenon, while regional population had dropped dramatically from disease and slave raiding (Sheridan 1981). Nevertheless, these densities may provide insights toward the nature of settlement pattern that Cushing (1892:154) could still observe at Mesa Grande: ". . . of the most extensive ancient settlement we had yet seen. . . . Before us, toward the north, east, and south, a long series of elevations which I at once recognized as house mounds, lay stretched out in seemingly endless succession. . . ."

# LEVELS OF HOHOKAM ORGANIZATION

## THE COURTYARD GROUP

Although spatially patterned structures within sites had been identified (Doyel 1974; Wasley and Johnson 1965; Di Peso 1956), Preclassic Hohokam settlement was perceived until recently as generally unstructured. At the residential level, only unoccupied public areas at large villages were recognized. For instance, Haury (1976:173) observed that at Snaketown there was ". . . no grain or even loosely organized plan in overall arrangement of houses with respect to each other, or in relation to refuse mounds." Spacing between houses, confusing superposition of structures over long spans, and scarcity of excavated site plans of comprehensive size undoubtedly delayed pattern recognition. It was the painstaking reanalysis of the excavated site plan at Snaketown by Wilcox (Wilcox et al. 1981) that stimulated recent rapid progress in household definition.

The basic residential structure at Snaketown involved from two to six houses opening onto a courtyard or common work area of approximately 250 sq m. Wilcox (Wilcox et al. 1981) found this arrangement to become more formalized through the Sacaton phase. Discovery of the courtyard group has influenced or structured analysis for most subsequent excavations in which any appreciable segment of a site plan has been recovered (e.g., Wilcox 1987c; Wilcox and Sternberg 1983:136, 156, 168; Howard 1982, 1985; Elson 1986; Henderson 1987a, 1987b; Gregory 1983; Doelle et al. 1987; Huntington 1986).

Later researchers have proposed additional facilities that may be associated with the courtyard group such as trash deposits, ramadas, pits, and burials (Henderson 1987a, 1987b; Howard 1982; Gregory 1983; Sires 1985). Another avenue of research emphasis has been discrimination of typical or differential activities within and between residences. Among this category are disposal behaviors (Rice 1987a, 1987b); productive specialization (Huntington 1986; Elson 1986; Rice 1987a), and stylistic differentiation (Henderson 1987b).

There is widespread agreement on interpretation of the house cluster or courtyard group as an aggregation of occupants linked by kinship. Equation of individual structures with nuclear families and clusters of structures with an extended family is frequent. Elaborations on this generalized interpretation allow for variability in group constituency. Wilcox (Wilcox et al. 1981:166) and Howard (1982, 1985:314) point to generational differences among structure occupants at given points in time and over time. Howard (1985) identified rules of residence as the cohesive social force promoting cluster persistence.

The size and long-term continuity of the cluster is attributed by both Doelle (Doelle et al. 1987) and Henderson (1987b) to the success of a prominent household head in attracting and maintaining the cohesion of other nuclear families.

Basic to all of these interpretations are two assumptions: (1) Most structures within the cluster or courtyard group replicate the function of residence for a nuclear family; and (2) Multiple structures of this type were occupied simultaneously. These assumptions do not conflict with additional structures of dissimilar, mainly nonresidential functions in the clusters, a possibility strongly suggested by ethnographic structural diversity. For example, Doelle (1983) describes a historic Papago house cluster near Nolic occupied by a single woman, with each of three structures serving a different function. Likewise, Russell (1975:155–157) describes Piman storage and other structures of distinctly aboriginal style as the normal accompaniment of household residences.

In a courtyard group or household cluster composed of eight or ten structures, it is possible to envision more than one contemporaneous habitation structure, one or two of a specialized nature, and perhaps the same number of unoccupied houses that pertain to the earlier end of the occupation. With such possible total numbers, it is reasonable to consider issues such as recruitment by an effective leader. However, a large proportion of clusters defined to date encompass no more than three or four structures. In such cases, it seems particularly critical to demonstrate replication of residential function and absolute contemporaneity if a cluster of nuclear families is to be convincingly proposed. Henderson's (1987a, 1987b) use of a regression formula involving ceramic attributes and absolute dates, Wallace's (Doelle et al. 1987) fine-grain seriation of red-on-brown ceramics, and Elson's (1986) sherd refitting study are all imaginative attempts to deal with the knotty problem of contemporaneity between houses.

## SUPRAHOUSEHOLD UNITS

Social units that incorporate several courtyard groups have been variously termed suprahousehold units (Wilcox 1987c), village segments (Henderson 1987a, 1987b; Howard 1985), loci (Rice et al. 1987a, 1987b), and precincts (Doelle et al. 1987). In at least a number of instances (Henderson 1987:10), communal elements shared by suprahousehold units include a central open area of common use, facilities such as *hornos* or pit ovens, a trash mound, and cemetery. However, there are acknowledged exceptions to these arrangements, such as dispersed burials rather than a cemetery concentration (Anderson 1986:192), or cemetery plots associated with particular courtyards (Gregory 1983).

Perhaps even more than residential proximity, the use of separate and associated cemeteries suggests generational continuity in a corporate group or lineage. Such groups are seen as becoming more formalized after the Pioneer period as a response to the requirements of pooled labor, access to land, and inheritance of land under conditions of canal irrigation (Cable and Doyel 1987; Henderson 1987b). Structural evidence for similar groups also occurs in areas where riverine canals do not form the basis of subsistence systems (e.g., Doelle et al. 1987; Rice 1987c).

With growing populations occupying the same locale over time, better defined corporate groups represent a possible mechanism by which well-watered land was apportioned among inhabitants. Simultaneously, lineages may have provided a larger work force for agricultural intensification. Canal irrigation per se need not be the necessary cause; floodwater and runoff field complexes may entail improvements and labor investment that make land a heritable commodity. With these techniques, too, there are limited amounts of prime land requiring subdivision among users.

Historically, village membership rather than kinship appears to have been a strong Piman principle in obtaining access to even irrigated land. For example, Russell (1975:88) records plot distribution along new canals to persons contributing construction labor. A village committee of six, who organized the undertaking, took the best plots and allocated the rest. Broad patterns of tenure, including flexible bilateral arrangements, among Pimans and other rancheria peoples do not closely parallel the more stringently clan-based Puebloan systems of ownership and use rights; the role of corporate groups among the Hohokam has yet to be established. Some shared facilities have been defined, but as yet there are few attempts to examine resource sharing and allocation or differentiation in production and consumption within a courtyard group or suprahousehold unit (see Huntington 1986; Rice 1987c as examples of exceptions).

## SITE LEVEL

Courtyard groups and suprahousehold units can be seen as idealized building blocks of Hohokam sites. Sires (1985) has equated isolated courtyard groups with the smallest site size, which he has termed the farmstead. Hamlets are equivalent to suprahousehold units. Sites of large size are multiples of these latter units. In most sites, there are structures, burials, and facilities remaining after these categories have been identified, as well as individual sites that appear less consistent with such models.

Other discussions of site structure have been developed around spatial arrangements of public areas. The existence of large central plazas was recognized by Haury (1976) and Wasley and Johnson (1965). Wilcox (Wilcox et al. 1981:140) showed persistence of this feature from the late Pioneer at Snaketown and occurrences (Wilcox and Sternberg 1983) at other sites. Positioning of public architecture around the edges of the plaza and concentric arrangement of suprahousehold units out from this center were first described for

Snaketown (Wilcox et al. 1981:140) and later for other sites (e.g., Howard 1982; Wilcox and Sternberg 1983; Doelle et al. 1987; Henderson 1987a, 1987b). The continuation of this general site layout was studied intensively by Gregory (Gregory and Nials 1985; Gregory 1987) for the Classic period, resulting in the definition of patterned spatial relationships and orientations among mounds, ballcourts, and other elements of public architecture.

Prior to the Classic period, large sites usually have been considered additive accumulations of units present at smaller sites other than in the unique presence of public architecture. It has been suggested that large structures functioned in site-level integration as facilities for communal gatherings, in keeping with the use of Pima community houses. Clear differentiations have not been observed among Preclassic residential structures on the basis of placement or contents. However, at Snaketown, Nelson (1981) has quantified dissimilar proportions of exotic and well-crafted ("prestige") goods among cemeteries.

Formal site layouts involving public architecture are commonly related to social organization at the higher level of the community. These issues are most relevant for the Classic period when the greatest amount of architectural elaboration and differentiation can be documented. There is a divergence in interpretive realms at this point between intrasite and multisite organizational models. Kinship or what is usually termed social structure is the referent for lower orders of spatial relationship. For higher levels, political bases have been emphasized.

## COMMUNITY LEVEL

A growing number of Hohokam investigators are exploring ways of defining supravillage interactive organizations that satisfied the requirements for mating, risk management, labor procurement, craft production, and so forth. Even the largest and most nucleated Hohokam sites appear to have had limited populations, typically numbering in the hundreds rather than thousands. Appreciable segments of Hohokam population can be accounted for in dispersed rancherias wherever comprehensive survey is available. Communities embody institutions that integrate these groups into bounded territorial units centered on pivotal sites. It is particularly critical to understand the integrative mechanisms in view of distributions of total population.

Ballcourts (Wilcox and Sternberg 1983), platform mounds (Gregory and Nials 1985; Gregory 1987), and primary villages (Doelle et al. 1985) have been identified as community focal points. Since ballcourts and platform mounds are assumed to mark replicates of integrative nodes, community definition can be approximated by boundaries equidistant from consecutive centers. The primary village is an alternative concept that relies more on unique site magnitude (Doelle et al. 1985), a comparative measure that can still be acquired in areas where disturbance may have obscured public architecture and no older records of such features exist.

Distribution and spacing of public architecture have suggested regularities in the size of integrated areas. Such studies draw heavily upon early maps of larger sites and canals prior to widespread erasure during the last 50 years. An average distance of 5.5 km was found to separate predominantly Preclassic ballcourts in the Phoenix Basin, with probable wider spacing in more poorly documented areas elsewhere (Wilcox and Sternberg 1983:195). Higher orders of ballcourt integration are suggested by multicourt sites, presumably reflecting coordination in ritual observation and possible associated social interactions such as those concerning mate exchange (Wilcox and Sternberg 1983).

The spacing of sites with platform mounds along shared Salt and Gila canal systems has similarly been studied (Gregory and Nials 1985). Such sites are separated by an average distance of 5 km, a figure remarkably similar to the 5.5 km distance for ballcourts. These averages are derived from an only partially overlapping set of sites with both forms of public architecture. The convergence is highly suggestive of continuity in a basic integrative unit size between the Sedentary and Classic periods. Because tendencies can be seen in linear distance between centers along canals or canal systems, regularity in this dimension may define an optimal distance over which agricultural travel (e.g., Crown 1987:154; Chisholm 1979:127) and day-to-day communications concerning canal function could be carried out within a single community or between adjacent community centers.

In the core areas, canals provide a spatial and relational starting point for identifying groups of sites that interact as a community. Indeed, an influential early definition of the community concept (Doyel 1974, 1980) involved a hierarchy of settlement types in which sites along each canal network represented an irrigation community. Common use of the system created a basis for sociopolitical integration embodied at larger administrative sites or centers. The term community, in this sense, encompasses several multisite organizational units at the level of the ballcourt or platform mound community. Before the Classic period, the largest sites on canal systems tend to be centrally located (Nicholas and Neitzel 1984), while later they are located at the ends. There is some agreement among researchers (Upham and Rice 1980; Nicholas and Neitzel 1984; Gregory and Nials 1985; Crown 1987) that by the Classic period these largest sites were differentiated to some degree from the other large settlements in a community hierarchy.

A current analysis of a canal-based community introduces factors in addition to site size, public architecture, and spacing. Howard (1987) documents differential access to trade ceramics, grooved axes, turquoise, and possibly obsidian and shell between the preeminent site of Mesa Grande and lesser sites with and without public architecture along the Lehi Canal. Mesa Grande is the largest site (over 2.5 sq. km), with the largest and most varied public architecture, the only known high-status burials, and the greatest amount of trade goods. A second site category contains public architecture, averages about 500,000 sq m in extent, but unfortunately is associated with no excavated data. Smaller sites lacking mounds and ballcourts, make up, by far, the greatest number of sites within the system and have low frequencies of trade goods.

Hohokam communities in regions lacking extensive riverine irrigation cannot be explained by interaction occasioned by shared networks, nor are settlement expressions necessarily similar. Basic descriptions of communities in such areas are few and mostly fragmentary. Greater potential for understanding the role and distribution of dispersed populations may exist in non-core basins since there is less coincidence with intense modern development. However, the expansive character of these communities entails large-scale settlement recording.

Regional survey in the Tucson and Picacho basins (P. Fish et al. 1985; S. Fish et al. 1989) have revealed settlement clusters concentrated along major basin floor drainages and in mountain flank bands. The greatest detail for such settlements is available near the vicinity of Marana, Arizona. Separate Preclassic ballcourt communities in each of these locations are similar in size (70 and 57 sq km) and include a variety of site sizes and types. Community locations correspond to year-round sources of domestic and agricultural water, in the form of optimal water table locales on the Santa Cruz River and on Tortolita Mountain pediments.

The two earlier communities coalesce by the early Classic period, spanning the basin from river to mountain. A central platform mound site, supplied by a canal, was constructed in a poorly watered and previously unused portion of the intervening bajada or valley slope. Six zones of functionally and topographically differentiated settlement can be defined within the 146 sq km community (S. Fish et al. 1989: Figure 9.6). These extend from the Tucson Mountains to the river to the lower Tortolita Mountain slopes, encompassing almost the full range of Tucson Basin environments. Some important elements in community configuration include the central site with platform mound and compounds (Zone 1), lesser compound sites (Zones 4 and 5), habitation sites without compounds (Zones 1, 4, 5, 6), *trincheras* sites with residential and agricultural features (Zone 6), large communal agricultural fields devoted primarily to the cultivation of agave (Zone 2), and large nonresidential sites devoted to intensive saguaro cactus exploitation (Zone 3).

A case can be made for a three-tiered settlement hierarchy based on site size, architecture, and ceramics (S. Fish et al. 1989). The four largest sites (greater than 500,000 sq m) are distinguished by nonlocal ceramics, notably higher consumption of decorated types, compounds and, in one case, a mound. Intermediate-sized sites (150,000 to 350,000 sq m) contain cobble outlines of surface structures. More than three-fourths of the Classic period residential sites fall into a small category (less than 100,000 sq m) with no visible architectural remains. The mound site is optimally situated for centrality in the community but not in a location of maximal subsistence potential, suggesting an important role for exchange in community integration. Internal differentiation in patterns of productivity and settlement similarly seems to characterize other noncore communities (Doelle et al. 1985; Rice 1987c) and, perhaps to a lesser degree, some core area ones as well (Crown 1987; Cable and Mitchell 1987; Howard 1987).

Quantitative assessment of Hohokam communities and their segments is problematic both in terms of area and population, and can only be approached through rough estimates. Nevertheless, even coarse-scale measures show some interesting regularities. Mound spacing appears relatively regular within the Phoenix area as a whole, as well as along individual canals (see Gregory 1987:185, fig. 1). If it is assumed that communities integrate all adjacent space, whether irrigated or not, the average territory integrated by each of the 23 mounds in this area is roughly 40 sq km. Each of the six mound sites in the Classic Casa Grande community on the Gila (Crown 1987) also integrates approximately 40 sq km.

Another general trend for the Salt and Gila basins involves magnitudes of irrigated acreage. Recent refined estimates place land irrigated from the Salt River at approximately 21,500 ha (Nials, Gregory, and Graybill 1989) or an average of 935 ha per platform mound community. Within the Casa Grande system on the Gila, recent estimates of 6,250 ha (Crown 1987:155) result in a comparable average of 1,040 ha incorporated by each mound locality. Irrigated acreage in Classic communities, like mound spacing along canals, may involve regular communication concerning canal administration, water delivery, and travel to fields (Crown 1987; Gregory and Nials 1985). Fairly restricted ranges for both irrigated acreage and total integrated territory may reflect convenient distances for routine transport of crops and gathered resources.

Convergences in irrigated acreage may also point to consistency or optimal size in a more elusive and vital community parameter: population. Estimates of supportable population may be derived using figures for Pimans given by Castetter and Bell (1942:54). By this analogy, a family of five subsisted on 0.86 to 2.15 ha. In the area integrated by a mound and containing about 1,000 ha of irrigated land, 2,300 to 5,800 persons might have been supported (for all 23 mound communities in the Phoenix area, totals range from 53,000 to 133,000 persons).

Although reasonably derived modalities per mound community can be cited for integrated area and irrigable acreage (and, by more speculative inference, population), these must be regarded as very general averages incorporating a degree of individual variation. For example, Crown (1987) finds a correlation between size of the mound site in the Gila community and amount of irrigable acreage. However, her extremes for community totals by two different means of estimation are only 1,801 and 1,889 ha.

Direct comparison is difficult between the few well-documented communities away from the core area and those within it. For example, Doelle,

Huntington, and Wallace (1987:77) locate primary Preclassic villages about every 3 km along the Santa Cruz, a closer spacing than for ballcourt sites, which were every 5.5 km along canals in the core. The territory of each primary village probably contained riverine canals of limited comparative scale. However, villages along the Santa Cruz probably integrated greater amounts of lateral hinterland. Due to differences in subsistence potential, integrated territory in these cases may be more variable than integrated population.

A second comparison can be made between the 40 sq km associated with Classic mound sites along the Gila and Salt, and 147 sq km for the Marana mound. With a high proportion of nonirrigated agriculture at Marana, a substantially larger territory might well be required to support a population equivalent to that around each Phoenix Basin mound. However, population estimates are particularly difficult to determine for noncore settlement types. In addition, appropriate levels of comparison for sociopolitical function are unclear. The Marana community, with internal settlement hierarchy, might correspond more closely to the irrigation community as a whole rather than to an individual mound site unit within it.

The issue of comparative sociopolitical organization between the lower Salt and middle Gila basins and the substantial remainder of the Hohokam domain is poorly understood at present. Uncertainties begin at the most basic levels for integrative configurations expressed by ballcourts and mounds. Puebloan patterns suggest unilineal kinship principles as a basis for integrative structure, while southern rancheria organization features flexible bilateral kinship and a stronger political role for the secular principle of territorial affiliation. Since Hohokam cultural remains encompass a broad geographic area and a major division between riverine irrigation and alternative farming technologies, variation is possible in the degree and mode of social differentiation.

Whatever the nature of underlying organization, it is clear that an abstract structural model for multisite integration, symbolized in public architecture, was held by groups in both core and noncore subareas. The model evolved in generalized synchroneity, if not in every detail, from the period marked by ballcourts as the major architectural expression to the period of mound predominance. Primacy of the core area in development of integrative forms and attendant public architecture is usually assumed. However, centers elsewhere are not well documented and early mound development is also documented away from the core in instances such as the Gatlin site (Wasley and Johnson 1965).

## HOHOKAM TRAJECTORIES

Development of complexity as expressed by settlement hierarchies and social linearization can be seen as basically progressing through the Classic period, although individual communities may have begun and ended, and temporary reversals may have occurred in the developmental histories of subareas. The perception of an overall trend combines elements pertaining to belief systems and sociopolitical organization.

When adobe surface structures are enclosed by compound walls, many embody spatial attributes and relationships paralleling the courtyard groups of the Preclassic period (Sires 1987). Larger agglomerations of rooms within compound walls in the late Classic period, as clearly illustrated at Los Muertos (Haury 1945) and La Ciudad (Wilcox 1987a), may have an additive nature, incorporating several equivalents of the courtyard group in a replication of the suprahousehold unit. At the same time, functional differentiation among structures or rooms progressed. For example, the functionally specialized storage rooms within the Escalante compound (Doyel 1974) have no easily identified Preclassic counterparts.

Figurines, palettes, censers, and other specialized artifacts with presumed ritual function are widely, if not uniformly, distributed within sites and among cremations in the earlier part of the Hohokam sequence. Such artifacts denoting noncentralized or individualistic participation become more elaborated into the Sedentary period and then disappear completely. Preclassic dispersion of ritual observance throughout the population has been replaced by the late Sedentary period.

A trend toward exclusion, with later indications of hierarchical specialists, is seen in mound architecture. The earliest adobe-capped Snaketown phase mounds are not secluded from the rest of the site in any way. Palisades are added during the Sedentary period, beginning the spatial differentiation between participants in mound activities and the general public. These are followed first by post-reinforced walls and then by massive adobe compound walls during the Classic period. Smaller and then larger Classic structures atop mounds and within the surrounding compounds bespeak public-oriented activity by small numbers of socially differentiated actors. Storage, residential, and possibly ritual functions for these structures imply an overlay of administrative or redistributive roles for mound complex participants. Formalization in layout of public architecture during this time appears to correlate with the crystallization of activity by specialists on behalf of the public.

The association of integrative symbols of the community with particular social groups is an important innovation in Classic social organization for which a precursor form cannot be clearly identified. Ballcourts are not linked with residential structures or any material evidence identifying socially differentiated participants. The same is true of Preclassic mounds prior to the late Sedentary period. Residential function for earlier structures within mound compounds has been questioned (Gregory 1987). Later in the period, residence both on mounds and within their compounds is clear from a number of sites (Doyel 1974; Wilcox 1987a; Gregory 1987). Compound walls demarcate personnel in internal precincts whose institutional roles are presently obscure.

It is unknown whether there were multiple bases for social differentiation in Hohokam society such as religious, administrative, and mercantile, or the designation of a generalized elite for some degree of privilege and authority by a single principle such as the ranked lineage.

Trends toward intersite hierarchy and greater territorial integration are apparent. Little tangible evidence of integration exists for the Pioneer period, but by its end the first caliche-capped mounds have appeared. Some sites are distinguished by ballcourts in the early Colonial period, and during this same interval, larger sites along Salt and Gila canal networks show the beginning of primacy. Mound sites serve as centers in the Classic period, with a tendency for principal sites to emerge near the terminus of canal systems. Outside the Salt and Gila valleys, areally extensive communities integrated by single mounds are likely equivalents of units involving entire canal lines.

Continuation of sociopolitical trends can be traced from early to late Classic period communities. Nucleation becomes intensified at late Classic platform mound sites, producing the densest concentrations of surface artifacts and the largest aggregations of structures as at Los Muertos. These trends hold within any single region, although absolute measures may vary from subarea to subarea. Likewise, the most massive instances of public architecture are constructed during this time: Mesa Grande, Pueblo Grande, and Casa Grande. Some researchers (e.g., Upham and Rice 1980; Nicholas and Nietzel 1984; Doelle and Wallace, this volume) have suggested that the size of integrated territories increases into the late Classic as well.

## THE ENIGMATIC HOHOKAM

The Hohokam stand out as particularly enigmatic among prehistoric culture groups in the Southwest. The roots and structure of their social organization remain elusive and difficult to classify. Hohokam society is most clearly defined by the archaeological record at the level of households and then again at an uppermost level expressed in the distribution of communal architecture. Principles and roles generating the social fabric that connected these levels are poorly understood.

Because the primary rationales for social order are unclear, the Hohokam cannot be conclusively evaluated according to current modalities of cultural form and evolution. The result is a continuing lack of consensus in Hohokam archaeology concerning basic aspects of sociopolitical interpretation. Simultaneous usage of contrastive terms for organizational character such as hierarchical and egalitarian or tribe and chiefdom, can be found among different scholars. In part, this situation reflects ongoing debates in Southwestern archaeology and the discipline as a whole, but it also reflects the unique background of Hohokam studies.

By comparison with the Puebloan Southwest, the Hohokam area suffers from a deficit of critical ethnographic and historic insights, as well as from the absence of an explicit iconographic record. The Mesoamerican flavor of ritual artifacts and public architecture is particularly difficult to link with appropriate social correlates. These influences set off the Hohokam from other Southwestern traditions and undoubtedly contribute to recurring perceptions of "un-Southwestern" complexity. In spite of the undisputed Mesoamerican origin of these elements, the Hohokam incorporated them in a selective manner. For instance, unlike groups in the Mississippian tradition of eastern North America, they did not adopt the associated Mesoamerican iconography and material items emphasizing political dominance, warfare, and human sacrifice. It is thus clear that close analogies with the well-documented societies of central Mexico are questionable. Early historic observations of relevance in adjacent northwestern Mexico are limited; Piman ethnography offers minimal insight into the social context of these intriguing elements.

One of the greatest challenges in Hohokam archaeology is a refined definition of organizational principles and integrative structure. These are well understood at present only in the sense of spatial patterns, and mainly with reference to architectural features. Detailed distributional studies of artifacts represent a largely unexploited avenue for further research, although Hohokam disposal and mortuary behavior present difficulties in such pursuits. Detailed and quantitative artifactual distributions are needed from small sites, but it is from the larger ones that such information is most critical and difficult to obtain. Reuse over time creates a complicated record and only fragments of many significant settlements have escaped destruction. Careful investigation is warranted at the few relatively intact sites and innovative approaches are needed at the others.

## REFERENCES CITED

Ackerly, Neal, Jerry Howard, and Randall H. McGuire
  1987  *La Ciudad Canals: A Study of Hohokam Irrigation Systems at the Community Level.* Arizona State University Anthropological Field Studies 17.
Anderson, Keith
  1986  Hohokam Cemeteries as Elements of Settlement Structure and Change. In *Anthropology of the Desert West: Essays in Honor of Jesse D. Jennings,* edited by Carol Condie and Don Fowler. University of Utah Press, Salt Lake City.
Bolton, Herbert E.
  1936  *Rim of Christendom: A Biography of Eusbio Francisco Kino.* Macmillan, New York.
Browne, John R.
  1869  *Adventures in the Apache Country: A Tour through Arizona and Sonora, with Notes on the Silver Region of Nevada.* Harper and Brothers, New York.
Cable, John, and David Doyel
  1987  Pioneer Period Village Structure and Settlement Pattern in the Phoenix Basin.

In *The Hohokam Village: Site Structure and Organization*, edited by David Doyel, pp. 21–70. Southwestern and Rocky Mountain Division of the American Association for the Advancement of Science. Glenwood Springs, Colorado.

Cable, John, and Douglas Mitchell
1987   La Lomita Pequena in Regional Perspective. In *Excavations at La Lomita Pequuna: A Santa Cruz/Sacaton Phase Hamlet in the Salt River Valley*, edited by Douglas Mitchell. Soil Systems Publications in Archaeology 10.

Castetter, E. F., and W. H. Bell
1942   *Pima and Papago Indian Agriculture*. University of New Mexico Press, Albuquerque.

Chisholm, M.
1979   *Rural Settlement and Land Use: An Essay on Location*. Hutchinson and Company, London.

Ciolek-Torrello, Richard, Martha Callahan, and David Greenwald
1988   *Hohokam Settlement along the Slopes of the Picacho Mountains: The Brady Wash Sites*. Museum of Northern Arizona Research Paper 35.

Cordell, Linda S.
1989   History and Theory on Reconstructing Southwestern Sociopolitical Organization. In *The Sociopolitical Structure of Prehistoric Southwestern Societies*, edited by S. Upham, K. Lightfoot, and R. Jewett, pp. 33–54. Westview Press, Boulder.

Crown, Patricia L.
1987   Classic Period Hohokam Settlement and Land Use in the Casa Grande Ruin Area, Arizona. *Journal of Field Archaeology* 14:147–162.

Cushing, Frank H.
1890   Preliminary Notes on the Origin, Working Hypotheses, Preliminary Researches of the Hemenway Southwestern Expedition. *Congres International des Americanistes*, pp. 151–194. Berlin.
1892   The Hemenway Southwestern Archaeological Expedition. Manuscript on file. Hayden Library, Arizona State University, Tempe.

Di Peso, Charles
1956   *The Upper Pima of San Cayetano del Tumacacori: An Archaeological Reconstruction of the Ootam of Pimeria Alta*. The Amerind Foundation 7.

Dobyns, Henry
1963   Indian Extinction in the Middle Santa Cruz River Valley, Arizona. *New Mexico Historical Review* 38:163–181.
1981   *From Fire to Flood: Human Destruction of Sonoran Desert Riverine Oases*. Ballena Press Anthropological Papers 20.

Doelle, William H.
1983   *Archaeological and Historic Investigations at Nolic, Papago Indian Reservation, Arizona*. Institute for American Research Anthropological Paper 2.
1985   The Southern Tucson Basin Rillito-Rincon Subsistence, Settlement and Community Structure. In *Proceedings of the 1983 Hohokam Symposium*, edited by A. E. Dittert and D. E. Dove, pp. 183–198. Arizona Archaeological Society Occasional Paper 2.

Doelle, William H., A. Dart, and H. D. Wallace
1985   *The Southern Tucson Basin Survey*. Institute for American Research, Technical Report 85-3.

Doelle, William H., Frederick W. Huntington, and Henry D. Wallace
   1987   Rincon Phase Reorganization in the Tucson Basin. In *The Hohokam Village: Site Structure and Organization*, edited by David Doyel, pp. 71–96. Southwestern and Rocky Mountain Division of the American Association for the Advancement of Science. Glenwood Springs, Colorado.
Doyel, David
   1974   *Excavations in the Escalante Ruin Group, Southern Arizona*. Arizona State Museum Archaeological Series 37.
   1980   Hohokam Social Organization and the Sedentary to Classic Transition. In *Current Issues in Hohokam Prehistory: Proceedings of a Symposium*, edited by David Doyel and Fred Plog, pp. 23–40. Arizona State University Anthropological Research Paper 23.
Elson, Mark D.
   1986   *Archaeological Investigations at the Tanque Verde Wash Site, a Middle Rincon Settlement in the Eastern Tucson Basin*. Institute for American Research Anthropological Papers 7.
Ezell, Paul
   1983   History of the Pima. In *Handbook of North American Indians*, vol. 10, Southwest, edited by Alfonso Ortiz, pp. 149–160. Smithsonian Institution Press, Washington, D.C.
Fewkes, Jesse Walter
   1912   Casa Grande, Arizona. *28th Annual Report of the Bureau of Ethnology, 1906–1907*, pp. 25–179. Washington, D.C.
Fish, Paul R., and Suzanne K. Fish
   1984   Agricultural Maximization in the Sacred Mountain Basin. In *Prehistoric Agricultural Strategies in the Southwest*, edited by Suzanne K. Fish and Paul R. Fish, pp. 147–169. Arizona State University Anthropological Research Papers 33.
Fish, Paul R., Suzanne K. Fish, and John Madsen
   1985   Northern Tucson Basin Survey: Research Summary and Recommendations for the Marana Complex. In *A Supplemental Class III Archaeological Survey of the Phase A, Reach 3 Corridor, Tucson Aqueduct, Central Arizona Project*, edited by John Czaplicki and A. G. Rankin, pp. 83–90. Arizona State Museum Archaeological Series 165.
Fish, Suzanne K., Paul R. Fish, and John Madsen
   1985   A Preliminary Analysis of Settlement and Agriculture in the Northern Tucson Basin. In *Proceedings of the 1983 Hohokam Symposium*, edited by A. E. Dittert and D. E. Dove, pp. 75–100. Arizona Archaeological Society Occasional Paper 2.
   1989   Classic Period Hohokam Community Integration in the Tucson Basin. In *The Sociopolitical Structure of Prehistoric Southwestern Societies*, edited by Steadman Upham, Kent Lightfoot, and Roberta Jewett, pp. 237–268. Westview Press, Boulder.
Ford, Richard I.
   1981   Gardening and Farming before A.D. 1000: Patterns of Prehistoric Cultivation North of Mexico. *Journal of Ethnobiology* 1:6–27.
Grebinger, Paul R.
   1971   *Hohokam Cultural Development in the Middle Santa Cruz Valley, Arizona*. Ph.D. Dissertation, Department of Anthropology, University of Arizona, Tucson.

Gregory, David
  1982   Technical Proposal: Archaeological Data Recovery at Las Colinas (AZ T:12:10,
         ASM) and AZ T:12:38 (ASM). Manuscript on file, Arizona State Museum,
         University of Arizona, Tucson.
  1983   Excavations at the Siphon Draw Site (AZ U:10:6). In *Hohokam Archaeology along
         the Salt-Gila Aqueduct, Central Arizona Project*, vol. 4: Village Sites on Queen
         Creek and Siphon Draw, edited by L. S. Teague and P. L. Crown. *Arizona
         State Museum Archaeological Series 150.*
  1987   The Morphology of Platform Mounds and the Structure of Classic Period
         Hohokam Sites. In *The Hohokam Village: Site Structure and Organization*, edited
         by David Doyel, pp. 183–210. Southwestern and Rocky Mountain Division
         of the American Association for the Advancement of Science. Glenwood
         Springs, Colorado.
Gregory, David, and Fred Nials
  1985   Observations Concerning the Distribution of Classic Period Hohokam Plat-
         form Mounds. In *Proceedings of the 1983 Hohokam Conference*, edited by A. E.
         Dittert and D. E. Dove, pp. 373–388. Arizona Archaeological Society Occa-
         sional Paper 2.
Haury, Emil W.
  1945   *The Excavation of Los Muertos and Neighboring Ruins in the Salt River Valley,
         Southwestern Arizona*. Papers of the Peabody Museum of American Archae-
         ology and Ethnology 24.
  1956   Speculations on Prehistoric Settlement Patterns in the Southwest. In *Prehis-
         toric Settlement Patterns in the New World*, edited by G. R. Willey, pp. 3–10.
         Viking Fund Publications on Anthropology 23.
  1976   *The Hohokam: Desert Farmers and Craftsmen*. University of Arizona Press, Tuc-
         son.
Henderson, T. Kathleen
  1987a  *Structure and Organization at La Ciudad*. Arizona State University Anthropo-
         logical Field Studies 18.
  1987b  The Growth of a Hohokam Village. In *The Hohokam Village: Site Structure and
         Organization*, edited by David Doyel, pp. 97–126. Southwestern and Rocky
         Mountain Division of the American Association for the Advancement of Sci-
         ence. Glenwood Springs, Colorado.
Howard, Jerry B.
  1982   Hohokam Community Organization at La Ciudad de Los Hornos. Manuscript
         on File, Department of Anthropology, Arizona State University, Tempe.
  1985   Courtyard Groups and Domestic Cycling: A Hypothetical Model of Growth.
         In *Proceedings of the 1983 Hohokam Symposium*, edited by A. E. Dittert and D.
         E. Dove. Arizona Archaeological Society Occasional Paper 2.
  1987   The Lehi Canal System: Organization of a Classic Period Community. In *The
         Hohokam Village: Site Structure and Organization*, edited by David Doyel, pp.
         211–222. Southwestern and Rocky Mountain Division of the American As-
         sociation for the Advancement of Science. Glenwood Springs, Colorado.
Huntington, Fredrick W.
  1986   *Archaeological Investigations at the West Branch Site: Early and Middle Rincon
         Occupation in the Southern Tucson Basin*. Institute for American Research An-
         thropological Paper 5.

Kirkby, Ann V. T.
   1973   *The Use of Land and Water Resources in the Past and Present Valley of Oaxaca.*
          University of Michigan Museum of Anthropology Memoir 5.
Kowalewski, S. A.
   1980   Population-Resource Balances in Period I of Oaxaca. *American Antiquity* 45:151–
          164.
Martin, Paul S. and Fred Plog
   1973   *The Archaeology of Arizona: A Study of a Southwest Region.* Natural History Press,
          New York.
Masse, W. Bruce
   1976   *The Hohokam Expressway Project: A Study of Prehistoric Irrigation in the Salt River
          Valley, Arizona.* Arizona State Museum, University of Arizona, Tucson.
   1981   Prehistoric Irrigation Systems in the Salt River Valley, Arizona. *Science* 214:408–
          415.
   1987   *Archaeological Investigations of Portions of the Las Acequias–Los Muertos Irrigation
          System.* Arizona State Museum Archaeological Series 176.
McGuire, Randall H.
   1987   *Death, Society, and Ideology in a Hohokam Community: Colonial and Sedentary
          Period Burials from La Ciudad.* Arizona State University Office of Cultural Re-
          source Management Report 68.
Midvale, Frank
   1968   Prehistoric Irrigation in the Salt River Valley, Arizona. *The Kiva* 34:28–32.
Nabhan, Gary
   1985   Native Crop Diversity in Aridoamerica: Conservation of Regional Gene Pools.
          *Economic Botany* 39:387–399.
Nelson, Richard S.
   1981   *The Role of a* Pochteca *System in Hohokam Exchange.* Ph.D. Dissertation, De-
          partment of Anthropology, New York University, New York.
Nials, Fred L., David Gregory, and Donald Graybill
   1989   Salt River Streamflow and Hohokam Irrigation Systems. In *The 1982–1984
          Excavations at Las Colinas: Environment and Subsistence,* edited by Carol Heath-
          ington and David Gregory, pp. 59–78. Arizona State Museum Archaeological
          Series 162.
Nicholas, Linda and Gary Feinman
   1989   A Regional Perspective on Hohokam Irrigation on the Lower Salt River Valley,
          Arizona. In *The Sociopolitical Structure of Prehistoric Southwestern Societies,* edited
          by Steadman Upham, Kent Lightfoot, and Rachel Most, pp. 199–236. West-
          view Press, Boulder.
Nicholas, Linda, and Jill Neitzel
   1984   Canal Irrigation and Sociopolitical Organization in the Lower Salt River Val-
          ley: A Diachronic Analysis. In *Prehistoric Agricultural Strategies in the Southwest,*
          edited by Suzanne K. Fish and Paul R. Fish, pp. 161–178. Arizona State
          University Anthropological Research Papers 33.
Patrick, H. R.
   1903   The Ancient Canal Systems and Pueblos of the Salt River Valley, Arizona.
          *Bulletin of the Phoenix Free Museum* 1.
Perez de Ribas, Andres
   1968   *My Life Among the Savage Nations of New Spain,* translated by Thomas Robert-
          son. The Ward Ritchie Press, Los Angeles.

Plog, Fred
    1980   Explaining Culture Change in the Hohokam Preclassic. In *Current Issues in Hohokam Prehistory: Proceedings of a Symposium*, edited by David Doyel and Fred Plog, pp. 4–22. Arizona State University Anthropological Research Papers 23.
Rice, Glen
    1982   La Ciudad Archaeological Project: A Proposal for Data Recovery. Manuscript on File, Department of Anthropology, Arizona State University, Tempe.
    1987a  La Ciudad: A Perspective on Hohokam Community Systems. In *The Hohokam Village: Site Structure and Organization*, edited by David Doyel, pp. 127–158. Southwestern and Rocky Mountain Division of the American Association for the Advancement of Science. Glenwood Springs, Colorado.
    1987b  *The Hohokam Community of La Ciudad.* Arizona State University Office of Cultural Resource Management Report 69.
    1987c  *Studies in the Hohokam Community of Marana, Arizona.* Arizona State University Anthropological Field Studies 15.
    1989   A Design for Salado Research: Roosevelt Platform Mound Study. Manuscript on file, Department of Anthropology, Arizona State University, Tempe.
Russell, Frank
    1975   *The Pima Indians.* Re-edition of the 1908 Bureau of American Ethnology Annual Report, 1904–1905. University of Arizona Press, Tucson.
Sheridan, Thomas
    1981   Prelude to Conquest: Yaqui Population, Subsistence, and Warfare during the Protohistoric Period. In *The Protohistoric Period in the North American Southwest*, edited by David Wilcox and W. B. Masse, pp. 71–93. Arizona State University Anthropological Research Paper 24.
Sires, Earl W., Jr.
    1985   Hohokam Architecture and Site Structure. In *Hohokam Archaeology Along the Salt-Gila Aqueduct, Central Arizona Project*, edited by L. S. Teague and P. L. Crown, pp. 115–139. Arizona State Museum Archaeological Series 150.
    1987   Hohokam Architectural Variability and Site Structure during the Sedentary-Classic Transition. In *The Hohokam Village: Site Structure and Organization*, edited by David Doyel, pp. 171–182. Southwestern and Rocky Mountain Division of the American Association for the Advancement of Science. Glenwood Springs, Colorado.
Southworth, Clay H.
    1915   Exhibits Relating to the Pima Indians as Collected During Work Connected with the Gila River Surveys of 1914–15, vol. 1. Phoenix Area Office, Bureau of Indian Affairs, Trust Protection. Manuscript on file, Arizona State Museum, University of Arizona, Tucson.
    1919   *History of Irrigation on the Gila River.* Hearings before the Committee on Indian Affairs, House of Representatives, 66th Congress, 1st Session, vol. 2. U.S. Government Printing Office, Washington.
Turney, Omar A.
    1929   *Prehistoric Irrigation in Arizona.* Arizona State Historian, Phoenix.
Underhill, Ruth
    1939   *Social Organization of the Papago Indians.* Columbia University Press, New York.
Upham, Steadman, and Glen Rice
    1980   Up the Canal without a Pattern: Modeling Hohokam Interaction and Ex-

change. In *Current Issues in Hohokam Prehistory: Proceedings of a Symposium,* edited by David Doyel and Fred Plog, pp. 78–105. Arizona State University Anthropological Research Papers 23.

Wasley, William W., and Alfred E. Johnson
  1965  *Salvage Archaeology in the Painted Rocks Reservoir, Western Arizona.* Anthropological Papers of the University of Arizona 9.

Wilcox, David
  1987a  *Frank Midvale's Investigation of the Site of La Ciudad.* Arizona State University Anthropological Field Studies 18.
  1987b  Hohokam Social Complexity. Paper presented in the Symposium "Cultural Complexity in the Arid Southwest: The Hohokam and Chacoan Regional Systems," organized by P. Crown and J. Judge. School of American Research, Santa Fe.
  1987c  New Models of Social Structure at C. C. Di Peso's Palo Parado Site. In *The Hohokam Village: Site Structure and Organization,* edited by David Doyel, pp. 223–248. Southwestern and Rocky Mountain Division of the American Association for the Advancement of Science. Glenwood Springs, Colorado.

Wilcox, David R., Thomas R. McGuire, and Charles Sternberg
  1981  *Snaketown Revisited: A Partial Cultural Resource Survey, Analysis of Site Structure, and an Ethnohistoric Study of the Proposed Hohokam-Pima National Monument.* Arizona State Museum Archaeological Series 155.

Wilcox, David, and Charles Sternberg
  1983  *Hohokam Ballcourts and Their Interpretation.* Arizona State Museum Archaeological Series 160.

Woodbury, Richard B.
  1960  The Hohokam Canals at Pueblo Grande, Arizona. *American Antiquity* 26:267–270.

# ·5·

# HOHOKAM MATERIAL CULTURE AND BEHAVIOR: THE DIMENSIONS OF ORGANIZATIONAL CHANGE

*Jill Neitzel*

The interpretive focus of material culture studies in archaeology has traditionally been culture historical, using the distributions of artifacts to define the temporal and spatial limits of their makers. However, over the past several decades, the problem of the behavioral significance of man's material creations has begun to be addressed by both anthropologists and archaeologists (Fenton 1974; Kluckhohn et al. 1971; Kristiansen 1984; Lechtman 1977; Lemonnier 1986; Leone 1973, 1982; Merrill 1968). Material culture studies have consequently been transformed from routine exercises in artifact description and classification to a challenging new approach for understanding how prehistoric populations lived.

This transformation is clearly evident in Hohokam research. The prehistoric occupants of south-central Arizona left a rich array of cultural materials, from impressive architecture and sophisticated irrigation works to finely made painted pottery and elegant shell jewelry. As late as 1976 when Haury's classic monograph on Snaketown was published, these Hohokam remains were interpreted almost exclusively from a culture-historical perspective. In addition to his primary goal of resolving controversies about the Hohokam chronology, Haury's (1976) other major objective in his Snaketown excavations seems to have been to produce a comprehensive description of Hohokam material culture, focusing on the changes that characterized each phase in his proposed temporal sequence.

Since the publication of Haury's (1976) monograph, the pace of archaeological investigations in south-central Arizona has accelerated, resulting in a virtual explosion in the amount of prehistoric data available for study. These data have been used to reevaluate the conclusions derived from previous work, as seen in the ongoing debate about Hohokam chronology (see Dean, this volume), and to address a wide range of new research issues. The one question that has linked all of the latter efforts has been how the study of Hohokam material culture can be expanded beyond the fairly straightforward description and classification of objects to provide insights into Hohokam behavior (Doyel 1985:20).

The behavioral issue that has dominated Hohokam research over the past decade has been the changing organization of the prehistoric populations of south-central Arizona. This work began over a decade ago with a series of evaluations of the long-accepted view that the Hohokam were egalitarian (e.g., Doyel 1979, 1980; McGuire 1983, 1987; Upham and Rice 1980; Wilcox et al. 1981; Wilcox and Shenk 1977; Wilcox and Sternberg 1983). With the conclusion that a hierarchically organized sociopolitical system was present certainly in the Classic period, probably in the Sedentary period, and perhaps even earlier, more recent investigations have been directed towards documenting the nature of this organizational change and explaining why it occurred.

The purpose of this paper is to show how material culture studies can contribute to our understanding of organizational change among the Hohokam. Three dimensions of change are considered: (1) craft specialization, (2) labor investment in public construction, and (3) elaboration of ritual. After an examination of the theoretical and methodological issues that affect the study of each of these topics, relevant data from the Hohokam core area are summarized.

## THEORETICAL AND METHODOLOGICAL CONSIDERATIONS

The longstanding and ultimate goal of anthropologists, including those archaeologists who study the Hohokam, has been to explain societal variation and change. The most productive approach for accomplishing this goal involves the identification and comparison of the major dimensions of change that together comprise the overall process of cultural evolution (Blanton et al. 1981). Three processes that are especially amenable to study through material culture analyses are considered here.

## CRAFT SPECIALIZATION

One dimension of cultural evolution is the specialization of labor. Occupational specialization has been found to be positively correlated with population growth, urbanization, social stratification, political complexity, and agricultural intensification (Dow 1985; Ember 1963; Naroll 1956; Tatje and Naroll 1973). Archaeological studies of specialization have generally focused on the appearance of craft specialists. Craft specialists are individuals who manufacture material, nonagricultural projects for use by others and who are remunerated in some way for this activity (Tatje and Naroll 1973). They may be independent specialists who are self-employed, providing either utilitarian goods or items of wealth in response to consumer demand (Brumfiel and Earle 1987). Or, they may be attached specialists who produce wealth items for elite patrons (Brumfiel and Earle 1987).

Degree of craft specialization is generally measured on a three-part scale representing societies with no specialists, part-time specialists, and full-time specialists (Muller 1984; Rice 1987). Part-time specialists devote only a portion of their time to craft production and the remainder to subsistence activities. Full-time specialists produce more goods at a relatively high, constant rate year-round and receive the bulk of their subsistence as payment.

Various evolutionary typologies have attempted to incorporate this tripartite division of degree of craft specialization (e.g., Fried 1967; Service 1962). While egalitarian societies generally lack craft specialists, part-time specialists have been associated with ranked societies or simple chiefdoms and full-time specialists have been associated with complex chiefdoms and states. In addition, states have the most kinds of craft specialists and the greatest numbers of individuals filling these roles.

This correlation between degree of specialization and organizational complexity reflects the economic as well as the political significance of craft specialization. Economically, the presence of craft specialists of any kind reflects a society's ability to support individuals who are not directly involved in subsistence activities. Politically, the presence of attached specialists reflects the efforts of leaders to control the production of wealth items.

Brumfiel (1987) has argued that the wealth items produced by attached specialists should be viewed as political capital (see also Brumfiel and Earle 1987). These items generally symbolize a leader's special status and in some cases his connections with the supernatural world. As a result, they can be used for two related purposes. First, the wealth items can legitimize the leader's role. Second, they can be used to attract allies and reward followers. Thus, through the skillful manipulation of the wealth objects produced by the attached specialists he supports, a leader can increase his power. It is due to this manipulation that major political transformations are often accompanied by major changes in craft production.

One impediment to understanding the role of craft specialization in cultural evolution is evaluating the degree and kind of specialization in different prehistoric contexts (Muller 1984; Peebles and Kus 1977; Rice 1987). Most of the archaeological indicators do not distinguish part-time from full-time specialization or independent from attached specialists. The best evidence comes from state-level societies where the large-scale production that occurs with full-time specialization may be evidenced by workshops, stockpiles of raw materials, large deposits of production waste, and storage facilities for completed craft goods (Becker 1973; Evans 1978; Feinman 1985; Haviland 1974; Minnis 1988; Muller 1984; Rice 1984; Rowlands 1971; Spence 1985; Stark 1985; Tosi 1984; Yerkes 1983). Unfortunately, such evidence may require extensive excavations for detection.

Many studies have focused on two other types of data. First, when manufacturing debris and finished artifacts are not evenly distributed within a settlement of any level of organizational complexity, this may be evidence that not every household participated in craft production (Tosi 1984). Second, standardization or elaboration of the artifacts themselves may indicate that production was restricted in some way (Feinman 1985; Rice 1981). Standardization is the reduction in variety of such attributes as raw materials, manufacturing techniques, size, shape, and decoration. It has generally been associated with the large-scale production of utilitarian and lesser valued items in highly stratified or state-level societies (Feinman 1985; Peebles and Kus 1977; Rice 1981). Elaboration is the increase in variety of these same attributes. It occurs with the production of valuable elite and ceremonial goods in simple chiefdoms as well as in more highly stratified and state-level societies (Rice 1981).

## LABOR EXPENDITURES

Large-scale construction is another characteristic that has been associated with the development of complex societies (Service 1962:170; White 1959:297). Two types of building activity can occur: (1) facilities related to the process of agricultural intensification such as irrigation canals, and (2) public architecture such as temples, pyramids, and administrative buildings (Price 1984). Both types of public works are significant because their scale reflects a society's ability to mobilize, support, and coordinate labor beyond the household and community level (Peebles and Kus 1977).

In general, the number and scale of construction projects undertaken by a society reflect its degree of organizational complexity as well as its population size and amount of surplus production. For example, more highly developed sociopolitical systems can build more extensive irrigation works

(Adams 1974; Hunt and Hunt 1976, 1978; Lees 1973, 1974a, 1974b; Mitchell 1973; Moseley 1974; Wittfogel 1957). Similarly, societies with greater sociopolitical complexity tend to produce public structures of greater size with more costly raw materials, more decoration, and greater diversity in forms and specialized functions (Flannery and Marcus 1971; McGuire and Schiffer 1982; Spencer 1987).

The major difference between agricultural facilities and public architecture is in the kinds of expenditures that they represent (Price 1984). Hydraulic projects are clearly capital investments because the costs that are incurred in their construction are mitigated by the resulting increase in agricultural productivity. In contrast, ceremonial and administrative structures produce no goods directly, although they may serve as collection points for offerings.

Both types of construction have political payoffs. The increased surplus produced by irrigation facilities can be used by elites to finance their political activities (Earle 1978). Public architecture is a highly visible symbol of the elite's political power, wealth, status, and often their connections with the supernatural (Flannery and Marcus 1971; McGuire and Schiffer 1983). Both of these functions are similar to those performed by the products of attached craft specialists.

In an effort to clarify the relationship between large-scale construction projects and sociopolitical development, a series of studies has attempted to estimate the labor requirements of construction (Ashbee and Cornwall 1961; Atkinson 1961; Bradley 1984; Chang 1968:205; Erasmus 1965; Pozorski 1980; Renfrew 1973; Startin and Bradley 1981; Webb 1987). Man-hour estimates have been derived by measuring the sizes of a structure's various components and then using work rates obtained from field experiments to calculate the costs of procuring and preparing raw materials and completing various stages in the construction process.

While the accurate reconstruction of labor costs is difficult (Earle 1987a; McGuire 1983), analyses of British earthworks and New World mounds have all produced the same conclusion (Ashbee and Cornwall 1961; Atkinson 1961; Erasmus 1965; Minnis 1989; Muller 1987; Pozorski 1980; Renfrew 1973). Highly centralized organizations with large pools of full-time laborers are not a necessary prerequisite of large-scale construction projects (Kaplan 1963).

The critical variable seems to be the duration of construction activity (Earle 1987a; Erasmus 1965; Kaplan 1963; Pozorski 1980). A society with minimal sociopolitical differentiation and a small pool of part-time labor could erect a monumental structure by accretion over a long period. However, any shortening in the duration of building necessarily entails increased labor costs as well as greater administrative capabilities.

These results indicate that while large-scale construction is generally correlated with sociopolitical complexity, a monumental structure cannot automatically be interpreted as evidence that the society in question was highly centralized or that its population and level of surplus production were large.

Nevertheless, the organizational significance of a monumental structure can be evaluated if calculations are done using reliable data with good temporal control (e.g., Pozorski 1980; Webb 1987).

## RITUAL ELABORATION

Ritual elaboration is another dimension of change in the overall process of cultural evolution. Ritual activity consists of highly patterned, repetitive behaviors that are performed in certain specified circumstances (Bloch 1986:184; Drennan 1976, 1983a, 1983b; Kertzer 1988; Rappaport 1971a, 1971b). Because ritual activity is often determined by religious beliefs, it can communicate and sanctify social information. Thus, so-called rituals of sanctification can ensure the acceptance of social messages by reinforcing them with the sacred authority of the supernatural world (Drennan 1976, 1983a, 1983b). Ritual activity changes during the process of cultural evolution because the kinds of messages that need to be communicated within a society change (Rappaport 1971a, 1971b).

Drennan (1976, 1983a, 1983b) has identified two important transitions in the elaboration of ritual. The first is the establishment of sedentary, agricultural villages. With movement no longer an option for settling disputes and with the reliance on a narrower, human-controlled resource base, more group decisions have to be made and accepted by all members. These decisions are more likely to be accepted if they are made within the context of ritual events.

The second transition discussed by Drennan (1983b) is the emergence of larger scale, ranked societies. With the vertical as well as horizontal differentiation of society, more decisions need to be made and more messages need to be communicated. Ritual legitimizes both the hierarchical system of group decision making and the greater power, status, and wealth of the individuals occupying the upper tiers of that hierarchy (see Bloch 1986:190–191; Cohen 1969; Friedel 1981; Geertz 1985; Kertzer 1988).

Archaeologists can study these major transitions through the remains of artifacts and structures that had ritual functions (Drennan 1976; Flannery 1976). For example, the increased importance of ritual in sedentary, agricultural villages is evidenced in Mesoamerica by the appearance of permanent, ceremonial buildings and the proliferation of clay figurines (Drennan 1976, 1983b). The buildings suggest that group ritual increased in frequency and regularity and that it entailed a greater social investment. Also, the fact that these buildings could not have held all village members at one time suggests that access was restricted in some way. The distribution of high numbers of figurines throughout the villages has been interpreted as evidence that individual households frequently participated in ritual activities.

With the development of ranked societies, the further elaboration of ritual is reflected in larger and more elaborate ceremonial structures and increasing variety of ritual artifacts (Drennan 1976, 1983b). As ritual increases in importance, structures may assume monumental proportions and display formalized layouts with religious significance. Ritual artifacts may be made of rare or foreign materials or decorated with symbols associated with the supernatural world.

Neither the ritual architecture nor artifacts of ranked societies can be separated from the domain of politics (Earle 1987b; Friedel 1981; Goldman 1970). Political leaders mobilize the labor necessary to build monumental structures, engage in the long-distance trading relationships to obtain exotic raw materials, and employ the craft specialists who apply symbolic decorations to ritual objects. By controlling and manipulating the construction of ritual architecture and the production of ritual artifacts, political leaders demonstrate their ties to the supernatural and thus legitimize and enhance their power. Political power is justified because it is seen as sacred power; and those leaders who are able to demonstrate the most sacred power, as manifested materially in ritual architecture and artifacts, are able to strengthen their political positions. Consequently, the process of sociopolitical development from ranked societies to complex chiefdoms and states is marked not only by increased vertical differentiation of the leadership hierarchy but also by the elaboration of ritual behavior.

## SUMMARY

The process of cultural evolution consists of a number of interrelated processes of change. Three of these processes are especially significant for the development of increasingly complex sociopolitical organizations. The emergence of craft specialization, the increased labor investment in public architecture, and the elaboration of ritual represent potential strategies for leaders to increase their political power. Products of craft specialists and public construction projects can increase a leader's wealth which in turn can be used for political gain. Products of craft specialists and public construction projects can also demonstrate a leader's connections to the supernatural world which in turn can legitimize political power by equating it with sacred power. Through the skillful manipulation of craft production, public construction, and ritual behavior, a leader can legitimize a hierarchical social structure and strengthen his position within it. As a result, sociopolitical development can occur.

## HOHOKAM CRAFT SPECIALIZATION

In the Hohokam area the problem of craft specialization has been addressed by two sets of researchers. Several early investigators whose primary concerns were artifact description and culture-historical reconstruction suggested that serrated projectile points (Wasley 1966) and red-on-buff pottery (Schroeder 1966:699, in Weaver et al. 1973:68) were produced by specialists.

More recently, archaeologists interested in documenting the changing organization of Hohokam society have treated the study of craft specialization as a means for monitoring increasing sociopolitical complexity (e.g., Doyel 1979, 1980). As a result of their efforts, the list of artifacts thought to have been made by specialists has grown. The items include utilitarian goods, status markers, and ritual paraphernalia.

## UTILITARIAN ARTIFACTS

The study of specialization in the manufacture of utilitarian objects is complicated by two factors. The first is the identification of which artifacts were in fact utilitarian.[1] For example, while ceramic vessels, textiles, and axes certainly served practical functions, some investigators have suggested that they were associated with persons of high status (Abbott 1984, 1985; Howard 1987; Wilcox 1987). Second, some utilitarian items, such as tabular knives, were used in the production of other crafts. Thus, their high frequency at a site may be evidence of their use in craft production rather than of their own manufacture (Teague 1984:215–216).

### Hohokam Red-on-buff Pottery

Red-on-buff pottery has traditionally been used to identify and date Hohokam sites. While considerable effort has been invested in classifying this pottery into a sequence of types (Gladwin et al. 1937; Haury 1976), questions about ceramic production have been addressed only recently. Evidence for ceramic production within the core area has been found at only a few sites (Haury 1976; Kisselburg 1987a, 1987b; Rafferty 1982; Seymour and Schiffer 1987).[2] As a result, investigators have asked whether red-on-buff pottery was mass produced at only a few manufacturing centers and then traded throughout the Hohokam region (Doyel 1980; Haury 1976; Schroeder in Weaver et al. 1973:68).

Efforts to answer this question have produced ambiguous results. One technological analysis has documented compositional diversity for red-on-buff ceramics from different sites (Weisman 1987). Other analyses have documented a high degree of compositional homogeneity (Abbott 1984; Crown 1984a). While diversity suggests localized production, the interpretation of homogeneous patterns is more difficult. Three possible causes for uniformity are: (1) potters at different sites were using the same clay and temper sources, (2) the clays and tempers from different sources were compositionally similar, or (3) ceramics made at one or a few sites were widely exchanged. Further complicating efforts to understand the nature of Hohokam ceramic exchange are the results of stylistic analyses that have revealed spatial patterns suggesting localized pottery production (Crown 1984b).

The question of whether specialists produced red-on-buff ceramics has been addressed for only the Colonial period occupation at La Ciudad and the

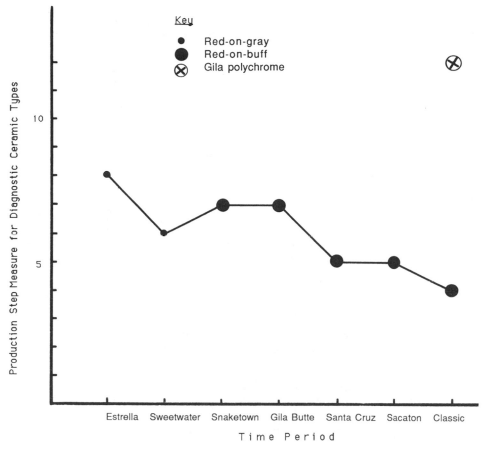

Figure 5.1    *Labor investment in traditionally defined Hohokam decorated ceramic types.*

Sedentary occupation at Snaketown. At La Ciudad, evidence for ceramic manufacture was evenly distributed among courtyards, a pattern which would be expected if there was no specialization (Kisselburg 1987a, 1987b, 1987c). Conversely, at Snaketown a limited number of households were associated with a ceramic production area, suggesting some degree of household specialization (Seymour and Schiffer 1987).

Only tentative evidence exists for changes in the organization of ceramic production. Haury (1976:210) has suggested that the artistic peak occurred during the Santa Cruz phase when the greatest variety of vessel forms and decorative motifs were employed. In addition, it seems that there was a change in the amount of labor invested in the production of individual pots. When I applied Feinman et al.'s (1981) production step measure to the traditionally defined types, I found a decline in labor investment beginning in the Santa Cruz phase and continuing through the Classic period (Fig. 5.1). This decline could be associated with a shift to specialized production. The production step measures also indicate that while the red-on-buff type made during the Classic period exhibits the lowest score of all of the decorated types, its contemporary, Gila Polychrome, exhibits the highest score. These two extremes in labor investment may reflect a change in the organization of ceramic production as well as in the demands of different categories of users (e.g., elites vs. commoners).

### Textiles

Hohokam textile production in the core area certainly predates the Classic period.[3] Cloth fragments, floral remains, and artifacts associated with textile production have all been found in Colonial and Sedentary period contexts. However, based on the frequency of spindle whorls, Wilcox (1987) argues that the level of production at this time was low. Distributional analyses of knives, spindle whorls, and plummets from the Colonial period occupation of La Ciudad suggest that this low-level production was not conducted by specialists (Kisselburg 1987a, 1987b, 1987c).

In the late Sedentary period, the Hohokam made a major technological innovation, a new type of spindle whorl that could be used to produce the finer threads necessary for gauze and weft-wrap openwork weaving (Kent 1957, 1983; King 1965; Wilcox 1987). This innovation was followed by a dramatic increase in textile production during the Classic period as indicated by the intensification of agave and cotton cultivation (Gasser and Miksicek 1985) and the increased frequency of textile manufacturing implements (Wilcox 1987). The clear association of these two sets of evidence with platform mound sites suggests some elite control of textile production. According to Wilcox (1987), elites may have collected textiles as tribute from village households or produced the textiles themselves. I would suggest a more likely alternative—the textiles were manufactured at the platform mounds by attached specialists employed by the elites.

### Tabular Knives

The Hohokam used tabular knives to process agave for textile production (Bernard-Shaw 1984). Possible functions of the knives include harvesting agave plants, scraping pulp from leaves, and extracting fibers (Kisselburg 1987a, 1987b, 1987c). The temporal trends in knife production parallel those exhibited by the other categories of evidence associated with textile manufacture. Knives increase in frequency during the late Sedentary period and reach their peak in the Classic period (Bernard-Shaw 1984).

Two types of evidence suggest that the production of tabular knives was carried out by specialists working at only a few locations (Bernard-Shaw 1984). First, these artifacts are highly standardized both in their raw materials and manufacturing techniques. Second, high frequencies of tabular knives, including caches of unused knives, have been recovered from a few Classic period platform mound sites. This pattern could indicate that knife production took place at these settlements. Alternatively, the pattern could indicate that knives were simply being used at the platform mounds for textile production (Teague 1984).

## Axes

Axes were made throughout the Hohokam sequence with their peak production occurring during the Classic period (Haury 1976:291). From the start, Hohokam axes were well made. However, during the Santa Cruz phase, their form was simplified, a change that coincided with the beginnings of the increase in axe production.

Although the axe was apparently used for the practical purpose of cutting wood (Haury 1976:292), its higher frequency at Classic period platform mound sites also suggests the possibility of a status-related function (Howard 1987; Teague 1984). Evidence for the production of axes at platform mound sites is provided not only by their higher frequency but also by the presence of caches of unused axes (Doyel 1974; Howard 1987).

## STATUS MARKERS

Status markers are objects that convey messages about the social position of their owners. To communicate these messages, artifacts must be highly visible and clearly associated with specific individuals (see Wobst 1977). In addition, since the purpose of markers of high status is to symbolize the greater wealth and power of their owners, these objects are usually valuable either in terms of the raw materials or the labor invested in their manufacture (Earle 1987b). Among the Hohokam, the artifacts that satisfy these criteria are items of jewelry made of shell and stone.

### Shell Jewelry

After red-on-buff pottery, the artifact for which the Hohokam are perhaps best known is shell jewelry. The Hohokam used a variety of shell species obtained primarily from the Gulf of California to make beads, pendants, bracelets, rings, perforated shells, and mosaics. Each period in the Hohokam sequence was marked by an increase in shell working (Gladwin et al. 1937; Haury 1976; Howard 1985; McGuire and Howard 1987). The artistic peak was in the Sedentary period when the greatest variety of techniques and shell species were used to produce the greatest variety of ornament types with the most elaborate decoration. The peak in quantity was in the Classic period.

Shell ornaments began to function as status markers sometime during the Colonial period. At the Colonial period occupation of La Ciudad, shell is uniformly distributed, suggesting that ornaments of this material conveyed no special social meaning (Kisselburg 1985). However, McGuire and Howard (1987; McGuire 1985) cite three sets of evidence from other Colonial and Sedentary period sites that support a different conclusion. First, during these two periods, shell is not evenly distributed among sites. Larger settlements have proportionately greater quantities. Second, most finished Colonial and Sedentary period shell artifacts have been recovered from ritual contexts of cremations and artifact caches. Finally, these artifacts are not evenly distributed among cremations. At Snaketown, only 20–25 percent of the cremations contained shell artifacts. This pattern suggests that some individuals, presumably those with high status, had preferential access to shell.

This role of shell as a status marker seems to have changed in the Classic period when shell artifacts were no longer consistently associated with high-status burials (McGuire and Howard 1987). McGuire and Howard (1987) postulate that only the rare, high value shell artifacts such as mosaics, *Pecten* pendants, etched shell, painted shell, and *Strombus* shell trumpets functioned as status markers at this time and that their exchange linked the local elites of different areas. The more common, lower value shell artifacts such as bracelets, beads, and cut-shell pendants were distributed by elites to their followers, serving as political payments rather than as status markers.

As the function of shell ornaments changed, so did the organization of production and exchange. During the Colonial and Sedentary periods, most shell artifacts were traded into the core area from the western Papagueria (Howard 1985; McGuire and Schiffer 1982). Shell artifact production in the core was extremely rare. The most convincing evidence recovered to date comes from the Colonial period occupation of La Ciudad (Kisselburg 1985) and from Colonial and Sedentary period contexts at Snaketown (Haury 1976). The concentration of this evidence in just two features at La Ciudad (Kisselburg 1985) and six houses at Snaketown (Seymour and Schiffer 1987:587) suggests that shell production in the core may have been a specialized activity. Howard (1985) has hypothesized that the rarer, more elaborate forms were produced at Snaketown, while the more common forms were imported from the Papagueria. McGuire and Howard (1987) have also suggested that the production loci at Snaketown may represent an effort by the high-status residents of this major center to control the production of the ornaments that symbolized their special social position.

During the Classic period, shell artifact production was clearly established within the core area as well as other parts of the Hohokam region (Howard 1985; McGuire and Howard 1987). In the core, evidence of shell production can be found at a number of large platform mound sites, including Los Hornos, La Ciudad, and Mesa Grande. McGuire and Howard (1987; McGuire 1985) suggest that specialized craftsmen may have been working for the high-status individuals who resided at these sites and who controlled the acquisition of shell.

This hypothesized shift to specialized production within the core area coincided with three other changes: (1) the greatest production of shell ornaments in terms of volume, (2) the end of the strong association of these ornaments with high-status burials, and (3) changes in the appearance of these artifacts. They became more standardized, less elaborate, and in the case of the most common ornament, the *Glycymeris* bracelet, less labor intensive. Zoomorphic motifs disappeared and geometric designs, which were probably easier and thus less costly to execute, became dominant.

### Stone Jewelry

The Hohokam also made stone beads and pendants (Gladwin et al. 1937). These ornaments are present throughout the sequence but occur in the greatest numbers and the most forms in the Sedentary period. This period was also marked by an increase in raw material types. Previously, only turquoise had been used. During the Sedentary period, jewelry also began to be manufactured from steatite, schist, and argillite.

Raw material seems to have determined whether or not stone ornaments were status markers. For example, at La Ciudad, schist pendants are evenly distributed, suggesting that these items of jewelry did not have any social function in communicating status (Kisselburg 1985, 1987a). However, turquoise exhibits differential distributions both within and between sites during the Colonial, Sedentary, and Classic periods. At both La Ciudad and Snaketown, finished turquoise artifacts are not evenly distributed (Kisselburg 1985; Nelson 1981; Seymour and Schiffer 1987); and the platform mound site of Mesa Grande contains proportionately more turquoise than other sites in its settlement system (Howard 1987). These patterns suggest that certain members of Hohokam society had preferential access to turquoise ornaments. Evidence for the specialized production of stone jewelry has been recovered from the Colonial period occupation of La Ciudad where schist pendant production seems to have been concentrated in a single courtyard (Kisselburg 1985).[4]

## RITUAL OBJECTS

Hohokam archaeologists have identified a series of objects as having ritual functions based primarily on their recovery from mortuary contexts. These artifacts include figurines, palettes, censers, and projectile points. Specialist production has been suggested for all of these items except figurines.

### Palettes

Hohokam palettes were made from the Pioneer through Sedentary periods. They are considered to have had ritual function due to their recovery from cremation contexts (Haury 1976; Kisselburg 1987a; McGuire 1987). In addition, lead silicate residues have been found on their surfaces (Hawley 1947). This substance liquifies and turns red when heated. Hawley postulates that the melting of lead silicate on palettes was part of Hohokam cremation ritual.

Initially, palettes were simply flat slabs of hard crystalline rock. Borders were not added until late in the Pioneer period. During the early Colonial period, the adoption of the softer raw material of schist was accompanied by an increase in production and changes in form. These changes included the thinning of the palette, the squaring of its corners, a greater distinction between the border and mixing surface, and the decoration of the border. The Santa Cruz phase was the peak of palette production. Palettes occur most frequently at this time, and they exhibit "the greatest range in form, the highest technical skill in manufacture, and extensive use of sculpturing" (Gladwin et al. 1937:123). During the succeeding Sedentary period, the number of palettes declined markedly as did the overall quality of the workmanship. By the Classic period, palettes ceased to be made. Suggestive evidence that palettes were made by specialists has been recovered from the Colonial period occupation of La Ciudad where schist debitage was concentrated within one cluster of households (Kisselburg 1987a).

## Stone Censers

The ritual function of stone censers is suggested by their recovery from cremation contexts (McGuire 1987) and their hypothesized function as incense burners. Hohokam censers are usually found in association with palettes (Haury 1976:288–289) and exhibit similar temporal patterns (Gladwin et al. 1937). They were made from the Pioneer to Sedentary periods. Plain and incised forms were produced throughout the Pioneer period with simple relief carvings of animals beginning to be added as decoration by the Colonial period. Censer production peaked, both in quantity and artistic elaboration, during the Santa Cruz phase. Incised designs virtually disappear at this time with approximately two-thirds of the Santa Cruz vessels being decorated with relief carvings of both realistic and conventionalized animals. The decline in censer production in the Sedentary period was accompanied by the reappearance of incised designs. The few Sedentary vessels with relief carving depict extremely conventionalized life forms.

The only suggestive evidence for the specialized production of censers comes from the artifacts themselves. The relief carvings used to decorate Santa Cruz phase censers would have required such a high degree of artistic skill that their execution by craft specialists seems likely.

## Projectile Points

Hohokam projectile points can be divided into two general types (Crabtree 1973). The first is small, simple points made of a variety of raw materials for utilitarian purposes. The second is more elaborate points made primarily of chert and chalcedony. Their elongated forms with barbed or serrated edges probably precluded practical use. The serrated points first appear in the early Colonial period, increase dramatically in frequency in the Santa Cruz and Sacaton phases, and then virtually disappear in the Classic period.

The ritual function of projectile points in general has been suggested by their recovery from burials. At the Colonial period occupation of La Ciudad, more projectile points were recovered from cemeteries than from habitation areas (Kisselburg 1987a). The strongest association with cemeteries is evidenced by the serrated points that have been recovered almost exclusively from cremations (Haury 1976). The number of these serrated points varies considerably with a few cremations containing hundreds (e.g., Wasley and Johnson 1965).

Evidence for the specialized production of projectile points takes two forms. First, projectile points are differentially distributed both within and between sites. At the Colonial period occupation of La Ciudad, the distribution of points within the habitation area suggests that production was occurring within a single courtyard (Kisselburg 1987a). During the Classic period, projectile points seem to be differentially associated with platform mound sites (Teague 1984). Second, Crabtree (1973) has described the lack of formal variation among serrated points—large numbers are exact duplicates of one another. This fact, together with the results of his reconstruction of the serrated point manufacturing process, led Crabtree to conclude that these points were made by a small number of highly skilled stone-working specialists.

## Figurines

The figurine is the most ubiquitous Hohokam ritual artifact. Most Hohokam figurines are clay representations of humans (Gladwin et al. 1937; Haury 1976). They have been viewed by archaeologists as ritual artifacts for three reasons. First, their presence in Colonial and Sedentary period cremation contexts suggests that they played a role in funerary rites (Wilcox 1987; Wilcox and Sternberg 1983). Second, a large proportion depict females, some of whom are either pregnant or carrying infants (Thomas and King 1985). These female figurines suggest an interest in fertility. The fact that they were made of clays from canals and wells suggests that the figurines may have had a role in efforts to enhance agricultural fertility. Finally, Hohokam figurines exhibit certain similarities with early Mesoamerican figurines whose function has been interpreted as ceremonial (Drennan 1976; Haury 1976).

Hohokam figurines were made throughout the pre-Classic period, although their numbers, appearance, and archaeological contexts changed through time (Gladwin et al. 1937). Approximately 90 percent of the figurines recovered from Snaketown date to the Pioneer period. They were recovered primarily from trash contexts and were crudely made with stylized heads, slit eyes, and little decoration.

As their numbers declined during the Colonial period, their appearance became more elaborate (Gladwin et al. 1937; Haury 1976). They had incised facial features, appliqued clothing, and occasionally painted designs. These artifacts have been recovered almost entirely from cremations. This shift in contexts may signify a change in the ritual role of figurines. In general, the distribution of figurines among cremations is fairly uniform. However, the presence of figurine caches in only some cremations suggests social differentiation (Thomas and King 1985). These caches consist of human figures as well as clay models of houses, ceramic vessels, grinding stones, and other items that were arranged to depict scenes of ceremonial significance.

The decline in frequency continued throughout the Sedentary period; figurines were no longer made by the start of the Classic period (Gladwin et al. 1937; Haury 1976). A major change in appearance occurred in the Sedentary period with many figurines consisting only of realistically modelled heads that were apparently attached to bodies made of perishable material. Also found at this time were figurines depicted in a seated position and decorated with red paint. Virtually all of these Sedentary period figurines have been recovered from cremation contexts.

Figurines represent the only Hohokam ritual artifact whose production has not been attributed to the efforts of specialists. Experiments by Thomas and King (1985) have demonstrated that a single figurine would have taken only 10–15 minutes to produce. The time associated with models of houses and artifacts would have been only a few minutes. Thomas and King calculate that all of the objects found in one of the cremation caches could have been made by one individual in 5–8 hours. Thus, figurine production does not seem to have been a labor intensive activity, and the diversity in the appearance of the figurines made in the Pioneer and Colonial periods suggests that it was not a specialized activity. Only during the Sedentary period, when figurine production was low, does there seem to have been standardization with some of the realistic heads being extremely uniform in style (Gladwin et al. 1937:234).

## OVERALL TRENDS

The development of craft specialization among the Hohokam was marked by several significant changes in the kinds of products made by specialists. Specialists produced ritual objects during the Colonial period, status markers during the Sedentary period, and both status markers and utilitarian goods in the Classic period (Table 5.1).

During the Pioneer period, the dominant ritual artifact was the figurine, for which there is no evidence of specialization (Table 5.1). However, the decline in the frequency of figurines in the Colonial period was matched by increases in the frequencies and elaboration of three other ritual artifacts, palettes, censers, and projectile points. There is evidence that each of these objects was made by specialists. While the production of projectile points continued at a relatively high level during the Sedentary period, palettes and censers exhibit a marked decline in numbers as well as workmanship.

The specialized production of status markers in the core area seems to have followed that of ceremonial items (Table 5.1). During the Colonial period, there is evidence of household specialization in the manufacture of schist

Table 5.1    *Peak Production of Different Types of Artifacts*

| PERIOD | TYPE OF ARTIFACT | | |
| --- | --- | --- | --- |
| | *Ritual* | *Status* | *Utilitarian* |
| *Pioneer* | figurines | | |
| *Colonial*[1] | palettes | | red-on-buff ceramics[5] |
| | censers | | |
| | serrated projectile points[2] | | |
| *Sedentary* | serrated projectile points[2] | shell jewelry[3] | |
| | | stone jewelry | |
| *Classic* | | shell jewelry[4] | textiles |
| | | | tabular knives |
| | | | axes |

1 all peaks in Santa Cruz phase
2 unclear which period had greatest production
3 artistic peak
4 quantity peak
5 artistic peak according to Haury 1976

pendants, but these items do not seem to have marked status. Shell orna-ments, which did serve as status markers, were manufactured outside the core area in the western Papagueria.

It was not until the Sedentary period, when the manufacture of ceremonial items declined, that specialized production of status markers began in the core area (Table 5.1). The shell ornaments of this period exhibit the greatest variety of form and the most elaborate decoration, including zoomorphic designs. While the majority of these items continue to be imported from the western Papagueria, there is evidence of production, possibly specialized, in the core area. For stone ornaments, the greatest numbers and the greatest diversity of forms occurred during the Sedentary period. While it seems likely that these items were also manufactured locally by specialists, no clear evi-dence has yet been found.

The only utilitarian object that may have been produced by specialists prior to the Classic period is red-on-buff pottery. There is no evidence for specialization during the Colonial period, although Haury (1976) has iden-tified the Santa Cruz phase as the time of the greatest artistic achievement in the manufacture of Hohokam decorated ceramics. It has been argued that during the Sedentary period, red-on-buff pottery was mass produced at only a few manufacturing centers (Doyel 1980), which seems to imply some degree of specialization. However, empirical evidence for the presence of specialists has yet to be found.

The Classic period was marked by major changes in Hohokam craft pro-duction (Table 5.1). While ceremonial items of the earlier periods are com-pletely absent, there is evidence for the specialized manufacture of both status markers, such as stone and shell jewelry, and utilitarian goods, such as axes, tabular knives, and textiles. Craft production no longer seems to have been an activity in which individual households specialized at the village level. Rather, it occurred at platform mound sites, presumably under the auspices of high-status individuals. In the case of shell ornaments and textiles, this organizational change was accompanied by increased productivity. Stylistic changes also occurred. The textiles of this period exhibit the greatest variety of weaving techniques, and Classic period shell ornaments were more standardized and less elaborate. The increased production of shell artifacts was apparently facilitated by a decrease in the labor required for each object.

# HOHOKAM LABOR INVESTMENT

The material remains of the Hohokam include three types of structures whose numbers and sizes raise questions about how much labor was involved in their construction. These structures are the irrigation canals that supported the Hohokam agricultural economy and the ballcourts and platform mounds that were the focal points of Hohokam ceremonial life. Estimates of the amount of manpower and the degree of administrative supervision required for the building of each can provide further insights into the dynamics of organizational change in Hohokam society.

## CANAL IRRIGATION

The Hohokam built an extensive network of canals in the core area. Construction began in the Pioneer period and continued throughout the prehistoric sequence with the irrigation systems reaching their maximum extent in the Classic period. The most construction occurred in the Lower Salt River valley where archaeologists have mapped 14 major canal systems with an aggregate length of more than 360 mi (Nicholas 1981; Turney 1929).

The question of how much labor was required to build these canals has been answered in different ways as views about the nature of Hohokam sociopolitical organization have changed. Two early studies by Woodbury (1961) and Haury (1976) produced actual manpower estimates. They concluded that the labor requirements of canal construction were not great and that this construction was handled cooperatively by egalitarian villages. More recently, with the growing body of evidence that the Hohokam were hierarchically organized, Woodbury and Haury's views on the low labor costs of canal construction have been challenged (Neitzel 1987; Nicholas and Feinman 1989; Nicholas and Neitzel 1984). However, the conclusion that canal construction required considerable labor as well as a hierarchical organization has not yet been supported by any labor calculations.

In order to evaluate these opposing positions on the labor requirements of canal construction, I calculated the total volume of soil excavated per year

Table 5.2  *Estimated Volumes of Soil Excavated for Hohokam Canals in the Lower Salt River Valley (cu m/year)*

| PERIOD | Main Canals | Secondary Canals | Lateral Canals | Total |
|---|---|---|---|---|
| Pioneer (A.D. 300–700) | 3,621 | 513 | 48 | 4,182 |
| Colonial (A.D. 700–950) | 9,532 | 2,593 | 271 | 12,396 |
| Sedentary (A.D. 950–1150) | 8,774 | 4,100 | 514 | 13,388 |
| Classic (A.D. 1150–1450) | 4,089 | 3,835 | 388 | 8,312 |

Table 5.3  *Estimated Work Crew Sizes for Construction of All Hohokam Canals in the Lower Salt River Valley (people/day)*

| PERIOD | Work year-round | Work 6 months/year | Work 3 months/year |
|---|---|---|---|
| Pioneer (A.D. 300–700) | 11 | 23 | 46 |
| Colonial (A.D. 700–950) | 34 | 68 | 136 |
| Sedentary (A.D. 950–1150) | 37 | 73 | 147 |
| Classic (A.D. 1150–1450) | 23 | 45 | 91 |

for the canals in the Lower Salt River valley (Table 5.2).[5] Soil volume was assumed to be an approximate measure of labor investment. My results indicated that the amount of labor was not constant in each of the four time periods. Rather, there was an almost threefold increase between the Pioneer and Colonial periods, a small increase in the Sedentary period, and a substantial decrease in the Classic period. In addition, the different kinds of canals exhibited different patterns of change. For example, during the Sedentary period, the volume of earth excavated for new main canals decreased while the volume of excavated soil increased more than one and a half times for secondary canals and almost doubled for lateral canals.

When I converted the soil volume estimates into manpower estimates,[6] the results suggested that if construction was a year-round activity that occurred continuously throughout the prehistoric sequence, then relatively small and presumably cooperative groups could have constructed all of the canals in the Lower Salt River valley (Table 5.3). However, if construction took place during only part of the year (6 months or 3 months), then beginning in the

Table 5.4    *Estimated Work Crew Sizes for Construction of Individual Pioneer Period Canal*
*Systems in the Lower Salt River Valley (people/day)\**

| Duration of<br>Construction | Work<br>year-round | Work<br>6 months/year | Work<br>3 months/year |
|---|---|---|---|
| Lifetime one leader<br>(30 years) | 12–41 | 24–82 | 48–164 |
| Lifetimes three successive<br>leaders (100 years) | 4–12 | 4–24 | 16–48 |
| Entire Pioneer Period<br>(400 years) | 1–3 | 2–6 | 4–12 |

*ranges defined by smallest and largest Pioneer period canal systems

Colonial period and continuing throughout the rest of the sequence, work crew size would have been large enough to require some sort of formalized leadership for coordination and supervision.

These labor estimates would increase even more dramatically if the number of years during which construction occurred was reduced. The assumption that canal building occurred at a constant rate throughout every year of each period may not be a reasonable one. Instead, it may be more likely that major building episodes occurred during the lifetimes of individuals whose leadership qualities enabled them to motivate others to undertake large-scale projects. To illustrate how the amount of time during which construction occurred can affect labor estimates, I performed two sets of calculations, one for all canal systems built in the Pioneer period and the other for a single canal system in all periods.

For the Pioneer period, the interval when canal construction first began and each system was clearly independent of the rest, I calculated the labor force sizes necessary for the construction of each system during successively shorter intervals of time. These intervals were the entire duration of the Pioneer period (400 years), the lifetimes of three successive leaders (100 years), and the lifetime of a single leader (30 years) (Table 5.4). My results indicate that if construction occurred year-round throughout the duration of the Pioneer period, then only a few laborers would have been necessary to excavate each of the Pioneer canal systems. However, many more workers would have been necessary if construction was not a year-round activity or if it occurred during only a limited portion of the Pioneer period. Thus, even in this initial period, which was characterized by the least construction, work crews of 50 individuals or more may have been necessary to excavate a single canal system.

Work crew size would have increased substantially in subsequent periods if construction occurred in major episodes rather than continuously. My labor calculations for Nicholas's (1981) canal system #2 in the southern part of the valley illustrate this point (Fig. 5.2). In contrast to the valleywide pattern, this

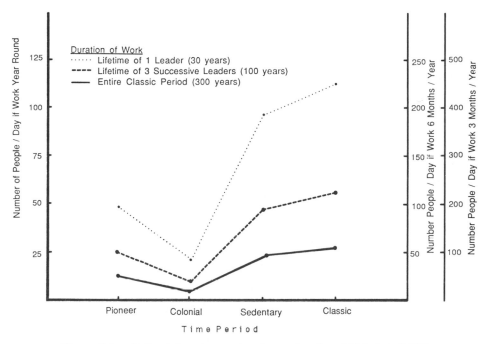

Figure 5.2    *Estimated work crew sizes for construction of Nicholas's (1981)
            canal system #2.*

system, which served the major Classic period settlement of Los Muertos, exhibits major increases in construction during both the Sedentary and Classic periods. During these two periods, work crew size estimates range from a low of 14 people, if construction occurred year-round throughout the entire duration of the Sedentary period, to a high of 450 people if construction occurred 3 months per year for 30 years during the Classic period. The organizational requirements of the latter estimate would have been qualitatively greater than those of the former estimate.

There are several reasons why the figures presented here should be viewed as conservative. First, the maps from which these figures were derived (Nicholas and Feinman 1989) may not show all of the main and secondary canals (Ackerly et al. 1987:115) and probably show only a small fraction of the lateral canals that delivered water to fields (see Herskovitz 1981; Masse 1976, 1981). Second, these figures reflect only initial construction activity and not the ongoing labor investment in canal maintenance. Archaeological investigations have revealed that canals had to be reexcavated periodically to remove accumulated silt (Ackerly et al. 1987; Haury 1976). In addition, entirely new channels may have been constructed in areas where existing canals were made nonfunctional by the shifting channel of the Lower Salt River (Ackerly et al. 1987). Labor would also have been necessary to build and repair intake structures at the river and diversion structures at canal branches (Ackerly et al. 1987; Haury 1976). Finally, if repairs to either canals or ancillary structures became necessary at key points in the agricultural cycle, then they would have had to be done quickly, which would have required a large, easily mobilized labor crew.

## BALLCOURTS

The most frequent form of Hohokam public architecture is the ballcourt, an oval-shaped depression surrounded by an earthen embankment. While archaeologists continue to debate what specific activities occurred within ballcourts, there is a general consensus that these activities had religious significance. Proposed activities have included ritual ballgames similar to those documented for Mesoamerica (Gladwin et al. 1937; Haury 1976; Wilcox and Sternberg 1983) and ceremonial dances (Ferdon 1967). Evidence for the religious function of ballcourts is found in their consistent orientation and placement relative to other ceremonial structures (Wilcox and Sternberg 1983). Wilcox (1987) has argued that the orientation of ballcourts indicates that the timing of their usage depended on astronomical events.

Ballcourt construction involved the building of an earthen embankment around an elliptical-shaped area (Wilcox and Sternberg 1983). This task was generally accomplished by excavating soil within the defined area and then piling it around the perimeter. Sometimes the size of the embankment was increased by adding soil from adjacent borrow pits or more distant locations. At some large courts, such as those at Snaketown and Casa Grande, this building process was done in installments. Completion of the ballcourt involved the smoothing of the interior floor, occasionally the addition of rock facings to the embankment, and the plastering of the embankment.

LeBlanc (1986:119) has stated that ballcourts did not take much labor to build. However, analyses by Wilcox have suggested that this conclusion may not be true for the largest ballcourts (Wilcox and Sternberg 1983). Wilcox's examination of the sizes of ballcourt embankments has indicated that individual construction episodes at the two largest known ballcourts required considerable labor. At Casa Grande, sufficient dirt for any one construction episode could not have been obtained from the immediately adjacent borrow pits. Thus, labor costs would have included not only the excavation of soil but also its transport to the building site. At Snaketown, the first construction episode produced an embankment that was slightly larger than the total volume of the Casa Grande embankment. Thus, the labor requirements of this one building episode were greater than those of any other Hohokam ballcourt.

The labor requirements of ballcourt construction become clearer when size estimates for earthen embankments are translated into manpower estimates.[7] The results of my analyses indicate that ballcourt construction was a much less labor-intensive activity than canal construction. The estimated aggregate

Table 5.5  *Estimated Work Crew Sizes for Construction of Hohokam Ballcourts (people/day)*

| Duration of Construction | Smallest Ballcourt (Snaketown 53 cu m) | Average Ballcourt (337 cu m) | Largest Ballcourt* (Snaketown 4,216 cu m) |
|---|---|---|---|
| 1 week | 8 | 48 | 602 (201/stage) |
| 2 weeks | 4 | 24 | 301 (100/stage) |
| 4 weeks | 2 | 12 | 151 (50/stage) |
| 8 weeks | 1 | 6 | 75 (25/stage) |

*this ballcourt was built in 3 stages ($\bar{x}$ = 1,405 cu m/stage)

volume of all of the ballcourts in the entire core area was 36,958 cu m, which is less than 1 percent of the aggregate volume of all of the canals in the lower Salt River Valley alone.

The aggregate volume of ballcourts would have required only 50 person days of work per year over the 750 years of the Colonial, Sedentary, and Classic periods. However, ballcourt construction was probably episodic rather than continuous with most being excavated within a limited amount of time. Thus, any understanding of the labor requirements of court construction requires a consideration of the amount of time over which construction occurred. Labor requirements increase as the amount of time decreases. For example, the average Hohokam ballcourt had an estimated volume of 337 cu m that could have been excavated by 6 individuals working every day for a period of eight weeks or 48 individuals working for a period of just one week (Table 5.5). In terms of organization, work crews of 6 and 48 individuals have different requirements. The smaller groups were probably able to operate cooperatively and the larger groups required some kind of supervision.

There seems to have been quite a range in the sizes of Hohokam ballcourts and thus in the labor requirements for their construction (Table 5.5). The smallest and largest known courts within the core area were both recorded at the site of Snaketown (Gladwin et al. 1937). The smallest, which dates to the Sedentary period, could have been built in a week by only 8 individuals (Table 5.5). In contrast, the largest court, which dates to the Colonial period and which was built in three stages, would have required 25 individuals working for a period of eight weeks to complete just one phase of construction (Table 5.5). If one building episode was completed in just a week, then the efforts of almost 200 people would have been necessary.

In order to look at change in labor investment through time, I made the assumption that each ballcourt was constructed during the earliest period assigned to it by Wilcox and Sternberg (1983). The temporal breakdown indicates that the peak of construction in the core area was the Colonial period

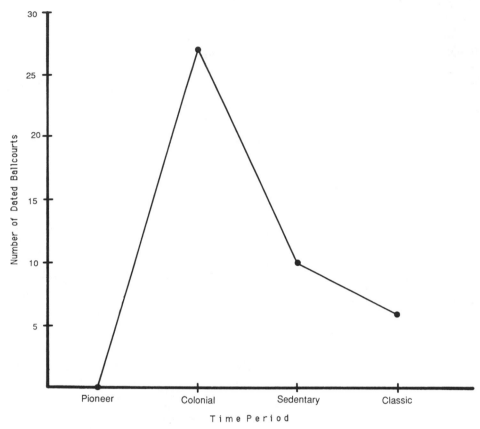

Figure 5.3    *Ballcourt construction through time in the Hohokam core area.*

when over 60 percent of the 43 dated courts were built (Fig. 5.3). The Sedentary and Classic periods each exhibit progressive declines in court building activity. In addition, both the sizes of the largest courts and the ranges of court sizes are considerably smaller in the Sedentary and Classic periods (Fig. 5.4). Thus, the labor requirements of court construction decreased through time as indicated by both the number of courts and the sizes of the largest courts.

It should be noted that these labor reconstructions are based solely on estimates of how much effort would have been required to excavate the volumes of soil that comprise ballcourt embankments. Some researchers may argue that Hohokam workers could have dug more per day than the one cubic meter per person figure used here (see Erasmus 1965). However, the resulting lower labor estimates would have to have other construction costs added to them. Additional effort would have been required to move excavated soil from the ballcourt interior, surrounding borrow pits, and more distant areas to the embankment. More labor would then have been necessary to

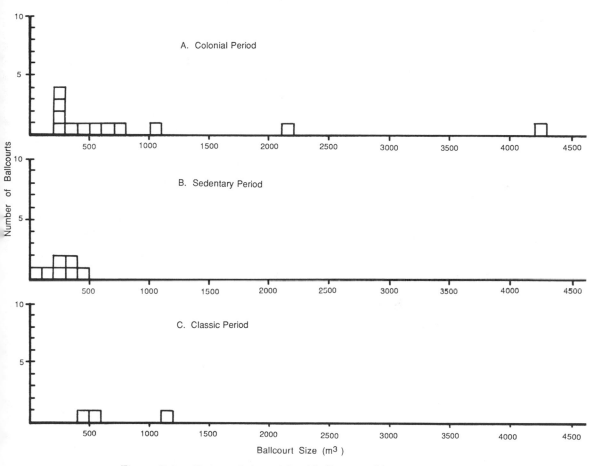

Figure 5.4    *Estimated sizes of dated ballcourts with measurements.*

form the embankment and cover it with plaster. The floor of the ballcourt would also have to be smoothed and occasionally rock facings added to the embankment. Given these additional labor costs, it could be argued that the figures presented here represent minimal estimates of how much labor was required for ballcourt construction.

## PLATFORM MOUNDS

Another type of public architecture built by the Hohokam is the platform mound. Unlike ordinary trash mounds that were formed by the gradual accumulation of garbage, platform mounds represent purposeful construc-tions that were intended to serve specific social functions. These functions are thought to have been ceremonial as indicated by the consistent placement of mounds within sites, their association with ballcourts, and beginning in the late Sedentary period, their restricted access (Gregory 1987; Wilcox et al.

1981). In addition to their ritual functions, Classic period mounds also served as the locations of elite residences (Doyel 1981; Wilcox 1987).

Mound building began during the late Pioneer and Colonial periods with the construction of relatively small mounds. The numbers and sizes of these structures increased in the Sedentary period. However, the Classic period was the time when the overwhelming majority of mounds, including the largest mounds, were built. According to Gregory (1987), most of this Classic period building occurred during the Soho phase dating from A.D. 1150–1300.

Changes in the sizes of mounds were also accompanied by changes in construction techniques (Gregory 1987). The earliest mounds were simply small piles of dirt or rubbish that were covered with a caliche adobe plaster (Haury 1976). These mounds were periodically enlarged; by the late Sedentary period, some were surrounded by wooden pallisades (for example, Mound 16 at Snaketown). A new construction technique adopted in the Soho phase was to build massive, rectangular-shaped caliche adobe walls, fill the interior with trash or soil, plaster the top, and then build one or a few nonresidential pithouses on this surface (Doyel 1974; Hammack and Hammack 1981). Like the earlier mounds, these Soho phase platforms were periodically enlarged. Their final sizes varied considerably, ranging from less than 1,000 cu m to as high as 40,000 cu m (Doyel, personal communication; Minnis 1989; Wilcox and Shenk 1977). The two major modifications that were made during the Civano phase were the construction of: (1) complexes of residential rooms on the tops of the mounds, and (2) compound walls around the bases of the mounds.

Most previous efforts to consider the amount of labor required to build the Hohokam mounds have focused on the sizes of these structures. Some have concluded that substantial manpower was involved (Bartlett et al. 1986; Doyel 1974). However, LeBlanc (1986:119) has stated that the pre-Classic period mounds did not require much labor. With regards to the Classic period mounds, Minnis (1989) has made two observations. First, these mounds were not that large in comparison to mounds found in other areas, such as the southeastern United States. Second, many of the Classic period mounds were built in stages. Thus, Minnis has suggested that the labor requirements for their construction may not have been that great.

While no actual labor estimates have yet been calculated for Hohokam platform mounds, Wilcox has estimated how much manpower was involved in the construction of the Great House at Casa Grande (Wilcox and Shenk 1977). This multistory structure was built in a single episode; its lower level resembles a platform mound. According to Wilcox, a large work force and a sophisticated social organization would not have been necessary to complete the Great House. Based on his calculations, Wilcox concludes that the entire structure could have been built by 15–20 families working full time over a three-month period. However, he raises the question of whether or not these families would have been willing to work continuously for this amount of time. This question is especially pertinent if the individuals who eventually resided in the Great House were elite members of Hohokam society rather than the families who built the structure.

In order to evaluate the alternative views on how much labor was required to build the Hohokam platform mounds, I used the sizes of the mounds to derive minimal manpower estimates. Like the earlier labor calculations for irrigation canals and ballcourts, I assumed that one person could excavate one cubic meter per day. Again, while other investigators may choose to use faster work rates for excavating the soil and trash used to form the mounds (Erasmus 1965), the additional costs of transporting these materials to the construction site and using them to form the structure make this figure appear to be a reasonable one (see Pozorski 1980).

There are several other methodological considerations that complicate efforts to use mound volume as an indicator of labor investment. First, while total mound volume may reflect overall manpower requirements, it is usually not a good measure of how much labor was invested at any one time. Since most mounds were built in stages, labor calculations must be derived from the volume added during each stage. However, the resulting figures may still not provide an accurate representation of manpower costs because later stages in a mound's construction often involved major alterations and sometimes the destruction of earlier stages (e.g., Mound 39 at Snaketown). The labor involved in such renovations would not be reflected in estimates derived from measures of volume alone.

Another methodological consideration is that labor estimates derived from the volume added during different stages of mound building do not include other major construction costs. For pre-Classic period mounds, the primary additional cost was the application of caliche adobe surfaces, with a wooden pallisade occasionally being erected around the mound. For Classic period mounds, the additional labor requirements were much greater: constructing buttressing walls, applying caliche adobe surfaces, building pithouses or complexes of adobe rooms on the tops of the mounds, and erecting an adobe compound wall around the base of the mound. As a result of these additional costs, any labor estimates derived from volume alone, especially those derived for Classic period mounds, should be regarded as gross approximations that define a minimal level of labor expenditure.

### The Snaketown Mounds

Data from Snaketown illustrate the change in labor requirements for mound construction during the pre-Classic period (Figs. 5.5–5.6).[8] This site contains eight mounds that were intentionally built around a central plaza (Wilcox et al. 1981). Mound construction at Snaketown began during the Snaketown phase with two episodes of building at one mound (#40) and one episode at another (#29) (Fig. 5.5). This construction was small in scale with the largest episode requiring approximately 20 workers to complete in one week. Con-

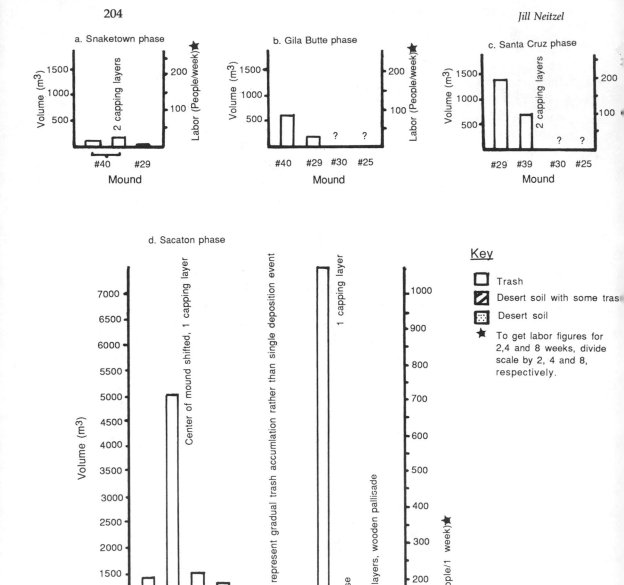

Figure 5.5    *Volume added during each construction stage at mounds surrounding plaza at Snaketown.*

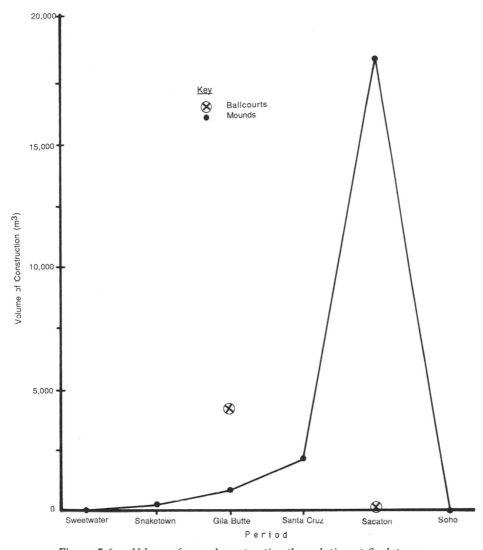

Figure 5.6    *Volume of mound construction through time at Snaketown.*

struction continued at these two mounds in the Gila Butte phase; the volume added to each mound exceeded that of the largest building episode of the previous phase (Fig. 5.5).

During the Santa Cruz phase, construction continued at one of the existing mounds (#29) and was initiated at another (#39) (Fig. 5.5). Again, the volume added at both of these structures was greater than that of the largest building episode of the preceding phase. Completion of the largest addition in one week would have required the labor of approximately 200 individuals.

While mound construction exhibited a steady increase during the Snaketown through Santa Cruz phases, there was a dramatic increase of almost ten times during the Sacaton phase (Fig. 5.6). Construction took place at seven of the eight mounds surrounding the plaza (Fig. 5.5). The volume added to these mounds ranged from a low of 20 cu m for initial construction at Mound 16 to a high of 7,500 cu m at Mound 38. The median addition of 1,300 cu m would have required approximately the same amount of labor (200 people working for one week) as the largest building episode of the preceding phase. The largest construction episode during the Sacaton phase would have required more than 1,000 people working for one week, approximately 500 people working for two weeks, or approximately 250 people for one month. Clearly, the labor requirements during the Sacaton phase were high, especially if several mounds were built simultaneously. Not only was substantial manpower required, but some kind of administrative supervision would have been required to coordinate the efforts of laborers whose numbers ranged in the hundreds.

## CLASSIC PERIOD MOUNDS

Data from three excavated platform mounds can be used to estimate Hohokam labor investment in the Classic period (Figs. 5.7–5.8).[9] These mounds, Escalante Ruin (Doyel 1974, 1981), Mound A at La Ciudad (Wilcox 1987), and Mound 8 at Las Colinas (Bartlett et al. 1986; Hammack 1969; Hammack and Hammack 1981), were each built in the Soho phase. Complexes of habitation rooms were added to their tops and compound walls around their bottoms in the Civano phase. In terms of their overall size, they range from 1,200–2,300 cu m. However, none was the product of a single construction episode. At Escalante Ruin, a very small mound was built prior to the formation of the final mound; at Mound A of La Ciudad, there were at least three phases of construction. Mound 8 at Las Colinas was built in two major episodes, each of which occurred in 2–3 stages.

The volume that was added in each of the construction episodes at these mounds varied considerably (Fig. 5.7). The median addition was approximately 350 cu m, which could have been built by 50 people working for one week, 25 people working for two weeks, or 13 people working for a month. The largest construction episode occurred at Escalante Ruin where 2,200 cu m were added at one time. Completion of this work would have required the labor of 312 people in one week, 156 people in two weeks, 78 people in one month, and 39 people in two months. Again, the larger work crew size necessary for completion in shorter intervals would have required greater administrative supervision.

These Classic period construction episodes were not dramatically larger than those that occurred at any one time at the pre-Classic mounds at Snaketown. In fact, the median Classic period addition of 350 cu m is almost one-fourth the size of the median Sacaton phase addition of 1,300 cu m at Snaketown. However, these volume comparisons alone do not provide a reliable

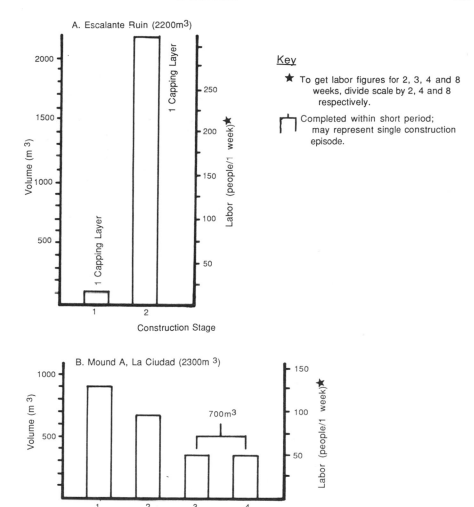

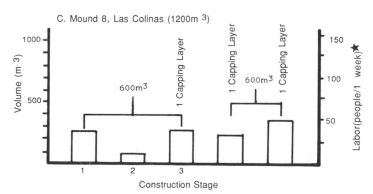

Figure 5.7    *Volume added during each construction stage at three Classic period platform mounds.*

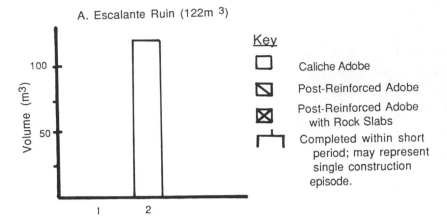

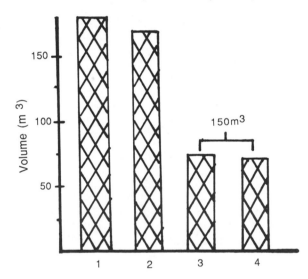

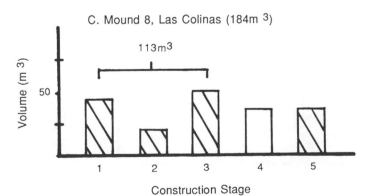

Figure 5.8    *Wall volume added at each construction stage at three Classic period platform mounds.*

basis for examining changes in the amount of labor invested by the Hohokam in mound construction. During the Classic period, mound construction involved not only the addition of volume to the structure and the application of a caliche adobe cap (as in the pre-Classic period), but also the building of massive buttressing walls around the perimeter of the structure and usually in its interior as well.

The labor costs of this wall construction would have been substantial. They would have included the excavation of soil, the transport of soil and water to the site, the mixing of these materials to form adobe, and finally the formation of the wall. In those cases where walls were reinforced with posts (e.g., Mound 8, Las Colinas), trees would have to be cut, transported to the site, and placed in holes dug in the ground. At Mound A of La Ciudad, rocks were also transported to the site and added to the body and surface of the buttressing walls. Thus, when the costs of building buttressing walls are considered, the labor invested in mound construction seems to have increased significantly between the Sedentary and Classic periods.

This conclusion is reinforced by two other observations. First, some Classic period platform mound sites had more than one mound. For example, at La Ciudad, there was a second mound that has been destroyed and whose size is unknown. At Las Colinas, there were at least three other mounds in addition to Mound 8, which was the smallest of the group. The total volume of these recorded mounds at Las Colinas was almost 20,000 cu m (Minnis 1989). Thus, the labor estimates calculated for Mound 8 at Las Colinas represent less than 10 percent of the total amount of effort that was invested in mound construction at this one site during the 150 years of the Soho phase.

The second observation reinforcing the conclusion that the Hohokam increased their labor investment in mound construction during the Classic period is that the three structures considered here are all at the low end of the range of sizes that has been recorded for Classic period platform mounds. The smallest recorded mound in the core area is the 800 cu m mound in Compound B of Casa Grande (Wilcox and Shenk 1977). At the other extreme, the largest recorded mounds at Pueblo Grande and Mesa Grande have estimated sizes of 35,000–40,000 cu m (Doyel, personal communication). These latter volumes are approximately 20 times greater than those of Escalante Ruin, Mound A at La Ciudad, and Mound 8 at Las Colinas.

Although both Pueblo Grande and Mesa Grande were probably built in stages (Hayden 1957; Placona 1979; Stewart 1967), the labor invested in their individual construction episodes must have been substantial (Tables 5.6–5.7). If mound expansion occurred in relatively small increments, then this construction would have occurred frequently in order to complete the mounds within the 150 years of the Soho phase. For example, if additions occurred in 500 cu m increments, then 80 such additions, which is equivalent to one construction episode every two years, would have been necessary to complete the mound. Work crew size would have ranged from approximately 70 in-

Table 5.6    *Timing of Hypothetical Construction Stages at 40,000 cu m Soho Phase Platform*
             *Mound*

| Size of addition (cu m) | Number of additions to complete in 150 years | Interval between additions (years) |
|---|---|---|
| 500 | 80 | 2 |
| 1,000 | 40 | 4 |
| 2,500 | 16 | 9 |
| 5,000 | 8 | 19 |
| 10,000 | 4 | 38 |

Table 5.7    *Estimated Work Crew Sizes for Hypothetical Construction Stages at 40,000 cu m*
             *Soho Phase Platform Mound*

| Duration of Construction | Size of Addition | | | | |
|---|---|---|---|---|---|
|  | 500 cu m | 1,000 cu m | 2,500 cu m | 5,000 cu m | 10,000 cu m |
| 1 week | 71 | 143 | 357 | 714 | 1429 |
| 2 weeks | 36 | 71 | 179 | 357 | 714 |
| 1 month | 18 | 36 | 89 | 179 | 357 |
| 2 months | 9 | 18 | 45 | 89 | 179 |
| 4 months | 5 | 9 | 22 | 45 | 89 |
| 6 months | 3 | 6 | 14 | 27 | 55 |
| 1 year | 1 | 3 | 7 | 14 | 27 |

dividuals, if all construction for one episode was done in a week, to approximately 10 individuals if the work was spread out over a two-month period.

Larger additions to the mounds would have required fewer construction episodes with more time between them (Table 5.6). However, they would have also required larger labor crews whose sizes would have depended on the amount of time within which construction was completed (Table 5.7). For example, if construction at Pueblo Grande and Mesa Grande occurred in 5,000 cu m increments, then only eight building episodes, or one episode every 20 years, would have been necessary. However, the number of workers that would have been necessary to complete the work would have been approximately 700 if the work for each episode was done in a week, almost 200 if work was done in a month, and almost 30 if work was spread out over six months.

These figures indicate that a relatively small labor force could have built Pueblo Grande and Mesa Grande if these mounds were built in small increments or if the duration of each construction episode was as long as six months or a year. However, larger additions or shorter building periods would have required more workers, perhaps numbering in the hundreds. Work crews of this size would have required some degree of administrative supervision. It

Table 5.8    *Total Volume of Hohokam Construction (cu m)*

| PERIOD | Irrigation Canals (Salt River Valley only) | Ballcourts* (entire core) | Platform Mounds** (entire core) |
|---|---|---|---|
| Pioneer (A.D. 300–700) | 1,672,660 | 0 | virtually none |
| Colonial (A.D. 700–950) | 3,099,010 | 16,091 | some, small |
| Sedentary (A.D. 950–1150) | 2,677,480 | 3,203 | more, larger |
| Classic (A.D. 1150–1450) | 2,493,450 | 2,861 | 148,000 |
| Total | 9,942,600 | 22,155+ | 148,000+ |

*These figures include only those ballcourts with dates in Wilcox and Sternberg's (1983) compilation. The aggregate size of the undated courts is approximately 14,803 cu m.

**These figures represent extremely gross estimates; the size of the average platform mound was assumed to be 2000 cu m. A total of 41 Classic period platform mounds have been recorded for the core, two of which are known to have been 35,000–40,000 cu m in size. So, total volume was obtained by multiplying 2,000 by 39 and then adding 70,000 (for the two large mounds) to the total.

should be emphasized that these figures presented for Pueblo Grande and Mesa Grande reflect only the effort required to form the volume of these mounds. Substantially more labor would have been necessary to build the buttressing walls.

## OVERALL TRENDS

Estimates of the amount of labor required to build prehistoric structures must be interpreted with caution. Such estimates are usually derived from data that are never as complete as the archaeologist would like; they require assumptions about the rates at which prehistoric workers performed various construction tasks and the spans of time during which these tasks were completed. Nevertheless, the labor estimates derived here reveal some significant trends for the study of Hohokam organizational change.

First, canal excavation was the most labor-intensive Hohokam construction activity throughout the prehistoric sequence (Tables 5.8–5.9). The manpower devoted to canal building was several thousand times greater than that invested in ballcourts and platform mounds. Each period in the sequence was marked by the progressive expansion of the canal systems with the maximum extent reached in the Classic period. However, this expansion did not occur at a constant rate. The greatest increase in construction activity occurred between the Pioneer and Colonial periods; the time of the most building was during the Sedentary period.

The two types of ceremonial structures exhibit completely opposite temporal patterns. Most ballcourt construction occurred in the Colonial period,

Table 5.9    *Estimated Labor Investment in Hohokam Construction (people days/year)*

| PERIOD | Irrigation Canals (Salt River Valley only) | Ballcourts* (entire core) | Platform Mounds (entire core) |
|---|---|---|---|
| Pioneer (400 years) | 4,182 | 0 | virtually none |
| Colonial (250 years) | 12,396 | 64 | a little |
| Sedentary (200 years) | 13,387 | 16 | more |
| Classic (300 years) | 8,312 | 10 | 493 |
| Total | 21,699 | 90 + | 493 + |

the time when the most dramatic increase in canal building was also taking place. In each of the succeeding periods, ballcourt construction declined. In contrast, only a few, small mounds were built in the Colonial period. More construction took place during the Sedentary period, and substantially more in the Classic period.

The overall size ranges of ballcourts and platform mounds overlap. Substantially less soil was used to form the average ballcourt (337 cu m) than any of the completed mounds considered here. However, the largest known ballcourt at Snaketown was almost six times larger than the aggregate volume of all of the mounds surrounding the site's plaza at any one time. After just one of its three construction stages, this ballcourt had a greater volume than Mound 8 at Las Colinas. At full size, its volume was greater than that of Mound A at La Ciudad and of Escalante Ruin.

These volume estimates indicate that some ballcourts, specifically the large ones built during the Colonial period, required more labor than contemporaneous as well as perhaps some later mounds. However, direct comparisons of labor investment cannot be made based on volume alone because the later mounds had the additional costs of constructing buttressing walls. Thus, while the Snaketown ballcourt may have been larger in volume than Mound 8 at Las Colinas, Mound A at La Ciudad, and Escalante Ruin, the manpower required to build at least the latter two of these mounds may have been greater due to their walls.

Evaluating the relative labor costs of building the large ballcourt at Snaketown and the three Classic period platform mounds considered here is difficult. However, it is clear that through time, the manpower invested in mound construction exceeded that invested in ballcourt construction. As the numbers of new ballcourts declined in the Sedentary and Classic periods, so did their sizes. In contrast, as the numbers of platform mounds increased in the Classic period, so did their size. This trend in mound construction culminated with Pueblo Grande and Mesa Grande, which were ten times larger than the largest known ballcourt at Snaketown. Even when the additional manpower required for wall construction is not considered, the labor and administrative costs of building these two mounds were clearly qualitatively greater than those of the largest ballcourts.

The most important variable for which data are lacking in all of these labor estimates is the span of construction time. As noted previously, the shorter the work time, the larger the work force necessary to complete construction. However, considering the sizes of these various projects and the fact that they often occurred simultaneously, the labor resources and administrative capabilities of the Hohokam seem to have been quite impressive.

## CEREMONIAL ELABORATION

The changing organization of ritual activity has only recently begun to be recognized as a significant component in the process of Hohokam sociopolitical development. While archaeologists will never be able to reconstruct the content of this activity, they can monitor its material manifestations. The major material correlates have already been mentioned in the earlier discussions of craft specialization and labor investment. Ritual artifacts include palettes, censers, projectile points, and figurines. Ritual architecture includes ballcourts and platform mounds.

The primary evidence for ritual activity during the Pioneer period consists of crudely made, stylized figurines that have been recovered from trash deposits. Other ritual artifacts include simple palettes and censers. Ceremonial architecture is lacking except for two very small mounds at Snaketown. These mounds date to the end of the period and would have required minimal effort to build.

Two major changes in Hohokam ceremonial life occurred during the Colonial period. The first was a new emphasis on mortuary practices that involved cremating the dead and placing ritual artifacts in cremation contexts. The second change was the appearance of community or even intercommunity ceremonies at ballcourts. While the timing of mortuary rituals would have been unpredictable, being determined by the deaths of particular individuals, the ceremonies that took place at ballcourts seem to have been calendrically scheduled events (Wilcox 1987; Wilcox et al. 1981).

During the Sedentary period, Hohokam ceremonial life became more formalized and community oriented. The previous emphasis on cremation rituals and the numbers and workmanship of the artifacts that had played an integral part in these rituals declined. In contrast, ceremonies associated with ballcourts continued, and ceremonies at platform mounds increased in importance. The focus of ceremonial activities at these public structures suggests an increasing emphasis on calendrically scheduled events that involved community as well as intercommunity participants (Wilcox 1987; Wilcox et al. 1981).

During the Classic period, the changes in Hohokam ceremonial life begun in the preceding period continued, culminating in the clear association of high-status individuals with platform mounds. The virtual absence of ritual artifacts and the enormous investment in mound construction evidence the replacement of individual-oriented cremation ritual by formalized and calendrically scheduled community and intercommunity ceremonies. These ceremonies took place at complexes of structures consisting of both ballcourts, most of which had been built previously, and newly constructed platform mounds (Gregory 1987). As in the preceding period, this Classic period mound construction occurred in multiple stages that may have been part of the rituals conducted at these structures. However, the scale of building as indicated by the numbers of mounds, their sizes, and their construction techniques was greater than previously.

Access to the ceremonial activities that took place on the Classic period mounds seems to have become increasingly restricted. In the Soho phase, the erection of nonresidential pithouses on the tops of mounds would have impeded ground-level visibility of any activities taking place there. In the Civano phase, access was restricted even further by the replacement of the pithouses by complexes of rooms on the tops of the mounds and the construction of compound walls along with other ground-level rooms around the bases of the mounds.

## CONCLUSION

This paper has attempted to show how material culture studies can contribute to our understanding of organizational change among the Hohokam. Three dimensions of change were considered: (1) craft specialization, (2) labor investment, and (3) elaboration of ritual. The results are summarized below.

Several important shifts were documented in the production of Hohokam craft goods. Specialization began during the Colonial period, with some types of goods, such as palettes, shell jewelry, and ceramics, becoming increasingly elaborated in the Colonial and Sedentary periods. This elaboration may be a manifestation of the competitive variety that Rice (1981) has associated with the development of sociopolitical differentiation in ranked societies. In addition, the shift in emphasis from the specialized production of ceremonial items (palettes and censers) to status markers (shell jewelry and perhaps decorated ceramics) may signify changes in the underlying basis of sociopolitical differences.

Rice (1981) has predicted that when ranked societies develop to the extent that they become truly stratified, then changes can be expected in specialized craft production. Highly valued craft goods may still be elaborately decorated, but goods that have lower value or are mass produced will be standardized. This prediction seems to hold for the Classic period Hohokam whose specialized craft production was concentrated at platform mound sites and was presumably done under the auspices of the elite residents of these settlements. The specialized products included the highly standardized utilitarian items of axes and tabular knives as well as the standardized and mass produced status-related good of shell jewelry. The changes in the production of shell ornaments between the Sedentary and Classic periods may indicate that these objects had been devalued in some way, perhaps being used by elites to distribute to their followers rather than to mark their own status (see Davis 1985; Frankenstein and Rowlands 1978).

The consideration of the Hohokam investment in public construction demonstrated that canal excavation required the most manpower. The progressive growth of the irrigation system through time is a measure of both the process of agricultural intensification as well as changes in the organization of Hohokam society. For example, greater investments in canal construction are possible only if the necessary manpower can be mobilized. Individuals have to be diverted from their own subsistence activities and must be fed during this time, thus requiring an agricultural surplus. In addition, once the work force surpasses a certain size, administrators are needed to plan, coordinate, and supervise construction activities. The labor estimates derived here indicate that this organizational change probably began during the Colonial period and continued throughout the rest of the prehistoric sequence.

Even though less labor was invested in the building of ballcourts and platform mounds, this labor is significant for the same reasons as that invested in canal construction. First, it evidences the availability of a surplus to support workers not involved in subsistence activities. Second, the amount of labor that would have been required to build the largest of the ceremonial structures suggests the presence of some type of administrative apparatus to plan, coordinate, and supervise construction activities. One important difference between canals and the ceremonial structures is that while the latter may have had some indirect consequences in terms of subsistence productivity or security, they were not in and of themselves capital investments that directly resulted in greater agricultural yields.

The construction of ballcourts and platform mounds is also important because it evidences the process of ceremonial elaboration among the Hohokam. This process began during the Colonial period when the first ballcourts were built. The occurrence of ceremonies at these specially designated locations may reflect the initial separation of ritual from everyday activities. Various researchers have suggested that these ceremonies had integrative functions (Wilcox 1987; Wilcox and Sternberg 1983). I would also argue that while the expansion of canal irrigation during the Colonial period would have allowed emerging leaders to increase their economic resources, involvement in ceremonial activities would have legitimized their positions of authority. Participation in ballcourt ceremonies as well as in the cremation rituals in which the products of craft specialists were used (e.g., palettes, censers, projectile points) would have enabled aspiring leaders to demonstrate their ties with the supernatural and thus to justify and even enhance their own status.

The construction of both ballcourts and platform mounds during the Sedentary period evidences further ceremonial elaboration among the Hohokam. The consistent placement of these two types of structures in relation to one another (Wilcox et al. 1981) suggests that their respective ceremonies may have been interrelated. However, during the Sedentary period the importance of mounds seems to have surpassed that of ballcourts. While existing ballcourts continued to be used, the number and sizes of new ballcourts declined. In contrast, there was a marked increase in mound building, measured by both the numbers and sizes of mounds.

Other changes in ceremonial life are evidenced by the decreasing importance of cremation ritual and the shift in the kinds of goods being produced by craft specialists from ritual artifacts to markers of high status. In addition, participation in ceremonies became more restricted through time. Not only could relatively small numbers of individuals fit on the tops of the increasingly important mounds, but some of these mounds had pallisades built around their bottoms.

These changes in ceremonial life during the Sedentary period were probably related to the expanding scale of Hohokam society as well as the processes of agricultural intensification and sociopolitical differentiation. The increasing population, incorporation of more communities into individual settlement systems, and growing economic dependence on irrigation agriculture would have required more formalized societal integration. Such integration could have been accomplished through the emergence of a leadership hierarchy and the development of a ceremonial cycle that brought communities together and reinforced the authority of leaders.

One final shift in the process of ceremonial elaboration occurred during the Classic period—elite residences began to be built on the tops of platform mounds. Apparently, as elites increased their social distance from other members of Hohokam society (Doyel 1980; Gregory and Nials 1985; Matthews et al. 1893; Upham and Rice 1980; Wilcox 1979), they became more closely associated with symbols of the supernatural world. By residing on the tops of platform mounds that had a ceremonial function and that were larger, more costly to build, and less accessible than earlier mounds, high-status leaders could not only demonstrate in a very visible way the extent of their power, but could also make that power appear supernaturally sanctioned.

The ceremonial elaboration that occurred throughout the Hohokam sequence, culminating in the developments of the Classic period, should not be viewed as a simple by-product of other demographic, economic, and organizational changes. Instead, changes in ritual may have played an integral role in the overall process of Hohokam cultural evolution. The manipulation of both the political economy and religious ceremonies may have been successful strategies for aspiring leaders attempting to increase and consolidate their power. By promoting the expansion of canal irrigation and subsidizing craft specialists, these leaders could increase the wealth that provided the economic basis of their political power. This power could in turn be legitimized and even enhanced by using participation in ceremonies to demonstrate close ties with the supernatural world. The long-term result of all of these activities was the increasing complexity of Hohokam society.

# NOTES

1. Evidence for the production of ground stone artifacts is not discussed here for two reasons (see Hoffman et al. 1985). First, ground stone manufacturing sites have not been located inside the core area. Second, it is not clear whether specialists worked at the sites that have been located in the northern periphery or whether these sites simply represent specialized activity areas that were utilized by entire communities.

2. For a discussion of the evidence for ceramic production outside the core area, see Huntington 1986; Kisselburg 1987d; Wallace and Heidke 1986.

3. For a discussion of the evidence for textile production outside the core area, see Fish et al. 1985 and Kisselburg 1987d.

4. For a discussion of the evidence for stone jewelry production at a Classic period platform mound site located outside the core area, see Kisselburg 1987d.

5. The canal calculations were done using maps produced for the Pioneer, Colonial, Sedentary, and Classic periods by Nicholas (see Nicholas and Feinman 1989). The aggregate lengths of the main, distribution, and lateral canals were measured for each period. Then, the amount of new construction for each type of canal was calculated for each period by subtracting the aggregate length of the preceding period from that of the period of interest. To obtain the total volume of dirt excavated for each type of canal, the mean width and depth of main, distribution, and lateral canals were calculated using the size ranges defined by Nicholas (1981). In the volume calculations, it was assumed that the shapes of the canals were halfway between rectangular and triangular. The formula used for the volume calculations was:

VOLUME = .75 (aggregate length new main canals) (mean main canal width = 8.1 m) (mean canal depth = 2.9 m) +
.75 (aggregate length new distribution canals) (mean distribution canal width = 3.4 m) (mean distribution canal depth = 1.6 m) +
.75 (aggregate length new lateral canals) (mean lateral canal width = 1.2 m) (mean lateral canal depth = .8 m)

6. To convert the soil volume estimates into manpower estimates, the assumption was made that a single worker could excavate one cubic meter of soil per day (see Pozorski 1980; Woodbury 1961). Then, for each period, the total volume estimates were divided by the number of years in that period to determine how much soil would have been excavated per year if canal construction was continuous. The resulting

figures were then divided by 365 to see how large a work crew would have been necessary to complete this construction activity if the crew worked every day of the year. Similar calculations were done for work periods of six months and three months per year.

7. The ballcourt calculations were done using length, width, and depth measurements recorded by Wilcox and Sternberg (1983). The earthen berm around each ballcourt was assumed to be a symmetrical trapezoid. The formula used to calculate the volume of the berm was:

$V = pi(h)/4(WL - wl)$ where
  $V$ = volume
  $h$ = depth
  $W$ = exterior width (assumed to be measured from outer edges of two crests)
  $L$ = exterior length (assumed to be measured from outer edges of two crests)
  $w$ = interior width (assumed to be measured at base)
  $l$ = interior length (assumed to be measured at base)

For those courts with incomplete measurements, the missing data were estimated using the average ratio of interior and exterior dimensions. The mean interior to exterior width ratio for all recorded courts was .63. The mean interior to exterior length ratio for all recorded courts was .78. For those courts without a depth measurement, the average depth for all recorded courts (1.25 m) was used. The calculations for the average court volume were done using the mean values of each dimension for which Wilcox had recorded data (mean exterior length = 36.7 m; mean exterior width = 21.4 m; mean interior length = 32.3 m; mean interior width = 13.7 m). For the calculation of the aggregate volume of all recorded courts in the core area, the average court volume of 337 cu m was applied to the courts that had no measurement data.

To convert the soil volume estimates into manpower estimates, I assumed that a single worker could excavate one cubic meter per day (see Pozorski 1980; Woodbury 1961). Then, I calculated the sizes of the work crews that would have been necessary to complete each court within varying amounts of time.

8. The measurements for the pre-Classic period mounds at Snaketown were taken from maps, stratigraphic profiles, and descriptions published by Haury (1976; Gladwin et al. 1937). The shapes of the mounds were assumed to be ovoid. The formula used to approximate their volumes during each stage of construction was:

$V = pi(h)/8(LW + lw)$ where
  $V$ = volume
  $h$ = height
  $L$ = length of base
  $W$ = width of base
  $l$ = length of top
  $w$ = width of top

9. The measurements for the Classic period mounds of Escalante Ruin, Mound 8 at Las Colinas, and Mound A at La Ciudad were taken from maps, stratigraphic profiles, and descriptions published by Doyel (1974, 1981), Hammack and Hammack (1981), and Wilcox (1987). The shapes of the mounds were assumed to be trapezoidal. The formula used to approximate their volumes during each stage of construction was:

$V = h/2(LW + lw)$ where
  $V$ = volume
  $h$ = height

L = length of base
W = width of base
l = length of top
w = width of top

The formula used to approximate the wall volume added during each construction stage was:

V = hLW where
V = volume
h = height
L = aggregate length
W = width

# ACKNOWLEDGMENTS

This paper would never have been written without the encouragement of several individuals whom I would like to thank here. The original stimulus for this research came from George Gumerman who invited me to participate in the Hohokam seminar and who assigned me the task of writing an overview on Hohokam material culture and technology. Gary Feinman helped me to understand the potential of this topic for contributing something new to our understanding of the Hohokam. Perry Susskind of Connecticut College's Department of Mathematics guided me in applying the proper formulas in my various calculations. Both Randy McGuire and Willett Kempton gave me extensive editorial suggestions that improved the content, organization, and presentation of the paper. Adele Hagar drafted the figures, and Anita Allen typed the tables. Finally, I would like to acknowledge the contribution of my son Rueben Kempton. His imminent birth gave the seminar an added dimension of excitement and his subsequent arrival made the completion of this paper a longer process than I ever anticipated.

# REFERENCES CITED

Abbott, D. R.
   1984   A Technological Assessment of Ceramic Variation in the Salt-Gila Aqueduct
          Area: Toward a Comprehensive Documentation of Hohokam Ceramics. In
          *Hohokam Archaeology along the Salt-Gila Aqueduct, Central Arizona Project*, vol.
          8, Material Culture, edited by L. S. Teague and P. L. Crown, pp. 3–117.
          Arizona State Museum Archaeological Series 150.
   1985   Spheres of Intra-Cultural Exchange and the Ceramics of the Salt-Gila Aque-

duct Project. In *Proceedings of the 1983 Hohokam Symposium*, Part II, edited by A. E. Dittert and D. E. Dove, pp. 419–438. Arizona Archaeological Society Occasional Paper 2.

Ackerly, N. W., J. B. Howard, and R. H. McGuire
  1987  *La Ciudad Canals: A Study of Hohokam Irrigation Systems at the Community Level.* Arizona State University Anthropological Field Studies 17.

Adams, R. McC.
  1974  Historic Patterns of Mesopotamian Agriculture. In *Irrigation's Impact on Society*, edited by T. Downing and M. Gibson, pp. 1–6. Anthropological Papers of the University of Arizona 25.

Ashbee, P., and I. W. Cornwall
  1961  An Experiment in Field Archaeology. *Antiquity* 35(138):129–134.

Atkinson, R. J. C.
  1961  Neolithic Engineering. *Antiquity* 35(140):292–299

Bartlett, M. H., T. M. Kolaz, and D. A. Gregory
  1986  *Archaeology in the City: A Hohokam Village in Phoenix, Arizona.* University of Arizona Press, Tucson.

Becker, M.
  1973  Archaeological Evidence for Occupational Specialization among the Classic Period Maya at Tikal, Guatemala. *American Antiquity* 38(4):396–406.

Bernard-Shaw, M.
  1984  The Stone Tool Assemblage of the Salt-Gila Aqueduct Project Sites. In *Hohokam Archaeology along the Salt-Gila Aqueduct, Central Arizona Project*, vol. 8, Material Culture, edited by L. S. Teague and P. L. Crown, pp. 373–443. Arizona State Museum Archaeological Series 150.

Blanton, R., S. Kowalewski, G. Feinman, and J. Appel
  1981  *Ancient Mesoamerica: A Comparison of Change in Three Regions.* Cambridge University Press, Cambridge.

Bloch, M.
  1986  *From Blessing to Violence: History and Ideology in the Circumcision Ritual of the Merina of Madagascar.* Cambridge University Press, Cambridge.

Bradley, R.
  1984  *The Social Foundations of Prehistoric Britain: Themes and Variations in the Archaeology of Power.* Longman, London.

Brumfiel, E.
  1987  Elite and Utilitarian Crafts in the Aztec State. In *Specialization, Exchange, and Complex Societies*, edited by E. M. Brumfiel and T. K. Earle, pp. 102–118. Cambridge University Press, Cambridge.

Brumfiel, E. M., and T. K. Earle
  1987  Specialization, Exchange, and Complex Societies: An Introduction. In *Specialization, Exchange, and Complex Societies*, edited by E. M. Brumfiel and T. K. Earle, pp. 1–9. Cambridge University Press, Cambridge.

Chang, K. C.
  1968  *The Archaeology of China.* Yale University Press, New Haven.

Cohen, A.
  1969  Political Anthropology: The Analysis of the Symbolism of Power Relationships. *Man* 4(2):215–235.

Crabtree, D. E.
  1973  Experiments in Replicating Hohokam Points. *Tebiwa* 16(1):10–45.

Crown, P. L.

1984a An X-ray Florescence Analysis of Hohokam Ceramics. In *Hohokam Archaeology along the Salt-Gila Aqueduct, Central Arizona Project*, vol. 8, Material Culture, edited by L. S. Teague and P. L. Crown, pp. 277–310. Arizona State Museum Archaeological Series 150.

1984b Design Variability in Salt-Gila Aqueduct Red-on-Buff Ceramics. In *Hohokam Archaeology along the Salt-Gila Aqueduct, Central Arizona Project*, vol. 8, Material Culture, edited by L. S. Teague and P. L. Crown, pp. 205–248. Arizona State Museum Archaeological Series 150.

Davis, D. D.

1985 Hereditary Emblems: Material Culture in the Context of Social Change. *Journal of Anthropological Archaeology* 4(3):149–176.

Dow, M. M.

1985 Agricultural Intensification and Craft Specialization: A Nonrecursive Model. *Ethnology* 24(2):137–152.

Doyel, D. E.

1974 *Excavations in the Escalante Ruin Group, Southern Arizona*. Arizona State Museum Archaeological Series 37.

1979 The Prehistoric Hohokam of the Arizona Desert. *American Scientist* 67:544–554.

1980 Hohokam Social Organization and the Sedentary to Classic Transition. In *Current Issues in Hohokam Prehistory*, edited by D. E. Doyel and F. Plog, pp. 23–40. Arizona State University Anthropological Research Papers 23.

1981 *Late Hohokam Prehistory in Southern Arizona*. Gila Press, Scottsdale.

1985 Current Directions in Hohokam Research. In *Proceedings of the 1983 Hohokam Symposium*, Part I, edited by A. E. Dittert and D. E. Dove, pp. 3–26. Arizona Archaeological Society Occasional Paper 2.

Drennan, R. D.

1976 Religion and Social Evolution in Formative Mesoamerica. In *The Early Mesoamerican Village*, edited by K. V. Flannery, pp. 345–368. Academic Press, New York.

1983a Ritual and Ceremonial Development in the Early Village Level. In *The Cloud People: Divergent Evolution of the Zapotec and Mixtec Civilizations*, editd by K. V. Flannery and J. Marcus, pp. 30–32. Academic Press, New York.

1983b Ritual and Ceremonial Development at the Early Village Level. In *The Cloud People: Divergent Evolution of the Zapotec and Mixtec Civilizations*, edited by K. V. Flannery and J. Marcus, pp. 46–50. Academic Press, New York.

Earle, T. K.

1978 *Economic and Social Organization of a Complex Chiefdom: The Halelea District, Kaua'i, Hawaii*. University of Michigan, Museum of Anthropology Anthropological Papers 63.

1987a Chiefdoms in Archaeological and Ethnohistorical Perspective. *Annual Review of Anthropology* 16:279–308.

1987b Specialization and the Production of Wealth: Hawaiian Chiefdoms and the Inka Empire. In *Specialization, Exchange, and Complex Societies*, edited by E. M. Brumfiel and T. K. Earle, pp. 64–75. Cambridge University Press, Cambridge.

Ember, M.

1963 The Relationship between Economic and Political Development in Non-Industrial Societies. *Ethnology* 2(2):228–248.

Erasmus, C. J.
  1965  Monument Building: Some Field Experiments. *Southwestern Journal of Anthropology* 21(4):277–301.
Evans, R. K.
  1978  Early Craft Specialization: An Example from the Balkan Chalcolithic. In *Social Archaeology: Beyond Subsistence and Dating*, edited by C. Redman et al., pp. 113–129. Academic Press, New York.
Feinman, G. M.
  1985  Change in the Organization of Ceramic Production in Pre-hispanic Oaxaca, Mexico. In *Decoding Prehistoric Ceramics*, edited by B. A. Nelson, pp. 195–223. Southern Illinois University Press, Carbondale.
Feinman, G. M., S. Upham, and K. G. Lightfoot
  1981  The Production Step Measure: An Ordinal Index of Labor Input in Ceramic Manufacture. *American Antiquity* 46(4):871–884.
Fenton, W. N.
  1974  The Advancement of Material Culture Studies in Modern Anthropological Research. In *The Human Mirror: Material and Spatial Images of Man*, edited by M. Richardson, pp. 15–36. Louisiana State University Press, Baton Rouge.
Ferdon, E. N.
  1967  The Hohokam "Ballcourt": An Alternative View of Its Function. *The Kiva* 33(1):1–14.
Fish, S. K., P. R. Fish, and J. H. Madsen
  1985  A Preliminary Analysis of Hohokam Settlement and Agriculture in the Northern Tucson Basin. In *Proceedings of the 1983 Hohokam Symposium*, Part I, edited by A. E. Dittert and D. E. Dove, pp. 75–101. Arizona Archaeological Society Occasional Paper 2.
Flannery, K. V.
  1976  Contextual Analysis of Ritual Paraphernalia from Formative Oaxaca. In *The Early Mesoamerican Village*, edited by K. V. Flannery, pp. 333–345. Academic Press, New York.
Flannery, K. V., and J. Marcus
  1971  Evolution of the Public Building in Formative Oaxaca. In *Cultural Continuity and Change: Essays in Honor of James Bennett Griffin*, edited by C. Cleland, pp. 205–221. Academic Press, New York.
Frankenstein, S., and M. J. Rowlands
  1978  The Internal Structure and Regional Context of Early Iron Age Society in South-western Germany. *University of London Institute of Archaeology Bulletin* 15:73–112.
Fried, M. H.
  1967  *The Evolution of Political Society: An Essay in Political Anthropology*. Random House, New York.
Friedel, D. A.
  1981  Civilization As a State of Mind. In *The Transition to Statehood in the New World*, edited by G. D. Jones and R. R. Kautz, pp. 187–227. Cambridge University Press, Cambridge.
Gasser, R., and C. Miksicek
  1985  Specialists: A Reappraisal of Hohokam Exchange and the Archaeobotanical Record. In *Proceedings of the 1983 Hohokam Symposium*, Part II, edited by A. E. Dittert and D. E. Dove, pp. 483–498. Arizona Archaeological Society Occasional Paper 2.

Geertz, C.
1985    Centers, Kings, and Charisma: Reflections on the Symbolics of Power. In *Rites of Power: Symbolism, Ritual and Politics Since the Middle Ages,* edited by S. Wilentz, pp. 13–38. University of Pennsylvania Press, Philadelphia.

Gladwin, H. S., E. Haury, E. B. Sayles, and N. Gladwin
1937    *Excavations at Snaketown: Material Culture.* University of Arizona Press, Tucson.

Goldman, I.
1970    *Ancient Polynesian Society.* University of Chicago Press, Chicago.

Gregory, D. A.
1987    The Morphology of Platform Mounds and the Structure of Classic Period Hohokam Sites. In *The Hohokam Village: Site Structure and Organization,* edited by D. E. Doyel, pp. 183–210. American Association for the Advancement of Science, Glenwood Springs, Colorado.

Gregory, D. A., and F. L. Nials
1985    Observations Concerning the Distribution of Classic Period Platform Mounds. In *Proceedings of the 1983 Hohokam Symposium,* Part I, edited by A. E. Dittert and D. E. Dove, pp. 373–388. Arizona Archaeological Society Occasional Paper 2.

Hammack, L. C.
1969    A Preliminary Report of the Excavations at Las Colinas. *The Kiva* 35(1):11–28.

Hammack, L. C., and N. S. Hammack
1981    Architecture. In *The 1968 Excavations at Mound 8, Las Colinas Ruins Group, Phoenix, Arizona,* edited by L. C. Hammack and A. P. Sullivan, pp. 15–86. Arizona State Museum Archaeological Series 154.

Haury, E. W.
1976    *The Hohokam: Desert Farmers and Craftsmen.* University of Arizona Press, Tucson.

Haviland, W. A.
1974    Occupational Specialization at Tikal, Guatemala: Stone Working–Monument Carving. *American Antiquity* 39(3):494–496.

Hawley, F. G.
1947    The Use of Lead Minerals by the Hohokam in Cremation Ceremonials. *Southwestern Journal of Anthropology* 3(1):69–77.

Hayden, J. D.
1957    *Excavations, 1940 at University Indian Ruin, Tucson, Az.* Southwestern Monuments Association Technical Series 5.

Herskovitz, R. M.
1981    AZ U:9:46: A Dual Component Hohokam Site in Tempe, Arizona. *The Kiva* 47(1–2).

Hoffman, T. L., D. E. Doyel, and M. D. Elson
1985    Ground Stone Tool Production in the New River Basin. In *Proceedings of the 1983 Hohokam Symposium,* Part II, edited by A. E. Dittert and D. E. Dove, pp. 655–686. Arizona Archaeological Society Occasional Paper 2.

Howard, A. V.
1985    A Reconstruction of Hohokam Interregional Shell Production and Exchange within Southwestern Arizona. In *Proceedings of the 1983 Hohokam Symposium,* Part II, edited by A. E. Dittert and D. E. Dove, pp. 459–467. Arizona Archaeological Society Occasional Paper 2.

Howard, J. B.
  1987   The Lehi Canal System: Organization of a Classic Period Community. In *The Hohokam Village: Site Structure and Organization*, edited by D. E. Doyel, pp. 211–222. American Association for the Advancement of Science, Glenwood Springs, Colorado.
Hunt, E., and R. C. Hunt
  1978   Irrigation, Conflict, and Politics: A Mexican Case. In *Origins of the State: The Anthropology of Political Evolution*, edited by R. Cohen and E. Service, pp. 69–123. ISHI, Philadelphia.
Hunt, R. C., and E. Hunt
  1976   Canal Irrigation and Local Social Organization. *Current Anthropology* 17(3):389–411.
Huntington, F. W.
  1986   *Archaeological Investigations at the West Branch Site: Early and Middle Rincon Occupation in the Southern Tucson Basin*. Institute for American Research Anthropological Papers 5.
Kaplan, D.
  1963   Men, Monuments, and Political Systems. *Southwestern Journal of Anthropology* 19(4):397–410.
Kent, K. P.
  1957   The Cultivation and Weaving of Cotton in the Prehistoric Southwestern United States. *Transactions of the American Philosophical Society*, n.s. 47(3).
  1983   *Textiles of the Prehistoric Southwest*. University of New Mexico Press, Albuquerque.
Kertzer, D. I.
  1988   *Ritual, Politics, and Power*. Yale University Press, New Haven.
King, M. E.
  1965   Appendix C: Prehistoric Textiles from the Gila Bend Area. In *Salvage Archaeology in Painted Rocks Reservoir, Western Arizona*, edited by W. W. Wasley and A. E. Johnson, pp. 110–114. Anthropological Papers of the University of Arizona 9.
Kisselburg, J. A.
  1985   Spatial Distribution of Stone and Shell Jewelry at La Ciudad, AZ T:12:37(ASU). In *Proceedings of the 1983 Hohokam Symposium*, Part II, edited by A. E. Dittert and D. E. Dove, pp. 525–530. Arizona Archaeological Society Occasional Paper 2.
  1987a  Specialization and Differentiation: Non-Subsistence Economic Pursuits in Courtyard Systems at La Ciudad. In *The Hohokam Village: Site Structure and Organization*, edited by D. E. Doyel, pp. 159–170. American Association for the Advancement of Science, Glenwood Springs, Colorado.
  1987b  The Economy of Community Systems at La Ciudad. In *The Hohokam Community of La Ciudad*, edited by G. E. Rice, pp. 69–86. Office of Cultural Resource Management Report No. 69.
  1987c  Categories of Special and Unusual Artifacts at La Ciudad. In *Specialized Studies in the Economy, Environment, and Culture of La Ciudad*, edited by J. A. Kisselburg, G. E. Rice, and B. L. Shears, pp. 181–200. Arizona State University Anthropological Field Studies 20 (1–2).
  1987d  Economic Specialization in the Community System at Marana. In *Studies in*

*the Hohokam Community of Marana*, edited by G. E. Rice, pp. 143–160. Arizona State University Anthropological Field Studies 15.

Kluckhohn, C., W. W. Hill, and L. W. Kluckhohn
  1971  *Navajo Material Culture.* Harvard University Press, Cambridge.
Kristiansen, K.
  1984  Ideology and Material Culture: An Archaeological Perspective. In *Marxist Perspectives in Archaeology*, edited by M. Spriggs, pp. 72–100. Cambridge University Press, Cambridge.
LeBlanc, S.
  1986  Aspects of Southwestern Prehistory, A.D. 900–1400. In *Ripples in the Chichimec Sea: New Considerations of Southwestern-Mesoamerican Interactions*, edited by F. J. Mathien and R. H. McGuire, pp. 105–134. Southern Illinois University Press, Carbondale.
Lechtman, H.
  1977  Style in Technology: Some Early Thoughts. In *Material Culture: Styles, Organization, and Dynamics of Technology*, edited by H. Lechtman and R. S. Merrill, pp. 3–20. West Publishing, St. Paul.
Lees, S. H.
  1973  *Sociopolitical Aspects of Canal Irrigation in the Valley of Oaxaca.* University of Michigan, Memoirs of the Museum of Anthropology 5.
  1974a Hydraulic Development As a Process of Response. *Human Ecology* 2(3):159–175.
  1974b The State's Use of Irrigation in Changing Peasant Society. In *Irrigaton's Impact on Society*, edited by T. E. Downing and M. Gibson, pp. 123–128. Anthropological Papers of the University of Arizona 25.
Lemonnier, P.
  1986  The Study of Material Culture: Toward an Anthropology of Technical Systems. *Journal of Anthropological Archaeology* 5(2):147–186.
Leone, M. P.
  1973  Archaeology as the Science of Technology: Mormon Town Plans and Fences. In *Research and Theory in Current Archaeology*, edited by C. L. Redman, pp. 125–150. John Wiley and Sons, New York.
  1982  Some Opinions about Recovering Mind. *American Antiquity* 47(4):742–760.
Masse, W. B.
  1976  *The Hohokam Expressway Project: A Study of Prehistoric Irrigation in the Salt River Valley, Arizona.* Arizona State Museum Contribution to Highway Salvage Archaeology in Arizona 43.
  1981  Prehistoric Irrigation Systems in the Salt River Valley, Arizona. *Science* 214:408–415.
Matthews, W. J. W. Wortman, and J. S. Billings
  1893  Human Bones of the Hemenway Collection in the U.S. Army Medical Museum. *Memoir of the National Academy of Sciences* 6(7):141–286.
McGuire, R. H.
  1983  Breaking Down Cultural Complexity: Inequality and Heterogeneity. In *Advances in Archaeological Method and Theory*, vol. 6, edited by M. B. Schiffer, pp. 91–142. Academic Press, New York.
  1985  The Role of Shell Exchange in the Explanation of Hohokam Prehistory. In *Proceedings of the 1983 Hohokam Conference*, Part II, edited by A. E. Dittert and D. E. Dove, pp. 47–479. Arizona Archaeological Society Occasional Paper 2.

1987   *Death, Society, and Ideology in a Hohokam Community: Colonial and Sedentary Burials from La Ciudad.* Arizona State University OCRM Report 58.

McGuire, R. H., and A. V. Howard
1987   The Structure and Organization of Hohokam Shell Exchange. *The Kiva* 52(2):113–146.

McGuire, R. H., and M. B. Schiffer
1982   *Hohokam and Patayan: Prehistory of Southwestern Arizona.* Academic Press, New York.
1983   A Theory of Architectural Design. *Journal of Anthropological Archaeology* 2(3):277–303.

Merrill, R. S.
1968   The Study of Technology. *International Encyclopedia of the Social Science* 15:576–589.

Minnis, P. E.
1988   Four Examples of Specialized Production at Casas Grandes, Northwestern Chihuahua. *The Kiva* 53(2):181–193.
1989   The Casas Grandes Polity in the International Four Courners. In *The Sociopolitical Structure of Prehistoric Southwestern Societies,* edited by S. Upham, K. Lightfoot, and R. A. Jewett, pp. 269–305. Westview Press, Boulder.

Mitchell, W. P.
1973   The Hydraulic Response: A Reappraisal. *Current Anthropology* 14(5):532-534.

Moseley, M. E.
1974   Organizational Preadaptation to Irrigation: The Evolution of Early Water Management Systems in Coastal Peru. In *Irrigation's Impact on Society,* edited by T. E. Downing and M. Gibson, pp. 77–82. Anthropological Papers of the University of Arizona 25.

Muller, J.
1984   Mississippian Specialization and Salt. *American Antiquity* 49(3):489–507.
1987   Salt, Chert, and Shell: Mississippian Exchange and Economy. In *Specialization, Exchange, and Complex Societies,* edited by E. M. Brumfiel and T. K. Earle, pp. 10–21. Cambridge University Press, Cambridge.

Naroll, R.
1956   A Preliminary Index of Social Development. *American Anthropologist* 58(4):687–715.

Neitzel, J. E.
1987   The Sociopolitical Implications of Canal Irrigation: A Reconsideration of the Hohokam. In *Coasts, Plains and Deserts: Essays in Honor of Reynold J. Ruppe,* edited by S. W. Gaines, pp. 205–211. Arizona State University Anthropological Research Papers 38.

Nelson, R. S.
1981   *The Role of a Pochteca System in Hohokam Exchange.* Unpublished Ph.D. dissertation, Department of Anthropology, New York University.

Nicholas, L. M.
1981   *Irrigation and Sociopolitical Development in the Salt River Valley, Arizona: An Examination of Three Prehistoric Canal Systems.* Unpublished M.A. thesis, Department of Anthropology, Arizona State University.

Nicholas, L. M., and G. M. Feinman
1989   A Regional Perspective on Hohokam Irrigation in the Lower Salt River Valley,

Arizona. In *The Sociopolitical Structure of Prehistoric Southwestern Societies*, edited by S. Upham, K. G. Lightfoot, and R. A. Jewett, pp. 199–235. Westview Press, Boulder.

Nicholas, L. M., and J. E. Neitzel
1984    Canal Irrigation and Sociopolitical Organization in the Lower Salt River Valley: A Diachronic Analysis. In *Prehistoric Agricultural Strategies of the Southwest*, edited by S. Fish and P. Fish, pp. 161–178. Arizona State University Anthropological Research Papers 33.

Peebles, C., and S. Kus
1977    Some Archaeological Correlates of Ranked Societies. *American Antiquity* 42(3):421–448.

Placona, J.
1979    *A Report on the Mesa Grande Ruin: Excavations, Chronology, Research Goals, and Problems*. Unpublished M.A. thesis, Department of Anthropology, Arizona State University.

Pozorski, T.
1980    The Early Horizon Site of Huaca de los Reyes: Societal Implications. *American Antiquity* 45(1):100–110.

Price, B.
1984    Competition, Productive Intensification and Ranked Society: Speculations from Evolutionary Theory. In *Warfare, Culture, and Environment*, edited by R. B. Ferguson, pp. 209–240. Academic Press, New York.

Rafferty, K.
1982    *Sociopolitical Organization in the Desert Southwest: The Hohokam of the Gila Butte Region, South-central Arizona*. Unpublished Ph.D. dissertation, Department of Anthropology, State University of New York, Stony Brook.

Rappaport, R. A.
1971a   Ritual, Sanctity and Cybernetics. *American Anthropologist* 73(1):59–76.
1971b   The Sacred in Human Evolution. *Annual Review of Ecology and Systematics* 2:23–44.

Renfrew, C.
1973    Monuments, Mobilization and Social Organization in Neolithic Wessex. In *The Explanation of Culture Change: Models in Prehistory*, edited by C. Renfrew, pp. 539–558. University of Pittsburgh Press, Pittsburgh.

Rice, P. M.
1981    Evolution of Specialized Pottery Production: A Trial Model. *Current Anthropology* 22(3):219–240.
1984    The Archaeological Study of Specialized Pottery Production: Some Aspects of Method and Theory. In *Pots and Potters: Current Approaches in Ceramic Archaeology*, edited by P. M. Rice, pp. 45–54. University of California Institute of Archaeology Monograph 24.
1987    *Pottery Analysis: A Sourcebook*. University of Chicago Press, Chicago.

Rowlands, M. J.
1971    The Archaeological Interpretation of Prehistoric Metalworking. *World Archaeology* 3(2):210–221.

Schroeder, A. H.
1966    Pattern Diffusion from Mexico into the Southwest after A.D. 600. *American Antiquity* 31(5):683–704.

Service, E. R.
  1962   *Primitive Social Organization: An Evolutionary Perspective.* Random House, New
         York.
Seymour, D. J., and M. B. Schiffer
  1987   A Preliminary Analysis of Pithouse Assemblages from Snaketown, Arizona.
         In *Method and Theory for Activity Area Research: An Ethnoarchaeological Approach,*
         edited by S. Kent, pp. 549–603. Columbia University Press, New York.
Spence, M. W.
  1985   Specialized Production in Rural Aztec Society: Obsidian Workshops of the
         Teotihuacan Valley. In *Contributions to the Archaeology and Ethnohistory of Greater
         Mesoamerica,* edited by W. J. Folan, pp. 76–125. Southern Illinois University
         Press, Carbondale.
Spencer, C. S.
  1987   Rethinking Chiefdoms. In *Chiefdoms in the Americas,* edited by R. D. Drennan
         and C. A. Uribe, pp. 369–389. University Press of America, Lanham, Mary-
         land.
Stark, B. L.
  1985   Archaeological Identification of Pottery Production Locations: Ethnoarchaeo-
         logical and Archaeological Data in Mesoamerica. In *Decoding Prehistoric Ce-
         ramics,* edited by B. A. Nelson, pp. 158–194. Southern Illinois University Press,
         Carbondale.
Startin, W., and R. J. Bradley
  1981   Some Notes on Work Organisation and Society in Prehistoric Wessex. In
         *Astronomy and Society During the Period 4000–1500 b.c.,* edited by C. Ruggles
         and A. Whittle, pp. 289–296. British Archaeological Reports 88.
Stewart, K. M.
  1967   Excavations at Mesa Grande: A Classic Period Hohokam Site in Arizona. *The
         Masterkey* 41(1):14–25.
Tatje, T. A., and R. Naroll
  1973   Two Measures of Societal Complexity: An Empirical Cross-Cultural Compar-
         ison. In *A Handbook of Method in Cultural Anthropology,* edited by R. Naroll and
         R. Cohen, pp. 766–833. Columbia University Press, New York.
Teague, L. S.
  1984   The Organization of Hohokam Economy. In *Hohokam Archaeology along the
         Salt-Gila Aqueduct, Central Arizona Project,* vol. 9: Synthesis and Conclusions,
         edited by L. S. Teague and P. L. Crown, pp. 187–249. Arizona State Museum
         Archaeological Series 150.
Thomas, C. M., and J. H. King
  1985   Hohokam Figurine Assemblages: A Suggested Ritual Context. In *Proceedings
         of the 1983 Hohokam Symposium,* Part II, edited by A. E. Dittert and D. E. Dove,
         pp. 687–732. Arizona Archaeological Society Occasional Paper 2.
Tosi, M.
  1984   The Notion of Craft Specialization and Its Representation in the Archaeolog-
         ical Record of Early States in the Turanian Basin. In *Marxist Perspectives in
         Archaeology,* edited by M. Spriggs, pp. 22–52. Cambridge University Press,
         Cambridge.
Turney, O.
  1929   *Prehistoric Irrigation in Arizona.* Arizona State Historian, Phoenix.

Upham, S., and G. Rice
  1980   Up the Canal without a Pattern: Modeling Hohokam Interaction and Ex-
         change. In *Current Issues in Hohokam Prehistory*, edited by D. E. Doyel and F.
         Plog, pp. 78–105. Arizona State University Anthropological Research Papers
         23.

Wallace, H. D., and J. Heidke
  1986   Ceramic Production and Exchange. In *Archaeological Investigations at the Tanque
         Verde Wash Site: A Middle Rincon Settlement in the Eastern Tucson Basin*, edited
         by M. D. Elson, pp. 233–270. Institute for American Research Anthropological
         Papers 7.

Wasley, W. W.
  1966   Classic Period Hohokam. Paper presented at the 31st Annual Meeting of the
         Society for American Archaeology, Reno.

Wasley, W. W., and A. E. Johnson
  1965   *Salvage Archaeology in Painted Rocks Reservoir, Western Arizona*. Anthropological
         Papers of the University of Arizona 9.

Weaver, D. E., S. S. Burton, and M. Laughlin
  1973   *Proceedings of the 1973 Hohokam Conference*. Contributions to Anthropological
         Studies 2.

Webb, M. C.
  1987   Broader Perspectives on Andean State Origins. In *The Origins and Development
         of the Andean State*, edited by J. Haas, S. Pozorski, and T. Pozorski, pp. 161–
         167. Cambridge University Press, Cambridge.

Weisman, R.
  1987   Pioneer to Sedentary Ceramic Technology at La Ciudad. In *Specialized Studies
         in the Economy, Environment, and Culture of La Ciudad*, edited by J. A. Kisselburg,
         G. E. Rice, and B. L. Shears, pp. 1–40. Arizona State University Anthropo-
         logical Field Studies 20(1–2).

White, L. A.
  1959   *The Evolution of Culture: The Development of Civilization to the Fall of Rome*.
         McGraw-Hill, New York.

Wilcox, D. R.
  1979   The Hohokam Regional System. In *An Archaeological Test of Sites in the Gila
         Butte–Santan Region, South-central Arizona*, edited by G. Rice, pp. 77–116. Ari-
         zona State University Anthropological Research Papers 18.
  1987   *Frank Midvale's Investigation at the Site of La Ciudad*. Arizona State University
         Anthropological Field Studies 19.

Wilcox, D. R., T. R. McGuire, and C. Sternberg
  1981   *Snaketown Revisited*. Arizona State Museum Archaeological Series 155.

Wilcox, D. R., and C. Sternberg
  1983   *Hohokam Ballcourts and Their Interpretation*. Arizona State Museum Archaeo-
         logical Series 160.

Wilcox, D. R., and L. O. Shenk
  1977   *The Architecture of the Casa Grande and Its Interpretation*. Arizona State Museum
         Archaeological Series 115.

Wittfogel, K.
  1957   *Oriental Despotism*. Yale University Press, New Haven.

Wobst, H. M.
  1977   Stylistic Behavior and Information Exchange. In *Papers for the Director: Research*

*Essays in Honor of James B. Griffin*, edited by C. E. Cleland, pp. 317–342. University of Michigan, Museum of Anthropology Anthropological Papers 61.

Woodbury, R.

   1961   A Reappraisal of Hohokam Irrigation. *American Anthropologist* 63(3):550–560.

Yerkes, R. K.

   1983   Microwear, Microdrills, and Mississippian Craft Specialization. *American Antiquity* 48(3):499–518.

# •6•

# HOHOKAM CULTURAL EVOLUTION IN THE PHOENIX BASIN

▼▼▼▼▼▼▼▼▼▼▼▼▼▼▼▼▼▼▼▼▼▼▼▼▼▼▼▼▼▼▼▼▼▼▼▼▼▼▼▼▼▼▼▼▼▼▼▼▼▼▼▼▼▼

## David E. Doyel

The Hohokam became archaeologically recognizable around the time of Christ (Cable and Doyel 1987a); some would say earlier (Haury 1976), and some would say later (Wilcox and Shenk 1977; Schiffer 1982). The early Hohokam pattern of small pithouse villages, grooved and decorated pottery, agriculture, and cremation burial is contained primarily within the Phoenix Basin. By the early Colonial period, a Hohokam presence can be identified in more geographically and environmentally diverse areas (Doyel 1980; Masse 1980a). The maximum distribution of the Hohokam interaction sphere dates to the Sedentary period (A.D. 900–1050) and encompassed roughly 65,000 sq km (40,000 sq mi) in area from the Verde Valley in the north to the New Mexico border on the east and the international border on the south to Gila Bend on the west (Fig. 6.1; Doyel 1979; Gumerman and Haury 1979:75). If the upper Tonto Creek-Flagstaff-Prescott areas are included, another 8,000 sq km (5,000 sq mi) could be added to the above figure (Haury 1976, fig. 1.2).

A conceptual structure of core and periphery recognizes that the Hohokam

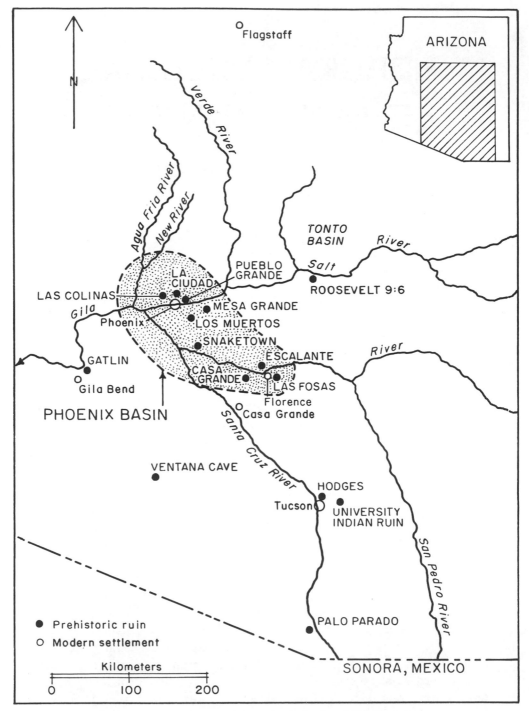

Figure 6.1    *Phoenix Basin region and selected Hohokam sites.*

cultural pattern underwent its greatest elaboration in the "core" areas along the major rivers contained within the Phoenix Basin (Doyel and Plog 1980; Wilcox 1985a). The Phoenix Basin terminology has recently been used interchangeably with the core area or Gila–Salt Valley (Wilcox 1979). Areas outside of the Phoenix Basin were related to the Hohokam, but were often characterized by less complexity. Recent research suggests that the core-periphery model masks significant local variation and does not provide sufficient conceptual rigor or flexibility for modern purposes (Wilcox 1979, 1985a; Masse 1980b; Fish 1983). Others state that the core-periphery dichotomy contains inherent bias toward the core while minimizing the role of the peripheries in Hohokam cultural dynamics (Lerner 1985; Wood 1985).

Questions remain about the relationship between the Hohokam and the historic populations inhabiting the same region. Because the Pima-Papago did not express significant complexity in social organization, it has been argued that the Hohokam also lacked tendencies towards social complexity (Woodbury 1961; Haury 1976). These ethnographic groups did have "ditch bosses" to manage irrigation, war chiefs for organizing battle, and they held village council meetings in large community houses often located adjacent to public plazas. While some even question the Hohokam-Pima continuum (Masse 1981; Doelle 1981), it remains common practice for researchers to use Pima-Papago analog models for Hohokam subsistence and economy.

It should be realized, however, that the Hohokam and Pima represent systems of very different scales. Furthermore, most northern Pima ethnography was recorded long after the introduction of winter wheat and livestock, infectious diseases, significant population reduction, and other historic period changes. The Pima did not build hundreds of miles of canals, over 225 ballcourts, and over 45 platform mounds, did not have an economic system encompassing over 65,000 sq km, and did not possess either the population levels or the complex settlement hierarchies recorded for the Hohokam. The Hohokam sequence reveals a dynamic record of growth and decline not to be understood by the use of static, historically based analog models (Doyel 1979:550).

## HOHOKAM CULTURAL ECOLOGY

Issues focusing on relationships among environment, subsistence, and society have been associated with Hohokam research since the turn of the century (Huntington 1914). Early research investigated the role of irrigation and its social implications (Haury 1936; Woodbury 1961). Haury (1950) identified regional variation among the "Desert" and "River" Hohokam, based in part on environmental influences on culture patterns. Other concepts, such as "riverine extensions" and core and periphery, were also grounded in cultural-ecological relationships (see papers in Doyel and Plog 1980).

The size, scale, and location of projects undertaken within the past two decades have for the first time created an opportunity to develop truly regional perspectives on Hohokam cultural dynamics. Survey and excavation have produced an information explosion on Hohokam land use, subsistence, resource distributions, and other data relevant to Hohokam cultural ecology. The Bureau of Reclamation alone has surveyed almost 700 sq mi, recorded 3,900 sites, and excavated over 10 percent of them (Tom Lincoln, personal communication, 1988; see Doyel 1985 for a recent summary).

Both Haury (1976) and I (Doyel 1984a) have noted the correspondence between the Hohokam range and the distribution of the Sonoran Desert environment in Arizona. The desert rivers proved adaptable to canal irrigation, which resulted in a stable settlement pattern unmatched elsewhere in the Southwest. When viewed in macroscale, however, it appears that adaptation through diversity was more characteristic of the Hohokam sequence. All periods of occupation within the Phoenix Basin reflect both riverine and nonriverine land-use patterns. Special-use agricultural farmsteads and field-houses have been identified in the Salt River Valley and its tributaries (Cable and Doyel 1985; Doyel 1984b; Doyel and Elson 1985) as well as in nonriverine localities (Teague and Crown 1983–1984), although the relative frequencies of such specialized sites through time have not been adequately studied. A wide range of water control facilities and agricultural strategies are known to exist within the region, which were integrated into local systems as conditions permitted (Teague and Crown 1983–1984; Masse 1979; Fish and Fish 1984). Hunting and resource gathering were also utilized to a degree, dependent on both local resource availability and annual conditions.

During the 1970s, emphasis was placed on cultural and environmental interaction as a primary mechanism for Hohokam cultural change (Weaver 1972; Grebinger 1971; Doyel 1981). During the 1980s, a perspective on the Hohokam as resourceful "environmental managers" and "masters of the desert" had developed (Teague and Crown 1983–1984; Fish 1983). There is no doubt that the Hohokam were resourceful managers and competent engineers; archaeological research has documented their diverse strategies for harnessing the energy of the Sonoran Desert through technology, resource exchange, and organizational diversity.

A recent study, however, asks how well could the Hohokam respond to catastrophic environmental events falling outside the normal range of variation? A reconstruction of flow patterns in the Salt River based upon tree-ring data and historical climatology has been completed by Nials, Gregory, and Graybill (1986). Encompassing the time period between the eighth and fourteenth centuries, the study concludes that serious problems due to increased river flow levels may have occurred on at least eight occasions of sufficient strength to damage head gates, wash out canal banks, and alter the flow of water in the riverbed. They further propose that flows at A.D. 899 and 1352 had devastating effects, resulting in system disuse, abandonment, and population relocation; some of the other flows *could* have had similar effects. Independent verification of prehistoric flooding in the Phoenix Basin has been obtained through geological research (Partridge and Baker 1987; Fuller 1987).

## PIONEER PERIOD: AGRICULTURE AND SEDENTISM IN SOUTHERN ARIZONA

Research undertaken during the past decade has had significant impacts on a number of traditional issues, including Hohokam origins and the timing and phase structure of the Pioneer period (Huckell 1984a; Huckell and Huckell 1988; Cable and Doyel 1987a, 1987b; Fish et al. 1987). Were the Hohokam immigrants from Mesoamerica, bringing with them an advanced economy structured by irrigation agriculture, or were they the descendants of the Cochise hunting and gathering tradition of southern Arizona (Gladwin 1948; DiPeso 1956; Schroeder 1965, 1966; Haury 1943, 1957, 1962; see Doyel 1986 for a summary)? The ruling hypothesis supported a migration from Mesoamerica. In contrast, Haury argued that certain similarities such as projectile points, the use of cremation, and incipient agriculture suggested a connection between the preceramic Cochise and the Hohokam.

Haury's second excavation at Snaketown encouraged him to reverse his long-held position on Hohokam origins. He then proposed that the earliest Vahki phase included irrigation agriculture, new crop varieties, an advanced ceramic technology, a fired-clay figurine assemblage, large square houses, the trough metate, and an advanced crafts industry, including the use of marine shell that had been brought by the Hohokam into southern Arizona from some unknown source in Mesoamerica (Haury 1976). His model differed from the rest, however, in that he retained the early date of 300 B.C., while others had postulated a post-A.D. 500 entry date for the Hohokam.

Researchers have since questioned the Mesoamerican migration model for the Hohokam based on theoretical grounds, data reanalysis, and new data (Cable and Doyel 1987a; Doelle 1985; Doyel 1988c; Fish et al. 1987; Plog 1980; Wilcox 1979). Until recently the lack of regional perspectives due to an absence of data had been a major limiting factor in Hohokam studies. The acquisition of new data bearing on the Archaic-Pioneer period transition, and thus Hohokam origins, must rank near the top of exciting new developments in Hohokam archaeology.

A cultural sequence can now be outlined which suggests that early Hohokam developments resembled the cultural trajectories identified for the Mogollon and Anasazi. Increasing documentation for a transitional phase between the terminal late Archaic and the Vahki phase currently questions the position that the Hohokam were technologically advanced immigrants

Table 6.1    *Attributes of the Late Archaic and Early Hohokam Phases*

| Late Archaic | Red Mountain | Vahki |
|---|---|---|
| 600 B.C.–A.D. 1 | A.D. 1–A.D. 300 | A.D. 300–450/500 |
| Small, circular houses | Small, square houses | Small, rectangular houses; large, square communal houses |
| Small villages or hamlets (up to 10 houses) | Small villages, increased site density | Large villages with plazas; segmented village plans |
| Near-river bottom site locations | Same | Same |
| Upland villages | Upland hamlets | Inferred |
| Incipient agriculture | Floodplain agriculture | Increased reliance on corn agriculture; diversion technology |
| Storage and roasting pits | Inferred | Inferred |
| Large, notched points | Same | Small, barbed points |
| Basin metate and handstone | Shallow basin metate | Trough metate and mano |
| Flexed inhumation; cremation also known | Flexed inhumation | Inhumation and cremation |
| No pottery | Sand-tempered brown ware pottery | Vahki Plain, Vahki Red, brown and red ware pottery |
| Clay figurines | Inferred | Developed clay figurine complex |

from Mexico. Rather, the existence of a pre-Vahki–Red Mountain phase supports the position that the Hohokam, like other major southwestern cultures, developed out of an Archaic culture base.

## THE LATE ARCHAIC-EARLY PIONEER PERIOD SEQUENCE: 600 B.C.–A.D. 500

Significant late Archaic occupations have been reported from east-central Arizona as well as the San Pedro and middle Santa Cruz river drainages (Huckell 1984a, 1984b; Whalen 1971). A number of these sites have yielded evidence of incipient agriculture and small village settlement patterns (Huckell and Huckell 1988). In Phoenix, a transitional phase has been described (the Red Mountain phase) that bridges the late Archaic and the Vahki phase of the Pioneer period (Morris 1969; Cable and Doyel 1987a). The contrasting attributes used to define the late Archaic, Red Mountain, and Vahki phases are presented in Table 6.1 (see also Cable and Doyel 1987a:56).

Several terminal late Archaic sites have been reported from southeastern Arizona. Groups of pithouses and inhumation burials occur in conjunction with evidence for agriculture. Pithouses are subcircular in plan, often containing large subfloor pits, but lack formal floor features and roof-wall support systems. Huckell reported two houses from the Rosemont area that measure 21.6 sq m and 8.2 sq m in floor area (Huckell 1984a:54, 83). The Matty Canyon site (AZ EE:2:30 ASM) and the Pantano Wash site also may represent similar settlements. Excavations at Matty Canyon have identified numerous houses, burials, bell-shaped and straight-sided roasting pits, and rock-filled hearths (Eddy and Cooley 1983:17; Huckell 1984a; Hemmings, Robinson, and Rogers 1968). The presence of flexed inhumation burials suggests behavioral continuity with the earlier Archaic periods (Sayles 1945, 1983).

Macrobotanical and pollen analysis have amply documented the presence of corn in late Archaic sites (Huckell and Huckell 1988; Current Research, *American Antiquity* 51:864). Late Archaic lithic assemblages in southeastern Arizona are characterized by basin metates, grinding slabs, nutting stones, mortars and pestles, and oval handstones (Sayles 1983:128). The presence of large projectile points suggests a continued reliance on hunting. Huckell (1984a:260) has proposed a subsistence-settlement model for the terminal late Archaic in southeastern Arizona that envisions semipermanent or permanent agricultural villages located along major streams and dispersed rancherias in upland zones.

The Red Mountain phase is represented by a single house (16 sq m in floor area) at Pueblo Patricio in central Phoenix. The architecture is more formalized than that of the late Archaic, but the form can be seen as deriving from these houses (Cable and Doyel 1987a, fig. 9). A number of other sites also contain Red Mountain or equivalent phase components, including Snaketown (Haury 1976), Red Mountain (Morris 1969), the Stricklin site (Kenny 1987), Arizona EE:3:10 in Matty Canyon (Eddy and Cooley 1983:23–24), and the Peñasco phase components at the Cave Creek and San Simon sites in southeastern Arizona (Sayles 1945). The Red Mountain site assemblage includes flexed inhumation burial, a basin metate grinding assemblage, corner-notched projectile points, and a small square house, all of which suggest the presence of a Red Mountain phase component (see Cable and Doyel 1987b for further discussion).

An early pottery phase was recognized by Sayles (1945:14) at Cave Creek Village. The complex consisted of deep basin metates, handstones, notched projectile points (Sayles 1945, plate x:d,e), and side-flexed inhumations. Pottery recovered included Alma Plain and a fugitive-slipped variant of San Francisco Red. Peñasco phase houses range between 9 and 12 sq m in floor area, and exhibit both subsquare and oval floor plans.

Cave Creek Village may be typical of an early pottery horizon village site. Seven houses, numerous rock-filled ovens, and burials were distributed over an area of about 37,000 sq m. At San Simon Village, nine possible Peñasco phase houses were identified in two areas of similar size to that described for Cave Creek. It can be proposed that late Archaic village size would have

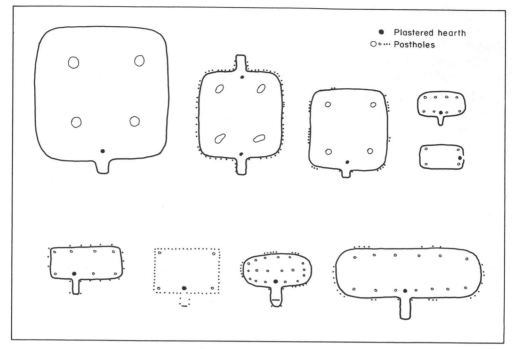

Figure 6.2    *Large, square communal (LSC) houses were constructed dur-*
*ing the Pioneer period and served as the dwellings of leaders*
*and as meeting places. Top row: three LSC houses and two*
*smaller, average-size units. Lower row: two Colonial (left)*
*and two Sedentary period houses. House sizes are relative.*
*(Adapted from E. Haury 1976, fig. 3.28.)*

been in the range of seven to ten houses. The presence of two house clusters
at San Simon Village may indicate either a sequence of occupation or the
presence of several social groups.

Both the Red Mountain and Peñasco phases share close relationships with
sites dating to the terminal late Archaic horizon. Bostwick and Shackley (1987)
have identified similarities between Archaic and Hohokam chipped stone
assemblages, while Ann Howard (1987) has shown that Archaic and Pioneer
period shell assemblages reveal general continuities. Szuter and Bayham (1987)
have suggested that Pioneer period faunal assemblages are more similar to
late Archaic patterns than to post-Pioneer faunal assemblages.

The Vahki phase contrasts sharply with these earlier phases. At Pueblo
Patricio, domestic houses were small rectangular structures, while Haury
reports only the large (his P-4 type) houses for the Vahki phase at Snaketown.
The large Vahki (Pioneer period type 4) houses averaged 85 sq m in area and
were built using a massive construction style including four large interior
roof support beams (Fig. 6.2; Haury 1976:72). The Vahki houses at Pueblo
Patricio averaged 16 sq m in floor area and were constructed in typical Ho-

hokam fashion with small interior and perimeter floor support beams (Cable et al. 1985:45–55). Given the addition of small houses, the large square Vahki-type houses (hereafter referred to as LSC houses for large, square communal) can be argued to represent communal or ceremonial buildings, as Sayles (in Gladwin et al. 1937:82) and Gladwin (1948:118) have suggested. The presence of hearths and domestic artifacts in the LSC structures, however, suggests that they may also have housed domestic groups. A possible analog is represented by the Cocopa, wherein band leaders lived in large structures capable of accommodating 40 to 50 people for community meetings (Kelly 1977:46; Cable and Doyel 1987b).

Both the large and small Vahki house types exhibited clay-lined hearths and patterned roof support systems; entryways were sturdily constructed, further indicating a greater degree of permanence than earlier houses. Wilcox and others (1981:143) have suggested that the LSC houses at Snaketown exhibit interrelated spatial orientations across the great central plaza, while Cable and Doyel (1987a) have proposed that a *sequence* of LSC house occupations occurred in this area during the Pioneer period. It is probable that several of these large pithouses were contemporary, suggesting that some form of segmentary social organization was emerging during the Vahki phase. The presence of LSC houses is documented for at least six sites in the Salt River Valley (Cable and Doyel 1987a:61–64).

Some 25 of the poorly dated, small, square- and rectangular-shaped houses excavated at Snaketown are candidates for a pre-Vahki-Red Mountain phase occupation (Cable et al. 1985:247–255). Large, notched projectile points were also found there, further supporting a late Archaic or Red Mountain presence (Gladwin et al 1937, plates 93, 94). The existence of a lengthy pre-Vahki plainware horizon provides evidence for a local ceramic development, which suggests that the temporally later and finely made Vahki Red and Vahki Plain pottery represent specialized types developed from a local tradition, rather than appearing as a full-blown imported ceramic technology.

Haury (1976) has stated that cremation burial was the typical Vahki phase burial practice, but this is not supported by available evidence. Early Pioneer period "cremations" at Snaketown were represented by ash stains with a few associated sherds, while flexed burials have also been reported from other sites (Morris 1969:51; Cable et al. 1985). Both cremation and flexed inhumation are known from preceramic (Haury 1957) and early Hohokam time periods (Ives and Opfenring 1966). Inhumation appears to have been the dominant pattern during the earlier phases while cremation gradually became dominant by the early Colonial period.

Direct evidence of agricultural technology for the Vahki phase is lacking, but the permanence of houses, the presence of segmental social organization, and higher population levels suggest that more intensive production systems had developed by this time. Floodwater farming was the primary agricultural strategy prior to the Snaketown phase (Gladwin et al. 1937:56–57; Wilcox

1979; Cable and Doyel 1985, 1987b). Floodwater farming can be intensified by employing water control strategies such as diversion dams, ditches, and levees to increase the amount of cultivated land (Castetter and Bell 1951). Unfortunately, subsequent land use and natural forces such as flooding would erase any traces of these ephemeral systems. The trough metate and accompanying mano grinding complex appears during the Vahki phase at Pueblo Patricio and at Snaketown, further suggesting a trend towards increased agriculture; the Archaic horizon slab and basin metates and the oval-shaped handstone complex are also represented.

Robert Hard has recently studied the relative reliance on corn agriculture by various ethnographic and prehistoric populations (Hard 1988). Statistical and other data indicate that relative agricultural dependence can be approximated by calculating the mean length of manos used to grind corn. Four categories of relative dependence were established, ranging from none-to-low dependence for assemblages averaging under 11 cm in length up to a high degree of agricultural dependence for assemblages averaging over 20 cm in mano length (Hard 1988, table 4).

These criteria were applied to the mano assemblage recovered from the Block-24 East project at the site of Pueblo Patricio in central Phoenix (Cable et al. 1985:161). Five complete manos were recovered from Vahki phase houses. These specimens average 10.1 cm in length, while the average weight is 728 gm. According to the scale developed by Hard, this would suggest a relative agricultural dependence of none-to-low for the Vahki phase Hohokam located along the Salt River at Pueblo Patricio. Other avenues of investigation, however, such as the macrobotanical remains (corn remains were abundant), the lithic assemblage, settlement pattern, and other data sources do not support this assessment based on mean mano length. Whether this disparity is due to the small sample size, whether the local population was somewhat technologically retarded, or whether the measure as developed through Hard's research requires reconsideration is not known at this time.

It may be instructive to note that the remainder of the mano assemblage from Pueblo Patricio (Block-24 East) dating between the later Estrella and Snaketown phases (n = 10) has a mean length of 13.3 cm and an average weight of 843 gm. These data suggest a none-to-moderate placement on Hard's relative dependence scale, and indicate some directionality towards increased agriculture in the Pueblo Patricio grinding assemblage through time. Hard's data from Snaketown, apparently dating to a later temporal horizon, reveal a mean mano length of 20.8 cm (n = 105), suggesting a high degree of dependency on corn agriculture. Relative to the Snaketown data, it would appear that while agriculture was becoming increasingly important, the Pioneer period Hohokam at Pueblo Patricio were still involved in a broad-based economy including gathering, hunting, and agriculture.

During the Pioneer period, the Phoenix Basin Hohokam may have maintained a flexible settlement pattern consisting of more-or-less permanent vil-

Figure 6.3    *A Sedentary period Hohokam farmstead in New River. (Il-*
*lustration by C. Cooperrider from Doyel and Elson 1985,*
*fig. 5.13.)*

lages containing pithouses and summer dispersion of a segment of the
population into smaller agricultural and other specialized hamlets composed
of specialized and ephemeral structures (Cable and Doyel 1985, 1987a). Many
Hohokam agricultural field structures strongly resemble the small, bent-pole,
oval- to round-shaped dwellings of the Archaic period Cochise (Fig. 6.3).

## REGIONAL VARIATION IN THE
## ARCHAIC-PIONEER TRANSITION

The current difficulties in modeling terminal late Archaic and early ceramic
horizon settlement and subsistence patterns is attributable to a combination
of historical and natural factors. Due to research bias, logistical concerns, and
other factors, archaeological research has tended to focus on the primary
drainages in the desert region (the Salt, Gila, San Pedro, and Santa Cruz
rivers). It is becoming apparent, however, that the early horticulturalists often
preferred upland site locations that combined a broad-based subsistence strategy with slow-moving water and cienegalike environments, such as the Matty
Canyon site. Other transitional sites now known to exist (Red Mountain,
Stricklin, and Milagro) are also located in the better watered upland zones
surrounding the Phoenix Basin. A second complicating factor involves the
recent alluvial history of the Santa Cruz River. Archaic period sites containing
corn remains have been inadvertently discovered under deep alluvium along
the river near Tucson (Fish et al. 1987), suggesting that this important aspect

of Archaic settlement systems may not be observable by standard survey techniques. Archaic period materials located along the major rivers may also be concealed by subsequent Hohokam occupations (Doelle 1985).

Much additional research is needed to identify the variation in site location and agricultural strategies involved in the transition to agriculture in the Sonoran Desert region. Was there a period of time when upland locations were preferred for villages, while seasonal movement was undertaken to near-river locations to practice floodplain agriculture? Such a model may be relevant to an explanation of the presence and content of the Gila Dune site, a large Archaic site located near the transition between the mountainous upland and desert portions of the eastern Gila Basin (Fish n.d.). Through time, this terminal late Archaic site location strategy apparently became reversed, with permanent villages located along the major rivers and specialized sites located in the upland zones.

In contrast, Mike Berry (1985:305) has recently suggested that the late Archaic occupation (San Pedro stage) in southeastern Arizona is so different from the preceding stages of the Cochise culture that an intrusion by immigrant populations is indicated, a position apparently receiving support from Bruce and Lisa Huckell (1988). Inspection of diversity in late Archaic projectile point morphology may suggest the presence of several different populations in the region (Roth and Huckell 1988).

While the above questions remain unanswered, it may be stated that the Archaic to Pioneer transition in southeastern Arizona, the Tucson Basin, and the Phoenix Basin appears to have been an uneven developmental process. Substantial late Archaic occupations have been documented for southeastern Arizona and the Tucson Basin (Whalen 1971; Huckell 1984a; Doelle 1985). A Red Mountain–Peñasco horizon also has been reported for the Tucson Basin (Fish et al. 1986:570), while the early phases of the Pioneer period are not well represented (Wallace and Craig 1986). The Phoenix Basin, however, contains numerous early Pioneer period occupations but lacks a substantial late Archaic occupation. While these differences may be more apparent than real, a comparison of the various drainage patterns of the region may provide an explanation for these findings.

Drainages in the Tucson Basin are characterized by relatively narrow channels and intermittent flow. These conditions are acceptable for the practice of floodwater farming, and probably would not have limited the expansion of late Archaic populations. In contrast, the larger Salt and Gila rivers are subject to extreme discharge events, making them more difficult to control using simple floodwater farming techniques. Once more intensive farming techniques were developed, however, the large floodplains in the Phoenix Basin would have become attractive, which may explain the presence of a Red Mountain horizon.

Over time, population growth in the Phoenix Basin would have encouraged the development of large-scale irrigation through further experimentation with water control techniques. Population growth promoted group segmentation and more complex social organization, leading to the patterns described for the Vahki phase. Lower population levels in the Tucson Basin would not have encouraged social development, thus creating a less distinct early Pioneer period (Cable and Doyel 1987b). The model presented herein is density dependent, but does not use population pressure to explain change. Rather, it emphasizes the potential of improved agricultural technology to increase carrying capacity; in this regard, the model supports the research undertaken by Boserup (1965).

## THE RED-ON-GRAY HORIZON:
### A.D. 450–600

The Estrella-Sweetwater time period can be referred to as the "red-on-gray horizon" after the deeply grooved and painted pottery characteristic of these phases. This is done for convenience and does not question the sequence of the phases. Sites dating to this horizon have been recorded within the Phoenix Basin and elsewhere (Haury 1976; Wilcox 1979; Ives and Ophenring 1966; Eddy and Cooley 1983; Fish et al. 1987). Site location appears to favor a near-river setting, which would suggest a continuing focus on floodplain agriculture (Cable and Doyel 1985:297–302). The presence of large, stemmed and notched projectile points indicates the continued importance of hunting, while desert plant resources also contributed significantly to the diet (see Schroeder 1940 for a similar view).

Only 13 houses dating to the Estrella and Sweetwater phases were excavated during the two projects at Snaketown; both large and small houses were recorded (Haury 1976:46). An interesting trend can be seen in the construction of the LSC houses: they became increasingly smaller through time. While the Vahki phase LSC houses at Snaketown averaged 85 sq m in area, a LSC house in central Phoenix dating between A.D. 485 and 540 measures only 33 sq m (Cable and Doyel 1987a:38, 62). The late Pioneer period LSC houses at Snaketown range between 25 and 49 sq m in floor area. A LSC house measuring about 30 sq m was recently excavated at Los Hornos, while a somewhat larger one was excavated in 1987 near Las Acequias; these sites are located along the Salt River in the Tempe-Mesa area. While still larger than average domestic houses (16–22 sq m), the reduced size of the LSC houses suggests a change in function focusing on maximum group size. The reduction in size combined with increased numbers of these houses may indicate increasing population segmentation during the red-on-gray horizon, accompanied by a relocation of group ceremonies to extramural plaza areas (Cable and Doyel 1985).

## PIONEER PERIOD INTERACTION,
## EXCHANGE, AND COSMOLOGY

From the earliest horizon, the Hohokam reveal an interest in exotic materials and items of adornment. Two species of marine shell as well as *Glycymeris* shell bracelet fragments were recovered from the Red Mountain phase
house in central Phoenix (A. Howard 1985a:170). At Snaketown, nine species
of shell were associated with Vahki through Sweetwater materials, while over
350 bracelets and ten pieces of turquoise were recovered (Haury 1976:298,
308–314). Also found were numerous sherds of imported pottery, most of
which was San Francisco Red, suggesting interaction with populations to the
east and the northeast (Haury 1976:328).

The presence of marine shell indicates knowledge of people and places
to the south and west. This may be an ancient connection, as the Archaic
period people traded in the same dominant species of shell used by the
Hohokam (A. Howard 1987). The early use of turquoise and, inferentially,
shell mosaic, the incising of pottery, and the plaza-oriented plans of the early
ceramic horizon village sites suggest other connections with the south. The
widespread use of quartered design fields as decoration on pottery reflects
knowledge of the ancient world-quarters cosmological concepts of Mesoamerica (Kelley 1966; DiPeso 1974). This appearance may correlate with the
transmission of new varieties of agricultural crops and associated ceremonial
knowledge (Kelley 1966:102). Cotton and beans probably became established
crops among the Hohokam during the Vahki phase and the subsequent red-
on-gray horizon (Haury 1976; Fish et al. 1987; Gasser and Kwiatkowski, this
volume).

Another well-documented Hohokam tradition is the production and ceremonial use of clay figurines. While crude clay human figurines have been
reported from late Archaic contexts (Huckell 1984a), the use of figurines becomes greatly accelerated during the Vahki phase. Over 1,000 human figurines
were recovered from the site of Snaketown (Haury 1976:255). Approximately
90 percent of these date between the Vahki and Snaketown phases, leading
Wilcox (Wilcox 1987a:154) to label the Pioneer period as the age of the figurine.
It is clear, however, that figurines remain an important component of Hohokam ritual through the Colonial and mid-Sedentary periods.

Haury has suggested that the figurines could represent a cult associated
with agriculture. The presence of sexual characteristics, including pregnant
females (Fig. 6.4; Haury 1976:357) and infants, would suggest in interest in
fertility. Wilcox has argued that the figurines represent a form of ancestor
worship, and that they were possibly associated with a ritual ball game (Wilcox
and Sternberg 1983). Hohokam figurines were made in a wide variety of
forms and sizes, complete with a range of posture, costume, and ornamentation. Thomas and King (1985) have described several remarkable figurine
assemblages dating to the Colonial period. Through detailed analysis of fig-

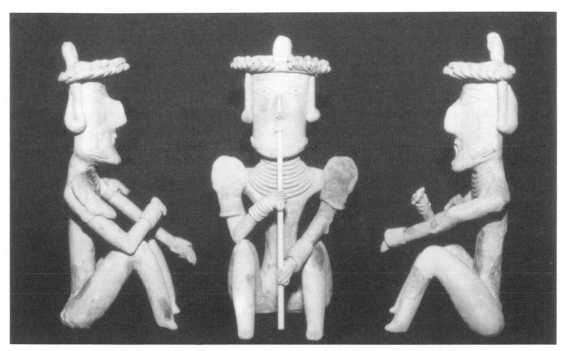

Figure 6.4    *Restored early Colonial period Hohokam fired clay figurines. Figurines are approximately 16 cm high. (Photo courtesy of Matt Thomas and Barbara Moulard.)*

urine parts and accompanying items (including household furniture and architectural elements), they argue that the figurines represent an ideological complex associated with the cremation ritual, having rebirth and productivity as embedded themes. Because Hohokam figurines undergo changes in style as well as a significant change in context of discovery between the Pioneer and later periods (trash versus cremation), it is entirely possible that they also underwent concomitant changes in function and ritual contexts through time.

While other southwestern populations made figurines, the Hohokam are unique in the sheer numbers, styles, and variety involved. To this extent, they again reflect Mesoamerican affinity, suggesting that shared religious and ceremonial belief systems were most likely involved (Kelley 1966:101). Comparisons have been made with the activity scenes found in the west Mexican figurine tradition (Thomas and King 1985:729; Haury 1976). Similarities to figurines of the Chupicuaro culture exist, including the use of headdresses, ear-plugs, elongated heads with enhanced eyes, arm pads, jewelry, and painted body decoration (Porter-Weaver 1981, plate 3c). For that matter, similarities also exist among Hohokam figurines and those recovered from the Valley of Mexico and the Gulf Coast (McGregor 1965:153; Ekholm 1944).

Much discussion has focused on the transmission mechanisms of these materials and concepts between the Hohokam and populations to the south. While some have proposed the movement of Mesoamerican populations into southern Arizona (Gladwin 1948; DiPeso 1956; Schroeder 1966; Haury 1976), others speak of transient contacts with traders (Doyel 1980) or contacts directed by organized traders (Schroeder 1966, 1981; Kelley 1980; DiPeso 1974). The presence of new crop varieties, associated ceremonial knowledge, brightly plumed birds (Haury 1976:346–347), and other items suggests that more than transient contacts were involved. It is possible that Mesoamerican-based trading parties were operating within the southern fringes of the American Southwest (the northern frontier of Mesoamerica) by A.D. 300, and that these traders acted as "cultural mediators" between the Hohokam and more advanced populations to the south (Weigand et al. 1977; Pailes 1988).

## COLONIAL AND SEDENTARY PERIODS: A.D. 600–1050

### EMERGING COMPLEXITY: A.D. 600–700

Events of the red-on-gray horizon soon culminated in fundamental changes in the structure of Hohokam society. The Snaketown phase witnessed an impressive number of "firsts," best known from the site of Snaketown. Here, the first trash mounds and the first capped, flat-topped mounds appear (Mound 40), along with evidence of a house cluster–courtyard residential pattern (Haury 1976:81; Wilcox et al. 1981:204). Decorated pottery is transformed from the dull red-on-gray into a light colored, red-on-buff ware, while vessel shapes and design styles show more diversity. Cremation is established as the preferred form of burial, and the death ritual became clearly associated with ornate stone palettes, censers, and figurines (Haury 1976). One loss during the Snaketown phase should be noted: the LSC houses were no longer constructed, suggesting that large group events had now moved to exterior plaza and mound areas (large houses did reappear after 900, but their frequency and function remain problematic). Domestic houses seem to increase in size, perhaps indicating a need for more storage space or that family size was growing due to increased sedentism (Cable and Doyel 1985, 1987a).

It is probable that irrigation was a strong factor in reducing residential mobility during the Snaketown phase. The stability of agricultural field locations and the labor costs associated with canal construction and maintenance stimulated more cooperation and economic ties among family groups. A similar process is documented for the Gila Pima-Maricopa during the nineteenth century as they came to rely more on irrigation (Hackenberg 1961).

Regionally, deployment of irrigation technology opened new agricultural lands on the terraces removed from the river floodplains (Wilcox and Shenk 1977; Greenwald and Ciolek-Torrello 1987). In the Salt River Valley, irrigation

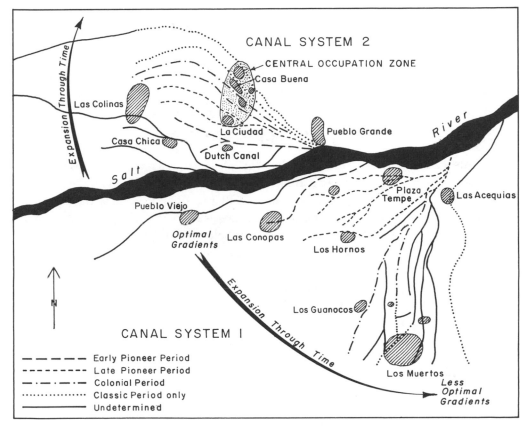

Figure 6.5    *Partial map of canal systems in the Salt River Valley showing*
*expansion away from the river over time. (Modified from map*
*by J. Howard 1988, fig. 5.13.)*

features and villages were at first located near the river and then expanded
through time (Fig. 6.5; Cable and Doyel 1985; J. Howard 1988). Small villages
were also founded in outlying regions (Doyel 1980; Doyel and Elson 1985;
Haury 1932; Masse 1980a, 1980b; Weed 1972).

The innovations dating to the Snaketown phase had lasting effects on the
Hohokam. Canal irrigation, large sedentary villages, increased ritual elaboration, and population growth and segmentation all become apparent in the
archaeological record, suggesting a time of rapid cultural change and growing
cultural complexity. Due to poor temporal control, it is difficult to identify a
"prime mover" if such existed; it is likely that these and other forces were
linked in complex feedback relationships (Cable and Doyel 1985:300–303). The
earlier existence of the LSC houses, representative of a decision-making authority, combined with increasing technological knowledge, are of interest in
this regard.

Snaketown phase subsistence, settlement, and society were more similar to later than to earlier phases, and it now appears preferable to consider the Snaketown phase as the *real* beginning of the Colonial period. The new pottery styles, cremation ritual complex, courtyard–house cluster living pattern, ornate handicrafts, mound construction, and other aspects of Snaketown phase culture bespeak of a growing communal identity markedly different from other southwestern cultural traditions.

## THE HOHOKAM VILLAGE: SITE STRUCTURE

Interest in the structure of Hohokam village sites is apparent from the earliest phases of research (Cushing 1890; Fewkes 1909, 1912; Gladwin et al. 1937). For a period of 40 years between 1940 and 1980, little new data were added, with several notable exceptions (Hayden 1957; Wasley and Johnson 1965). In 1985, the first-ever symposium was held on the structure of Hohokam villages (Doyel 1987a); other studies have also become available (Wilcox et al. 1981; Teague and Crown 1983–1984; Sires 1985; Rice 1984, 1987; J. Howard 1982, 1985; Gregory 1983; Henderson 1987).

While recognizing several land-use patterns such as ceremonial, plaza, and habitation areas, Haury felt that Hohokam villages were structured much like the sprawling rancherias recorded among the historic Pima of the area. He did observe clustering of some houses at Snaketown, but cites problems in establishing "simultaneous occupancy" of the structures (Haury 1976:77). In a subsequent study of the site, Wilcox not only suggested the presence of clusters of houses but also observed that the site as a whole retained a basic pattern of organization throughout the sequence (Wilcox et al. 1981).

Data from additional sites were needed to test this newly developing model of village structure. Excavations along the Salt-Gila Aqueduct doubled the inventory from Snaketown, yielding 196 architectural features from 18 sites (Sires 1985:117). Other recent excavations have greatly increased the sample size and distribution of architectural features found in Hohokam village sites (Doyel 1987a).

It is now established that size, shape, orientation, and construction of Hohokam pre-Classic period pithouses found at village sites exhibit patterning within a definable range. Groups of individual houses were found to be clustered around exterior courtyards (or simply yards). These house groups tended to maintain their integrity over time as houses were added or abandoned (Wilcox et al. 1981; J. Howard 1982, 1985). Most houses were utilized for multiple purposes including storage and habitation, while some specialized structures were also present (Huntington 1986; Rice 1987), which may be related to exchange or to other factors such as redistribution (Baar 1982).

Courtyard groups often had communal cooking ovens (*hornos*), trash mounds, and cemeteries associated. It is estimated that each courtyard-house group contained between 16 and 20 individuals (Wilcox et al. 1981:180; Gregory 1983:158). Clusters of these courtyard-house groups deployed around an outside activity area or plaza containing trash areas, ovens, and cemeteries are referred to as village segments (J. Howard 1982) and may represent corporate descent groups. Hohokam villages are composed of repeated clusters of such village segments that are spatially separated from other such units. At large villages, these units are often located around a great central plaza containing public architectural features (Fig. 6.6).

Hohokam villages of the A.D. 600–1050 time period probably contained several hundred individuals, while large sites such as Snaketown may have contained between 500 (Wilcox 1987a:155, 160) and 2,000 people (Haury 1976:77). Research has demonstrated that while many patterns have been identified in Hohokam village sites, it should be remembered that not all villages are expected to exhibit identical patterns or sequences. Each Hohokam community had its own developmental history and should be considered as a unique set of temporal and historical events within a regional context (Gregory and Nials 1985).

## CEREMONY AND SYMBOL

By the Gila Butte phase, ballcourts were constructed at numerous village sites, both within and outside of the Phoenix Basin (Doyel 1980; Wilcox and Sternberg 1983). The large court at Snaketown could have accommodated 500 people on its massive embankments, which measure 5 m in height and over 60 m in length, representing the largest ballcourt ever constructed by the Hohokam (Wilcox 1987a:154). By A.D. 1050, over 225 ballcourts are known to have been constructed, with 40 percent of them located within the Phoenix Basin (Wilcox 1985a). The number and size of courts varied from village to village, suggesting a hierarchical structure within the system. The distribution of ballcourts and Hohokam artifacts documents expansion of the system as well as probable changes in the regional interaction network through time (Doyel 1980; Wilcox and Sternberg 1983). New designs reflective of Mesoamerican styles appeared on Gila Butte Red-on-buff pottery (Kelley 1966). The figurine tradition became transformed by the Santa Cruz phase, indicating changes in ritual practices, perhaps due to increased participation in new religious cults emanating from central Mexico, similar but perhaps not identical to those described by DiPeso (1974).

The construction of ballcourts along with the continued use of capped mounds reflects greater emphasis on public architecture and group ceremonialism. The cremation ritual became even more elaborate, while increasing numbers of discrete cemetery areas in sites indicate greater population segmentation. A new ceremony, focusing on the production of saguaro wine (historically associated with rain-making), appears near a mound group at Snaketown and continues into the Classic period (Haury 1976; Doyel 1974, 1981; Underhill 1946). These developments underscore the continuing elab-

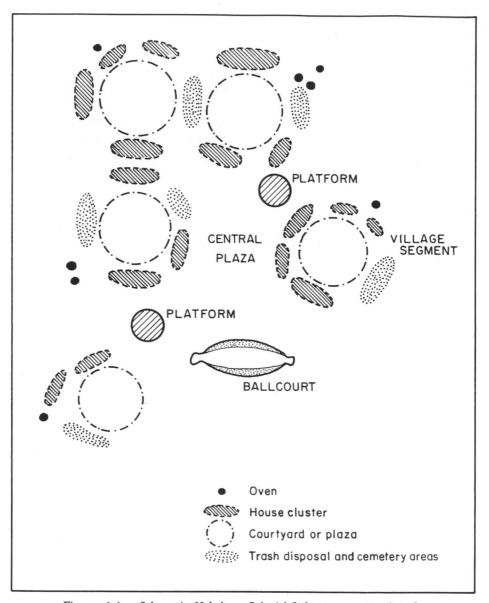

Figure 6.6    *Schematic Hohokam Colonial-Sedentary community plan*
*showing village segments and architectural features. (Mod-*
*ified from map by J. Howard 1988, Fig. 5.13.)*

oration of Hohokam ceremonialism, suggesting the emergence of new positions of power and authority.

During this period, Snaketown attained a concentric site structure, consisting of a ring of mounds and ballcourts surrounding the ancient great
central plaza (Fig. 6.7; Wilcox and Sternberg 1983; Wilcox 1987a). The presence

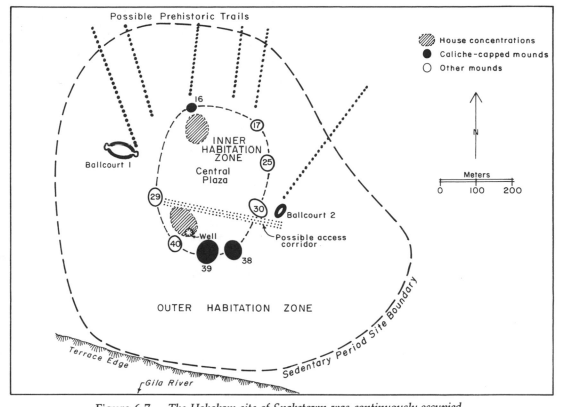

Figure 6.7    *The Hohokam site of Snaketown was continuously occupied*
*from the time of Christ to* A.D. *1075. By the Sacaton phase,*
*the site exhibited a concentric pattern of spatial relationships*
*between mounds, ballcourts, habitation units, and plaza areas.*
*(Modified from a map in Wilcox, McGuire, and Sternberg*
*1981, fig. 5.5.)*

of variable cremation assemblages, restricted distributions of exotic artifacts, and the presence of large houses located in the central site area, some of them used to store objects of wealth, further underscores the presence of a privileged group of individuals (Doyel 1981, 1988a; Nelson 1986). It is probable that other regional centers, such as the Grewe site, Pueblo Grande, Las Colinas, Cashion, and the Gatlin site, had developed similar village plans. Large village sites with ballcourts also became evenly spaced within the Phoenix Basin, a pattern that survived into the Classic period (Wilcox 1979; Nicholas and Neitzel 1983; Fish and Fish, this volume).

## EXCHANGE AND INTERACTION

Hohokam interaction networks reach their greatest distributions during the Colonial and Sedentary periods (Crown, this volume; Doyel 1979, 1988a).

The amount and diversity of resource materials present document active local, regional, and interregional exchange networks. Nonlocal resource materials include mosaic mirrors, shell, and copper bells from Mesoamerica, obsidian, chert, quartz, and other stone for the production of stylized projectile points and blades, andesite and quartz-basalt for ground stone tools, exotic pottery from all four directions, but especially from the north, and numerous exotic materials used for jewelry, pigment, and ceremonial purposes (Doyel 1987b, 1988a, 1989; Haury 1976; Gladwin et al. 1937; Crown 1985). Thousands of worked shell artifacts and finely made projectile points, along with stylized stone palettes, censers, effigies, and evidence for ceramic and ground stone tool production, argue for the presence of craft specialists at some regional centers and outlying resource locations (Crabtree 1973; Doyel 1988a; Doyel and Elson 1985; Haury 1976; A. Howard 1985b).

Interregional contacts with other populations included the Kayenta and Cibola Anasazi, Mountain and Mimbres Mogollon, Dragoon, Trincheras, Yuman, and coastal California groups (Crown 1985; Doyel 1988a). It is probable that between A.D. 900 and 1050, the Hohokam and Chaco regional systems represented overlapping interaction spheres along the Little Colorado River between Flagstaff and Holbrook (Doyel 1987b; Fowler et al. 1987). Shell has been found in Kayenta, Chaco, and Mogollon sites, along with stone palettes and other Hohokam artifacts; perhaps cotton textiles, agave products, lac, pigments, and other desert resources were also involved in Hohokam exchange networks.

The Hohokam ballcourt system was instrumental in orchestrating and regulating both local and long-distance exchange and served as a primary source of horizontal social integration within the regional system. Ballcourts have also been found in non-Hohokam sites from Wupatki to Point of Pines, in some cases in association with cremation burials (Doyel 1981; Wilcox and Sternberg 1983), suggesting that attempts were made to introduce new socioreligious concepts to non-Hohokam populations. Some interregional exchange activities were sponsored by elites as a way of acquiring wealth to increase their status and power among various reference groups, as indicated by the rich burials at Snaketown, Gatlin, Grewe, and other sites in the Phoenix Basin (Nelson 1986).

The dynamics of regional expansion during this time period require additional study. While the Gladwinian model (Wilcox 1979) postulated the movement of Hohokam populations out from the Phoenix Basin during the Colonial period, it remains difficult in specific cases to ascertain whether people are actually moving or whether the process reflects the deployment of an economic system across multiple local group territories. The replication of Hohokam material culture and architecture at sites such as Roosevelt 9:6 (Haury 1932) and in the San Carlos area (Mitchell 1986:25–40) strongly supports population movement; other assemblages from Flagstaff and the Upper Verde Valley, east along the Mogollon Rim and into southeastern Arizona could represent frontier or cultural contact situations with non-Hohokam populations (DiPeso 1956; Doyel 1984a:159, 162); specialized functions such as mining or other resource acquisition could be involved in these cases.

# CLASSIC PERIOD: A.D. 1050–1400

## VILLAGE PATTERNS

Between A.D. 1050 and 1100, Hohokam architectural and village settlement patterns began a transition to Classic period forms, wherein variation on several themes was the rule. Domestic architecture consisted of both above-ground and pithouse forms, and greater use of post-reinforced and solid adobe wall construction styles was characteristic of this period. Construction of massive platform mounds probably had begun by this time, as seen in the Gatlin site mound (Gregory 1987). Also occurring were an increase in the production of red ware pottery, a decrease in the production of red-on-buff pottery, an emphasis on urn cremation burial, a decrease in the frequency of ornate artifacts, and a weakening of the regional ballcourt system. This phase remains poorly documented, but has been reported from Pueblo Grande, Las Colinas, and Sacaton 9:6 (Hayden 1957; Gregory and Heathington 1986; Gladwin 1957; DiPeso 1974). The term "Santan phase" suggested by past researchers is utilized herein for this transitional phase, which contains elements of both the earlier Sacaton and the later Soho phase patterns.

During the Soho phase (A.D. 1175–1300), villages consisted of clusters of houses and mounds, often surrounded by rectangular-shaped walled enclosures made of adobe called compounds (Fewkes 1912; Haury 1945).The compound enclosure may have derived from the palisaded structures surrounding earlier platform mounds, or from a need to demarcate social space more clearly. Pithouses and surface structures built with adobe, wood, and stone were constructed (Doyel 1974). Sires (1987:173) has proposed a developmental model that outlines the transition from clusters of pithouses to compounds containing plazas (courtyards), pithouses, and surface structures. While variation exists, the number of houses within a compound is often similar to the number of pithouses in the earlier courtyard pattern, suggesting some organizational continuity. Most, if not all, of the massive-walled platform mounds reached their maximum size during this phase.

Civano phase (A.D. 1300–1400) village and architectural patterns basically represent elaborations on the themes defined during the Soho phase. Wall construction became more massive, contiguous rooms became common, and multistoried buildings were constructed. More functional differentiation is seen at some sites, such as at Escalante, where storage, habitation, and ceremonial rooms have been identified (Doyel 1974, 1981). Central site compounds containing mounds, such as at Las Colinas and Pueblo Grande, appear to

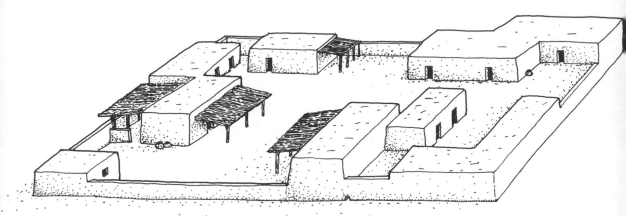

Figure 6.8    *Many Classic period villages consisted of from one to twenty walled compounds. This reconstruction of a compound shows an arrangement of house units, porch-ramadas, and small courtyard areas. (Modified from a drawing by Ben Mixon in S. Baar 1982, fig. 8.)*

have been remodeled and expanded on multiple occasions, with mound enlargement, resurfacing, and new compound construction being identifiable goals. The culmination of the Classic period platform mound architectural tradition can be seen in the still-standing Casa Grande, a four-story structure, the basal floor of which is a platform mound; a similar structure was excavated by Cushing at Pueblo Grande (Wilcox and Shenk 1977; Wilcox and Doyel 1985; Doyel 1987c). Most Hohokam of the Civano phase, however, did not live in big houses or on mounds, or perhaps even in compounds, and a wide range of domestic architectural patterns has been documented (Fig. 6.8; Sires 1985; J. Howard 1988; Baar 1982).

Clusters of sites forming communities continue into the Classic period. Settlement variation increases and becomes more hierarchical in nature, with at least four to five different levels represented (Doyel 1980:37). Classic period villages can be large in size, containing up to 30 compounds, such as Los Muertos (Haury 1945) and Casa Grande (Wilcox and Shenk 1977), or they can be quite small, such as Escalante (Doyel 1974, 1981; Gregory 1987). The population at Escalante was estimated to be around 100 people, while Los Muertos may have had a population approaching 1,000 people (Haury 1976; Wilcox et al. 1981).

## CEREMONY AND SYMBOL

The Classic period witnessed new directions in ceremony and symbol, including new forms of architecture, burial pattern, and ceramics. After A.D. 1050, much of the highly ornate material culture of the Hohokam disappeared,

including the carved stone and modeled clay effigy forms, the stylized ceremonial projectile points, the pallete-censer complex, and other handicrafts
(Doyel 1980). The rejection of these traditional ceremonial items further underscores the changing patterns of ceremony and symbol. This change is also
represented by the shift from ballcourts to platform mounds as a dominant
theme in monumental architecture. Earlier forms of capped mounds and
artificial platform mounds are present during the era of the ballcourt; thus
the platform mound can be seen to have undergone numerous phases of
development (Doyel 1974:175–176). The ballcourt system may have met a
more abrupt demise between A.D. 1050 and 1200. For a while, however, the
ballcourt and platform mound features appear to have overlapped in time as
aspects of late Sedentary to early Classic Hohokam ceremonial life (Gregory
1987).

The Soho phase was the era of platform mound and compound construction. Some earlier mounds, such as Mound 8 at Las Colinas, were enclosed
by massive rectangular-shaped adobe walls, a technique that characterizes all
known platform mound construction after A.D. 1200 (Gregory 1987:188). The
two largest mounds, Mesa Grande and Pueblo Grande, were indeed massive,
measuring 100 m by 50 m and containing 35,000 cu m of fill. Others, such as
Escalante, were much smaller and equal in size to earlier mounds such as
Gatlin with approximately 2,000 cu m of fill. Initially, these mounds were
ceremonial in function and contained only limited evidence of surface architecture. The mound surface at Escalante first contained a single structure
represented by a Sacaton phase pithouse floor plan (Doyel 1974). The mound
surfaces were probably used for ceremonial dances, while the structures were
used for storage of ritual objects; limited habitation may also have occurred.
Similar findings are reported from Pueblo Grande (Hayden 1957) and La
Ciudad (Wilcox 1987b).

Between A.D. 1250–1325, the function of the mounds became residential,
with numerous adobe-walled rooms built on the mound surfaces (Doyel 1974;
Gregory 1987), suggesting a consolidation of power on the part of the local
elites. The remaining populations were housed in off-mound compounds and
in outlying units. This pattern culminated in the construction of the Casa
Grande around A.D. 1325 (Wilcox and Shenk 1977; Long et al. 1987). Wilcox
(1987a) has argued that the Casa Grande was probably used as an elite residence wherein astronomical observations could be made, suggesting further
elaboration of the Hohokam calendrical system. He has also noted that the
village of Casa Grande, like Snaketown, retained a concentric settlement plan,
with various compounds located around the great central compound containing the Casa Grande; a similar village plan was present at Los Muertos
(Fig. 6.9). Other large villages, however, such as those along the Salt River
in Phoenix, do not always reveal this concentric structure but appear to be
more influenced by the structure of the irrigation systems (Gregory and Nials
1985).

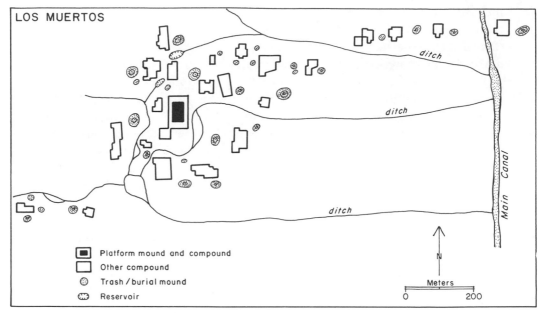

Figure 6.9    *Some Classic period sites still exhibit the concentric settlement*
             *plan observed in pre-Classic sites such as Snaketown. The*
             *large village of Los Muertos shows this pattern of compounds*
             *around a central compound containing a large mound, while*
             *other compounds were situated along a canal entering the*
             *village. (Modified from maps by E. Haury 1945, fig. 2, and*
             *D. Gregory 1987, fig. 8.)*

Several inhumation burials were found at Snaketown along with the more numerous cremation burials dating to the Sacaton phase (Haury 1976). These burials presage the inhumation (noncremation) burials, which increase in frequency during the Soho phase of the Classic period. In fact, all of the Soho phase burials recovered from the Escalante Ruin Group were inhumations (Doyel 1974), while variable patterns are reported from other sites (Hayden 1957; Johnson 1964). Associated with these burials was a new type of polished, slipped, and smudged interior pottery called Gila Red (Schroeder 1940, 1952; Haury 1945). This smudged and polished red pottery probably developed from the unsmudged red and smudged plain ware of the pre-A.D. 1050 horizon (Abbott 1983; Doyel 1974, 1980). Cremation also continues to be practiced throughout the Classic period, often occurring in variable assemblages with inhumations (Fink 1988a). It is my opinion that these variable burial patterns symbolize the breakdown of traditional practices and the presence of competing belief systems and shifting preferences, rather than being uniformly reflective of status and role differentiation. Changing perceptions about the death ritual were clearly a part of the Sedentary to Classic transition (Doyel 1981; Wilcox and Sternberg 1983), and continued to remain in flux throughout the Classic and into the protohistoric periods.

## EXCHANGE AND INTERACTION

Current evidence suggests that Classic period exchange systems were active but variable on a regional level; some networks became truncated while others were reorganized (Doyel 1988a). Ground stone tools made of imported (New River?) andesite and quartz basalt still accounted for 25 percent of the Las Colinas ground stone assemblage (Doyel and Elson 1985). Obsidian becomes more common (Bostwick and Shackley 1987; Teague and Crown 1984, vol. 9). Trade networks for shell acquisition were reorganized, and some villages such as Pueblo Grande became production centers for shell artifacts (A. Howard 1985b). A variety of exotic minerals were still acquired (Doyel 1987b). Tabular knives greatly increase in frequency due to their use in processing agave; these knives and stone axes were probably made at a limited number of sites and then circulated through the system.

Intrusive ceramics also reflect changes in regional interaction. It should be recognized that exotic pottery was *never* common in the Hohokam region. Of 2,500,000 sherds recovered from numerous Hohokam sites, only 2,172 (0.0009 percent) were non-Hohokam trade sherds (Doyel 1989). My recent reanalysis of the trade pottery at Pueblo Grande (excluding the Salado polychromes) suggests that a trade ware vessel entered the village on an average of once every seven years between A.D. 700 and 1400. At the same time, however, 100 ceramic types from numerous areas have been identified, indicating that many different traditions were represented.

Crown (1985, 1987:158) has proposed that the major river systems in south-central Arizona acted as boundaries to interregional ceramic exchange. Recent analysis of a larger sample demonstrates this not to be the case (Doyel 1988a, 1989). In a pattern nearly identical to some Salt River Valley sites, Snaketown was receiving a variety of Tusayan-Kayenta pottery dating between 700 and 1050. Snaketown, however, does not contain temporally later types, such as Tusayan Black-on-red, Sosi Black-on-white, or Holbrook Black-on-white, all of which are common at Las Colinas and Pueblo Grande in the Salt River Valley. These data indicate that Snaketown was abandoned around A.D. 1050 or shortly thereafter, a date supported by the low frequency of red ware recovered and by a recent reanalysis of archaeomagnetic dates (Eighmy and Doyel 1987). The absence of Kayenta Polychrome and Kayenta Black-on-white in the Salt River Valley further suggests that Hohokam connections with the Verde Valley and Kayenta areas underwent alteration between A.D. 1250 and 1300 (Schroeder 1952). The near absence of widely traded pottery types dating between A.D. 1150 and 1300, such as Tularosa Black-on-white and St. John's

Polychrome, further suggests a reduction in interregional trade during the Soho phase.

The Civano phase witnessed additional changes in ceramic interaction patterns. Jeddito Black-on-yellow, Salado polychromes, and Tanque Verde Red-on-brown became popular; the last two types may have been manufactured in the Phoenix Basin (Crown and Bishop 1986; Doyel and Haury 1976). Local variation appears to have been present, however, as White Mountain Red Ware and corrugated brown ware are present at Pueblo Grande (Doyel 1989). None of these types are common as burial offerings, which are primarily plain and red wares (Abbott 1983; Doyel 1974). These data reveal an interesting change, since intrusive pottery vessels predating A.D. 1100 are almost always associated with burials at large village sites.

Prior to the Classic period, Hohokam exchange systems are thought to have been associated with the ballcourt system (Doyel 1981, 1988a; Wilcox and Sternberg 1983; Wilcox 1987a). Since this system became inoperative by or before A.D. 1200, exchange systems must have been restructured during the later phases of the Classic period. It is probable that much of the interregional exchange of exotic products, such as shell, minerals, and some of the pottery, was controlled by the occupants of the platform mounds, but more research is needed to clarify these issues (Doyel 1988a; Teague and Crown 1984; Wilcox 1987b).

Regional dynamics outside the Phoenix Basin between 1050 and 1300 are unclear. Numerous local phases have been documented in the Tonto, Verde, Tucson, San Pedro, Santa Cruz, and other areas, suggesting marked localization of cultural patterns (Doyel 1981). It is likely that ritual and economic ties with these areas became severed or altered at this time, leaving the Phoenix Basin somewhat circumscribed. Competition over resources may have led to warfare as indicated by local depopulation (New River–Cave Creek) and the construction of hilltop boulder sites throughout the region (Spoerl and Gumerman 1984; Wilcox 1985b).

An argument can be made for expansion of the Hohokam interaction sphere during the Civano phase. Platform mound communities appear in the Tonto Basin, Santa Cruz, Papagueria, and San Pedro drainages by A.D. 1300 (Hayden 1957; Doelle and Wallace 1988; Wood 1985). At the same time, ceramic evidence from the Salt River Valley suggests a sharp reduction in contacts with the Verde Valley and Kayenta regions (Schroeder 1952; Doyel 1988a). A question in need of additional research is: How were the fourteenth-century pueblos located between Flagstaff and Zuni acquiring considerable amounts of shell? While many of the forms appear similar to Hohokam examples (see Pilles 1987:10), the presence of macaws at these sites (rare in southern Arizona at this time) may suggest that the trade connection was east along the Mogollon Rim and south to Casas Grandes (DiPeso 1974). Alternatively, the Hohokam could have traded shell through the mound communities in the Tonto Basin and then north to the pueblo areas.

# RECAPITULATION: HOHOKAM CULTURE CHANGE IN THE PHOENIX BASIN

To summarize, a brief overview of the Phoenix Basin Hohokam sequence is presented, with some of the more salient hallmarks listed chronologically in Table 6.2. Some possible causes for the identified changes are also provided. It should be noted that little significance can be attached to variations in chronologies of 25 or even 50 years, due to the poor resolution of available dating techniques. This situation is positive, however, given that ten years ago most chronologies were concerned with centuries and not decades!

The Pioneer period (A.D. 1–600) includes four phases, during which time the semisedentary Archaic populations incorporated agriculture into their hunting and gathering economy. The basic technologies of water control, processing domesticated foodstuffs, architectural elaboration, and storage were developed. After a lengthy plain ware horizon, polished red ware and decorated pottery were manufactured. By the Vahki phase, the large communal/ceremonial (LSC) house system appeared, along with village plazas in the context of population growth and segmentation. A village-farming economy was present by the end of this period. Figurines were prominent components of the socioreligious system. Through a complex feedback process including improved technology and organizational change, the shift to agriculture placed the Hohokam on an intensification spiral that would last for a period of over 1,000 years.

Major innovations in social organization, ritual systems, the arts, and technology occurred during the Colonial and Sedentary periods (A.D. 600–1050). The earlier phases (Snaketown-Gila Butte) witnessed the development of large settled villages and an evolving cultural identity including complex architectural and ritual systems and a new style of decorated pottery. The development of irrigation agriculture placed a premium on labor, which encouraged an increased birthrate and the inflow of labor, as the system expanded beyond the Phoenix Basin through a network of ballcourt communities. Arts and crafts industries flourished through the development of craft specialization, encouraged by village leaders who by now had developed an elite sphere of interaction, as illustrated by the elaborate cremation burials and architectural developments at numerous sites. Villages were evenly spaced along the major river systems due to economic and personnel flow innovations. Many of the canals in the Salt River Valley became consolidated, including the Pueblo Grande–La Ciudad–Las Colinas megacommunity (System Two). Some settlements were strategically located relative to trade routes, such as Gatlin, Snaketown, Cashion, Azatlan, and Hodges (Doyel 1988a). The Hohokam interaction sphere reached its maximum expansion during this period and included ties with Chaco Canyon to the north and Mesoamerica to the south. Perhaps the reorganization and dispersion occurring in some

Table 6.2    *Diachronic Listing of Developmental Characteristics for the Phoenix Basin Hohokam*

| Period | Date | Phase | Characteristics | Site |
|---|---|---|---|---|
| Reservation | 1870 | | Variable architecture, ki, sandwich adobe, and wood frame; village and rural settlement; reduced agriculture, wage labor; population dislocation. | Sacaton Santan Olberg Maricopa |
| | 1750 | Blackwater | Bachi phase plus wheat and other introduced crops; horses, cattle, and other introduced animals; metal implements; nucleated (defensive) villages; irrigation; extensive trade, slave raiding. | Casa Blanca to Casa Grande Ruins area |
| | 1450 | Bachi | Shallow pit houses, round house or ki?; red ware; dispersed rancheria settlement pattern; mixed subsistence patterns; Salt River Valley depopulated. | Picacho area Batki |
| Post-Classic | 1400 | Polvoron | Shallow pit houses, red ware and polychrome; obsidian; irrigation and other farming techniques utilized. | Las Colinas Casa Buena Grand Canal El Polvoron Brady Wash |
| | 1300 | Civano | Big houses, mounds occupied, polychrome pottery, reduced buff ware, large communities, specialization. | Los Muertos Casa Grande Pueblo Grande Mesa Grande |
| | 1200 | | Compound architecture, increased red ware, reduced buff ware, extended burials and cremation, mounds, reduced trade, system reorganization. | Escalante Sites Marana |
| | 1150 | Soho | | |
| | 1100 | | Platform mounds; transitional architecture (pithouse and adobe-walled houses); reduced buff ware, increased red ware; | Pueblo Grande Sacaton 9:6 Las Colinas |

*(continued)*

Mesoamerican states after A.D. 600 can in some way be related to the elaboration of Hohokam sociocultural patterns occurring in the Colonial period and early Sedentary periods.

After A.D. 1050, a number of changes signal the coming of a new era, symbolized by the abandonment of Snaketown and other ancestral sites. Platform mounds were constructed in numerous communities and red ware pottery production increased while buff ware pottery decreased. Domestic architecture underwent a transition but included large pithouses and pit-

Table 6.2   *continued*

| Period | Date | Phase | Characteristics | Site |
|---|---|---|---|---|
| Classic | 1050 | Santan | new ritual systems; defensive sites; variable burial pattern; reduction in craft arts. | |
| | 1000 | Sacaton | Formal village plans; early platform mounds; some canals consolidated; interregional exchange, maximum regional system expansion. | Snaketown Gatlin Las Colinas Cashion |
| Sedentary | 900 | | | Azatlan |
| | 800 | Santa Cruz | Craft specialization and ritual elaboration; agricultural intensification; some canals consolidated. | Citrus Beardsley Canal Pueblo Grande La Ciudad Las Canopas |
| | 700 | Gila Butte | Ballcourts; population growth; expansion. | Snaketown Grewe Buttes Dam Site |
| Colonial | 600 | Snaketown | Large villages; irrigation; cremation; buff ware, evolving ritual system, house clusters, capped mounds. | |
| | | Sweetwater | | Snaketown Pueblo Grande |
| | 500 | Estrella | Decorated pottery; evolving technology; beans, cotton. | |
| | 400 | | | |
| | 300 | Vahki | Communal houses, plazas; polished red ware; improved cultigens, diversion technology; shell and turquoise; trough metate and mano; small points; clay figurines. | Snaketown Pueblo Patricio Red Mountain |
| | 200 | | | |
| | 100 | | | |
| Pioneer | A.D. 1 | Red Mountain | Semisedentary; evolving technology; small houses; agriculture; large projectile points, shell jewelry, plain ware. | Snaketown Pueblo Patricio Red Mountain |

houses built partially of adobe as well as solid-walled structures. Less is presently known about this time period because of poor archaeological visibility and the vertical stratigraphy present in many mounds constructed after A.D. 1050. Urn cremation increased in frequency, but a variable pattern including inhumation may have been present. The arts and crafts industries underwent a reduction and reorientation, and the ballcourt system became inoperative by A.D. 1200. The cause or causes of the changes that occurred between A.D. 1050 and 1200 in the Hohokam region remain poorly understood, much like the seemingly simultaneous reorganization of the Chaco regional system located to the north. Environmental change, shifting trade and alliance networks, the severing of trade with Mesoamerica, and other explanations have been proposed.

By the Soho phase (A.D. 1175–1300), a pattern of massive platform mounds surrounded by compounds was present; riverine villages became clusters of compounds and house groups, indicating increasing social distance and a more hierarchical social system. Interregional trade was reorganized; shell, stone, and other utilitarian products survived while exotic pottery reduced in frequency. Specialized production of polished red ware continued to increase at the expense of buff ware, and red ware was usually associated with both inhumation and cremation burials. All of these events predate the arrival of the Salado polychrome series, which has an unexplained distribution restricted to the late phases of the Classic period. Given that the Paquime phase at Casas Grandes cannot be shown to predate A.D. 1275 (Dean and Ravesloot 1988), it is difficult to attribute the developments in the Phoenix Basin to this source. Intrusions by Toltec-related populations, decreased interregional interaction, and environmental change have been suggested to have occurred during this phase.

The Civano phase (A.D. 1300–1400) came on the heels of a long drought followed by massive flooding in the Phoenix Basin, as postulated by Nials, Gregory, and Graybill (1986). Behavior oriented towards social control through ritual elaboration and a concern for agricultural production resulted in the construction of the Casa Grande by struggling local elites. Increasingly restricted social space, increased storage space in some sites, the continued incorporation of some canal systems, and the hierarchical structure of settlement systems all suggest a pattern of increasing social differentiation. The platform mound-elite organizational system was soon truncated, however, marking the end of a long-standing cultural tradition.

Sires (1983, 1985) has recently described the Polvoron phase, which is thought to represent the latest documented prehistoric occupation of the Phoenix Basin. The assemblage found at the site of El Polvoron is known from several other localities in the region (see below); architectural assemblages deemphasize the use of adobe and consist of single-unit pithouses found in groups without enclosing compounds. High frequencies of Salado polychromes and red ware pottery are accompanied by Hopi yellow wares, red-on-brown wares, and low frequencies of buff ware. Marine shell is represented, and obsidian is common. A variable burial assemblage is documented. Irrigation may have been practiced at some sites. This phase is thought to be transitional between the Classic period and the less complex cultural patterns of the protohistoric period.

It could be argued that the Polvoron phase is little more than an updated version of the Bachi phase, suggested by the Gladwins over 50 years ago (Gladwin and Gladwin 1935:256–259). Unfortunately, the Polvoron phase con-

cept appears to have been hastily developed, as it mixes assemblages traditionally attributed to the Civano phase, such as those of the Escalante Ruin
and other materials. Nevertheless, given that Polvoron has been rapidly adopted
and utilized by numerous authors, the most realistic approach may be to
simply hope that subsequent research will clarify and better define the phase.

By creating a short phase for the immediately post-Classic period assemblages in the Phoenix Basin, it becomes possible to refine the Gladwins's
theoretical concept of the Bachi phase. The definitive attributes of this phase
are small, brush and "clay" houses, "degenerate" pottery, and a rancheria
settlement pattern. This seems to be a description of the Polvoron phase
without the vestiges of the Classic period, namely Salado polychromes, other
pottery types, and obsidian. The term Bachi phase is herein suggested for
the post-Classic occupation of the Phoenix Basin dating between the Polvoron
phase and the Spanish entrada (A.D. 1450–1750).

Several other post-Bachi phases are listed on Table 6.2, primarily to extend
the Phoenix Basin sequence into modern times. The Blackwater phase defines
that remarkable period of time (A.D. 1750–1870) after the coming of the Spanish when the Gila Pima began growing irrigated wheat and acquired horses.
Wheat provided the Pima a new and prolific winter crop, while the horse
played an integral role in the development of a highly integrated militaristic
society among the Pima to combat the invading Apache (Ezell 1983; Sheridan
1988; Doyel 1988b). The Blackwater phase, which will eventually be divisible
into smaller time units, ends when the Apache are quelled and the Mexican
and Anglo immigrants cut off the life-giving waters of the Gila River to the
Pima fields located to the west of Adamsville. The post-1870 period marks
the decline of agriculture among the Gila Pima. Socioeconomic reorganization
and strong acculturative pressures characteristic of the American reservation
system are introduced.

## REGIONAL DYNAMICS

### SYNCHRONIC VARIATION

The recognition of synchronic variation within subregional and local populations is critical to a more complete understanding of Hohokam prehistory.
It can be said that communities consisting of clustered settlements were present in the Phoenix Basin from the Colonial through the Classic periods. These
communities differed in both scale and economic organization. Synchronic
variation in subsistence practices (irrigation, flood water, or dry farming agriculture, gathering or hunting) has already been suggested. Adaptation to
environmental variation would predictably vary according to local resource
availability, group size, and the socioeconomic orientation of the population.

The organizational feature of a community may have been a ballcourt, an irrigation system, or a platform mound. All of these features possess the common feature of communal labor and cooperation. Community size and morphology also differed along a single drainage, as is clearly illustrated by the 1929 Turney map of the Salt River Valley (Gregory and Nials 1985). Most drainages contain site hierarchies, consisting of primary villages, hamlets, farmsteads, fieldhouses, and specialized resource extraction sites. Primary villages contain formal site plans, public or monumental architecture, residential units, and cemetery areas, while lesser villages may contain a small ballcourt and more vernacular architectural patterns, such as sites in the Buttes Dam and Painted Rocks Reservoir areas (Debowski et al. 1976; Wasley and Benham 1968; Wasley and Johnson 1965).

Numerous strategies were developed to adapt to the unsettled environmental and social conditions of the fourteenth century in the Phoenix Basin. Subsistence intensification and specialization occurred, as documented by extensive irrigation networks, rock pile farming systems, agave production sites, and cactus fruit gathering camps. In some areas, the size of communities was enlarged through time to increase diversity and facilitate distribution.

Numerous stone forts were constructed around (but few within) the Phoenix Basin, leading some to propose Hohokam hegemony over neighboring populations, while the structure and directionality of these defensive patterns has yet to be empirically determined (DiPeso 1956; Wilcox 1985a; Doelle and Wallace 1988; see Fish and Fish 1989 for further discussion). Judging from the variety and quantity of materials recovered from village sites, however, Hohokam exchange systems remained active throughout the sequence.

## SUBSISTENCE AND SETTLEMENT VARIATION: THREE EXAMPLES

The Salt River Valley represented one of the most densely populated regions in the American Southwest and also contained the largest irrigation system in aboriginal North America. Most irrigation systems contained more than one site cluster. While a valleywide level of organization has not been empirically identified, some form of supracommunity organization must have existed. The Salt River Valley communities were highly integrated and represent a specialized farming adaptation. Canal corridors were utilized to grow crops of agave, cholla, and other plant products to supplement variable yields of farm produce. High ratios of cactus and other desert resources found at riverine sites may also indicate the operation of food exchange or redistribution systems (Gasser and Kwiatkowski, this volume). Major flood events or other natural environmental processes such as soil salinization and water logging would have dramatic, if not catastrophic, effects on this adaptive strategy. The Salt River Hohokam may eventually be shown to have violated the "diversity promotes stability rule," which often dictated human survival in the arid Southwest. It remains a mystery why the Salt River Valley was depopulated, if not abandoned, at the time of the Spanish entrada.

Crown (1987) has described a different adaptive pattern for the Gila River Hohokam near Casa Grande Ruins. Here, due to the lower discharge rates, topographic and other variables, a more diversified adaptation was developed. Multivillage irrigation systems and regular site spacing were present, but the scale and the population of the Gila Valley system was much smaller. Agricultural strategies including irrigation, run-off, and dry farming were practiced, along with hunting and gathering. Natural catastrophies such as floods would have been buffered somewhat through this adaptive diversity.

Some communities in the Santa Cruz and San Pedro river valleys had developed alternative economic strategies. Higher average rainfall levels relative to the Phoenix Basin supported extensive rock pile dry farming systems in the San Pedro River Valley and neighboring drainages. The community of Marana to the west in the Santa Cruz drainage developed an adaptation based upon run-off agriculture and specialization in the production of agave and agave products. The large size of this community captured more diversity while balancing risk (Fish and Fish, this volume). Although ballcourts, a canal, and later a small platform mound were present at this community, the organization of the economy was not based upon irrigation. Furthermore, since the Santa Cruz and the San Pedro rivers derive from a different watershed than the Gila and Salt, they may not have been subjected to the same flood events proposed for the Phoenix Basin Hohokam. Nonetheless, Marana was abandoned by A.D. 1300 and local reorganization is evident.

## POPULATION

Even after the recent surge in fieldwork, quantitative data on regional population sizes remain lacking. This is due to problems inherent in the nature of Hohokam settlements, for example, pithouse architecture, dispersed residential patterns, and the changing use of space through time (Doyel 1980). Schroeder (1940:20) has stated that the maximum Salt River Valley population was between 80,000 and 200,000, based upon his estimates of available agricultural land. Haury (1976:356) has suggested a *total* Phoenix Basin population (including the Salt and Gila rivers) of under 60,000 for the Classic period and half this number for the Colonial-Sedentary population.

With an emphasis on sedentism and intensive agriculture, it is theoretically possible that the Phoenix Basin population could have doubled between A.D. 600 and 1300 (LeBlanc 1986:107). Given current site data, however, the doubling of the population between the Sedentary and Classic periods is questionable; population deployment as opposed to real growth may account for many of the observed changes. A constant growth curve would also be precluded by suggested impacts on agricultural production due to massive flooding and destruction of agricultural systems. If we assume that 45 platform

mound communities existed in the Phoenix Basin during the Classic period
and that these communities contained an average of 500 people (a figure I
cannot completely defend and is probably too high), the net result is 22,500.
If we double this figure to account for undiscovered and outlying sites, the
result is 45,000, or somewhat below Haury's openly speculative estimate of
60,000 for the Phoenix Basin. As stated elsewhere (Doyel 1980:39), I see no
compelling evidence for a significant increase in population between the Sedentary and Classic periods for the eastern Gila Basin, the work of Teague and
Crown notwithstanding (1984, vol. 9:150–152). Until some systematic quantitative work is accomplished, however, population dynamics will continue
to be a vexing problem in Hohokam studies.

## THE TRANSITION TO HISTORY

Like elsewhere in the American Southwest between A.D. 1350 and 1450,
numerous large villages in the Phoenix Basin were abandoned. Explanations
for the abandonment of the Hohokam villages include a variety of environmental (flood, soil salinization, deteriorating climate) and sociocultural causes
(internal warfare, cessation of trade, shifting centers of power, domination
by Casas Grandes). While DiPeso (1956, 1974) and more recently other scholars
(Reff 1988; Dobyns 1988) have attempted to extend the Civano phase beyond
A.D. 1600 in order for it to meet its demise through introduced European
diseases, there remains no reliable archaeological evidence to support this
claim (Doyel 1981:75–76, 1988b; Eighmy and McGuire 1988). Reasons other
than strictly external factors must be investigated for the fading of Civano
phase culture and other southwestern regional traditions by A.D. 1400.

While some scholars have doubted that a Hohokam-Pima continuum exists
(Doelle 1981; Masse 1981), at least three lines of investigation may suggest
otherwise. Recent excavations have demonstrated that simple brush and adobe-
covered structures represent the latest architectural features present at numerous sites in the Phoenix Basin dating to the late fourteenth and fifteenth
centuries, including Las Colinas (Hammack and Sullivan 1981), Pueblo Grande
and Casa Grande, Compound F (Hayden 1957), Casa Buena (J. Howard 1988),
Grand Canal Ruin (Mitchell 1988), and El Polvoron (Sires 1983). It now appears
that by A.D. 1400, the resident populations returned to less complex architectural, settlement, and economic patterns (Doyel 1981:78; Sires 1985). Excavations have also identified what appears to be overlapping architectural
traditions between the Hohokam and the Pima, including pithouses, ramadas,
and special function facilities (Doyel 1988b).

Numerous material and behavioral parallels can be identified that link
the Hohokam and the Pima, including but not limited to the use of council
houses, public plazas, ball games, similar ceramic types, and numerous subsistence practices (Haury 1976; Doyel 1981; Ezell 1963, 1983). Recent exca-

vations at late Classic period cemetery sites in Phoenix have revealed striking parallels in mortuary behavior between the Pima-Papago and the Hohokam (J. Howard 1988; Mitchell 1988). Similarities include seated burials, log cribs, open (not backfilled) burial pits, benches in pits, clustered burials, the use of hematite, the presence of personal possessions and food remains, and other historically documented traits (Russell 1975; Brew and Huckell 1987). These late Classic cemeteries have also revealed the use of both inhumation and cremation, a pattern consistent with historic records (Ezell 1963, 1983).

A key to understanding the transition to history in the Hohokam region resides in the issue of population reconstruction (Doelle 1981; Ezell 1983; Doyel 1988b). According to Haury (1976:356) and Ezell (1983:152), the early historic Pima population for the Phoenix Basin was between 3,000 and 5,000 people. If an estimate of between 30,000 and 60,000 is used for the Classic period, it is obvious that a significant population reduction occurred between A.D. 1400 and 1700. Population loss of this magnitude undoubtedly rendered disfunctional many of the density-dependent characteristics of earlier phases.

The process of population reduction in the Phoenix Basin during and after the Civano phase has not been adequately characterized. Was it a gradual process, much as it was elsewhere in the Southwest (LeBlanc 1986:122)? Can Pima legends regarding warfare and population dislocation at the end of the Classic period be verified through archaeological research (DiPeso 1956; Hayden 1987:322)? Fink (1988b) has recently suggested that the Hohokam may have been the victims of their own technology by transmitting infectious diseases through their systems of canals and reservoirs. While currently lacking empirical support, such a condition would surely have had a major impact on the dense, highly integrated communities in the Salt River Valley. Phoenix Basin populations may also have been further impacted by introduced European diseases carried unknowingly up the trade routes from Mesoamerica after A.D. 1525 (Riley 1987). By the time of the arrival of these new vectors, however, the Classic period was already history. These new diseases may have further reduced the resident populations prior to the coming of the Spanish (Ezell 1983). The contact period Pima pattern along the Gila River and in the Picacho Peak area, consisting of residential mobility, small villages containing brush structures, subsistence diversification, and deemphasis on stored crops, appears to represent an adaptation to a significant population reduction beginning during the late prehistoric period and continuing into historic times. Additional research should shed new light on these important historical issues.

## ACKNOWLEDGMENTS

I would like to express my appreciation to the Bureau of Reclamation and to the organizers for the opportunity to participate in the Amerind Foundation seminar and to the staff for their warm hospitality provided while there. While not necessarily representing their viewpoints, conversations with John Cable, Jeff Dean, Paul Fish, Emil Haury, Bob Gasser, Dave Gregory, Jerry Howard, Bruce Masse, and Dave Wilcox have influenced my thinking on various matters. Todd Bostwick and Thom Hulen provided valuable assistance during the production process. The City of Phoenix is acknowledged for administrative support.

# REFERENCES CITED

Abbott, David R.
1983    A Technological Assessment of Ceramic Variation in the Salt-Gila Aqueduct Area: Toward a Comprehensive Documentation of Hohokam Ceramics. In *Hohokam Archaeology Along the Salt-Gila Aqueduct, Central Arizona Project*, edited by L. S. Teague and P. L. Crown, pp. 3–118. Arizona State Museum Archaeological Series 150(8).
Baar, Sam
1982    Post-Sedentary Hohokam Architectural Units. Paper presented at the Annual Meeting of the Society for American Archaeology, Minneapolis.
Berry, Michael S.
1985    The Age of Maize in the Greater Southwest: A Critical Review. In *Prehistoric Food Production in North America*, edited by R. Ford, pp. 279–307. Anthropological Papers 75, Museum of Anthropology, The University of Michigan.
Boserup, Ester
1965    *The Conditions of Agricultural Growth*. Aldine, Chicago.
Bostwick, Todd, and M. Steven Shackley
1987    Settlement Strategies and Lithic Technology: An Examination of Variability in Hunter-Gatherer and Agriculturalist Chipped Stone Assemblages in the Sonoran Desert. Paper presented at the 1987 Hohokam Conference, Tempe.
Brew, Susan A., and Bruce B. Huckell
1987    A Protohistoric Piman Burial and a Consideration of Pima Burial Practices. *The Kiva* 52:163–191.
Cable, John S., K. S. Hoffman, D. E. Doyel, and F. Ritz (editors)
1985    *City of Phoenix, Archaeology of the Original Townsite: Block 24-East*. Soil Systems Publications in Archaeology 8. Phoenix.
Cable, John S., and David E. Doyel
1985    Hohokam Land-use Patterns along the Terraces of the Lower Salt River Valley: The Central Phoenix Project. In *Proceedings of the 1983 Hohokam Symposium*, edited by A. E. Dittert, Jr. and D. E. Dove, pp. 263–310. Arizona Archaeological Society Occasional Paper 2. Phoenix.
1987a   Pioneer Period Village Structure and Settlement Pattern in the Phoenix Basin. In *The Hohokam Village: Site Structure and Organization*, edited by D. E. Doyel, pp. 21–71. American Association of the Advancement of Science, Glenwood Springs, Colorado.

1987b The Archaic to Hohokam Transition: A View from the Pioneer Period. Paper presented at the 1987 Hohokam Conference, Tempe.

Castetter, E. F., and W. N. Bell
1951 *Yuman Indian Agriculture.* Inter-American Studies III, University of New Mexico Press, Albuquerque.

Crabtree, Don E.
1973 Experiments in Replicating Hohokam Points. *Tebiwa* 16(1):10–45.

Crown, Patricia L.
1985 Intrusive Ceramics and the Identification of Hohokam Exchange Networks. In *Proceedings of the 1983 Hohokam Conference,* edited by A. E. Dittert, Jr., and D. E. Dove, pp. 439–458. Arizona Archaeological Society Occasional Paper 2. Phoenix.
1987 Classic Period Hohokam Settlement and Land Use in the Casa Grande Ruins Area, Arizona. *Journal of Field Archaeology* 14:147–162.

Crown, Patricia L., and R. L. Bishop
1987 Convergence in Ceramic Manufacturing Traditions in the Late Prehistoric Southwest. Paper presented at the 52nd Annual Meeting of the Society for American Archaeology, Toronto.

Cushing, Frank H.
1890 Preliminary Notes on the Origin, Working Hypothesis, and Primary Researches of the Hemenway Southwestern Archaeological Expedition. *Congres International des Americanistes, Compte-rendu de la septieme session,* pp. 151–194. Berlin.

Dean, Jeffrey, and J. Ravesloot
1988 The Chronology of Cultural Interaction within the Gran Chichimeca. Paper presented at Charles C. DiPeso Retrospective, the Amerind Foundation, Dragoon. In press.

Debowski, Sharon S., A. George, R. Goddard, and D. Mullon
1976 *An Archaeological Survey of the Buttes Reservoir.* Arizona State Museum Archaeological Series 93. Tucson.

DiPeso, Charles C.
1956 *The Upper Pima of San Cayetano del Tumacacori: An Archaeo-Historical Reconstruction of the Ootam of Pimeria Alta.* The Amerind Foundation 7. Dragoon.
1974 *Casas Grandes: A Fallen Trading Center of the Gran Chichimeca.* The Amerind Foundation 9. Dragoon.

Dobyns, Henry F.
1988 Comments on Prehistoric to Historic Transitions. Paper presented at the Southwest Symposium, Tempe.

Doelle, William H.
1981 The Gila Pima in the Seventeenth Century. In *The Protohistoric Period in the North American Southwest,* A.D. *1450–1700,* edited by D. R. Wilcox and W. B. Masse, pp. 57–70. Anthropological Research Papers 24. Arizona State University, Tempe.
1985 *Excavations at the Valencia Site, a Pre-Classic Hohokam Village in the Southern Tucson Basin.* Institute for American Research Anthropological Papers 3. Tucson.

Doelle, William H., and Henry Wallace
1988 The Transition to History in Pimeria Alta. Paper presented at the Southwest Symposium, Tempe.

Doyel, David E.
   1974   *Excavations in the Escalante Ruin Group, Southern Arizona.* Arizona State Museum Archaeological Series 37. Tucson.
   1979   The Prehistoric Hohokam of the Arizona Desert. *American Scientist* 67:544–554.
   1980   Hohokam Social Organization and the Sedentary to Classic Transition. In *Current Issues in Hohokam Prehistory,* edited by D. E. Doyel and F. Plog, pp. 23–40. Anthropological Research Papers 23. Arizona State University, Tempe.
   1981   *Late Hohokam Prehistory in Southern Arizona.* Contributions to Archaeology 2. Gila Press, Scottsdale.
   1984a  From Foraging to Farming: An Overview of the Pre-Classic in the Tucson Basin. *The Kiva* 49:147–166.
   1984b  Sedentary Period Hohokam Paleo-economy in the New River Drainage, Arizona. In *Prehistoric Southwestern Agricultural Strategies,* edited by P. R. Fish and S. K. Fish, pp. 35–52. Anthropological Research Papers 33. Arizona State University, Tempe.
   1985   Current Trends in Hohokam Research. In *Proceedings of the 1983 Hohokam Symposium,* edited by A. E. Dittert, Jr. and D. E. Dove, pp. 3–26. Arizona Archaeological Society Occasional Paper 2. Phoenix.
   1986   The Hohokam: A Short History of Research. In *Emil W. Haury's Prehistory of the American Southwest,* edited by J. Reid and D. E. Doyel, pp. 193–210. The University of Arizona Press, Tucson.
   1987a  (editor) *The Hohokam Village: Site Structure and Organization.* American Association for the Advancement of Science, Glenwood Springs, Colorado.
   1987b  The Role of Commerce in Hohokam Society. Paper prepared for "Cultural Complexity in the Arid Southwest," School of American Research, Santa Fe. On file, Pueblo Grande Museum, Phoenix.
   1987c  Pueblo Grande National Landmark Celebrates a Centennial. *Masterkey* 64(4):3–11.
   1988a  Hohokam Exchange and Interaction. In *Cultural Complexity in the Arid Southwest,* edited by W. J. Judge and P. L. Crown. School of American Research, Santa Fe. In press.
   1988b  The Transition to History in Northern Pimeria Alta. In *Columbian Consequences,* vol. 1, edited by D. H. Thomas. Smithsonian Institution Press, Washington, D.C. In press.
   1988c  Interpreting Prehistoric Cultural Diversity in Southern Arizona. Paper presented at the Charles C. DiPeso Retrospective, the Amerind Foundation, Dragoon. In press.
   1989   Prehistoric Inter-regional Ceramic Exchange in the Phoenix Basin. Paper presented at the Annual Meeting of the Society for American Archaeology, Atlanta.
Doyel, David E., and Mark D. Elson (editors)
   1985   *Hohokam Settlement and Economic Systems in the Central New River Drainage, Arizona.* Soil Systems Publications in Archaeology 4. Phoenix.
Doyel, David E., and Emil W. Haury (editors)
   1976   The 1976 Salado Conference. *The Kiva* 42:1–134.
Doyel, David E., and Fred Plog (editors)
   1980   *Current Issues in Hohokam Prehistory.* Anthropological Research Papers 23. Arizona State University, Tempe.

Eddy, F. W., and M. E. Cooley
1983 *Cultural and Environmental History of the Cienega Valley, Southeastern Arizona.* Anthropological Papers of the University of Arizona 43.

Eighmy, Jeffrey L., and David E. Doyel
1987 A Reanalysis of First-Reported Archaeo-magnetic Dates from the Hohokam Area, Southern Arizona. *Journal of Field Archaeology* 14:331–342.

Eighmy, Jeffrey L., and R. McGuire
1988 *Archaeomagnetic Dates and the Hohokam Phase Sequence.* Archaeometric Laboratory Technical Series 3. Colorado State University, Ft. Collins, Colorado.

Ekholm, Gordon F.
1944 *Excavations at Tampico and Panuco in the Huasteca, Mexico.* Anthropological Papers of the American Museum of Natural History 37(5).

Ezell, Paul H.
1963 Is There a Hohokam-Pima Culture Continuum? *American Antiquity* 29:61–66.
1983 History of the Pima. In *Handbook of North American Indians,* vol. 10, Southwest, edited by Alfonso Ortiz, pp. 149–160. Smithsonian Institution, Washington, D.C.

Fewkes, J. Walter
1909 Prehistoric Ruins of the Gila Valley. *Smithsonian Miscellaneous Collections* 5(4):403–436. Washington, D.C.
1912 Casa Grande, Arizona. *Twenty-eighth Annual Report of American Ethnology.* Washington, D.C.

Fink, T. M.
1988a The Human Skeletal Remains from the Grand Canal Ruins. In *Archaeological Investigations at the Grand Canal Ruins: A Classic Period Site in Phoenix, Arizona,* edited by D. Mitchell. Soil Systems Publications in Archaeology 12. Phoenix. In press.
1988b The Prehistoric Irrigation Canals and Reservoirs of Southern Arizona and their Possible Impact on Hohokam Health. Manuscript on file, Soil Systems, Inc., Phoenix.

Fish, Paul R.
1983 Hohokam Prehistory, Manuscript on file, Arizona State Museum, Tucson.
n.d. Gila Dunes: A Chiricahua Stage Site near Florence, Arizona. Manuscript on file, Department of Anthropology, Arizona State University, Tempe.

Fish, Paul, and Suzanne Fish
1989 Hohokam Warfare from a Regional Perspective. In *Cultures in Conflict.* University of Calgary Press, Calgary.

Fish, P. R., S. K. Fish, A. Long, and C. Miksicek
1986 Early Corn Remains from Tumamoc Hill, Southern Arizona. *American Antiquity* 51:563–572.

Fish, P. R., S. K. Fish, J. Madsen, C. Miksicek, C. Szuter, and J. Field
1987 A Long-Term Pioneer Adaptation in the Tucson Basin. Paper presented at the 1987 Hohokam Conference, Tempe.

Fish, Suzanne, and Paul Fish (editors)
1984 *Prehistoric Agricultural Strategies in the Southwest.* Anthropological Research Paper 33. Arizona State University, Tempe.

Fowler, A. P., J. Stein, and R. Anyon
1987 An Archaeological Reconnaissance of West-Central New Mexico: The Anasazi Monuments Project. Manuscript on file, New Mexico State Historic Preservation Office, Santa Fe.

Fuller, J. E.
  1987   *Paleoflood Hydrology of the Alluvial Salt River, Tempe, Arizona.* Master's thesis, Department of Geosciences, University of Arizona, Tucson.
Gladwin, Harold S.
  1948   *Excavations at Snaketown IV: Review and Conclusions.* Medallion Papers 38. Gila Pueblo, Globe.
  1957   *A History of the Ancient Southwest.* Bond-Wheelwright Co., Portland, Maine.
Gladwin, Harold S., E. W. Haury, E. B. Sayles, and Nora Gladwin
  1937   *Excavations at Snaketown, Material Culture.* Medallion Papers 25. Gila Pueblo, Arizona.
Gladwin, Winifred, and Harold S. Gladwin
  1935   *The Eastern Range of the Red-on-buff Culture.* Medallion Papers 16. Gila Pueblo, Globe.
Grebinger, Paul
  1971   *Hohokam Cultural Development in the Middle Santa Cruz River Valley, Arizona.* Unpublished Ph.D. dissertation, Department of Anthropology, University of Arizona, Tucson.
Greenwald, David H., and Richard Ciolek-Torrello
  1987   An Early Hohokam Canal System on the First Terrace of the Salt River. Paper presented at the 1987 Hohokam Conference, Tempe.
Gregory, David A.
  1983   Excavations at the Siphon Draw Site. In *Hohokam Archaeology along the Salt-Gila Aqueduct, Central Arizona Project*, vol. 4, pt. 1, edited by L. S. Teague and P. L. Crown. Arizona State Museum Archaeological Series 150. Tucson.
  1987   The Morphology of Platform Mounds and the Structure of Classic Period Hohokam Sites. In *The Hohokam Village: Site Structure and Organization*, edited by D. E. Doyel, pp. 183–210. American Association for the Advancement of Science, Glenwood Springs, Colorado.
Gregory, David A., and C. Heathington (editors)
  1986   *The 1982–84 Excavations at Las Colinas.* Arizona State Museum Archaeological Series. Tucson. In press.
Gregory, David A., and Fred Nials
  1985   Observations Concerning the Distribution of Classic Period Hohokam Platform Mounds. In *Proceedings of the 1983 Hohokam Symposium*, edited by A. E. Dittert, Jr., and D. E. Dove, pp. 373–388. Arizona Archaeological Society Occasional Paper 2. Phoenix.
Gumerman, George J., and Emil W. Haury
  1979   Prehistory: Hohokam. In *Handbook of North American Indians*, vol. 9, Southwest, edited by Alfonso Ortiz, pp. 75–90. Smithsonian Institution Press, Washington, D.C.
Hackenberg, Robert A.
  1961   *Aboriginal Land Use and Occupancy of the Pima-Maricopa Community.* Report to the U.S. Department of Justice, vols. I and II. On file, Arizona State Museum Library, Tucson.
Hammack, Laurens C., and Alan P. Sullivan
  1981   *The 1968 Excavations at Mound 8, Las Colinas Ruins Group, Phoenix, Arizona.* Arizona State Museum Archaeological Series 154. Tucson.
Hard, Robert J.
  1988   Agricultural Dependence in the Mountain Mogollon and Other Southwestern Regions. Paper presented at the Southwest Symposium, Tempe.

Haury, Emil W.

1932    *Roosevelt 9:6, A Hohokam Site of the Colonial Period.* Medallion Papers 11. Gila Pueblo, Globe.

1936    The Snaketown Canal. *University of New Mexico Bulletin* 296, *Anthropological Series* 1(5):48–50. University of New Mexico, Albuquerque.

1943    A Possible Cochise-Mogollon-Hohokam Sequence. In *Proceedings of the American Philosophical Society* 86:260–263. Philadelphia.

1945    *The Excavation of Los Muertos and Neighboring Ruins in the Salt River Valley, Southern Arizona.* Papers of the Peabody Museum of American Archaeology and Ethnology 24(1). Cambridge.

1950    *The Stratigraphy and Archaeology of Ventana Cave.* Reprinted in 1975, The University of Arizona Press, Tucson.

1957    An Alluvial Site on the San Carlos Indian Reservation, Arizona. *American Antiquity* 23(1):2–27.

1962    The Greater American Southwest. In *Courses Toward Urban Life,* edited by R. J. Braidwood and G. R. Wiley, pp. 106–131. Aldine, Chicago.

1976    *The Hohokam: Desert Farmers and Craftsmen.* The University of Arizona Press, Tucson.

Hayden, Julian D.

1957    *Excavations, 1940, At University Indian Ruin, Tucson, Arizona.* Southwestern Monuments Association, Technical Series 5. Gila Pueblo, Globe.

1987    The Vikita Ceremony of the Papago. *Journal of the Southwest* 29:273–324.

Hemmings, E. T., M. D. Robinson, and R. N. Rogers

1968    Field Report on the Pantano Site (Arizona EE:2:50). Manuscript on file. Additional Site File Information, Arizona State Museum, Tucson.

Henderson, T. Kathleen

1987    Structure and Organization at La Ciudad. *Anthropological Field Studies* 18. Office of Cultural Resource Management, Arizona State University, Tempe.

Howard, Ann

1985a   The Block 24-East Prehistoric Shell Assemblage. In *City of Phoenix Archaeology of the Original Townsite,* edited by J. S. Cable, K. S. Hoffman, D. E. Doyel, and F. Ritz, pp. 169–182. Soil Systems Publications in Archaeology 8. Phoenix.

1985b   A Reconstruction of Hohokam Interregional Shell Production and Exchange within Southwestern Arizona. In *Proceedings of the 1983 Hohokam Conference,* edited by A. E. Dittert, Jr., and D. E. Dove, pp. 459–472. Arizona Archaeological Society Occasional Paper 2. Phoenix.

1987    Late Archaic and Pioneer Period Shell Utilization: An Examination of Early Shell Production and Exchange within Arizona. Paper presented at the 1987 Hohokam Conference, Tempe.

Howard, Jerry B.

1982    Hohokam Community Organization at La Ciudad de los Hornos. Paper presented at the Society for American Archaeological meetings, Minneapolis.

1985    Courtyard Groups and Domestic Cycling: A Hypothetical Model of Growth. In *Proceedings of the 1983 Hohokam Symposium,* edited by A. E. Dittert, Jr., and D. E. Dove, pp. 311–326. Arizona Archaeological Society Occasional Paper 2. Phoenix.

Howard, Jerry B. (editor)
  1988   *Excavations at the Casa Buena Site, City of Phoenix.* Soil Systems Publications in
         Archaeology 11. Phoenix.
Huckell, Bruce B.
  1984a  *The Archaic Occupation of the Rosemont Area, Northern Santa Rita Mountains,
         Southeastern Arizona.* Arizona State Museum Archaeological Series 147. Tuc-
         son.
  1984b  The Paleo-Indian and Archaic Occupation of the Tucson Basin: An Overview.
         *The Kiva* 49:133–146.
Huckell, Bruce B., and Lisa W. Huckell
  1988   Crops Come to the Desert: Late Preceramic Agriculture in Southeastern Ari-
         zona. Paper presented at the 53rd Annual Meeting of the Society for American
         Archaeology, Phoenix.
Huntington, Ellsworth
  1914   *The Climatic Factor in Arid America.* Carnegie Institution Publication 192, Wash-
         ington, D.C.
Huntington, Frederick
  1986   *Archaeological Investigations at the West Branch Site.* Institute for American Re-
         search Anthropological Papers 5. Tucson.
Ives, J. C. and D. J. Opfenring
  1966   Some Investigations into the Nature of the Early Phases of the Hohokam
         Culture. Report submitted to the National Science Foundation, Washington,
         D.C.
Johnson, Alfred E.
  1964   Archaeological Excavations in Hohokam Sites of Southern Arizona. *American
         Antiquity* 30(2):145–161.
Kelley, J. Charles
  1966   Mesoamerica and the Southwestern United States. In *The Handbook of Middle
         American Indians,* edited by G. Willey and G. Ekholm, pp. 95–111. The Uni-
         versity of Texas Press, Austin.
  1980   Comments on the Papers by Plog, Doyel, and Riley. In *Current Issues in
         Hohokam Prehistory,* edited by D. E. Doyel and F. Plog, pp. 49–66. Anthro-
         pological Research Papers 23. Arizona State University, Tempe.
Kelly, William H.
  1977   *Cocopa Ethnography.* Anthropological Papers of the University of Arizona 29.
         University of Arizona Press, Tucson.
Kenny, Brian
  1987   The Stricklin Site: A Transitional Site in the Hohokam Northern Periphery.
         Paper presented at the 1987 Hohokam Conference, Tempe.
LeBlanc, Steven A.
  1986   Aspects of Southwestern Prehistory: A.D. 900–1400. In *Ripples in the Chichimec
         Sea,* edited by F. J. Mathien and R. McGuire, pp. 105–134. Southern Illinois
         University Press, Carbondale.
Lerner, Shereen
  1985   A Re-evaluation of the Hohokam Periphery: Fact or Fiction? In *Proceedings of
         the 1983 Hohokam Symposium,* edited by A. E. Dittert, Jr. and D. E. Dove, pp.
         499–510. Arizona Archaeological Society Occasional Paper 2. Phoenix.
Long, A., J. Andresen and J. Klein
  1987   Construction of the Casa Grande by Sequential High Precision C-14 Dating.
         *Geoarchaeology* 2:217–222.

Masse, W. Bruce
  1979 An Intensive Survey of Prehistoric Dry Farming Systems near Tumamoc Hill in Tucson, Arizona. *The Kiva* 45:141–186.
  1980a The Hohokam of the Lower San Pedro and the Papagueria: Continuity and Variability in Two Regional Populations. In *Current Issues in Hohokam Prehistory*, edited by D. E. Doyel and F. Plog, pp. 205–223. Anthropological Research Papers 23. Arizona State University, Tempe.
  1980b *Excavations at Gu Achi: A Reappraisal of Hohokam Settlement and Subsistence in the Arizona Papagueria*. Western Archaeological Center Publications in Anthropology 12. National Park Service, Tucson.
  1981 A Reappraisal of the protohistoric Sobaipuri Indians of Southeastern Arizona. In *The Protohistoric Period in the North American Southwest, A.D. 1450–1700*, edited by D. R. Wilcox and W. B. Masse, pp. 28–56. Anthropological Research Papers 24. Arizona State University, Tempe.

McGregor, John C.
  1965 *Southwestern Archaeology*. University of Illinois Press, Urbana.

Mitchell, Douglas E.
  1986 *Hohokam, Mogollon and Western Pueblo Settlement Systems in the San Carlos River Valley, Arizona*. Archaeological Research Service, Inc., Tempe.

Mitchell, Douglas E. (editor)
  1988 *Archaeological Investigations at the Grand Canal Ruins: A Classic Period Site in Phoenix, Arizona*. Soil Systems Publications in Archaeology 12. Phoenix.

Morris, Donald M.
  1969 Red Mountain: An Early Pioneer Period Hohokam Site in the Salt River Valley of Central Arizona. *American Antiquity* 34:40–54.

Nelson, Richard S.
  1986 Pochtecas and Prestige: Mesoamerican Artifacts in Hohokam Sites. In *Ripples in the Chichimec Sea*, edited by F. J. Mathien and R. H. McGuire, pp. 154–182. Southern Illinois University Press, Carbondale.

Nials, Fred, D. A. Gregory, and D. A. Graybill
  1986 Salt River Streamflow and Hohokam Irrigation Systems. In *The 1982–1984 Excavations at Los Colinas*, vol. 5. Arizona State Museum Archaeological Series 162. Tucson. In press.

Nicholas, Linda, and J. Neitzel
  1983 Canal Irrigation and Socio-Political Organization in the Lower Salt River Valley: A Diachronic Analysis. In *Prehistoric Agricultural Strategies in the Southwest*, edited by S. K. Fish and P. E. Fish, pp. 161–178. Anthropological Research Papers 33. Arizona State University, Tempe.

Pailes, Richard A.
  1988 Elite Formation and Inter-Regional Exchange in Peripheries. Paper presented at the Southwest Conference, Tempe.

Partridge, J., and V. Baker
  1987 Paleoflood Hydrology of the Salt River, Arizona. *Earth Surface Processes and Landforms* 12:109–125.

Pilles, Peter J., Jr.
  1987 The Sinagua: Ancient People of the Flagstaff Region. *Exploration*, pp. 2–12. School of American Research, Santa Fe.

Plog, Fred T.
  1980 Explaining Culture Change in the Hohokam Preclassic. In *Current Issues in Hohokam Prehistory*, edited by D. E. Doyel and F. Plog, pp. 4–22. Anthropological Research Papers 23. Arizona State University, Tempe.

Porter-Weaver, Muriel
    1981    *The Aztecs, Maya, and Their Predecessors*. Academic Press, New York.
Reff, Dan
    1988    Old World Diseases in the Protohistoric Period. Paper presented at the South-
            west Symposium, Tempe.
Rice, Glen
    1984    The Organization of Hohokam Communities during the Pre-Classic Period.
            *American Archaeology* 4:194–206.
Rice, Glen (editor)
    1987    *The Hohokam Community of La Ciudad*. Anthropological Field Studies 69. Office
            of Cultural Resource Management, Arizona State University, Tempe.
Riley, Carroll
    1987    *The Frontier People*. University of New Mexico Press, Albuquerque.
Roth, Barbara J., and Bruce Huckell
    1988    Cortaro Points and Cultural Complexity in the Late Archaic. Paper presented
            at the 53rd Annual Meeting of the Society for American Archaeology, Phoenix.
Russell, Frank
    1975    *The Pima Indians*. The University of Arizona Press, Tucson.
Sayles, Edwin B.
    1945    *The San Simon Branch*. Medallion Papers 34. Gila Pueblo, Globe.
    1983    *The Cochise Cultural Sequence in Southeastern Arizona*. Anthropological Papers
            of the University of Arizona 42. Tucson.
Schiffer, Michael B.
    1982    Hohokam Chronology: An Essay on History and Method. In *Hohokam and
            Patayan, Prehistory of Southwestern Arizona*, edited by Randall H. McGuire and
            Michael B. Schiffer, pp. 299–344. Academic Press, New York.
Schroeder, Albert H.
    1940    *A Stratigraphic Survey of Pre-Spanish Trash Mounds in the Salt River Valley, Arizona*.
            Master's thesis, University of Arizona, Tucson.
    1952    The Bearing of Ceramics on Developments in the Hohokam Classic Period.
            *Southwestern Journal of Anthropology* 8(3):320–335.
    1965    Unregulated Diffusion from Mexico into the Southwest Prior to A.D. 700.
            *American Antiquity* 30:297–309.
    1966    Pattern Diffusion from Mexico into the Southwest after A.D. 600. *American
            Antiquity* 31:683–704.
    1981    How Far Can a Pochteca Leap without Leaving Footprints? In *Collected Papers
            in Honor of Erik Kallerman Reed*, edited by A. H. Schroeder, pp. 43–64. Papers
            of the Archaeological Society of New Mexico 6. Albuquerque.
Sheridan, Thomas E.
    1988    Kino's Unforeseen Legacy: The Material Consequences of Missionization. *The
            Smoke Signal*, pp. 151–167. Tucson Corral of the Westerners, Tucson.
Sires, Earl W., Jr.
    1983    Excavations at El Polvoron. In *Hohokam Archaeology along the Salt-Gila Aqueduct,
            Central Arizona Project*, edited by L. S. Teague and P. L. Crown. Arizona State
            Museum Archaeological Series 150(4). Tucson.
    1985    Hohokam Architecture and Site Structure. In *Hohokam Archaeology along the
            Salt-Gila Aqueduct, Central Arizona Project*, edited by L. S. Teague and P. L.
            Crown, pp. 115–139. Arizona State Museum Archaeological Series 150(9).
            Tucson.

1987   Hohokam Architectural Variability and Site Structure During the Sedentary-Classic Transition. In *The Hohokam Village: Site Structure and Organization*, edited by D. E. Doyel, pp. 171–182. American Association for the Advancement of Science, Glenwood Springs, Colorado.

Spoerl, Patricia, and George Gumerman
1984   *Prehistoric Cultural Development in Central Arizona: Archaeology of the Upper New River Region*. Center for Archaeological Investigations Occasional Paper 5. Southern Illinois University, Carbondale.

Szuter, Christine R. and Frank E. Bayham
1987   Faunal Exploitation During the Late Archaic and Pioneer Periods. Paper presented at the 1987 Hohokam Conference, Tempe.

Teague, Lynn S., and Patricia L. Crown (editors)
1983–  *Hohokam Archaeology Along the Salt River Aqueduct*. Arizona State Museum
1984   Archaeological Series 150 (1–9). Tucson.

Thomas M., and J. King
1985   Hohokam Figurine Assemblages: A Suggested Ritual Context. In *Proceedings of the 1983 Hohokam Symposium*, edited by A. E. Dittert, Jr. and D. E. Dove, pp. 687–732. Arizona Archaeological Society Occasional Paper 2. Phoenix.

Underhill, Ruth M.
1946   *Papago Indian Religion*. Columbia University Press, New York.

Wallace, H. D., and D. Craig
1986   Tucson Basin Hohokam: Chronological Considerations. Paper presented at the second Tucson Basin Conference, Tucson.

Wasley, William W., and Alfred E. Johnson
1965   *Salvage Archaeology in Painted Rocks Reservoir, Western Arizona*. Anthropological Papers of the University of Arizona 9. Tucson.

Wasley, William, and B. Benham
1968   Salvage Excavations in the Buttes Dam Site. *The Kiva* 33(4):244–279.

Weaver, Donald E., Jr.
1972   A Cultural-Ecological Model for the Classic Hohokam Period in the Lower Salt River Valley. *The Kiva* 38(1):43–52.

Weed, Carol S.
1972   The Beardsley Canal Site. *The Kiva* 38:57–94.

Weigand, P. C., G. Harbottle, and E. Sayre
1977   Turquoise Sources and Source Analysis: Mesoamerica and the Southwestern U.S.A. In *Exchange Systems in Prehistory*, edited by T. K. Earle and J. E. Ericson, pp. 15–34. Academic Press, New York.

Whalen, Norman K.
1971   *Cochise Culture Sites in the Central San Pedro Drainage, Arizona*. Unpublished Ph.D. dissertation, Department of Anthropology, The University of Arizona, Tucson.

Wilcox, David R.
1979   The Hohokam Regional System. In *An Archaeological Test of the Sites in the Gila Butte–Santan Region, South-central Arizona*, edited by G. Rice, D. Wilcox, K. Rafferty and J. Schoenwetter, pp. 77–116. Anthropological Research Papers 18. Arizona State University, Tempe.
1985a  Preliminary Report on New Data on Hohokam Ballcourts. In *Proceedings of*

the 1983 Hohokam Conference, edited by A. E. Dittert, Jr. and D. E. Dove, pp. 641–654. Arizona Archaeological Society Occasional Paper 2. Phoenix.

1985b Hohokam Warfare. Paper presented at the Annual Meeting of the Society for American Archaeology, Denver.

1987a The Evolution of Hohokam Ceremonial Systems. In *Astronomy and Ceremony in the Prehistoric Southwest*, edited by J. Carlson and W. J. Judge, pp. 149–168. Papers of the Maxwell Museum of Anthropology 2. Albuquerque.

1987b *Frank Midvale's Investigation of the Site of La Ciudad.* Anthropological Field Studies 19. Office of Cultural Resource Management, Arizona State University, Tempe.

Wilcox, David R., and D. E. Doyel

1985 Maximum Extent and Site Structure of the Pueblo Grande. Manuscript on file, Pueblo Grande Museum. Phoenix.

Wilcox, David R., T. R. McGuire, and C. Sternberg

1981 *Snaketown Revisited.* Arizona State Museum Archaeological Series 155. Tucson.

Wilcox, David R., and L. Shenk

1977 *The Architecture of the Big House and Its Interpretation.* Arizona State Museum Archaeological Series 115. Tucson.

Wilcox, David R., and Charles Sternberg

1983 *Hohokam Ballcourts and Their Interpretation.* Arizona State Museum Archaeological Series 160. Tucson.

Wood, J. Scott

1985 The Northeastern Periphery. In *Proceedings of the 1983 Hohokam Conference,* edited by A. E. Dittert, Jr. and D. E. Dove, pp. 239–262. Arizona Archaeological Society Occasional Paper 2. Phoenix.

Woodbury, Richard B.

1961 A Reappraisal of Hohokam Irrigation. *American Anthropologist* 63:550–560.

# •7•

# THE CHANGING ROLE OF THE TUCSON BASIN IN THE HOHOKAM REGIONAL SYSTEM

▼▼▼▼▼▼▼▼▼▼▼▼▼▼▼▼▼▼▼▼▼▼▼▼▼▼▼▼▼▼▼▼▼▼▼▼▼▼▼▼▼▼▼▼▼▼▼▼▼▼▼▼▼▼▼

*William H. Doelle*
*Henry D. Wallace*

H istorically the Tucson Basin has played a limited role in shaping our understanding of the Hohokam, but the thesis of this paper is that the Tucson Basin represents an ideal laboratory for monitoring change in the Hohokam regional system. Unlike the Phoenix Basin where large irrigation systems represented major capital investments that structured and constrained the options for change, the subsistence and social systems of the Tucson Basin appear to have been more flexible. As a result, several major settlement pattern changes can be documented in the archaeological record, and they serve to highlight times of transition in the Tucson Basin. While the causes of these transitions may not have been the same in the Phoenix Basin, the magnitude of some of the Tucson Basin changes suggests that *regional-level* effects could be expected.

The authors accept the general notion of a Hohokam regional system that was characterized by a core-periphery contrast, as proposed by Wilcox (1979a; Wilcox et al. 1981; Wilcox and Sternberg 1983). Such a model must not, however, employ a simplistic assumption that the peripheral areas were dependent on the core to initiate change and innovation. On the contrary, the core-periphery relationship is shown to have been a dynamic one, and ultimately the Tucson Basin may have emerged as a regional center in its own right in the latest prehistoric times.

This paper follows several important themes through time. The first is the definition of the Tucson Basin as a distinctive component of the Hohokam regional system. In particular, the degree of variation between the Hohokam of the Tucson and Phoenix basins is addressed. It is also necessary to explore the meaning of this regional variation. The second theme is the rapid pace of change that is increasingly evident in Hohokam prehistory. Our approach to this task is to focus on the changing structure of the Hohokam village in the Tucson Basin. We examine some of the social units that comprised Hohokam villages and consider how they were integrated. We also address how village structure and integrative mechanisms changed; in general we find a trend of increasing social differentiation over time. A final theme that emerges from this discussion is the increasing importance of the Tucson Basin to the development of Hohokam archaeology.

# CHRONOLOGY

After reevaluating the Hohokam chronology following the second excavations at Snaketown, Emil Haury was still convinced that the fabric of Hohokam society had evolved very gradually over a long period of time (Haury 1976:340). The much more compressed temporal perspective for the Hohokam that has emerged over the past decade indicates that, counter to Haury's impression of long, gradual cultural development, the Hohokam were characterized by a dynamic way of life. Figure 7.1 shows the relationship of the period and phase names for the Tucson and Phoenix basins (see Wallace and Craig [1988] for a fuller discussion of Tucson Basin chronology).

# DEFINING REGIONAL VARIATION:
# PERSPECTIVES FROM CERAMIC STUDIES

Archaeologists have long appreciated the value of prehistoric pottery as a source of temporal information and for documenting exchange and interaction over space. Hohokam ceramics have proved particularly useful in defining differences between the Tucson and Phoenix basins. Three separate approaches to this problem are presented in this section. First, a combination of petrographic and typological data from well-controlled excavated contexts are used to argue that the Tucson Basin Hohokam manufactured a distinctive local red ware from very early in the ceramic period. Second, a distributional

THE CHANGING ROLE OF THE TUCSON BASIN

| Period | Phoenix Basin Phase | Tucson Basin Phase |
|--------|---------------------|---------------------|
| Classic | Civano<br>Soho | Tucson<br>Tanque Verde |
| Sedentary | Sacaton | Rincon |
| Colonial | Santa Cruz<br>Gila Butte | Rillito<br>Cañada del Oro |
| Pioneer | Snaketown<br>Sweetwater<br>Estrella<br>Vahki | Snaketown<br>Sweetwater<br>————<br>———— |

Figure 7.1    *Tucson and Phoenix basin phase names and their chronological placement.*

study of contemporaneous Tucson and Phoenix basin types is presented for the Rillito through Tanque Verde phases (Santa Cruz through Soho phases in Phoenix). Third, a more refined distributional study that compares quantitative data from controlled contexts allows the identification of a rather striking pattern of variation in the frequency of Phoenix Basin buff wares relative to local brown wares in the northern and southern portions of the Tucson Basin.

## THE EARLY CERAMIC PERIOD

A recent development in the Tucson Basin is that an early red ware horizon is now recognized. Current studies are describing the variability within this red ware (Huckell et al. 1987; Heidke 1989a), and there is already conclusive petrographic evidence that these red wares were made in the Tucson Basin. Available dates for red ware contexts in the Basin are limited and somewhat variable. The El Arbolito site (Huckell et al. 1987) is an early site, with four radiocarbon samples yielding a corrected average of A.D. 256–530 (two sigma). To date, the most consistent and well-controlled contexts are from five pithouses at the Lonetree site, AZ AA:12:149 (Bernard-Shaw 1989b). The weighted average of these five samples is A.D. 644 ± 33 years (Bernard-Shaw and Heidke 1989:2). At neither El Arbolito nor Lonetree do red wares co-occur with diagnostic decorated types such as Estrella Red-on-gray, Sweetwater Red-on-gray, or Snaketown Red-on-buff, though they do co-occur with these types at Tucson Basin sites such as Redtail (Bernard-Shaw 1989c) and the

Dairy site (P. Fish, personal communication). It seems likely then, that pure "red ware-plain ware" assemblages date relatively early, with red wares that are associated with Pioneer and early Colonial diagnostic types representing the later end of this red ware tradition.

Isabel Kelly (1978) used the Cañada del Oro phase as the point where the ceramics of the Tucson Basin diverged sufficiently from those of the Phoenix Basin to merit a separate, though largely parallel, system of types. There have been new data regarding these early Tucson Basin ceramics that have become available in recent years (Craig 1989a; Deaver 1984; Doelle and Wallace 1986; Heidke 1989a, 1989b), and in one interesting development, Wallace (Doelle and Wallace 1986:10) concluded that nearly half of the sherds that Isabel Kelly selected to illustrate her Cañada del Oro type were actually Gila Butte Red-on-buff. Using new criteria for distinguishing between these two types, Heidke (1989b) has found that none of the Cañada del Oro ceramics from the Redtail site are incised, whereas Gila Butte Red-on-buff shows incising in roughly 85 percent of the cases in the Phoenix Basin (Crown 1984:231; Deaver 1984:284; Haury 1965:188, 1976:213). In a small sample from the Redtail site, Heidke (1989b) has also found that the Snaketown Red-on-buff bowls (presumed to have been made in the Phoenix Basin) were incised at frequencies comparable to the 50–65 percent range reported for Snaketown (Haury 1965:191, 1976:216). On the other hand, incising was observed on only 10 percent of the Snaketown Red-on-brown bowls (presumed to have come from the Tucson Basin). Finally, a sherd of Estrella Red-on-gray recovered from the Redtail site was reviewed petrographically by Heidke (Bernard-Shaw and Heidke 1989). He found that it matched a local sand source that differs markedly from the Phoenix Basin descriptions of the type. Taken together, these data on Cañada del Oro, Snaketown, and Estrella decorated types and Tortolita Red suggest that Kelly's (1978) traditional model must now be rejected and that decorated ceramics were being produced from the inception of the Hohokam decorated ceramic tradition in the Tucson Basin. This conclusion alters the common perception of direct Phoenix Basin involvement early in the development of the Tucson Basin system, though it does not negate the significance of exchange and the transmission of design styles and the information they may encode.

## THE SPATIAL DISTRIBUTION OF TUCSON AND PHOENIX BASIN DECORATED TYPES

As an artifact class, Hohokam decorated ceramics provide a relatively high degree of temporal control, they are reasonably common to abundant on almost all Hohokam sites, and type-level information is available from a broad regional sample of sites. Therefore, if ceramic types are used with caution they can provide reasonable temporal controls for an overview of changing patterns of interaction.

This review uses survey data because of the large number of sites and the

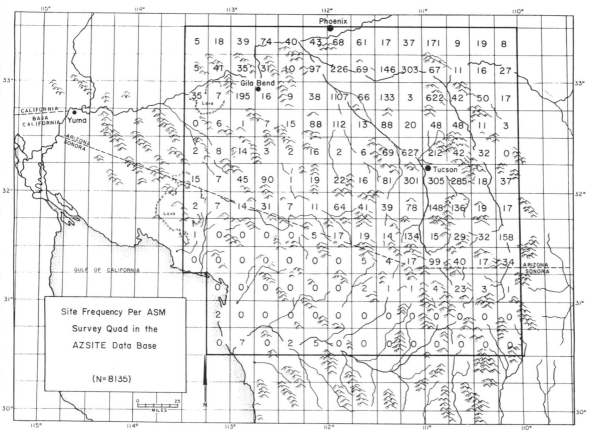

Figure 7.2    *Number of sites per 15-minute quadrangle from the Arizona*
*State Museum AZSITE computerized data file (February 1988).*

broad spatial coverage that survey information provides. The computerized
site files (AZSITE) at the Arizona State Museum contained 8,135 sites in
February 1988 for the area reviewed for this paper (Fig. 7.2). Despite the great
increase in excavations throughout the Hohokam region, the excavated data
base cannot match the survey data for obtaining a broad regional perspective.
The procedure employed involved mapping the frequency of occurrence of
archaeological sites that contain a particular pottery type for each 7.5 minute
quadrangle in the study region. Those frequency classes were used to help
define spatial patterns visually on a series of maps. The frequency classes
serve to identify low (2–9), moderate (10–19), and high (≥20) frequencies of
sites with a particular ceramic type. Because areas of concentration were of
primary interest, quadrangles with only a single site were not plotted. These
data provide a general perspective on the spatial extent of a variety of ceramic
types over time. This exercise suffers from the fact that survey coverage is
not even over the entire southern portion of the state, but the nature of the
results obtained suggests that this is not a severe problem.

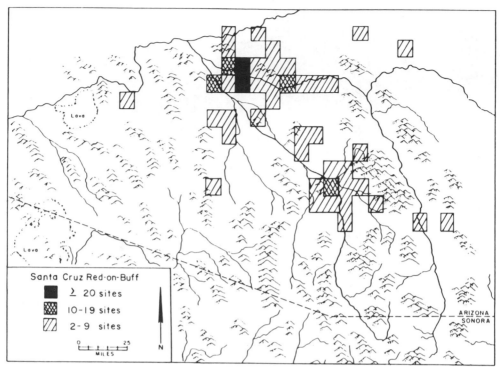

Figure 7.3     *Distribution of Santa Cruz Red-on-buff pottery in southern Arizona.*

The paired maps presented here display the distributions of sites with ceramic types that are believed to be roughly contemporaneous. Though specific production locations cannot be identified, it is a relatively safe assumption that Santa Cruz, Sacaton, and Casa Grande red-on-buff ware were produced in the Phoenix Basin and that Rillito and Rincon red-on-brown ware were produced in the Tucson Basin. Recent work suggests that it cannot be assumed that the type Tanque Verde Red-on-brown was all made in the Tucson Basin. Crown's work at Las Colinas (Crown et al. 1988) documents local production of this type in the Phoenix Basin. Macroscopic inspection of limited additional samples from Phoenix Basin sites suggests that the sherds examined were not from the Tucson area.

Figures 7.3–6 demonstrate that the Tucson Basin is an area of overlap for buff ware and brown ware distributions. The buff ware distribution is centered in the Phoenix Basin and has its southern terminus in the Tucson Basin. The brown ware distribution is centered in the Tucson Basin and extends southward. Given that the buff ware production was somewhere in the Phoenix Basin, these maps document a substantial exchange of buff ware into the Tucson Basin during the Rillito and Rincon phases. In addition, Figures 7.4 and 7.6 make it clear that it was not decorated pottery from the Tucson Basin that was being exchanged in order to obtain these buff wares.

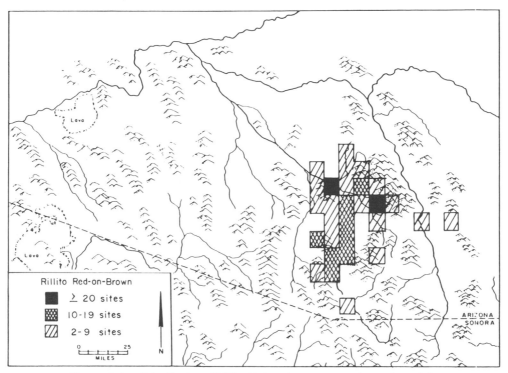

Figure 7.4     *Distribution of Rillito Red-on-brown pottery in southern Arizona.*

The Classic period decorated types shown in Figures 7.7 and 7.8 show a very different pattern than was the case in Preclassic times. Casa Grande Red-on-buff has a substantially restricted range. It is almost totally absent from the Tucson Basin, even from excavated contexts. This is not surprising because it is known that the frequency of this buff ware type drops sharply even in the Phoenix Basin, with red ware frequencies showing a substantial rise in the Phoenix Basin during the Classic period.

Interpreting the Tanque Red-on-brown distribution (Fig. 7.8) requires caution because the place of manufacture is not well controlled and because of the persistence of this type throughout the Classic period. If the Tanque Verde Red-on-brown data are considered to be a general measure of "interaction" rather than exchange, an interesting conclusion is reached. The imitation of a style from the Tucson Basin by Phoenix Basin potters is a rather dramatic reversal of the substantial movement of Phoenix Basin pots to Tucson in slightly earlier times.

Knowledge of the production location for particular ceramic types allowed inferences of commodity movement in early times and the movement of ideas in later times. These two kinds of interaction raise the possibility that if there was a social boundary of some sort between the Tucson and Phoenix basins,

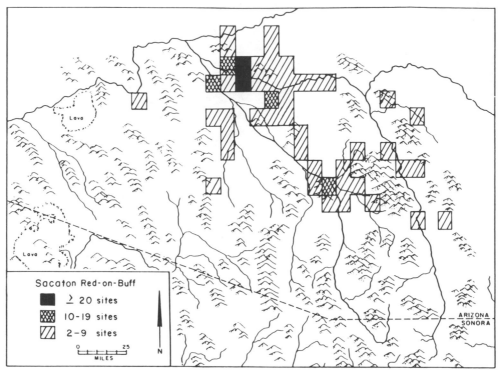

Figure 7.5     *Distribution of Sacaton Red-on-buff pottery in southern Ari-*
                *zona.*

then the nature of that boundary probably changed over time. It was interest
in the nature of this boundary that led Wallace (1987, 1988a) to use ceramic
data from Rillito (Santa Cruz) times as a means for empirically defining the
boundary of the Tucson Basin.

## REFINING BOUNDARY DEFINITIONS: AN EXAMPLE
## FROM THE RILLITO PHASE

Different material items were probably exchanged for different reasons by
the prehistoric Hohokam. Therefore, a distributional study of another class
of material culture might not yield the exact same results as a ceramic distributional study. Aware of this problem, Wallace reasoned that ceramics were
an appropriate starting point for exploring boundary issues. Therefore, he
assembled information on ceramic type frequencies for as many Colonial
period sites as possible south of the Gila River in southern Arizona (Wallace
1987, 1988a). From these data it was found that the overall frequency of
decorated ceramics varied within a relatively narrow range (around 10 percent
of the total assemblage) for Santa Cruz (Rillito) phase contexts within this
sample. Therefore, the relative percentages of Rillito Red-on-brown and Santa

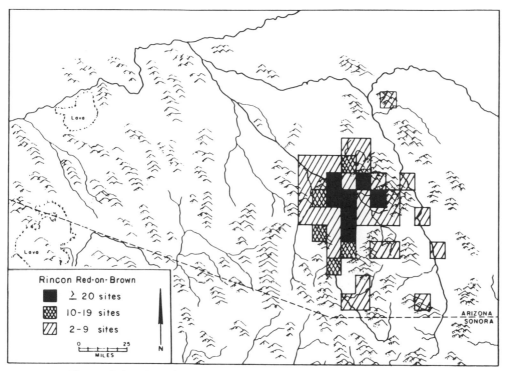

Figure 7.6    *Distribution of Rincon Red-on-brown pottery in southern Arizona.*

Cruz Red-on-buff was used to define a ceramic boundary for the Tucson Basin (Fig. 7.9). The frequencies of other nonlocal types were also taken into consideration for establishing the southern (Trincheras Purple-on-red) and eastern (San Simon wares) ceramic boundaries (see Wallace [1987, 1988a] for more detail). Furthermore, this boundary is conceptualized as having changed over time.

Within the Tucson Basin, a striking pattern in the relative frequencies of Santa Cruz Red-on-buff is observed (Fig. 7.9). The southern and southwestern sites have much lower percentages of buff ware than sites in the northern and eastern portions of the basin. Such a pattern might at first seem to be due to a distance fall-off from the source(s) of the buff ware coming from the north. However, the buff ware percentages increase once more as one proceeds south and southeast out of the Tucson Basin; therefore, a simple fall-off model cannot account for this patterning. The data are particularly striking when one considers the close proximity of the Hodges and St. Mary's sites (less than 7 km apart) and their dramatically different percentages of buff ware (54 percent compared to less than 6 percent). Thus, variation in frequency of contemporaneous decorated types can serve to define a boundary for the Tucson Basin, but also it has revealed an unexpected pattern of variation within the Tucson Basin.

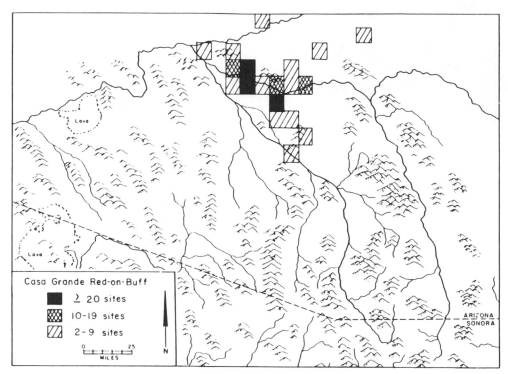

Figure 7.7     *Distribution of Casa Grande Red-on-buff pottery in southern Arizona.*

## DISCUSSION

Research carried out in 1937 and 1938 in the Tucson Basin (Kelly 1978) served to define this area as a distinctive variant of the Hohokam culture that was then being explored by researchers from Gila Pueblo (Haury 1932; Gladwin et al. 1965). Thereafter, however, only limited research was carried out in the Tucson area. Some who did work here tended to assume that the Hohokam of the Tucson area were essentially the same as the Hohokam of the Phoenix Basin (e.g., Grebinger 1971). Others (e.g., DiPeso 1956) saw rather sharp cultural differences between the two areas. The three examples considered above provide evidence that the prehistoric residents of the Tucson Basin participated in the same overall system with the Phoenix Basin Hohokam. However, they were a distinctive entity from earliest times. Furthermore, the pace of change and the direction of influence and interaction were not always constant. In later sections, a number of the issues raised here are explored in more detail.

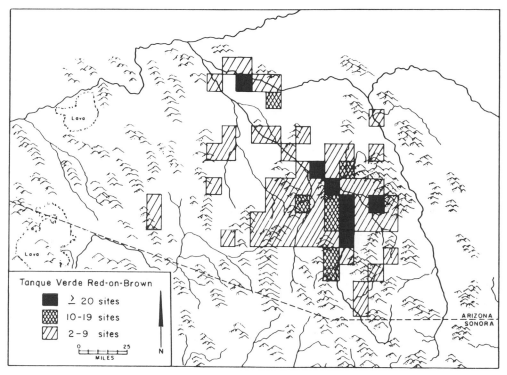

Figure 7.8    *Distribution of Tanque Verde Red-on-brown pottery in south-*
*ern Arizona.*

# SETTLEMENT PATTERNS: AN OVERVIEW
# OF SOCIAL CHANGE

Two keys to developing a new perspective on change in the Tucson Basin
have been a vastly expanded survey coverage and the refinement of the
ceramic typology for the Rincon phase. This refinement process was initiated
by Greenleaf (1975), but it has been taken much farther by Wallace in a series
of studies (1985, 1986a, 1986b, 1986c). Archaeological surveys initiated in the
last decade have resulted in the inventory of hundreds of square miles (Buttery
1986; Craig and Wallace 1987; Dart 1987; Doelle, Dart, and Wallace 1985; Doelle
and Wallace 1986; Downum et al. 1986; Elson and Doelle 1987; Fish, Fish, and
Madsen 1985). Settlement pattern changes in the southern Tucson Basin are
considered in some detail in order to gain an overview of the changing Tucson
Basin social system.

## CAÑADA DEL ORO PHASE

The limited number of temporal diagnostics for this time period make
inferences about site types somewhat difficult, but there is evidence for at

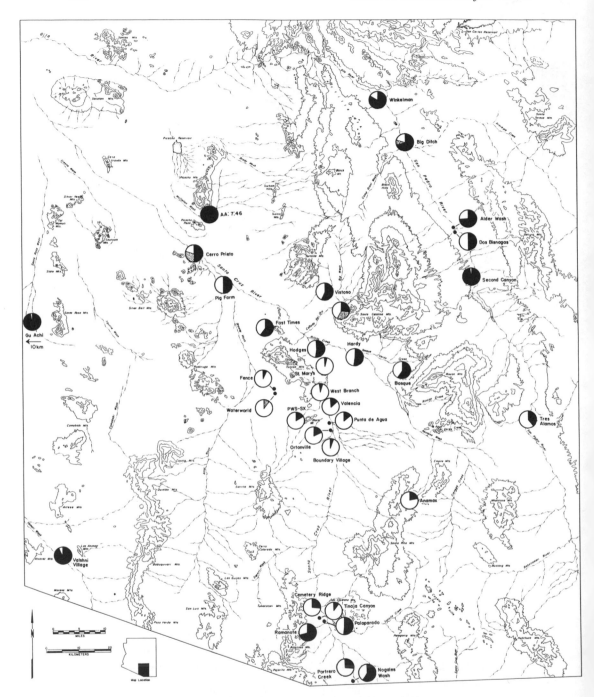

Figure 7.9   *Boundary of the Tucson Basin based on relative percentages of Santa Cruz Red-on-buff and Rillito Red-on-brown pottery from sites with sufficient data. Black represents the percentage of Santa Cruz Red-on-buff; white represents the percentage of Rillito Red-on-brown; stippling represents estimated percentages of Santa Cruz Red-on-buff.*

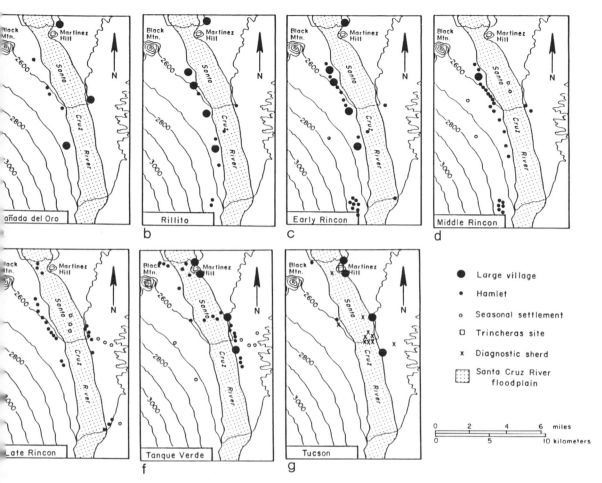

Figure 7.10    *Changing settlement pattern over time in the southern Tucson Basin.*

least three ballcourts in the southern Tucson Basin during the Cañada del
Oro phase (Fig. 7.10a). Each of the ballcourt sites and several other Cañada
del Oro sites have evidence of Pioneer period occupations as well.

## RILLITO PHASE AND EARLY RINCON SUBPHASE

The number of sites and the quantity of diagnostics at individual sites
increases dramatically for the Rillito phase (Fig. 7.10b), and for the most part
the Early Rincon map indicates both continuity and a further increase in the
number of sites occupied (Fig. 7.10c). Four large villages are known, and three
of these had at least one ballcourt. Many of the large villages have hamlets
located in close proximity to them, and all the large villages were quite evenly

spaced along the Santa Cruz. The apparent decline of the former ballcourt village on the east side of the Santa Cruz meant that population was concentrated largely on the western margin of the river.

## MIDDLE RINCON SUBPHASE

As Figure 7.10d shows, the settlement pattern in the southern Tucson Basin was very different during the Middle Rincon subphase. Rather than well-defined large villages with associated hamlets, settlement was much more dispersed. There was an almost continuous band of small settlements along the western margin of the Santa Cruz floodplain. These changes are dramatic in both their magnitude and their suddenness, and available evidence indicates that a disruption in the floodplain environment along the southern Santa Cruz River was a major causal factor acting to trigger them (Doelle et al. 1987).

Waters (1987) argues that the Santa Cruz River in the southernmost Tucson Basin was a discontinuous arroyo during Middle Rincon times. It was characterized by deep downcutting in its southern extent that would have reduced or destroyed the agricultural potential of that area. Just a few miles to the north, however, a fan delta situation was created where waters slowed and spread out and the soil that was eroded from upstream was deposited. Such a setting would have been ideal for floodwater farming. In this scenario, the environmental change had a strongly differential impact on the northern and southern portions of the southern Tucson Basin, and these differences correspond very closely to the observed changes in settlement pattern.

Similar settlement pattern changes are now documented at three other large villages located along the Santa Cruz River during the same time period. The cases include the nearby Valencia (Elson and Doelle 1986) and West Branch (Craig 1989a, 1989b; Huntington 1986) communities and the Los Morteros community (Bernard-Shaw 1989a; Wallace 1990) at the northern end of the Tucson Mountains. Two settlements in the northern Tucson Basin (Craig 1989c; Elson and Doelle 1987) located on tributaries to the Santa Cruz also were reorganized in the Middle Rincon subphase, as was the nonriverine area just west of Black Mountain in the southern Tucson Basin (Dart 1987). There is some indication that changes in the Santa Cruz hydrology played a role in changes in the canal system at Los Morteros (Bernard-Shaw 1989a), which may indicate that arroyo cutting was occurring broadly across the Tucson Basin. However, it is likely that the settlement pattern shift in these diverse areas had a strong social component as well as environmental causes.

## LATE RINCON SUBPHASE

The Late Rincon subphase was a time of further rapid change (Fig. 7.10e). There was continued occupation in many of the small settlements on the west side of the Santa Cruz, but in general this area lost population. At the same time there is evidence of population increase on the east side of the Santa Cruz and to a limited extent in the Santa Cruz River floodplain. Of special significance, Late Rincon ceramics have been recovered from several large roasting pits that are associated with extensive rock pile features in the non-riverine area immediately east of the Santa Cruz. In the northern Tucson Basin similar feature complexes have been firmly established as locations of agave cultivation and processing (Fish, Fish, Miksicek, and Madsen 1985).

Waters (1987) noted that the discontinuous arroyo of Middle Rincon times continued through the Late Rincon subphase. It is possible that a cienega environment was developing in the vicinity of Martinez Hill by this subphase, but in general the magnitude of the environmental change was relatively minor.

## TANQUE VERDE PHASE

During the Tanque Verde phase there was a substantial shift in settlement pattern in the southern Tucson Basin (Fig. 7.10f). The population shift from the west to the east side of the river continued with increasing intensity, though the net effect was probably a stable population size when both sides of the river are considered.

Equally dramatic in the southern Tucson Basin is the very large area of rock pile features in nonriverine settings east of the Santa Cruz River. Recent survey in this area has documented 15 very large roasting pits from 10 to 16 m in diameter. In all cases these roasting pits are associated with Tanque Verde Red-on-brown pottery; a few also have some Late Rincon sherds. It appears that a substantial subsistence effort was invested in the cultivation of agave, and possibly other crops, in these nonriverine settings. The availability of large expanses of suitable land for such nonriverine agriculture, and its near absence on the west side of the Santa Cruz (except around Black Mountain), may have been a significant factor in the population shift from the west to the east side of the Santa Cruz. The distribution of these large roasting pits is suggestive that some communities were specializing in the production of particular subsistence resources, for they cluster almost exclusively around the southernmost Tanque Verde phase large village, the Zanardelli site (Wright and Gerald 1950; Doelle, Dart, and Wallace 1985).

## TUCSON PHASE

Further striking changes in settlement pattern occurred during the Tucson phase. There is a strong trend toward aggregation into a few large villages. Equally striking is the apparent decline in the use of the nonriverine agricultural features that were so important during Tanque Verde times. Figure 7.10g shows the distribution of Tucson phase sites and diagnostic sherds in the southernmost Tucson Basin. Identification of sites from this time period is complicated by the fact that only relatively rare polychrome and intrusive types are firmly diagnostic to the Tucson phase. But Figure 7.10g shows that such ceramics do occur throughout the floodplain of the Santa Cruz. For this reason it is considered significant that none of the roasting pits and rock pile features in the nonriverine zone have produced Tucson phase diagnostics. A significant decline in local population is one mechanism that might be responsible for a process of agricultural de-intensification (Boserup 1965) that is suggested by the absence of late Classic diagnostics in the nonriverine field systems east of the Zanardelli site. However, throughout the Tucson Basin, population appears to have been concentrated in a few locations that were likely the most favorable environmental settings (Wallace and Holmlund 1984). Furthermore, the very high density of Tucson phase material culture at sites such as Martinez Hill, Zanardelli, and BB:13:120, does not support a hypothesis of population decline. It is essential that new research be carried out within local late Classic sites in order to better assess the frequency of Tuscon phase pithouses and the relative intensity of occupation within the large, relatively compact sites that are known for the period.

## DISCUSSION

The shift to the Classic period has long been recognized as a major transformation in Hohokam prehistory. The southern Tucson Basin settlement pattern data supports this conclusion, but it has also helped to identify an earlier transformation of major magnitude. The cause of this mid-Sedentary period settlement pattern shift may have an environmental component, but its broad spatial extent along with dramatic changes in ceramics, household size, mortuary practices, the ballcourt system, and exchange patterns both within and outside the Tucson Basin all argue that regional-level social changes were taking place. Having sketched the broad outline of prehistoric change in the Tucson Basin, it is necessary to develop a framework within which to understand these changes. The approach taken is to focus on the structure and social dynamics of the Hohokam village. Then, in later sections we examine three major research issues where Tucson Basin archaeology provides new insights about the Hohokam regional system.

## THE HOHOKAM VILLAGE AND THE STUDY OF
## PREHISTORIC CHANGE

A common critique from the 1970s of Hohokam archaeology was that it relied on research from a few large sites as its information base. One of the revolutions of the past decade is that there is now both survey and excavation data from a range of site types over a broad region. Contrary to the 1970s critiques, it is now apparent that it was the small sample size, not the focus on large villages, that was a weakness of earlier Hohokam archaeology. Regional settlement pattern studies (Dart 1987; Doelle, Dart, and Wallace 1985; Fish, Fish, and Madsen 1985; Upham and Rice 1980; Wilcox 1979a) and even nonsite archaeology (Doelle 1976; Goodyear 1975), reaffirm the need to focus on the Hohokam village in order to understand the prehistory of this desert region. The village appears to have been the level at which most social and political decision making occurred among the Hohokam (Doelle 1988).

The origin of the Hohokam village is not a central topic here, but the issue requires brief discussion. There is increasing evidence for the Hohokam village having strong roots in the Late Archaic period. Clusters of small, circular pithouses that are associated with abundant evidence of maize are documented at numerous localities in the Tucson Basin and vicinity (Huckell 1988). Dates for these small settlements range from about 800 B.C. to as late as A.D. 400. Several locations have yielded evidence of cemeteries in association with such early settlements. Fish et al. (1988) have even argued that the Late Archaic settlements in the Tucson Basin represent fully sedentary villages. It seems more likely that there was a general temporal trend from Late Archaic through Pioneer period Hohokam times of increasing sedentism. However, there is considerable spatial and temporal variation in the degree of sedentism that is evident within Hohokam villages, with some of the more arid areas never achieving full sedentism. It seems advisable, therefore, to consider sedentism as a variable that must be measured empirically for different sites and time periods.

The village was critical to survival in the desert, but the dynamics of adapting to the desert environment and the social relations between communities appear to have resulted in constant change. There have been great strides in documenting this change, but we are at the early stages of trying to explain it. In the next two sections we outline what is known about the structure and integration of the Hohokam village. Our goal is to introduce a framework within which to examine change in the remainder of the paper.

## HOHOKAM VILLAGE STRUCTURE

The work of numerous researchers over the past decade has led archaeologists to change from the perspective that Hohokam villages were loosely structured clusters of individual pithouses to one that recognizes several structural levels within the village. Future research is likely to establish further refinements to our understanding of the Hohokam village, but at present we find it useful to consider three structural levels: the household, the village segment, and the village.

### The Household

From our perspective, the household is the basic unit of production and consumption (Netting et al. 1984; Wilk and Netting 1984; Wilk and Rathje

1982). The key value of the household concept is that it is defined in behavioral terms rather than in terms of kinship or other intangibles. Thus it is a highly appropriate concept to apply to the archaeological record. Different Hohokam archaeologists have approached the issue of identifying the household somewhat differently (e.g., Henderson 1986; Howard 1982, 1985; Huntington 1986; Rice 1987a; Wilcox et al. 1981), but there is a general consensus that Preclassic Hohokam pithouses frequently were oriented around a common open space, or courtyard. In addition, there is evidence that there was a range in household size. Some consisted of only a single pithouse, whereas others may have encompassed multiple pithouses (Howard 1985), though the issue of the absolute contemporaneity of different houses around an open courtyard presents difficult archaeological problems. For the Classic period, a more formal architectural pattern where several rooms open onto a private, walled courtyard has been noted by archaeologists working in widely dispersed areas within the Hohokam region (Doyel 1977a; Franklin 1980; Hayden 1957; Sires 1987).

### The Village Segment

Several researchers have pioneered the exploration of levels of organization between the household and the village (e.g., Craig 1987; Henderson 1986; Howard 1985). There is still no consensus on terminology, nor is it clear how many intermediate organizational levels may ultimately be of relevance to the understanding of the Hohokam village. In this discussion we use the term village segment to refer to groups of two or more households that were spatially clustered, frequently around a small plaza, and maintained communal facilities such as large roasting pits or a separate cemetery area. It seems likely that village segments represent corporate groups that interacted closely and shared a common social identity. Hayden and Cannon (1982) argue that corporate groups are a highly appropriate level on which to focus archaeological investigation because such groups are not subject to the same degree of idiosyncratic variation as are households. Research on this level of the Hohokam social system is just beginning, but it appears that it will be highly productive.

### The Village

The village has long been the focus of Hohokam archaeology. Many large villages that contained clusters of large mounds and dense artifact scatters were consistently discovered on early archaeological surveys. Villages were also where public architecture such as ballcourts, platform mounds, and compounds were located. Thus, it has not been difficult to appreciate the importance of the village for the understanding of Hohokam archaeology. But recent research has led to an awareness of much greater complexity in village structure. In addition, the rapid pace of change in the structure of the Hohokam village has only recently been perceived. For researchers interested in this change, the central issues are the ways in which these different structural levels were integrated and how those means of integration changed over time.

## INTEGRATION OF THE HOHOKAM VILLAGE

Our principal concern here is the identification of a set of mechanisms of social integration that can be identified and monitored through time with the available data on Hohokam villages in the Tucson Basin. Ideally, this would include a discussion of leadership patterns, ritual practices, and evidence for exchange of multiple classes of commodities at the three levels of organizational structure just described. However, the availability of high quality survey data for all time periods, and the lack of detailed excavation data for all but the Sedentary period, make it necessary to work largely at the village level. On some topics, though, consideration of multiple levels of organization is possible.

## DISCUSSION

There are variable amounts of information of varying quality, and the three topics that are addressed in the remainder of this paper are diverse. As a result, a somewhat eclectic methodology is taken, but the Hohokam village and its changing structure provide a linking theme. The village is the locus of information about public architecture, Hohokam burial practices, and ceramic production and exchange. Furthermore, spatial distributions of villages provide evidence regarding population growth and changing patterns of regional relationships. The topics explored in the sections that follow are: (1) social integration and interaction in the late Colonial period, (2) the major reorganization that took place in the mid-Sedentary period in the Tucson Basin, and (3) the trend toward increasing social differentiation during the Classic period. Within each of these sections a consideration of issues affecting village structure is presented along with data addressing the specific research question.

# SOCIAL INTEGRATION AND INTERACTION
# IN THE LATE COLONIAL PERIOD

The Rillito (Santa Cruz) phase was a time of florescence throughout the Hohokam regional system. In addition, the existing data base is relatively good for this phase. In this section we review the evidence for population growth during the Rillito phase, describe the Colonial period ballcourt system in the Tucson Basin, and discuss models of late Colonial period socioeconomic interaction.

## POPULATION GROWTH DURING THE RILLITO PHASE

Information on population size is important for addressing issues of social change. While current data do not allow actual population estimates to be made, it is possible to consider on a more refined relative scale whether substantial population increase is indicated for the Colonial period in the Tucson Basin. Data presented by Mayberry (1983), for example, show that there was almost a fivefold increase in site frequency in the Tucson Basin between the Cañada del Oro and Rillito phases. A more recent tabulation from the Arizona State Museum's computerized AZSITE files showed a four-fold increase between these phases (Dart and Doelle 1988). These data provide a useful starting point for addressing the issue of population increase.

In a recent article, Nichols and Powell (1987) discuss some pitfalls of demographic reconstruction using archaeological data. In particular, they address situations where large sites, large numbers of sites, or both conditions in combination, result from the actions of relatively few persons. Seasonal occupations, short occupation spans, and reoccupation of the same area are three specific mechanisms that they discuss. The present discussion addresses such factors to the extent possible.

Only a few large-scale excavations have been completed at Colonial period sites (e.g., Ferg et al. 1984; Kelly 1978; Layhe 1986), though several relevant examples are still under analysis at present (e.g., Bernard-Shaw 1989b; Cza-plicki and Ravesloot 1989). Therefore, this discussion relies most heavily on data from surface contexts, which are supplemented with excavation data. Fortunately, new data on occupation span are available for 10 of the 24 large villages considered here (Table 7.1), and 6 more have at least some excavation data.

Variation in site occupation span and seasonality of occupation can be controlled to a degree by focusing this inquiry upon a specific class of site, the large village. Such villages are believed to have been the primary locus of the Hohokam community prior to Middle Rincon times (Doelle 1988). Furthermore, although permanency of occupation at large villages is a hypothesis that has not been adequately tested, the potential pitfall of "counting" the same population more than once is largely avoided by such a focus.

Rather than consider only site frequency, newly collected data allow the frequency of large samples of temporally diagnostic ceramics to be examined. Figures 7.11 and 7.12 show two classes of sites that have been identified within the sample of large villages. Sites in the first group (Fig. 7.11) all had an initial occupation during the Pioneer period that continued through the Colonial period and frequently into the Sedentary period. These data indicate that continuity of occupation is generally the case for the Tucson Basin large villages until late in Preclassic times. This fact lowers the probability that sequential occupations of different large villages are being classed as contemporaneous.

Table 7.1    *Known Tucson Basin Large Villages with Data on Ballcourts and Site Occupation Span (sites with two ballcourts are listed twice)*

| Site Number | Site Name | Length (m) | Orientation | Dating Source* | Site Occupation Span |
|---|---|---|---|---|---|
| *Large Courts* | | | | | |
| BB:9:1 | Romero | 54 | N050E | 1 | Sweetwater through Tucson |
| BB:9:104 | Sleeping Snake | 46 | N157E | 7 | Rillito through Tanque Verde |
| AA:12:57 | Los Morteros | 64 | N130E | 2 | Rillito through Tanque Verde |
| AA:12:18 | Hodges | 61.5 | N105E | 3 | Sweetwater through Tanque Verde |
| BB:13:15 | Valencia | 56 | N162E | 4 | Sweetwater through Late Rincon |
| BB:13:7 | Martinez Hill | 56 | N009E | 5 | Sweetwater through Rincon |
| BB:13:232 | Unnamed | 51 | N-S | 8, 9 | Snaketown through Cañada del Oro, Rincon through Tanque Verde |
| BB:13:221 | Boundary Village | 69 | N111E | 6 | Sweetwater or Snaketown through Early Rincon |
| *Indeterminate Courts* | | | | | |
| AA:12:73 | Huntington | ? | ? | 16 | Snaketown through Tanque Verde |
| *Small Courts* | | | | | |
| AA:11:4 | Robles Wash | 22.4 | N080E | 15 | Cañada del Oro through Tanque Verde |
| AA:8:184 | Derrio Wash | 26.5 | N078E | 15 | Rillito(?) through Tanque Verde |
| BB:5:5 | Rainbows End | 20 | N045E | 7 | Rillito through Middle Rincon |
| BB:9:88 | Honey Bee | 30.5 | N032E | 7, 17 | Snaketown through Tanque Verde |
| BB:9:1 | Romero | 25.3 | N024E | 1 | Estrella through Tucson |
| AA:16:49 | Dakota Wash | 20 | N-S | 10, 18 | Estrella through Rillito, Tanque Verde reoccupation |
| AA:16:94 | Waterworld | 23.3 | N077E | 11 | Rillito |
| BB:13:7 | Martinez Hill | 28.5 | N104E | 5 | Estrella through Rincon |
| BB:13:16A | Punta de Agua | 40 | N-S | 6 | Rillito through Tanque Verde |
| BB:13:16C | Punta de Agua | 34.5 | N077E | 6 | Cañada del Oro through Late Rincon, Tucson reoccupation |
| EE:2:105 | Ballcourt | 24.8 | N035E | 12 | Cañada del Oro through Early Rincon |
| *Large Sites without Known Courts* | | | | | |
| AA:12:51 | Stewart Brickyard | | | 5 | Sweetwater through Rillito |
| BB:9:14 | Hardy | | | 13 | Sweetwater through Late Rincon |
| BB:14:22 | Bosque | | | 9 | Snaketown through Middle Rincon |
| BB:14:2,3 | Pithouse Village | | | 5 | Sweetwater through Tanque Verde |
| AA:16:26 | Saint Mary's | | | 14 | Snaketown through Middle or Late Rincon |
| BB:13:17 | Julian Wash | | | 9 | Snaketown through Rincon |
| BB:13:202 | Ortonville | | | 6 | Snaketown through Late Rincon |

*Citations for dating sources: 1, Elson and Doelle 1987; 2, Lange 1989; 3, Kelly 1978; 4, Elson and Doelle 1986; 5, Arizona State Museum site files; 6, Doelle and Wallace 1986; 7, Craig and Wallace 1987; 8, Doelle, Dart, and Wallace 1985; 9, Unpublished data at Center for Desert Archaeology; 10, Craig, 1988; 11, Czaplicki and Ravesloot 1989; 12, Ferg et al. 1984; 13, Gregonis 1989; 14, Jacobs 1979; 15, John Madsen and David Wilcox personal communication 1988; 16, Huntington 1912; 17, Craig 1989c; 18, Craig 1989b.

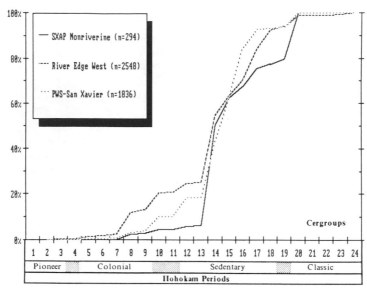

Figure 7.11    *Occupational histories of early large villages in the Tucson Basin.*

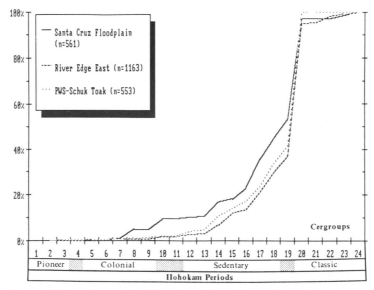

Figure 7.12    *Occupational histories of "later" large villages in the Tucson Basin.*

The sites in Figure 7.12 show that a second group of sites represents large villages that were established during the Colonial period, especially the Rillito phase. The establishment of new large villages with apparent continuity of most other large villages appears to be good evidence for population increase during the Colonial period. Two of these sites, Waterworld and Sleeping

Snake, were established in areas without direct access to permanent water. Thus there are suggestions that the prime areas along the major river systems had been utilized by the Rillito phase, thereby forcing further expansion to occur in less optimal environmental settings.

For some sites in Figures 7.11 and 7.12, the spatial distribution of diagnostic ceramic types over the site has been examined. Intensive mapping and surface collection at the Valencia and Romero sites showed that the Rillito and Early Rincon diagnostics were maximally scattered over the site area and within the site area, numerous high density areas were present that were identifiable as trash concentrations or mounds (Elson and Doelle 1986, 1987). Similar patterns were documented at the Honey Bee and Sleeping Snake sites (Craig 1987). Thus, in addition to continuity of occupation, many sites show a maximum intensity of occupation in the Rillito or Early Rincon phases. All of these factors support the proposition that population was growing in the Colonial and possibly early Sedentary periods in the Tucson Basin.

That the Colonial period was a time of population growth in the Tucson Basin is certainly not counter to the conventional wisdom about this time period, but this review provides more empirical support for this proposition than has been possible in the past. A question that has not been adequately addressed is: What caused population growth during this time period? Several factors can be suggested. First, in the southernmost Tucson Basin, Waters (1987) has documented improved conditions for floodwater farming within the Santa Cruz River floodplain. The spatial extent of these floodplain conditions needs to be better established before this can be considered a primary causal factor, however, for this phenomenon has thus far been documented within only a limited study area. Second, there is evidence of the introduction of new corn varieties into other parts of the Hohokam area in Santa Cruz times (Cutler and Blake 1976:365–366). In the Tucson Basin, excavations at the Dakota Wash site established that all early Colonial period maize was of a more primitive type (Miksicek 1989). Therefore, it is likely that Rillito phase samples will be required in order to document the time of introduction of new maize varieties into the Tucson Basin. A third factor to consider is that the new social system indicated by the wide distribution of Hohokam ballcourts was a contributing factor to population growth. As an integrative mechanism, the ballcourt system may have functioned to resolve disputes, encourage cooperative labor and surplus production, and generally favor larger family size for the larger labor pool that it would represent. As additional excavation of Colonial period sites is completed, it will be important to refine and test hypotheses regarding the magnitude and causes of population growth.

## COLONIAL PERIOD BALLCOURTS IN THE TUCSON BASIN

Until recently, very few ballcourts were known at Preclassic sites in the Tucson Basin, but 20 ballcourts are now documented (Table 7.1). Dating of these ballcourts is imprecise because few have been excavated; however, several patterns are suggestive. First, many of the sites in Table 7.1 have continuous occupation spans from at least the late Pioneer through the Colonial periods. Second, excavations at three courts have established that they date at least as early as the Rillito phase (Craig 1989a; Czaplicki and Ravesloot 1989; Kelly 1978). Finally, a large ballcourt was discovered recently at BB:13:232, a site where surface collections yielded moderate quantities of Snaketown and Cañada del Oro phase ceramics, but very little from the Rillito phase. Even without excavation, then, BB:13:232 appears to have a high likelihood to be a Cañada del Oro phase ballcourt.

In his important synthesis of data on Hohokam ballcourts, Wilcox (Wilcox and Sternberg 1983:193) reported only four courts that dated to the Gila Butte phase (equivalent to the Cañada del Oro phase in the Tucson Basin). The broad spatial distribution of those courts led Wilcox to infer that early ballcourts tended to be widely separated from one another. Subsequent data are beginning to suggest that the network character of the Hohokam ballcourt system that Wilcox (Wilcox and Sternberg 1983:194) attributes largely to the late Colonial and Sedentary periods, may have developed quite quickly. The possible Cañada del Oro ballcourt just discussed and the fact that many of the Tucson Basin ballcourt sites have strong early Colonial occupations are suggestive of a rapid spread of the ballcourt system over the Hohokam region. Furthermore, ballcourts at Los Solares (McGuire 1987) in the Phoenix Basin and at the Rock Ball Court site near Gila Bend (Wasley and Johnson 1965) were both built and abandoned during the Gila Butte phase.

A plot of the frequency of Tucson Basin ballcourts by length shows a strong bimodal distribution into small and large size classes (Fig. 7.13). However, examination of the spatial distribution of these two size classes of ballcourts (Fig. 7.14) does not reveal an obvious pattern; courts of both sizes are widely distributed. This diversity of size and temporal data for Tucson Basin ballcourts is similar to that documented by Wilcox (Wilcox and Sternberg 1983) for the entire Hohokam system, and it raises questions regarding the function of ballcourts in Hohokam society.

## THE ROLE OF BALLCOURTS IN THE
## LATE COLONIAL SOCIOECONOMIC SYSTEM

Most researchers seem to agree with the basic premise presented by Wilcox (1979a:111; Wilcox and Sternberg 1983:189–217) that ballcourts served an integrative function, tying various levels of the Hohokam settlement hierarchy together. This includes intervillage relationships, the integration of communities within local systems, and ultimately the integration of multiple local systems within the Hohokam regional system. From Wilcox and Sternberg's (1983:213) perspective, the ballcourt data indicate an economically integrated

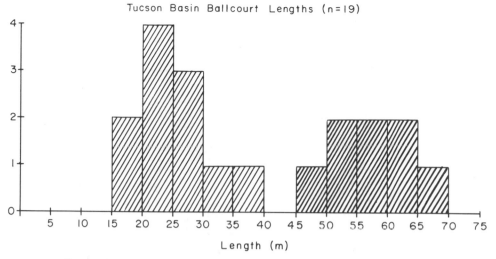

Figure 7.13     *Bimodal size distribution of Tucson Basin ballcourts as a basis for identifying "large" and "small" ballcourts.*

system at each level of the settlement hierarchy. Although they note the possibility of seasonal trade fairs or markets, in general they conceptualize exchange as occurring within the framework of affinal relationships rather than through a market economy. They suggest that:

> To transfer food or other goods in bulk from one place to another in a short time, the Hohokam would have needed such a system [one that entailed a seasonal round of ballcourt ceremonies]. The obligation to produce goods or services for ceremonies, when harnessed to a scheduled round of ceremonial events among a set of nearby communities would have created periodic pools of goods and the motivation to carry them to another place as gifts or presentations in a continuing series of reciprocal exchanges. . . . All of these exchanges could have been handled at the domestic group level, though the heads of some of these groups may have also acted on some occasions for larger social aggregates [Wilcox and Sternberg 1983:213].

Wilcox and Sternberg's (1983) model also incorporates levels of exchange beyond that cited here. Elite goods are apparently seen to follow a different pattern of exchange than bulk commodities, though specific mechanisms and expected patterns of distribution are not explained. Wilcox and Sternberg (1983:51) clearly argue against a true redistributive economy characterized by central places with warehouse storage given the lack of any archaeological supporting data or appropriate ethnographic models (Wilcox and Sternberg 1983:51).

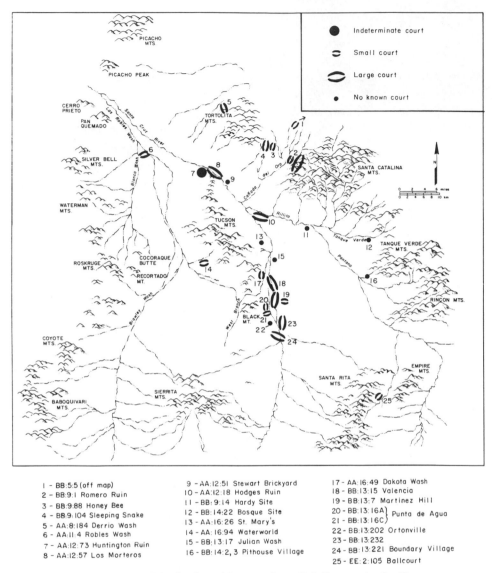

| | | |
|---|---|---|
| 1 - BB:5:5 (off map) | 9 - AA:12:51 Stewart Brickyard | 17 - AA:16:49 Dakota Wash |
| 2 - BB:9:1 Romero Ruin | 10 - AA:12:18 Hodges Ruin | 18 - BB:13:15 Valencia |
| 3 - BB:9:88 Honey Bee | 11 - BB:9:14 Hardy Site | 19 - BB:13:7 Martinez Hill |
| 4 - BB:9:104 Sleeping Snake | 12 - BB:14:22 Bosque Site | 20 - BB:13:16A } Punta de Agua |
| 5 - AA:8:184 Derrio Wash | 13 - AA:16:26 St. Mary's | 21 - BB:13:16C } |
| 6 - AA:11:4 Robles Wash | 14 - AA:16:94 Waterworld | 22 - BB:13:202 Ortonville |
| 7 - AA:12:73 Huntington Ruin | 15 - BB:13:17 Julian Wash | 23 - BB:13:232 |
| 8 - AA:12:57 Los Morteros | 16 - BB:14:2, 3 Pithouse Village | 24 - BB:13:221 Boundary Village |
| | | 25 - EE:2:105 Ballcourt |

Figure 7.14    *Distribution of large and small ballcourts in the Tucson Basin and vicinity.*

Teague (1984) has attempted to identify the nature of economic interactions of the Hohokam in the Phoenix Basin and Gila Bend areas through an evaluation of ratios of various artifact classes at platform mound, ballcourt, and other habitation sites. She evaluates the data utilizing the basic economic distinctions of Polanyi (reciprocity, redistribution, and market economy) and concludes that for the Preclassic, "the ballcourt system . . . does not appear to have been economically significant to the Hohokam except, perhaps, as the site of ritual exchange between families and individuals" (Teague 1984:238).

She states that "the basic level of down-the-line exchange (probably rooted in reciprocal relationships) seems to have coexisted with more clearly bounded and, in some cases centralized networks. Common but reasonably valuable items, like decorated ceramics, might have traveled in virtually all the networks existing at one time" (Teague 1984:237).

Such debate between Hohokam researchers regarding the economic role of ballcourts is concerned largely with the function of ballcourts on intervillage relations. While Wilcox's argument is both plausible and appealing, it is in need of substantial testing. Similarly, Teague's (1984) arguments are not sufficiently thorough to have discredited Wilcox's model. Given this situation, we offer a consideration of the role of ballcourts on the intravillage level. This aspect of ballcourts has not been ignored entirely by other researchers, but we argue that it has at least been underemphasized.

We propose to make a crude estimate of the labor required for ballcourt construction in comparison to a common activity performed at the household level, construction of a pithouse. In this manner at least a relative scale for assessing the labor management requirements of ballcourt construction can be obtained. There are not good data on the volume of earth that was excavated during the construction of most Tucson Basin ballcourts, but we can use the surface area of the courts as a relative measure of that volume and by extension as a relative measure of labor requirements. Based on this, the average surface area of small ballcourts was approximately 286 sq m, with an average of 1,276 sq m for large courts. A logical standard of comparison is the area of a pithouse, for this type of feature was commonly constructed by the Hohokam, presumably with labor recruited from the household. Figures vary for different sites and time periods, but a mean of about 20 sq m seems reasonable. This means that ballcourts represent a range from 14 to over 60 times the level of effort that individual households were commonly investing in architectural endeavors.

Two very general implications can be safely drawn from this exercise. First, ballcourts imply an effective mechanism to organize labor at a level above the household. Given that nearly all late Colonial period large villages in the Tucson Basin are now known to have had ballcourts, it seems most likely that the labor for ballcourt construction would have been mobilized at the village level. Second, ballcourts can probably be viewed as indicators that a population threshold had been reached by a related set of villages. The conditions of general increase in population within the Tucson Basin and the evidence for larger village size indicate the availability of a potential source of labor for ballcourt construction, maintenance, and use, and they imply a greater need for social integration. This is a much more general level of inference regarding ballcourts than has generally been made by Hohokam archaeologists, but it appears to be a cautious one that will not lead us too far astray pending further research on ballcourt function.

# THE ROLE OF EXCHANGE IN THE LATE COLONIAL
# SOCIOECONOMIC SYSTEM

The most striking result of the buff ware distributional analysis presented earlier is without question the identification of an area in the southern portion of the Tucson Basin that is marked by low frequencies of Santa Cruz Red-on-buff. Considering the relatively constant decorated ceramic percentages obtained for sites all across the basin, it can be seen that the buff ware present in other portions of the northern Basin was displaced by Rillito Red-on-brown in the southern Tucson Basin, not added to it. This means that there are higher frequencies of Rillito Red-on-brown in this area than elsewhere in the basin, a finding consistent with the hypothesis of localized ceramic production. To determine how much more common Rillito Red-on-brown is on these sites, an odds ratio (see Knoke and Burke 1980:10) was calculated using frequency data published by Wallace (1987, 1988a). The ratios of Rillito Red-on-brown to Santa Cruz Red-on-buff for each case with accurate counts were calculated and then averaged for the northern basin and the southern basin. These values were then divided as follows:

$$\text{Odds Ratio} = \frac{\text{Southern Basin Brown}}{\text{Southern Basin Buff}} \div \frac{\text{Northern Basin Brown}}{\text{Northern Basin Buff}}$$

$$= (782/119) \div (846/850)$$
$$= 6.6 / 1.0$$
$$= 6.6$$

Thus, Rillito Red-on-brown sherds, on the average, are 6.6 times more common on sites in the southern basin as on sites in the northern basin. In order to evaluate the significance of this differential spatial distribution, at least three topics must be discussed. First, general issues of ceramic production and exchange must be assessed. The second issue is the nature of social relations between the Tucson and Phoenix basins, and the third issue is the nature of social relations within the Tucson Basin.

## Ceramic Production and Exchange: Some General Issues

There are two different decorated ceramic types involved in the spatial patterning under consideration, and there are some general issues that merit discussion for each type in order to properly evaluate the meaning of these data. First, it is well established that the buff ware and brown ware types were made in the Phoenix and Tucson basins, respectively, but it would be useful to know how many production locations there were for these decorated wares. Decorated ceramic production could have occurred on a continuum from highly centralized (e.g., production at a single village) to highly dispersed (e.g., production by every household), and the interpretation of archaeological distributions of materials is greatly aided by an understanding of the context in which production took place.

Second, it is important to establish a framework for considering the value of these different types of pottery. The value that was placed on a particular item would have affected what people would have been willing to exchange for it, and it would have affected the ways in which the vessel was used once it was obtained. Value cannot be determined precisely, but a general consideration of this issue is useful.

Third, it is necessary to consider the contexts within which decorated ceramic types were used by the prehistoric Hohokam. Were these items confined only to elite contexts or did they circulate with items that were used broadly regardless of one's level in the social system? Once these three general topics have been considered, we return to the issues of prehistoric socioeconomic relations that are our central concern.

## Decorated Ceramic Production

There is often an assumption of village, or site-level autonomy employed by archaeologists, particularly when considering ceramic production. Plog (1980; Braun and Plog 1982) has seriously questioned this general assumption, and there is increasing evidence that production of decorated ceramics was not carried out by every Hohokam household (Abbott 1984; Wallace and Heidke 1986). For the Phoenix Basin, the best evidence for decorated ceramic manufacture comes from sites such as Snaketown (Haury 1976) and the Gila Butte site (Rafferty 1982). The term "centralized production" employed by Abbott (1984) implies very few loci of production. Such a model would be appropriate if further study were to show that the Snaketown–Gila Butte area was producing all of the buff ware, for example. A more realistic model might be that production occurred at a series of settlements or village segments across the Phoenix Basin. This "limited production" model represents a level of production somewhere between true single-village production and the more general pan-regional production often assumed in the literature. Furthermore, such a model could account for the spatial variability in ceramic design encountered by Crown (1984) in the Queen Creek and Gila River areas. If understanding of exchange and many other issues related to Phoenix Basin ceramics is to advance, it will be critical to resolve which of these models are closest to reality, for they have dramatically different implications.

In the Tucson Basin some progress is being made toward the resolution of this issue. In the western Tucson Basin, strong evidence for ceramic production on a scale of sufficient magnitude to be supplying a large proportion of the decorated wares at several sites in the eastern Basin has been reported (see Wallace and Heidke 1986:247). In addition, the evidence suggests that the sites located south of the Valencia site on the Santa Cruz River may have been involved in a separate exchange system and, at least at Punta de Agua, were definitely producing decorated pottery (Rincon Red or Rincon Polychrome) in the Middle Rincon subphase. A variety of data suggest that the Middle Rincon pattern was preceded by a long history of ceramic production in the same area.

No evidence for Rillito phase ceramic production has been gathered for the northern or eastern Tucson Basin although a strong Rillito phase component has been documented at Hodges (Kelly 1978; Whittlesey 1986) and surface collections have been made on other sites (Elson and Doelle 1987; Lange 1989; Craig and Wallace 1987). In contrast, there is good evidence for Rillito phase ceramic production in the southern portion of the basin where Middle Rincon production was later centered. Craig (1989a) reports finding pieces of ceramic temper (Catalina gneiss and schist) in excavations at the Dakota Wash site (AA:16:49), implying continuity in production at this locality at least through the Sedentary period (see Huntington 1986). Pieces of temper were also recovered from surface contexts at the Valencia and Ortonville sites (Elson and Doelle 1986), both of which are large early villages with strong Rillito phase components. At the site complex west of Black Mountain, Dart (1987) reports finding a large number of polishing stones on sites that have mixed Rillito through Middle Rincon components.

In summary, a "limited production" model for decorated ceramics appears to best fit the data for the Tucson Basin for at least the late Colonial and the early half of the Sedentary periods. The possibility of a similar model being appropriate for the Phoenix Basin has been suggested, but convincing empirical support for any model in the Phoenix Basin is lacking at present.

### The Value and Cultural Context of Hohokam Decorated Ceramics

These issues are considered together due to their close relationship and to the limited amount of data for addressing them. For the archaeologist, a reasonable way to approach the question of the value of a prehistoric item is to consider the relative amount of labor that is required for the production and distribution of that item. Abbott (1984) used such an approach in his consideration of Hohokam plain, red, and buff wares. Based on the number of production steps involved, he concluded that the value of plain ware would have been the lowest and buff ware the highest. Buff ware is considered by Abbott (1984) to have been equivalent to fine china in modern society in terms of its use for domestic purposes and in terms of its exchange value. Evidence on the recovery contexts of buff ware ceramics in the Tucson Basin supports this general view of its prehistoric value as well.

There are no data to support the position of Wallace and Holmlund (1982) that buff ware was an elite trade commodity, and Wallace (1987, 1988a) provides a detailed discussion to counter Whittlesey's (1986) argument that Santa Cruz Red-on-buff was present primarily in cremation contexts at the Hodges site. Buff ware is found on both large and small sites and it is distributed in all types of contexts within sites. It seems most likely that a Santa Cruz Red-on-buff vessel would have had a slightly higher value than a local pot, due at a minimum to the higher transportation costs of the nonlocal vessel. However, it is unlikely that it was so valuable or limited in function as to preclude the average household from acquiring and utilizing it for domestic purposes. The occurrence of this type in similar contexts in neighboring areas such as the San Pedro Valley (Franklin 1980; Masse 1980; Tuthill 1947) and the Nogales area (DiPeso 1956; Grebinger 1971; Doyel 1977b) implies a similar role in each area where it was introduced as a trade ware. The lack of evidence that this type is recovered only from high status or ceremonial contexts is significant in evaluating its spatial distribution, for it suggests that the systems involved in its transport were not restricted to "elite" or "prestige" spheres of exchange. The same conclusion would appear to hold for the red-on-brown decorated wares from the Tucson Basin, as they are found widely distributed in all types of sites and in diverse contexts within sites.

### Social and Economic Relations between the Tucson and Phoenix Basins

The presence of substantial quantities of Santa Cruz Red-on-buff pottery in the Tucson Basin and vicinity raises the question of the nature of the social relations between these two subregions of the Hohokam regional system. The similarities in form and style between Santa Cruz Red-on-buff and the Tucson Basin type, Rillito Red-on-brown, are striking. Considered along with similarities in other classes of material culture, participation in a shared cultural system is the minimum level of relationship that must be drawn. The degree of material dependence on the Phoenix Basin probably was not all that great, however. For example, even though buff ware frequencies are high in the northern Tucson Basin when they are calculated as a percentage of the decorated assemblage, they are only about 5 percent of the *total* ceramic assemblage. Using procedures and assumptions similar to those detailed by Wallace and Heidke (1986), we have made an "order of magnitude" estimation that annual consumption of buff ware vessels in the Tucson Basin probably numbered in the hundreds, not the thousands. Relatively few potters in the Phoenix Basin could have met this demand with little difficulty. Therefore, the really interesting question raised by the differential distribution of buff ware in the northern and southern Tucson Basin is: What kinds of local conditions are likely to have caused this pattern?

### Social and Economic Relations within the Tucson Basin

The economics of ceramic production in the Tucson Basin probably played a key role in the observed distribution of decorated ceramics. The presence of an anomalously low frequency of intrusive buff ware in the same area where most of the decorated ceramics for the basin may have been produced seems more than coincidental. Thus the availability of large numbers of decorated vessels near their sites of production in the southern Tucson Basin would have served to give them a much lower "cost" than an imported buff ware. This would help account for the higher frequency of brown ware in the southern Tucson Basin, but there are two elements of the distribution data that remain problematic.

First, it is curious that there are relatively high frequencies of buff ware in the Nogales area south of Tucson, for this implies that the buff ware somehow bypassed the economic system of the southern Tucson Basin. Second, the abruptness of the transition between the northern and southern Tucson Basin patterns of decorated frequency is difficult to explain. Several possibilities to address these problems are considered.

The first hypothesis is tied to the economics of pottery production. The limited production model for the Tucson Basin means that southern Tucson Basin potters would have a relatively low-value item to exchange if they wanted to obtain Phoenix Basin buff wares. The logical sources for buff wares for these people would be the residents of the northern Tucson Basin. Furthermore, why should a southern Tucson Basin potter pay a premium price for a buff ware when all that would be gained was an item that was the functional equivalent of the pottery that he or she could make? One motivation for such a transaction might be to obtain an item that could be exchanged again to more distant parties who valued it even more. This hypothesis accounts for the abruptness of the transition between the northern and southern Tucson basins by postulating that the transition zone is the transition between producers and nonproducers of decorated ceramics. It accounts for the very low buff ware frequencies in the southern Tucson Basin by postulating that buff wares were only rarely consumed in that location; they were traded again to parties farther to the south.

The second hypothesis postulates a degree of social differentiation between the northern and southern Tucson basins. Fall-off models employed by archaeologists to assess the types of exchange systems implied by different spatial distributions of material culture assume that the costs of production and transport are key factors affecting the movement of goods. The present spatial pattern, which runs counter to a simple fall-off model, suggests that additional cultural factors may have to be considered. It is possible, for example, that the southern Tucson Basin represents an interacting social system that had become at least somewhat differentiated from the northern Tucson Basin. It may be that only a limited level of population (or number of villages) could be incorporated into an interaction system. With population growth, new villages would enter the interaction system, leading to a process of differentiation.

A preliminary test of these models is provided by the existing data that were already reviewed. They indicated a lack of evidence for decorated ceramic manufacture in the northern Tucson Basin during the Colonial period. A more intensive study directed at this issue will be necessary to fully evaluate these hypotheses, however.

## SUMMARY

The developments of the Colonial period were dramatic throughout the Hohokam regional system, and the Tucson Basin participated very directly in those developments. The distribution of Phoenix Basin ceramics and the ballcourt system are strong indicators of the rapid spread of a common cultural system and the maintenance of continued interaction. However, the Tucson Basin Hohokam system was different from the Phoenix Basin in a number of ways, and those differences were to become increasingly marked during the subsequent Sedentary period.

# THE MID-SEDENTARY PERIOD
# REORGANIZATION

The review of settlement pattern data already provided evidence for a major reorganization of the Tucson Basin Hohokam during the middle of the Sedentary period. In this section a focus on the Valencia site, a large ballcourt village in the southern Tucson Basin, further illustrates this reorganization and it provides insight into some aspects of village structure that were changing. This is supplemented by a discussion of excavated Rincon phase sites. Changes in the role of ballcourts as integrative mechanisms, transformations of the role that households played in the social and economic system, changes in burial ritual, and shifts in patterns of ceramic production and exchange are all considered.

## CHANGING VILLAGE STRUCTURE AT THE
## VALENCIA SITE

Excavation data from the Valencia site come from a road right-of-way along the western margin of the site (Doelle 1985a), but intensive surface collections from most of the site and testing of the southern component (Elson and Doelle 1986) help place those excavations in context, as does other research in the immediate vicinity (Betancourt 1978; Bradley 1980; Downum and Dart 1986; Ravesloot 1984; Sense 1980).

The Valencia site testing project employed a 25 m grid system that was tied-in to a detailed contour map (Fig. 7.15). The surface collection methods that were used (Elson and Doelle 1986:8–10) yielded roughly a 40 percent sample of high-information artifacts like decorated ceramics, plain ware rims, and shell. Only about 8 percent of lower-information artifacts, like plain ware body sherds and lithic debitage, were collected. The surface collection at the Valencia site yielded nearly 23,000 artifacts. Major features defined from surface observation include 16 trash mounds, 12 trash concentrations, and a

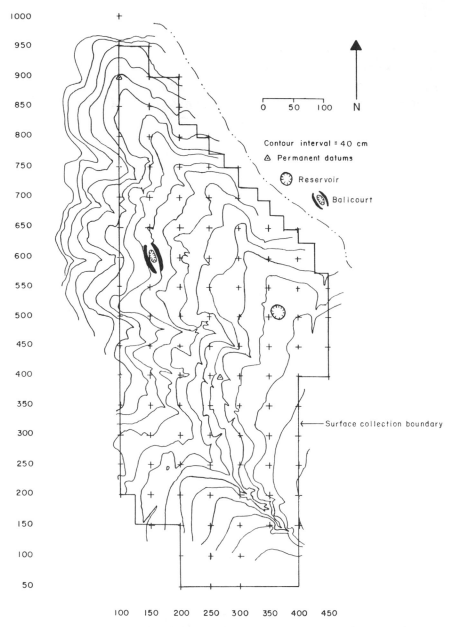

Figure 7.15    *Surface features and grid system at the Valencia site in the southern Tucson Basin.*

ballcourt. In addition, a small reservoir was visible as a surface depression, and its function was determined through trenching.

Studies of artifact distributions revealed three additional features or activity areas. First, cremated human bone was found to be highly concentrated on the east-central portion of the site allowing the identification of a large

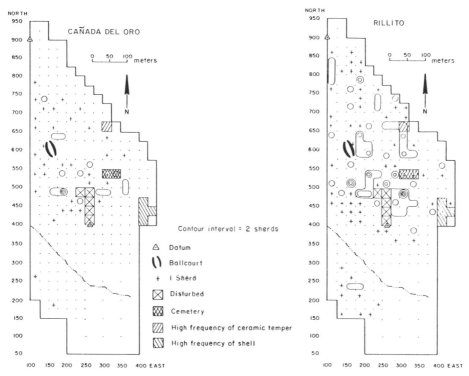

Figure 7.16    *Surface distribution of Colonial period diagnostic ceramic types for the central portion of the Valencia site.*

cemetery. Second, an area on the far eastern periphery of the site showed a particularly high frequency of worked and unworked shell. This suggests a possible workshop area, though excavation would be required to test this inference due to the overall low frequency of shell on the site surface. Third, a very large concentration of gneiss that was imported from the northern side of the Tucson Basin for use as ceramic temper was found on a trash mound on the northeast side of the site. The distribution of temporal diagnostics is the only basis for assigning dates to these special use areas. Because this is an imprecise method, these special use areas are shown on each of the maps in Figures 7.16 and 7.17.

The 40 percent sample of decorated ceramics on the site surface amounted to some 3,610 sherds. Of these, 1,503 (42 percent) could be assigned to a Cergroup (Cergroups represent temporally sequenced groups of ceramic types), and 812 (22 percent) could be identified to a specific phase or subphase. The phase data (Table 7.2) show a significant Pioneer period occupation, particularly when the low frequency of decorated ware production during the early Hohokam phases is considered. The increase in Cañada del Oro ceramics would likely be even greater if better criteria for identifying the diagnostic types for this phase were available, but the highest frequency of diagnostics

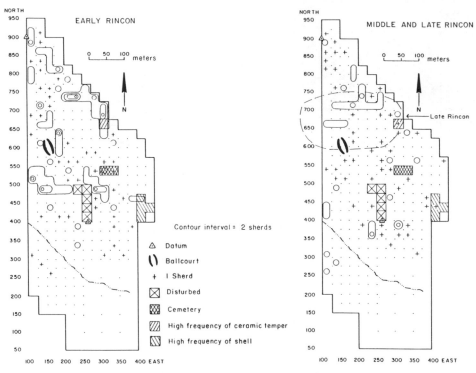

Figure 7.17    *Surface distribution of Sedentary period diagnostic ceramic
types for the central portion of the Valencia site.*

Table 7.2    *Diagnostic Ceramics Recovered from the Surface of the Valencia Site*

| Phase or Subphase | Count | Percent |
|---|---|---|
| Tanque Verde | 2 | 0.2 |
| Late Rincon | 22 | 2.7 |
| Middle Rincon | 151 | 18.6 |
| Early Rincon | 269 | 33.1 |
| Rillito | 260 | 32.0 |
| Cañada del Oro | 87 | 10.7 |
| Snaketown | 19 | 2.3 |
| Sweetwater | 2 | 0.2 |
| TOTAL | 812 | 99.8 |

is clearly for Rillito and Early Rincon times (Fig. 7.16). The Middle Rincon
subphase appears to represent a significant decline in the intensity of occupation at Valencia (Fig. 7.17), particularly given the fact that this time period
was probably longer than the Early Rincon subphase (Doelle 1985a:272) and
it was probably characterized by higher frequencies of decorated ceramics

Table 7.3    *Diagnostic Ceramics Recovered from Surface and Subsurface Contexts at the Southern Component of the Valencia Site*

| Phase or Subphase | Count | Percent |
|---|---|---|
| Tanque Verde | 1 | 2.6 |
| Late Rincon | 1 | 2.6 |
| Middle Rincon | 8 | 21.1 |
| Early Rincon | 5 | 13.2 |
| Rillito | 20 | 52.6 |
| Cañada del Oro | 3 | 7.9 |
| TOTAL | 38 | 100.0 |

(Elson and Doelle 1986:56; Dart 1987:95). The Valencia site was abandoned by the end of the Late Rincon subphase.

Craig (1987) developed the concept of mound groups as an empirical means for identifying possible prehistoric social groups using data from intensive surface collections. His approach was to identify clusters of trash mounds and trash concentrations and then to examine the temporal variation within the different deposits. In general he found that the deposits within a mound group showed similar temporal patterns. He reasoned, therefore, that there was a likelihood that social groups that persisted over time had occupied the areas identified as mound groups. For the Valencia site, a refinement of Craig's approach is proposed. We plot the distribution of the diagnostics from particular time periods, and then employ the assumption that high density areas identify probable trash disposal areas. In many cases these high density areas are visible mounds even today, but some are too subtle to distinguish without the carefully controlled surface collection techniques that were employed at the Valencia site. The second refinement is to connect the probable trash deposits that are indicated by higher frequencies of diagnostics with straight lines. The area bounded by the polygons that result from this exercise are hypothesized to roughly approximate the occupation area of a past social group.

Fortunately, there are several lines of evidence to support such a procedure. First, at the southern component of the Valencia site, backhoe trenching served to supplement the intensive surface collection. The intensity of occupation of this southern component appears to have been less than the area around the ballcourt, and the resulting low frequency of diagnostics requires a slight modification to the approach that is used on the rest of the site. This modification is based on the fact that this is largely a single component occupation. The majority of the surface and subsurface ceramics recovered from this component date to the Rillito phase (Table 7.3). Only 8 of the 18 pithouses could be dated based on artifacts recovered during testing, and 6 of those dated to the Rillito phase. Thus, it is likely that the majority of the undated houses would be placed in the Rillito phase if they were excavated. Therefore,

316                                                       *William H. Doelle and Henry D. Wallace*

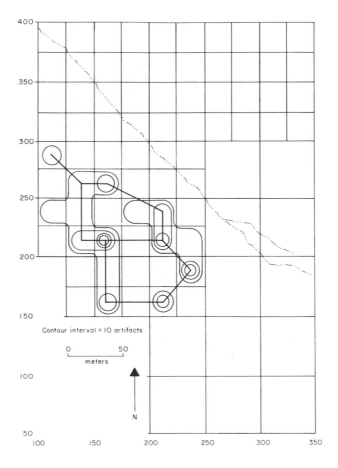

A. Village segments defined by surface data.

Figure 7.18    *Possible Rillito phase village segments defined with surface
data and verified through backhoe trenching at the southern
component of the Valencia site.*

if total artifact density is plotted, then an approximation of a contemporaneous
set of trash deposits can be defined. As Figure 7.18a shows, our method
serves to define two enclosed polygons. Similarly, the results of the backhoe
trenching define two clusters of buried pithouses (Fig. 7.18b), though there
is a slight spatial offset to the areas defined by the two methods.

The two social groups that are hypothesized as present are outlined by
75 m diameter circles, based on Wallace's (1988b) observation that village
segments tend to have a maximum size that is not expected to be greater
than 75 m. Furthermore, it is interesting to note that many of the closed
polygons defined on the basis of surface diagnostics from the Valencia site
(Fig. 7.19) are also approximately 50 to 75 m in diameter. These data add
strong support to the assumption that a reasonable approximation of the size

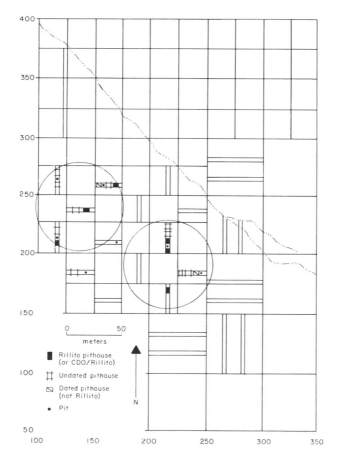

B. Village segments defined by backhoe trenching.

and distribution of past social units is being delineated with this analysis method (see also Craig 1989c). This approach is employed here as a means for examining changing village structure over time.

For the Rillito phase, it is striking how an interlocking network of polygons of roughly equivalent size is definable. Also, two apparent communal features are in evidence; a large cremation area on the eastern side of the site and a large ballcourt on the west side. The nearly continuous occupation by these hypothesized social units, and the sharing of at least these two communal areas is suggestive of a high degree of coherence of social action on the level of the village. This evidence is consistent with our earlier discussion regarding the important functions of ballcourts on the intravillage level.

The changes evident for the Early Rincon subphase are very interesting. Rather than uniformity in the size of polygons, they are of variable size, and along the northeast edge of the site the trash concentrations appear more linear. The cremation area shows continued use, and there are indications of

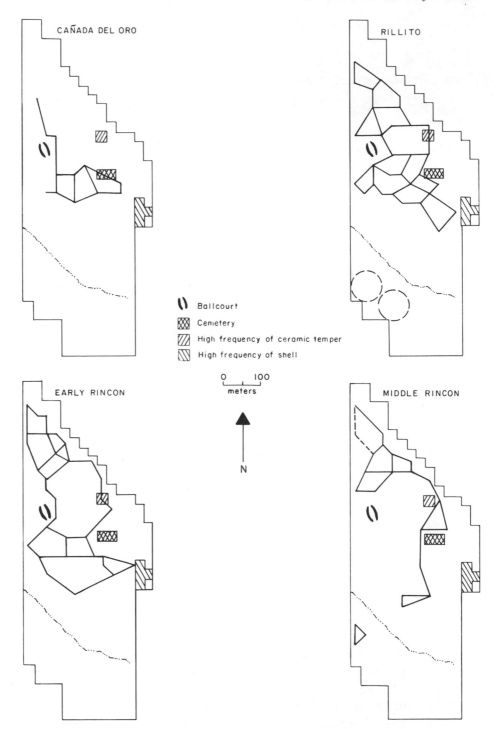

Figure 7.19    *Networks of polygons derived by connecting inferred trash*
*deposits. The polygons serve to identify possible social groups*
*at the Valencia site.*

a large open area in the center of the site. This latter feature is evident on the ground, and it is inferred to represent a plaza. Thus, the patterning of the polygons suggests a northern and a southern cluster of population around a central plaza. The other two communal features, the ballcourt and the cemetery, are located at the west and east margins of the plaza area, respectively.

For the Middle Rincon subphase, the southern cluster of population almost disappears, and the northern cluster is substantially reduced. It is of interest that the only area where multiple polygons are produced by this analysis method for the Middle Rincon subphase is also the only area where evidence of Late Rincon occupation was recovered at the Valencia site. This suggests that there was a continuity in the occupation of this northern portion of the site through Middle and Late Rincon times, though the population trend was clearly downward.

It is necessary to examine a somewhat larger area to understand the pattern of Middle and Late Rincon times. While there was population decline at the site center, four new settlements were founded immediately to the north (Fig. 7.20). Given the apparent close synchronization of these population shifts it seems most likely that the settlements shown in Figure 7.20d for Middle Rincon represent the redistribution of the Early Rincon population that was present at the Valencia site.

## THE CHANGING BALLCOURT SYSTEM
## IN THE TUCSON BASIN

It has already been argued that the ballcourt system in the Tucson Basin had developed in the Cañada del Oro phase and achieved a florescence during the Rillito phase. Despite indications of greater longevity in the Phoenix area, in the Tucson Basin there is a variety of evidence that the ballcourt system had collapsed or was in significant decline by the Middle Rincon subphase.

First, of the 20 known sites with ballcourts in the Tucson Basin (Table 7.1), 5 had been completely abandoned by the Early Rincon subphase or earlier. Second, at the Valencia site, the mid-Sedentary period shifts in population location clearly represent a substantial change in village organization. During Cañada del Oro through Early Rincon times, settlement had been concentrated around the ballcourt, extending a maximum of 700 m north-south. The subsequent settlement dispersal over a north-south distance of 2.1 km does not prove that the ballcourt was abandoned, but at a minimum it suggests that the function of the ballcourt had changed by Middle Rincon times. The ideology and activities associated with the ballcourt apparently did not continue to function as a centralizing force for village residential patterns at the Valencia site. Third, at both Romero (Elson and Doelle 1987) and the two Punta de Agua courts (Doelle 1987), similar patterns of residential shifts away from the ballcourts are documented for the Middle Rincon subphase. In sum-

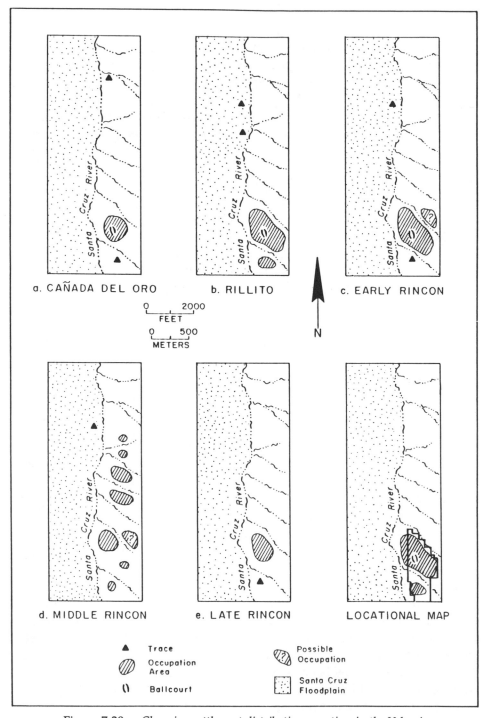

Figure 7.20    *Changing settlement distribution over time in the Valencia community.*

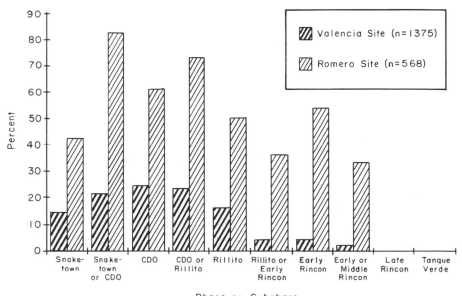

Figure 7.21    *Changing buff ware frequency over time at the Valencia and Romero sites. Percentages are of total decorated ceramics calculated independently for each site and time period.*

mary, the data suggest that the ballcourt system was at least in substantial decline by Middle Rincon times, and abandonment of the system must be considered as a possibility.

## THE DECLINING IMPORTATION OF BUFF WARES
## TO THE TUCSON BASIN

Figure 7.21 shows how buff ware frequencies changed over time at the Valencia and Romero sites, large ballcourt villages from the southern and northern Tucson Basin, respectively. This figure also confirms that the differential buff ware frequencies for the northern and southern portions of the Tucson Basin, which were considered in detail for the Rillito phase in an earlier section, have long temporal continuity. The lack of a precise temporal correlation between the Tucson and Phoenix Basin decorated wares complicates the documentation of this trend of declining importation of buff wares, but it is clear that such wares were absent after the middle of the Middle Rincon subphase at the Tanque Verde Wash site (Wallace 1986a). It is possible that importation of buff wares continued somewhat longer in the northern Tucson Basin than in the south, but for the entire Tucson Basin this practice had virtually ceased by the Late Rincon subphase.

In at least one site in the northeastern Tucson Basin, this decline in buff ware importation during the Middle Rincon subphase has been shown to coincide with an increase in local production of pottery (Heidke 1988). The implications of these two trends are considered further in the discussion section that follows.

## CHANGING BURIAL PRACTICES

A recent reassessment (Doelle 1987) of the Punta de Agua site complex originally reported by Greenleaf (1975) indicates that burial ritual underwent changes within the same time frame as changes in ballcourt use at that site. The latest ceramics in the small Punta de Agua cemetery, which was excavated completely, were dated to the first half of the Middle Rincon subphase. At the Valencia site the cremation area defined from surface evidence (see Figs. 7.16 and 7.17) is located in an area that has evidence of a high intensity of occupation in Early Rincon times and earlier, but has a low frequency of Middle and Late Rincon material. Excavation data from Middle and Late Rincon sites provide additional support for the observation that burial customs were changing during the Rincon phase.

At the West Branch site only a few cremations were discovered, and their spatial distribution was suggestive that interments were being made in the immediate periphery of individual households. Huntington (1986) has made a rather detailed argument regarding the importance of intentional burning of houses as part of the Hohokam burial ritual at the West Branch site. This pattern has been observed at other sites (Doelle 1985a; Elson 1986; Greenleaf 1975), and Doelle (1985b) has presented evidence that house burning tends to be more common in Middle and Late Rincon contexts in the Tucson Basin.

## DISCUSSION

Numerous social changes for the Tucson Basin Hohokam during the Sedentary period have just been reviewed. The decline of the ballcourt system, a dramatic drop off in the rate of importation of buff ware, and changes in burial practices were emphasized. Changes during the Colonial period were found to correlate with a time of population increase, but the role of population in the mid-Sedentary period shift has yet to be addressed. In addition, the changing role of the household and a possible shift in the importance of ritual as an integrating force in the Hohokam village are considered as important factors that can help account for the large-scale changes that are apparent.

It is proposed that changes in the ballcourt and burial ritual may be part of a larger shift to a more secular-based system, which replaced an earlier system where power and authority were derived largely from the sacred realm. If power and authority can be achieved through secular means, such as the more effective control of a labor force, then it is to be expected that greater behavioral diversity between social groups will be the rule. For example, innovations may be adopted relatively quickly by some groups. Such an occurrence may account for the rapid adoption of changes in ceramic layout that appeared suddenly during Middle Rincon times (Wallace 1986c). Also, the development of the system of red ware production that is represented by Rincon Red involves a very sudden shift. Yet within a relatively short time this new ware was widely traded and manufactured over the Tucson Basin (see Wallace and Heidke 1986). These occurrences suggest that the Rincon phase may be particularly productive for the application of economic models of social change.

One such economic model has been proposed by Huntington (1986, 1988), who was concerned with explaining variation in household size during the Middle Rincon subphase at the West Branch site (see also Elson 1986). He was particularly interested in accounting for the largest households, and his economic adaptation model was derived from the works of Wilk and Netting (Wilk 1982; Wilk and Rathje 1982; Wilk and Netting 1984; Netting 1982). Wilk and Rathje (1982:632) observed, "Large households have the potential for greater flexibility in dealing with very diverse or scattered economic opportunities that require simultaneous labor." Huntington (1988:216) proposes that:

> This inherent flexibility in large groups requires the leadership of a powerful individual—the head of the household—who can schedule the labor of the group members in an efficient manner. In addition, because a number of tasks are performed simultaneously, it becomes necessary to pool the goods produced for distribution to individuals within the household. Thus, membership in a large group affords access by each individual to a wider range of resources than would otherwise be available. This differential access provides an incentive for each member of the household to remain a part of the group.

Huntington (1988) cites increasing subsistence diversity at the West Branch site as one factor favoring larger household size in the Middle Rincon subphase. Environmental stress, which was discussed as a factor in the settlement pattern changes during the Middle Rincon subphase, would be a factor favoring diversification and pooling of resources within larger households. Furthermore, economic change is indicated by the pattern of declining import of nonlocal ceramics, and the concomitant increase in local ceramic production. Finally, evidence from the Valencia site and other large villages indicates that this hypothesized change in the leadership roles of household heads was occurring at the same time that village-level integrative mechanisms such as the ballcourt and village-level mortuary practices were falling into disuse. It has been suggested (Doelle et al. 1987) that the heads of the largest households very likely assumed leadership over larger social units, such as one or more village segments. It is also likely these conditions fostered greater competition between these intermediate-level social units and that the break up of large villages may have served to lessen internal conflict through spatial separation.

It is not clear that population increase was a significant variable in these mid-Sedentary period changes. A substantial increase in site frequency during the Rincon phase has been the basis for inferring population increase (e.g., Mayberry 1983), but the nature of the mid-Sedentary reorganization requires careful assessment of settlement pattern data. The break up of the large ball-court villages into multiple smaller settlements and the establishment of new seasonally occupied sites to exploit special resources (see Craig 1988; Huntington and Bernard-Shaw 1989) are two trends that suggest that the increase in sites for the Middle Rincon subphase is largely due to greater dispersal of the same population that was more aggregated in earlier times. Thus, it appears that population growth is not likely to have been a significant causal factor in the mid-Sedentary period reorganization. However, it is clear that the transition to the Hohokam Classic period was a long-term process that was initiated early in the Rincon phase and had major effects on the distribution of the existing population.

## INCREASING SOCIAL DIFFERENTIATION
## DURING THE CLASSIC PERIOD

Although most recent research in the Tucson Basin has focused on the Preclassic period, there is still a large amount of evidence that indicates a trend of increasing social differentiation during the Classic period. Early excavations provided a great deal of information about the Hohokam Classic period in the Tucson Basin (Gabel 1931; Haury 1928; Hayden 1957; Kelly 1978), which was supplemented somewhat by work in the 1960s and early 1970s (Grebinger 1971; Hammack n.d.; Zahniser 1966). However, there has been only limited excavations at Classic period sites during the recent explosion of contract-funded research (Douglas 1989; Ravesloot 1987; Rice 1987b; Slawson 1988). Fortunately, there have been numerous intensive surveys that have helped clarify our understanding of Classic period settlement patterns (Craig and Stephen 1985; Craig and Wallace 1987; Dart 1987; Doelle and Wallace 1986; Doelle, Dart, and Wallace 1985; Elson and Doelle 1987; Fish, Fish, and Madsen 1985), but a well-balanced data set is still lacking for the Tucson Basin Classic period.

### AN OVERVIEW OF THE CLASSIC PERIOD
### IN THE TUCSON BASIN

Due to the lack of intensive new research, this discussion does not consider village structure to the same extent as was possible for earlier time periods.

However, issues related to the organization of the Classic period Hohokam in the Tucson Basin are briefly addressed by temporal phase in order to document the trend toward increasing social differentiation.

### The Tanque Verde Phase

After the many changes of the mid-Sedentary period, it is likely that the Late Rincon subphase represents the period of time when a new pattern was crystallizing. In that sense, the Late Rincon subphase is viewed as a time of change that may have had more in common with the later Tanque Verde phase than it did with the earlier Middle Rincon subphase. This is evident in the settlement pattern data for the southern Tucson Basin that was discussed earlier (Fig. 7.10). However, some continuities are also evident.

In a previous paper (Doelle, Wallace, and Huntington 1985), we argued that the structure of Tanque Verde phase sites may derive from the village segments ("precincts") that were evident in Middle Rincon Hohokam sites (Doelle et al. 1987). In particular, the idea was advanced that those households that emerged as dominant within a village segment (through control over the scheduling and allocation of labor as discussed for Middle Rincon times), may have achieved wealth and power beyond that of others. Such households and those closely associated with them may have been the ones that planned and implemented the construction of the compounds, or enclosing walls, that were first built in the Tanque Verde phase.

It was also during the Tanque Verde phase that the first platform mound construction occurred in the Tucson Basin at the Marana mound. The platform mound at Marana was operative during the early Classic period, and the presence of multiple compounds in the vicinity of the mound indicates that multiple village segments were living in a relatively nucleated setting. Paul Fish (this volume) argues that Marana represented a substantial increase in the area integrated into a single community, and that the mound was the key focus for such development. A similar pattern of nucleation is indicated at the Zanardelli site in the southern Tucson Basin (Doelle, Dart, and Wallace 1985), but platform mounds appear to have been established largely during the late Classic period at locations other than Marana in the Tucson Basin (see Wallace and Holmlund 1982, 1984).

It is interesting to note the contrasts between the very "public" nature of the Hohokam ballcourt and the increasing evidence of a more "private" focus for Hohokam platform mounds. First, nearly all Hohokam platform mounds are found within compound walls. Furthermore, Gregory (Gregory 1987; Gregory and Nials 1985) has documented that within those compounds, palisades frequently surrounded Hohokam platform mounds. Finally, during the late Classic period, most platform mounds in the Phoenix Basin became the locations where a portion of the population lived elevated above the rest of the village. A trend towards the development of a socially segregated elite portion of the society in multiple localities is suggestive of increasing social differentiation.

A strong contrast that is evident between the Preclassic and Classic periods is the sharpness with which the boundaries of groups below the village level were defined. In Preclassic times, spatial factors, such as orientation of doorways, placement of trash disposal and activity areas, and distance between residential areas, were used to demarcate social boundaries. By the Classic period, however, compound walls of stone or adobe were used to enclose the houses and activity areas of at least some of the residents of the larger settlements. Such walls could have served multiple purposes. The authors suggest that one important function was to establish and maintain social boundaries within Classic period Hohokam society.

Another theme evident in the Tanque Verde phase occupation of the Tucson Basin is that there was substantial spatial variation as documented by a number of variables. First, for example, is frequency of the dominant decorated ware Tanque Verde Red-on-brown. Sites along the Santa Cruz and Rillito rivers show very high frequencies of this ceramic type, whereas it is very low on sites around the Tortolita Mountains (Paul Fish, personal communication; Craig and Stephen 1985) and on the Romero Ruin along the Cañada del Oro drainage (Elson and Doelle 1987).

Second, at sites in the eastern Tucson Basin corrugated ceramics are common. They seem to be locally manufactured, but they are also indicators of probable ties toward the east (see Fig. 7.22). These types are rare at sites in the western portions of the Basin.

Third, areas that were intensively occupied in earlier times were largely abandoned. This is seen most clearly in the southern Tucson Basin where settlement shifted from the west to the east side of the Santa Cruz (see Fig. 7.10). Also, along Tanque Verde Wash there was a shift in the focus of occupation to new locations (see Elson 1986), as well as an intensification of occupation nearby in the foothills of the Catalina and Rincon mountains.

It seems likely that there were increasing opportunities for social differentiation, both within individual communities and between communities. There was increasing variation in household size, and some households distinguished themselves from others residentially in compounds and perhaps through more material goods (see Rice 1987b for some examples). Variability in burial practices and the absence of clear ritual material items or facilities suggest that there may not have been the same degree of ritual control over competition and social differentiation that may have characterized earlier times. On the contrary, it seems most likely that the ideology of the Classic period may have encouraged competition and striving for differentiation. These are the kinds of conditions that could be expected to foster conflict between villages or between groups of allied villages.

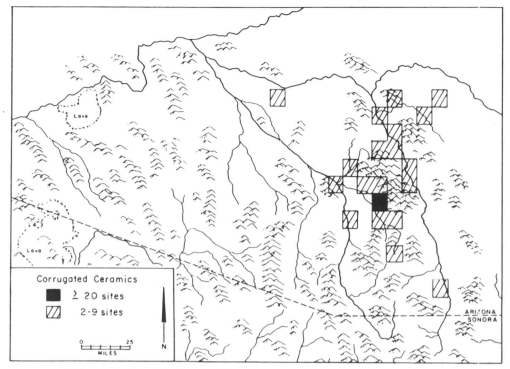

Figure 7.22    *Distribution of corrugated wares in southern Arizona.*

## The Tucson Phase

Temporal resolution for the late Classic period in the region is based largely on the dating of a few ceramic types, particularly Gila Polychrome and Tonto Polychrome (see Doelle and Wallace 1989 for a distribution map), Tucson Polychrome (Fig. 7.23), and in the Tucson Basin, Sells Red is most abundant in the Tucson phase (Fig. 7.23), though it has a longer temporal span in the Papagueria. Current information on Gila Polychrome from Casas Grandes (Ravesloot et al. 1986) and other areas where it has been found in datable contexts supports A.D. 1300 for a start date with an end date uncertain but not prior to A.D. 1400 (Lekson 1984:56–57; Ravesloot et al. 1986).

The latest dates for Gila Polychrome from within the Hohokam area are primarily archaeomagnetic determinations based on the undocumented DuBois curve. Eighmy and Doyel (1988) recently reevaluated the DuBois dates and developed a procedure for converting them to the Southwest master curve. Dates from the early and mid-1300s were pushed later into the late 1300s and post-1400 period. However, Eighmy and Doyel point out that there are insufficient data points on the curve for this period of time to make any positive determinations. This deficiency in the archaeomagnetic curve has been ignored in some recent studies, and it would behoove us all to take note of it.

The distribution of platform mounds has been mapped for the Phoenix

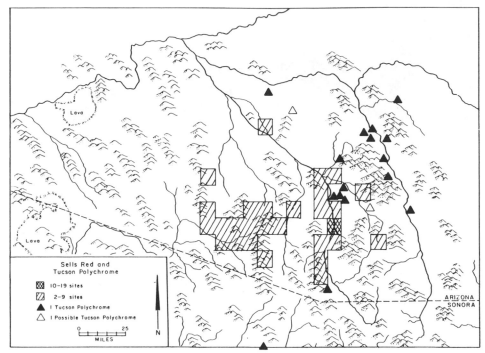

Figure 7.23    *Distribution of Sells Red and Tucson Polychrome in southern Arizona.*

Basin by Gregory and Nials (1985), and in this paper we expand the study south of the Gila to the Santa Cruz River, San Pedro River, and the Papagueria (Fig. 7.24). Figure 7.24 groups known mounds into four different subregional systems. First, the Phoenix Basin contains the largest number of mounds and, as Gregory and Nials (1985) have noted, the mounds are regularly spaced along the canal systems and the rivers. Second, in the Tucson Basin, the known mounds occur in two general localities, both of which may have contained multiple mounds (Gabel 1931; Wallace and Holmlund 1984; Julian Hayden, personal communication 1983). A mound reported by Fewkes (1909), but not relocated in recent times, raises the possibility that additional mounds were present along the Santa Cruz but have been destroyed by urban Tucson. Third, a relatively newly explored area at the edge of the Papagueria around the Coyote Mountains has revealed a large cluster of mounds, as well as the excavated Jackrabbit site (Scantling 1940). Fourth, the lower San Pedro exhibits a string of mound sites, some of which have been destroyed (Carpenter n.d.).

The most dramatic patterning discernible in the data presented here relates to the contrasts between the settlement patterns of the Phoenix Basin and the surrounding systems to the south, east, and west. Following a brief general discussion of warfare, three lines of evidence are reviewed in support of the hypothesis that an increase in Hohokam warfare was initiated by the early Classic period (Doelle and Wallace 1989; Wilcox 1979b, 1989).

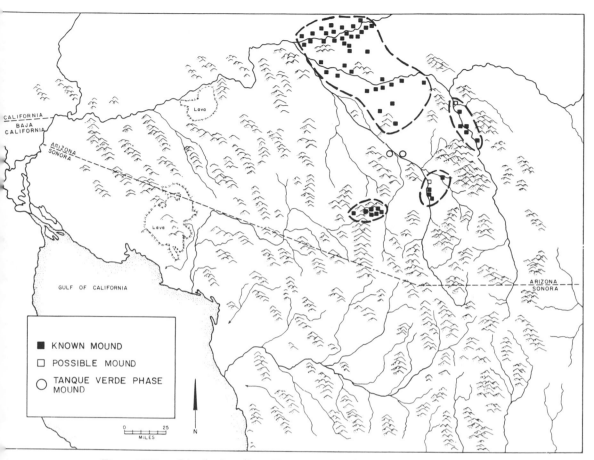

Figure 7.24     *Distribution of Late Classic period platform mounds in southern Arizona.*

## EVIDENCE FOR WARFARE IN THE CLASSIC PERIOD

The data review already presented has shown that there are clear trends in Classic period Hohokam society that suggest increasing social differentiation both within individual settlements and between groups in different subregions of the Hohokam area. But how strong is the evidence that these differences were of a magnitude to lead to warfare?

Few topics generate such heated discussion among archaeologists as warfare does. It is necessary, therefore, to outline the theoretical context within which we place our discussion of warfare. Ferguson (1984) provides a definition of warfare that identifies several key issues. He considers war as "organized, purposeful group action, directed against another group that may or may not be organized for similar action, involving the actual or potential application of lethal force" (1984:5). Of critical importance in this definition is the fact that warfare "is a *social* activity, carried out by *groups* of people"

(1984:5). Wilcox (1989) focuses on this same issue when he states: "The conditions that must be present for warfare to exist are social group identities based on shared interests distinct from and in conflict with the interests of other populations." After a review of some of the general trends in the Tanque Verde and Tucson phases of the Classic period, the evidence for warfare is addressed.

Ferguson's definition of warfare is important in that it does not require actual conflict. It recognizes that the *threat* of lethal force can be a very important social force. Therefore, as we approach the limited archaeological data that are available for the Hohokam Classic period, we are not necessarily searching for evidence of battles, violent deaths, mass graves, or other indicators of large-scale casualties. Such events, even if they occurred among the Hohokam, were probably very rare and their archaeological visibility would likely be low (see Vencl 1984 for a review of this issue). Therefore, we begin this review of the archaeological record by searching for spatial indicators in settlement pattern data that may be indicators of responses to threats. Furthermore, we examine the distribution of ceramic diagnostics to identify possible patterns of interaction or barriers to exchange.

The first line of evidence that raises the possibility of hostile relationships is the gap between the Phoenix Basin platform mound system and the other three. Within this space are two platform mounds that were abandoned during the early Classic period. Furthermore, two hillside villages, or *trincheras* sites, are present—Los Morteros and Cerro Prieto—both of which are thought to have had a defensive motivation for construction (Craig and Douglas 1984; Downum 1986; Wallace 1983). All of these sites were abandoned prior to the late Classic, along with numerous smaller sites in their vicinities, which is interpreted as possible retraction of territories as hostilities increased during the Classic period.

Figure 7.24 clearly illustrates that there are spatial gaps between all of the platform mound systems; therefore it is necessary to examine decorated pottery assemblages as indicators of interaction as our second line of evidence. The data show that the Coyote Mountains and Tucson Basin share Sells Red and the lower San Pedro and the Tucson Basin share Tucson Polychrome (Fig. 7.23). However, Sells Red does not reach the San Pedro and Tucson Polychrome does not appear to reach the Coyote Mountains. From this one can infer that the Tucson Basin was interacting with both the Coyote Mountains and the lower San Pedro. It is significant that *both* Sells Red and Tucson Polychrome are rare in the Phoenix Basin, for this indicates an exchange barrier of some sort. One might be tempted to argue on the basis of Tanque Verde Red-on-brown being a common "intrusive" in the Phoenix Basin, that exchange was occurring between the areas. However, recent examinations of Tanque Verde Red-on-brown from Phoenix Basin sites indicates that many of these "intrusives" may have been produced in the Phoenix area (Crown et al. 1988) and are therefore not necessarily indicative of peaceful commerce.

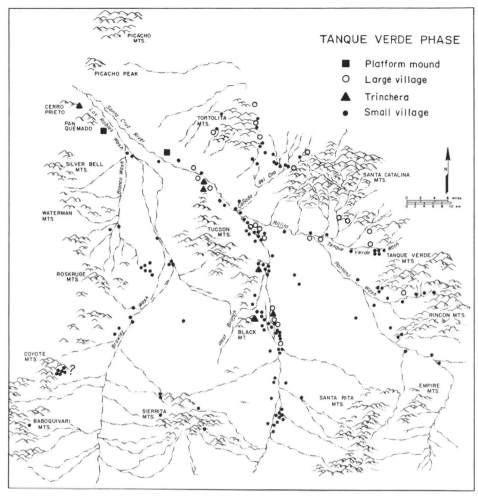

Figure 7.25    *Tanque Verde phase settlement distribution in the Tucson Basin and vicinity.*

The third line of evidence is settlement patterns within the four platform mound systems. A defensive posture is most clearly in evidence along the lower San Pedro. Unlike other areas, at least four of the mounds in this system are situated on high alluvial mesas overlooking the river in what may easily be interpreted as defensive locations, particularly since Preclassic settlements in this area are located on low terraces adjacent to the river.

In the Tucson Basin a defensive response may be indicated by a marked tendency for populations to aggregate in just a few localities. Figures 7.25 and 7.26 display the sharp contrasts in Tucson Basin settlement pattern between the Tanque Verde and Tucson phases. The large-scale abandonment of the northern Tucson Basin and the clustering of population around University Ruin, Martinez Hill, and near the Rillito–Santa Cruz junction are

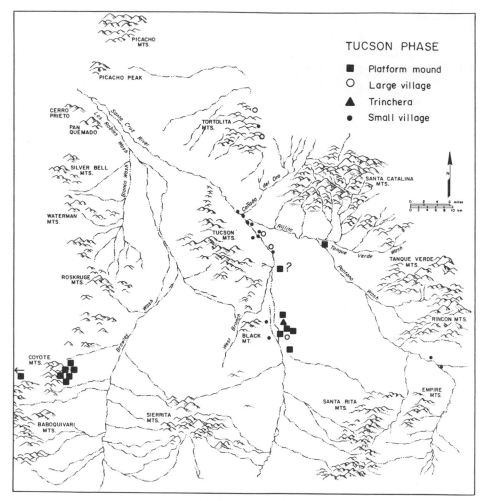

Figure 7.26    *Tucson phase settlement distribution in the Tucson Basin and vicinity.*

notable. The large agglomerated villages have the appearance to the authors of representing the densest and largest settlements for any time period in the region, and it is reasonable to suggest that there was *not* an overall population decrease between the early and late Classic periods in this area. Recent work in the Picacho Mountain area (Ciolek-Torrello and Wilcox 1988; Czaplicki 1984) documents intensive late Classic occupation at numerous sites at the northern edge of this proposed "buffer zone." Thus it is unlikely that this buffer zone resulted from a simple environmental cause, such as a large-scale abandonment of sites in nonriverine settings.

The aggregation of settlement seen in the Tucson Basin may also have occurred in the Avra/Altar Valley at the same time given the very large site complex that surrounds the Coyote Mountains near Kitt Peak. In this area there are at least six and perhaps as many as eight platform mounds within several miles of one another.

The Phoenix Basin in the late Classic period contrasts sharply with the other regional systems considered here in that there was not an obvious defensive posture to the settlement system. Although many large sites were present, they are not necessarily indicative of any major change from the early Classic period system. If anything, current data on the platform mound distribution and development (Gregory and Nials 1985) suggest that continuity from late Sedentary through late Classic times was common in the Phoenix area. This continuity in site structure is absent in the other areas under consideration.

In conclusion, the available data reveal some interesting patterns. On a very general level, all of the settlement systems examined share common elements such as platform mounds and Roosevelt Red Ware. Beyond that, however, a sharp contrast has been identified between the Phoenix Basin and at least three local settlement systems to the south. The hypothesis presented here to account in part for these contrasts is that there was increasing warfare between Hohokam populations in southern Arizona during the Classic Period. The authors view large villages as the primary locus of Hohokam social and political action; therefore it seems premature to propose that entire local systems were organized in opposition to one another. Rather it is more likely that leaders from large villages may have been allied with some villages and hostile toward others. There may also have been considerable flux in these relationships over time. To learn how actions at the village level could result in the observed settlement patterns and exchange patterns will require substantial further research. The authors believe that warfare will be an important component of models that ultimately account for these patterns.

## THE TRANSITION TO HISTORY

Consideration of the transition to history in the study area must deal with a time gap of some 300 years. Given the major changes that are known to have occurred within that time period, it is with caution that we approach the issue of accounting for the intervening years. It is in the Salt-Gila area that the prehistoric archaeology and the seventeenth-century documents show the greatest contrast. There has been new data relevant to the end of the Salt-Gila platform mounds—in particular the El Polvoron phase proposed by Sires (1984) and the evidence by Nials, Graybill, and Gregory (1989) that one or more major floods may have occurred on the Salt River in the mid-1300s, providing a mechanism that could have triggered a collapse of the social and settlement system in this area. Since we still lack sufficient data to fully reconstruct the settlement system during and after this time of collapse, we therefore can say little about the pattern of such a collapse. For example, was it sudden and regionwide, or was it gradual and variable in different areas? Even considering the weakness of the dating evidence for the late Classic period in the Phoenix Basin, all indications are that the collapse of the Phoenix Basin platform mound system occurred within prehistoric times, and European diseases could not have been a primary factor.

If our interpretations of warfare and increasing regionalization in the Hohokam system during the Classic period are correct, then a collapse of one portion of the Phoenix system may have had strong internal effects and yet not have greatly affected the surrounding regions. Thus there could have been significant differences between the cultural trajectory of Phoenix and those of its neighbors. Furthermore, we would expect that a greater degree of cultural continuity after the Classic period would be more likely in the surrounding areas that were not directly affected by the events in the Phoenix Basin.

The major sources of information on the Hohokam region for the early historic period are the late seventeenth-century documents of Father Kino and his associates. Mapping of key variables derived from these documents serves to outline a regional system during the 1690s with population most concentrated in the Tucson Basin (see Doelle and Wallace 1989). Unlike prehistoric times, the Gila River area was probably a low-density frontier setting and the Salt River was not even permanently inhabited. It is still one of the great challenges to Hohokam archaeology to document the collapse of the Hohokam system and the emergence of the Piman system that has been so briefly noted here.

# CONCLUSIONS

The dramatic reversals of the roles of the Tucson and Phoenix areas by early historic times rather neatly underscores our point that the simplistic application of a core-periphery model is no longer appropriate in Hohokam archaeology. In closing, there are two points that bear final emphasis, and they relate to the two meanings in the title of our chapter.

First, we have shown that the Tucson Basin has been a distinctive component of the Hohokam regional system since the Pioneer period. Furthermore, both internal relations and the relationship with the Phoenix Basin and other areas within the regional system have been dynamic, not static. These changes had complex causes, and while we do not yet fully understand those causes, progress toward that goal is being made.

Second, we have tried to communicate some of the aspects of Tucson Basin archaeology that make it important to Hohokam archaeology as a research endeavor. Several aspects of the archaeological record in the Tucson Basin have inherent strengths that allow insights that are not as obvious or accessible in other areas. For example, extensive regional survey in very recent times, combined with flexible settlement-subsistence strategies in prehistoric times, serve to make major transformations in the local system readily apparent. The settlement pattern shift in the mid-Sedentary period is an important example. It was shown earlier that this involved changes in relations with the Phoenix Basin, so the magnitude of the Tucson Basin changes raise the question of whether comparable reorganizations took place in other portions of the Hohokam regional system. A leadership role for the Tucson Basin within Hohokam archaeology has taken a long time to develop, but it is a legitimate role and one that should be productive into the future.

# REFERENCES CITED

Abbott, David R.
  1984   A Technological Assessment of Ceramic Variation in the Salt-Gila Aqueduct Area. In *Hohokam Archaeology along the Salt-Gila Aqueduct, Central Arizona Project*, vol. 8, pp. 3–118. Material Culture, edited by Lynn S. Teague and Patricia L. Crown, Arizona State Museum Archaeological Series 150. University of Arizona, Tucson.
Bernard-Shaw, Mary
  1989a   *Archaeological Investigations at Los Morteros, AZ AA:12:57 (ASM), Locus 1, in the Northern Tucson Basin*. Institute for American Research Technical Report 89-9. Tucson.
  1989b   *Archaeological Investigations at the Lonetree Site, AZ AA:12:120 (ASM), in the Northern Tucson Basin*. Center for Desert Archaeology Technical Report 90-1. Tucson.
  1989c   *Archaeological Investigations at the Redtail Site, AZ AA:12:149 (ASM), in the Northern Tucson Basin*. Center for Desert Archaeology Technical Report 89-8. Tucson.
Bernard-Shaw, Mary, and James Heidke
  1989   Early Ceramic Production in the Tucson Basin: Evidence from the Lonetree and Redtail Sites. Paper presented at the Arizona Archaeological Council Spring Meeting and Symposium, March 31, 1989, Flagstaff.
Betancourt, Julio L.
  1978   *Cultural Resources within the Proposed Santa Cruz Riverpark Archaeological District*. Arizona State Museum Archaeological Series 125. University of Arizona, Tucson.
Boserup, Esther
  1965   *The Conditions of Agricultural Growth*. Aldine Publishing Co., Chicago.
Bradley, Bruce A.
  1980   *Excavations at Arizona BB:13:74, Santa Cruz Industrial Park, Tucson, Arizona*. CASA Papers 1. Complete Archaeological Service Associates, Oracle, Arizona.
Braun, David P. and Stephen Plog
  1982   Evolution of "Tribal" Social Networks: Theory and Prehistoric North American Evidence. *American Antiquity* 47:504–525.

Buttery, Cynthia E.
   1986   An Archaeological Survey of the Santa Rita Experimental Range. Paper pre-
          sented at the Second Tucson Basin Conference, Tucson.
Carpenter, Alice
   n.d.   Unpublished field notes on the archaeology of the lower San Pedro River
          and Oracle area, Arizona. Copy on file at the Center for Desert Archaeology,
          Tucson.
Ciolek-Torrello, Richard S., and David R. Wilcox
   1988   *Hohokam Settlement along the Slopes of the Picacho Mountains,* vol. 6, Synthesis
          and Conclusions. Museum of Northern Arizona Research Paper 35. Flagstaff.
Craig, Douglas B.
   1987   Intra-site Settlement Patterns. In *Prehistoric Settlement in the Cañada del Oro
          Valley, Arizona. The Rancho Vistoso Survey Project,* by Douglas B. Craig and
          Henry D. Wallace, pp. 83–100. Institute for American Research Anthropo-
          logical Papers 8. Tucson.
   1988   *Archaeological Investigations at Sun City Vistoso.* Institute for American Research
          Technical Report 87-9. Tucson.
   1989a  *Archaeological Investigations at AA:16:49 (ASM), The Dakota Wash Mitigation.*
          Anthropology Series Archaeological Report 14. Pima Community College.
          Tucson. In preparation.
   1989b  *Archaeological Testing at the Dakota Wash Site, AZ AA:16:49 (ASM).* Center for
          Desert Archaeology Technical Report 88-5. Tucson. In preparation.
   1989c  *Archaeological Testing at Honey Bee Village, AZ BB:9:88 (ASM).* Institute for
          American Research Technical Report 89-6. Tucson.
Craig, Douglas B., and John E. Douglas
   1984   Architectural Variability and Community Structure at Cerro Prieto (AZ AA:7:11).
          Paper presented at the 49th Annual Meeting of the Society for American
          Archaeology, Portland.
Craig, Douglas B., and David V. M. Stephen
   1985   *Archaeological Investigations in the Eastern Tortolitas: Results of Phase III of Tortolita
          Mountains Archaeological Project.* Manuscript on file, Pima Community College
          Center for Archaeological Field Training, Tucson.
Craig, Douglas B., and Henry D. Wallace
   1987   *Prehistoric Settlement in the Cañada del Oro Valley, Arizona: The Rancho Vistoso
          Survey Project.* Institute for American Research Anthropological Papers 8.
          Tucson.
Crown, Patricia L.
   1984   Design Variability in Salt-Gila Aqueduct Red-on-Buff Ceramics. In *Hohokam
          Archaeology along the Salt-Gila Aqueduct, Central Arizona Project,* vol. 8, *Material
          Culture,* edited by Lynn S. Teague and Patricia L. Crown, pp. 205–248. Ari-
          zona State Museum Archaeological Series 150. University of Arizona, Tucson.
Crown, Patricia L., Larry A. Schwalbe, and J. Ronald London
   1988   X-Ray Fluorescence Analysis of Materials Variability in Las Colinas Ceramics.
          In *The 1982–1984 Excavations at Las Colinas,* vol. 4, *Material Culture,* by David
          R. Abbott, Kim E. Beckwith, Patricia L. Crown, R. Thomas Euler, David A.
          Gregory, J. Ronald London, Marilyn B. Saul, Larry A. Schwalbe, Mary Ber-
          nard-Shaw, Christine R. Szuter, and Arthur W. Vokes, pp. 29–72. Arizona
          State Museum Archaeological Series 162. University of Arizona, Tucson.

Cutler, Hugh C., and Leonard W. Blake
  1976  Corn from Snaketown. In *The Hohokam: Desert Farmers and Craftsmen. Excavations at Snaketown, 1964–1965*, by Emil W. Haury, pp. 365–366. University of Arizona Press, Tucson.

Czaplicki, Jon S. (compiler)
  1984  *Class III Survey of the Tucson Aqueduct Phase A Corridor Central Arizona Project.* Arizona State Museum Archaeological Series 165. University of Arizona, Tucson.

Czaplicki, Jon S., and John C. Ravesloot (Editors)
  1989  *Hohokam Archaeology Sites along Phase B of the Tucson Aqueduct, Central Arizona Project.* Arizona State Museum Archaeological Series 178. 3 volumes. University of Arizona, Tucson.

Dart, Allen
  1987  *Archaeological Studies of the Avra Valley, Arizona for the Papago Water Supply Project. Volume 1: Class III Archaeological Surveys on the Tohono O'odham Indian Reservation.* Institute for American Research Anthropological Papers 9. Tucson.

Dart, Allen, and William H. Doelle
  1988  *The Pima County Archaeological Inventory Project.* Institute for American Research Technical Report 87-11. Tucson.

Deaver, William L.
  1984  Pottery. In *Hohokam Habitations Sites in the Northern Santa Rita Mountains*, by Alan Ferg, Kenneth C. Rozen, William L. Deaver, Martyn D. Tagg, David A. Phillips, Jr., and David A. Gregory, pp. 237–419. Arizona State Museum Archaeological Series 147. University of Arizona, Tucson.

DiPeso, Charles C.
  1956  *The Upper Pima of San Cayetano del Tumacacori.* Amerind Foundation Publication 7. Dragoon, Arizona.

Doelle, William H.
  1976  *Desert Resources and Hohokam Subsistence: The CONOCO-Florence Project.* Arizona State Museum Archaeological Series 103. University of Arizona, Tucson.
  1985a  *Excavations at the Valencia Site, a Preclassic Hohokam Village in the Southern Tucson Basin.* Institute for American Research Anthropological Papers 3. Tucson.
  1985b  The Southern Tucson Basin: Rillito-Rincon Subsistence, Settlement, and Community Structure. In *Proceedings of the 1983 Hohokam Symposium*, edited by Alfred E. Dittert, Jr., and Donald E. Dove, pp. 183–198. Arizona Archaeological Society Occasional Paper 2. Phoenix.
  1987  A View of the Avra Valley from the Southern Tucson Basin. In *Archaeological Studies of the Avra Valley, Arizona, for the Papago Water Supply Project*, by Allen Dart, pp. 321–372. Institute for American Research Anthropological Papers 9. Tucson.
  1988  Preclassic Community Patterns in the Tucson Basin. In *Recent Research on Tucson Basin Prehistory: Proceedings of the Second Tucson Basin Conference*, edited by William H. Doelle and Paul R. Fish, pp. 277–312. Institute for American Research Anthropological Papers 10. Tucson.

Doelle, William H., Allen Dart, and Henry D. Wallace
  1985  *The Southern Tucson Basin Survey: Intensive Survey along the Santa Cruz River.* Institute for American Research Technical Report 85-3. Tucson.

Doelle, William H., Frederick W. Huntington, and Henry D. Wallace
  1987   Rincon Phase Community Reorganization in the Tucson Basin. In *The Hohokam
         Village: Site Structure and Organization*, edited by David E. Doyel, pp. 71–96.
         American Association for the Advancement of Science, Denver.
Doelle, William H., Henry D. Wallace, and Frederick W. Huntington
  1985   Classic Period Community Structure in the Tucson Basin. Paper presented at
         the 50th Annual Meeting of the Society for American Archaeology, Denver.
Doelle, William H., and Henry D. Wallace
  1986   *Hohokam Settlement Patterns in the San Xavier Project Area, Southern Tucson Basin*.
         Institute for American Research Technical Report 84-6. Tucson.
  1989   The Transition to History in Pimeria Alta. In *Proceedings of the First Southwest
         Symposium*, edited by Paul Minnis. Westview Press. In press.
Douglas, John E.
  1989   *Archaeological Investigations at AA:16:44 (ASM)*. Department of Archaeology,
         Pima Community College, Tucson. In preparation.
Downum, Christian E.
  1986   The Occupational Use of Hill Space in the Tucson Basin: Evidence from Linda
         Vista Hill. *The Kiva* 51:219–232.
Downum, Christian E., and Allen Dart
  1986   *Archaeological Studies at AZ BB:13:223 (ASM) and Nearby Sites in the Santa Cruz
         Industrial Park, Tucson, Arizona*. Institute for American Research Technical
         Report 86-3. Tucson.
Downum, Christian E., Adrianne Rankin, and Jon S. Czaplicki
  1986   *A Class III Archaeological Survey of the Phase B Corridor, Tucson Aqueduct, Central
         Arizona Project*. Arizona State Museum Archaeological Series 168. University
         of Arizona, Tucson.
Doyel, David E.
  1977a  *Classic Period Hohokam in the Escalante Ruin Group*. Unpublished Ph.D. dis-
         sertation, Department of Anthropology, University of Arizona, Tucson.
  1977b  *Excavations in the Middle Santa Cruz Valley, Southeastern Arizona*. Contributions
         to Highway Salvage Archaeology in Arizona 44. Arizona State Museum, Tuc-
         son.
Eighmy, Jeffrey L., and David E. Doyel
  1988   A Reanalysis of First Reported Archaeomagnetic Dates from the Hohokam
         Area, Southern Arizona. *Journal of Field Archaeology* 14:331–342.
Elson, Mark D.
  1986   *Archaeological Investigations at the Tanque Verde Wash Site, a Middle Rincon Set-
         tlement in the Eastern Tucson Basin*. Institute for American Research Anthro-
         pological Papers 7. Tucson.
  1988   Household Interaction and Differentiation at the Tanque Verde Wash Site, a
         Middle Rincon Hamlet in the Eastern Tucson Basin. In *Recent Research on
         Tucson Basin Prehistory: Proceedings of the Second Tucson Basin Conference*, edited
         by William H. Doelle and Paul R. Fish, pp. 87–107. Institute for American
         Research Anthropological Papers 10. Tucson.
Elson, Mark D., and William H. Doelle
  1986   *The Valencia Site Testing Project: Mapping, Intensive Surface Collecting, and Limited
         Trenching of a Hohokam Ballcourt Village in the Southern Tucson Basin*. Institute
         for American Research Technical Report 86-6. Tucson.

1987   *Archaeological Survey in Catalina State Park with a Focus on the Romero Ruin.* Institute for American Research Technical Report 87-4. Tucson.

Ferg, Alan, Kenneth C. Rozen, William L. Deaver, Martyn D. Tagg, David A. Phillips, Jr., and David A. Gregory
1984   *Hohokam Habitation Sites in the Northern Santa Rita Mountains.* Arizona State Museum Archaeological Series 147(2). University of Arizona, Tucson.

Ferguson, R. Brian
1984   Introduction: Studying War. In *Warfare, Culture, and Environment,* edited by R. Brian Ferguson, pp. 1–82. Academic Press, New York.

Fewkes, Jesse W.
1909   Prehistoric Ruins of the Gila Valley. *Smithsonian Miscellaneous Collections* 5(4):403–436.

Fish, Suzanne K., Paul R. Fish, and John Madsen
1985   A Preliminary Analysis of Hohokam Settlement and Agriculture in the Northern Tucson Basin. In *Proceedings of the 1983 Hohokam Symposium,* edited by Alfred E. Dittert, Jr., and Donald E. Dove, pp. 75–100. Arizona Archaeological Society Occasional Papers 2. Phoenix.
1988   The Archaic Period. Paper delivered at the First Southwest Symposium, Tempe.

Fish, Suzanne K., Paul R. Fish, Charles H. Miksicek, and John Madsen
1985   Prehistoric Agave Cultivation in Southern Arizona. *Desert Plants* 7:107–112.

Franklin, Hayward H.
1980   *Excavations at Second Canyon Ruin, San Pedro Valley, Arizona.* Contributions to Highway Salvage Archaeology in Arizona 60. Arizona State Museum, Tucson.

Gabel, Norman
1931   *Martinez Hill Ruins: An Example of Prehistoric Culture of the Middle Gila.* Unpublished Master's thesis, Department of Anthropology, University of Arizona, Tucson.

Goodyear, Albert C., III
1975   *Hecla II and III. An Interpretive Study of Archaeological Remains from the Lakeshore Project, Papago Reservation, South Central Arizona.* Anthropological Research Paper 9. Arizona State University, Tempe.

Gladwin, Harold S., Emil W. Haury, E. B. Sayles, and Nora Gladwin
1965   *Excavations at Snaketown: Material Culture.* Medallion Paper 25. Gila Pueblo, Globe, Arizona.

Grebinger, Paul F.
1971   *Hohokam Cultural Development in the Middle Santa Cruz Valley, Arizona.* Unpublished Ph.D. dissertation, Department of Anthropology, University of Arizona, Tucson.

Gregonis, Linda M.
1989   *The Hardy Site at Fort Lowell Park.* Arizona State Museum Archaeological Series 175. University of Arizona, Tucson. In preparation.

Greenleaf, J. Cameron
1975   *Excavations at Punta de Agua in the Santa Cruz River Basin, Southeastern Arizona.* Anthropological Papers 26. University of Arizona, Tucson.

Gregory, David A.
1987   The Morphology of Platform Mounds and the Structure of Classic Period Hohokam Sites. In *The Hohokam Village: Site Structure and Organization,* edited by David E. Doyel, pp. 183–210. American Association for the Advancement

of Science, Southwestern and Rocky Mountain Division, Glenwood Springs, Colorado.

Gregory, David, and F. Nials
   1985   Observations Concerning the Distribution of Classic Period Hohokam Plat-
          form Mounds. In *Proceedings of the 1983 Hohokam Conference,* edited by A.
          Dittert and D. Dove, pp. 373–388. Arizona Archaeological Society Occasional
          Paper 2. Phoenix.

Hammack, Nancy S.
   n.d.   An Analysis of Ceramic Vessels from the Mortuary Pits, Arizona, AA:12:46,
          Rabid Ruin, Tucson, Arizona. Manuscript on file, Arizona State Museum
          Archives, University of Arizona, Tucson.

Haury, Emil W.
   1928   *The Succession of House Types in the Pueblo Area.* Unpublished Master's thesis,
          Department of Anthropology, University of Arizona, Tucson.
   1932   *Roosevelt 9:6 a Hohokam Site of the Colonial Period.* Medallion Papers 1. Gila
          Pueblo, Globe, Arizona.
   1965   Pottery Types at Snaketown. In *Excavations at Snaketown: Material Culture,* by
          Harold S. Gladwin, Emil W. Haury, E. B. Sayles, and Nora Gladwin, pp.
          169–229. Medallion Papers 25. Gila Pueblo, Globe. Originally published 1937,
          University of Arizona, Tucson.
   1976   *The Hohokam: Desert Farmers and Craftsmen. Excavations at Snaketown, 1964–
          1965.* University of Arizona, Tucson.

Hayden, Julian D.
   1957   *Excavations, 1940, at the University Indian Ruin, Tucson, Arizona.* Southwestern
          Monuments Association Technical Series 5. Globe, Arizona.

Hayden, Brian, and Aubrey Cannon
   1982   The Corporate Group as an Archaeological Unit. *Journal of Anthropological
          Archaeology* 1:132–158.

Heidke, James
   1988   Ceramic Production and Exchange: Evidence from Rincon Phase Contexts.
          In *Recent Research on Tucson Basin Prehistory: Proceedings of the Second Tucson
          Basin Conference,* edited by William H. Doelle and Paul R. Fish, pp. 387–410.
          Institute for American Research Anthropological Papers 10. Tucson.
   1989a  Ceramic Analysis. In *Archaeological Investigations at the Lonetree Site, AZ AA:12:120
          (ASM), in the Northern Tucson Basin,* by Mary Bernard-Shaw. Institute for
          American Research Technical Report 89-9. Tucson. In preparation.
   1989b  Ceramic Analysis. In *Archaeological Investigations at the Redtail Site, AZ AA:12:149
          (ASM), in the Northern Tucson Basin,* by Mary Bernard-Shaw. Institute for
          American Research Technical Report 89-8. Tucson.

Henderson, T. Kathleen
   1986   *Site Structure and Development at La Ciudad: A Study of Community Organization.*
          Unpublished Ph.D. dissertation, Department of Anthropology, Arizona State
          University, Tempe.

Howard, Jerry B.
   1982   Hohokam Community Patterns at La Ciudad de los Hornos. In *The Archaeology
          of La Ciudad de los Hornos,* edited by David Wilcox and Jerry Howard. Manu-
          script on file, Arizona State University, Tempe.
   1985   Courtyard Groups and Domestic Cycling: A Hypothetical Model of Growth.
          In *Proceedings of the 1983 Hohokam Symposium,* edited by Alfred E. Dittert, Jr.

and Donald E. Dove, pp. 311–326. Arizona Archaeological Society Occasional Paper 2. Phoenix.

Huckell, Bruce B.
1988   Late Archaic Archaeology of the Tucson Basin: A Status Report. In *Recent Research on Tucson Basin Prehistory: Proceedings of the Second Tucson Basin Conference*, edited by William H. Doelle and Paul R. Fish, pp. 57–80. Institute for American Research Anthropological Papers 10. Tucson.

Huckell, Bruce B., Martyn D. Tagg, and Lisa W. Huckell
1987   *The Corona de Tucson Project: Prehistoric Use of a Bajada Environment*. Arizona State Museum Archaeological Series 174. University of Arizona, Tucson.

Huntington, Ellsworth
1912   The Physical Environment of the Southwest in Pre-Columbian Days. *Records of the Past* 11(3):128–141.

Huntington, Frederick W.
1986   *Archaeological Investigations at the West Branch Site: Early and Middle Rincon Occupation in the Southern Tucson Basin*. Institute for American Research Anthropological Papers 5. Tucson.
1988   Rincon Phase Community Organization. In Recent Research in Tucson Basin Prehistory: *Proceedings of the Second Tucson Basin Conference*, edited by William H. Doelle and Paul R. Fish, pp. 207–224. Institute for American Research Anthropological Papers 10. Tucson.

Huntington, Frederick W., and Mary Bernard-Shaw
1989   *Rincon Phase Seasonal Occupation in the Northeastern Tucson Basin*. Technical Report 90-2. Center for Desert Archaeology, Tucson. In preparation.

Jacobs, Mike
1979   The St. Mary's Hospital Site. *The Kiva* 45:119–130.

Kelly, Isabel T.
1978   *The Hodges Ruin: A Hohokam Community in the Tucson Basin*. Anthropological Papers 30. University of Arizona, Tucson.

Knoke, David, and Peter J. Burke
1980   *Log-Linear Models*. Sage Publications, Beverly Hills.

Lange, Richard (compiler)
1989   *1979–1983 Testing at Los Morteros (AZ AA:12:57 ASM), A Large Hohokam Village Site in the Tucson Basin*. Archaeological Series 177. Cultural Resource Management Division, Arizona State Museum, University of Arizona, Tucson.

Layhe, Robert W. (editor)
1986   *The 1985 Excavations at the Hodges Site Pima County, Arizona*. Arizona State Museum Archaeological Series 170. University of Arizona, Tucson.

Lekson, Steven H.
1984   Dating Casas Grandes. *The Kiva* 50:55–60.

Masse, W. Bruce
1980   The Hohokam of the Lower San Pedro Valley and the Northern Papaguería: Continuity and Variability in Two Regional Populations. In *Current Issues in Hohokam Prehistory*, edited by David Doyel and Fred Plog, pp. 205–223. Anthropological Research Papers 23. Arizona State University, Tempe.

Mayberry, James D.
1983   The Hohokam and Protohistoric Periods. In *An Archaeological Assessment of the Middle Santa Cruz River Basin, Rillito to Green Valley, Arizona, for the Proposed Tucson Aqueduct Phase B, Central Arizona Project*, by Jon S. Czaplicki and James D. Mayberry, pp. 27–62. Arizona State Museum Archaeological Series 164. University of Arizona, Tucson.

McGuire, Randall H.

    1987   A Gila Butte Ballcourt at La Ciudad. In *The Hohokam Community of La Ciudad,* edited by Glen E. Rice, pp. 69–110. Office of Cultural Resource Management Report 69. Arizona State University, Tempe.

Miksicek, Charles H.

    1989   Plant Remains. In *Archaeological Investigations at AZ AA:16:49 (ASM), the Dakota Wash Mitigation,* by Douglas B. Craig, pp. 197–218. Anthropology Series, Archaeological Report 14. Pima Community College, Tucson. In preparation.

Netting, Robert McC.

    1982   Some Home Truths on Household Size and Wealth. *American Behavioral Scientist* 25(6).

Netting, Robert McC., Richard R. Wilk, and Eric J. Arnould (editors)

    1984   *Households: Comparative and Historical Studies of the Domestic Group.* University of California Press, Berkeley.

Nials, Fred L., David A. Gregory, and Donald A. Graybill

    1989   Salt River Streamflow and Hohokam Irrigation Systems. In *The 1982–1984 Excavations at Las Colinas,* vol. 5, Studies of Prehistoric Environment and Subsistence, edited by David A. Gregory and Carol Anne Heathington. Archaeological Series 162. Cultural Resource Management Division, Arizona State Museum, University of Arizona, Tucson. In preparation.

Nichols, Deborah L., and Shirley Powell

    1987   Demographic Reconstructions in the American Southwest: Alternative Behavioral Means to the Same Archaeological Ends. *The Kiva* 52:193–208.

Plog, Stephen

    1980   Village Autonomy in the American Southwest: An Evaluation of the Evidence. In *Models and Methods in Regional Exchange,* edited by R. E. Fry, pp. 135–146. Society for American Archaeology Papers 1. Washington, D.C.

Rafferty, Kevin

    1982   Hohokam Micaceous Schist Mining and Ceramic Specialization: An Example from Gila Butte, Arizona. *Anthropology* 6(1–2):199–222.

Ravesloot, John C.

    1984   *Archaeological Testing within the Santa Cruz Industrial Park, Tucson, Arizona.* Institute for American Research Technical Report 84-2. Tucson.

Ravesloot, John C. (editor)

    1987   *The Archaeology of the San Xavier Bridge Site (AZ BB:13:14), Tucson Basin, Southern Arizona.* Arizona State Museum Archaeological Series 171. University of Arizona, Tucson.

Ravesloot, John C., Jeffrey S. Dean, and Michael S. Foster

    1986   A New Perspective on the Casas Grandes Tree-Ring Dates. Paper presented at the 4th Mogollon Conference, Tucson.

Rice, Glen E.

    1987a  *A Spatial Analysis of the Hohokam Community of La Ciudad.* Anthropological Field Studies 16. Arizona State University, Tempe.

Rice, Glen E. (editor)

    1987b  *Studies in the Hohokam Community of Marana.* Anthropological Field Studies 15. Arizona State University, Tempe.

Scantling, Frederick H.

    1940   *Excavations at the Jackrabbit Ruin, Papago Indian Reservation, Arizona.* Unpublished Master's thesis, Department of Anthropology, University of Arizona, Tucson.

Sense, Richard
  1980   *Archaeological Investigations: Santa Cruz Riverpark, Drexel to Irvington Roads.* Archaeological Resources, Tucson.
Sires, Earl W., Jr.
  1984   Excavations at El Polvoron. In *Hohokam Archaeology along the Salt-Gila Aqueduct, Central Arizona Project,* vol. 4, Prehistoric Occupation of the Queen Creek Delta, edited by Lynn S. Teague and Patricia L. Crown, pp. 221–356. Arizona State Museum Archaeological Series 150. University of Arizona, Tucson.
  1987   Hohokam Architectural Variability and Site Structure during the Sedentary-Classic Transition. In *The Hohokam Village: Site Structure and Organization,* edited by David E. Doyel, pp. 171–182. American Association for the Advancement of Science, Denver.
Slawson, Laurie V.
  1988   The Classic Period Continental Site, AZ EE:1:32. In *Recent Research on Tucson Basin Prehistory: Proceedings of the Second Tucson Basin Conference,* edited by William H. Doelle and Paul R. Fish, pp. 135–144. Institute for American Research Anthropological Papers 10. Tucson.
Teague, Lynn S.
  1984   The Organization of Hohokam Economy. In *Hohokam Archaeology along the Salt-Gila Aqueduct, Central Arizona Project,* vol. 9, Synthesis and Conclusions, edited by Lynn S. Teague and Patricia L. Crown, pp. 187–250. Arizona State Museum Archaeological Series 150. University of Arizona, Tucson.
Tuthill, Carr
  1947   *The Tres Alamos Site on the San Pedro River, Southeastern Arizona.* The Amerind Foundation Publication 4. Dragoon, Arizona.
Upham, S., and G. Rice
  1980   Up the Canal without a Paddle: Modeling Hohokam Interaction and Exchange. In *Current Issues in Hohokam Archaeology,* edited by David Doyel and F. Plog, pp. 78–105. Anthropological Research Papers 23, Arizona State University, Tempe.
Vencl, Sl.
  1984   War and Warfare in Archaeology. *Journal of Anthropological Archaeology* 3:116–132.
Wallace, Henry D.
  1983   The Mortars, Petroglyphs, and Trincheras on Rillito Peak. *The Kiva* 48:137–246.
  1985   Decorated Ceramics. In *Excavations at the Valencia Site: A Preclassic Hohokam Village in the Southern Tucson Basin,* by William H. Doelle, pp. 81–135. Institute for American Research Anthropological Papers 3. Tucson.
  1986a  Decorated Ceramics. In *Archaeological Investigations at the Tanque Verde Wash Site: A Middle Rincon Settlement in the Eastern Tucson Basin,* by Mark D. Elson. Institute for American Research Anthropological Papers 7. Tucson.
  1986b  Decorated Ceramics. In *Archaeological Investigations at the West Branch Site: Early and Middle Rincon Occupation in the Southern Tucson Basin,* by Frederick W. Huntington, pp. 123–164. Institute for American Research Anthropological Papers 5. Tucson.
  1986c  *Rincon Phase Decorated Ceramics in the Tucson Basin: A Focus on the West Branch Site.* Institute for American Research Anthropological Papers 1. Tucson.

1987   Regional Context of the Prehistoric Rancho Vistoso Sites: Settlement Patterns and Socioeconomic Structure. In *Settlement in the Cañada del Oro Valley, Arizona. The Rancho Vistoso Survey Project*, by Douglas B. Craig and Henry D. Wallace, pp. 117–166. Institute for American Research Anthropological Papers 8. Tucson.

1988a  Ceramic Boundaries and Interregional Interaction: New Perspectives on the Tucson Basin Hohokam. In *Recent Research on Tucson Basin Prehistory: Proceedings of the Second Tucson Basin Conference*, edited by William H. Doelle and Paul R. Fish, pp. 313–348. Institute for American Research Anthropological Papers 10. Tucson.

1988b  Mitigation Plan for the Los Morteros Site, AA:12:57, and Results of the Phase 1 Excavations. Manuscript on file. Institute for American Research, Tucson.

1990   *Archaeological Investigations at the Los Morteros Site, AZ AA:12:57 (ASM), and Sites AZ AA:12:146 (ASM) and AZ AA:12:147 (ASM): Late Colonial Through Early Classic Period Occupation in the Northern Tucson Basin*. Technical Report 90-1. Center For Desert Archaeology, Tucson.

Wallace, Henry D., and Douglas B. Craig
1988   A Reconsideration of the Tucson Basin Hohokam Chronology. In *Recent Research on Tucson Basin Prehistory: Proceedings of the Second Tucson Basin Conference*, edited by William H. Doelle and Paul R. Fish, pp. 9–29. Institute for American Research Anthropological Papers 10. Tucson.

Wallace, Henry D., and James Heidke
1986   Ceramic Production and Exchange. In *Archaeological Investigations at the Tanque Verde Wash Site: A Middle Rincon Settlement in the Eastern Tucson Basin*, by Mark D. Elson, pp. 233–270. Institute for American Research Anthropological Papers 7. Tucson.

Wallace, Henry D., and James P. Holmlund
1982   The Classic Period in the Tucson Basin. Manuscript on file, Arizona State Museum Library, University of Arizona, Tucson.

1984   The Classic Period in the Tucson Basin. *The Kiva* 49:167–194.

Wasley, William W., and Alfred E. Johnson
1965   *Salvage Archaeology in Painted Rocks Reservoir, Western Arizona*. Anthropological Papers 9. University of Arizona Press, Tucson.

Waters, Michael R.
1987   Holocene Alluvial Geology and Geoarchaeology of AZ BB:13:14 and the San Xavier Reach of the Santa Cruz. In *The Archaeology of the San Xavier Bridge Site (AZ BB:13:14), Tucson Basin, Southern Arizona*, edited by John C. Ravesloot, pp. 39–60. Arizona State Museum Archaeological Series 171. University of Arizona, Tucson.

Whittlesey, Stephanie M.
1986   The Ceramic Assemblage. In *The 1985 Excavation at the Hodges Site, Pima County, Arizona*, edited by Robert W. Layhe, pp. 61–126. Arizona State Museum Archaeological Series 170. University of Arizona, Tucson.

Wilcox, David R.
1979a  The Hohokam Regional System. In *An Archaeological Test of Sites in the Gila Butte–Santan Region, South-Central Arizona*, by Glen Rice, David Wilcox, Kevin Rafferty, and James Schoenwetter, pp. 77–116. Anthropological Research Paper 18. Arizona State University, Tempe.

1979b  Warfare Implications of Dry-Laid Masonry Walls on Tumamoc Hill. *The Kiva* 45:15–38.

1989  Hohokam Warfare. In *Cultures in Conflict: Current Archaeological Perspectives*, edited by Dianna Claire Tkaczuk and Brian C. Vivian, pp. 163–172. Proceedings of the 20th Annual Conference Chacmool, the Archaeological Association of the University of Calgary, Calgary.

Wilcox, David R., Thomas R. McGuire, and Charles Sternberg

1981  *Snaketown Revisited.* Arizona State Museum Archaeological Series 155. University of Arizona, Tucson.

Wilcox, David R., and Charles Sternberg

1983  *Hohokam Ballcourts and Their Interpretation.* Arizona State Museum Archaeological Series 160. University of Arizona, Tucson.

Wilk, Richard R.

1982  *Agriculture, Ecology, and Domestic Organization among the Kekchi Maya.* Ph.D. dissertation, University of Arizona. University Microfilms, Ann Arbor.

Wilk, Richard R., and Robert McC. Netting

1984  Households: Changing Forms and Function. In *Households: Comparative and Historical Studies of the Domestic Group*, edited by Robert McC. Netting, Richard R. Wilk, and Eric J. Arnould, pp. 1–28. University of California Press, Berkeley.

Wilk, Richard R., and William L. Rathje

1982  Household Archaeology. In *Archaeology of the Household: Building a Prehistory of Domestic Life*, edited by Richard R. Wilk and William L. Rathje, pp. 617–639. American Behavioral Scientist 25.

Wright, Barton A., and Rex E. Gerald

1950  The Zanardelli Site. *The Kiva* 16(3):8–15.

Zahniser, Jack L.

1966  Late Prehistoric Villages Southeast of Tucson, Arizona, and the Archaeology of the Tanque Verde Phase. *The Kiva* 31:103–204.

# •8•

# ON THE OUTSIDE LOOKING IN: THE CONCEPT OF PERIPHERY IN HOHOKAM ARCHAEOLOGY

▼▼▼▼▼▼▼▼▼▼▼▼▼▼▼▼▼▼▼▼▼▼▼▼▼▼▼▼▼▼▼▼▼▼▼▼▼▼▼▼▼▼▼▼▼▼▼▼▼▼▼▼▼▼▼▼▼▼

## *Randall H. McGuire*

M ost contemporary archaeologists work with an explicit concept of a Hohokam core surrounded by areas that are in some sense peripheral to that core. The Phoenix Basin is generally regarded as the core and the rest of the Hohokam range as the periphery. This core-periphery contrast has been extremely resilient, originating about 60 years ago and continuing, often in modified form, through several major theoretical shifts in Hohokam archaeology. The contrast clearly has some reality in the archaeological record of the Hohokam, but it also has become a framework that shapes the creation of that record.

This framework particularly affects our interpretations of areas labeled peripheral. Archaeologists have a marked tendency to see developments in these peripheral areas as originating in and dependent upon what happens in the core. The movement of styles, products, and items are often assumed to be one way—from the core out. These peripheries are somehow viewed as incapable of existing, at least as Hohokam, apart from the core. Archaeologists may discuss the core without reference to the peripheries, but they seldom discuss peripheries without reference to the core.

Using the examples of the Papagueria, the Middle Verde Valley, and the Trincheras culture of northern Sonora, I wish to discuss the development of the concept of periphery and how it has shaped our interpretations of these regions. The three regions will be briefly described, the historical development of the concept of core and periphery will be discussed, and the usefulness of the concept critically evaluated. Finally, this evaluation leads to a reappraisal of temporal and spatial relationships in the Hohokam system from the outside looking in.

## THREE HOHOKAM PERIPHERIES

Prehistorians have variously classified and described the peripheries of the Hohokam and only a few attempts exist that consider the entire region systematically (Gladwin et al. 1936; DiPeso 1956, 1979; Schroeder 1960, 1979; Haury 1976; Gumerman and Haury 1979; Wilcox and Sternberg 1983; Neitzel 1984; Teague 1984). Hohokam archaeologists have not divided the tradition into a set of commonly accepted named branches such as exist for the Anasazi tradition. They do, however, recognize a set of subareas that correspond to major basins and river valleys. These areas include the Tucson Basin, Gila Bend, the Papagueria, the San Pedro River, the Safford area, the Agua Fria River, the Middle Verde River, the Upper Santa Cruz River, and the Phoenix Basin (Fig. 8.1). Researchers working within these areas will often further subdivide them and recombining or promoting some of these smaller units would produce a different list of subareas.

Hohokam prehistorians generally consider the Phoenix Basin to be the core area of the Hohokam and the other subareas to be peripheries. As Figure 8.1 reflects, some researchers would limit the core designation to the riverine areas within the Phoenix Basin and treat the nonriverine portions of the basin as an internal periphery (Wilcox and Sternberg 1983:219–220). The most elaborate expressions of the Hohokam tradition occur in the Phoenix Basin, including the largest sites, the biggest ballcourts and platform mounds, the most extensive irrigation networks, the most lavish ritual objects, and the highest percentage of red-on-buff pottery. Most of these occur in the peripheral areas but they are less elaborate and appear later than in the core.

When researchers start in the Phoenix Basin and look out at the peripheries, they cannot help but be struck by the similarities between the Phoenix Basin and the other subareas. Upon examining these similarities they easily conclude that the Phoenix Basin was a "hot" area of cultural development and the source of a common cultural pattern or economy. If researchers start with peripheral areas and look in, they encounter more diversity than the shared similarities of the core. The prehistory of three peripheries, the Pa-

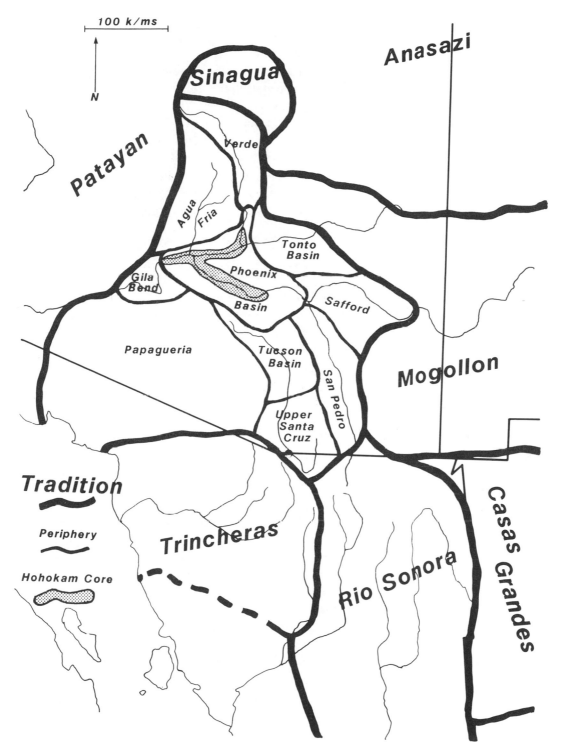

Figure 8.1    *The Hohokam regional system at the beginning of the Sacaton period.*

pagueria, the Middle Verde Valley, and the Trincheras region, illustrates the variability that existed within the system.

Hohokam archaeologists often interpret these three peripheries as having different cultural and economic relationships to a Phoenix Basin core. The Papagueria is generally regarded as a peripheral area within the Hohokam tradition for its entire Formative period prehistory. Many archaeologists see the Middle Verde region as first a periphery of the Hohokam tradition and then later as the southern edge of the Sinagua culture. The relationship of the Trincheras culture of northern Sonora to the Hohokam is highly controversial; some scholars claim this area is part of the Hohokam tradition and others maintain it was a separate tradition. As these debates suggest, the three areas are quite distinct from each other in spite of their shared status as Hohokam peripheries.

## THE PAPAGUERIA

The Papagueria includes the modern Tohono O'odham Nation, the lands west of the reservation to the Colorado River, and the area north and west of Caborca in Sonora, Mexico. Like today, the prehistoric population occurred primarily in the eastern half of the region. There are no permanent flowing rivers or streams in the Papagueria and precipitation ranges from about 10 in annually at the eastern edge of the region to less than 3 in at the western edge.

Aboriginal agriculturalists, lacking perennial streams, practiced *ak-chin* agriculture. This strategy involves the careful placement of fields and features to capitalize on storm runoff (Nabhan 1979). In the Papagueria the frequency of areas suitable for this technique decline from east to west following the rainfall gradient. In the eastern Papagueria modern Papagos built elaborate systems of canals and diversion dams to distribute water over large areas and the late prehistoric peoples of the region may have also done so (Withers 1973). Aboriginal varieties of corn yield the same productivity per acre with either canal irrigation or *ak-chin* methods, but *ak-chin* agriculture involves greater risk, with historically reported crop failures occurring up to three years in a row (Castetter and Bell 1942:44).

In both the core area and in the Papagueria foraging for wild plants provided a significant portion of the subsistence base in all periods. Several analyses suggest that the dependence on agriculture increased through time in both regions but that in all time periods gathering was of greater importance in the Papagueria than in the core (Plog 1980:109; McGuire and Schiffer 1982:237).

Very few archaeologists worked in the Papagueria before the late 1960s (Gladwin and Gladwin 1929; Fraps 1936; Ives 1936; Hoover 1941; Ezell 1954). The University of Arizona Papagueria project carried out in the late 1930s and early 1940s on the Tohono O'odham Nation provides the earliest definition of the Papagueria as a region, and it developed the currently used phase sequence (Scantling 1940; Haury 1950; Withers 1973). Since the late 1960s, federal contracts have generated a considerable amount of research, primarily on the Tohono O'odham Nation (Stewart and Teague 1974; Goodyear 1975; Stacy 1975, 1977; Raab 1976; Rosenthal et al. 1978; McGuire and Mayro 1978; Huckell 1979; Doelle 1980; Masse 1980; Anderson 1982). Julian Hayden (1970, 1972) has completed extensive surveys in the Sierra Pinacate, but virtually no other work has been done in the Mexican portion of the Papagueria.

Hohokam occupation of the region extends from the Pioneer through the Classic period. Cultural development is not uniform over the area and the region might usefully be broken down into two parts: a western section, including the Santa Rosa Wash drainage and extending to the Colorado River, and an eastern section that extends off the Tohono O'odham Nation into the Avra Valley. The eastern section, especially south and east of Sells and on the east flanks of the Baboquivari Mountains, was more densely populated and compounds and platform mounds were present in the later periods. The people of the western section participated heavily in the shell trade and throughout the sequence lived in scattered rancheria settlements of pithouses.

Most of our information on the Archaic of the Papagueria comes from the site of Ventana Cave (Haury 1950). At this site Haury found stratified deposits dating from the late Pleistocene through the present. Haury identified the terminal Archaic phase in the cave as San Pedro Cochise and the artifact assemblage greatly resembles San Pedro Cochise remains from southeastern Arizona.

The earliest Hohokam remains in the Papagueria date to the Snaketown phase and appear in the Santa Rosa Wash drainage. Ventana Cave yielded a handful of Pioneer period types including Estrella Red-on-gray and Sweetwater Red-on-gray (Haury 1950:353). Masse (1980:306–307), Raab (1976), and Brown (1976:14) located Snaketown Red-on-buff sherds at large multicomponent village sites. Finally, marine shell, which probably crossed the Papagueria, occurs in the earliest (Vahki phase) deposits at Snaketown (Haury 1976:308). Pioneer period remains in the Papagueria consist of widely scattered sherds and possibly habitation sites along the Santa Rosa Wash. At present no Pioneer period architectural features have been identified or excavated in the region.

During the Colonial period small Hohokam pithouse settlements existed throughout the modern Tohono O'odham Reservation area. The earliest excavated architectural features in both the eastern and western sections of the reservation are from the late Colonial period Vamori phase. In the eastern section, excavators have found typical Hohokam pithouses with effigy palettes, stone bowls, and serrated projectile points. Along the Santa Rosa Wash Hohokam-style pithouses also occurred, but palettes and finely carved stone bowls have not been located. Throughout the Papagueria painted pottery accounts for less than 5 percent of assemblages during the Colonial period and over half of this pottery was Santa Cruz Red-on-buff. The only burial from this period is a flexed inhumation at Valshni Village, near Sells (Withers 1973:36). In the western section of the reservation extensive deposits of worked shell, mainly manufacture waste, occur with late Colonial ceramics, but very little shell occurs in the eastern section and there is no evidence of shell jewelry manufacture (McGuire and Howard 1987).

The Sedentary period witnessed an expansion of Colonial period trends. The split between an eastern section with a more elaborated material assemblage and a western section with more shell and evidence of shell manufacture continues into this period. Larger villages occur, principally in the Santa Rosa Wash and around Sells, and researchers have reported more sites from this period than the previous Colonial period. Painted pottery continues to make up a small portion of the assemblage in the eastern section of the reservation but the composition of the assemblage has changed. The Tucson Basin type Rincon Red-on-brown occurs more frequently than Sacaton Red-on-buff, representing more than 50 percent of painted ceramics. In the western section painted pottery is more common, accounting for up to 11 percent of the ceramic assemblage, and the relative frequency of red-on-buff sherds declines, even though Sacaton Red-on-buff remains the most common painted type. Researchers have not reported Hohokam public architecture, ballcourts, or capped mounds from any Papaguerian sites of this or the previous period.

The archaeology of the region changes dramatically in the Classic period. Sites greatly outnumber those of earlier periods in the Papagueria (McGuire and Schiffer 1982:193–194). Pithouses continue to be occupied, but in the eastern section compounds and platform mounds appear. Scantling (1940) excavated one platform mound and associated compound at the Jackrabbit Ruin east of Sells. Surveys along the east flanks of the Baboquivari Mountains have located at least four platform mounds dating to this period. Classic period ceramics from both the eastern and western sections are brown wares; Tanque Verde Red-on-brown and a distinctive red ware called Sells Red become the most common types. Burial practices include primary cremation and extended inhumation in the western section and extended inhumation and urn cremation in the eastern section. Evidence for shell jewelry continues in the west, with little shell at all in the east.

A new site type, *cerros de trincheras*, appears at the beginning of this period or the end of the previous period. These *cerros de trincheras* consist of isolated hills covered with terraces, walls, and sometimes compounds. Excavations in the Tucson Basin indicate that many of the terraces served as platforms for pithouses (Fraps 1936; Downum 1986) and some may have been used to grow agave (Fish et al. 1984). These sites appear to represent hillside villages whose occupants engaged in the wide range of activities we would expect at habitation sites. The most probable reason for their location on steep isolated hills, often with curtain walls and walled entrances, is defense (Fontana et al. 1959; Wilcox 1979; Wallace and Holmlund 1984:180).

The Papagueria lies between the Phoenix Basin and the major source of Hohokam shell—the Gulf of California. The presence of Gulf of California shell in Pioneer period contexts in the Phoenix Basin suggests that the Hohokam may have crossed or occupied the region before the Snaketown phase. In the Colonial, Sedentary, and Classic periods, pithouse village sites in the Santa Rosa Wash area and west contain large quantities of debitage from the manufacture of shell jewelry but few finished artifacts. The exchange of shell jewelry is the most obvious economic link between the Phoenix Basin core and the Papaguerian periphery.

The historic occupants of the Papagueria, the Tohono O'odham, lived in scattered villages and practiced *ak-chin* agriculture. The largest of these villages numbered several hundred persons in the eighteenth century. These people were the westernmost extension of the upper Pima and spoke a mutually intelligible language with the O'odham of the Tucson Basin, San Pedro River, Gila River, and northern Sonora. The Spanish never successfully missionized the Papagueria and effective European domination of the area came only in the nineteenth century.

## THE MIDDLE VERDE VALLEY

The Middle Verde River Valley lies north of Phoenix, Arizona and contains the modern towns of Cottonwood, Camp Verde, and Perkinsville. The Black Mountains force the Verde River into a series of canyons near its confluence with the east Verde River, and these canyons mark the divide between the Middle and Lower Verde rivers.

The Middle Verde Valley is the northernmost island of the Sonoran Desert in Arizona. To the north of the valley rises the Mogollon Rim and a rapid progression from lower Sonoran cactus-palo verde communities to Ponderosa pine occurs. The pine-covered Black Mountains and higher elevation grasslands to the south separate the Sonoran Desert of the Middle Verde region from the main expanse of the Sonoran Desert.

The Verde River flows year-round but has a relatively narrow floodplain flanked by high terraces and hills making an aboriginal irrigation system like that of the prehistoric Phoenix Basin impossible. However, researchers have located small aboriginal canal systems and extensive runoff farming systems (Breternitz 1960; Fish and Fish 1984).

Archaeological research in the Middle Verde Valley has been sporadic since the end of the last century (Mindeleff 1896), although several late pueblos in the valley were excavated during the first half of this century (Fewkes 1912; Caywood and Spicer 1935; Spicer and Caywood 1936; Dixon 1956; Hartman 1976). Hohokam archaeology has been limited to excavations by Breternitz (1960), Fish (1974), and McGuire (1977), and Paul and Suzanne Fish (1984) also completed studies of agricultural systems in the valley during the 1980s. The boom in contract work of the 1970s and 1980s hardly touched this region.

No Late Archaic sites have been excavated or reported on from the Middle Verde Valley. Fish and Fish (1977:12), however, report San Pedro Cochise-style projectile points in private collections from the region.

Breternitz (1960:7–8) discovered two oval to rectangular preceramic pit-houses in two large multicomponent sites. Very little material was associated with these houses and temporal assignment is tenuously based on the presence of oval manos, grinding slabs, and the absence of pottery. These houses may belong to a widespread transitional Archaic to formative Red Mountain phase as described by Cable and Doyel (1987). If they are Red Mountain phase, we do not presently have any substantial evidence for a subsequent Vahki phase of the area. Researchers have found a handful of Pioneer period Hohokam ceramics in the Middle Verde Valley, but presently they have not identified any single component Pioneer period sites or excavated any Pioneer period structures.

Large villages with ballcourts, mounds, and Hohokam-style pithouses clearly exist in the Verde Valley by the Colonial period. Excavators have also found pithouses in the Sinagua style in these same settlements, apparently contemporary with the adjacent Hohokam-style houses. A wide range of site sizes exists; large sites with 100+ pithouses occur along with sites of as few as 2 pithouses. Ballcourts and mounds at some sites, such as the Verde Ball Court site, may identify ritual and political centers in the valley. The only two burials recorded from this period are inhumations (Breternitz 1960:18). Canal irrigation was present during this time.

The artifact assemblage exhibits a number of Hohokam traits including shell jewelry and palettes. The plain ware from the period is a paddle-and-anvil produced brown ware, Verde Brown, which some researchers treat as a variant of Gila Plain (Breternitz 1960:11) and other researchers place within the Alameda Brown Wares from the Flagstaff area (Colton 1958; McGuire 1977:21–22; Fish and Fish 1977:13). Hohokam painted ceramics include Gila Butte Red-on-buff and Santa Cruz Red-on-buff, but these never make up more than 40 percent of the painted ceramics. Anasazi ceramics comprise the other 60 percent. Painted ceramics in general comprise a small portion of the collection, about 1.4 percent to 2.0 percent of any assemblage. If Wingfield Plain is treated as a Hohokam ware, then Hohokam ceramics comprise 22.7 percent of all the ceramics recovered from this period (data in Fish et al. 1980, table 1).

Generally, during the Sedentary period villages get larger and the basic pattern of the previous Colonial period remains. Ballcourts were present in at least eight sites (Wilcox and Sternberg 1983:119) and mounds in at least three sites. All 11 burials from this period are cremations. The percentage of Hohokam pottery in the collections, however, declines to 15.1 percent for all ceramics and 8 percent for painted types. The percentage of painted pottery in the assemblages increases to 5–6 percent. The floodplain appears to have been heavily irrigated by this time with most of the areas in reach of gravity-fed canals.

In the Classic period the archaeology of the valley changes so much that it is generally identified with a different archaeological tradition, the Sinagua (Pillas 1981). Villages grow from clusters of pithouses to contiguous-roomed, cobble-walled pueblos. These pueblos seem to be the culmination of trends starting with cobble-walled pithouses and pithouses, still present in some sites (Fish and Fish 1977:15–17). Site locations shift from the terraces next to the river, to bluffs and hills overlooking the rivers. Pueblos vary in size from a few rooms to several hundred, but none possesses clear examples of public architecture such as ballcourts. These pueblos are often associated with extensive dry farming and irrigation systems (Fish and Fish 1984). Ceramic assemblages are dominated by Sinagua red wares with the only painted pottery being intrusive Anasazi types. The 450+ burials from this period are all inhumations. Local artisans made Hohokam-style shell jewelry (principally bracelets) in the larger pueblos (Howard 1985).

When the first Spanish passed through the Middle Verde Valley in the sixteenth century they encountered scattered groups of Yavapai. These Yuman speakers did not live in permanent settlements and farmed only a few scattered parcels of exceptionally well watered land (Schroeder 1974).

## TRINCHERAS

The Trincheras tradition of northern Sonora included an area stretching from around the international border on the north, to Puerto Libertad on the south, and from the Rio Sonoita on the west to the Rio San Miguel on the east (Alvarez 1985). Sites of this culture centered on the river system of the Rio Magdalena, Rio Altar, and Rio Concepción.

Archaeological research in the region includes several expansive surveys (Sauer and Brand 1931; Wasley 1968; Bowen n.d.), a variety of limited excavations (Johnson 1963; Robles 1973, n.d.), and several excavations along the boundary between Trincheras and Hohokam traditions (DiPeso 1956; Doyel 1977; Jácome 1986). The most intensive survey to date is the 1988 Altar Valley project (McGuire and Villalpando 1989) and the most intensive excavations are Beatriz Braniff's (1985, 1988), near Caborca and on the Rio San Miguel.

A major debate has concerned whether or not these archaeological remains should be considered a separate tradition or Hohokam. Some archaeologists, such as Haury (1950:547) and Johnson (1963:182–185), include the Trincheras in the Hohokam tradition, but others, such as DiPeso (1979:158, 1983) and Braniff (1985), regard it as a separate tradition. In early historic times O'odham (Piman) groups occupied the Trincheras area and the southern half of the Hohokam area.

The development of the Trincheras tradition broadly parallels that of the Hohokam. Initially, this population occupied shallow pithouses much like the Hohokam and appears to have been heavily involved in the shell trade—as indicated by raw shell and waste at the site of La Playa on the Rio Magdalena. Trincheras people produced shell bracelets using a different manufacturing technique than the Hohokam, but their purple-on-red pottery exhibits numerous stylistic parallels to Hohokam wares.

In the fourteenth and fifteenth centuries they built massive *cerros de trincheras* along the major rivers. These sites can be quite large, covering up to one-half of a square kilometer with 40 to 50 terraces. The range of features and overall layout of the Sonoran *cerros de trincheras* appears similar to those in the Papagueria and the Tucson Basin, but they are more common and often larger in Sonora.

Our research in the Rio Altar suggests that the Trincheras may be best considered a separate tradition in its early stages and included as a part of the southern Arizona tradition in the later prehistoric period (McGuire and Villalpando 1989). The earliest ceramic sites in the Altar are settlements with shallow pithouses and cremation burial, but other aspects of their material culture do not resemble Hohokam. The pottery includes a very reddish plain ware and Trincheras Purple-on-red. Both of these types often exhibit scraping marks on their interior indicating a coil-and-scrape manufacture technique. (The scraping marks on the interior of Trincheras pottery have often been misinterpreted as "brushing." Scraping the wet clay vessel with a straight-edged tool would produce these marks because the tool would drag bits of temper along the surface.) Trincheras sites of this period lack certain key Hohokam traits including ballcourts, censers, and palettes. These sites often contain non-Hohokam material items such as rectangular ground-stone *mocajetes* and drop-ended manos and narrow metates.

This period can be divided internally and corresponds to Bowen's (n.d.) phases II and III. Trincheras ceramics from this period occur in Colonial and Sedentary period Hohokam sites. This period probably dates between A.D. 700 and 1300.

The most numerous sites in the Altar Valley date to the subsequent period that Hinton (1955) initially called the Plain ware period. The material culture of these sites greatly resembles other late prehistoric assemblages from the Papagueria, Tucson Basin, and San Pedro River Valley in southern Arizona. The plain ware is a polished, paddle-and-anvil brown ware, which is very similar to the plain ware of southern Arizona. A polished red ware similar to Sells Red accompanies this plain ware. No locally produced painted ware comparable to the Tanque Verde Red-on-brown of southern Arizona occurs. Settlements are still shallow pithouses but the local population also built *cerros de trincheras*. Shell manufacture waste occurs on sites of this period suggesting a continued involvement in the shell trade. Burials include both urn cremations and inhumations (Robles n.d.). Intrusive pottery is principally Salado polychromes and Casas Grandes Polychrome, suggesting that these sites date from A.D. 1300 to 1450.

The protohistoric assemblage in the valley is essentially the same as in southern Arizona (Masse 1981; Doelle and Wallace, this volume). The plain ware pottery is thin, finger impressed, and unpolished. It differs from San Pedro Valley Whetstone Plain primarily in color and nonplastic inclusions. Projectile points were small and triangular with basal notches. Oval to square outlines of rock provide the only surface indication of houses in this period.

O'odhams (Pimas) occupied the valley when the Jesuits entered in the seventeenth century, and modern villages exist at all but one of the valley's Jesuit mission locations. The aboriginal population in the valley when Kino arrived numbered between 1,000 to 1,500 but fell to only a few hundred in the early nineteenth century. The indigenous O'odham were gradually replaced by Tohono O'odham from the Papagueria. The most recent Native American sites in the valley are late nineteenth-century Tohono O'odham rancherias.

## COMPARING THE THREE PERIPHERIES

Throughout the history of Hohokam archaeology all three of these regions have been regarded as peripheral to a core Phoenix Basin Hohokam, and their prehistories have largely been interpreted in relation to this core area. Despite this shared status, the patterns of material culture, sequence of development, and relationship to the core differ greatly for each area.

Hohokam-style material culture appears in each of these areas at some point in their prehistory, but beyond this similarity the development of each area is quite different. In the Middle Verde Valley, Hohokam traits appear early in the sequence but never make up a majority of the material culture. In the late prehistoric period, most prehistorians would consider the area to be Sinagua, not Hohokam. In the Papagueria, the earliest formative ceramics and architecture were virtually identical to core area assemblages. Through time the artifact assemblage of the region looks increasingly like that of the Tucson Basin rather than the core area. The Trincheras materials are initially distinctive from the core, but in the late prehistoric period the archaeology of the area greatly resembles that of the Papagueria and the Tucson Basin. At no time does the archaeology of the Trincheras area mirror that of the core.

# THE CORE-PERIPHERY CONCEPT
# IN HOHOKAM ARCHAEOLOGY

Archaeologists have interpreted the relationship between each periphery and the core in various ways, but have never assumed that all three had the same relationship to the core. Initially, the core-periphery contrast was drawn in terms of diffusions and migrations from a cultural core and later in terms of economic interconnections and dependencies.

## THE HOHOKAM AS AN ETHNIC GROUP

The core-periphery contrast originates with Harold Gladwin's definition of the Hohokam in the 1920s and 1930s (Gladwin and Gladwin 1934). This is what Wilcox (1980) has called the Gladwinian moden of the Hohokam. This model conceptualizes the Hohokam as a distinct culture that originated in a single place and then migrated and diffused out. This Hohokam culture flourished in southern Arizona during the Pioneer, Colonial, and Sedentary periods. During the Classic period, an intrusive group, the Salado, dominated the area and then departed at the end of this period leaving the Hohokam to become the Pima. By the logic of this model the core area was that region with the purest collection of "Hohokam traits," while peripheral areas would have admixtures of other traits or adulterated versions of the pure traits.

Gila Pueblo initiated field research in the Southwest to define the core and periphery of the Hohokam. Gladwin sent survey crews to the far corners of the region: Texas, California, Chihuahua, and Sonora. Pottery was identified as the primary trait of interest; systematic collections of sherds were made at the archaeological sites and the percentages of different types of pottery were calculated. The core area would have the highest percentage of red-on-buff pottery and peripheral areas would have a majority of Hohokam traits. Based on these criteria, the Trincheras culture was placed outside the Hohokam tradition and both the Papagueria and the Middle Verde were identified as peripheral to the Hohokam core (Gladwin and Gladwin 1929, 1935).

Gladwin's use of the single-culture, core-periphery model to define the Hohokam differed from the assumptions used in the definition of the Anasazi and Mogollon cultures. In the Anasazi definition, perhaps because of the ethnic and linguistic diversity of modern Pueblos, no initial assumption of a core or single cultural identity was made. At the same time that Gladwin was defining the Hohokam, archaeologists were dividing the Anasazi into distinct branches, often assumed to be ancestral to specific modern Pueblo groups. Concurrently, defining the Mogollon culture, there was also no concept of a central core, and an almost immediate attempt was made to define interrelated but distinct branches. The primary scholars of the Hohokam (among them Gladwin and Haury) also worked with the Mogollon and the Anasazi, but did not apply this one-culture, core-periphery model to these areas.

The one-culture view of the Hohokam provided the framework for the first intensive field research in the Papagueria, the University of Arizona Papagueria project of the 1930s and 1940s. This project provided new data that began to define the differences between the Papagueria and the Phoenix

Basin. Haury (1950:546–548) accounted for these differences by an analogy to the riverine-dwelling Pima and the desert-dwelling Papago, the ethnographically documented O'odham division. This division between desert and riverine Hohokam posited an initial Hohokam settlement of the Papagueria followed by a process of environmentally influenced cultural drift whereby the desert branch diverged from the riverine. Haury's scheme evokes environmental and adaptive differences to account for the variation between a Papaguerian periphery and the core, while maintaining a vision of the Hohokam as a single cultural group.

Haury derived his concept of the O'odham from late nineteenth- and twentieth-century ethnographies and his own experience. This modern O'odham world included the Pima on the Salt and Gila rivers and the Tohono O'odham in the Papagueria. Haury treated the Gila River Pima and their cousins who had moved to the Salt River in the 1870s as the core of Pima culture. The Tohono O'odham were regarded as a conservative population on the peripheries of the O'odham world.

Gladwin (1942, 1948) recanted his original one-culture view at about the same time that Haury was formulating the riverine-desert contrast. Gladwin proposed that the Pioneer period manifestations at Snaketown were not Hohokam. He linked these materials instead to a Mogollon origin, with a Hohokam intrusion in the Colonial and Sedentary periods and finally a Salado intrusion in the Classic period.

Important challenges to the one-culture view came in the 1950s from Albert Schroeder (1960, 1979) and Charles DiPeso (1956, 1979). These men still worked in an "archaeological-culture-equals-ethnic-group" framework but divided the archaeology of southern Arizona into two cultural groups. Gladwin's cultural core became an intrusive ethnic group, the Hohokam, that dominated or displaced an indigenous population, the Hakataya for Schroeder and the O'otam for DiPeso. Both Schroeder and DiPeso followed Gladwin's revisions and identified the Pioneer period in the Phoenix Basin with their indigenous populations. The Hohokam entered the Phoenix Basin in the Colonial period and dominated the indigenous population until the Classic period when the Hohokam departed or were absorbed and the local culture reasserted itself. These views gave the peripheries more autonomy and raised issues of power and domination in prehistoric southern Arizona.

These new syntheses resulted in part from greater work in regions identified as peripheries and from a commitment to these areas on the part of the researchers involved. Both DiPeso and Schroeder approached the archaeology of southern Arizona from outside the Phoenix Basin looking in, rather than from inside the Phoenix Basin looking out, as Gladwin and Haury had.

DiPeso focused his work primarily to the east and south of the Tucson Basin. His concept of the O'odham was historical and based in the O'odham world of the late seventeenth century. He recognized that the center of this world extended from the Tucson Basin south to the Rio Concepción-Altar-

Magdalena drainage in Sonora. The Gila River Pima and Papago and the Hohokam core lay at the peripheries of this O'odham range. In the 1950s DiPeso sent Thomas Hinton (1955) to the Altar Valley in Sonora to try and link the Trincheras culture to this scheme of prehistory and history. In this world, the Phoenix Basin was a periphery, an area that gained prominence only because of the intrusion of a dominant foreign group.

Schroeder focused much of his work to the west and north of the Phoenix Basin and tied his prehistory to a Yuman present. The ancestral Yumans, the Hakataya of the Middle Verde Valley, accepted the Hohokam cultural overlay then shed it to go back to their Hakataya origins.

In the 1950s and 1960s Haury maintained the one-culture view, despite the revisionism of Gladwin and the challenges of Schroeder and DiPeso (Haury 1976). In 1964 he returned to Snaketown, which he regarded as "a likely candidate for the original and parent Hohokam village" (Haury 1976:9). He countered the arguments of a non-Hohokam Pioneer period by showing that all the elements of Hohokam culture were in place at Snaketown by the Pioneer period. He postulated that migrants from Mexico introduced the Hohokam tradition to Arizona at the beginning of the Vahki phase and that these migrants then expanded to the limits of the Sonoran Desert. He also retained the idea of a Salado intrusion to account for the Classic period.

Haury's one-culture view manifested itself in the study of peripheral areas in the late 1950s. Breternitz (1960) interpreted the Colonial and Sedentary period occupants of the Middle Verde Valley as Hohokam, even identifying the local plain ware as a variant of Gila Plain. In the Trincheras region, Johnson (1963) made similar claims identifying the region as the southernmost extension of the Hohokam. In both of these cases, researchers gave priority to those aspects of the region's archaeology that resembled core features and minimized the distinctive characteristics of each area.

## HOHOKAM CULTURAL ECOLOGY

In the late 1960s and early 1970s a major theoretical shift occurred in Hohokam archaeology when adaptation replaced culture as the key concept. This shift fundamentally altered the nature of investigations, placing the emphasis on reconstructing the prehistoric adaptation of regions corresponding to river valleys and basins rather than more expansive questions of cultural boundaries and migrations. The researchers of this period accepted the one-culture view of the Hohokam and even rejected the intrusion of a Salado culture in the Classic period. By denying the existence of the migrations and ethnic shifts previously used to explain change in the region, these investigators forced the consideration of adaptive factors as primary. The core-periphery contrast remained but receded in importance as the prehistoric cultural ecology of naturally bounded regions became the primary concern.

Some researchers used a cultural-ecological stance, either directly or indirectly, to explain the core-periphery model (Gumerman et al. 1976).

For the first time, peripheral areas such as the Papagueria and the Middle Verde were looked at primarily in terms of themselves. The growth of contract archaeology in the 1970s and a spate of federally funded construction projects on the Tohono O'odham Reservation produced a growing number of contract reports that focused primarily on adaptation in the Papagueria and less on the Papagueria's place in the Hohokam world (Stewart and Teague 1974; Goodyear 1975; Stacy 1975, 1977; Raab 1976; Rosenthal et al. 1978; Huckell 1979). Bruce Masse (1980), in his report on the site of Gu Achi on the Santa Rosa Wash, questioned the desert-riverine Hohokam contrast and asserted that the Papaguerian Hohokam were Hohokam, not different from those in the Phoenix Basin. In the Verde Valley, a series of reports sought to reconstruct prehistoric adaptation in the region and played down the importance of cultural migrations to the prehistory of the valley (Fish 1974; McGuire 1977; Fish and Fish 1984).

## THE HOHOKAM REGIONAL SYSTEM

The core-periphery contrast was reexamined by Wilcox and Shenk (1977) and then reasserted itself as a central focus of Hohokam archaeology at the 1978 Society for American Archaeology session on Hohokam archaeology in Tucson (Doyel and Plog 1980). The organizers of this session divided the papers into those pertaining to the core and those pertaining to the periphery. In this new manifestation, the nature of the core-periphery contrast had seemingly changed. The geographic areas identified as core and periphery remained essentially the same, but the basis of the contrast no longer rested in concepts of cultural diffusion or migration. Instead, recent researchers see the contrast as a manifestation of some combination of ceremonial, economic, or political relations of dependency.

David Wilcox's conceptualization of a Hohokam regional system has been the major intellectual force revitalizing a core and periphery distinction in Hohokam archaeology (Wilcox 1980; Wilcox and Shenk 1977; Wilcox et al. 1981; Wilcox and Sternberg 1983). Wilcox (1980) rejected the Gladwinian concept of the Hohokam as a single ethnic, linguistic, or cultural group. He proposed instead that we discuss the Hohokam as a regional system and shift debate away from discussion of who the Hohokam were to considerations of the systematic relations and interactions of the system (Wilcox 1980). In his initial formulations Wilcox retained the idea of a Hohokam core within the Phoenix Basin surrounded by areas that were in some sense peripheral. Recently he has moved away from this "basin-centric" perspective to see more evidence for local development (Wilcox 1987c).

In his study of ballcourts, Wilcox elaborated the model, identifying a core area, an inner periphery, an intermediate periphery, and a far periphery based

on the distribution of ballcourts (Wilcox and Sternberg 1983:219–220). Wilcox
restricted the core to the riverine areas of the Gila and Salt rivers within the
Phoenix Basin and labeled the nonriverine areas of the basin as the inner
periphery. The intermediate periphery included the principal river valleys
surrounding the Phoenix Basin, the Tucson Basin, the Middle Verde, Gila
Bend, and San Pedro Valley. The far periphery was the Tonto Basin, Papagueria, Safford Valley, the Flagstaff area, northern Sonora, southeastern Arizona, and Point of Pines. Wilcox postulates that the ritual associated with the
ballcourts was the glue that held the system together. Ideology and ceremonial
exchange linked the system and the Phoenix Basin gained its centrality because the ritual originated there.

According to Wilcox and Sternberg (1983:242), the Hohokam regional system collapses at the end of the Sedentary period when peripheral populations
abandon the ballcourts. By A.D. 1300 the core became the western member
of a Saladoan interaction sphere stretching to Casas Grandes on the southeast.
Wilcox suggests that this Saladoan interaction sphere was a "weakly integrated system of exchange among a large series of small-scale regional systems" (Wilcox and Sternberg 1983:244). He explicitly identifies the Tucson
Basin as a periphery of this Saladoan sphere and his discussions suggest that
he would also classify the Middle Verde, Papagueria, and Trincheras as peripheries.

The notion of a Hohokam regional system with a Phoenix Basin core and
surrounding peripheries quickly came to dominate Hohokam studies (Doyel
and Plog 1980; Crown 1984; Teague 1984; Cable and Doyel 1987; Gregory and
Nials 1985; Howard 1985; McGuire and Howard 1987; Neitzel 1984). This new
perspective opened up new models and theories that sought to once again
link the development of subregions in the Hohokam to the Phoenix Basin.
Most of these new models tended to emphasize economic linkages rather
than maintain the central interest in ideology and ritual that characterizes
Wilcox's formulations.

In the Papagueria, new survey data and the revised core-periphery contrast led to major revisions in the interpretation of Papaguerian prehistory.
In the late 1970s, a series of projects in the western Papagueria located sites
dating from the Colonial through the Classic periods with large amounts of
shell debitage on them (Rosenthal et al. 1978; McGuire and Mayro 1978;
Huckell 1979). Such sites had been reported earlier but were identified as the
camps of shell gathering expeditions from the core. It became apparent in
the 1970s that these were in fact pithouse settlements. Incorporating these
new data in the economic core-periphery framework, several researchers posited that the Papagueria, from Santa Rosa Wash west, was an economic periphery trading shell for food (Doelle 1980; Teague and Baldwin 1978; McGuire
and Schiffer 1982; McGuire and Howard 1987). Recently, investigators at the
Gila Butte phase site of Shelltown have carried this perspective to its extreme,

claiming that the people of the Papaguerian were shell merchants engaged in a market exchange (Marmaduke and Martynec n.d.).

The Middle Verde River Valley had long been regarded as culturally intermediate between the Hohokam and the Sinagua (Pillas 1981). Under the new model this intermediacy was reinterpreted in economic terms. Various authors have linked the appearance of a Hohokam material culture assemblage in the valley to exchange between the core and the Sinagua of Flagstaff (Fish et al. 1980; McGuire and Downum 1982). These archaeologists postulated trading outposts, trading expeditions, and down-the-line trade networks to account for the Hohokam traits in the valley and around Flagstaff.

In the new core-periphery contrast, peripheral areas have been redefined in terms of their relations to the core. The Papagueria and the Trincheras are discussed principally as shell suppliers for the Hohokam core, the Middle Verde as trade middlemen connecting the Hohokam and the Sinagua. These economic linkages are seen as creating and influencing political and cultural changes in the regions. The general assumption seems to be that cultural relations and similarities follow from these economic relations.

## A CRITICAL EVALUATION OF THE CORE-PERIPHERY CONCEPT

The core-periphery concept, as currently constituted in Hohokam archaeology, tends to emphasize economic and political relationships. Causative statements concerning cultural change originate in changes in the economic and political relations between cores and peripheries. Many researchers see change in peripheries such as the Papagueria, Middle Verde, and the Trincheras as emanating from changes in the core, Phoenix Basin, area.

This perspective leads to a map of the Hohokam world very similar to the map produced under the diffusionary Gladwinian model. Consequently, the individual perspectives of many Hohokam archaeologists are a mix of earlier diffusionary ideas and the new economic, political view. Most Hohokam archaeologists would suggest that there is an underlying empirical reality to the core-periphery perspective for which the two core-periphery concepts offer alternative, competing, or complementary explanations. Unfortunately, in many of our considerations, the words regional system are simply substituted for culture and very little else is changed.

The renewed emphasis on a core-periphery contrast has opened up Hohokam archaeology to a whole set of new and significant ideas. Most importantly it has shifted us from the myopia of individual valleys and basins and forced us to consider broad-scale patterns of change across the whole of the Sonoran Desert and throughout the Southwest. We have once again started to ask questions about broad patterns of change previously only accounted for by reference to diffusion and migration. We have framed these questions in terms of economic and political dependencies and relations of power. After a decade of use it has, however, become apparent, even to a strong advocate of the perspective such as myself, that a critical reevaluation of it is needed. Such reevaluation needs to consider the limitations of any scheme that rates some areas as "hot" innovators and others as "cold" recipients.

The most obvious problem with classificatory terms such as core and periphery is that they link areas in terms of a specified set of similarities, but in doing so can mask or hide important variation among regions placed in the same category. Studies such as Crown's (1984) of intrusive pottery in the Phoenix Basin have shown that the core was not a uniform area but subdivisible into different spheres of interaction presumably with different relations to each peripheral area.

The regional perspective of researchers has a big impact on how the variation will be standardized. It is in the peripheries that the homogenization of variation is most apparent. The Papagueria, Middle Verde, and Trincheras culture share little in common other than being seen as somehow less Hohokam than the Phoenix Basin. They could just as easily be identified as separate identities in terms of their ecological, cultural, and material content. Wilcox's attempt to divide the peripheries into subcategories based primarily on distance from the core only partially solves this classificatory problem. By consistently starting our considerations from the core, from the inside looking out, we obscure variation in the peripheries and potentially ignore linkages between the peripheries that do not emanate from the core.

If we think of the Hohokam in terms of a core-periphery model, then the work of Immanuel Wallerstein (1974, 1980) and his world systems theory would appear attractive. Wilcox (1986, 1987a, 1988) has invoked Wallerstein because world systems theory shows how a social system can be defined in terms of a division of labor that unites different ethnic groups in cores, peripheries, and semi-peripheries to define a larger social system. Wilcox's interest in a division of labor among the Hohokam is well founded, but he may err by linking this interest to Wallerstein's ideas. Wilcox's own formulations are far richer and less economically based than the world systems theory he wishes to draw on. The application of world systems theory to the Hohokam case could be seriously misleading. The changes in the Hohokam regional system over time do not fit with the expectations of the theory. This lack of fit should alert us to the fact that something other than relations of economic dependency linked the Hohokam regional system.

World systems theory holds that diverse peripheries will become more alike and less different economically, politically, and culturally, due to their shared economic relationship to a core. The concept of periphery has analytical value because of this convergence. Once a world system incorporates a region, the relationship of that periphery to the core will shape its development and therefore the core-periphery relationship becomes the key to understanding changes in the periphery.

Hohokam prehistory offers little evidence of such functional convergence. The pattern of change, in fact, contradicts the predictions of world systems theory. Peripheral areas have very similar looking Archaic manifestations and look most like each other and the core at the beginning of the Colonial period. Over time these areas diverge from each other and the core rather than converge. The Papagueria and the Middle Verde Valley start the Colonial period with red-on-buff pottery, Hohokam-style pithouses, and other Hohokam material manifestations. By the Classic period the material culture of both regions was greatly different from each other and from the Phoenix Basin.

Hohokam prehistory lacks functional convergence because southern Arizona was never as economically or politically integrated as the world systems model assumes. Few archaeologists would argue that large-scale, long-distance trade in basic commodities existed among the prehistoric Hohokam. Even the models of food trade into the Papagueria do not require that the amount be more than a fraction of total subsistence to buffer irregular supplies in the local environment. Furthermore, in this case the Papaguerian peoples may have traveled to the food in times of stress rather than the other way around. The technology available to move foodstuffs would have allowed the regular redistribution of foodstuffs over distances of 50 to 60 km (Lightfoot 1979; Hassig 1988:64). Food redistribution networks could have covered areas of 7,800 to 11,232 sq km. All of the Hohokam peripheries shown on Figure 8.1 are approximately this size except the Papagueria and the Trincheras, which are considerably larger.

The Hohokam peripheries such as the Middle Verde, Tonto Basin, Tucson Basin, Agua Fria, had to have been primarily self-provisioning. The Hohokam must have forged the connections in their regional system primarily through the exchange of precious items. Trade in these goods will link areas producing cultural convergence and dependencies that form the locus of cultural change.

Such trade will not, however, lead to large-scale functional convergence and uniform peripheries because the local economic-ecological relations remain primary. We cannot arrive at an adequate understanding of cultural change in large regions without integrating trade in precious items with local economic relations. To do this we must once again emphasize the difference among peripheries without denying the interconnections.

## SHIFTING CORES AND PERIPHERIES

Wilcox proposed the concept of a Hohokam regional system to direct us away from models of cultural migration and to focus our research on the interconnections and relations that made up the system. Wilcox's formulation would allow for a prehistory with multiple and shifting cores and multiple and shifting peripheries. Such a dynamic picture of Hohokam prehistory has not developed because the major syntheses have continued to start and end from the perspective of the Phoenix Basin. By placing the Phoenix Basin at the center of the intellectual problem, it becomes a core long before it was and remains one long after it ceased to be. Current conceptualizations of the Hohokam regional system tend to maintain the one-culture view of Gladwin and Haury even though they alter the terminology and advocate different mechanisms of change in the system. A better understanding of Hohokam prehistory might be obtained by standing on the outside and looking in, that is, by reviving the perspective taken by DiPeso.

Recent studies of the Archaic and early Formative periods in southern Arizona and northern Sonora suggest a common adaptation and cultural pattern over the entire region (Huckell 1984a, 1984b; Cable and Doyel 1987; Doyel, this volume). San Pedro phase Cochise sites existed throughout southern Arizona and northern Sonora providing a common Archaic base for later developments. Agriculture appears at the end of this phase with the introduction of small settlements, each containing a few circular pithouses in the Tucson Basin and southeast Arizona. Cable and Doyel (1987) define a subsequent Red Mountain phase, which has pottery, floodplain agriculture, and small rectangular pithouses. Sites of this phase occur over a large area from southeast Arizona, into the Phoenix Basin, and possibly to the Middle Verde.

In the transition from the Archaic to the Formative, the Phoenix Basin did not appear as a core area. The earliest evidence of settlements comes from the Tucson Basin and southeast Arizona. This basic small settlement agricultural pattern was adopted over a very large area, larger than the later Hohokam regional system.

Doyel (this volume) discusses in detail the development of the Hohokam cultural pattern in the Phoenix Basin during the Pioneer period. In areas such as the Middle Verde, Tucson Basin, and the Papagueria we have very little evidence for this time period, probably because the earlier cultural patterns continue until the Snaketown phase. The Hohokam regional system originates in the Colonial period with the expansion of a cluster of traits including ballcourts, red-on-buff pottery, palettes, finely made stone bowls, shell jewelry, and cremation burial. In the Middle Verde, the local agricultural population adopted much of the Hohokam tradition, but the bulk of their material culture continued to follow a local pattern. In the Santa Rosa Wash area of the Papagueria, the Hohokam assemblage is virtually indistinguishable from that of the Phoenix Basin and the first settlements are Snaketown phase in age. All of this suggests an actual migration of peoples. The Trincheras tradition apparently lay beyond the reach of the Hohokam regional system.

Figure 8.2 illustrates the late Colonial period–early Sedentary period distribution of a variety of traits that have been used to define the Hohokam regional system. These include red-on-buff pottery, ballcourts, shell jewelry, palettes, and stone effigy vessels. The distributions of all these materials suggest a center or core in the Phoenix Basin. They do not, however, suggest

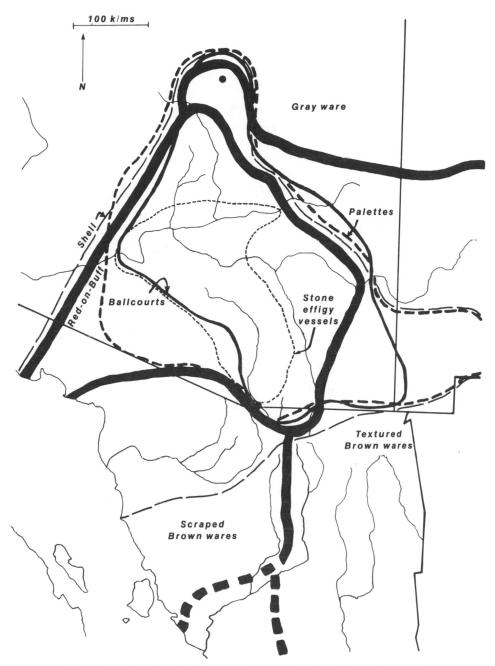

Figure 8.2    *Distribution of Hohokam material culture in the Sedentary period.*[1]

a hard-bounded system and we must assume that each had a different position in the system. Some, such as shell and palettes, have a much wider distribution than the traditional boundaries of the Hohokam, while stone effigy vessels and a variety of less common items, such as etched shell, have a more restricted distribution.

General agreement appears to exist among Hohokam archaeologists that the Hohokam regional system collapses or is reorganized at the end of the Sedentary period and the beginning of the Classic. In the Middle Verde, Papagueria, and the Trincheras, major alterations occur at this time in the material culture assemblage and adaptation. In the Middle Verde, ballcourts are abandoned and the cultural pattern becomes an extension of the Sinagua to the north. Both the Papagueria and the Trincheras become more like each other and the Tucson Basin.

Figure 8.3 illustrates the late prehistoric (A.D. 1300–1450) distribution of several traits that have been used by archaeologists as cultural markers in this period. A number of frequently discussed attributes, including extended inhumation, polished red ware, and shell jewelry, are not plotted because they would extend over the entire map. The trait distributions for this period do not give the impression of a single regional system with a Phoenix Basin core.

Clearly by this time period it does not make sense to speak of a Hohokam regional system, and applying the term Hohokam to all of the areas previously in the system can only confuse our research efforts. Wilcox proposed that a new Saladoan interaction sphere came into being at this time and that the Tucson Basin was peripheral to that system (Wilcox and Sternberg 1983). Minnis (1989) has advanced a compatible model for a Saladoan interaction sphere based on the idea of peer polity interaction. Peer polity interactions do not involve clear asymmetries of power and are strongest between nearby populations. He posits a chain of interacting polities stretching from Casas Grandes northwest to the Tonto Basin and then southwest to the Phoenix Basin. He further suggests that these polities engaged in warfare between collaborating or competing polities in the interaction sphere (Minnis 1989:303). The Tucson Basin and the Papagueria lay outside this sphere in Minnis's model.

I would accept this notion of a string of competing and cooperating polities that formed a Saladoan interaction sphere but would suggest that the formation of this sphere put in motion a process of ethnogenesis that created an O'otam culture. Ethnogenesis is a process whereby kin-based communities create a culture and cultural identity to resist more powerful elite-based polities (Diamond 1974; Gailey 1987; Patterson 1987). This O'otam culture, defined by the distribution of Sonorna brown wares, developed in southern Arizona and northern Sonora with the Tucson Basin as its center. The development of the Saladoan interaction sphere, ethnogenesis of an O'otam culture, and the collapse of the Hohokam regional system could have been

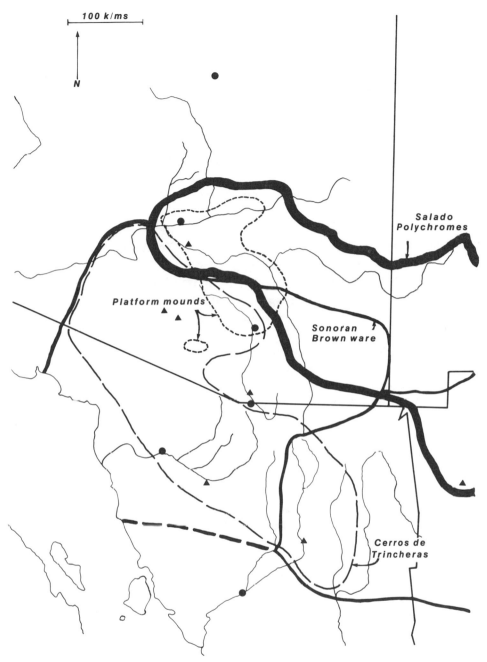

Figure 8.3    *Distribution of selected traits in southern Arizona and northern Sonora in late prehistoric times.*[2]

a response to an increasingly powerful Phoenix Basin (see also Wilcox 1979, 1989).

A comparison of Figures 8.2 and 8.3 suggest a rather dramatic and sudden transformation in southern Arizona prehistory. It was such a comparison that led earlier researchers to seek explanations for the change in the migrations of people. Such a comparison is, however, misleading because the transformation was not sudden but rather a matter of small quantitative changes building up to a major qualitative shift at the end of the Sedentary followed by a hundred years or more of reoganization. Peripheral areas such as the Middle Verde and the Papagueria began to diverge from the core area cultural pattern from the Colonial period onwards.

We can see these small shifts in the prehistory of the Tucson Basin, the Papagueria, and the Trincheras. Red-on-buff ceramics remain the dominant type in the Tucson Basin until the Rillito phase when the local brown ware style begins to dominate in the southern half of the basin (Doelle and Wallace, this volume). In the eastern Papagueria, red-on-brown frequencies exceed red-on-buff in the Sedentary period. In both the western Papagueria and the Trincheras area, Sonoran brown wares become the dominant ceramic types only in the Classic period.

The development of Saladoan and O'otam regional systems in the late prehistoric period might be taken to indicate a declining role for the Phoenix Basin. The basin appears to have lost its hot status as a center of innovation and becomes a cultural periphery receiving innovation. This perception is not consistent with economic and political developments in the basin that suggest increased production and increased social differentiation. In the Classic period the irrigation system reaches its greatest extent, villages include elite residences on mounds, and at least one specialized administrative center, Casa Grande, exists.

We need to consider the possibility that the Hohokam regional system, Saladoan interaction sphere, and O'otam culture were fundamentally different types of social formations. The Hohokam system was based on an ideological and ritual complex shared by agricultural peoples principally in the northern Sonoran desert (a la Wilcox and Sternberg 1983). The complex originated in the Phoenix Basin and the Hohokam of the Phoenix Basin exploited the centrality gained from this complex and the productive potential of the basin to grow in power and influence in the region. We see the evidence for this process in the early appearance of ballcourt ritual, red-on-buff pottery styles, and other Hohokam culture in the Phoenix Basin and in its subsequent spread over most of the Arizona portion of the Sonoran desert. The growth of large communities in the Phoenix Basin such as Snaketown, and the increased production resulting from expansion of irrigation systems, could have threatened surrounding peripheries and newly developing core areas (i.e., the Tucson Basin and potentially the Tonto Basin). A growing Phoenix Basin may have tried to draw people out of the peripheries or use its centrality in the religion to influence or exert control over the peripheries (Wilcox and Sternberg 1983:240–242). The collapse of the system would have resulted from these peripheries and developing cores reorganizing themselves to answer this expansion. The results of this reorganization were at least two very different types of regional social formations.

Wilcox described the Saladoan interaction sphere as a weakly integrated system of exchange between smaller regional systems (Wilcox and Sternberg 1983). He later identified a system of elite and possibly marriage exchanges that would have linked the system (Wilcox 1987a). Such systems of elite exchange and intermarriage could have linked the competing elite of the culturally very different centers of the Phoenix Basin, Tonto Basin, and Casas Grandes.

Such elite alliance and ideological systems were common in Mesoamerica and often incorporated very different cultural and ethnic groups. Described by a number of authors, the elite of different polities intermarried and maintained an elite culture (including material items) more like each other than their followers (Marcus 1973; Blanton et al. 1981; Hassig 1985). Such systems of elite interaction existed in the absence of an overarching political system that linked the groups. Two levels of material culture existed in these systems. All of the groups in the system shared a style of polychrome pottery and set of special elite goods. Each group differed in terms of utility pottery and other utilitarian material items determined by adaptive and ethnic factors.

The Salado interaction sphere exhibits a similar pattern both in terms of orgnaization and material culture. The regions involved in the sphere include the largest and most complex sites existing in the Southwest at that time. These sites, such as Casa Grande and Casas Grandes include evidence of elite residences and elite burials. No overarching political system linked the different regions in the system and various polities probably existed within regions such as the Phoenix Basin (Gregory and Nials 1985). The material culture of the sphere includes a shared polychrome style and set of elite goods, turquoise on shell mosaic, copper bells, macaws, *Strombus* shell trumpets, turquoise, asbestos, and some types of shell beads. Utilitarian items including pottery, however, tended to vary among regions depending on cultural and environmental factors.

This Saladoan interaction sphere was bounded on the north by a series of fortified hills stretching from the Agua Fria region, east to the Lower Verde Valley, and on the south by *cerros de trincheras* from the Gila Bend south and east to the San Pedro River Valley. In these areas the populations reorganized themselves in opposition to the power centers of the Saladoan system.

Warfare patterns may have been similar to those recorded for the aboriginal Yuma of Arizona and California (Kroeber and Fontana 1986) and the Cahita (Yaqui and Mayo) of Sonora (Spicer 1980). In both these cases raiding and warfare were major factors structuring settlement patterns, ideology, and social organization. Small polities led by chiefs could use alliances with other polities to gather forces of several hundred to a thousand special warriors, fight in well-organized ranks ordered by weaponry (spearmen, clubmen, and archers), and strike at distances of over 200 miles. They raided and fought for revenge, to take captives, and to take territory. Large empty spaces opened up as a result of this fighting, and villages were frequently burned. We see similar evidence in southern Arizona, northern Sonora, and northwest Chihuahua. Intensive survey in the Tucson Basin has revealed empty spaces of up to 15 miles between Classic Period settlements (Fish and Fish, this volume; Doelle and Wallace, this volume). Burned houses and rooms are common on sites throughout the region (Casas Grandes was sacked), as are skeletons with trauma injuries, and there is evidence for trophy skulls and human sacrifice at Casas Grandes (DiPeso 1974; Minnis 1989; Wilcox 1989). As Fish and Fish (1989) have pointed out, there is no iconography of violence in southern Arizona but then neither was there among the Yuma or Cahita. Yuma and Cahita villages were not fortified but rather depended upon war chiefs and their warriors for protection. The fortified hills of central Arizona and the *cerros de trincheras* of southern Arizona and northern Sonora could have served as defensible settlements for peoples who lacked elite-based military organizations and alliances.

The basis of organization on these peripheries of the Saladoan interaction sphere was most likely ethnicity or a shared cultural identity, that is, the establishment of a basic us-them opposition, which served to unify the population against the threat of encroachment. Such systems existed on the edges of the elite systems of Mesoamerica, where in the absence of a well-defined elite hierarchy, people organized themselves along ethnic lines to oppose elite-based polities (Hassig 1985, 1988; Brumfiel 1988). In these types of social formations, material culture functions as ethnic boundary markers, as suggested by Wobst (1977) and observed by Weissner (1983) for the Kung! San.

In the O'otam region this process of ethnogenesis probably built on already established linguistic distinctions. It developed slowly from the Colonial period through the end of the Sedentary period when these quantitative changes culminated in the qualitative change producing the Classic period. We see this process manifest in the gradual changes in style and other aspects of material culture away from a core Hohokam pattern in the Papagueria and Tucson Basin and in the development of a common material pattern with the Trincheras area. During the Classic period the O'otam were flanked on the north by the great houses of the Phoenix Basin and on the east by Casas Grandes. The boundaries of the O'otam region correspond very closely to the distribution of the historic O'odham, and in the Papagueria and the Trincheras regions the archaeological evidence suggests a continuum of occupation through the protohistoric period (Haury 1950; Hayden 1970; Hinton 1955; Goodyear 1977; Masse 1980; Braniff 1985). As DiPeso (1956, 1979, 1983) pointed out, the range of variability in the material culture of the late prehistoric O'otam system compares favorably with the variation in early historic O'odham material culture.

The O'otam region does not appear to have been made up of linked polities. Only in the Tucson Basin and at Cerros de Trincheras does the density and scale of settlement suggest that polities with elite leadership might have existed. Even these centers pale, however, in comparison to the settlements of the Phoenix Basin, Tonto Basin, and Casas Grandes region. Outside of these centers there are only scattered villages and *cerros de trincheras* of middling size. As Wilcox (1987b) notes there is little evidence of systemic linkages among the O'otam above the local level, and most local areas must have been, for the most part, socially, ritually, and economically self-sustaining. The trade in shell did, however, continue and Bowen (n.d.) has suggested that the populations in the Altar-Magdalena-Concepción drainage began large-scale exchange of shell into the Tucson Basin in the Classic Period. The two largest population centers of the O'otam, the Tucson Basin and Cerros de Trincheras, may have been linked by this trade and owe their special character to it. In the Middle Verde and Agua Fria areas a similar process may have taken place. We might still have need of a more limited version of Schroeder's Hakataya concept to include the Middle Verde, Agua Fria, and Prescott traditions.

The Salado interaction sphere collapsed in the mid- to late 1400s. When the Spanish arrived, scattered populations of hunters and gatherers occupied the Tonto Basin and the Casas Grandes region. The Salt River was unoccupied and the Gila River was the northern fringe of the O'odham world. In the O'otam region, people stopped building compounds, platform mounds, and *cerros de trincheras*. They began to live in more scattered, smaller communities with more ephemeral houses. These people did not perish in the Salado collapse, but instead, became the O'odham culture that greeted the Spaniards when the power centers of the Salado system, Casa Grande and Casas Grandes, stood as forlorn ruins.

The contrast between core and periphery remains a useful one for the prehistory of southern Arizona and northern Sonora, useful as long as we treat the relationships implied in the contrast as variable and dynamic. The prehistory of the region is too complex to be accounted for by one regional system or tradition. The Hohokam regional system existed during the Colonial and Sedentary periods but not before or after. In the late prehistoric period at least two (Salado and O'otam) and maybe three (Hakataya) regional social formations developed together. The relations that internally structured these systems were probably fundamentally different despite the fact that each developed because of the existence of the others. All were certainly different from the Hohokam regional system that preceded them.

We may ultimately best understand these changes by standing on the outside and looking in. When we frame our research questions in terms of the Phoenix Basin and look out, we create a false perspective in which the Phoenix Basin is core to our explanation, even if it was not core in a prehistoric world. When we stand on the outside and look in, the perspective encourages us to look for the impacts of shifting cores and different regional social formations on our peripheries.

## ACKNOWLEDGMENTS

A number of people assisted me in the preparation of this paper. I would like to thank the other participants in the Amerind Foundation Advance Seminar on the Hohokam for a very enjoyable and stimulating week. Russell Weisman pointed out that the so-called brushing in Trincheras pottery was in fact scraping marks. George Gumerman, David Wilcox, and Ann Stahl reviewed the paper and supplied me with many helpful comments. My collaborator in the Altar Valley project, Elisa Villalpando, covered my absence from the field during February of 1988, so that I could attend the advanced seminar. Our work in the Altar Valley was supported by NSF grant BNS-8703515.

## NOTES

1. Data in figure 8.2 was compiled from a variety of sources. Shell: McGuire and Howard; ballcourts: Wilcox and Sternberg 1983; palettes and stone effigy vessels: DiPeso 1956, Withers 1973, Wasley and Johnson 1965, Johnson and Wasley 1966, Greenleaf 1975, Doyel 1977, Kelly 1978, Masse 1980, Rosenthal et al. 1978, Doyel and Elson 1985, Wasley and Bentham 1968, Weed and Ward 1970, Weed 1972, LeBlanc 1983; red-on-buff pottery: Gladwin and Gladwin 1935. The distribution of red-on-buff pottery is based on those sources where it comprises fifty percent or more of the assemblage.

2. Data in figure 8.3 was compiled from a variety of sources. Salado polychromes: Doyel and Haury 1976, Franklin 1980; *cerros de trincheras:* Braniff 1985; platform mounds: Gregory and Nials 1985, Doelle and Wallace this volume; Sonoran brown ware: Ezell 1954, Braniff 1985. The distribution of Salado polychromes is based on sites where these types comprise fifty percent or more of the painted ceramics. The distribution of Sonoran brown wares is based on sites where it is the predominate plain ware.

# REFERENCES CITED

Alvarez, Ana María
  1985  Sociedades Agrícolas. In *Historia General de Sonora*, vol. 1, edited by J. C. Montané, pp. 225–262. Gobierno del Estado de Sonora, Hermosillo.

Anderson, Keith
  1982  Hohokam Community and Social Identity: View From a Sand Papago Cemetery. In *Anthropology of the Desert West: Essays in Honor of Jesse D. Jennings*, edited by D. D. Fowler. University of Utah Press, Salt Lake City.

Blanton, Richard E., Stephen A. Kowalewski, Gary Feinman, and Jill Appel
  1981  *Ancient Mesoamerica*. Cambridge University Press, Cambridge.

Bowen, Thomas
  1976  *Seri Prehistory: The Archaeology of the Centeral Coast of Sonora, Mexico*. Anthropological Papers of the University of Arizona 27. Tucson.
  n.d.  A Survey and Re-evaluation of the Trincheras Culture, Mexico. Manuscript on file, Arizona State Museum, Tucson.

Braniff, Beatriz
  1985  *La Frontera Protohistorica Pima-Opata en Sonora, Mexico*. UNAM, México.
  1988  Observations on the Elites of the Pimeria and Opateria in Prehispanic Times. Paper presented at the Southwest Symposium, Tempe.

Breternitz, David A.
  1960  *Excavations at Three Sites in the Verde Valley, Arizona*. Museum of Northern Arizona Bulletin 34. Flagstaff.

Brown, Patricia Eyring
  1976  An Archaeological Survey of the Vaiva Vo Kohatk Road, Papago Indian Reservation, Southern Arizona. Manuscript on file, Department of Anthropology Arizona State University, Tempe.

Brumfiel, Elizabeth M.
  1988  Factions, Class, and Inter-Ethnic Alliance at Late Postclassic Xaltocan. Paper presented at the 46th International Congress of Americanists, Amsterdam.

Cable, John S. and David E. Doyel
  1987  Pioneer Period Village Structure and Settlement Pattern in the Phoenix Basin. In *The Hohokam Village: Site Structure and Organization*, edited by D. E. Doyel, pp. 21–71, American Association for the Advancement of Science.

Castetter, Edward F., and Willis H. Bell
  1942  *Pima and Papago Indian Agriculture*. University of New Mexico Press, Albuquerque.

Caywood, Louis R., and Edward H. Spicer
  1935  *Tuzigoot, the Excavation and Repair of a Ruin on the Verde River Near Clarkdale, Arizona*. Field Division of Education, National Park Service, Berkeley.

Colton, Harold S.
  1946  *Pottery Types of the Southwest*. Museum of Northern Arizona Ceramic Series 3C. Flagstaff.
  1958  Pottery Types of the Southwest: Wares 14, 15, 16, 17, and 18. Museum of Northern Arizona Ceramic Series 30. Flagstaff.

Crown, Patricia L.
  1984  Ceramic Vessel Exchange in Southern Arizona. In *Hohokam Archaeology Along*

the Salt Gila Aqueduct Central Arizona Project, vol. 9, edited by L. S. Teague and P. L. Crown, pp. 251–304. Arizona State Museum Archaeological Series 150. Tucson.

Diamond, Stanley
1974  *In Search of the Primitive: A Critique of Civilization.* E.P. Dutton Books.

DiPeso, Charles C.
1956  *The Upper Pima of San Cayetano del Tumacacori.* Amerind Foundation Publications 7. Dragoon.
1979  Prehistory: Southern Periphery. In *Handbook of North American Indians,* vol. 9, edited by Alfonso Ortiz, pp. 152–161. Smithsonian Institution, Washington, D.C.
1983  The Northern Sector of the Mesoamerican World System. In *Forgotten Places and Things,* edited by A. E. Ward, pp. 11–22. Center for Archaeological Studies, Albuquerque.

Dixon, Keith A.
1956  *Hidden House, A Cliff Ruin in Sycamore Canyon, Central Arizona.* Museum of Northern Arizona Bulletin 29. Flagstaff.

Doelle, William H.
1980  *Past Adaptive Patterns in the Western Papaguería: An Archaeological Study of Non-Riverine Resource Use.* Ph.D. dissertation, Department of Anthropology, University of Arizona, Tucson.

Downum, Christian E.
1986  The Occupational Use of Hill Space in the Tucson Basin: Evidence From The Linda Vista Hill. *The Kiva* 51(4):219–232.

Doyel, David E.
1977  *Excavations in the Middle Santa Cruz River Valley, Southeastern Arizona.* Contribution to Highway Salvage Archaeology in Arizona 44. Arizona State Museum, Tucson.

Doyel, David E., and Mark D. Elson
1985  *Hohokam Settlement and Economic Systems in the Central New River Drainage, Arizona.* Soil Systems Publications in Archaeology 4. Phoenix.

Doyel, David, and Emil W. Haury (editors)
1976  The 1976 Salado Conference. *The Kiva* 42(1).

Doyel, David, and Fred Plog (editors)
1980  *Current Issues in Hohokam Prehistory.* Arizona State University Anthropological Research Paper 23. Tempe.

Ezell, Paul H.
1954  An Archaeological Survey of Northwestern Papaguería. *The Kiva* 19(2–4):1–26.

Fewkes, Jesse W.
1912  Antiquities of the Upper Verde River and Walnut Creek Valleys, Arizona. *Bureau of American Ethnology, 28th Annual Report,* pp. 181–220. Washington, D.C.

Fish, Paul R.
1974  Prehistoric Land Use in the Perkinsville Valley. *The Arizona Archaeologist* 8:1–36.

Fish, Paul R., and Suzanne K. Fish
1977  *Verde Valley Archaeology: Review and Perspective.* MNA Research Paper 8. Flagstaff.

1984 Agricultural Maximization in the Sacred Mountain Basin. In *Prehistoric Agricultural Strategies in the Southwest*, edited by P. R. Fish and S. K. Fish, pp. 147–160. Arizona State University Anthropological Research Papers 33. Tempe.

1989 Hohokam Warfare From a Regional Perspective. In *Cultures in Conflict: Current Archaeological Perspectives*, edited by D. C. Tkaczuk and B. C. Vivian, pp. 152–162. The Archaeological Association of the University of Calgary, Calgary.

Fish, Paul R., Peter J. Pillas, and Suzanne K. Fish

1980 Colonies, Traders, and Traits: The Hohokam in the North. In *Current Issues in Hohokam Prehistory*, edited by David Doyel and Fred Plog, pp. 151–175. Arizona State University Anthropological Research Papers 23. Tempe.

Fish, Suzanne K., Paul R. Fish, and Christian Downum

1984 Hohokam Terraces and Agricultural Production in the Tucson Basin. In *Prehistoric Agricultural Strategies in the Southwest*, edited by P. R. Fish and S. K. Fish, pp. 55–71. Arizona State University Anthropological Research Papers 33. Tempe.

Fontana, Bernard L., J. Cameron Greenleaf, and Donnely D. Cassidy

1959 A Fortified Arizona Mountain. *The Kiva* 25(4):41–52.

Franklin, Hayward Hoskins

1980 *Excavations at Second Canyon Ruin, San Pedro Valley, Arizona.* Contribution to Highway Salvage Archaeology in Arizona 60. Arizona State Museum, Tucson.

Fraps, Clara Lee

1936 Blackstone Ruin. *The Kiva* 2(3):9–12.

Gailey, Christine Ward

1987 Culture Wars: Resistance to State Formation. In *Power Relations and State Formation*, edited by T. C. Patterson and C. W. Gailey, pp. 35–56. American Anthropological Association, Washington, D.C.

Gladwin, Harold S.

1942 *Excavations at Snaketown III: Revisions.* Medallion Papers 30, Gila Pueblo, Globe.

1948 *Excavations at Snaketown IV: Review and Conclusions.* Medallion Papers 38, Gila Pueblo, Globe.

Gladwin, Harold S., and Winifred Gladwin

1929 *The Red-on-buff Culture of the Papaguería.* Medallion Papers 4. Globe.

1934 *A Method for the Designation of Cultures and Their Variations.* Medallion Papers 15. Globe.

1935 *The Eastern Range of the Red-on-buff Culture.* Medallion Papers 14. Globe.

Gladwin, Harold S., E. W. Haury, E. B. Sayles, and Nora Gladwin

1936 *Excavations at Snaketown I: Material Culture.* Medallion Papers 25. Globe.

Goodyear, Albert C., III

1975 *Hecla II and III: An Interpretive Study of Archaeological Remains From the Lakeshore Project.* Arizona State University Anthropological Research Papers 9. Tempe.

1977 The Historical and Ecological Position of Protohistoric Sites in the Slate Mountains, South Central Arizona. In *Research Strategies in Historical Archaeology*, edited by S. South, pp. 203–239, Academic Press, New York.

Greenleaf, J. Cameron

1975 *Excavations at Punta de Agua in the Santa Cruz River Basin, Southeastern Arizona.* University of Arizona Anthropological Papers 26. Tucson.

Gregory, David, and Fred Nials

1985 Observations Concerning the Distribution of Classic Period Hohokam Platform Mounds. In *Proceedings of the 1983 Hohokam Symposium,* edited by A. E. Dittert, Jr. and D. E. Dove, pp. 373–388. Phoenix Chapter of the Arizona Archaeological Society, Phoenix.

Gumerman, George C., and Emil W. Haury
  1979   Prehistory: Hohokam. In *Handbook of North American Indians,* vol. 9, edited by Alfonso Ortiz. Smithsonian Institution. Washington, D.C.

Gumerman, George C., Carol S. Weed, and John S. Hanson
  1976   *Adaptive Strategies in a Biological and Cultural Transition Zone: The Central Arizona Ecotone Project.* University Museum Studies 6. Southern Illinois University, Carbondale.

Hartman, Dana
  1976   *Tuzigoot: An Archaeological Overview.* MNA Research Paper 4. Flagstaff.

Hassig, Ross
  1985   *Trade, Tribute, and Transportation.* University of Oklahoma Press, Norman.
  1988   Structure and Growth of the Aztec Empire. Paper presented at the Annual Meetings of the Society for American Archaeology, Phoenix.

Haury, Emil W.
  1950   *The Stratigraphy and Archaeology of Ventana Cave.* University of Arizona Press, Tucson.
  1976   *The Hohokam: Desert Farmers and Craftsmen.* University of Arizona Press, Tucson.

Hayden, Julian D.
  1970   Of Hohokam Origins and Other Matters. *American Antiquity* 35:87–94.
  1972   Hohokam Petroglyphs of the Sierra Pinacate, Sonora, and the Hohokam Shell Expeditions. *The Kiva* 37:74–84.

Hinton, Thomas B.
  1955   A Survey of Archaeological Sites in the Altar Valley, Sonora. *The Kiva* 21(3–4):1–12.

Hoover, J. W.
  1941   Cerros de Trincheras of the Arizona Papagueria. *The Geographical Review* 2:229–239.

Howard, Ann Valdo
  1985   A Reconstruction of Hohokam Interregional Shell Production and Exchange Within Southern Arizona. In *Proceedings of the 1983 Hohokam Symposium,* edited by A. E. Dittert, Jr. and D. E. Dove, pp. 459–472. Phoenix Chapter of the Arizona Archaeological Society, Phoenix.

Huckell, Bruce B.
  1979   *The Cornet Real Project: Archaeological Investigations on the Luke Range, Southwestern Arizona.* Arizona State Museum Archaeological Series 129. Tucson.
  1984a  The Paleo-Indian and Archaic Occupation of the Tucson Basin. *The Kiva* 49(3–4):133–146.
  1984b  *The Archaic Occupation of the Rosemont Area, Northern Santa Rita Mountains, Southestern Arizona.* Arizona State Museum Archaeological Series 147. Tucson.

Ives, Joseph C.
  1936   A Trinchera Near Quitovaquita, Sonora. *American Anthropologist* 38:257–259.

Jácome, Felipe Carlos
  1986   *The Nogalas Wash Site.* Pimería Alta Historical Society, Nogales.

Johnson, Alfred E.
    1963    The Trincheras Culture of Northwestern Sonora. *American Antiquity* 29(4):174–
            186.
Johnson, Alfred E., and William W. Wasley
    1966    Archaeological Excavations Near Bylas Arizona. *The Kiva* 31(4):205–253.
Kelly, Isabel T.
    1978    *The Hodges Ruin: A Hohokam Community in the Tucson Basin.* Anthropological
            Papers of the University of Arizona 30, Tucson.
Kroeber, Clifton B., and Bernard L. Fontana
    1986    *Massacre on the Gila.* University of Arizona Press, Tucson.
LeBlanc, Steven A.
    1983    *The Mimbres People.* Thames and Hudson, New York.
Lightfoot, Kent G.
    1979    Food Redistribution Among Prehistoric Pueblo Groups. *The Kiva* 44(4):319–
            340.
Marcus, Joyce
    1973    Territorial Organizations of the Lowland Classic Maya. *Science* 180:911–916.
Marmaduke, W. S., and R. Martynec
    n.d.    Productive Specialization and the Hohokam Shell Trade. Manuscript on file,
            Arizona State Museum, Tucson.
Masse, W. Bruce
    1980    *Excavations at Gu Achi.* Western Archaeological Center Publications in Ar-
            chaeology 12. National Park Service, Tucson.
    1981    A Reappraisal of the Protohistoric Sobaipuri Indians of Southeastern Arizona.
            In *The Protohistoric Period in the North American Southwest, A.D. 1450–1700,* edited
            by D. R. Wilcox and W. B. Masse, pp. 28–56. Arizona State Museum Ar-
            chaeological Series 24. Tempe.
McGuire, Randall H.
    1977    *The Copper Canyon–McGuireville Investigations in the Middle Verde Valley, Arizona.*
            Contribution to Highway Salvage Archaeology in Arizona 45. Arizona State
            Museum, Tucson.
McGuire, Randall H., and Christian E. Downum
    1982    A Preliminary Consideration of Desert-Mountain Trade Relations. In *Mogollon
            Archaeology: Proceedings of the 1980 Mogollon Conference,* edited by P. H. Beckett
            and Kira Silverbird, pp. 111–122. Acoma Books, Ramona.
McGuire, Randall H., and Ann Valdo Howard
    1987    The Structure and Organization of Hohokam Shell Exchange. *The Kiva* 52(2):113–
            146.
McGuire, Randall H., and Linda Mayro
    1978    *Papago Wells Project: Archaeological Surveys Near Kaka and Stoa Pitk, the Papago
            Reservation.* Arizona State Museum Archaeological Series 120. Tucson.
McGuire, Randall H., and Michael B. Schiffer
    1982    *Hohokam and Patayan: The Archaeology of Southwestern Arizona.* Academic Press,
            New York.
McGuire, Randall H., and María Elisa Villalpando
    1989    Prehistory and the Making of History in Sonora. In *Columbian Consequences
            I: Archaeological and Historical Perspectives on the Spanish Borderlands West,* edited
            by D. H. Thomas, pp. 159–177. Smithsonian Institution Press, Washington,
            D.C.

Mindeleff, Cosmos
  1896   Aboriginal Remains in the Verde Valley, Arizona. *Bureau of American Ethnology Thirteenth Annual Report*, pp. 179–261. Smithsonian Institution, Washington, D.C.
Minnis, Paul E.
  1989   The Casas Grndes Polity in the International Four Corners. In *The Sociopolitical Structure of Prehistoric Southwestern Societies,* edited by Steadman Upham, K. G. Lightfoot, and R. A. Jewett, pp. 269–305, Westview Press, Boulder.
Nabhan, Gary Paul
  1979   The Ecology of Floodwater Farming in Arid Southwestern North America. *Agro-Ecosystems* 5:245–255.
Neitzel, Jill E.
  1984   The Organization of the Hohokam Regional System. *American Archaeology* 4(3):207–216.
Patterson, Thomas C.
  1987   Tribes, Chiefdoms, and Kingdoms in the Inca Empire. In *Power Relations and State Formation,* edited by T. C. Patterson and C. W. Gailey, pp. 117–127, American Anthropological Association, Washington, D.C.
Pillas, Peter J.
  1981   The Southern Sinagua. *Plateau* 53(1):6–17.
Plog, Stephen
  1980   Hohokam Exchange, Subsistence, and Interaction: Some Comments. In *Current Issues in Hohokam Prehistory,* edited by David Doyel and Fred Plog, pp. 106–112. Arizona State University Anthropological Research Papers 23. Tempe.
Raab, Mark L.
  1976   *The Structure of Prehistoric Community Organization at Santa Rosa Wash.* Ph.D. dissertation, Department of Anthropology, Arizona State University, Tempe.
Robles, Manuel
  1973   El Arroyo Bacoachi y el Trafico de Concha Trincheras. Manuscript on file Centro Regional de Noroeste de INHA, Hermosillo.
  n.d.   Un Sitio de la Cultura Trincheras en el Valle del Río Altar. Manuscript on file, Centro Regional de Noroeste de INHA, Hermosillo.
Rosenthal, E. Jane, Douglas R. Brown, Marc Severson, and John B. Clonts
  1978   *The Quijotoa Valley Project.* National Park Service, Western Archaeological Service, Tucson.
Sauer, Carl O., and Donald D. Brand
  1931   Prehistoric Settlements of Sonora with Special Reference to *Cerros de Trincheras.* University of California Publications in Geography 5(3):67–148.
Scantling, Frederick H.
  1940   Excavations at the Jackrabbit Ruin, Papago Indian Reservation, Arizona. Master's thesis, Department of Anthropology, University of Arizona, Tucson.
Schroeder, Albert H.
  1960   *The Hohokam, Sinagua, and Hakataya.* Society for American Archaeology Archives of Archaeology 5.
  1974   *A Study of Yavapai History.* Indian Claims Commission Docket no. 22E. Garland Publishing Inc., New York.
  1979   Prehistory: Hakataya. In *Handbook of North American Indians,* vol. 9, edited by Alfonso Ortiz, pp. 100–107. Smithsonian Institution, Washington, D.C.

Spicer, Edward H.
1980    *The Yaqui: A Cultural History.* University of Arizona Press, Tucson.
Spicer, Edward H. and Louis R. Caywood
1936    *Two Pueblo Ruins in West Central Arizona.* University of Arizona Social Science
        Bulletin 10. Tucson.
Stacy, Valeria Kay Pheriba
1975    Archaeological Survey in the Arizona Papagueria. *The Kiva* 40:11–18.
1977    Activity Patterning at Cerros De Trincheras in South Central Arizona. *The
        Kiva* 43:11–18.
Stewart, Yvonne, and Lynn S. Teague
1974    *An Ethnoarchaeological Study of the Vekol Copper Mining Project.* Arizona State
        Museum Archaeological Series 49. Tucson.
Teague, Lynn S.
1984    The Organization of Hohokam Economy. In *Hohokam Archaeology Along the
        Salt-Gila Aqueduct Central Arizona Project,* vol. 9, edited by L. S. Teague and
        P. L. Crown, pp. 187–250. Arizona State Museum Archaeological Series 150.
        Tucson.
Teague, Lynn S., and Anne R. Baldwin
1978    *Painted Rock Reservoir Project Phase 1: Preliminary Survey and Recommendations.*
        Arizona State Museum Archaeological Series 126. Tucson.
Wallace, Henry D., and James P. Holmlund
1984    The Classic Period in the Tucson Basin. *The Kiva* 49(3–4):167–194.
Wallerstein, Immanuel
1974    *The Modern World-System I.* Academic Press, New York.
1980    *The Modern World-System II.* Academic Press, New York.
Wasley, William W.
1968    Archaeological Survey in Sonora, Mexico. Paper presented at the Annual
        Meeting of the Society for American Archaeology, Santa Fe.
Wasley, William W., and Blake Benham
1968    Salvage Excavations in the Buttes Dam Site, Southern Arizona. *The Kiva*
        33(4):244–279.
Wasley, William W., and Alfred E. Johnson
1965    *Salvage Archaeology in Painted Rocks Reservoir Western Arizona.* Anthropological
        Papers of the University of Arizona 9. Tucson.
Weed, Carol S.
1972    The Beardsley Canal Site. *The Kiva* 38(2):57–94.
Weed, Carol S., and Albert E. Ward
1970    The Henderson Site: Colonial Hohokam in North Central Arizona. *The Kiva*
        36(2):1–12.
Weissner, Polly
1983    Style and Social Information in Kalahari San Projectile Points. *American An-
        tiquity* 48(2):253–276.
Wilcox, David R.
1979    Implications of Dry Laid Masonry Walls on Tumamoc Hill. *The Kiva* 45(1–
        2):15–38.
1980    The Current Status of the Hohokam Concept. In *Current Issues in Hohokam
        Prehistory,* edited by D. E. Doyel and Fred Plog, pp. 236–242. Arizona State
        University Anthropological Research Papers 23. Tempe.
1986    A Historical Analysis of the Problem of Southwestern-Mesoamerican Con-

nections. In *Ripples in the Chichimec Sea: New Considerations of Southwestern-Mesoamerican Interactions*, edited by F. J. Mathian and R. H. McGuire, pp. 9–45. Southern Illinois University Press, Carbondale.

1987a  *Frank Midvale's Investigation of the Site of La Ciudad*. Anthropological Field Studies 16. Arizona State University, Tempe.

1987b  New Models of Social Structure at C. C. DiPeso's Paloparedo Site. In *The Hohokam Village: Site Structure and Organization*, edited by D. E. Doyel, pp. 72–85. American Association for the Advancement of Science.

1987c  Hohokam Social Complexity. Paper presented at the Advanced Seminar on Cultural Complexity in the Arid Southwest: The Hohokam and Chaco Regional Systems, School of American Research, Santa Fe.

1988  The Regional Context of the Brady Wash and Picacho Peak Area Sites. In *Hohokam Settlements Along the Slopes of the Picacho Mountains*, edited by Richard Ciolek-Torrello and D. R. Wilcox, pp. 244–267, MNA Research Paper 35(6). Museum of Northern Arizona, Flagstaff.

1989  Hohokam Warfare. In *Cultures in Conflict: Current Archaeological Perspectives*, edited by D. C. Tkaczuk and B. C. Vivian, pp. 163–172. The Archaeological Association of the University of Calgary, Calgary.

Wilcox, David R., Thomas R. McGuire, and Charles Sternberg
1981  *Snaketown Revisited*. Arizona State Museum Archaeological Series 155. Tucson.

Wilcox, David R., and Lynette O. Shenk
1977  *The Architecture of the Casa Grande and its Interpretation*. Arizona State Museum Archaeological Series 115. Tucson.

Wilcox, David R., and Charles Sternberg
1983  *Hohokam Ballcourts and Their Interpretation*. Arizona State Museum Archaeological Series 160. Tucson.

Withers, Arnold M.
1973  Excavations at Valshni Village, Arizona. *The Arizona Archaeologist* 7. Arizona Archaeological Society Inc., Phoenix.

Wobst, H. Martin
1977  Stylistic Behavior and Information Exchange. In *Papers for the Director: Research Essays in Honor of James B. Griffen*, edited by C. E. Cleland, pp. 317–342. University of Michigan, Museum of Anthropology, Anthropological Papers 61, Ann Arbor.

# •9•

# THE ROLE OF EXCHANGE AND INTERACTION IN SALT-GILA BASIN HOHOKAM PREHISTORY

*Patricia L. Crown*

This paper explores exchange in material goods and the interaction of the Hohokam with contemporaneous populations. Several points are emphasized here: (1) Exchange and interaction in southern Arizona have a long history, predating the period traditionally defined as Hohokam; (2) Linkages between populations in southern Arizona and their neighbors become more visible archaeologically through time as increasing frequencies of clearly identifiable exotic goods both enter and leave the Hohokam area; (3) A Hohokam regional system can be defined on the basis of architecture and artifactual evidence; (4) Materials may have moved through this regional system in different spheres of exchange; and (5) A variety of procurement strategies were employed to obtain goods from outside of the Hohokam area. These points reveal that, although the Hohokam could attain self-sufficiency, at no time were they self-contained.

# EXPLORING EXCHANGE AND INTERACTION
# IN THE PAST

Located in an area rich in comestibles, arable land, and building materials, but generally deficient in luxury items and valued raw materials, the Hohokam had to develop ties with surrounding populations to obtain such resources. Even though they could achieve self-sufficiency, economic, social, and political ties were probably important in assuring biological and social reproduction of the group (Braun and S. Plog 1982; Sahlins 1972). The archaeological record in the Southwest presents compelling evidence for the movement of goods into and out of the Hohokam area, but any attempt at interpreting such evidence for past interactions must take into consideration the inherent limitations of this record.

There are a number of problems encountered in any attempt at elucidating prehistoric exchange relationships. In particular, it is difficult to identify exchange items and to evaluate what these mean in terms of interaction among groups. Reasonable inferences concerning exchange relationships require information on what items are exotic, where these materials came from, possible mechanisms for the movement of goods from one place to another, and the attendant implications for broader issues of interaction between groups. Most studies of Hohokam exchange undertaken in recent years have involved obvious exotic artifacts and raw materials, that is, items that do not occur naturally in the Hohokam area. Hence, researchers have concentrated on examining the distribution of such items as intrusive ceramics, macaws, copper bells, obsidian, shell, and turquoise. Items less easily identified as exotic, such as many lithic materials or red-on-buff ceramics, have been given little attention.

Compositional analysis simplifies identification of exotic items. In particular, it increases our ability to document what items are foreign to a particular assemblage and occasionally results in identification of the actual source of individual items or classes of items. Compositional studies of Hohokam materials include studies of copper bells (Root 1937:276–277; Hawley 1953), obsidian (Brown 1982; Bostwick and Shackly 1987; Ebinger 1984), turquoise (Colberg-Sigleo 1975; Haury 1976:277–278; Ravesloot 1987:151), and ceramics (Crown 1984c; Crown, Schwalbe, and London 1985; Crown and Bishop 1987; Doyel 1977; Doyel and Elson 1985; Weisman 1985). Yet even here, the researchers examined relatively small samples of these materials, including primarily types of materials clearly exotic to the area, with the analyses aimed at discerning actual sources. Despite an increase in the number of such studies in recent years, relatively few ceramic and lithic sourcing studies have been completed and these have concentrated on a small sample of the total universe of collected materials.

The fact that empirically based studies must concentrate almost exclusively on nonperishable items represents a limiting factor as well. Textiles, basketry, foodstuffs, and other perishable items very likely were exchanged (e.g., Gasser and Miksicek 1985; Plog 1986; Wilcox 1987), but they are rarely preserved and recovered, and are difficult to attribute to source. Exchange in nonmaterial goods, such as information and services, or marriage partners, is impossible to document or demonstrate directly from the archaeological record.

Studies of exchange are generally tied to broader issues of prehistoric interaction. To evaluate adequately the significance of exchanged items for understanding prehistoric interaction, we must consider not only exchange, production, and consumption of materials and artifacts, but the social context and meaning of the exchanged goods (Earle 1982; Hodder 1982). A major question concerns how much interaction is recognizable in the archaeological record, when not all interaction involves exchange and not all exchange involves material items. Interaction may take the form of conflict, negotiation, coordination, or casual contact, as well as exchange. The material we *recognize* as exotic reflects only a minute proportion of the actual interactions that occurred prehistorically. Furthermore, the identification of a source for an exotic does not demonstrate contact between the producer and the recipient of that exotic in particular, nor does it illuminate the nature of the interaction in general. We are left then with evidence of only a biased sample of the total exchanges that took place prehistorically and no means to evaluate the representativeness of that sample for assessing prehistoric interaction in southern Arizona.

## A TEMPORAL PERSPECTIVE ON EXCHANGE IN SOUTHERN ARIZONA

Most archaeologists would now argue for continuity in the populations occupying southern Arizona from at least the late Archaic. Any discussion of exchange and interaction through time in this area would be incomplete without consideration of the evidence for interaction among Archaic populations. Not only is this evidence generally informative about the nature of interaction during this period, but it is likely that patterns established during the Archaic variably endured and influenced the patterns of interaction that developed in succeeding centuries.

Excavations in southern Arizona have revealed evidence for horticulture (maize and probably beans), pithouse architecture, storage features, trash accumulations, cemeteries, and a fully developed ground stone industry dating to 1000–500 B.C. (Huckell 1987). Although the earliest ceramic vessels appear later in time, there is clear evidence for sedentary horticulturalists in southern Arizona before the advent of pottery production. Shell ornaments (Huckell 1987) and obsidian (Doyel, this volume), both exotics in the area, occur in these Archaic contexts. In addition, corn and beans both represent species introduced into the Southwest from Mesoamerica. Huckell (1987) proposes that these domesticates arrived via river drainages off the western slopes of the Sierra Madre to southeastern Arizona river valleys. It is not clear if this movement involved migration of populations or simply adoption of agriculture by indigenous hunters and gatherers (Huckell 1987:17). Clay fig-urines also occur in late Archaic contexts, possibly as a result of the diffusion of ideas concerning their meaning and manufacture from Mesoamerica (Huck-ell 1984). Even at this early time, we have strong evidence for movement of goods and ideas into southern Arizona from other areas. Movement of such items need not have involved formalized exchange networks, but certainly implies at least casual contacts between the southern Arizona populations and their neighbors to the south.

The poorly known Red Mountain phase (pre-A.D. 300) is characterized by the earliest pottery in southern Arizona, a sand-tempered plain brown ware. The derivation and precise timing for initial pottery production are disputed, although traditionally the idea for pottery manufacture is thought to have diffused from Mesoamerica (LeBlanc 1982:27).

By the Vahki phase (A.D. 300–500), a red-slipped ware was also manufac-tured at Hohokam sites. Carved and perforated shell ornaments, turquoise mosaics, and a variety of nonlocal minerals also occur in Vahki phase contexts. Possible sources are known for many of the minerals, exhibiting considerable geographic spread (Doyel 1987; Wood 1985). The earliest squash and cotton remains have been recovered from Vahki contexts (Fish et al. 1987; Haury 1976), as have the earliest palettes; all may indicate the movement of ideas from Mesoamerica (Haury 1976:289), continuing the trend first identified in the late Archaic. The first recognizable intrusive pottery appears, including San Francisco Red from the Mogollon area and Trincheras Purple-on-red from the south (Haury 1976:328). It is also during the Vahki phase that we find the earliest documented evidence for Hohokam artifacts outside of the Hohokam area. Vahki Red sherds have been identified at two sites in northern Arizona, and 43 sherds of Vahki Plain were recovered at Crooked Ridge Village in the Point of Pines area (Crown 1984a:272–273). At the end of the Vahki phase, then, Southwestern artifactual assemblages reveal movement of material goods or contact between the Hohokam and groups to the south (shell, Trincheras pottery in Hohokam sites, squash), east (Mogollon pottery in Hohokam sites, Hohokam pottery in Mogollon sites, turquoise?, exotic minerals in Hohokam sites?), and north (Hohokam pottery in northern sites).

At about A.D. 500, the Hohokam first manufactured decorated pottery, signaling the beginning of the Estrella phase. Deposits assigned to this phase and to the remainder of the Pioneer period (ending at approximately A.D. 800) provide additional evidence for interaction. The items described previ-ously continued to appear in Hohokam sites. The earliest remains of macaws and parrots, both native to Mesoamerica, have been recovered from Pioneer period contexts (Haury 1976). Intrusive pottery in Hohokam sites includes

Mogollon decorated, red and plain wares, and Trincheras types (Crown 1984a). Irrigation systems and the earliest capped trash mounds may indicate continued Mesoamerican influence on Hohokam architectural traditions and subsistence technology (Haury 1976). Items manufactured in the Hohokam area and found in other portions of the Southwest during the late Pioneer period include pottery recovered in northern, eastern, and southern Arizona. Shell ornaments of possible Hohokam manufacture also occur in other portions of the Southwest (McGuire and Howard 1987).

By the Colonial period (A.D. 775–1000), new items appear in the Salt-Gila Basin, including iron-pyrite mosaic mirrors from Mesoamerica (Haury 1976). Recent research has demonstrated that ground stone artifacts were manufactured of basalt found in the New River area and then transported to the Salt-Gila Basin (Doyel and Elson 1985) beginning in the late Colonial period. Intrusive pottery reveals interaction with groups in the Kayenta-Tusayan, Mimbres, east-central Arizona, and southern Arizona areas (Crown 1984a). Single sherds of possible highland Mesoamerican origin were recovered in Gila Butte and Santa Cruz contexts at Snaketown as well (Haury 1976:345). The first ballcourts appear, once again suggesting diffusion from Mesoamerica (Wilcox and Sternberg 1983). Outside of the Salt-Gila Basin, Hohokam ceramics occur as intrusives at sites in northern, eastern, western, and southern Arizona. Stone palettes and shell artifacts of probable Hohokam manufacture also occur in sites outside of the Basin (Doyel 1987).

The variety and quantity of material exchanged during the Sedentary period (A.D. 1000–1150) exceeded that of any previous period. In addition to the items described previously, *Strombus* trumpets, modeled spindle whorls, and copper bells appear for the first time, all of Mesoamerican origin. Intrusive ceramics appear from a broader geographic area than any preceding phase (Crown 1984a), and include six sherds of Mesoamerican origin (Nelson 1986:170–171). The first completely artificial platform mounds indicate continuing architectural influence from Mesoamerica. Pottery interpreted as Salt-Gila Basin Hohokam manufacture occurs over a broader area than during any other time period. Sacaton phase pottery appears throughout most of Arizona and on the California and northern Mexican coasts (Crown 1984a:294). Shell artifacts of purported Hohokam manufacture occur over an area greater than for any other time period (McGuire and Howard 1987).

The Classic period (A.D. 1150–1350) witnessed changes in the nature and extent of exotic materials in the Salt-Gila Basin. Certain items of Mesoamerican origin, such as pyrite mosaic mirrors, apparently were no longer brought into the Salt-Gila Basin, while other items, notably macaws (Rea 1981:298; Sires 1983a:560), copper bells (Nelson 1986:162–163), and *Strombus* trumpets (Gladwin et al. 1937:147) continued to appear in low frequencies at Hohokam sites. The appearance of compound architecture and *comales* may signal continued borrowing of technology and ideas from Mesoamerica. The proportion of shell increased in Hohokam sites during the Classic period (McGuire and

Howard 1987). Intrusive ceramics represent fewer geographic areas of the Southwest, although sherds from the Hopi area, east-central Arizona, the Mimbres area, and the Tonto Basin occur. The proportion of intrusives entering the Basin declined in the Soho phase and then rose again during the Civano phase. The greatest proportion of intrusives are red-on-brown ceramics, traditionally assumed to come from the Tucson Basin. However, a recent x-ray fluorescence analysis of red-on-brown "intrusive" ceramics from the Hohokam site of Las Colinas suggests that at least some of this material is in fact a local copy rather than intrusive (Crown, Schwalbe, and London 1985). These findings call into question all of the red-on-brown "intrusives" in the Salt-Gila Basin and suggest that additional work is needed to determine how much of this material is actually intrusive. The number of identifiable Salt-Gila Basin Hohokam ceramics declines dramatically in other portions of the Southwest, although a few sherds were recovered at sites in the Papagueria and in eastern Arizona.

A final phase has been posited for the end of the Hohokam sequence, the Polvoron phase (A.D. 1350–1450/1500) (Sires 1983b). The Polvoron phase shares many characteristics with the preceding Civano phase, so that it is difficult to distinguish Polvoron phase contexts at multicomponent sites in the absence of independent absolute dates. The single component El Polvoron site thus largely forms the basis for evaluating exchange during the Polvoron phase. Exotics change in quantity rather than form. Obsidian use increased dramatically, yet the frequency of other nonlocal minerals declined in comparison to sites occupied during the Classic (Sires 1983b:315). Shell also declined in frequency from the preceding Classic period. Intrusive ceramics include material from the Hopi area, and eastern and southern Arizona.

This brief chronological overview of Hohokam exchange materials reveals that the populations of the Greater Southwest interacted and exchanged items over a 2,000-year period prior to the arrival of Europeans in the area. The material evidence indicates that the Hohokam had direct or indirect (through goods or ideas only) contact with populations representing virtually all recognized culture areas in the Greater Southwest. Such contact is most clearly reflected in the presence of nonlocal material goods. While nonperishable material objects provide a basis for tracking exchange in a cursory fashion, these items probably moved along routes that existed primarily to facilitate exchange involving mates (Wilcox 1987), food, services, and information, or interaction in the absence of exchange. More often than not, material goods themselves may have been only symbolic of, or incidental to, less visible, yet fundamentally important, modes of interaction. Interestingly, the items critical to the development and survival of Hohokam culture appeared largely during the Archaic to Vahki phases, and included the primary crops grown in the area throughout the remainder of the sequence. Virtually all of the items and ideas subsequently introduced into the area were luxury goods or exotic versions of items also manufactured within the Basin. In the following section, I review models of Hohokam exchange that have attempted to move beyond the objects to the processes responsible for their occurrence in Hohokam sites.

## MODELS OF HOHOKAM EXCHANGE AND INTERACTION

Over the last century, researchers working in the Hohokam area have documented the magnitude and variety of exchange into and out of the Hohokam area. In recent years, researchers have turned toward exploring the possible mechanisms for achieving access to these goods, the scale of the economic network thus indicated, and the nature and extent of interactions with surrounding populations.

Prehistorians frequently address the question of exchange from the vantage point of specific artifact classes. A number of studies have concentrated on shell artifact production and exchange in the Hohokam area (Howard 1983, 1985; McGuire 1985, 1987; McGuire and Howard 1987; Seymour 1985, 1988; Vokes 1984).

McGuire and Howard (1987) argue that the Salt-Gila Basin Hohokam obtained shell artifacts manufactured in the Papagueria during the Colonial and Sedentary periods. In the middle and late Sedentary, manufacture of shell artifacts was undertaken in the Salt-Gila Basin as well, and by the Classic, procurement of raw shell and manufacture of the artifacts may have been controlled by elites within the Basin. They identify high-value (etched shell, *Pecten vogdesi* pendants, *Strombus* trumpets, shell mosaics, and painted shell) and low-value (*Glycymeris* bracelets) shell artifacts and argue that exchange in high-value shell linked elites in the Salt-Gila Basin with elites outside, while low-value shell linked elites with dependents within the region. Exchange of shell items might have occurred in conjunction with other activities: marriages, rites of passage, rituals, payment of social fines.

In examining the prehistory of the Papagueria, McGuire (1987) argues that kinship was the dominant means for establishing rights to resources and labor. Pre-Classic Papaguerian settlements provided finished shell objects in return for food from the Salt-Gila Basin populations. Pre-Classic elites located in the Salt-Gila Basin maintained their positions by redistributing these finished shell objects for social transactions, including debts. By the Classic period, the elites had gained control over both the manufacture and distribution of shell jewelry as a greater supply of raw shell became available from both the Trincheras area and the Papagueria. This led to increasing inequalities in the Classic period. This system collapsed at the end of the Classic when intensification of agricultural production exceeded the capabilities of a kin-based mode of production to resolve conflicts over water availability. The dependency relationship of the Salt-Gila Basin and the Papagueria thus grew through exchange of valuable jewelry for food.

In a detailed analysis of Snaketown house floor assemblages, Seymour (1988) argues that individuals living in separate residential areas procured the raw materials and manufactured and distributed shell ornaments on a part-time basis. She argues further that these materials were exchanged with individuals within Snaketown and perhaps between communities. Although her sample of houses was primarily Sacaton phase in date, shell production debris was present in the earliest strata at the site suggesting that this pattern had greater time depth than she was able to demonstrate (1988:19). She believes that evidence is lacking for production and distribution of craft items involving a formal redistribution system, a class of elites, or centralized pro-duction system at Snaketown (1988:25). Rather, the producing groups con-trolled the exchange of items, such as finished shell ornaments, and this exchange served to promote social identity and reinforce interaction networks or alliances. Interdependence between communities based on shared water resources may have provided a basis (or need) for distribution of other re-sources. Finally, she suggests that the localized distribution of exotics within Snaketown may indicate that long distance exchange was coordinated through trade partnerships between specific residential kin-based groups at the site and individuals in specific geographic areas. The existence of such partner-ships may have led to the differential distribution of exotics (turquoise, pyrite mirrors, and copper bells) (1988:30).

Other studies have examined exchange and interaction by assessing ce-ramic production and exchange within and between sites. Abbott (1984) in-vestigated Hohokam buff, red, and plain ware production and exchange within the Salt-Gila Basin. He argued that plain ware had the lowest value of these wares, was manufactured in the greatest number of locales, and was ex-changed through reciprocal relationships. By contrast, buff and red wares had higher exchange values, were manufactured in fewer locations, and were exchanged through formalized relationships between socially distant parties (Abbott 1984). Crown's (1984b) work with the stylistic attributes of the buff wares led to much the same conclusions: production at a few centers with exchange from those centers. A compositional analysis revealed sufficient variability to suggest local production of plain ware (Crown 1984c); no inter-pretation of how the vessels might have been exchanged was provided in this study.

Wallace (1987) examined the distribution of Santa Cruz Red-on-buff as an intrusive in the Tucson Basin. He found that buff ware frequencies are low in the area where red-on-brown ceramics are known to have been manufac-tured (the southern Tucson Basin), and high throughout the remainder of the Basin. Wallace notes that these distributions indicate that buff ware was either not equally valued or equally available throughout the Basin, and that simple down-the-line reciprocal exchange cannot account for the relative frequencies of buff ware to brown ware found. Doelle and Wallace (this volume) postulate that the ballcourt system provided a mechanism for moving Salt-Gila Basin buff ware into the Tucson Basin. They provide two possible interpretations of the patterning found: either the distribution of buff ware intrusives resulted from the position of the southern Tucson Basin sites at the southern terminus of the ballcourt system with increased cost of buff ware stimulating local production of brown ware; or, the southern Tucson Basin represented a social system interacting in a distinct manner from the northern Tucson Basin.

In a study of Tucson Basin Hohokam ceramic production and exchange, Wallace and Heidke (1986:268–269) argued that exchange within and between communities occurred at least partially through trade partnerships. These partnerships linked families in largely exclusive, hereditary relationships that existed in either egalitarian or prestige contexts.

Lindauer (1988) examined red-on-buff vessel exchange and posited that different vessel forms had different social meanings and were exchanged by different mechanisms. Using a large sample of complete vessels dating primarily to the Sacaton phase, he hypothesized four mechanisms of exchange for these vessels: prestige goods exchange for animal effigy vessels; balanced reciprocity for a specific jar form possibly used to contain valued liquids; generalized reciprocity; and redistribution through gambling. Generalized reciprocity and redistribution through gambling were most difficult to document using available data, and although he argues for their presence in Hohokam exchange interactions, he was unable to provide material evidence in support of this contention. Redistribution associated with specialized and centralized production was not supported by his data. Lindauer's work provides a thorough examination of the assumptions behind the discernment of various mechanisms of exchange.

Studies of intrusive ceramics in the Salt-Gila Basin and Hohokam ceramics outside this area provide additional evidence for differential spatial distribution of ceramics (McGuire and Downum 1982; Crown 1984a; Doyel 1987). McGuire and Downum examined the distribution of Kayenta ceramics within the Salt-Gila Basin and the distribution of Hohokam shell in the Flagstaff area. They suggested that Kayenta ceramics were traded in a down-the-line network due to a correlation of Kayenta ceramics with distance and a lack of correlation with site size. By contrast, they found that shell occurred in disproportionately high frequencies at larger sites, regardless of distance from source. Thus, during the Colonial and Sedentary periods, large settlements apparently had preferential access to shell artifacts.

I noted discontinuities in the distributions of intrusive ceramics within the basin and suggested that these were due to the presence of separate exchange networks operating contemporaneously within the Salt-Gila Basin (Crown 1984a). On the basis of available data, it was suggested that the major drainages served as boundaries between these networks, so that from the Gila Butte through the Soho phases, the Salt River populations received intrusives primarily from the north and west, populations between the Salt and Gila received intrusives from the east, and occupants of sites south of the Gila received intrusives from the south. The quantity of material declined during the Soho phase, and new exchange "territories" replaced the old ones during the Civano. By the Polvoron phase, the few remaining sites had essentially the same intrusives, indicating the breakdown of specifically bounded exchange territories that existed during the previous phases. On the basis of differences in vessel forms and types, it was argued that Hohokam ceramics were exchanged primarily as containers for some valued commodity. By contrast, intrusives coming into the Basin appear to have been the valued objects themselves. No interpretation of the mechanisms behind exchange in these vessels was provided. However, an examination of relative frequencies of intrusives in relation to site function (position in the site hierarchy) revealed no relationship between presence of ballcourts/platform mounds and number of intrusives. Thus, intrusives do not appear to have been redistributed from centralized locations (1984a:292). On the basis of these same data, Lindauer (1988:66–67) suggested that intrusives found in Hohokam sites were obtained either through the exchange of prestige goods or to cement social contacts, but that Hohokam vessels found elsewhere were primarily containers and may have been exchanged through balanced reciprocity.

Doyel (1987) reevaluated these results on the basis of new information. He concluded that the patterning seen was due, at least in part, to sampling problems and differences in temporal ranges for materials from the three areas within the basin. However, his results do confirm a significantly higher frequency of Kayenta/Tusayan ceramics at sites north of the Salt River, a higher frequency of Mogollon/Mimbres ceramics between the Salt and Gila Rivers, and a higher frequency of southern Arizona ceramics south of the Gila River (1987:41).

In contrast to studies of specific artifact classes, Gasser and Miksicek (1985) addressed the difficult question of exchange in foodstuffs. They examined differences in the kinds and frequencies of economic plant remains on a regional basis and found anomalies that could not be explained on the basis of topographic or farming conditions. They argued that populations within particular areas specialized in the production of agave, little barley, hedgehog cactus, saguaro products, or cotton for exchange to promote intergroup cooperation. This exchange in food would have facilitated exchange in other forms of goods, a position which contrasts with the suggestions of Ford (1972) and Doelle (1980) that exchange in material objects promoted food exchange among Southwestern groups (see also Pires-Ferreira and Flannery 1976:290; Rappaport 1968:106).

While the studies described thus far examined only a single class of object, several researchers have attempted to integrate data on multiple artifact types. Perhaps the most ambitious study of Hohokam exchange undertaken to date is that of Nelson (1981, 1986). Nelson posited a "prestige" sphere of exchange that would include both Mesoamerican items and other "valuable" items. He examined the frequency and distribution of probable Mesoamerican artifacts in Hohokam sites, including copper bells, pyrite mirrors, intrusive ceramics, and macaws or parrots. He then compared the distributions of these items with other rare objects (*Pecten vogdesi* pendants, shell overlay, shell trumpets, black steatite objects, asbestos, standardized arrowpoints, human head figurines, carved bone hairpins, legged vessels) in Hohokam contexts. He concluded that during the Colonial and Sedentary periods exchange in prestige goods from Mesoamerica involved a Hohokam elite. The degree of social differentiation reflected by "prestige sphere" exchange increased from the Colonial to the Sedentary periods. He posited an alliance or "other specialized relationship" between a few Hohokam elites and certain individuals or groups in Mesoamerica (Nelson 1986:178). This system declined by the Classic period, when Mesoamerican intrusives lack any distinctive patterning in terms of context, distribution, or associations.

Nelson argued that the exchange relationships between Hohokam and Mesoamerican individuals or groups were "qualitatively different" from those between the Hohokam and other Southwestern societies, at least during the Sedentary period. The Classic period patterning is interpreted as indicative of a relatively egalitarian society or an economy in which "prestige goods were widely accessible and moved through the same sphere as subsistence goods" (Nelson 1986:157–158).

Teague (1984) attempted a general examination of Hohokam economic interactions by examining the relationships between artifact frequencies and site function. Through comparisons of the ratios of particular artifact types at platform mound, ballcourt, and other habitation sites, she evaluated the presence of reciprocal, redistributive, and market economic interactions. Settlement distributions provided a means for evaluating the presence of central places having central functions in the economy. Teague argues that pre-Classic exchange was not centralized. The ballcourt system may have provided a mechanism for ritual exchanges between families and individuals, but ballcourt sites were not "central places." During the Sedentary, a few sites with platform mounds, or destined to have them later, became loci of centralized distribution of some commodities. Multiple exchange networks with different boundaries existed in the Hohokam area during the late Sedentary and Classic periods for the movement of different commodities. Some items, such as locally available rocks used in manufacturing lithic artifacts, were obtained by direct access. Some ceramic types (phyllite-tempered plain ware, red-on-buff, and red ware) were manufactured at a few locales and exchanged through down-the-line exchange, "probably rooted in reciprocal relationships" (Teague 1984:237). In contrast, nonlocal lithic materials (turquoise, serpentine, argillite, jet, and obsidian) and shell occurred in their greatest frequency and variety at Sedentary and Classic period platform mound sites, and sites that later developed into platform mound sites. She argues that this pattern is indicative of centralized distribution of these materials from the platform mound (and protoplatform mound) sites. Ritual paraphernalia (asbestos, copper bells, pyrite mirrors, *Strombus* trumpets, inlaid and etched shell) were moved through a network that involved an elite functioning at platform mound sites, which limited and controlled their distribution. The role of the platform mound sites in controlling exchange increased during the Classic, with increased access to exotics. The platform mound system collapsed at the end of the Civano phase, and although some commodities disappeared, others are more evenly distributed across sites after this time.

Examining the distribution of ballcourts throughout the Greater Southwest, Wilcox (1979; Wilcox and Sternberg 1983) argued that ballcourts served an integrative function for the entire Hohokam area. The ballcourt system was initiated to facilitate movement in exotics from outside the Salt-Gila Basin. Local systems of ballcourts were central to a calendrical round of ceremonial events among communities that witnessed reciprocal exchanges between domestic groups. At a higher level, the network of ballcourt communities was economically integrated, probably involved in fewer transactions of goods of greater value than the local systems. At this higher level, elite households probably exchanged rare exotics (copper bells, pyrite mirrors, macaws, shell trumpets, and rubber balls). Periodic exchanges between elites of different local systems cemented marriages and alliances and encouraged negotiation of disputes (Wilcox and Sternberg 1983:212–214). Wilcox also argued that the rare exotics listed above were transferred from Mesoamerica along a corridor of Tepiman speakers through exchange between high-status individuals (1983:227). This economic network collapsed in the eleventh or twelfth century, resulting in loss of access to the rare exotics and perhaps abetting the regional system collapse at A.D. 1100–1150. The Soho phase witnessed a collapse and reorganization of the regional and economic systems, with participation of the Hohokam area in a Salado regional system after A.D. 1300. The Salado regional system was a "weakly integrated system of exchange among a large series of small-scale regional systems" (Wilcox and Sternberg 1983:244). Integration occurred through alliances of individuals (or councils) representing each small regional system (Wilcox and Sternberg 1983:245).

Finally, Doyel (1987) completed a comprehensive overview of the role of exchange in Hohokam society. He posited the existence of three different spheres of exchange or levels at which different types of objects circulated through the system. The first, or prestige, sphere, involved exchange in Mesoamerican items, certain minerals, obsidian, and "high-value" shell products. He argued that this sphere of exchange is only known to have operated during the pre-Classic, A.D. 800–1100. A second, social sphere of exchange might have included low-value shell, pottery, textiles, baskets, and other objects that might have served in payment of social debts or obligations. Such a social sphere might link elites and dependents within regions. Finally, a "utilitarian" sphere of exchange might have served to move ground stone tools, raw materials, and tabular knives. He also argued for an incipient level of market exchange during the pre-Classic, functioning primarily at sites with ballcourts and central plazas. He suggested that subsistence products were not centrally controlled and redistributed, but that exchange in prestige items (shell, pottery, minerals) might have been regulated during the late pre-Classic through Classic by the occupants of sites with platform mounds (1987:76–77). The Classic period was characterized by a retraction in population to the Salt-Gila Basin. Numerous products ceased to occur in Hohokam sites, and obsidian increased in frequency. Doyel argued that these changes signaled a collapse in the Sedentary period regional system and a reduction in exchange with outside groups. The Civano phase might represent a return to greater complexity with the Hohokam involved in a broader interaction sphere with a reinstated prestige sphere of exchange (possibly Salado; see Wilcox 1987).

These models provide contradictory views of Hohokam exchange and interaction. Several models suggest considerable complexity in the organization of exchange of goods into the Hohokam area (Doyel 1987; McGuire 1987; McGuire and Howard 1987; Nelson 1986; Teague 1984; Wilcox and Sternberg 1983), while others posit substantially less complexity in accounting for the presence of the same items (Crown 1984a; Seymour 1988; Wallace and Heidke 1986). Virtually all of the models suggest some type of alteration in Hohokam exchange networks between the Sedentary and Classic periods, although the nature of this change is seen by some as indicative of increasing complexity (McGuire and Howard 1987; Teague 1984), and by others as decreasing complexity (Doyel 1977, 1980; Nelson 1986).

## SPHERES OF EXCHANGE:
## AN OVERVIEW AND CRITIQUE

Two major points emerge from this review of previous interpretations. First, the distributions and frequency of each commodity must be independently examined and interpreted before comparisons between commodities are made; a single model will not explain all of the varieties of exchange present in the Hohokam area. Second, the quantities of many exotics recovered are small (often less than 100 items) and the contexts excavated to date in the Hohokam area are of questionable representativeness. It is important that we compare, interpret, and speculate, but it is just as important that we recognize the limitations of both the data base and available interpretive constructs.

It is possible, however, to combine many of the models presented above to derive a single version of the Hohokam system. Beginning with pre-Classic exchange and interaction, most of these researchers suggest that exchange involved different spheres, or levels, of exchange in which goods or services of different types or values were exchanged. They posit the existence of an "elite" or prestige sphere of exchange, which involved movement of non-utilitarian goods related to wealth, status, role, or ritual. The existence of such a sphere of exchange is inferred on the basis of several lines of evidence, all involving the presence of nonutilitarian goods that: (1) have limited contexts of production; (2) were either difficult to produce or obtain; (3) were important to ceremonial or social occasions; and (4) have been recovered differentially between and within sites, particularly within caches or burials (Lindauer 1988:293). Goods hypothesized to have been exchanged within a prestige sphere during the pre-Classic include copper bells, pyrite mirrors, macaws, shell mosaics, etched shell, *Pecten vogdesi* pendants, painted shell, *Strombus* trumpets (Nelson 1986; McGuire and Howard 1987; Doyel 1987), intrusive ceramics, and animal effigy vessels (Lindauer 1988). Most of these items would have been manufactured outside of the Hohokam area and introduced into the area through reciprocal exchange between Hohokam elites and elites from surrounding areas (Nelson 1986; McGuire and Howard 1987). Many of the shell items might have been obtained directly by Hohokam elites from the Papagueria (McGuire 1987). Such items legitimized elite status or were used in social transactions, and may have been taken out of circulation periodically in order to increase their value (Lindauer 1988).

The second or social sphere (Doyel 1987) involved exchange of nonutilitarian goods, with somewhat limited nonlocal or localized production or source areas, that were important in cementing social transactions or payments of social debts (Doyel 1987; McGuire 1987). Such items might include shell bracelets, beads, cut pendants (McGuire and Howard 1987), turquoise, obsidian, serpentine, jet, red-on-buff ceramics (Teague 1984), intrusive ceramics, textiles, basketry (Doyel 1987), and argillite and steatite (David A. Gregory, personal communication). Such goods would be exchanged from elites to "dependents" within a region through redistribution.

The third or utilitarian sphere (Doyel 1987) would involve exchange of items related to subsistence or daily activities, produced at many places using raw materials with a broad availability. Such items would be exchanged between socially close individuals or trading partners (Wallace and Heidke 1986). These items probably included plain ware vessels, locally available stone materials, and probably foodstuffs.

Although this interpretation of pre-Classic Hohokam exchange and interaction combines the views of a number of researchers, not all would concur with this view. Seymour has recently argued strongly against the level of complexity implied by such a model, stating that "there is no support at Snaketown for a formal redistributive system, a class of elites, or a centralized production system" (1988:25). It is important then to examine more closely the existing evidence for these spheres of exchange, particularly the prestige sphere.

It has been argued that prestige sphere objects were used as social valuables in transactions validating major life transitions or in legitimizing the power of an elite by symbolically signaling their status (McGuire and Howard 1987; Nelson 1986). According to Nelson, ". . . objects which symbolize or communicate something about a status or role which is held by only a few individuals may not circulate very widely, especially if that status is ascribed rather than achieved" (1986:157). The existence of an elite among the pre-Classic Hohokam has been predicated in large measure on the presence and distribution of these so-called "elite goods." For instance, Nelson's (1986) test for the existence of an elite versus egalitarian society involved examination of the distribution of Mesoamerican and rare local materials and artifacts both within and between Hohokam sites. With the exception of a few rare locally manufactured objects, the items considered high value, or prestige sphere objects, come from Mesoamerica. Their inclusion in the list of prestige sphere objects was based on this source and on their differential distribution both within sites in the Hohokam area and in "ritual" contexts (burials/caches) in these sites. For instance, McGuire and Howard (1987:125–126) argued that certain shell objects had a higher value based on their low frequency and their differential distribution in ritual contexts.

Two aspects of this argument warrant closer examination: the sample size of prestige material relative to the function hypothesized, and the possibility that other interpretations would explain the frequencies and distributions of these data equally well. The facts are that certain items, both Mesoamerican and locally manufactured, occur in low frequencies and often (although not exclusively) in caches or burials. I examine first the question of whether the sample size is appropriate for the interpretations made.

If the so-called elite sphere items served primarily to legitimize the power of an elite, or to provide the owners with status, they should be a recognized and recognizable symbol, that is, there must be a consensus as to the symbolic or actual value of the object. To legitimize power or status, such objects should then occur in highly visible contexts associated with the individual seeking power and with sufficient frequency to be recognizable as a symbol of that power. They would probably be items of personal adornment and quite possibly occur as a prescribed set of items, perhaps as part of a costume. We might then expect true symbols of elite status to occur not only differentially within and between sites (in sites with ballcourts, plazas, or platform mounds, and within burials, caches, mounds, and ballcourts), but also in sufficient numbers to support the view that these objects were shared symbols of wealth, power, or status, and were valued accordingly.

By the same token, if these elite sphere items served in transactions validating major life transitions, we would again anticipate a frequency in keeping with the frequency of major life transitions. If, for example, it is important to exchange a copper bell as part of a marriage ceremony, copper bells should occur in a quantity roughly equivalent to the number of elite marriages in a given time period.

Table 9.1 lists many commonly suggested Sedentary period "prestige goods"

Table 9.1    *Sedentary Period Prestige Goods from the Salt-Gila Basin*

| Item | Number | Sites | Contexts |
|------|--------|-------|----------|
| Shell trumpets | 2 | Snaketown | 1 trash, 1 cremation |
|  | ? | Grewe? | cremations? |
| Etched shell[1] | under 30 | Snaketown | cremations, trash |
| Painted shell[1] | under 10 | Snaketown | cremations, trash |
| Shell overlay[2] | 492–493 | Snaketown | cremations, caches, trash |
| *Pecten vogdesi* pendants[2] | 800–900 | Snaketown | cremations, caches, trash |
|  |  | Grewe |  |
| Copper bells | 28 | Snaketown | House 6G: 8 |
| Pyrite mosaic mirrors | 31[3] | Snaketown | cremations, mound, house |
|  | 14 | Grewe | cremations, offertory area |
| Macaws | — | — | — |
| Mesoamerican pottery | 5 sherds | Snaketown | trash, house floor |
|  | 3 sherds | Grewe | ? |
|  | 1 vessel | Cashion | cremation |
| Animal effigy vessels[4] | 9 vessels | Snaketown | caches, cremations |
|  | 4 vessels | Grewe | ? |
|  | 1 vessel | Cashion | ? |

[1]includes all Sedentary period Hohokam sites examined by Nelson (1981)
[2]counts include Colonial and Sedentary period contexts at all sites examined by Nelson (1981)
[3]estimated by Nelson (1986:168)
[4]vessel frequencies provided by Lindauer (personal communication 1988)
(Data derived from Crown 1984a; McGuire and Howard 1987; Nelson 1981, 1986; and Dr. Owen Lindauer, personal communication, 1988)

found at sites in the Salt-Gila Basin (Lindauer 1988; McGuire and Howard 1987; Nelson 1981, 1986). There are admittedly many problems with the sample of excavated and reported materials, but these are the data available at the present time. Apart from shell overlay and *Pecten* pendants, the total number of objects is remarkably low, particularly when context of recovery is taken into account. Thus, although 28 copper bells were recovered from Snaketown, all came from a single structure and were part of a single necklace (Haury 1976:278). Given a 200-year duration for the Sacaton phase, the actual quantity of this material in use at any one time would have been even lower. All of the Mesoamerican pottery and the overwhelming majority of the pyrite mosaic mirrors occur as fragments, raising the possibility that these items entered the Basin in fragmentary form, as has been suggested for some intrusive pottery (Crown 1984a:289).

The extreme localization of these materials at three sites in the basin (Snaketown, Cashion, and Grewe) is intriguing. To some degree this may be a sampling problem, but the fact that these materials repeatedly occur at these same sites and only these sites suggests that Snaketown, Cashion, and Grewe attracted objects that simply were not present (or perhaps accessible to the populations) elsewhere.

Do these distributions and numbers match the expectations of a "prestige goods" exchange model? The low frequencies of material dating to a 200-year time period suggest that, if elites brought this material to these sites, they were not particularly successful at acquiring valuables. Since symbols of power would need to be visible, recognizable items readily identifiable by all "non-elites," the highly localized distribution and low number of individual items calls the efficiency of these objects as symbols of power or status into question. These objects would certainly be recognized as foreign and as oddities, but any meaning or value attached to them might be less clear. Individuals with a clear status, otherwise supported, might have owned and worn these items as part of a costume, but the items themselves probably did not imbue that individual with power. Rather than the individual acquiring status through ownership of these items, the items might have acquired status through association with individuals already possessing power. This is an important distinction. Status symbols are necessary identifiers that communicate information about status or role; these objects may simply have been exotic ornaments. Alternatively, if these items were needed to validate major life transitions, these transitions must not have occurred with any frequency during the Sedentary period.

All we truly know then, is that some objects with a low frequency in Hohokam sites in general, occur at a few large Hohokam sites primarily in burial and offertory contexts. This fact admits several equally plausible interpretations, the currently popular "prestige sphere" model being only one. The possibility should be considered that many of the "prestige sphere" objects were so rare in Hohokam society that their final disposition reflects the difficulty in obtaining them and the value placed on that rarity rather than their use as symbols of elite status or use in social transactions. Alternatively, they might be items that functioned in specific ceremonies or rituals and might be considered community property (Pires-Ferreira and Flannery 1976:289). Underhill (1939:71–72) notes village ownership of sacred objects among the Papago, and these supernaturally acquired items were kept in hiding away from the settlement (see also Haury 1976:190). The recovery of the necklace of copper bells, together with asbestos, 30 *Pecten vogdesi* pendants, a steatite bowl, and 60 vessels from a Sacaton phase structure at Snaketown (Structure 6G:8) (Nelson 1986; Seymour 1988:16; Seymour and Schiffer 1987:572) may indicate use of this material as community ritual paraphernalia. Drennan (1976:357) suggests that such foreign, rare, and unusual objects might help in inducing religious experiences by their mysterious nature. A third possibility is that these goods may occur at Snaketown, Grewe, and Cashion because these were among the largest Hohokam settlements with the greatest number of people and "ritual" features in the Salt-Gila Basin. In effect, the more people in the settlement, the greater the diversity of outside contacts, the more frequent and more focal the ritual activities, and the greater the opportunity for the rare, unusual artifacts to occur. Perhaps most importantly, we should recognize that since other commodities reached the Salt-Gila Basin by different means, there is no reason why we should expect all of these rare items to have reached the Basin through a single mechanism or source.

As a final note, the occurrence of these items in ritual versus nonritual contexts needs to be examined more cautiously. For instance, McGuire and Howard (1987:125) argued that if shell were strictly an item of personal ornamentation (as Haury [1976:321] suggested), then intact shell artifacts should be common in de facto and primary refuse in household contexts. Alternatively, if shell had value as a status-religious object it should occur in ritual contexts. Indeed they found that "most finished, unbroken shell artifacts from Colonial-Sedentary period sites in the Phoenix Basin have been recovered from ritual contexts, principally from cremations and artifact caches" (1987:126). The problem with this argument is that there are very few de facto or primary refuse contexts in Hohokam sites (Seymour and Schiffer 1987). Most whole, unbroken objects of almost any type occur in cremations or caches simply because of the nature of these deposits: the items were intentionally deposited in a manner that dictated their recovery in complete or reconstructible form. Except in cases of destruction by fire, Hohokam pithouses and courtyards generally produce remarkably few whole objects. A large portion of whole and reconstructible vessels also comes primarily from burials and caches, but this has not been taken to indicate that they were prestige goods, or that their function was primarily ritual in nature. Shell ornaments were highly portable and intended for personal adornment, so that it is unlikely that whole shell artifacts would be left in houses or courtyards except by accident. The differential *distribution* of these items within burials and caches is a more interesting and informative pattern (McGuire and Howard 1987:126) than their *occurrence* in burials and caches.

The concept of a Hohokam elite should not be dismissed out-of-hand, but I believe that the extremely low number of so-called prestige goods should lead to a reexamination of our arguments in support of the existence of such an elite. Apart from ongoing exchange (or expeditions) for raw or finished shell objects, it also calls into question the existence of formal and ongoing exchange transactions with groups in Mesoamerica. Interaction obviously occurred intermittently over a long period of time between the Hohokam and groups to the south, but the magnitude of most of the material exchanged is a small foundation upon which to link a local and Mesoamerican elite. Other lines of evidence need to be examined before a strong and lasting picture of Hohokam social organization emerges.

The existence of separate social and utilitarian exchange spheres should be evaluated more closely as well. It is hard to demonstrate that items from one "sphere" would not be exchanged for items from another, and if this were not the case, the concept of different "spheres" of exchange is not appropriate to the Hohokam economy.

## THE ORGANIZATION OF EXCHANGE

Regardless of the existence of differing spheres of exchange, raw materials and finished goods entered and left the basin, and it is important to examine the mechanisms responsible and how these materials circulated within the basin exchange network. There is considerable evidence for different types of items entering and leaving this network by different means. The recovery of Hohokam red-on-buff ceramics at major shell and salt collecting locales along the California and Gulf of California coasts and near a salt mine in southern Nevada (Crown 1984a) suggests that these materials might have been acquired directly through expeditions to the source. The presence of Hohokam petroglyphs along trails to the Adair Bay area in Sonora reinforces this possibility (Hayden 1972). Other materials were probably acquired through down-the-line exchange from the source, as has been suggested for locally available stone materials (Teague 1984) and Kayenta pottery (McGuire and Downum 1982). Shell might have been acquired from the Papagueria or Trincheras areas, with the Hohokam serving as middlemen to distribute the shell to other portions of the Southwest (McGuire and Howard 1987:130). Hohokam materials interpreted as indicating the presence of trading outposts occur at the Stove Canyon site (Neely 1974), Winona Village (Fish, Pilles, and Fish 1980), the Perkinsville site (Fish and Fish 1977), and Walnut Creek Village (Morris 1970; Doyel 1987). Hakataya structures excavated at the site of Las Colinas in the Salt-Gila Basin, and dating to the late Sedentary to mid-Soho phases (David A. Gregory, personal communication, 1988), may represent "trading outposts" as well.

Perhaps most significantly, the system of ballcourts found throughout much of the Southwest has been postulated as a mechanism for movement of goods, as well as people for labor, in a calendrical round (Wilcox and Sternberg 1983). This model suggests that the ballcourt system provided a ritual context for both exchange of items and interaction, and that the alliances formed were as important as the goods obtained. Close overlap in the distribution of Hohokam ballcourts, red-on-buff pottery, and shell ornaments, either manufactured in the Salt-Gila Basin (Seymour 1988) or distributed from there (McGuire and Howard 1987), reinforces the notion that the ballcourt system was somehow tied to exchange of Hohokam goods outside of the Salt-Gila Basin (Fig. 9.1). The distributions thus provide a means for approximating the boundaries for a Hohokam regional system (Crown 1987b; Wilcox 1979, 1980; see also McGuire, this volume), "a number of interacting but geograph-

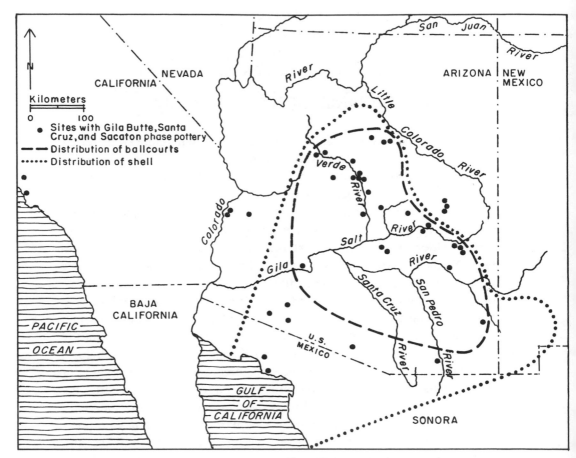

Figure 9.1     *Distribution of Hohokam ballcourts, shell, and red-on-buff*
*ceramics outside the Salt-Gila Basin. Sources: ballcourts (Wilcox*
*1988); ceramics (Crown 1984a); shell (McGuire and Howard*
*1987).*

ically separate communities that were dependent on each other through the
exchange of goods and services" (Judge 1984:8).

Both the movement of goods and the shared ideology suggested by the
presence of the ballcourts indicate that the degree of interaction among groups
participating in this regional system was greater than their interaction with
groups outside. The way that the system functioned is not clear, yet as suggested by Wilcox and Sternberg (1983), whatever ritual or activity occurred
at the ballcourts probably drew population from surrounding areas and provided a mechanism for interaction and exchange. However, despite the common presence of the ballcourt, sites with ballcourts differ in locally produced
material culture, site structure, and burial practices from one end of the system
to the other.

It thus appears to have been an acephalous system, with no single site or portion of the area encompassed by the regional system boundaries "in charge" of coordinating interaction and exchange. In a more organized system, we might anticipate a more homogeneous distribution of particular types of goods. This is not the case; the quantities and types of exotic goods recovered from particular sites vary considerably and appear to reflect both the position of that site in a hierarchy (multiple ballcourts, single ballcourts, no ballcourts) and the singular set of exchanges or interactions or alliances formed between the inhabitants of that site and other groups.

Examination of the distribution of intrusive ceramics suggests that the materials occurring at particular sites were strongly influenced by geographic proximity and ease of access between various populations. However, if simple down-the-line exchange from source were present, we would expect a clinal distribution in frequency of items from that source. Yet this is not the case, at least with most intrusive ceramics found in Hohokam sites; the major rivers appear to have served as only minimally porous boundaries, so that materials found in quantities on one side of the river fall off in frequency dramatically on the other side. For instance, there is no clear topographic reason why Mimbres ceramic vessels that reached the area between the Salt and Gila Rivers from some 300 km to the east were not moved an additional 40 km or less to sites north of the Salt River. Yet, while during the interval of its production, Mimbres pottery represents 30 percent of the intrusives found in sites between the Salt and Gila Rivers, it represents less than 1 percent of the intrusives from sites north of the Salt River (Doyel 1987). Sampling problems alone cannot explain such a discrepancy.

Hohokam populations simply did not interact or exchange materials equally with all surrounding populations. As indicated by the distribution of intrusives, the ties formed were due in part to proximity; but these patterns of interaction also appear to reflect networks developed perhaps as early as the Pioneer period and maintained through the pre-Classic. Thus, the populations located on the northern bank of the Salt River interacted and exchanged material goods most frequently with groups in western Arizona and in the Flagstaff/Prescott areas; populations between the Salt and Gila Rivers interacted primarily with Mogollon and Mimbres groups; and populations on the south bank of the Gila River interacted most often with groups in southern Arizona. The exact nature of the interactions between these differentially connected populations is not clear. While concurring with Doyel (1987, this volume) that our sample is woefully skewed and inadequate, I would observe that the current sample clearly indicates that pre-Classic Hohokam populations in the Salt-Gila Basin did not interact as a unified body or in a similar fashion with all other groups in the Southwest. Rather, consistent differences existed in the nature of interaction between Hohokam groups within the Basin and those Hohokam and non-Hohokam entities outside of the Basin. If these differences exist for intrusive ceramics, they probably also exist for other materials.

By the end of the Sedentary period, the regional system had collapsed, or at least altered dramatically. Smaller systems organized along major drainages and within the basins replaced the widespread exchange network represented by the pre-Classic regional system boundaries (McGuire and Howard 1987:134). Evidence for the manufacture of artifacts from imported raw materials increases within the Salt-Gila Basin, suggesting a greater emphasis on the exchange of raw materials rather than finished products. Manufacture of some items declines (red-on-buff pottery) or ceases (stone palettes, stone bowls, effigies, elaborate projectile points), but other items occur in greater numbers.

Some of the so-called elite sphere items found in the Sedentary period no longer occur in the Classic period (etched shell, pyrite mosaic mirrors), but most of these items occurred with greater frequency and wider distribution during the Classic period. Nelson (1986) has interpreted this pattern as indicative of a decline in the Hohokam elite prestige sphere of exchange to a relatively egalitarian society. Other researchers (McGuire and Howard 1987; Wilcox 1987) view this as part of a broader shift in the Southwest toward smaller and roughly equivalent exchange systems controlled by elites sharing a common set of symbols. I concur that the known Classic period distributions provide more powerful evidence for the use of these items in legitimizing status or as symbols of life transitions than do the Sedentary period distributions. Even distributions of exotics across sites do not necessarily evince equal status for everyone, and the presence of habitation structures on top of platform mounds demonstrates that not everyone *was* equal during the Civano phase (Gregory 1982). High-value items that might have served as symbols of status at this time include shell trumpets, turquoise mosaic artifacts, copper bells, and possibly textiles and macaws.

Other exchange items appear to have changed less in distribution and frequency. Low-value shell is more evenly distributed across sites and is less common in burial contexts (McGuire and Howard 1987). Red-on-buff ceramics were manufactured in low amounts, but red ware may have replaced red-on-buff pottery as a "higher value" exchange item (Abbott 1984).

Changes in the types and distributions of goods were accompanied by changes in the sources for those goods. Recognizable Salt-Gila Basin Hohokam ceramics occur less frequently outside of the Salt-Gila Basin. If, as suggested above, these ceramics were often exchanged in conjunction with the acquisition of other materials, such as shell and salt, the Classic period Hohokam ceramic distributions might indicate that certain raw materials were obtained through down-the-line exchange or middlemen rather than expedition to source. Shell may have been obtained most commonly from populations in the Trincheras area rather than the Papagueria (McGuire and Howard 1987:135). Former trading outposts outside the Salt-Gila Basin were abandoned by this

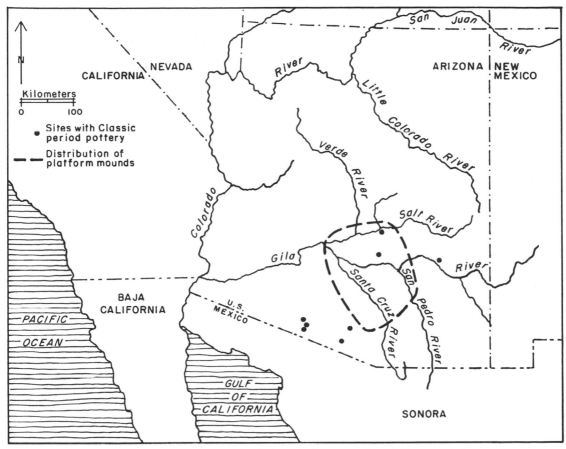

Figure 9.2     *Distribution of Hohokam platform mounds and Classic period red-on-buff ceramics outside the Salt-Gila Basin. Sources: platform mounds (Gregory and Nials 1985); ceramics (Crown 1984a).*

time. The Hakataya structures at Las Colinas were abandoned by approximately A.D. 1200–1250 (David A. Gregory, personal communication).

For the Classic period, the distribution of platform mounds and red-on-buff pottery provides some approximation of the area of most intense interaction between the Hohokam and surrounding groups (Fig. 9.2) (Crown 1987b). The distribution of platform mounds reveals an area greatly reduced from the considerably broader distribution of ballcourts. The number and areal distribution of intrusives outside of the Basin had also diminished from the Sedentary, although this may be due in part to the problem of distinguishing Salt-Gila Basin Hohokam red ware from other red ware manufactured at this time. Intrusive ceramics found within the Salt-Gila Basin during the early Classic decline in number, but originate in roughly the same areas as during the Sacaton phase. By the Civano phase, there was a more even distribution of intrusive types across the entire Salt-Gila Basin, suggesting essentially equal access to the ceramics regardless of geographic proximity to source (Crown 1984a:270). This pattern fits well with the distribution of other exotics in the Basin. The equivalent overlay of material does suggest that the pre-Classic trading partnerships or networks discussed above had broken down by the Civano phase and been replaced by other types of networks. Whether occupants of different portions of the Salt-Gila Basin took advantage of equivalent access to sources of materials for the first time or whether the mechanisms that brought items into the basin had changed is unclear. It does suggest however, that the occupants of the Salt-Gila Basin sites were dealing with surrounding groups in a more uniform manner, regardless of settlement locations within the basin.

By A.D. 1350–1400, the Salt-Gila Basin was largely abandoned, with small populations distributed at comparatively few sites. Interestingly, these sites exhibit high frequencies of some exotics, particularly obsidian and intrusive pottery, while other exotic minerals and shell declined. Polvoron phase assemblages included the same range of intrusive types regardless of site locale. Population at this time is sparse and distance between occupied sites relatively greater, so that interaction between groups within the basin was probably diminished from previous periods. The canals, always a major force integrating population at different sites, may or may not have continued to be utilized at this time period (Gregory and Nials 1985; Sires 1983b). It seems likely that the exotic materials found in the basin at this time were present due to the location of the Salt-Gila Basin between more populated areas to the north (Hopi, Tonto Basin) and south (Tucson) (Crown 1984a).

## SUMMARY AND CONCLUSIONS

From the late Archaic on, populations in the Salt-Gila Basin interacted with surrounding groups. The inhabitants of the basin never constituted a self-contained group, although they could have been economically self-sufficient. All of the crops and technology necessary to exploit the desert environment were present by the late Pioneer period. The exchange of materials and finished goods both within the Hohokam area and between the Hohokam and their neighbors after this time seems to have primarily provided the Hohokam with exotic items that were not essential to their physical well-being and probably served to develop economic, social, and political ties that were essential to their social well-being. As suggested by several researchers (Gasser and Miksicek 1985; McGuire 1987; Wilcox 1987), the Hohokam may have supplied food, raw cotton, or finished textiles to the groups they interacted with in addition to serving as middlemen in shell exchange in the Southwest. The vessels they exchanged, primarily jars, seem to have had value as containers rather than as objects, so that the contents (food, saguaro wine, salt?) were the items of exchange rather than the vessels themselves (Crown 1984a).

Different commodities were exchanged by different means, and no single model accounts for all of the varieties of exchange present among the Hohokam. A number of the models reviewed here posited the existence of a prestige sphere of exchange for the pre-Classic. The low sample size of the material included as prestige goods makes demonstration of the existence of such a sphere of exchange difficult, particularly since other interpretations can account for these same data.

Overlap in the distribution of shell, red-on-buff ceramics, and ballcourts in the Southwest provides a basis for defining a pre-Classic Hohokam regional system. Rituals occurring in association with the ballcourts probably encouraged interaction and exchange among communities, although the entire "system" never functioned as a unified polity. Rather, portions of the Salt-Gila Basin developed specific exchange and interaction networks (at least for ceramic vessels) early in the pre-Classic, and these networks endured into the early Classic period. The breakdown of the ballcourt system at the end of the Sedentary period eventually led to a smaller regional system, which can be defined on the basis of platform mounds and red-on-buff ceramics. A common set of symbols of status seems to have been in use over much of the Southwest at this time. Whether the Hohokam became part of a larger Salado regional system after A.D. 1300 (Wilcox and Sternberg 1983) remains to be explored. The earlier, distinct exchange networks had disappeared by A.D. 1300 and site location no longer seems to have affected the types of material found at the site. The remnant population in the Salt-Gila Basin after A.D. 1350–1400 continued to interact with surrounding groups.

If we were to rank intensity or frequency of interaction among the Hohokam, those individuals occupying a single house cluster (Wilcox, McGuire, and Sternberg 1981), would undoubtedly interact with greatest frequency. Above this level would be the inhabitants of a single settlement or village, followed by the inhabitants of sites along a single canal, designated an irrigation community (Crown 1987a; Doyel 1977). The irrigation systems forced and necessitated interaction in matters of construction, maintenance, and water allocation (Crown 1987a; Gregory and Nials 1985). Cooperation would have been a necessity for populations along a canal. Along the Salt River during the Classic period, at least, single sites irrigated land off of multiple canals, necessitating interaction and cooperation with populations at sites located on more than a single canal system (Nicholas and Neitzel 1983). This does not appear to have been the situation on the Gila River, where topography prevented the "stacking" of parallel canals away from the river (Crown 1987a; Gregory and Nials 1985). This difference in topography would have been reflected in differences in interaction patterns of populations along these drainages. The need for cooperation between populations occupying several

canals would have forced a greater degree of interaction and encouraged a
more overarching political structure to allocate water resources across several
canals along the Salt (Nicholas and Neitzel 1983). No such structure would
have been necessary on the Gila River and it is highly likely that each canal
system was essentially autonomous throughout the Hohokam occupation of
the area. Interaction undoubtedly occurred between populations utilizing
different irrigation systems along the river, but since they may have been
competing for sometimes scarce water resources, such interaction would not
necessarily have been friendly. It is for this reason that with larger samples
from more sites, I would anticipate finding that differences existed in the
types of exotic raw materials and objects found at sites occupying different
canal systems. If we were to rank degrees of similarity in assemblages, I
would expect sites on shared canals to be most similar, those on different
canals on the same side of the river to be next in similarity, sites on different
sides of the same river to follow, and sites on different rivers to be least
uniform. The Hohokam were never a unified group under a single political
body. The exchange and interaction that occurred was not uniform for all
inhabitants of the Salt-Gila Basin and the exotic items found in sites are the
product of the particular ties the populations at those sites had with surrounding groups. As described above, the sources for items and thus the
types and degrees of interaction changed through time. In some instances,
this was the result of events within the Hohokam area, and in others the
result of events external to the Hohokam.

## UNDERSTANDING HOHOKAM EXCHANGE
## AND INTERACTION: THE FUTURE

This paper demonstrates how limited our understanding of Hohokam
exchange is at the present time. A number of different types of studies are
needed to amplify this understanding. First, additional work needs to be
done to identify sources for the material found in Hohokam sites. Much of
the work that has already been done should be compiled and synthesized,
so that data files from individual projects are combined and reexamined.
Second, data on distributions of exotic items should be compiled for the
Southwest. The studies of macaws (Hargrave 1970), copper bells (Sprague
and Signori 1963; Sprague 1964), shell (Howard 1983; McGuire and Howard
1987), and intrusive ceramics (Crown 1984a, 1985; Doyel 1987) provide us
with a basis for evaluating how material moved through the broader exchange
networks in the Southwest, and the information exists to undertake such
studies with other artifact and raw material types. Overlays of these distributions provide information on exchange networks, and information on sources
for exotics should be examined relative to site function and location on irrigation systems or drainages. For instance, do sites with ballcourts or on

different irrigation networks exhibit different sources for obsidian or turquoise? Perhaps most importantly, we need larger and more representative data bases, and more precise temporal control. Contract projects have expanded the data base tremendously in recent years, but the excavated sites are not necessarily representative of the range of site types that exist. The very low frequency of "prestige sphere" items for the Sedentary period suggests that many of these items were indeed rarities in the Hohokam world. Our sample may be so skewed, however, that the real picture is obscured. Do more sites with materials like those at Snaketown, Grewe, and Cashion exist, or is this distribution of sites, with one south of the Gila, one between the rivers, and one north of the Salt, meaningful? And how can we look at exchange patterns in any meaningful fashion when we are still for the most part lumping material in 200-year time blocks?

The next decade promises to resolve many of the issues raised in this paper. As we have time to absorb, compare, and interpret the voluminous data collected in the last decade, our views of Hohokam exchange and interaction will be clarified. It is hoped that we will then be better able to unravel the intricacies of the Hohokam exchange systems, and ultimately the structure of Hohokam society.

## ACKNOWLEDGMENTS

I would like to express my gratitude to Dr. George Gumerman and Thomas Lincoln for organizing such a stimulating conference, and to the Amerind Foundation for providing such a wonderful setting in which to hold it. Owen Lindauer, Deni Seymour, and Randall McGuire kindly provided unpublished information that aided immeasurably in completing this study. David A. Gregory and Wirt H. Wills provided useful comments on this paper. Charles Sternberg drafted the figures in his inimitable style. My thanks to all of these individuals, but they are absolved of all association with the outcome.

## REFERENCES CITED

Abbott, David R.
    1984   A Technical Assessment of Ceramic Variation in the Salt-Gila Aqueduct Area: Toward a Comprehensive Documentation of Hohokam Ceramics. In *Hohokam Archaeology Along the Salt-Gila Aqueduct, Central Arizona Project*, vol. 8, Material Culture, edited by Lynn S. Teague and Patricia L. Crown, pp. 3–118. Arizona State Museum Archaeological Series 150. University of Arizona, Tucson.

Bostwick, Todd W., and M. Steven Shackley
   1987   Settlement Strategies and Lithic Technology: An Examination of Variability in Hunter-Gatherer and Agriculturalist Chipped Stone Assemblages in the Sonoran Desert. Paper presented at the 1987 Hohokam Symposium. Arizona State University, Tempe.
Braun, David P., and Stephen Plog
   1982   Evolution of "Tribal" Social Networks: Theory and Prehistoric North American Evidence. *American Antiquity* 47:504–525.
Brown, Patricia
   1982   Tracing Prehistoric Sources of Obsidian. In *Granite Reef: A Study in Desert Archaeology,* edited by Patricia Eyring Brown and Connie L. Stone, pp. 227–241. Anthropological Research Papers 28. Arizona State University, Tempe.
Colberg-Sigleo, Anne
   1975   Turquoise Mine and Artifact Correlations for Snaketown Site, Arizona. *Science* 189(4201):459–460.
Crown, Patricia L.
   1984a   Ceramic Vessel Exchange in Southern Arizona. In *Hohokam Archaeology Along the Salt-Gila Aqueduct, Central Arizona Project,* vol. 9, Synthesis and Conclusions, edited by Lynn S. Teague and Patricia L. Crown, pp. 251–304. Arizona State Museum Archaeological Series 150. University of Arizona, Tucson.
   1984b   Design Variability on Hohokam Red-on-buff Ceramics. In *Hohokam Archaeology Along the Salt-Gila Aqueduct, Central Arizona Project,* vol. 8, Material Culture, edited by Lynn S. Teague and Patricia L. Crown, pp. 205–247. Arizona State Museum Archaeological Series 150. University of Arizona, Tucson.
   1984c   An X-ray Fluorescence Analysis of Hohokam Ceramics. In *Hohokam Archaeology Along the Salt-Gila Aqueduct, Central Arizona Project,* vol. 8, Material Culture, edited by Lynn S. Teague and Patricia L. Crown, pp. 277–310. Arizona State Museum Archaeological Series 150. University of Arizona, Tucson.
   1985   Intrusive Ceramics and the Identification of Hohokam Exchange Networks. In *Proceedings of the 1983 Hohokam Symposium,* edited by A. E. Dittert, Jr. and D. E. Dove, pp. 439–458. Arizona Archaeological Society Occasional Paper 2. Phoenix.
   1987a   Classic Period Hohokam Settlement and Land Use in the Casa Grande Ruins Area. *Journal of Field Archaeology* 14:147–162.
   1987b   The Hohokam: Current Views of Prehistory and the Regional System. Paper presented at the Advanced Seminar, Cultural Complexity in the Arid Southwest: The Hohokam and Chacoan Regional Systems. School of American Research, Santa Fe.
Crown, Patricia L., Larry A. Schwalbe, and J. Ronald London
   1985   X-Ray Fluorescence Analysis of Materials Variability in Las Colinas Ceramics. In *Excavations at Las Colinas, Phoenix, Arizona,* vol. 4, Material Culture, edited by David A. Gregory. Arizona State Museum Archaeological Series 162. University of Arizona, Tucson.
Crown, Patricia L., and Ronald L. Bishop
   1987   The Manufacture of the Salado Polychromes. *Pottery Southwest* 14(4):1–4.
Doelle, William H.
   1980   *Past Adaptive Patterns in Western Papagueria: An Archaeological Study of Nonriverine Resource Use.* Ph.D. dissertation, University of Arizona, Tucson.

Doyel, David E.
   1977   *Classic Period Hohokam in the Escalante Ruin Group.* Ph.D. dissertation, Department of Anthropology, University of Arizona, Tucson.
   1980   Hohokam Social Organization and the Sedentary to Classic Transition. In *Current Issues in Hohokam Prehistory,* edited by David E. Doyel and Fred Plog, pp. 23–40. Anthropological Research Papers 23. Arizona State University, Tempe.
   1987   The Role of Commerce in Hohokam Society. Paper presented at the Advanced Seminar, Cultural Complexity in the Arid Southwest: The Hohokam and Chacoan Regional Systems. School of American Research, Santa Fe.

Doyel, David E., and Mark D. Elson
   1985   *Hohokam Settlement and Economic Systems in the Central New River Drainage, Arizona.* Publications in Archaeology 4. Soil Systems, Phoenix.

Drennan, Robert D.
   1976   Religion and Social Evolution in Formative Mesoamerica. In *The Early Mesoamerican Village,* edited by Kent V. Flannery, pp. 345–363. Academic Press, New York.

Earle, Timothy
   1982   Prehistoric Economics and the Archaeology of Exchange. In *Contexts for Prehistoric Exchange,* edited by Jonathan Ericson and Timothy Earle, pp. 1–11. Academic Press, New York.

Ebinger, Michael
   1984   X-ray Fluorescence Analysis of Hohokam Lithics. In *Archaeology Along the Salt-Gila Aqueduct, Central Arizona Project,* vol. 8, Material Culture, edited by Lynn S. Teague and Patricia L. Crown, pp. 445–452. Arizona State Museum Archaeological Series 150. University of Arizona, Tucson.

Fish, Paul, and Suzanne K. Fish
   1977   *Verde Valley Archaeology: Review and Perspective.* Museum of Northern Arizona Research Papers 8. Flagstaff.

Fish, Paul R., Suzanne K. Fish, John Madsen, Charles Miksicek, Christine Szuter, and John Field
   1987   A Long-term Pioneer Adaptation in the Tucson Basin. Paper presented at the 1987 Hohokam Symposium. Arizona State University, Tempe.

Fish, Paul R., Peter J. Pilles, Jr., and Suzanne K. Fish
   1980   Colonies, Traders, and Traits: The Hohokam in the North. In *Current Issues in Hohokam Prehistory,* edited by David Doyel and Fred Plog, pp. 151–175. Anthropological Research Papers 23. Arizona State University, Tempe.

Ford, Richard I.
   1972   Barter, Gift, or Violence: An Analysis of Tewa Intertribal Exchange. In *Social Exchange and Interaction,* edited by E. N. Wilmsen, pp. 21–45. Anthropological Papers 46. Museum of Anthropology, University of Michigan, Ann Arbor.

Gasser, Robert, and Charles Miksicek
   1985   The Specialists: A Reappraisal of Hohokam Exchange and the Archaeobotanical Record. In *Proceedings of the 1983 Hohokam Symposium,* edited by A. E. Dittert, Jr. and D. E. Dove, pp. 483–498. Arizona Archaeological Society Occasional Paper 2(2). Phoenix.

Gladwin, Harold S., Emil W. Haury, E. B. Sayles, and Nora Gladwin
  1937   *Excavations at Snaketown: Material Culture.* Medallion Papers 25. Gila Pueblo, Globe.
Gregory, David A.
  1982   The Morphology of Platform Mounds and the Structure of Classic Period Hohokam Sites. Paper presented at the 47th Annual Meeting of the Society for American Archaeology, Minneapolis.
Gregory, David A., and Fred L. Nials
  1985   Observations Concerning the Distribution of Classic Period Hohokam Platform Mounds. In *Proceedings of the 1983 Hohokam Symposium,* edited by Alfred E. Dittert, Jr. and Donald Dove, pp. 373–389. Arizona Archaeological Society Occasional Paper 2. Phoenix.
Hargrave, Lyndon L.
  1970   *Mexican Macaws: Comparative Osteology and Survey of Remains from the Southwest.* University of Arizona Anthropological Paper 20. Tucson.
Haury, Emil W.
  1976   *The Hohokam: Desert Farmers and Craftsmen.* University of Arizona Press, Tucson.
Hawley, Fred
  1953   The Manufacture of Copper Bells Found in Southwestern Sites. *Southwestern Journal of Anthropology* 9:99–111.
Hayden, Julian D.
  1972   Hohokam Petroglyphs of the Sierra Pinacate, Sonora and the Hohokam Shell Expeditions. *The Kiva* 37(2):74–83.
Hodder, Ian
  1982   Toward a Contextual Approach to Prehistoric Exchange. In *Contexts for Prehistoric Exchange,* edited by Jonathan Ericson and Timothy Earle, pp. 199–299. Academic Press, New York.
Howard, Ann Valdo
  1983   *The Organization of Interregional Shell Production and Exchange within Southwestern Arizona.* Master's thesis, Department of Anthropology, Arizona State University, Tempe.
  1985   A Reconstruction of Hohokam Interregional Shell Production and Exchange within Southwestern Arizona. In *Proceedings of the 1983 Hohokam Symposium,* edited by A. E. Dittert, Jr. and D. E. Dove, pp. 459–472. Arizona Archaeological Society Occasional Paper 2(2). Phoenix.
Huckell, Bruce B.
  1984   *The Archaic Occupation of the Rosemont Area, Northern Santa Rita Mountains, Southeastern Arizona.* Arizona State Museum Archaeological Series 147. University of Arizona, Tucson.
  1987   Agriculture and Late Archaic Settlements in the River Valleys of Southeastern Arizona. Paper presented at the 1987 Hohokam Symposium, Tempe.
Judge, W. James
  1984   New Light on Chaco Canyon. In *New Light On Chaco Canyon,* edited by David Grant Noble, pp. 1–12. School of American Research, Santa Fe.
LeBlanc, Steven
  1982   The Advent of Pottery in the Southwest. In Southwestern Ceramics: A Comparative Review, edited by Albert H. Schroeder, pp. 27–52. *The Arizona Archaeologist* 15. Arizona Archaeological Society, Phoenix.

Lindauer, Owen
  1988  *A Study of Vessel Form and Painted Designs to Explore Regional Interaction of the Sedentary Period Hohokam*. Ph.D. dissertation, Department of Anthropology, Arizona State University.
McGuire, Randall H.
  1985  The Role of Shell Exchange in the Explanation of Hohokam Prehistory. In *Proceedings of the 1983 Hohokam Symposium*, edited by A. E. Dittert, Jr. and D. E. Dove, pp. 473–482. Arizona Archaeological Society Occasional Paper 2(2). Phoenix.
  1987  The Papaguerian Periphery: Uneven Development in the Prehistoric Southwest. In *Polities and Partitions: Human Boundaries and the Growth of Complex Societies*. Edited by Kathryn M. Trinkaus, pp. 123–139. Anthropological Research Papers 37. Arizona State University, Tempe.
McGuire, Randall H., and Christian E. Downum
  1982  A Preliminary Consideration of Desert-Mountain Trade. In *Mogollon Archaeology: Proceedings of the 1980 Mogollon Conference*, edited by Patrick Beckett, pp. 111–122. Acoma Books, Ramona, N.M.
McGuire, Randall H., and Ann Valdo Howard
  1987  The Structure and Organization of Hohokam Shell Exchange. *The Kiva* 52(2):113–146.
Morris, Donald H.
  1970  Walnut Creek Village: A Ninth Century Hohokam-Anasazi Settlement in the Mountains of Central Arizona. *American Antiquity* 35(1):49–61.
Neely, James A.
  1974  *The Prehistoric Lunt and Stove Canyon Sites, Point of Pines, Arizona*. Ph.D. dissertation, Department of Anthropology, University of Arizona.
Nelson, Richard S.
  1981  *The Role of the Pochteca System in Hohokam Exchange*. Ph.D. dissertation, Department of Anthropology, New York University, New York.
  1986  Pochtecas and Prestige: Mesoamerican Artifacts in Hohokam Sites. In *Ripples in the Chichimec Sea, New Consideration of Southwestern-Mesoamerican Interactions*, edited by Frances Joan Mathien and Randall H. McGuire, pp. 154–182. Southern Illinois University Press, Carbondale.
Nicholas, Linda, and Jill Neitzel
  1983  Canal Irrigation and Sociopolitical Organization in the Lower Salt River Valley: A Diachronic Analysis. In *Prehistoric Agricultural Strategies in the Southwest*, edited by Suzanne K. Fish and Paul R. Fish, pp. 161–178. Anthropological Research Paper 33. Arizona State University, Tempe.
Pires-Ferreira, Jane W., and Kent V. Flannery
  1976  Ethnographic Models for Formative Exchange. In *The Early Mesoamerican Village*, edited by Kent V. Flannery, pp. 286–291. Academic Press, New York.
Plog, Stephen
  1986  Mesoamerican-Southwestern Relationships: Issues and Future Directions. In *Ripples in the Chichimec Sea*, edited by Frances Mathien and Randall H. McGuire, pp. 291–300. Southern Illinois University Press, Carbondale.
Rappaport, R. A.
  1968  *Pigs for the Ancestors: Ritual in the Ecology of a New Guinea People*. Yale University Press, New Haven.

Ravesloot, John C.
   1987   The Archaeology of the San Xavier Bridge Site: Summary and Conclusions.
          In *The Archaeology of the San Xavier Bridge Site (AZ BB:13:14) Tucson Basin,
          Southern Arizona*, edited by John C. Ravesloot, pp. 149–154. Arizona State
          Museum Archaeological Series 171. University of Arizona, Tucson.

Rea, Amadeo
   1981   Avian Remains from Las Colinas. In *1968 Excavations at Mound 8, Las Colinas
          Ruins Group, Phoenix, Arizona*, edited by Laurens Hammack and Alan Sullivan,
          pp. 297–302. Arizona State Museum Archaeological Series 154. University of
          Arizona, Tucson.

Root, W. C.
   1937   The Metallurgy of Arizona and New Mexico. In *Excavations at Snaketown:
          Material Culture*, by Harold S. Gladwin, Emil W. Haury, E. B. Sayles, and
          Nora Gladwin, pp. 276–277. Gila Pueblo Medallion Paper 25. Gila Pueblo,
          Globe.

Sahlins, Marshal
   1972   *Stone Age Economics*. Aldine, Chicago.

Seymour, Deni J.
   1985   Evidence for the Production and Distribution of Artifacts at Snaketown.
          Manuscript on file, Arizona State Museum Library, University of Arizona,
          Tucson.
   1988   An Alternative View of Sedentary Period Hohokam Shell Ornament Pro-
          duction. *American Antiquity* 53(4):812–828.

Seymour, Deni J., and Michael B. Schiffer
   1987   A Preliminary Analysis of Pithouse Assemblages from Snaketown, Arizona.
          In *Method and Theory for Activity Area Research: An Ethnoarchaeological Approach*,
          edited by Susan Kent, pp. 549–603. Columbia University Press, New York.

Sires, Earl W.
   1983a  Archaeological Investigations at Las Fosas (AZ U:15:19): A Classic Period
          Settlement on the Gila River. In *Hohokam Archaeology Along the Salt-Gila Aq-
          ueduct, Central Arizona Project*, vol. 6, Habitation Sites on the Gila River, edited
          by Lynn S. Teague and Patricia L. Crown, pp. 493–657. Arizona State Museum
          Archaeological Series 150. University of Arizona, Tucson.
   1983b  Excavations at El Polvoron (AZ U:15:59). In *Hohokam Archaeology Along the
          Salt-Gila Aqueduct, Central Arizona Project*, vol. 4, Village Sites on Queen Creek
          and Siphon Draw, edited by Lynn S. Teague and Patricia L. Crown. Arizona
          State Museum Archaeological Series 150. University of Arizona, Tucson.

Sprague, Roderick
   1964   Inventory of Prehistoric Copper Bells: Additions and Corrections. *The Kiva*
          30(1):18–24.

Sprague, Roderick, and Aldo Signori
   1963   Inventory of Prehistoric Southwestern Copper Bells. *The Kiva* 28(4):1–20.

Teague, Lynn S.
   1984   The Organization of Hohokam Economy. In *Hohokam Archaeology Along the
          Salt-Gila Aqueduct, Central Arizona Project*, vol. 9, Synthesis and Conclusions,
          edited by Lynn S. Teague and Patricia L. Crown, pp. 187–250. Arizona State
          Museum Archaeological Series 150. University of Arizona, Tucson.

Underhill, Ruth M.
   1939   *Social Organization of the Papago Indians*. Columbia University Contributions
          to Anthropology 30. New York.

Vokes, Arthur
   1984   Shell in the SGA Assemblages. In *Hohokam Archaeology Along the Salt-Gila Aqueduct, Central Arizona Project*, vol. 8, Material Culture, edited by Lynn S. Teague and Patricia L. Crown, pp. 463–574. Arizona State Museum Archaeological Series 150. University of Arizona, Tucson.

Wallace, Henry D.
   1987   Regional Context of the Prehistoric Rancho Vistoso Sites: Settlement Patterns and Socioeconomic Structure. In *Prehistoric Settlement in the Cañada del Oro Valley, Arizona: The Rancho Vistoso Survey Project*, by Douglas B. Craig and Henry D. Wallace, pp. 117–166. Institute for American Research Anthropological Papers 8. Tucson.

Wallace, Henry D., and James Heidke
   1986   Ceramic Production and Exchange. In *Archaeological Investigations at the Tanque Verde Wash Site: A Middle Rincon Settlement in the Eastern Tucson Basin*, by Mark D. Elson, pp. 233–270. Institute for American Research Anthropological Papers 7. Tucson.

Weisman, Russell
   1985   Style and Technology in the Development of Hohokam Red-on-buff Ceramics. Paper presented at the 85th Annual Meeting of the American Anthropological Association, Washington D.C.

Wilcox, David R.
   1979   The Hohokam Regional System. In *An Archaeological Test of Sites in the Gila Butte–Santan Region, South-Central Arizona*, edited by Glen Rice, pp. 77–116. Anthropological Research Papers 18. Arizona State University, Tempe.
   1980   The Current Status of the Hohokam Concept. In *Current Issues in Hohokam Prehistory*, edited by David E. Doyel and Fred Plog. Anthropological Research Papers 23. Arizona State University, Tempe.
   1987   *Frank Midvale's Investigation of the Site of La Ciudad*. Anthropological Field Studies 16. Arizona State University, Tempe.
   1988   The Mesoamerican Ballgame in the American Southwest. In *The Mesoamerican Ballgame*, edited by Vernon L. Scarborough and David R. Wilcox. University of Arizona Press, Tucson. In press.

Wilcox, David R., Thomas R. McGuire, and Charles Sternberg
   1981   *Snaketown Revisited: A Partial Cultural Resource Survey*. Arizona State Museum Archaeological Series 155. University of Arizona, Tucson.

Wilcox, David R., and Charles Sternberg
   1983   *Hohokam Ballcourts and Their Interpretation*. Arizona State Museum Archaeological Series 160. University of Arizona, Tucson.

Wood, Jon Scott
   1985   The Northeastern Periphery. In *Proceedings of the 1983 Hohokam Symposium*, edited by A. E. Dittert, Jr. and Donald Dove, pp. 239–262. Arizona Archaeological Society Occasional Paper 2. Phoenix.

# •10•

# FOOD FOR THOUGHT: RECOGNIZING PATTERNS IN HOHOKAM SUBSISTENCE

▼▼▼▼▼▼▼▼▼▼▼▼▼▼▼▼▼▼▼▼▼▼▼▼▼▼▼▼▼▼▼▼▼▼▼▼▼▼▼▼▼▼▼▼▼▼▼▼▼▼▼▼▼▼▼▼▼▼▼▼▼

*Robert E. Gasser*
*Scott M. Kwiatkowski*

## INTRODUCTION

There has been a quantum leap in our understanding of Hohokam subsistence during the past decade due to the excavations of several significant sites and site areas preceding rapid development in southern Arizona. As a result, our knowledge is in a state of flux. We are on the verge of knowing a great deal more than ever before, but are awaiting the results, synthesis, and publication of several major archaeological projects. While the Hohokam may still be thought of as desert farmers (Haury 1976) who grew maize as their primary crop, the current data are beginning to illuminate the rich regional and temporal diversity that characterized prehistoric Hohokam subsistence.

In this paper we will elaborate on the responses of the Hohokam to water availability, ecological setting, and their participation in an economic network that involved the procurement and production of plant resources. Intersite variability in Hohokam plant use and possible reasons for differential plant use will be emphasized. Some attention is also given to faunal studies. The goal has been to develop a set of expectations for recognizing patterns in Hohokam food use at a regional as well as site level. By creating a series of generalizations based on Hohokam archaeobotanical and zooarchaeological data and historic plant and animal use, we make the assumption that the set of conditions that create them are always uniform. The generalizations presented in this paper will probably not always hold true, but they might serve as a sounding board for future work.

From the outset we recognize that several problems are inherent in archaeobotanical data. Plant parts preserve differentially, depending on their structure and method of preparation (Begler and Keatinge 1979; Cohen 1975; Dennell 1976, 1979; Gasser and Adams 1981; Greenhouse et al. 1981; Munson et al. 1971). Modern contaminants can be accidentally introduced into a sample (Keepax 1977). Components of the prehistoric seed or pollen rain can also be preserved and misinterpreted as economically important (Minnis 1981). Bias can be introduced by small sample sizes, the comparison of noncomparable contexts, and different processing and analytical techniques. Finally, random variation may cause "patterns," overrepresentation, or underrepresentation that can skew the archaeobotanical record or lead to erroneous interpretations.

We have taken steps to minimize these biases. First, sites with fewer than 20 flotation samples have not been considered; most sites discussed are represented by 40 or more samples. A variety of sampled contexts are represented from each site. In addition, we have emphasized recent projects that have incorporated standardized techniques for the recovery and processing of samples, and interpretations have been based on an awareness of the sorts of potential biases discussed above. Also, most of the observations made in this paper are based on the presence of plant taxa that researchers have considered economic. For instance, only charred remains in flotation samples are considered prehistoric.

# INTERSITE VARIABILITY IN
# HOHOKAM SUBSISTENCE

## ETHNOGRAPHIC RECORDS

Several years ago while gathering informant data for the Walpi Archaeological project (Gasser 1981d), the senior author was impressed by a statement made by a Hopi man about plant use on the three Hopi mesas. He said something to the effect that "we all use many of the same plants, but those Hopi on each mesa use plants differently." I wondered why this should be the case, and was especially concerned about the implications of the statement for the archaeobotanical record. The Hopi gentleman was inferring that we could not use data from one village and assume that similar results would apply to other, even nearby, villages. Implicit in this assumption is that the only way to understand plant use is to study data bases from several sites within a region. There are microenvironmental differences between the mesas that create variability in the distribution of plant resources and farmers from each mesa tend to practice different horticultural techniques (Bradfield 1971). Thus, differences in the local availability of plants and in farming practices could cause variability in plant use.

There are also culturally induced reasons for differentiation between the Hopi mesas. For example, the residents of the three Hopi mesas also practice craft specialization; First Mesa is known for pottery production, Second Mesa for wicker basketry, and Third Mesa for plaited baskets. All Hopis have the potential to do any of these crafts, but they choose to be more specialized. Further, certain Hopis apparently choose to emphasize growing some plants while making a decision not to grow others because they know their neighbors on nearby mesas raise that plant. By selecting certain plants or crafts, and rejecting others, the Hopi have created a supply-and-demand system. This selection process also enhances group identification by maintaining tangible differences between recognized groups.

The Hopi are not the only indigenous people exhibiting regional variability in plant use. Within the Hohokam area, each of the three traditional O'odham groups (Papago or Tohono O'odham, Sand Papago or Hiach-eD O'odham, and Pima or Akimel O'odham) occupying the Sonoran Desert used plants and animals differently. Part of the reason for the differential use of plants was based on ecological setting. The following discussion of O'odham subsistence is primarily summarized from Crosswhite (1980, 1981), but is also based on work by Castetter and Bell (1942), Castetter and Underhill (1935), and Russell (1975).

The Akimel O'odham lived along the middle Gila River and practiced irrigation agriculture as early as the late 1700s (Doelle 1981). Over half of their diet during the mid-eighteenth century apparently was comprised of maize, beans, wheat, and other agricultural products (a list of the scientific and common names of the plants discussed in this paper is provided in Table 10.1). The remaining 40–45 percent of the estimated subsistence ratios was about half mesquite, and the remaining 20–25 percent was about equally divided between hunting and gathering as one unit, and fishing and trade as the other. Proximity to a steady source of water undoubtedly influenced their subsistence regime by allowing agriculture to become a prime economic component. Mesquite bosques were often adjacent to the Gila (Rea 1983) and again proximity encouraged increased reliance on a plant resource.

The Akimel O'odham received many nonlocal plant resources through trade. The Tohono O'odham brought saguaro seeds, dried fruit and saguaro syrup, agave syrup, flat roasted agave cakes and bundles of agave fibers, prickly pear syrup, wild gourd seeds, wild chili peppers, acorns, and bulbs of wild lily to the Akimel O'odham as trade items. The Tohono O'odham also traded labor, pottery, baskets, and a variety of other items.

Table 10.1    *Plants Mentioned in the Text*

| Common Name | Scientific Name |
| --- | --- |
| Agave | *Agave americana, Agave* sp. |
| Amaranth, Pigweed | *Amaranthus* sp. |
| Bristle Grass | *Setaria* sp. |
| Brome Grass | *Bromus* sp. |
| Canary Grass | *Phalaris caroliniana* |
| Cheno-am | Chenopodiaceae or *Amaranthus* sp. |
| Cholla | Cylindropuntia |
| Common Bean | *Phaseolus vulgaris* |
| Cotton | *Gossypium hirsutum* var. *punctatum* |
| Domesticated Grain Amaranth | *Amaranthus hypochondriacus* |
| Dropseed | *Sporobolus* sp. |
| Globemallow | *Sphaeralcea* sp. |
| Goosefoot | *Chenopodium* sp. |
| Hedgehog Cactus | *Echinocereus* sp. |
| Horse Purslane | *Trianthema portulacastrum* |
| Huauzontle | *Chenopodium nuttaliae* |
| Jack Bean | *Canavalia ensiformis* |
| Lima Bean | *Phaseolus lunatus* |
| Little Barley | *Hordeum pussillum* |
| Locoweed | *Astragalus* sp. |
| Maize, Corn | *Zea mays* |
| Monolepis | *Monolepis* sp. |
| Mesquite | *Prosopis velutina* |
| Mexican Crucillo | *Condalia warnockii* var. *kearneyana* |
| Panic Grass | *Panicum* sp. |
| Plantain | *Plantago* sp. |
| Potato Family | Solanaceae |
| Prickly Pear | Platyopuntia |
| Purslane | *Portulaca* sp. |
| Red Dye Amaranth | *Amaranthus cruentus* |
| Saguaro | *Carnegiea gigantea* |
| Sand Root | *Ammobroma sonorae* |
| Scarlet Runner Bean | *Phaseolus coccineus* |
| Seepweed | *Suaeda* sp. |
| Squash | *Cucurbita* sp. |
| Stick-leaf | *Mentzelia* sp. |
| Tansy Mustard | *Descurainia* sp. |
| Tepary Bean | *Phaseolus acutifolius* var. *latifolius* |
| Tobacco | *Nicotiana* sp. |
| Wheat | *Triticum sativum* |
| White-seeded Devil's Claw | *Proboscidea parviflora* var. *hohokamia* |
| Wild Chili Pepper | *Capsicum* sp. |
| Wild Gourd | *Cucurbita* sp. |
| Wild Lily | *Allium* sp. |

In contrast, most Tohono O'odham did not have access to a year-round source of water for agricultural purposes, and crops comprised only about 20 percent of their diet. Most crops were grown locally under floodwater conditions; some were obtained from the Akimel O'odham through trade and exchange of labor. Trade, gathering saguaro fruits, and hunting each accounted for roughly 20 percent of the estimated Tohono O'odham subsistence ratios during the mid-1700s with mesquite and other wild plants contributing the remaining 20 percent. The Tohono O'odham have historically been associated with two plants, the saguaro and the tepary bean; the name "Papago" derives from the tepary bean. They tended to live in a bi-locational residence pattern, spending their winters near springs in the mountains and their summers farming along floodplains. They would camp at large stands of saguaro for about three weeks before moving down to their summer villages. Thus, the Tohono O'odham seasonally took advantage of at least three major microenvironments, the mountains, bajadas, and floodplains. Each provided a different set of locally available resources.

During the mid-1700s and early 1800s, a group known as the Kohatk resided between the homelands of the Tohono O'odham and Akimel O'odham in an area south of the Gila River (Cable 1988b). They lived in permanent or at least semipermanent settlements and depended primarily upon *ak-chin* (alluvial fan) floodwater farming for a major portion of their subsistence. Recent archaeological investigations on the Ak-Chin Indian Reservation showed that the protohistoric Kohatk raised maize, squash, wheat, cotton, and white-seeded devil's claw in their floodwater fields (Gasser 1988a; Gish 1988; Miksicek 1988). This group also depended heavily on mesquite as a food source; archaeobotanical and archival data (Gasser and Jackson 1988) show that mesquite was probably abundant in the local environment at Ak-Chin during the protohistoric and early historic periods.

Another group, the Hiach-eD O'odham, lived on the fringes of the Hohokam area east of the Colorado River and in the Sierra Pinacate in northwestern Mexico. This group is characterized by one particular plant, the sand root, that was gathered as a wild plant staple (Crosswhite 1981; Nabhan 1980). The Hiach-eD O'odham had a subsistence regime that was distinct from other O'odham; these nomadic hunters and gatherers depended more on small and large game, fish, shellfish, and arthropods than plant foods. Crops were insignificant in Hiach-eD O'odham diet. Mesquite, other wild plants, and trade comprised the remainder of their subsistence.

Cable (1988b) provides us with more evidence of ethnic diversity in southern Arizona during the protohistoric and early historic period. He draws upon archival data to show that there were several distinct cultural groups living in the region. Certain ethnic groups were not always confined within contiguous areas. The Sobaipuri and Maricopa tended to live only in narrow bands along major drainages, yet the length of the area occupied along these riparian habitats could be extensive. In determining ethnicity, linguistic affinity and geographical location tended to be the major criteria used by the indigenes to separate themselves into different groups. Based on the historic record, we should expect that ethnic and regional differentiation extended into prehistory. This could result in distinct patterns of subsistence within Hohokam subgroups.

In sum, it could be expected that what we call the Hohokam recognized dialectic and regional variation among themselves, differentially adapted to their unique environments, and, like the Hopi, chose to express localized differences in subsistence pursuits and material culture. In addition, the Hohokam could have interacted with people from other ethnic groups who also occupied the region. For example, there appears to have been a Yuman group who lived with the Hohokam at Las Colinas (Gregory et al. 1988). Thus, when we refer to the Hohokam, we might not expect cultural homogeneity or pan-regional homogeneity in the subsistence base.

## INTERSITE VARIABILITY IN HOHOKAM ARCHAEOBOTANY

Regional and intersite differences in Hohokam plant use are readily apparent and have already been pointed out (Gasser and Miksicek 1985; Miksicek 1987). The following section elaborates the regional, and even local, variability in the use of foods by the Hohokam.

### Variability in Crop Production Based on Access to Water

Just as the historic Akimel O'odham who had access to a dependable source of water from the Gila River tended to rely more on crops than did other groups living further away from rivers, so apparently did the riverine Hohokam groups. For example, if one compares the importance values that Miksicek (1984c, table II.2.4, 77) attributed to maize from fieldhouses, farmsteads, and hamlets from the Queen Creek area to the importance values of maize from the same types of settlements along the Gila River, maize occurred more often at the sites along the Gila River. Using the same data, it is also apparent that the recovery of remains of agave, cotton, squash, and little barley grass was more prevalent at the Gila River sites vis-a-vis similar site types in the Queen Creek area.

*Maize*    Hypothetically, water availability should influence the ability of a group to practice successful maize agriculture. We might logically expect that if a site was close to permanent water, its occupants would be dependent upon maize and that dependence would taper off as site locations became more distant from permanent water. While there is some basis for this assumption (Table 10.2), maize presence values tend to be inconsistent within and among Hohokam subareas. Other factors, particularly stochastic processes, the use of multiple farming techniques, and the increased dependence on other crops probably account for much of this variability.

Table 10.2    *Presence Values of Maize and Agave for Certain Sites Mentioned in the Text*

| Region Site | Maize | Agave | Source |
|---|---|---|---|
| NORTHERN PERIPHERY | | | |
| New River Sites (40) | 53 | 0 | Gasser 1985b |
| SALT AND GILA RIVER VALLEYS | | | |
| Casa Buena (49) | 45 | 73 | Gasser 1988b |
| El Caserío (58) | 38 | 81 | Kwiatkowski 1989a |
| Grand Canal Ruins (96) | 38 | 93 | Kwiatkowski 1989b |
| La Ciudad (78) | 69 | 0* | Gasser 1981b |
| La Lomita Pequeña (47) | 23 | 89 | Kwiatkowski 1988b |
| Los Hornos (77) | 52 | 0* | Gasser 1982 |
| Escalante Ruin (28) | 64 | 0* | Gasser 1982 |
| Jones Ruin (44) | 36 | 0 | Miksicek 1984c |
| Las Fosas (69) | 40 | 48 | Miksicek 1984c |
| QUEEN CREEK AREA | | | |
| El Polvorón (50) | 38 | 2 | Miksicek 1984c |
| Frogtown S.C. (37) | 14 | 2 | Miksicek 1984c |
| Frogtown Sac. (35) | 26 | 4 | Miksicek 1984c |
| NONRIVERINE AREAS BETWEEN THE GILA RIVER AND THE TUCSON BASIN | | | |
| Brady Wash B (41) | 66 | 10 | Gasser 1988c |
| Brady Wash C (51) | 36 | 35 | Gasser 1988c |
| Brady Wash E (51) | 39 | 61 | Gasser 1988c |
| Brady Wash I (67) | 39 | 15 | Gasser 1988c |
| Brady Wash S (41) | 49 | 49 | Gasser 1988c |
| McClellan Wash (60) | 10 | 42 | Gasser 1988c |
| Picacho Pass (29) | 10 | 0 | Gasser 1988c |
| Va-pak (66) | 61 | 0 | Miksicek 1988, Gasser 1988a |
| Hind Site (55) | 49 | 2 | Hutira, in prep. |
| Shelltown (32) | 38 | 0 | Hutira, in prep. |
| Rancho Derrio (40) | 28 | 25 | Miksicek 1987 |
| Muchas Casas A (46) | 28 | 20 | Miksicek 1987 |
| Muchas Casas D (42) | 17 | 14 | Miksicek 1987 |
| Muchas Casas E (32) | 53 | 31 | Miksicek 1987 |
| Fastimes (41) | 37 | 0 | Kwiatkowski & Gasser 1989b |
| Hawk's Nest (42) | 26 | 2 | Kwiatkowski & Gasser 1989a |
| Waterworld (27) | 15 | 11 | Kwiatkowski & Gasser 1989c |
| TUCSON BASIN | | | |
| Dairy Site (100) | 64 | 11 | Miksicek 1987 |
| Dakota Wash (30) | 77 | 13 | Miksicek 1987 |
| West Branch (244) | 43 | 20 | Miksicek 1987 |
| Tanque Verde (186) | 60 | 18 | Miksicek 1987 |
| Cienega Site (120) | 14 | 11 | Miksicek 1987 |
| Hodges Ruin (27) | 59 | † | Huckell 1986 |

( ) Number of flotation samples used to calculate presence values.
*Samples analyzed prior to 1982, may have contained agave but was not identified.
†Found as a macroplant sample, not in the flotation samples.

In the northern periphery, the Hohokam who lived in the New River area (Doyel and Elson 1985) seem to have raised about as much maize as the Hohokam who lived in large permanent settlements along the Salt River (Gasser 1985b, table 7.6). Maize occurred in slightly over half of the flotation samples from New River (see Table 10.2). Gish (1985) found that maize pollen was also common at New River and in some instances, there were remarkably high maize pollen frequencies from single features.

The New River may have been a dependable source of water during the Colonial and Sedentary periods, but it probably did not carry nearly as much water as the Salt River. Why was maize recovered as often from some of the New River sites as it was from several sites in the Salt River Valley? One possible explanation is that the New River Hohokam utilized more than one agricultural technique. They apparently practiced a less intense form of irrigation agriculture compared to the Salt River Hohokam, but they also practiced multiple forms of floodwater agriculture (Green 1989; Rodgers 1985). By maximizing agricultural output through the application of multiple farming techniques, the New River Hohokam may have been able to raise enough maize to depend upon it as their staple. Thus, using a variety of farming techniques may offset the smaller amount of available river water.

Recent evidence from the New Waddell Dam project (Green 1989) shows regular occurrences of maize in Hohokam sites along both the Agua Fria and New River (Cummings 1989; Hutira 1989), but there is apparently more evidence of use of maize in the New River area. A variety of farming techniques were also practiced along the Agua Fria; apparently all were forms of floodwater agriculture (see also Nabhan 1983; Doolittle 1984). The Agua Fria is well below the terraces where most of the sites are located, which makes irrigation agriculture impossible in certain areas. For this reason Green (1989) believes that while maize could be grown locally, it was not as dependable a crop as it was along New River, where the shallow depth of the New River allows for overbank flooding and more arable land adjacent to its course.

In the Salt and Gila river valleys maize tends to occur in roughly 40 to 70 percent of the flotation samples (Table 10.2). The mean presence value for maize in these areas is 45 percent. Working on the assumption that maize is recovered from roughly half of the flotation samples from riverine sites, should we expect that lower values will consistently occur at nonriverine sites? No, just as in the northern periphery, other factors apparently influenced its use and recovery.

Another method of increasing agricultural productivity in a nonriverine environment was to practice *ak-chin*, or alluvial fan, farming. For instance, the late Pioneer/early Colonial period Hohokam who occupied Va-pak in the Ak-Chin area apparently grew quite a bit of maize (Table 10.2) and other crops (Gasser 1988a; Gish 1988; Miksicek 1988). Maize was also commonly recovered from Locus E at Muchas Casas (Table 10.2), another small village site located on an alluvial fan. However, data from other sites in the Marana area suggest that the use of maize was not as great. Sites on alluvial fans might be characterized as containing a variety of crops (Gasser 1988a; Miksicek 1987), rather than always having high maize values.

What about the nonriverine sites located near ephemeral watercourses where *ak-chin* farming apparently was not practiced? In these areas the occupants must have relied on simple overbank floodwater farming. Hypothetically, the recovery of maize from such sites should be the lowest. Based on the available data (Table 10.2), this assumption is true at a few sites (e.g., McClellan Wash, Picacho Pass, Waterworld) but does not hold for a number of sites along Brady Wash, within the Santa Rosa canal area, and in the Avra Valley. Even in such "marginal" areas, the recovery of maize is sometimes comparable to riverine sites. Generally speaking, it appears that most Hohokam tried to raise as much maize as possible, despite variability in ecological setting and water availability.

In the Tucson Basin maize agriculture appears to have been important (Table 10.2). The only site with less than a 40 percent presence value for maize in flotation samples was the Cienega site, a small farmstead at the base of the Santa Catalina Mountains. Perhaps this site is anomalous since the recovery of maize from other sites in the Tucson Basin is comparable to, or even greater than, the recovery of the taxon from sites along the Salt and Gila rivers.

*Agave*     Although charred agave was noted within *hornos* at Los Muertos as early as 1887 (Haury 1945:39), up until about 1982, no one recognized its remains in Hohokam flotation samples. Miksicek (1982) was the first to identify agave remnants within them. He (1984c, table II.2.4) also recognized its importance as a transplanted cultivar. Shortly thereafter its cultivation was recognized as associated with a series of rock pile features, roasting pits, and "mescal knives" on the slopes of certain bajadas in the upper Tucson Basin (Fish et al. 1985a, 1985b). Since then, charred agave remnants have been found at several sites. At least some of the cultivated Hohokam agave appears to have been *Agave murpheyi* (Fish et al. 1985a:109).

Evidence for agave cultivation by the Hohokam occurs within two seemingly disparate environmental zones. One of these is the bajadas of mountains in areas near where agave occurs naturally today (Fish et al. 1985b) and in habitation sites along ephemeral desert washes near those bajadas. For instance, the Hohokam who lived along Brady Wash west of the Picacho Mountains extensively utilized agave (Table 10.2). Agave may have been grown on the floodplains along Brady Wash; rock pile sites are nearby and agave may have been grown on the mountain bajadas as well. Agave did not occur in any of the Colonial period flotation samples from the Picacho Pass site located south of the Picacho Mountains, but remains of agave were in slightly over 40 percent of the late Sedentary/early Classic period samples from the nearby McClellan Wash site. In the latter area, agave was apparently cultivated in rock piles on the nearby bajadas (Ciolek-Torrello 1987). In certain nonriverine areas, agave cultivation appears to have provided an alternative to more extensive use of water-intensive crops such as maize.

Agave also seems to have been raised on or near floodwater farmed alluvial fans in the Marana area. Miksicek (1987, table 9.5) found fairly common occurrences of charred agave remains from Rancho Derrio and the different components of Muchas Casas (Table 10.2). But agave was not grown by the Hohokam in all nonriverine areas. For example, no agave was found in the New River sites, and only one feature at Ak-Chin contained agave (Miksicek 1988). In addition, agave was not abundant at Fastimes, Hawk's Nest, and Waterworld, located within the Tucson Aqueduct Project-Phase B corridor in the Avra Valley west of the Tucson Mountains or at the Hind site and Shelltown in the Santa Rosa area further north (Table 10.2).

The other locale where agave was apparently cultivated by the Hohokam is along major rivers. Miksicek (1984c, Table II.2.4) found that agave was common from Las Fosas, a hamlet along the Gila River (Table 10.2). Agave was much more common at farmsteads and hamlets along the Gila River than it was at similar site types along Queen Creek (Miksicek 1984c, Table II.2.4). Along the Salt River, agave was very common in the flotation samples from La Lomita Pequeña, the Grand Canal ruins, AZ U:9:24 (ASU) (Kwiatkowski 1988a), El Caserío, and Casa Buena (Table 10.2). At these Salt River sites the occurrences of agave exceeded 70 percent and were in as many as 90 percent of the samples. Lesser occurrences were noted from Las Colinas (Miksicek and Gasser 1989) and La Ciudad (Bohrer 1987).

In the Tucson Basin agave occurred in roughly 10–20 percent of the flotation samples from sites such as the Dairy site, the Dakota Wash site, the West Branch site, and the Tanque Verde Wash site (Table 10.2). The occupants of the Dairy site apparently utilized small alluvial fans for farming agave and other crops such as maize, while the occupants of the other sites probably farmed the floodplains of the Santa Cruz River and its tributaries.

In the bajada/ephemeral desert wash ecosystem, agave may have been used because it was a plant that grew nearby. Young agave plants could have been gathered at higher elevations in the wild and either transplanted in rock pile fields on the bajadas or taken to habitation sites along the floodplains and planted in field areas that did not receive much water. To a large extent, there may have been a need to adapt a wild plant because there may not have been enough water to always assure the successful harvest of conventional crops. In the desert areas where agave was commonly found in archaeological sites, maize was often uncommon or found in lesser frequencies than agave. Fish et al. (1985a) indicate that an area of rock pile fields in the upper Tucson Basin could be used to grow enough agave to supply the annual caloric requirements for 155 persons; agave may have been a mainstay in the diet of certain Hohokam who lived in these areas. Fish et al. (1985a) also provide us with reasons to believe that agave cultivation in the nonriverine areas may have been guided in part by local availabilty because rock pile sites are often near known natural communities of agave. Perhaps Hohokam in nonriverine areas that did not raise agave did not have local access to the plant.

In the riverine areas, a different situation occurred. The pattern that currently exists is that agave cultivation was considerably more prevalent along the major rivers, especially at certain sites in the Salt River Valley. Along the Gila and Salt rivers, the Hohokam had extensive canal systems and could bring river water to large fields of maize and other crops. However, the riverine areas were also more densely populated, and it may have been population pressure, and the knowledge that agave could be cultivated, that made the riverine Hohokam seek another principal crop. Fields of agave could have been located at the outer edges of canal irrigated fields; agave does not require as much water. Agave cultivation also has the advantage of not requiring much care once it is established and some species mature rather rapidly (McDaniel 1985). In addition, agaves reproduce vegetatively, making the task of reseeding unnecessary. Further, agave provided both a source of food and a source of cordage or fiber. Use of its fibers may have rivaled its food use. The riverine Hohokam may have acquired young agave plants through exchange; once they had it, the benefits of raising agave were enormous.

Part of the reasons for the differences in the occurrences of agave between the nonriverine and riverine sites could be due to differences in preparation and consumption behavior (Donaldson and Fish in press). For instance, it appears that many of the Hohokam farmers in the nonriverine areas raised agave away from the settlements and also apparently processed the agave in field sites, not in habitation sites. In the Salt River Valley, agave may have been grown closer to villages and may have been prepared within the village. Thus, such differences in behavior could account for the differences in the recovery of this taxa.

But why was there differential use of agave within riverine settings? Possibly because the Hohokam wanted to create differential availability in order to have a mechanism for exchange. Specialization in plant foods for exchange purposes was not limited to just agave (Gasser and Miksicek 1985).

*Cotton*    Cotton is a crop that needs a long growing season (150–180 days for modern cotton) with long, hot days, rich soil, and a sufficient amount of water; high yields of modern cotton can only be obtained with irrigation (Dennis and Briggs 1969:16; Ellwood 1954:11; Jones 1936). However, the Hohokam grew a variety of cotton (sometimes referred to as "Hopi cotton," *Gossypium hopi*) that could mature in about 85 days (Bohrer 1984:254; Lewton 1912:7; Jones 1936). Providing there is sufficient water available, southern Arizona is an ideal place to raise cotton because of its long, hot summers.

The archaeobotanical evidence from Hohokam sites shows that the distribution of cotton was not uniform (Table 10.3). Cotton seeds are almost never as common as maize or agave, but when they are found with any frequency, it is usually in large sites along the Gila or Salt rivers. To date, the

Table 10.3    *Some Charred Cotton Seed or Textile Occurrences at Hohokam Sites*

| Site | Total No. Seeds | x̄ No. Seeds per Sample | Presence Value (%) | Total No. Flotation Samples (No. Productive) | Date | Reference |
|---|---|---|---|---|---|---|
| SALT AND GILA RIVER VALLEYS | | | | | | |
| Snaketown | 20 | 0.465 | 21 | 43 | Sweetwater to Sacaton | Bohrer 1970 |
| La Ciudad | 2 (and 1 young fruit) | 0.004 | + | 533[a] | Early Colonial | Bohrer 1987 |
| Los Hornos | 1 | 0.250 | 25 | 4 (4) | Colonial | Large in Gasser 1980 |
| El Caserío | 5 | 0.071 | 5 | 70 (58) | Colonial | Kwiatkowski 1989a |
| Las Canopas | 1 | 0.036 | 4 | 28 (27) | Colonial | Gasser 1980 |
| Los Guanacos | (6 textile fragments) | | | | Colonial to Sedentary | Haury 1945 |
| AZ U:15:84 (ASM) | 2 | 2.000 | 100 | 1 (1) | Santa Cruz | Miksicek 1983f |
| Saguaro Site | (1 calyx fragment) | | | | Santa Cruz | Miksicek 1983e |
| La Lomita Pequeña | 69 | 0.986 | 4 | 70 (47) | Late Santa Cruz to Sacaton | Kwiatkowski 1988b |
| La Ciudad | 2 | 0.019 | 3 | 107 (78) | Sacaton and Sacaton/Classic? | Gasser 1981b |
| Las Colinas | (refer to text) | | | | Sacaton/Soho Transition | Miksicek pers. comm. |
| Jones Ruin | 14 | 0.318 | 23 | 44 (44) | Soho | Miksicek 1983c |
| Gopherette Site | 5 | 0.250 | 25 | 20 (20) | Soho | Miksicek 1983b |
| Escalante Ruin Group | 26 (and 1 textile fragment) | 0.929 | 43 | 28 (28) | Soho and Civano | Gasser 1981c |
| Casa Buena | 1 | 0.018 | 2 | 49 (56) | Soho and Civano | Gasser 1988b |
| AZ U:10:7 (PGM) | (2 seeds) | | | | Classic | Gasser 1976 |
| Grand Canal Ruins | 1 | 0.009 | 1 | 117 (96) | Classic | Kwiatkowski 1989b |
| Casa Grande | (numerous textile fragments) | | | | Classic | Fewkes 1912 |
| Las Acequias | (numerous textile fragments) | | | | Classic | Haury 1945 |
| Los Muertos | (raw cotton and 1 textile fragment) | | | | Classic | Haury 1945 |
| Double Butte Cave | (numerous textile fragments) | | | | Classic? | Haury 1945 |
| Las Fosas | 65 (and 260+ seeds in a macrobotanical sample) | 0.942 | 30 | 69 (69) | Civano | Miksicek 1983a |
| Junkyard Site | 4 | 0.250 | 25 | 16 (16) | Civano | Miksicek 1983d |
| La Ciudad | (431 seeds from 3 loci) | | | | Unknown | Gasser 1976 |

| Pueblo Grande | (7 seeds from 1 locus) | | | | Unknown | Gasser 1976 |
|---|---|---|---|---|---|---|
| QUEEN CREEK/SIPHON DRAW AREA | | | | | | |
| Siphon Draw | 1 (and 1 calyx) | 0.017 | 2 | 55 (60) | Santa Cruz | Miksicek 1984d |
| Frogtown | 6 | 0.061 | 6 | 99 (81) | Santa Cruz/Sacaton Transition to Sacaton | Miksicek 1984a |
| Rancho Sin Vacas | 1 | 0.167 | 17 | 6 (6) | Sacaton | Miksicek 1983h |
| Smiley's Well | 9 | 0.450 | 26 | 20 (19) | Late Sacaton/Soho | Miksicek 1983i |
| El Polvorón | 33 | 0.660 | 20 | 50 (50) | El Polvorón | Miksicek 1984b |
| NONRIVERINE AREAS BETWEEN THE GILA RIVER AND THE TUCSON BASIN | | | | | | |
| Gu Achi Sites | 3 | 0.103 | 7 | 29 (29) | Late Pioneer to Sedentary | Gasser 1981a |
| Ventana Cave | (69 textile fragments, 1 boll, and cotton yarn) | | | | Santa Cruz? to Civano | Haury 1950 |
| Waterworld | 4 | 0.085 | 11 | 47 (27) | Late Colonial | Kwiatkowski and Gasser 1989c |
| Muchas Casas | 12 | 0.100 | 5 | 120 (101) | Sedentary-Classic Transition | Miksicek 1987 |
| Marana Roasting Pits | * | * | 4 | 80 | Tanque Verde | Miksicek 1987 |
| McClellan Wash Site | 1 | 0.016 | 2 | 62 (52) | Soho | Gasser 1988c |
| Brady Wash, Locus B | 4 | 0.083 | 2 | 48 (41) | Soho | Gasser 1988c |
| Brady Wash, Locus C | 9 | 0.148 | 5 | 61 (58) | Classic | Gasser 1988c |
| Brady Wash, Locus E | 5 | 0.076 | 2 | 66 (60) | Late Classic | Gasser 1988c |
| Brady Wash, Locus I | 2 | 0.025 | 2 | 81 | Late Soho | Gasser 1988c |
| Brady Wash, Locus S | 3 | 0.068 | 7 | 44 (41) | Late Soho to Civano | Gasser 1988c |
| TUCSON BASIN | | | | | | |
| Dairy Site | * | * | 3 | 100 | Pioneer to Early Colonial | Miksicek 1987 |
| Dakota Wash | * | * | 5 | 30 | Early Colonial | Miksicek 1987 |
| Hodges Ruin | * | * | 33 | 27 | Rillito to Tanque Verde | Miksicek 1987 |
| West Branch | * | * | 3 | 244 | Early and Middle Rincon | Miksicek 1986a |
| Tanque Verde Wash | 8 | 0.043 | 2 | 186 (175) | Middle Rincon | Miksicek 1986c |
| Cienega Site | * | * | 3 | 120 | Middle Rincon | Miksicek 1986b |
| Dakota Wash Cremations | * | * | 9 | 11 | Tanque Verde | Miksicek 1987 |

Notes: Presence values are based on productive samples unless only the number of all samples was available. *Present but quantitative data not available. †Present in less than 1 percent of samples. a Approximate sample size.

highest presence value of cotton seeds from a site with more than 20 analyzed flotation samples comes from the Escalante Ruin group (Gasser 1977, 1981c) where they were the second most commonly occurring taxon, next to maize. At Escalante, cotton seeds occurred in a variety of contexts (different room types, in vessels, hearths, an ash dump, and a dog burial), which can be taken as evidence of widespread use. A rare charred fragment of a cotton textile was also found there.

Elsewhere, if cotton is present, it is generally found in less than 10 percent of the flotation samples. Thus, an occurrence (presence value) of cotton that exceeds 15 or 20 percent may perhaps indicate increased production of this resource. For example, the occurrences of cotton seeds from the Hodges Ruin in the lower Tucson Basin may indicate specialization for exchange purposes. Other examples of an unusual presence of cotton seeds were found at Las Fosas and at the Jones Ruin (Table 10.3) along the Gila River. By way of comparison, cotton seeds occurred in about 12 percent of the 490 productive flotation samples from Las Colinas (Miksicek and Gasser 1989). Cotton has been found in sites throughout much of the geographical area of the Hoho-kam, from the Salt River Valley to the lower Tucson Basin (Table 10.3). Cotton has also been found in nonriverine areas such as at Ak-Chin, Brady Wash, Gu Achi, and at Waterworld, but only in trace amounts.

In sum, wherever cotton occurs in over 15 or 20 percent of the flotation samples, it should be given attention as an indication of relatively substantial use of the plant and one should consider the possibility that it was raised in surplus for exchange purposes. Based on the available data, the likelihood of finding cotton as relatively common can be predicted by a site's proximity to a major river or canal system. It also appears that the Gila River was a center of cotton production. The Hohokam also raised cotton by floodwater farming, but apparently not to the same degree.

*Beans*    The earliest common beans found in a Hohokam site were in an Estrella phase context at Snaketown (Bohrer 1970). Domesticated beans (*Phaseolus vulgaris, P. lunatus, P. acutifolius* var. *latifolius, P. coccineus,* and *Canavalia ensiformis*) are relatively rare in most Hohokam sites, in fact, rare in most archaeobotanical assemblages from open air sites in the American Southwest. This is probably not due to their lack of use, but rather to their method of preparation—boiling until soft and then consumed in their entirety (see Munson et al. 1971), and their susceptibility to microbial destruction (Gasser and Adams 1981). Thus, whenever any beans are found, it is noteworthy.

Domesticated beans have been found at a few sites north of the Gila River. For example, they have been found at Escalante Ruin (Gasser 1981c), Grand Canal Ruins (Kwiatkowski 1989b), Las Canopas (Gasser 1982, table 1), Las Colinas (Miksicek and Gasser 1989), Snaketown (Bohrer 1970), and have recently been noticed by the junior author during archaeological testing at Pueblo Grande. However, the most common occurrences of beans are thus far restricted to the Tucson Basin and one could interpret the archaeobotanical record as evidence that the Tucson Basin was a regional center for raising beans.

Thus far the most common occurrences of beans have been found at the Tanque Verde Wash site (Miksicek 1986c; 1987, table 9.8). Tepary beans occurred in 32 percent of the 186 samples that Miksicek analyzed from the Tanque Verde Wash site; common beans were in 30 percent of the samples, and jack beans were in 11 percent. These occurrences were primarily from one catastrophically burned structure; however, this variety and presence of beans is truly outstanding. Other unusual occurrences of beans were found at the Dakota Wash site (Miksicek 1986d) where both teparies and common beans were found. For instance, common beans occurred in 5 of the 11 Tanque Verde phase flotation samples from the Dakota Wash site and tepary beans were in 3 of those samples (Miksicek 1986d). In addition, the macroplant contents of the Punta de Agua sites (Bohrer et al. 1969) are unique for the presence of tepary beans and jack beans in several storage jars. Common beans have also been found at the Dairy site (Miksicek 1987, table 9.8), the West Branch site (Miksicek 1986a), and the San Xavier Bridge site (Gasser 1987). Jack beans have been found at the Hodges Ruin (Huckell 1986; Kelly et al. 1978) and the West Branch site (Miksicek 1986a). Aside from the outstanding presence of beans at the Tanque Verde Wash site, it is probably significant that beans have occurred in most of the sites in the Tucson Basin that have been studied to date.

It is possible that microenvironmental factors (e.g., a slightly higher elevation and cooler temperatures than the Phoenix Basin, and more available moisture) enhanced the growth of beans in the Tucson Basin. It is also possible that cultural factors were involved, such as a decision on the part of the Tucson Basin Hohokam to emphasize bean production in order to better engage in trade, or the particular like of beans by a separate ethnic group. It will be remembered that the Tohono O'odham historically also relied heavily on beans, especially the tepary (Crosswhite 1980:5).

*Squash*    Like beans, squash seeds are rarely found at Hohokam sites. So far, the highest occurrence of squash seeds from a Hohokam site was found at the Dakota Wash site, especially within the Tanque Verde phase cremations (Miksicek 1986d). Squash seeds or rind fragments have also been found at sites in the Salt-Gila Aqueduct project area (Miksicek 1984c, table II.2.4) and at a few other sites, but always in low numbers. Evidence of squash is most commonly found through pollen analysis; even then, squash pollen is relatively rare. For example, Fish (1984:112) states that "Cucurbit pollen in SGA [Salt-Gila Aqueduct] Project samples fits a general pattern of sporadic occurrence and overall rarity in Hohokam samples. The record should not be interpreted as indicating limited use. . . ." Squash pollen did not occur in any of the Salt-Gila Aqueduct fieldhouse sites, but traces occurred in 5 of the 10 farmsteads and hamlets that were investigated (Fish 1984, table III.1.3). One would expect that squash pollen might be more common in the Gila River sites within the Salt-Gila project than in the Queen Creek sites, but the data are not convincing. Traces of squash pollen occurred in two of the four Queen Creek sites and in half of the six Gila River sites (Fish 1984, table III.1.3).

To date, the occurrences of squash seeds at Hohokam sites is sporadic. Occurrences of *Cucurbita* pollen (squash and possibly wild gourds) is more common, but never occurs in over 30 percent of the samples and is usually only found in trace amounts. When found, squash appears to often be associated with a variety of other cultivars (e.g., Miksicek 1987, 1988).

*Other Crops*    Bohrer (in press) has recently prepared a paper on wild plants cultivated or encouraged by the Hohokam in fields. These include agave, cholla, little barley grass, Mexican crucillo, tobacco, and a member of the potato family. In addition, Bohrer indicates that some of the wild Cheno-ams, other weedy annuals, and certain other native grasses may have been encouraged in agricultural fields. Little barley grass is one of the better known wild plants that was presumably cultivated by the Hohokam (Adams 1987; Bohrer 1984, 1987; Gasser 1981b, 1982). It has been most commonly recovered from sites north of the Gila River and rarely occurs in the Tucson Basin (Miksicek 1987, table 9.8; Table 10.4).

### Variability in Wild Plant Exploitation

Wild plant exploitation was perhaps more strictly governed by natural factors than cultural factors. However, like the indigenous groups who occupied the area in historic times, a few noncultivated wild plant foods were probably stockpiled and exchanged with groups who lived in other areas. Because nature played such a big part in the availability of wild plants, expectations can be generated about their distribution and use. Following are a few examples of what might be expected from the variable distribution of wild plants and human use of those taxa; others could undoubtedly be given.

*Cacti*    Cacti tend to grow better on well-drained soils and prefer the south-facing slopes of mountain bajadas. Therefore, it can be expected that cacti were aggregated (and more diverse) on bajadas in the past, just as they are today. Most cacti do not do well in compacted silty soils and they do not normally do well if given too much water. Therefore, the natural distribution of cacti increases toward the bajadas and is relatively low near floodplains.

The archaeobotanical record indicates that the Hohokam consumed several cactus fruits, especially saguaro, hedgehog cactus, and prickly pear (Gasser 1982, table 1; Miksicek 1984c, table II.2.4, 1987, tables 9.5 and 9.8). The Hohokam also relished cholla buds, as evidenced by the pollen record (Fish 1984, table III.1.3; Gish 1988). Limited activity sites are found in the bajadas that were probably used as specialized activity sites to gather the fruits and buds of different cacti (Goodyear 1975). In general, one could expect that the closer a Hohokam settlement was to a bajada, the more its inhabitants would exploit cacti (Cable and Mitchell 1988). For example, the McClellan Wash site was located on the lower bajada of the Picacho Mountains and yielded cactus seeds in over 30 percent of the productive flotation samples. Proximity to cactus resources undoubtedly influenced their use at this site. However, the archaeobotanical record shows us that such was not always the case.

For instance, the most common occurrence of saguaro seeds in any Hohokam site is presently from Snaketown on the Gila River. Saguaro seeds occurred in 88 percent of the macroplant samples from Snaketown (Bohrer 1970). Elsewhere, saguaro seeds rarely occur so often; however, they have been found in about 45 percent of the flotation samples from the Dakota Wash site (Miksicek 1986d) and were in slightly over 30 percent of the samples from the McClellan Wash site (Gasser 1988c). In another example, hedgehog cactus seeds occurred in 30 percent of the productive flotation samples from Los Hornos (Gasser 1982, table 1) and small cacti seeds occurred in 65 percent of all of the Sacaton/Soho flotation samples from Jones Ruin, a farmstead on the Gila River (Miksicek 1984c, table II.2.4).

Certain cactus products may have frequently been traded into riverine villages. In fact, they may have been traded in so often and in such high demand that their presence is outstanding at sites such as Snaketown. Thus, demand may outweigh natural availability, and where we might find an abundance of a wild product is not necessarily in the area that it is most abundant, but rather where the population was large and used to trading goods and foodstuffs. Of course, not all riverine sites yield evidence of much use of cacti.

Elsewhere, cactus foods may have attained importance in areas that were not particularly good for farming, even if those areas were not close to cactus aggregates. In such instances there may have been a need to seek out all available foods, and since cactus fruits and buds were within gathering distance, they may have been exploited more than at sites where more water for farming was available. As a case in point, the Colonial period occupants of the Hind site and Shelltown (Hutira, in prep.) within the Santa Rosa Canal corridor were able to raise maize (Table 10.2), but apparently grew few other cultivars. The only other cultivar at these two sites was a trace occurrence of agave, not enough to suggest that it was grown locally. As an alternative to heavy emphasis on crops, the Hohokam at the Hind Site and Shelltown apparently relied on wild plants, including cacti. Hedgehog cactus seeds were in over 30 percent, and saguaro seeds were in over 20 percent of the samples from the Hind site; prickly pear seeds were also present. Prickly pear seeds were in over 20 percent of the flotation samples from Shelltown; also present were lesser occurrences of hedgehog cactus and saguaro seeds (Hutira, in prep.).

*Mesquite*    Until historic times when cattle increased the distribution of mesquite by scarifying the seeds in their stomachs and depositing them over the landscape in their nutrient-rich dung (Humphrey 1974), the growth of mesquite probably was more restricted to semimesic habitats along watercourses, and where the water table was high. Huge mesquite bosques have been

Table 10.4    *Some Charred Little Barley Grass Grain Occurrences in Flotation Samples from Hohokam Sites*

| Site | Total No. Grains | x̄ Grains per Sample | Presence Value (%) | Total No. Samples (No. Productive) | Date | Reference |
|---|---|---|---|---|---|---|
| NORTHERN PERIPHERY | | | | | | |
| Ironwood Site | 3 | 0.150 | 10 | 20 (10) | Santa Cruz/Sacaton | Gasser 1985b |
| Carpet Site | 1 | 0.077 | 20 | 13 (5) | Mid-Sacaton | Gasser 1985b |
| Antelope Glyph Site | 1 | 0.036 | 5 | 28 (19) | Mid-Sacaton | Gasser 1985b |
| AZ N:16:46 (ASM) | 33 | 6.600 | 80 | 5 (5) | Sedentary? | Bohrer 1984 |
| AZ N:16:51 (ASM) | 1 | 0.500 | + | 2 (0)[a] | Sedentary? | Bohrer 1984 |
| SALT AND GILA RIVER VALLEYS | | | | | | |
| Snaketown | 20 | 0.465 | 21 | 43 | Vahki/Estrella to Santa Cruz | Bohrer 1970 |
| La Ciudad | 109 | 0.205 | 15 | 533[b] | Pioneer to Early Sedentary | Bohrer 1987 |
| La Ciudad | 89 | 0.832 | 44 | 107 (78) | Gila Butte to Classic? | Gasser 1981b |
| AZ U:15:84 (ASM) | 4 | 4.000 | 100 | 1 (1) | Santa Cruz | Miksicek 1983f |
| Junkyard Site | 8 | 0.500 | 19 | 16 (16) | Santa Cruz | Miksicek 1983d |
| | | | | | Sacaton and Civano | |
| La Lomita Pequeña | 6 | 0.086 | 11 | 70 (47) | Late Santa Cruz to Sacaton | Kwiatkowski 1988b |
| Las Colinas | (refer to text) | | | | Late Santa Cruz to Soho | Miksicek and Gasser 1989 |
| El Caserío | 50 | 0.769 | 24 | 65 (58) | Colonial | Kwiatkowski 1989a |
| Tempe Outer Loop | 3 | 0.008 | 1 | 358 | Colonial to Sedentary | Miksicek, pers. comm. |
| Gopherette Site | 3 | 0.150 | 5 | 20 (20) | Soho | Miksicek 1983b |
| Casa Buena | 2 | 0.036 | 4 | 56 (49) | Soho and Civano | Gasser 1988b |
| Las Fosas | 6 | 0.087 | 6 | 69 (69) | Civano | Miksicek 1983a |
| QUEEN CREEK/SIPHON DRAW AREA | | | | | | |
| Casas Pequeñas | 2 | 0.118 | 12 | 17 (17) | Gila Butte and Late Sacaton | Miksicek 1983g |

| Site | | | | | Period | Reference |
|---|---|---|---|---|---|---|
| Siphon Draw | 1 | 2 | 0.017 | 55 (60) | Santa Cruz | Miksicek 1984d |
| Frogtown | 5 | 5 | 0.051 | 99 (81) | Santa Cruz to Sacaton | Miksicek 1984a |
| Smiley's Well | 1[c] | 5 | 0.053 | 19 (19) | Late Sacaton/Soho | Miksicek 1983i |
| NONRIVERINE AREAS BETWEEN THE GILA RIVER AND THE TUCSON BASIN | | | | | | |
| Va-Pak | 2 | 5 | 0.027 | 73 (66) | Santa Cruz | Miksicek 1988 |
| Beeth-Ha-Ha-a | 1 | 7 | 0.056 | 18 (15) | Gila Butte/Santa Cruz | Miksicek 1988 |
| Picacho Pass Site | 1 | 3 | 0.031 | 32 (30) | Colonial | Gasser 1988c |
| Whip-it | 1 | 9 | 0.083 | 12 (11) | Colonial | Gasser 1988c |
| McClellan Wash Site | 8 | 4 | 0.129 | 62 (52) | Sedentary to Classic Transition | Gasser 1988c |
| Brady Wash, Locus B | 20 | 2 | 0.417 | 48 (41) | Soho | Gasser 1988c |
| Brady Wash, Locus C | 2 | 3 | 0.033 | 61 (58) | Classic | Gasser 1988c |
| Brady Wash, Locus H | 1 | 5 | 0.043 | 23 (20) | Sedentary | Gasser 1988c |
| Brady Wash, Locus S | 3 | 2 | 0.068 | 44 (41) | Late Soho to Civano | Gasser 1988c |
| TUCSON BASIN | | | | | | |
| Los Morteros | 3 | 13 | 0.125 | 24 | Rincon (?) | Holmlund pers. comm. 1988 |
| Los Morteros | 1 | 2 | 0.016 | 63 | Sedentary or Early Classic | Miksicek pers. comm. 1988 |

Notes:

Presence values are based on productive samples unless only the number of all samples analyzed was available.

[a] Grain found in pollen sample.

[b] Sample size and total number of charred little barley grass grains are approximate, and are based on data from Table 9.15, and Appendices 9A and 9B in Bohrer (1987). Actual number of samples and grains was probably higher. Two charred rachis joints and two charred rachis fragments were also found.

[c] Grain with adherent palea and lemma.

†Present in less than 1 percent of samples.

documented occurring along the Gila River (Rea 1983), and others occurred along the Salt River near what is today downtown Phoenix (General Land Office 1868). In addition, several large desert washes probably supported smaller stands of mesquite along their edges in the past. For example, Miksicek (1984c) has indicated that more mesquite was probably present in the Queen Creek and Gila River areas during the Hohokam occupation. The groundwater table in southern Arizona has been lowered considerably during historic times partly due to pumping for irrigation (Rea 1983). In the protohistoric and prehistoric past, the water table may have supported the growth of mesquite in places away from washes. For instance, at Ak-Chin the historic, geomorphic, and archaeobotanical records indicate that the water table was considerably higher and the growth of mesquite considerably enhanced compared to what it is today (Gasser and Jackson 1988; Schuster 1988). The presence of an alluvial fan that deposited its floodwaters on the area also contributed to the growth of mesquite at Ak-Chin. In sum, the preferred habitat of mesquite is one that receives more water than most desert areas; it is usually only dense where there is either nearby surface water or where there is a high water table (Shantz and Piemeisel 1924:758–759).

Mesquite pods undoubtedly were a wild plant staple of many Hohokam (Doelle 1976; Gasser 1982). Flotation data show that mesquite is often one of the three or four most common taxa recovered from sites (Gasser 1982, table 1). Since we know that the Hohokam liked mesquite pods, and tended to rely on them if locally available (cf. Felger 1977), it follows that the degree of use of mesquite by the Hohokam might be contingent upon its local availability. If well-watered areas with mesquite were near Hohokam sites, we should expect to find more mesquite from those sites vis-a-vis sites in more xeric environments.

Consideration has been given to the possibility that the Hohokam overexploited mesquite in areas around large villages, thereby diminishing its presence (Plog 1980:9). Crown (1984:93) tested Plog's assumption using the Salt-Gila Aqueduct archaeobotanical data and found that there was no evidence to support his idea in that area. She concluded that mesquite wood charcoal occurred at sites along Queen Creek and the Gila River throughout the occupation, and was most prevalent, in fact, during the terminal (El Polvorón phase) Classic period, a time when overexploitation might have diminished its use. Thus, degradation of the natural environment does not appear to have been an important problem (Crown 1984:93) and the presence of mesquite should be a viable indicator of available moisture and local availability. Therefore, the occurrences of mesquite should be greatest in riverine areas and should taper off in more xeric areas. Further, there might be variability in its presence within certain areas based on proximity to mesquite bosques. For instance, mesquite seeds and pod fragments were commonly found at Pueblo Patricio (Gasser 1985a) near an extensive historic mesquite bosque (Cable 1983) along the Salt River, but rarely occurred at La Lomita

Pequeña (Kwiatkowski 1988b) and El Caserío (Kwiatkowski 1989a) away from the bosque.

*Weedy Annuals*    Weedy annuals are forbs whose preferred habitat is disturbed ground; given a sufficient amount of water, they will flourish. Examples that grow in the Hohokam area are many of the Cheno-ams: pigweed, goosefoot, seepweed, and monolepis. Other weedy annuals are tansy mustard, horse purslane, purslane, locoweed, and globemallow. Disturbed ground that might harbor the enhanced growth of weedy annuals include agricultural fields, canal banks, abandoned structures, and floodplains.

In the Hohokam archaeobotanical record, Cheno-am pollen and the charred seeds of weedy annuals are ubiquitous. On a site specific basis, Cheno-ams seeds usually occur in at least 30 percent of the flotation samples but are often more common. Pollen spectra from Hohokam sites are often dominated by Cheno-ams.

The Hohokam probably ate the greens of weedy annuals when the plants were immature. During historic times, Cheno-am greens constituted one of the main articles of Pima subsistence, especially when available in the spring, and the people could stop relying just on stored foods (Castetter and Bell 1942:61). The record indicates that the Hohokam were also fond of the small seeds of weedy annuals; these were probably gathered en masse, parched, and ground into a multipurpose meal (Castetter 1935:15–16; Castetter and Bell 1942:61, 62; Russell 1975:68, 73, 78).

One also has to consider that not all of the remains of weedy annuals found in the archaeobotanical record were used by the Hohokam. A good deal of the Cheno-am pollen was probably part of the natural background pollen rain, and because some of these plants probably were growing within and around activity areas, their seeds might have been inadvertently included in features such as cooking pits and were subsequently charred (Minnis 1981). Despite the probability of a degree of prehistoric contamination, the archaeobotanical record nevertheless indicates examples of cultural use including numerous features scattered throughout the Hohokam area that contained relatively high amounts of seeds of charred weedy taxa. A few obvious caches have also been found. For instance, Miksicek (1987, appendix 9.1) recovered over 14 million tansy mustard seeds from one pithouse at Muchas Casas; about 25,000 amaranth seeds came from the same structure. Bohrer et al. (1969) identified large amounts of tansy mustard seeds, Cheno-am seeds, and stick-leaf (another weedy type) seeds from vessels within the Punta de Agua sites in the lower Tucson Basin. Most of these weeds were probably harvested on disturbed ground.

The Hohokam altered their surrounding environment primarily by establishing settlements and creating nearby fields, and thereby enhanced biotic diversity including the increased growth of weedy annuals. For example, the results of the Salt-Gila Aqueduct project show evidence for a considerable amount of ground disturbance around sites in that area and further suggest that the disturbance was beneficial to the plants as well as the Hohokam (Crown 1984; Fish 1984; Stein 1979). A historical example of ground disturbance beneficial to the biotic habitat has been documented by the creation and maintenance of Pima fields (Rea 1979).

Weedy annuals can be used as potential indicators of ground disturbance and, by extension, agricultural productivity. Minnis (1978:363), for example, has suggested that as more ground is disturbed, the growth of Cheno-ams will be enhanced. Therefore, increases in the occurrence of Cheno-ams can be used as indicators of periods of increased agricultural productivity.

There are, however, exceptions that suggest that Cheno-am production does not always increase at the same time as agricultural productivity. For example, there are indications of increased agricultural productivity through time at the Brady Wash sites (Gasser 1988c, table 28). Maize occurred in 25 percent of the pre-Classic sites in this area, in 49 percent of the Classic period sites, and in 56 percent of the late Classic period sites. Agave occurred in 23 percent of the pre-Classic sites, in 26 percent of the Classic period sites, and in 48 percent of the late Classic period sites. This seems to be good evidence of increased use of maize and agave through time. However, the occurrences of Cheno-ams decreased through time in the same site complex, occurring in 54 percent of the pre-Classic samples, in 21 percent of the Classic period samples, and in 19 percent of the late Classic period samples.

Tansy mustard appears to be more geographically restricted than the Cheno-ams by being far more common in Hohokam sites south of the Gila River than its occurrences further north. It was recovered rather frequently from sites in the Santa Rosa area (Hutira, in prep.), Marana area, and from sites in the lower Tucson Basin (Miksicek 1987, tables 9.5 and 9.8) but has not been found as often at sites further north (Gasser 1982, table 1, 1988c, table 28; Miksicek 1984c, table II.2.4). These data indicate that the Tucson Basin is distinctive for having more tansy mustard than most Hohokam areas.

Globemallow appears to be common at certain sites, especially at the Picacho Pass site and the McClellan Wash site where it occurred in about a quarter of the productive flotation samples (Gasser 1988c), but is not as common at most other sites. Where globemallow and other weedy taxa occur often, they may contribute to a "signature" of localized plant use.

Another weedy taxa that has a spotty geographical distribution is plantain. The Seri historically considered plantain seeds mixed with water a much relished food, ". . . the best food of all" (Felger and Moser 1985:354). Charred seeds from this plant, like tansy mustard, appear infrequently in Hohokam sites in the Salt River Valley and in the northern periphery (Gasser 1982, table 1, 1985b), but are more common at sites to the south, especially along Queen Creek (Miksicek 1984c, table II.2.4, the Gila River (Miksicek 1984c, table II.2.4), and Brady Wash (Gasser 1988c, table 28). The presence of plantain diminishes further south, however. Plantain was relatively rare in the Marana project samples (Miksicek 1987, table 9.5), in sites within the Avra Valley (Kwiatkowski and Gasser 1989a, 1989b, 1989c), and in sites within the lower Tucson Basin (Miksicek 1987, table 9.8). Thus, the only significant occurrences of plantain reported to date were between Queen Creek and Brady Wash. As such, plantain is a "signature" taxon of that area. An exception to the geographical patterning of plantain was noted by Kwiatkowski (1988a) at AZ U:9:24 (ASU) north of the Salt River in Tempe. However, some of the charred plantain seeds there were believed to be prehistoric weedy contaminants, due to a preponderance of plantain in the modern seed rain, and the lack of a historic analog for processing these seeds by exposure to fire.

Yet another weedy taxon exhibiting a limited geographical distribution is locoweed. This plant is usually absent or rare in flotation assemblages from Hohokam sites. However, two nearby, predominantly Colonial period sites in the lower Salt River Valley, La Ciudad (Bohrer 1987) and El Caserío (Kwiatkowski 1989a), contained abundances of charred locoweed seeds in various contexts. This plant was believed to be economically important at both sites, and as such might constitute an example of a temporally discrete local "signature" plant.

As we increase the archaeobotanical data base and refine our quantitative methods of looking at the distributions of certain weedy taxa, we will surely see other examples of restricted use of certain taxa. Much of the variability in distribution is probably caused from variability in the natural occurrences of these plants. However, the occurrences of some weedy taxa appear to be part of a larger pattern of the development of alternative exploitative strategies to overcome potential shortcomings in crop production.

*Grasses*     Charred grass grains are regularly found in Hohokam sites, but not in all sites and not in similar frequencies. They are often common enough to be interpreted as a food regularly used by the Hohokam. For example, charred grass grains occurred in almost 30 percent of the productive flotation samples from Los Hornos in the Salt River Valley and in 30 percent of the macroplant samples from Snaketown (Bohrer 1970; Gasser 1982, table 1) north of the Gila River. At the San Xavier Bridge site south of Tucson, charred grass grains occurred in almost 40 percent of the Tanque Verde phase samples and accounted for 30 percent of all charred economic plant parts from the Hohokam component of the site (Gasser 1987, table 18.4). Another strong presence of grasses was noted by Miksicek (1987, table 9.5) at the Marana sites, especially at Muchas Casas where dropseed was recovered from 38 to 48 percent of the flotation samples from the three loci at that site. Dropseed is commonly found at other Hohokam sites, but usually not in such high frequencies (Miksicek 1987, table 9.8). Unfortunately, many grass grains used by the Hohokam have not been identified to a more specific level. Aside from the previously mentioned little barley grass and dropseed grass, grasses that have been identified include brome grass, canary grass, panic grass, and bristle grass (Bohrer 1987, in press; Kwiatkowski 1989b).

**Variability at the Community Level**

Variability in plant use at large complex riverine sites might be expected because of increased social complexity. Should we expect such variability in nonriverine areas where it is assumed that social and economic systems were less complex? Further, should we expect variability in plant use within a particular nonriverine community? Based on analyses of two such areas, the answer to both questions is yes.

Gasser's (1988c) analysis from the Brady Wash site showed distinct differences among the macroplant assemblages from contemporary hamlets within that community. Controlling for comparable proveniences and similar sample sizes, the Brady Wash flotation analysis indicated that the occupants of some loci used a great deal of Cheno-ams, while the occupants of nearby hamlets did not. There were also distinct differences in the recovery of agave, maize, and mesquite from the different Brady Wash loci. Because potential sampling bias was reduced and there was no obvious difference in local plant availability within such a small area, it was presumed that the distinctions were due to cultural factors.

Miksicek's (1987) analysis of flotation samples from contemporaneous sites in the Hohokam community at Marana is another example of variability at the community level. There were distinct differences in the recovery of maize from the three loci at Muchas Casas as well as what appear to be significant differences in the presence of other taxa such as agave, amaranth, tansy mustard, globemallow, and saguaro. Thus, it appears that Hohokam hamlets within one community can exhibit variable plant use and it is assumed that these differences were enhanced by choice, perhaps to increase interaction with neighbors.

# DIACHRONIC VARIABILITY IN PLANT USE

Changes in the use of plants within Hohokam areas appear to have been minor when compared to the kind of regional variability discussed above. However, diachronic variability has been observed within five groups of domesticates or cultivars: agave, Cheno-ams, cotton, little barley grass, and maize. Evidence for an increasing dependence on nonagricultural resources during the Classic period will also be considered.

## AGAVE

An archaeological survey by Fish et al. (1985a) within the northern Tucson Basin found an increase in rock pile sites associated with Classic period habitation sites and Classic period artifacts. Because rock pile sites have been associated with agave horticulture in this area (Fish et al. 1985a:95, 1985b:107–109), it appears that agave cultivation may have become more important

Table 10.5   *Domesticated Cheno-am Types Found at Some Hohokam Sites*

| Site | Date | Taxon | Reference |
|---|---|---|---|
| Snaketown | Sacaton | *Amaranthus hypochondriacus* | Miksicek 1987 |
| AZ BB:13:224 (ASM) | mid to late Rincon | *Amaranthus hypochondriacus* | Miksicek 1987 |
| Grand Canal Ruins | Classic | *Amaranthus hypochondriacus* | Kwiatkowski 1989b |
| AZ AA:16:49 (ASM) Cremations | Tanque Verde | *Amaranthus hypochondriacus* | Miksicek 1987 |
| Las Fosas | Civano | *Amaranthus hypochondriacus* | Miksicek 1983a |
| Las Colinas | mid-Sedentary to post-Classic | *Amaranthus hypochondriacus* | Miksicek and Gasser 1989 |
| AZ AA:12:285 (ASM) | early Colonial | *Amaranthus cruentus?* | Miksicek 1987 |
| Rancho Derrio | Tanque Verde | *Amaranthus cruentus?* | Miksicek 1987 |
| AZ BB:9:143 (ASM) | middle Rincon | *Chenopodium nuttaliae* | Miksicek 1986c |
| AZ EE:2:107 (ASM) | middle Rincon | *Chenopodium nuttaliae* | Miksicek 1986c |
| Tanque Verde Wash | middle Rincon | *Chenopodium nuttaliae* | Miksicek 1986c |

during the Classic period in the northern Tucson Basin. Further support for this idea was found at the nearby Brady Wash site complex (Gasser 1988c), where charred agave remains became more prevalent in Classic period flotation samples compared to pre-Classic samples from the same area.

However, evidence for a corresponding increase in agave dependence during the Classic period in the lower Salt River Valley does not currently exist. It appears to have been an important resource at some sites within this area as early as the mid-Colonial period. Agave was present in at least 70 percent of the flotation samples from a number of sites recently analyzed within this area: the Colonial period hamlet of El Caserío, the late Colonial and Sedentary period hamlet of La Lomita Pequeña, the Civano phase compound at AZ U:9:24 (ASU), and the Classic period villages of Casa Buena and the Grand Canal Ruins (Table 10.2). Further, it may be speculated that the presence of numerous *hornos* at the site of Los Hornos, which had a large Colonial period component, probably indicates that agave was an important Preclassic food item there. Agave appears to have been commonly prepared in *hornos* (Mitchell and Kwiatkowski 1989).

## CHENO-AMS

Domesticated Cheno-ams are difficult to identify in flotation samples, and their pollen cannot be discriminated from other Cheno-ams. One of the primary characteristics used in the identification of grain amaranth seeds is their ivory color, which is lost upon charring (Miksicek 1983a:697). Miksicek has focused efforts toward the identification of possible domesticated Cheno-ams seeds at a number of Hohokam sites. He differentiates domesticated seeds primarily by their large size but also uses other morphological characteristics.

The presence of domesticated Cheno-ams appears to be primarily a mid-Sedentary through Classic period phenomenon (Bohrer in press; Miksicek 1987:208; Table 10.5). Miksicek provides two alternative explanations for their emergence. First, perhaps large-seeded varieties of locally occurring wild species were either unconsciously or deliberately selected. Mean seed size then should slowly increase through time. A second possibility is that the increase in seed size reflects a gradual introduction of domesticated types from further south combined with germplasm from local, wild relatives. In either case, these explanations reflect "significant levels of interaction between human and amaranth populations, beyond the simple act of collecting wild species for food" (Miksicek 1987:208).

## COTTON

The use of cotton by the Hohokam occurred as early as the Sweetwater phase at Snaketown (Table 10.3). Its use is well represented during the Colonial period, where it was present in sites within the lower Salt River Valley, the Tucson Basin, and the Queen Creek/Siphon Draw area. Its use continues throughout the Sedentary and Classic periods, and may have peaked during the Classic period in the Gila River area, particularly at large sites such as the Escalante Ruin group and Las Fosas.

Although variability in the use of cotton through time is not particularly striking, this plant is nevertheless temporally significant because the Hohokam area exhibits the greatest antiquity for the presence of its seeds in any region north of Mexico (Ford 1985:354). Although cotton products were present in the Kayenta Anasazi region as early as the eighth century A.D., Ford (1985:354) believes that the absence of bolls and seeds outside the Hohokam area prior to A.D. 1100 may indicate that cotton cordage and textiles were traded to the Anasazi and Mogollon before the plant was cultivated in these areas. The earliest presence of cotton seeds north of the Hohokam area apparently derives from Antelope House (Magers 1975) and the Mimbres area (Minnis 1985). Therefore, it appears that the Hohokam were the source for the early distribution of cotton cordage and textiles, and later for the distribution of its seed to the north and east.

## LITTLE BARLEY GRASS

Charred little barley grass grains have occurred most commonly within Colonial and Sedentary period contexts. They are relatively uncommon during both the Pioneer and Classic periods. Grains from this taxon have been recovered in Pioneer period proveniences only from Snaketown and La Ciudad (Table 10.4).

Charred little barley grass grains are often rare in Classic period contexts, especially within the lower Salt River Valley. In the lower Salt, no little barley grass was recovered from the Classic period Grand Canal Ruins, or the Civano phase site AZ U:9:24 (ASU), and a total of two "cf." grains were recovered in flotation samples from the Classic period site of Casa Buena. Barley was most common in the late Santa Cruz phase contexts at Las Colinas, although it continued to occur through the Soho phase (C. H. Miksicek, personal communication, 1988).

In the Gila River area, no charred little barley grass grains were recovered from the Classic period sites within the Escalante Ruin group or from El Polvorón. The current data appear to indicate that the use of little barley grass may have been important in the Queen Creek/Siphon Draw and Gila River areas longer than in other areas. As can be seen from Table 10.4, a number of sites in these areas contained charred grains from this grass in Classic period contexts.

It is unclear why little barley grass, which would have been a winter/early spring crop, apparently fell into disuse in the lower Salt River Valley during the Classic period. Presumably the harvest from such an incipient cultivar would provide a welcome addition during the leanest time of the year and during a period of high population densities. The current data do not suggest that its use was replaced by another resource, such as agave.

## MAIZE

There appears to be temporal variability in the races of maize used by the Hohokam. Archaic charred maize remains have been found at Tumamoc Hill (Fish et al. 1986) and from the Milagro site, Los Ojitos, and AZ EE:2:30 (ASM) (Huckell and Huckell 1988). These specimens resemble the modern race Chapalote (Wellhausen et al. 1952:54–58), a small-eared, 12–14 rowed popcorn. Grains that were probably from a Chapalote-like race, as well as those from other flinty types, were present in Vahki phase samples from Snaketown (Cutler and Blake 1976). Maize with larger grains, fewer rows, and more floury kernels, which resemble those used by the O'odham (Carter and Anderson 1945:315), were present by the Santa Cruz phase at Snaketown (Cutler and Blake 1976) and by the Rincon and Sacaton phases at several other Hohokam sites (Miksicek 1979, table 1).

On the regional level, good evidence for temporal changes in the dependence on maize has not yet been found. Gasser and Miksicek (1985:487) compared the ubiquity of ten commonly occurring plants at 15 Hohokam sites and concluded that "the only species that approaches uniform use is *Zea*, or maize, but its presence values still have a wide range." Further, maize agriculture appears to have been important from the beginning of the Hohokam sequence. For example, besides the Vahki phase maize from Snaketown, Cable (1988a) found that the presence values of maize from the Pioneer period component of Pueblo Patricio in present day Phoenix were comparable to those at later sites in the area. Finally, Mitchell (1989) has recently evaluated the evidence for the intensification of maize agriculture by comparing the presence values of maize from several pre-Classic and Classic period sites in the Salt River Valley and found no evidence for increased maize dependence through time.

## CLASSIC PERIOD PLANT
## RESOURCE DIVERSIFICATION

Hohokam archaeologists have postulated for over 30 years that the Classic period may have been a time of increasing dependence on nonagricultural resources (Doyel 1981:46). However, until recently archaeobotanical data have been too meager to convincingly address this question. The current data do not support such a trend. Doyel (1981) found no convincing evidence for increasing dependence on wild plant foods at the Escalante Ruin group, and Crown (1984:112) found that both the subsistence base and the agricultural technology remained relatively stable from the Gila Butte phase through the late Classic period in the Salt-Gila project area. Moreover, Mitchell (1989) has recently used linear regression analyses on pre-Classic and Classic period flotation data from both the Salt River Valley and the Salt-Gila project area. Plotting the number of taxa identified versus the total number of liters sampled, he found no strong pattern of increased taxonomic diversity through time.

## FAUNAL EXPLOITATION

Variability in the hunting and use of animals for meat protein by the Hohokam seems to have been as variable as plant use (Bayham and Hatch 1985; Hatch et al. 1987; James 1987; Szuter 1984). Most zooarchaeologists working in the Hohokam area find many of the same taxa present at sites, but in different proportions. Although a significant portion of most Hohokam faunal assemblages is usually unidentified, or identified only as mammal bone because of the vagaries of preservation, if one has to generalize about economic fauna, it can be stated that Lagomorpha, especially jackrabbits (*Lepus californicus, L. alleni*) and cottontails (*Sylvilagus audubonii*), are most common. Another order that is usually represented is the Artiodactyla, especially deer (*Odocoileus* spp.) and bighorn sheep (*Ovis canadensis*). Antelope (*Antilocapra americana*) were rarely hunted. Other mammals that are commonly found in Hohokam sites are rodents (Rodentia) but these are often interpreted as intrusive. Mammals (Mammalia) always constitute the bulk of a Hohokam faunal assemblage. Birds (Aves) and carnivores (Carnivora) are usually recovered, and were probably economic, but they comprise only a fraction of the total.

Based on their analysis of Sedentary period faunal evidence from the Miami Wash Project near Globe, two sites along Tonto Creek, and the nine New River sites, Bayham and Hatch (1985) found that upland Hohokam sites located close to optimal artiodactyl habitat contained a greater proportion of artiodactyls relative to lagomorphs. At these sites, the artiodactyl to lago-morph (A/L) proportions ranged from about 0.30 to 0.40. They also noted that the faunal material from the ceramic-bearing levels of Ventana Cave had A/L proportions of 1.40 to almost 1.80, evidence that Bayham (1982) inter-preted as activity specialization. Thus, certain Hohokam sites, at least spe-cialized activity sites, functioned as locales for the procurement and butchering of deer and other big game.

Artiodactyls are found at some large Hohokam villages, but not all. For example, Bayham and Hatch (1985) evaluated the Sedentary period faunal assemblage from Snaketown (Greene and Mathews 1976) and concluded that the A/L proportions were slightly less than 0.30. In contrast, Sedentary period villages and hamlets along the Salt-Gila Aqueduct (Szuter 1984) yielded A/L indices that were consistently less than 0.05; farmsteads and fieldhouses con-tained even less big game relative to the lagomorphs. This may indicate selective access to bigger game at the larger, more important Hohokam villages such as Snaketown. However, during the Classic period, there is evidence from the Salt-Gila Aqueduct villages that suggests that artiodactyls became more important in the diet, comparable to the recovery of that taxa from earlier contexts at Snaketown (Szuter 1984). At other village sites, such as La Ciudad in the Salt River Valley, the overwhelming majority of the identified bones were lagomorphs, especially jackrabbits (Hatch et al. 1987). At La Ciu-dad, the small number of prehistoric deer and the absence of bighorn sheep is unusual (Hatch et al. 1987:249).

In the Marana project area, James (1987) found that jackrabbits were the most common taxa in the late Sedentary–early Classic period sites; these were followed by bighorn sheep, deer, and cottontails. James found that the Marana lagomorph remains often lacked cranial elements and he postulated that the prehistoric hunters dismembered the heads of rabbits before using the meat inside of structures. In contrast, it appears that the skulls of bighorn sheep were used and were selected for nonfood uses at the habitation sites. Other-wise, James noted that most of the artiodactyl bone probably was a result of selective butchering, where only high meat-yielding body parts were trans-ported to residential sites.

Recently Szuter (in press) concluded that the Hohokam as horticulturalists modified their environment, and in so doing, adapted their hunting behavior to primarily exploit game that were preying on crops. Jackrabbits were a prime objective of garden hunting. They prefer barren fields or similar open habitats for a quick escape while cottontails prefer to hide in and roam near dense vegetation, such as along washes. Thus, the relative proportions of jackrabbits to cottontails may be partly influenced by areas cleared for fields; hypothetically, as more land is cleared for fields, the jackrabbit population will increase (Bayham 1976; Szuter in press). However, it also follows that when fully mature, some gardens may have temporarily been preferred habitats for cottontails because of the dense growth (Rea 1979).

To support her model of Hohokam garden hunting, Szuter (in press) discusses five major trends in Hohokam faunal exploitation: (1) a reliance on small and medium-sized mammals; (2) the use of rodents as food; (3) the presence of water-dependent taxa (sometimes including fish) at sites with an enhanced, culturally modified environment; (4) a diminished use of cottontails through time; and (5) differential use of jackrabbits and cottontails at farmsteads versus villages. Szuter posits that the occupation of farmsteads made less of an impact on the environment, which in turn meant that cottontails were more available. Hence, the occupants of farmsteads exploited more cottontails (relative to jackrabbits) than the occupants of villages because cottontails were more readily available at farmsteads.

In addition, Szuter (in press) concluded that as opposed to upland sites, body parts of large game (Artiodactyl) from most of the lowland Hohokam sites are primarily cranial and lower limb elements. She postulates that these bone elements were saved for ritual and utilitarian purposes. Hunting deer and other big game was more complex than hunting small and medium-sized mammals in gardens. Big game may have been hunted further afield, or as Bayham and Hatch (1985) suggest, may have been butchered at upland sites and selectively carried home by hunting parties or selectively traded into lowland sites.

Like plants, it appears that a variety of factors influenced Hohokam procurement of animals. Availability was a key factor as was the presence or absence of a modified environment. In addition, there may have been regional economic motives as well as the need for the nonfood uses of the resource.

## SUMMARY AND CONCLUSIONS

Based on what is presently known, intersite variability in the recovery of macroplant and pollen remains from Hohokam sites can be expected. We can also expect the archaeobotanical data to pattern to some extent based on (1) geographical area; (2) farming practices; (3) proximity to permanent water; or (4) proximity to other natural resources. In addition, it has been suggested that the Hohokam created a modified environment around their habitation sites and sometimes overcame constraints imposed by the natural distribution of certain plants by engaging in horticulture of wild plants. It is also argued that the Hohokam artificially induced variability in plant food resources by choosing to restrict the growth or gathering of certain plants while emphasizing others to create supply and demand mechanisms for exchange. Different ethnic groups probably comprised what we call the Hohokam, and each may have had certain food preferences that add to the variability found in the archaeobotanical record. Finally, potential sampling bias and stochastic processes inherent in archaeobotanical data may effect "patterns" found in the archaeobotanical record. Natural factors undoubtedly had their influence on Hohokam subsistence, but cultural factors provided a dimension to the variability that we see in the Hohokam archaeobotanical record.

Hohokam plant use varied by region and may have been effected by ethnic diversity. The occupants of some regions either specialized in certain plants for exchange, had access to certain wild taxa that were not widely available in other regions, were in environmental zones that were particularly well suited for growing certain crops, or were constrained by local environmental conditions.

The Hohokam who occupied the northern periphery appear to have been able to raise enough maize to supply relatively low populations. In many respects, the archaeobotanical record from the northern periphery looks similar to data from the Salt River Valley. Macroplant remains of maize and maize pollen are regularly found at habitation and fieldhouse sites along New River and the Agua Fria. The presence of other domesticated plants is not pronounced. There is little evidence that the Hohokam in the New River area grew agave; however, agave was commonly recovered from sites along the Agua Fria (Hutira 1989). The reasons for the difference in the use of agave between the two drainages appear to be due more to local topography than cultural factors. It is not presently possible to compare more detailed distinctions in plant use between the Agua Fria and New River.

The occupants of sites that were along New River and the Agua Fria used mesquite frequently, but Hohokam who lived along other smaller drainages in the northern periphery apparently did not use much mesquite. At smaller sites elsewhere in the area, the presence of maize is often lower and there may be evidence of specialization in a wild plant resource such as cholla (Bohrer 1984) or saguaro (Gasser 1983).

The Hohokam who lived in the Salt and Gila river valleys grew large amounts of maize and other crops; some of these may have been raised for exchange. Agave was a mainstay at certain riverine sites as early as the Colonial period; agave cultivation continued throughout the occupation span but appears to have been more prevalent in the Salt River than in the Gila River Valley. Oddly enough, agave horticulture appears to be more pronounced at the riverine sites than in more peripheral areas. This apparent difference may be due to differences in production and consumption behavior.

Weedy types are frequently found, often in over half of the botanical samples, indicating ground disturbance for agriculture and the importance placed on these taxa for food. Many of the Cheno-ams were probably tended by the Hohokam in fields, and some were domesticated forms. Remains of cacti are generally not plentiful in riverine sites but are always present. They were sometimes more extensively used by the occupants of sites in upper elevations yet some of the highest occurrences of cacti come from riverine sites that are distant from cactus resources. Riverine Hohokam may have been more involved in exchange networks and probably placed a high demand on cactus products. In addition, there are reasons to believe that the Hohokam who lived along the rivers may have been among the first to experiment with the cultivation of wild plants. Often times there are distinct differences between the macroplant assemblages from sites within each river valley; each site may have one or more "signature" taxa that set it off from the others.

Away from the rivers, floodwater farming was more often the principal method to raise crops, although there is evidence to suggest that some of the earliest occupants of the riverine areas practiced floodwater agriculture. The Hohokam who lived in nonriverine areas were able to sustain themselves in a manner similar to many of the riverine Hohokam, yet they did not always have the means to establish large population centers. Some nonriverine Hohokam farmed alluvial fans. Examples are the prehistoric occupants of the Ak-Chin area, the Marana area, and perhaps the Santa Rosa area. Other nonriverine Hohokam practiced simple overbank floodwater farming. Examples are found along Brady Wash, Gu Achi Wash, and McClellan Wash.

When access to alluvial fans was the principal method of floodwater farming, the Hohokam grew a variety of crops. For example, maize, squash, and cotton were raised at Ak-Chin prehistorically and more crops were added during the protohistoric and historic periods at Ak-Chin. At Marana, prehistoric crop diversity is even greater than at Ak-Chin. These farmers also appear to have placed a lot of emphasis on weedy taxa. The Hohokam at Ak-Chin commonly utilized mesquite because it was probably locally plentiful. At Marana, mesquite was less important because it was probably less abundant locally. The use of cacti was not pronounced in either area.

With overbank floodwater farming in nonriverine areas, sometimes (but not always) less emphasis was placed on crops and the crop "deficit" was made up by use of wild plants, some of which may have been tended. The weedy taxa and mesquite were utilized extensively if locally available. In some areas, such as along Brady Wash, maize, weedy taxa, agave, and mesquite were the predominant remains; these macroplant assemblages were sometimes distinguished by a rather unusual emphasis on the use of plantain. In the Santa Rosa Wash area, a similar pattern existed for maize, mesquite, and the weedy taxa, but agave apparently was not cultivated; at the Hind site and Shelltown, grasses, cacti, and an emphasis on weedy types (especially Cheno-ams, tansy mustard, purslane and horse purslane) apparently made up for not raising agave as a supplemental crop. A similar use of plants was found at sites such as Hawk's Nest, Fastimes, and Waterworld in the Avra Valley. Maize was raised in the Avra Valley but there is not much evidence for use of other cultivars. The presence of agave was minimal at Hawk's Nest, Fastimes, and Water World. Weedy types, grasses, and cacti apparently made up for the diminished use of cultivars.

Plant use was different in the Tucson Basin. Crops were important and several types were grown. It is not unusual to find maize, beans, squash, cotton, and agave at a permanent site there. The occurrences of beans in the Tucson Basin are unique for the Hohokam area as a whole. Not surprisingly, weedy annuals (including Cheno-ams and tansy mustard) were also important as was mesquite and a few cacti, especially saguaro. Like beans, the Tucson Basin sites appear to contain more tansy mustard than most sites further north. The Tucson Basin area is similar to the Salt and Gila river areas except that crop diversity is often more pronounced in the Tucson area, and the production of agave is slightly less than the Salt and Gila River areas.

It is hoped that this overview of variabilty in Hohokam plant use will help future researchers gauge what to expect from different areas and will aid in generating more refined methods to explore prehistoric plant use in southern Arizona.

# REFERENCES CITED

Adams, Karen
   1987    Little Barley (*Hordeum pusillum* Nutt.) as a Possible New World Domesticate. In *Specialized Studies in the Economy, Environment and Culture of La Ciudad*, Part III, edited by JoAnn Kisselburg, Glen Rice, and Brenda Shears, pp. 203–237. Arizona State University Anthropological Field Studies 20, Tempe.

Bayham, Frank E.
   1976    Faunal Exploitation. In *Desert Resources and Hohokam Subsistence: The CONOCO Florence Project*, by William H. Doelle, pp. 110–121. Arizona State Museum Archaeological Series 103. Tucson.
   1982    *A Diachronic Analysis of Prehistoric Animal Exploitation at Ventana Cave*. Unpublished Ph.D. dissertation, Department of Anthropology, Arizona State University, Tempe.

Bayham, Frank E., and Pamela Hatch
   1985    Archaeofaunal Remains from the New River Area. In *Hohokam Settlement and Economic Systems in the Central New River Drainage, Arizona*, edited by David E. Doyel and Mark D. Elson, pp. 405–436. Soil Systems Publications in Archaeology 4. Phoenix.

Begler, Elsie B., and Richard W. Keatinge
   1979    Theoretical Goals and Methodological Realities: Problems in the Reconstruction of Prehistoric Subsistence Economies. *World Archaeology* 11(2):208–226.

Bohrer, Vorsila L.
   1970    Ethnobotanical Aspects of Snaketown, a Hohokam Village in Southern Arizona. *American Antiquity* 35(4):413–430.
   1984    Domesticated and Wild Crops in the CAEP Study Area. In *Prehistoric Cultural Development in Central Arizona: Archaeology of the Upper New River Region*, edited by Patricia M. Spoerl and George J. Gumerman, pp. 183–259. Center for Archaeological Investigations Occasional Paper 5. Southern Illinois University, Carbondale.

1987      The Plant Remains From La Ciudad, A Hohokam Site in Phoenix. In *Specialized Studies in the Economy, Environment and Culture of La Ciudad, Part III*, edited by JoAnn Kisselburg, Glen Rice, and Brenda Shears, pp. 67–202. Arizona State University Anthropological Field Studies 20. Tempe.

in press   Recently Recognized Cultivated and Encouraged Plants Among the Hohokam. *The Kiva.*

Bohrer, Vorsila L., Hugh C. Cutler, and Jonathan D. Sauer

1969      Carbonized Plant Remains from Two Hohokam Sites, Arizona BB:13:41 and Arizona BB:13:50. *The Kiva* 35(1):1–10.

Bradfield, Maitland

1971      *The Changing Pattern of Hopi Agriculture.* Royal Anthropological Institute of Great Britain and Ireland.

Cable, John S.

1983      Environmental Background. In *City of Phoenix Archaeology of the Original Townsite Block 28-North*, edited by John S. Cable, Susan L. Henry, and David E. Doyel, pp. 11–41. Soil Systems Publications in Archaeology 2. Phoenix.

1988a    The Processes Leading to the Adoption of Agriculture in the Phoenix Basin, Arizona. Paper presented at the 53rd Annual Meeting of the Society for American Archaeology, Phoenix.

1988b    Who Were the Protohistoric Occupants of Ak-Chin: A Study Concerning the Relationship Between Ethnicity and Ceramic Style. Manuscript on file, Soil Systems, Inc., Phoenix.

Cable, John S., and Douglas R. Mitchell

1988      La Lomita Pequeña in Regional Perspective. In *Excavations at La Lomita Pequeña: A Santa Cruz/Sacaton Phase Farmstead in the Salt River Valley*, edited by Douglass R. Mitchell, pp. 395–446. Soil Systems Publications in Archaeology 10. Phoenix.

Cable, John S., and David E. Doyel

1985      The Pueblo Patricio Sequence: Its Implications for the Study of Hohokam Origins, Pioneer Period Site Structure and the Processes of Sedentism. In *City of Phoenix Archaeology of the Original Townsite, Block 24-East*, edited by John S. Cable, Kathleen S. Hoffman, David E. Doyel, and Frank Ritz, pp. 211–272. Soil Systems Publications in Archaeology 8. Phoenix.

Carter, George F., and Edgar Anderson

1945      A Preliminary Survey of Maize in the Southwestern United States. *Annals of the Missouri Botanical Garden* 32:297–317.

Castetter, Edward F.

1935      Uncultivated Native Plants Used as Sources of Food. *University of New Mexico Bulletin, Biological Series* 4(1), Albuquerque.

Castetter, Edward F., and Willis H. Bell

1942      *Pima and Papago Agriculture.* Interamericana Studies 1. University of New Mexico Press, Albuquerque.

Castetter, Edward F., and Ruth M. Underhill

1935      Ethnobiological Studies in the American Southwest II: The Ethnobiology of the Papago Indians. *University of New Mexico Bulletin, Biological Series* 4(3), Albuquerque.

Ciolek-Torrello, Richard

1987      *Hohokam Settlement Along the Slopes of the Picacho Mountains: The Picacho Pass Sites.* Museum of Northern Arizona Research Paper 35(3). Flagstaff.

Cohen, M. N.
1975    Some Problems in the Quantitative Analysis of Vegetable Refuse Illustrated by a Late Horizon Site on the Peruvian Coast. *Nawpa Pancha* 10–12:49–60.
Crosswhite, Frank S.
1980    The Annual Saguaro Harvest and Crop Cycle of the Papago, with Reference to Ecology and Symbolism. *Desert Plants* 2(1):3–61.
1981    Desert Plants, Habitat and Agriculture in Relation to the Major Pattern of Cultural Differentiation in the O'odham People of the Sonoran Desert. *Desert Plants* 3(2):47–76.
Crown, Patricia L.
1984    Hohokam Subsistence and Settlement in the Salt-Gila Basin. In *Hohokam Archaeology Along the Salt-Gila Aqueduct, Central Arizona Project*, vol. 9: Synthesis and Conclusions, edited by Lynn S. Teague and Patricia L. Crown, pp. 87–114. Arizona State Museum Archaeological Series 150. Tucson.
Cummings, Linda Scott
1989    Pollen Analysis for the Waddell Data Recovery Project: an Examination of the Subsistence Base from the Agua Fria and New River Drainages. In *Settlement, Subsistence, and Specialization in the Northern Periphery: The Waddell Project*, edited by Margarie Green, pp. 801–850. Archaeological Consulting Services, Ltd. Cultural Resources Report 65, vol. 2, Phoenix.
Cutler, Hugh C., and Leonard W. Blake
1976    Corn from Snaketown. In *The Hohokam: Desert Farmers and Craftsmen*, by Emil W. Haury, pp. 365–366. University of Arizona Press, Tucson.
Dennell, R. W.
1976    The Economic Importance of Plant Resources Represented on Archaeological Sites. *Journal of Archaeological Sciences* 3(3):229–247.
1979    Prehistoric Diet and Nutrition: Some Food for Thought. *World Archaeology* 11(2):121–135.
Dennis, Robert E., and R. E. Briggs
1969    Growth and Development of the Cotton Plant in Arizona. *The University of Arizona College of Agriculture Bulletin* A-64. Tucson.
Doelle, William H.
1976    *Desert Resources and Hohokam Subsistence: The CONOCO-Florence Project*. Arizona State Museum Archaeological Series 103. Tucson.
1981    A Gila Pima in the Late Seventeenth Century. In *The Protohistoric Period in the North American Southwest, A.D. 1450–1750*, edited by David R. Wilcox and W. Bruce Masse, pp. 57–70. Arizona State University Anthropological Research Paper 24. Tempe.
Donaldson, Marcia, and Suzanne Fish
in press Production and Consumption in the Archaeological Record: a Hohokam Example. *The Kiva*.
Doolittle, William E.
1984    Agricultural Change as an Incremental Process. *Annals of the Association of American Geographers* 74(1):124–137.
Doyel, David E.
1981    *Late Hohokam Prehistory in Southern Arizona*. Contributions to Archaeology 2. Gila Press, Scottsdale.

Doyel, David E., and Mark D. Elson (editors)
  1985    *Hohokam Settlement and Economic Systems in the Central New River Drainage,
          Arizona.* Soil Systems Publications in Archaeology 4. Phoenix.
Ellwood, Charles
  1954    *Growing Arizona Cotton.* University of Arizona Agricultural Experimental
          Station Circular 222. Tucson.
Felger, Richard S.
  1977    Mesquite in Indian Cultures of Southwestern North America. In *Mesquite:
          Its Biology in Two Desert Scrub Ecosystems,* edited by B. B. Simpson, pp. 150–
          176. Smithsonian Institution, US/IBP Synthesis Series, Dowden, Hutch-
          inson & Ross, Stroudsburg, Pennsylvania.
Felger, Richard S., and Mary Beck Moser
  1985    *People of the Desert and Sea: Ethnobotany of the Seri Indians.* University of
          Arizona Press, Tucson.
Fewkes, Jesse Walter
  1912    Casa Grande, Arizona. *Twenty-eighth Annual Report of the Bureau of American
          Ethnology 1906–1907,* pp. 25–179. Government Printing Office, Washington,
          D.C.
Fish, Suzanne K.
  1984    Agriculture and Subsistence Implications of the Salt-Gila Aqueduct Pollen
          Analysis. In *Hohokam Archaeology Along the Salt-Gila Aqueduct, Central Arizona
          Project,* vol. 7: Environment and Subsistence, edited by Lynn S. Teague
          and Patricia L. Crown, pp. 111–138. Arizona State Museum Archaeological
          Series 150. Tucson.
Fish, Paul R., Suzanne K. Fish, Austin Long, and Charles Miksicek
  1986    Early Corn Remains from Tumamoc Hill, Southern Arizona. *American An-
          tiquity* 51(3):563–572.
Fish, Suzanne K.
  1987    Marana Sites Pollen Analysis. In *Studies in the Hohokam Community of Mar-
          ana,* edited by Glen E. Rice, pp. 161–170. Arizona State University An-
          thropological Field Studies 15. Tempe.
Fish, Suzanne K., Paul R. Fish, Charles Miksicek, and John Madsen
  1985a   Prehistoric Agave Cultivation in Southern Arizona. *Desert Plants* 7(2):100,
          107–112.
Fish, Suzanne K., Paul R. Fish, and John Madsen
  1985b   A Preliminary Analysis of Hohokam Settlement and Agriculture in the
          Northern Tucson Basin. In *Proceedings of the 1983 Hohokam Symposium, Part
          I,* edited by Alfred E. Dittert, Jr. and Donald E. Dove, pp. 75–100. Phoenix
          Chapter, Arizona Archaeological Society, Occasional Paper 2. Phoenix.
Ford, Richard I.
  1985    Patterns of Prehistoric Food Production in North America. In *Prehistoric
          Food Production in North America,* edited by Richard I. Ford, pp. 341–364.
          Museum of Anthropology, University of Michigan Anthropological Papers
          75. Ann Arbor.
Gasser, Robert E.
  1976    *Hohokam Subsistence: a 2,000 Year Continuum in the Indigenous Exploitation of
          the Lower Sonoran Desert.* USDA Forest Service, Southwestern Region, Ar-
          chaeological Report 11. Albuquerque.
  1977    Further Analysis of Plant Remains from the Escalante Ruin Group. In *Classic*

*Period Hohokam in the Escalante Ruin Group,* by David E. Doyel, pp. 248–
256. Unpublished Ph.D. dissertation, Department of Anthropology, University of Arizona, Tucson.

1980     Meeting the Demands of Population Growth: a View from the Hohokam
         Archaeobotanical Record. Manuscript on file, Office of Cultural Resource
         Management, Department of Anthropology, Arizona State University, Tempe.

1981a    Gu Achi: Seeds Season and Ecosystems. In *Excavations at Gu Achi: A Reappraisal of Hohokam Settlement and Subsistence in the Arizona Papagueria,* by W.
         Bruce Masse, pp. 313–342. National Park Service, Western Archaeological
         Center Publications in Anthropology 12, Tucson.

1981b    Hohokam Plant Use at La Ciudad and Other Riverine Sites: the Flotation
         Evidence. In Archaeological Investigations, Testing at La Ciudad (Group
         III), West Papago-Inner Loop (I-10), Maricopa County, Arizona, by Ronald
         K. Yablon et al., pp. 341–380. Manuscript on file, Arizona Department of
         Transportation, Phoenix and Museum of Northern Arizona, Flagstaff.

1981c    The Plant Remains from the Escalante Ruin Group. In *Late Hohokam Prehistory in Southern Arizona,* by David E. Doyel, pp. 84–89. Gila Press Contributions to Archaeology 2. Scottsdale.

1981d    The Plant Remains from Walpi. In Walpi Archaeological Project—Phase II,
         vol. 7, Archaeobotanical Remains, by Robert E. Gasser and Linda J. Scott,
         pp. 1–326. Manuscript on file, National Park Service, San Francisco.

1982     Hohokam Use of Desert Plant Foods. *Desert Plants* 3(4):216–234.

1983     Float Samples from NA15,909, the Adobe Dam Site. In *Archaeological Investigations in the Adobe Dam Project Area,* by J. Simon Bruder, pp. 241–252.
         Museum of Northern Arizona Research Paper 27. Flagstaff.

1985a    Macrobotanical Analysis. In *City of Phoenix Archaeology of the Original Townsite, Block 24-East,* edited by John S. Cable, Kathleen S. Hoffman, David E.
         Doyel, and Frank Ritz, pp. 391–394. Soil Systems Publications in Archaeology 8. Phoenix.

1985b    Prehistoric Subsistence and Settlement in the New River Area. In *Hohokam
         Settlement and Economic Systems in the Central New River Drainage, Arizona,*
         edited by David E. Doyel and Mark D. Elson, pp. 317–342. Soil Systems
         Publications in Archaeology 4. Phoenix.

1987     Macrofloral Analysis. In *The Archaeology of the San Xavier Bridge Site (AZ
         BB:13:14) Tucson Basin, Southern Arizona,* edited by John C. Ravesloot, pp.
         303–318. Arizona State Museum Archaeological Series 171. Tucson.

1988a    Farming, Gathering, and Hunting at Ak-Chin: Evidence for Change, Seasonality, and Comparison. Manuscript on file, Soil Systems, Inc., Phoenix.

1988b    Casa Buena Flotation Analysis. In *Excavations at Casa Buena: Changing Hohokam Land Use Along the Squaw Peak Parkway,* edited by Jerry B. Howard,
         pp. 561–586. Soil Systems Publications in Archaeology 11. Phoenix.

1988c    Flotation Studies. In *Hohokam Settlement Along the Slopes of the Picacho Mountains: Environment and Subsistence,* vol. 5, edited by Donald E. Weaver, Jr.,
         pp. 143–235. Museum of Northern Arizona Research Paper 35. Flagstaff.

Gasser, Robert E., and E. Charles Adams
1981     Aspects of Deterioration of Plant Remains in Archaeological Sites: the Walpi
         Archaeological Project. *Journal of Ethnobiology* 1(1):182–192.

Gasser, Robert E., and J. Brantley Jackson
1988     The Modern and Historic Environment in the Ak-Chin Project Area. Manuscript on file, Soil Systems, Inc., Phoenix.

Gasser, Robert E., and Charles Miksicek
  1985      The Specialists: a Reappraisal of Hohokam Exchange and the Archaeo-
            botanical Record. In *Proceedings of the 1983 Hohokam Symposium, Part II*,
            edited by Alfred E. Dittert, Jr. and Donald E. Dove, pp. 483–498. Phoenix
            Chapter, Arizona Archaeological Society, Occasional Paper 2.
General Land Office
  1868      Survey Plat of Township 1 North, Range 1 East. Map on file, Bureau of
            Land Management, Phoenix.
Gish, Jannifer W.
  1985      Pollen from the New River Project, and a Discussion of Pollen Sampling
            Strategies for Agricultural Systems. In *Hohokam Settlement and Economic
            Systems in the Central New River Drainage, Arizona*, edited by David E. Doyel
            and Mark D. Elson, pp. 343–404. Soil Systems Publications in Archaeology
            4. Phoenix.
  1988      Ak-Chin Pollen Study, Central Arizona. Manuscript on file, Soil Systems,
            Inc., Phoenix.
Goodyear, Albert C., III
  1975      *Hecla II and III, an Interpretative Study of Archaeological Remains from the Lake-
            shore Project, Papago Reservation, South Central Arizona.* Arizona State Uni-
            versity Anthropological Research Paper 9. Tempe.
Green, Margarie, editor
  1989      *Settlement, Subsistence, and Specialization in the Northern Periphery: The Waddell
            Project.* Archaeological Consulting Services Ltd., Cultural Resources Report
            65, vols. 1 and 2, Phoenix.
Greene, J. L., and T. W. Mathews
  1976      Faunal Study of Unworked Mammalian Bones. In *The Hohokam: Desert
            Farmers and Craftsmen*, by Emil W. Haury, pp. 367–373. University of Ari-
            zona Press, Tucson.
Greenhouse, Ruth, Robert Gasser, and Jannifer Gish
  1981      Cholla Bud Roasting Pits: an Ethnoarchaeological Example. *The Kiva* 46(4):227–
            242.
Gregory, David A., William L. Deaver, Suzanne K. Fish, Ronald Gardiner, Robert W.
Layhe, Fred L. Nials, and Lynn S. Teague
  1988      *The 1982–1984 Excavations at Las Colinas. The Site and Its Features.* Arizona
            State Museum Archaeological Series 162(2). Tucson.
Hatch, Pamela, Steven R. James, and Frank E. Bayham
  1987      La Ciudad Faunal Assemblage. In *Specialized Studies in the Economy, Envi-
            ronment and Culture at La Ciudad, Part III*, edited by JoAnn E. Kisselburg,
            Glen E. Rice, and Brenda L. Shears, pp. 239–276. Arizona State University
            Anthropological Field Studies 20. Tempe.
Haury, Emil W.
  1945      *The Excavation of Los Muertos and Neighboring Ruins in the Salt River Valley,
            Southern Arizona.* Papers of the Peabody Museum of American Archaeology
            and Ethnology 24(1). Harvard University, Cambridge.
  1950      *The Stratigraphy and Archaeology of Ventana Cave.* Reprinted in 1975 by the
            University of Arizona Press, Tucson.
  1976      *The Hohokam: Desert Farmers and Craftsmen.* The University of Arizona Press,
            Tucson.

Huckell, Lisa W.
    1986      Botanical Remains. In *The 1985 Excavations at the Hodges Site, Pima County,
              Arizona,* edited by Robert W. Layhe, pp. 241–269. Arizona State Museum
              Archaeological Series 170. Tucson.
Huckell, Bruce B., and Lisa W. Huckell
    1988      Crops Come to the Desert: Late Preceramic Agriculture in Southeastern
              Arizona. Paper presented at the 53rd Annual Meeting of the Society for
              American Archaeology, Phoenix.
Humphrey, Robert R.
    1974      *The Desert Grassland: A History of Vegetational Change and an Analysis of Causes.*
              University of Arizona Press, Tucson.
Hutira, Johna
    1989      Flotation Analysis. In *Settlement, Subsistence, and Specialization in the Northern
              Periphery: The Waddell Project,* edited by Margarie Green, pp. 851–872. Ar-
              chaeological Consulting Services Ltd., Cultural Resources Report 65, vol.
              2, Phoenix.
    in prep. Macrofossil Analysis. In *Shelltown and the Hind Site: Hohokam Specialized
              Production and the Colonial Period Expansion,* edited by William S. Marmaduke
              and T. Kathleen Henderson. Northland Research, Inc., Flagstaff and Tempe.
James, Steven R.
    1987      Hohokam Patterns of Faunal Exploitation at Muchas Casas. In *Studies in
              the Hohokam Community of Marana,* edited by Glen E. Rice, pp. 171–196.
              Arizona State University Anthropological Field Studies 15. Tempe.
Jones, Volney H.
    1936      A Summary of Data on Aboriginal Cotton of the Southwest. In *Symposium
              on Prehistoric Agriculture,* edited by D. D. Brand, pp. 51–64. University of
              New Mexico Bulletin, Anthropological Series 1(5), Albuquerque.
Keepax, Carole
    1977      Contamination of Archaeological Deposits by Seeds of Modern Origin with
              Particular Reference to Use of Flotation. *Journal of Archaeological Sciences*
              4:221–229.
Kelly, Isabel T., James Officer, and Emil W. Haury
    1978      *The Hodges Ruin: A Hohokam Community in the Tucson Basin.* University of
              Arizona Anthropological Papers 30, Tucson.
Kwiatkowski, Scott M.
    1987      Flotation Results from the Krueger Site. In Archaeological Investigations
              at the Krueger Site (NA19,765) Pinal County, Arizona, by James B. Rodgers.
              Manuscript on file, Museum of Northern Arizona, Flagstaff.
    1988a     *The Effects of Postoccupational Disturbance on Archaeobotanical Data from AZ
              U:9:24 (ASU).* Unpublished M.A. thesis, Department of Anthropology,
              Arizona State University, Tempe.
    1988b     Flotation, Macrobotanical, and Charcoal Analyses. In *Excavations at La Lom-
              ita Pequeña: a Santa Cruz/Sacaton Phase Farmstead in the Salt River Valley,* edited
              by Douglas R. Mitchell, pp. 231–269. Soil Systems Publications in Archae-
              ology 10. Phoenix.
    1989a     El Caserío Flotation and Wood Charcoal Studies. In *El Caserío: Colonial
              Period Settlement Along the East Papago Freeway,* edited by Douglas R. Mitch-
              ell, pp. 143–178. Soil Systems Publications in Archaeology 14. Phoenix.
    1989b     The Paleoethnobotany of the Grand Canal Ruins: Results from Flotation,

Macrobotanical and Wood Charcoal Analyses. In *Archaeological Investigations at the Grand Canal Ruins: A Classic Period Site in Phoenix, Arizona*, edited by Douglas R. Mitchell, pp. 497–558. Soil Systems Publications in Archaeology 12. Phoenix.

Kwiatkowski, Scott M., and Robert E. Gasser

1989a    Macrofloral Analysis [Hawk's Nest]. In *Hohokam Archaeology Along Phase B of the Tucson Aqueduct Central Arizona Project, vol. 4: Small Sites and Specialized Reports*, edited by Jon S. Czaplicki and John C. Ravesloot, pp. 105–126. Arizona State Museum Archaeological Series 178(4). Tucson.

1989b    Macrofloral Analysis. In *Hohokam Archaeology Along Phase B of the Tucson Aqueduct Central Arizona Project, vol. 2: Excavatons at Fastimes (AZ AA:12:384) A Rillito Phase Site in the Avra Valley*, edited by Jon S. Czaplicki and John C. Ravesloot, pp. 277–302. Arizona State Museum Archaeological Series 178(2). Tucson.

1989c    Macrofloral Analysis. In *Hohokam Archaeology Along Phase B of the Tucson Aqueduct Central Arizona Project, vol. 3: Excavations at Waterworld (AZ AA:16:94) A Rillito Phase Ballcourt Village in the Avra Valley*, edited by Jon S. Czaplicki and John C. Ravesloot, pp. 287–304. Arizona State Museum Archaeological Series 178(3). Tucson.

Lewton, F. L.

1912    The Cotton of the Hopi Indians: A New Species of *Gossypium*. *Smithsonian Miscellaneous Collections* 60(6). Washington, D.C.

Magers, Pamela C.

1975    The Cotton Industry at Antelope House. *The Kiva* 41(1):39–48.

McDaniel, Robert G.

1985    Field Evaluations of Agave in Arizona. *Desert Plants* 7(2):57–60, 101.

Miksicek, Charles H.

1979    From Parking Lots to Museum Basements: the Archaeobotany of the St. Mary's Site. *The Kiva* 45(1–2):131–140.

1982    Macro-botanical Remains. In *Hohokam Archaeology Along the Salt-Gila Aqueduct Central Arizona Project*, vol. 1: Research Design, by Lynn S. Teague and Patricia L. Crown, pp. 155–161. Arizona State Museum Archaeological Series 150(1). Tucson.

1983a    Archaeobotanical Aspects of Las Fosas: A Statistical Approach to Prehistoric Plant Remains. In *Hohokam Archaeology Along the Salt-Gila Aqueduct, Central Arizona Project*, vol. 6: Habitation Sites on the Gila River, edited by Lynn S. Teague and Patricia L. Crown, pp. 671–700. Arizona State Museum Archaeological Series 150(6). Tucson.

1983b    Archaeobotanical Remains From the Gopherette Site. In *Hohokam Archaeology Along the Salt-Gila Aqueduct, Central Arizona Project*, vol. 6: Habitation Sites on the Gila River, edited by Lynn S. Teague and Patricia L. Crown, pp. 353–366. Arizona State Museum Archaeological Series 150(6). Tucson.

1983c    Archaeobotanical Remains From the Jones Ruin. In *Hohokam Archaeology Along the Salt-Gila Aqueduct, Central Arizona Project*, vol. 6: Habitation Sites on the Gila River, edited by Lynn S. Teague and Patricia L. Crown, pp. 143–145. Arizona State Museum Archaeological Series 150(6). Tucson.

1983d    Archaeobotanical Remains From the Junkyard Site. In *Hohokam Archaeology Along the Salt-Gila Aqueduct, Central Arizona Project*, vol. 6: Habitation Sites on the Gila River, edited by Lynn S. Teague and Patricia L. Crown, pp. 473–481. Arizona State Museum Archaeological Series 150(6). Tucson.

1983e   Carbonized Plant Remains From the Dust Bowl and the Saguaro Site. In *Hohokam Archaeology Along the Salt-Gila Aqueduct, Central Arizona Project*, vol. 6: Habitation Sites on the Gila River, edited by Lynn S. Teague and Patricia L. Crown, pp. 265–276. Arizona State Museum Archaeological Series 150(6). Tucson.

1983f   Flotation Results From AZ U:15:84. In *Hohokam Archaeology Along the Salt-Gila Aqueduct, Central Arizona Project*, vol. 6: Habitation Sites on the Gila River, edited by Lynn S. Teague and Patricia L. Crown, pp. 741–744. Arizona State Museum Archaeological Series 150(6). Tucson.

1983g   Plant Remains From Casas Pequeñas (AZ U:15:97). In *Hohokam Archaeology Along the Salt-Gila Aqueduct, Central Arizona Project*, vol. 5: Small Habitation Sites on Queen Creek, edited by Lynn S. Teague and Patricia L. Crown, pp. 209–220. Arizona State Museum Archaeological Series 150(5). Tucson.

1983h   Plant Remains From Rancho Sin Vacas (AZ U:15:62). In *Hohokam Archaeology Along the Salt-Gila Aqueduct, Central Arizona Project*, vol. 5: Small Habitation Sites on Queen Creek, edited by Lynn S. Teague and Patricia L. Crown, pp. 427–430. Arizona State Museum Archaeological Series 150(5). Tucson.

1983i   Plant Remains From Smiley's Well (AZ U:14:73, Locus A). In *Hohokam Archaeology Along the Salt-Gila Aqueduct, Central Arizona Project*, vol. 5: Small Habitation Sites on Queen Creek, edited by Lynn S. Teague and Patricia L. Crown, pp. 87–97. Arizona State Museum Archaeological Series 150(5). Tucson.

1984a   Archaeobotanical Remains From Frogtown. In *Hohokam Archaeology Along the Salt-Gila Aqueduct, Central Arizona Project*, vol. 4: Prehistoric Occupation of the Queen Creek Delta, edited by Lynn S. Teague and Patricia L. Crown, pp. 563–590. Arizona State Museum Archaeological Series 150(4). Tucson.

1984b   Flotation Samples and Macrofossils From El Polvorón. In *Hohokam Archaeology Along the Salt-Gila Aqueduct, Central Arizona Project*, vol. 4: Prehistoric Occupation of the Queen Creek Delta, edited by Lynn S. Teague and Patricia L. Crown, pp. 333–344. Arizona State Museum Archaeological Series 150(4). Tucson.

1984c   Historic Desertification, Prehistoric Vegetation Change, and Hohokam Subsistence in the Salt-Gila Basin. In *Hohokam Archaeology Along the Salt-Gila Aqueduct, Central Arizona Project*, vol. 7: Environment and Subsistence, edited by Lynn S. Teague and Patricia L. Crown, pp. 53–80. Arizona State Museum Archaeological Series 150(7). Tucson.

1984d   Macrofloral Remains From the Siphon Draw Site. In *Hohokam Archaeology Along the Salt-Gila Aqueduct, Central Arizona Project*, vol. 4: Prehistoric Occupation of the Queen Creek Delta, edited by Lynn S. Teague and Patricia L. Crown, pp. 179–204. Arizona State Museum Archaeological Series 150(4). Tucson.

1986a   Plant Remains. In *Archaeological Investigations at the West Branch Site: Early and Middle Rincon Occupation in the Southern Tucson Basin*, by Frederick Huntington, pp. 289–313. Institute for American Research Anthropological Papers 5. Tucson.

1986b   Paleoethnobotanical Analysis at the Cienega Site: a Middle Rincon Farmstead in the Eastern Tucson Basin. In *Archaeological Investigations at the*

*Cienega Sites*, edited by Frederick Huntington. Manuscript on file, Institute for American Research, Tucson.

1986c    Plant Remains from the Tanque Verde Wash Site. In *Archaeological Investigations at the Tanque Verde Wash Site*, edited by Mark D. Elson, pp. 371–394. Institute for American Research Anthropological Papers 7. Tucson.

1986d    Prehistoric Plant Remains from the Dakota Wash Site (AZ AA:16:49). Manuscript on file, Pima Community College, Tucson.

1987    Late Sedentary–Early Classic Period Hohokam Agriculture: Plant Remains from the Marana Community Complex. In *Studies in the Hohokam Community of Marana*, edited by Glen E. Rice, pp. 197–216. Arizona State University Anthropological Field Studies 15. Tempe.

1988    Pioneer to Present: Archaeobotanical Remains From Ak-Chin, Arizona. Manuscript on file, Soil Systems, Inc., Phoenix.

Miksicek, Charles H., and Robert E. Gasser

1989    Hohokam Plant Use at Las Colinas: the Flotation Evidence. In *The 1982–1984 Excavations at Las Colinas: Environment and Subsistence*, by Donald A. Graybill, David E. Gregory, Fred L. Nials, Suzanne K. Fish, Robert E. Gasser, Charles H. Miksicek, and Christine R. Szuter, pp. 95–115. Arizona State Museum Archaeological Series 162(5). Tucson.

Minnis, Paul E.

1978    Paleoethnobotanical Indicators of Prehistoric Environmental Disturbance. In *The Nature and Status of Ethnobotany*, edited by Richard I. Ford, pp. 347–366. Museum of Anthropology, University of Michigan Anthropological Papers 67. Ann Arbor.

1981    Seeds in Archaeological Sites: Sources and Some Interpretative Problems. *American Antiquity* 36:410–431.

1985    Domesticating People and Plants in the Greater Southwest. In *Prehistoric Food Production in North America*, edited by Richard I. Ford, pp. 309–339. Museum of Anthropology, University of Michigan Anthropological Papers 75. Ann Arbor.

Mitchell, Douglas R.

1989    Settlement Patterns and Social Organization for the Phoenix Area Classic Period. In *Archaeological Investigations at the Grand Canal Ruins: A Classic Period Site in Phoenix*, edited by Douglas R. Mitchell, pp. 859–878. Soil Systems Publications in Archaeology 12. Phoenix.

Mitchell, Douglas R., and Scott M. Kwiatkowski

1989    Functional Analysis of Hornos from Grand Canal Ruins. In *Archaeological Investigations at the Grand Canal Ruins: a Classic Period Site in Phoenix*, edited by Douglas R. Mitchell, pp. 169–207. Soil Systems Publications in Archaeology 12. Phoenix.

Munson, Patrick J., Paul W. Parmalee, and Richard A. Yarnell

1971    Subsistence Ecology of Scovill, a Terminal Woodland Village. *American Antiquity* 36:410–431.

Nabhan, Gary Paul

1980    *Ammobroma sonorae*, an Endangered Parasitic Plant in Extremely Arid North America. *Desert Plants* 2(3):188–196.

1983    *Papago Fields: Arid Land Ethnobotany and Agricultural Ecology*. Unpublished Ph.D. dissertation, Arid Land Resources Sciences, University of Arizona, Tucson.

Plog, Stephen
    1980    Hohokam Exchange, Subsistence and Interaction: Some Comments. In
            *Current Issues in Hohokam Prehistory: Proceedings of a Symposium*, edited by
            David Doyel and Fred Plog, pp. 106–112. Arizona State University An-
            thropological Research Papers 23. Tempe.
Rea, Amadeo M.
    1979    The Ecology of Pima Fields. *Environment Southwest* 484:8–13.
    1983    *Once a River: Bird Life and Habitat Changes on the Middle Gila*. University of
            Arizona Press, Tucson.
Rodgers, James B.
    1985    Prehistoric Agricultural Variability in the Hohokam Northern Periphery.
            In *Hohokam Settlement and Economic Systems in the Central New River Drainage,
            Arizona*, edited by David E. Doyel and Mark D. Elson, pp. 249–296. Soil
            Systems Publications in Archaeology 4. Phoenix.
Russell, Frank
    1975    *The Pima Indians*. Re-edition of the 26th Annual Report of the Bureau of
            American Ethnology, additional text by Bernard L. Fontana, University of
            Arizona Press, Tucson.
Schuster, Janette H.
    1988    The Ak-Chin Physical Environment: A Geological Perspective. Manuscript
            on file, Soil Systems, Inc., Phoenix.
Shantz, H. L., and R. L. Piemeisel
    1924    Indicator Significance of the Natural Vegetation of the Southwestern De-
            sert. *Journal of Agricultural Research* 28(8):721–802.
Stein, Pat H.
    1979    Hohokam Archaeology Along the Salt-Gila Aqueduct, Central Arizona Proj-
            ect. Manuscript on file, Museum of Northern Arizona, Flagstaff.
Szuter, Christine R.
    1984    Faunal Exploitation and the Reliance on Small Animals Among the Ho-
            hokam. In *Hohokam Archaeology Along the Salt-Gila Aqueduct, Central Arizona
            Project*, vol. 7: Environment and Subsistence, edited by Lynn S. Teague
            and Patricia L. Crown, pp. 139–170. Arizona State Museum Archaeological
            Series 150. Tucson.
    in press Hunting by Prehistoric Horticulturalists in the American Southwest. *The
            Kiva*.
Wellhausen, E. J., L. M. Roberts, and E. Hernandez X.
    1952    *Races of Maize in Mexico: Their Origin, Characteristics and Distribution*. The
            Bussey Institution, Harvard University, Cambridge.

# •11•

# HOHOKAM ARCHAEOLOGY IN THE EIGHTIES: AN OUTSIDE VIEW

▼▼▼▼▼▼▼▼▼▼▼▼▼▼▼▼▼▼▼▼▼▼▼▼▼▼▼▼▼▼▼▼▼▼▼▼▼▼▼▼▼▼▼▼▼▼▼▼▼▼▼▼▼▼▼▼▼▼

## *Gary M. Feinman*

The days are gone when our ideas about the Hohokam would languish for a decade or more awaiting new data and fresh interpretations (McGuire 1987:23).

We are in the midst of an exciting and productive period of research into the prehistory of the Hohokam region of southern Arizona. . . . Many questions are being asked and addressed which only a decade ago might have seemed unrealistic and unobtainable (Doyel 1987a:19).

The point of this discussion is not that there is some clear and unambiguous explanation of Hohokam culture change. On the contrary, it is that the study of the Hohokam is finally becoming very interesting, and very difficult (Teague 1984:315).

## INTRODUCTION

Several years ago, Bruce Trigger (1984) characterized archaeology as being at a crossroads. Sometimes, however, it appears more like a crossfire—the field pinned down between the pseudoscientific jargon of doctrinaire methodologists on one side, the sterile revisionism of 'arch-empiricists' on another, and the somewhat moralistic fables of an often data-free post-processualism on the third. Yet, for the majority of us who believe that contemporary archaeology must integrate solid empirical findings with sensible theories, whose interpretations cannot be typecast or pigeon-holed into simple deterministic "isms," and those who see our primary aim as the understanding of how different human behaviors have changed or remained relatively stable over time, there is great promise in this volume and, in general, in the tremendous advances in Hohokam archaeology over the last 15 years.

Fueled by much new fieldwork and energized by novel theoretical perspectives (as well as the declining importance of traditional trait-based diffusionism and migrationism), Hohokam studies have entered a new era. For a Mesoamericanist like myself, someone at the fringe of Southwestern studies but who lived and worked in Arizona roughly a decade ago, the rapidly changing climate of opinion is dramatic and exciting. Many viewpoints that were dogma or consensus in the 1970s have been challenged, expanded, modified, or supplanted. Yet, because the changes have been driven more frequently by new data than simply by polemic, there is reason for constructive debate and optimism. In 1978, Emil Haury (1980:113) acknowledged that Hohokam research was roughly 40 years behind Anasazi studies. Clearly, this is no longer so. For example, as evidenced here and elsewhere (Doyel 1987b), contemporary Hohokam research is at the forefront when it comes to conceptualizing and analyzing long-term societal change at multiple organizational scales, a research direction pioneered by Flannery (1976) in *The Early Mesoamerican Village*.

As the conference's *resident alien*, I have focused the remainder of this commentary on four key issues or areas of debate that I believe to be particularly relevant for archaeologists working both in southern Arizona and in other regions. I have endeavored to stress topics in which significant changes in interpretation have occurred over the last decade or so, subsequent to the last generation of areal syntheses (e.g., Haury 1976; Gumerman and Haury 1979). Obviously, I make no claim to have isolated all the recent theoretical, empirical, and methodological breakthroughs in Hohokam research, nor to have chosen the most significant topics for any other nonspecialist.

## HOHOKAM ORIGINS

Although the recent breakthroughs in Hohokam research largely reflect the tremendous increase in empirical knowledge (fostered by public archaeology), the contemporary perspective also owes much to theoretical shifts that led to diminished reliance on what Wilcox (1980:239) termed the "Gladwinian model of Hohokam prehistory." In a series of seminal papers, Wilcox (1979, 1980; see also Fish, Pilles, and Fish 1980) challenged the assumptions of the traditional trait-based (Doyel 1984:151), migrationist Gladwinian scheme, and suggested the adoption of a more 'relational' approach to past patterns of behavior (Wilcox 1988a). Is it merely happenstance that contemporary Hohokam studies now (1) question whether the Colonial period was a period of colonization, (2) emphasize spatial variation rather than homogeneity (Doyel 1985:19–20; Gasser and Kwiatkowski, this volume; Neitzel, this volume), (3) examine site plans with social relationships in mind (Doyel 1987b; Doelle and Wallace, this volume; Fish and Fish, this volume), (4) challenge the simple division between core and periphery (Crown, this volume; McGuire, this volume), (5) endeavor to define shifting relational boundaries (Crown, McGuire, and Neitzel, this volume), and (6) have taken a new look at Hohokam beginnings (Cable and Doyel 1987; Doyel, this volume)? I think not, and in a sense, these new agendas were set with the intellectual dissection and shift away from Gladwin's long-held framework.

A decade ago, Wilcox (1980:240) argued that "reliance on the Gladwinian model has led to a neglect of the relationship of pre-ceramic Archaic hunter-gatherers to the ceramic-producing sedentary villagers." Now, a new consensus, close to the first position advocated by Haury (1962:126), seems to have emerged. While maize and certain ceremonial concepts are recognized to have been adopted from the south (Wilcox and Sternberg 1983:225–228; Wilcox 1986a:138–139, 1987a), few any longer see Mesoamerican in-migration (Haury 1976) as the root cause for Hohokam beginnings. Rather, current emphasis is on a more indigenous development of Hohokam villages from local Archaic populations (Dean 1987:254; Doyel 1987a:7; Fish 1987:266). Doyel's (Cable and Doyel 1987; Doyel, this volume) definition of the Red Mountain material, providing a clearer transition between the late Archaic and Vahki, has strengthened this interpretation.

The establishment of sedentary villages, using distinctive red-on-buff pottery, can be viewed plausibly now as part of a long episode of material cultural divergence that began thousands of years earlier when the entire Southwest was part of a more widespread Paleoindian (and later Archaic) tradition (Haury 1950:535–536; Irwin-Williams and Haynes 1970; Irwin-Williams 1979). With the recent reworking of the Hohokam chronology (Dean, this volume), the Southwest's first pottery now appears to have been used over a broad area within a short temporal period (LeBlanc 1982a:28). The earliest Hohokam and Mogollon ceramics were similar brown wares, which were complemented by a red ware (Haury 1974:98; LeBlanc 1982a:39, 1982b:119). "Each area then produced a broad line red-on-brown (or gray) painted ware. Then in each case the designs became more complex and diverged in different directions" (LeBlanc 1982b:119). As Wilcox (1979, 1988a) has argued, the process of diversification and increasing localization in utilitarian artifact styles would seem to reflect greater residential stability, rising population densities, and the decreasing openness of interactive/mating networks (see Wobst 1974, 1976, 1977; Moore 1983).

Crown (1984:292) found that 82 percent of the identified exotic Pioneer period pottery at Snaketown was Mogollon, suggesting close interaction between these neighboring populations. In fact, Wilcox (1988b:251) has argued that "nothing identifiable as 'Hohokam' or 'Mogollon' cultural identity emerged until the sixth to seventh century A.D. Extra-large communal structures occur at Snaketown in the Vahki through Sweetwater phases (Cable and Doyel 1985, 1987) contemporaneously with comparable structures in sites of the Early Pithouse Period in southwestern New Mexico (Anyon 1984)." Later, by the Colonial period, grooving or incising on the exteriors of painted Hohokam bowls sharply distinguished these vessels from Mogollon wares (Wilcox and Sternberg 1983:229). Shortly thereafter, the cremation ritual, palettes, ballcourts, worked shell, and censers were adopted in southern Arizona, defining a regional cultural identity distinct from the rest of the Southwest (Doyel, this volume). At roughly the same time, less obvious (but nevertheless distinctive paste) differences began to distinguish the ceramics found in the Phoenix and Tucson basins, necessitating the use of alternative phase names for these Hohokam pottery complexes (something not required for earlier Sweetwater and Snaketown times) (Doyel 1984:152–153; see also Wilcox 1987b:238). Apparently, this increasing localization of red-on-buff ceramic styles through time was part of a process of differentiation that began early in the preceramic period and may have continued through the Sedentary period (Masse 1982; Wilcox 1987a).

The emerging alternative to the 'Gladwinian model' offers a new perspective on Hohokam beginnings and the prevailing dynamics of the Colonial period. It also places the transition from mobile hunting and gathering to sedentary villages in southern Arizona in a context similar to that seen elsewhere in the New World (e.g., Ford 1974; Flannery and Marcus 1983; Hantman 1984; Plog 1984; MacNeish 1986; Smith 1986). At the same time, it does not preclude the possibility that specific episodes of migration (inside the Hohokam world) occurred during the Colonial period or earlier (Doyel, this volume). Furthermore, although shifts in residential stability, population density, and networks of communication seem the principal basis for the increasing diversification, we do not know why the material cultural 'boundary' between Hohokam and Mogollon formed where it did. Why was this boundary evidently less permeable than that between different Hohokam populations? Clearly, this conference has shown that Hohokam ceramic varieties and lifeways were not simply restricted to contexts where irrigation was feasible, nor does cultural variation strictly mimic environmental diversity (e.g., Ferg and Huckell 1985; Fish and Nabhan, this volume). In addition, what specific factors account for the uneven pace of cultural differentiation, and what may have accounted for the advent of a more sedentary lifeway in *both* the Mogollon and Hohokam regions soon after the outset of our era? These and other related questions should provide research foci for the years ahead.

## MESOAMERICAN CONNECTIONS

For decades, Southwestern archaeologists have debated the role and importance of Mesoamerican contact in Hohokam development (see Kelley 1966; Wilcox 1986b). Too often this debate has been polarized between extreme 'isolationist' and 'migrationist' positions. The emerging evidence for Archaic through Hohokam continuity seems to weaken the likelihood that large-scale movements of people are required to account for the sharing of cosmological traditions between the Hohokam and populations to the south. At the same time, event-centered, *pochteca* models, which envision Mesoamerican traders spreading their ideologies and goods to the Southwest, remain largely untestable and unsupported. As Wilcox (1986b:30) has noted: *"pochteca* burials have been sought (Reyman 1978), but even if elaborate burials were found, would it be possible to prove the skeletons derive from a non-southwestern and mesoamerican population?" Is it then surprising that, given what we know, the pendulum of opinion is swinging toward a more 'isolationist' stance (Mathien and McGuire 1986)? In this vein, the question of southern connections was little discussed at the Dragoon seminar (but see Crown, Doyel, McGuire, this volume).

Clearly, the cultural and organizational differences between the Hohokam and the later prehispanic populations of Central Mexico, Oaxaca, and the Maya lowlands are obvious and rather marked to someone, like myself, who works south of Arizona. Furthermore, I question whether a technological innovation like canal irrigation (utilized independently by populations in so many global regions) should be considered a Mesoamerican 'trait' transmitted to the Hohokam, especially since some Mesoamerican populations did not (or only sparingly) utilize that specific technique of water control. Nevertheless, I find it difficult to ignore, as most 'isolationists' do, the rather significant ideological and ceremonial traditions shared at a generic level by the Southwest and Mesoamerica. In comparing (through ethnohistory and ethnography) the Aztec and the Pueblo, Elsie Clews Parsons (1974:137) found their ritual systems to be "strikingly similar" with the exception of blood sacrifice.

Perhaps the most appropriate question is how, without invoking Mesoamerican migration, do we account for the Hohokam adoption of maize, as well as such specific ideological conventions (associated with many prehispanic Mesoamerican peoples) as the ballgame, color-directional symbolism (Kelley 1966:98; Wilcox 1987a), a square, plaza-centered community plan (Wilcox 1987a), the ceremonial importance of caves (Fulton 1941), and certain astronomical beliefs and orientations (Wilcox 1987a, n.d.)? Although an 'isolationist' might attribute this shared tradition to the original cultural unity of the American Indian and the peopling of the New World, such a model neither would account for the items (maize, copper bells, turquoise) that actually were moved across these cultural regions, nor can it alone explain the extent of the similarity noted between Mesoamerica and the Southwest.

Although I will not evaluate the specifics of Wilcox's (1986a) 'Tepiman Connection,' his 'middle-ground' model that envisions down-the-line, network-like linkages between the Southwest and northern Mesoamerica, it has several strong attributes. A network of linkages (so that the ultimate connections are indirect) helps to account for the generic nature of Mesoamerican-Southwest shared beliefs (e.g., that the specific associations of color and direction were far from uniform [Riley 1963], or that the rubber ballgame was played on different courts). Furthermore, a network model, which envisions changing patterns of communication and interaction with episodes of relative permeability and closure between communities, helps to explain the temporal and spatial unevenness of 'Mesoamerican influence' in the Southwest. Certainly, such an interpretation is more parsimonious than numerous waves of migration, and it can subsume the flow of certain goods to the south.

A networklike model also can incorporate both the open, family-to-family linkages that are typical of mobile, low-density, rather egalitarian social systems, as well as prestige-chain exchanges that occur in more hierarchical contexts (Renfrew 1975). Through the Pioneer period, the southern Arizona-Mesoamerica connection seems to have involved largely the former, family-to-family linkages with utilitarian stone tool and pottery styles bearing broad decorative similarities over wide regions (Schroeder 1982). Later, during the Sedentary and Classic periods, a greater majority of the interconnections may have been handled through more restricted prestige exchanges. At that time, basic utilitarian artifact styles remained more regionally distinct (suggesting less household-to-household interaction), while goods like copper bells and turquoise were transferred over great distances.

That ritual, ceremonial, and cosmological knowledge as well as highly-decorated, rare, and exotic items are the kinds of information and goods that 'crossed the Chichimec Sea' is not surprising. After all, such traditions and precious items (as opposed to utilitarian goods) most frequently traversed great distances in the later (post-Archaic) pre-Columbian World (e.g., Helms 1979; Drennan 1983; Blanton and Feinman 1984).

Here, it is necessary to take a brief aside to question Crown's (this volume) empirical rejection of the prestige exchange model as applied to the Sedentary period in southern Arizona. Crown argues that the prestige goods, such as shell, exotic pottery, mirrors, copper bells, and macaws, could not have been used to define high status because they were too rare and restricted in distribution in the archaeological record. Yet, those artifacts found and reported are probably only a tiny fraction of the items that were actually in use centuries ago. Furthermore, if the prestige items were bountiful and evenly distributed archaeologically, one would not want to associate them with high status, which by definition is restricted to a small segment of the population. It seems to me that Crown's criteria for rejecting the prestige exchange model are exactly the test implications that one might call on to define or support it (Renfrew 1975).

## BONE IMPLEMENTS AND BLOOD SACRIFICE

If Southwestern peoples indeed shared in a Mesoamerican ideological tradition, then why was some form of bloodletting or sacrifice apparently not part of the former's ritual system (Parsons 1974)? As in Mesoamerica, were such conceptions modified or excised from Southwestern religious conceptions during the first centuries after European contact, yet prior to the ethnographic present? Or, did the Hohokam and Southwestern peoples simply hold different conceptions about human blood and its sacred importance? If the ballgame and color-directional symbolism were communicated north as posited, then it seems strange that long-standing and broadly distributed Mesoamerican associations of blood and auto-sacrifice with fertility and the maintenance of order in the universe also were not shared.

Based on sixteenth-century accounts, Mesoamericanist scholars have long known that the Aztec elite considered themselves responsible for keeping the cosmos in order through the offering of blood and hearts in sacrificial events (Anawalt 1982). Although Aztec human sacrifice, particularly during the last century before conquest, probably was carried out at an unprecedented scale (Berdan 1982:116), we now know that the historical basis for this tradition (including blood offerings, the ritual importance of blood, and self-immolation) was more than two millennia older than Aztec Tenochtitlán (Flannery and Marcus 1976; MacNeish 1981; Grove 1987) and very widespread (Anawalt 1982:42; Schele and Miller 1986). According to ethnohistoric accounts from Oaxaca (Marcus 1983), the northern Yucatán (Tozzer 1966), and Central Mexico (Nicholson 1971), auto-sacrificial rites were performed most commonly by men who drew blood from their ear lobes, tongues, and genitals, using sharpened bones, stingray spines, obsidian blades, stone knives, cactus spines, or long specially grown fingernails.

In the Quiche Maya Popol Vuh, a linguistic parallel has been noted between the word for bloodletting and that for the suckling or breast feeding of a child by its mother (Schele 1984:33; Stone 1985:25). Long ago, Seler (1904) noted a similar connection in the Borgia Group codices. Even contemporary Otomi myth tells of a girl "suckling" blood from her father for nourishment (Manrique C. 1969:716).

Admittedly, in the absence of documentary data, archaeological indicators for Hohokam bloodletting can neither be straightforward nor indisputable. We might as well forget long fingernails and stingray spines (which are not locally available). Obsidian blades are rare, and as in Mesoamerica, they could be used for a whole series of tasks. Cactus spines are a very likely and readily available implement for drawing blood (Cook de Leonard 1971:220), yet unfortunately they do not preserve well archaeologically and also were used for other purposes, such as sewing (Haury 1950, pl. 38).

But what about bone implements? Haury (1937:154; see also Kelly 1978:121;

Olsen 1981:291) long ago noted their relative rarity at Hohokam sites compared to northern Pueblos. Perhaps because of their limited number, they have received little analytical attention and have been grouped in rather inclusive categories. Thus, any suggestions regarding their past use runs great risk of lumping or combining implements that were not used for the same tasks. For Grasshopper and other Puebloan sites where bone tools were more numerous, Olsen (1979, 1980, 1981) has illustrated that these implements probably were used for a variety of tasks (including sewing, basketry, and hide working). Yet, she also found it difficult to determine function strictly from form, and that the variety of bone implements makes it very hard to separate them into clear and discrete classes.

Of most interest to this discussion are bone implements similar to those that Olsen (1979, 1981) categorized as awls and hair pins. While the former tend to be short and are made on bone from a wide range of species, the latter are long (generally made on leg bones), deliberately polished, and sometimes decoratively carved (in rare instances incrusted with turquoise) on the handle end (Woodward 1930; Haury 1976:303–304; see also Cosgrove and Cosgrove 1932 for Swarts Ruin). I will not devote much attention to the awls, because they likely were used for a diversity of activities (many of which were more mundane). Nevertheless, some Hohokam awls seem both too sharp and fragile to make particularly effective or long-lived utilitarian tools (Tuthill 1947:65; see also Kidder 1932:218 for a similar view on certain bone awls at Pecos). Other Hohokam awls (e.g., Haury 1937; Tuthill1 1947) are similar in form to pointed bone implements from Mesoamerica, presumed to be for bloodletting (e.g., Brady and Stone 1986:23).

Of greater interest are the so-called bone hairpins, which most analysts agree were not used as simple piercing tools (Haury 1945:160). Their current attribution as hairpins is based on rather skimpy grounds. Namely, in a few cases from across the Southwest (Fewkes 1927:214–215; Cummings 1940:63; DiPeso 1956:76), these worked bones have been recovered in burials close to the head of the deceased. Although the so-called hairpins frequently are found in burial contexts (Haury 1945:170, 1976:303–304), the relatively small proportion situated above the skull would seem to cast doubt on the notion that these objects merely served to adorn the hair. Such hairpins, when recovered in burial contexts, are just as likely not to be located near the head. For example, at Casa Grande, Fewkes (1912:145) found a bone implement (which he called a dirk) situated on the shoulder of a deceased, pointed toward the individual's heart, while at Guasave in Sinaloa, Ekholm (1942:43) found a similar bone implement (which he referred to as a dagger) in the hand of a male skeleton, who had been buried elaborately with many grave offerings.

Several other associations do not seem in concert with the simple hairpin interpretation for these bone objects. Although primarily found with males (Haury 1976:304), as are bloodletting implements in Mesoamerica, the hairpins at Snaketown also were recovered with several infant cremations. Furthermore, if they are simply hairpins, why are they often recovered in contexts with exotic goods and in unusually elaborate death assemblages (Haury 1945, 1976:304; Nelson 1981)? Nelson (1986:175) has noted their association with mosaic mirrors at Snaketown and the Grewe site. Also intriguing is the frequent occurrence, among the Hohokam (as well as elsewhere in the Southwest), of sharpened bone implements and hairpins with apparently sacred bundles (Cummings 1915:280; Haury 1950:440–441) and in ceremonial caves (Fulton 1941). Finally, if they are simply hairpins, why is more than one such object frequently found in the same burial (e.g., Haury 1976:303–304) and why are they sharpened?

Many Hohokam archaeologists have followed Fewkes (1927) and emphasized the knifelike properties of bone hairpins. For example, Haury (1976:304) frequently refers to them as 'daggerlike' hairpins. Citing Trik's (1963) description of an elite burial from Tikal's Temple I, Haury also draws an intriguing comparison between those Maya objects and the Snaketown hairpins. "One suspects that, like so many other traits of Hohokam culture, the homeland was to the south. Without implying the existence of a direct connection, the bone carvings of the Maya include ornate objects that probably were hair pins dating at least as early as the Classic period" (Haury 1976:304). While Haury rightly observed the formal and contextual similarities between these two sets of worked bone (allowing for the more intricate carvings often including hieroglyphic inscriptions on the Maya bones), he, as well as Trik, apparently were not aware that these Tikal bones almost certainly were associated with bloodletting. The Maya glyph for 'displaying one's blood' (Stuart 1984:17) is evident on two of the Tikal bones (Trik 1963:11). Likewise, remarkably similar objects are associated with Maya bloodletting in numerous contexts, including the depiction of the bloodletting act (using a 'hairpinlike' tool) on a Maya polychrome vase (Joralemon 1974). In at least one instance (Baudez and Mathews 1978:39), a Classic Maya tablet (from Palenque) depicts an individual with a bone daggerlike object in his hair; however this individual is thought to be a captive and has been explicitly associated with the letting of blood. In other words, a sharp object bound in the hair is not necessarily a 'hairpin,' as Cummings (1940:63) long ago recognized.

The Maya region is far from southern Arizona, and like Haury, I explicitly do not want to convey (or even imply) any notion of a direct link to the Southwest. Hence, it is important to note that bloodletting and long, sharpened bone objects in burial contexts seem to have a long history in Central Mexico (e.g., Tolstoy 1971). More importantly, Ekholm (1942:113) found three long, polished bone implements at Guasave (including the one in burial context noted above). He calls these objects 'daggers' and suggests that they were too thin and delicate to make practical tools. Further south at Amapa, Nayarit, Meighan (1976:124–125, 418) found two classes of bone implements. Although 'heavy awls' always were found in refuse, five 'light awls' were recovered in a single grave. Scarification and bloodletting also are mentioned in archival accounts of northeast Mexico (Taylor 1966:77).

Although this discussion probably has presented enough data to necessitate a reevaluation of whether Hohokam bone 'hairpins' were simply head ornaments, their actual use remains somewhat inferential. Nevertheless, the appearance of polished, sharpened bone implements in the Pioneer period (e.g., Haury 1976:303), along with four-directional symbolism, the ballgame (Wilcox 1987a), and an apparent concern with fertility (Doyel, this volume), suggests that these closely related conceptions may have diffused in concert (albeit in down-the-line fashion). Furthermore, the increasing number of these bone implements, and their closer association with pyrite mirrors and other ceremonial objects in Colonial and Sedentary contexts (Nelson 1986), indicates that (as in Classic and Postclassic Mesoamerica) this long-standing tradition could have acquired new meanings as other aspects of society changed (see Wilcox and Sternberg 1983:232–239). I should hasten to add that while the existence of an indirect Mesoamerican connection is recognized, these macro-regional linkages (as well as the goods and concepts that were transmitted) should not be assumed to be the simple stimuli or prime-movers for recognized episodes of temporal change in Hohokam social and economic organization.

## ORGANIZATIONAL SCALE AND SPATIAL VARIATION

Despite the numerous accomplishments of the Snaketown research (Gladwin et al. 1937; Haury 1976), even strong supporters (Masse 1982:71) now acknowledge that too much was generalized about "Hohokam ceramic art, culture history, and culture process . . . based on the evidence from a single site." In large part, through the late 1970s the Hohokam were modeled as one rather homogeneous system in space (and to a lesser degree in time) "with the available data often forced into artificial typological categories" (Doyel 1985:19). Perhaps, reflecting the continued adherence to this somewhat normative, trait-based framework (see Neitzel, this volume), a major symposium held in 1978 (Doyel and Plog 1980) contained surprisingly little direct discussion of village organization (Fish 1987:269) or of other Hohokam social units.

As Dean (1987) has noted previously, the last decade has witnessed an impressive and exciting transformation. At the Dragoon symposium, almost all of the papers described and interpreted spatial and temporal variation in the Hohokam regional system (Fish and Fish, Gasser and Kwiatkowski, McGuire, this volume). The movement away from traditional, normative archaeological units has led to an increasing emphasis on the definition, quantification, and interpretation of archaeological distributions and associations at several scales of analysis (Fish 1987). As McGuire (this volume; see also Crown 1985; Wilcox 1987c) has shown for the macroregional scale, the distributions of different artifact classes and features are neither simple nor uniform. As in Mesoamerica (see Blanton and Feinman 1984), a single core-periphery dichotomous structure is not maintained for the entire sequence.

At smaller scales of investigation, there is now the rich empirical foundation to compare and discuss socially linked canal systems (Gregory and Nials 1985), multisite irrigation communities (Howard 1987; Fish and Fish, this volume), diachronically variable settlement plans (Wilcox and Sternberg 1983; Doelle, this volume), as well as continuity and change in household organization (Sires 1987; Doyel, this volume). Doyel (this volume) reminds us that each Hohokam site seems to have its own distinctive occupational sequence, while settlement pattern studies show marked spatial variation in the hierarchical organization of different platform mound/canal systems (Bruder 1985; Gregory and Nials 1985; Crown 1987; Nicholas and Feinman, 1989).

One aspect of temporal variation that is particularly intriguing concerns changes in household organization during the Archaic-Pioneer period (Doyel, this volume). The initial transition from small circular to small square houses during the Red Mountain phase is what might be expected with increased sedentism and occupational continuity (Flannery 1972). As Doyel (this volume) implies, the subsequent emergence of a bimodal pattern of house size in the Vahki phase indicates a possible change in community integration, with the occupants of the large square houses perhaps becoming the focus for certain suprahousehold activities (for a parallel case, see Lightfoot and Feinman 1982).

In the Estrella and Sweetwater phases at Snaketown, basal organization (Johnson 1983) may have shifted again as settlement population apparently increased. More large square houses are found, but they are smaller in size than in the preceding Vahki phase. Doyel (this volume) suggests that village segmentation may have occurred, perhaps as an increasing number of households made it impossible for the inhabitants of a single large square house to coordinate the entire community. Extramural plazas, which appear at this time, may have been the focus of events that linked village segments. At the same time, some of the activities formerly carried out in the large houses may have shifted to the plazas, accounting for the decrease in the sizes of the former structures. This transition was continued at Snaketown during the following Snaketown phase. The development of the house cluster–courtyard residential pattern, the cessation of large square house construction, and the building of trash and flat-topped mounds (along with extramural plazas, and shortly thereafter ballcourts) signal both a possible change in the organization of basal units (from houses to house clusters), as well as the increasing importance and diversity of suprahousehold forms of integration (Cable and Doyel 1987; Wilcox 1987a).

The growing sophistication and general theoretical importance of contemporary Hohokam studies is best exemplified by the numerous strands of evidence from several scales of analysis that now can be brought to bear on the long-standing question of the Sedentary-Classic transition (Dean 1987:255–256). While Sires (1987) emphasizes basal unit continuity, focusing on the structure of courtyard clusters (Sedentary) and compounds (Classic), Gregory (1987), working at a different scale, details significant temporal shifts in Sedentary–early Classic platform mound construction, function, and distribution. At the same time, McGuire (1987:122) stresses a significant Sedentary-Classic shift in domestic architecture, such that "more marked differences in the quality, permanence, and elevation of the dwellings housing different social groups" are suggested for the Classic period. Several authors (McGuire and Howard 1987; Wilcox 1987a, 1987c; McGuire, this volume) have argued that major transitions in extraregional networks also took place at this time. The complexity of the evidence led LeBlanc (1986:120) to note that: "the Soho phase is difficult to explicate because of two opposing trends. On the one hand, the areal extent of the Hohokam was considerably diminished and also the level of external trade was probably lessened. On the other hand, the emerging elite probably became more institutionalized with increased authority and control."

Is this an enigma? Are some of the authors necessarily wrong? Not if one acknowledges that human socioeconomic systems may undergo different, yet simultaneous, transitions at several organizational scales. In the late Pioneer period at Snaketown, we surmised that the growth (and increasing importance) of the community in the regional system may have required organizational transformations both to larger basal units (courtyard groups) and to more formal kinds of suprahousehold organization. Likewise, during the Classic period, basal units may have retained roughly the same structure that they had in the Sedentary period (Sires 1987; Doyel, this volume), yet the degree of status differentiation between those units may have increased (McGuire 1987, this volume). At the same time, some platform mound/canal systems may have become more hierarchically (and perhaps centrally) organized (Gregory 1987, LeBlanc 1986), while the ties that interconnected such systems in the Phoenix Basin to each other, to other parts of the Hohokam regional system, and to elsewhere in the Southwest may have undergone significant transformations (Wilcox 1987a). From this perspective, LeBlanc's dilemma would meet more general expectations (see Kowalewski et al. 1983) that increasing centralization may coincide with decreasing boundary permeability (and hence in this case, a shrinking distribution of 'Hohokam' ceramics).

The expanding informational base for Hohokam studies allows (perhaps even demands) that we increase our terminological sophistication. To ask simply whether the Hohokam were a 'tribe' or a 'chiefdom' would seem to make little sense (as phrased), given the great temporal and spatial variation that existed, and the complexity of changes at various organizational levels that can be modeled. To assume that a hierarchically organized social system need be associated (by definition) with either redistribution or the centralized production of craft goods (Seymour 1988) would seem to be an arcane simplification (see Feinman and Neitzel 1984; Drennan and Uribe 1987; Earle 1987). Likewise, we must be especially careful to distinguish and properly use such concepts as complexity (vertical and horizontal), centralization, scale, and integration (e.g., Blanton et al. 1981; Johnson 1980, 1982). To conflate such terms (Crown, this volume) will only complicate our models and confuse our interpretations.

## PIMA-PAPAGO ANALOGY

Hohokam archaeologists long have recognized the organizational and demographic differences between the historic populations of southern Arizona and the earlier Hohokam (e.g., Gumerman and Haury 1979:90); however, at the same time, direct analogies with the Pima often have been used to reconstruct ancient Hohokam social formations (e.g., Woodbury 1961:556–557; Haury 1976:150–151). Clearly, as Speth (1988:203–204) has noted, analogies are essential to archaeology and serve as a critical starting point for hypothesis construction. Yet, given the extent of the differences and the historical discontinuity between the Hohokam and the more recent Pima-Papago, I frequently have wondered whether such analogies are a logical place on which to base or conclude Hohokam interpretations.

In the Maya region, an area closer to my own research, uncritical overreliance on ethnographic analogy led to several decades of misdirection and misinterpretation (e.g., Becker 1979). Hence, I was heartened by the very 'critical eye' that was given to the use of simple analogy by the conference participants (Doyel, Fish and Fish, Fish and Nabhan, this volume). The scalar contrasts drawn by Doyel (this volume) between the Hohokam and the Pima-Papago are rather striking. Yet, in a sense, the extent of the discontinuity is not so surprising if one considers some of the known forces (Old World diseases, domesticated animals, Apache raids, shifting precipitation cycles, European incursions, firearms and metal) that were at work during the intervening centuries (see also Doyel 1987a:7). In this vein, and given several recent efforts to model (through direct analogy) Hohokam settlement patterns, population, and water use, Fish and Nabhan's (this volume) observation that total historic Papago water requirements were increased tremendously to support domestic cattle in addition to humans is extremely important and would seem to require careful consideration.

## CONCLUSION

In archaeology, it is generally easier to "poke holes" than to synthesize, to criticize than to praise. Although this essay includes some of the former as well as the latter, the principal tone is meant to convey the current richness, vigor, optimism, and excitement in Hohokam studies. I have not even touched upon the prehispanic canal irrigation systems in the Phoenix Basin and the Tucson area (Fish and Fish, this volume), which are currently some of the best mapped in the world (prehistoric or historic). They potentially offer an excellent opportunity to examine long-standing hypotheses concerning water management and social organization. Any 'ivory tower' academician who uniformly doubts the general intellectual significance of government-sponsored (contract) archaeological research need look no further than southern Arizona for a striking counter-example. The Bureau of Reclamation and other governmental agencies deserve the thanks of the archaeological community for the solid empirical foundation that their support has helped to establish. In the context of increasingly sophisticated theoretical frameworks, this infusion of new information clearly has placed Hohokam research close to the forefront of American archaeology. This volume should help to disseminate that message to the rest of the field.

## ACKNOWLEDGMENTS

I would like to thank all the seminar participants for a most enjoyable and instructive session at the Amerind Foundation. Anne I. Woosley and Thomas R. Lincoln deserve very special recognition for having provided an atmosphere that was conducive to thoughtful communication and intellectual stimulation. A great acknowledgment is owed George J. Gumerman and the Bureau of Reclamation for the opportunity to exchange a week from a long cold Wisconsin winter for the stunning warmth of the Arizona desert in February, 1988.

## REFERENCES CITED

Anawalt, Patricia R.
   1982  Understanding Aztec Human Sacrifice. *Archaeology* 35:38–45.
Anyon, Roger
   1984  *Mogollon Settlement Patterns and Communal Architecture.* Unpublished Master's thesis, Department of Anthropology, University of New Mexico, Albuquerque.
Baudez, Claude F., and Peter Mathews
   1978  Capture and Sacrifice at Palenque. In *Tercera Mesa Redondo de Palenque,* edited by M. G. Robertson, pp. 31–40. University of Texas Press, Austin.

Becker, Marshall J.
  1979   Priests, Peasants, and Ceremonial Centers: The Intellectual History of a Model. In *Maya Archaeology and Ethnohistory*, edited by N. Hammond and G. R. Willey, pp. 3–20. University of Texas Press, Austin.
Berdan, Francis F.
  1982   *The Aztecs of Central Mexico: An Imperial Society*. Holt, Rinehart, and Winston, New York.
Blanton, Richard E., and Gary Feinman
  1984   The Mesoamerican World System. *American Anthropologist* 86:673–682.
Blanton, Richard E., Stephen A. Kowalewski, Gary Feinman, and Jill Appel
  1981   *Ancient Mesoamerica: A Comparison of Change in Three Regions*. Cambridge University Press, Cambridge.
Brady, James E., and Andrea Stone
  1986   Naj Tunich: Entrance to the Maya Underworld. *Archaeology* 39(6):18–25.
Bruder, J. Simon
  1985   Comments on Hohokam Settlement Patterns. In *Proceedings of the 1983 Hohokam Symposium*, Part I, edited by A. E. Dittert, Jr. and D. E. Dove, pp. 389–394. Arizona Archaeological Society Occasional Papers 2. Phoenix.
Cable, John S., and David E. Doyel
  1985   Hohokam Land-use Patterns Along the Terraces of the Lower Salt River Valley: The Central Phoenix Project. In *Proceedings of the 1983 Hohokam Symposium*, Part I, edited by A. E. Dittert, Jr. and D. E. Dove, pp. 263–310. Arizona Archaeological Society Occasional Papers 2. Phoenix.
  1987   Pioneer Period Village Structure and Settlement Pattern in the Phoenix Basin. In *The Hohokam Village: Site Structure and Organization*, edited by D. E. Doyel, pp. 21–70. Southwestern and Rocky Mountain Division of the American Association for the Advancement of Science, Glenwood Springs, Colorado.
Cook de Leonard, Carmen
  1971   Minor Arts of the Classic Period in Central Mexico. In *Handbook of Middle American Indians*, vol. 10, *Archaeology of Northern Mesoamerica*, Part 1, edited by G. F. Ekholm and I. Bernal, pp. 206–227. University of Texas Press, Austin.
Cosgrove, H. S., and C. B. Cosgrove
  1932   *The Swarts Ruin: A Typical Mimbres Site in Southwestern New Mexico*. Papers of the Peabody Museum of American Archaeology and Ethnology 15(1). Cambridge.
Crown, Patricia L.
  1984   Ceramic Vessel Exchange in Southern Arizona. In *Hohokam Archaeology Along the Salt-Gila Aqueduct, Central Arizona Project*, vol. 9, Synthesis and Conclusions, edited by L. S. Teague and P. L. Crown, pp. 251–303. Arizona State Museum Archaeological Series 150. Tucson.
  1985   Intrusive Ceramics and the Identification of Hohokam Exchange Networks. In *Proceedings of the 1983 Hohokam Symposium*, Part II, edited by A. E. Dittert, Jr. and D. E. Dove, pp. 439–458. Arizona Archaeological Society Occasional Papers 2. Phoenix.
  1987   Classic Period Hohokam Settlement and Land Use in the Casa Grande Ruins Area, Arizona. *Journal of Field Archaeology* 14:147–162.
Cummings, Byron
  1915   Kivas of the San Juan Drainage. *American Anthropologist* 17:272–282.

1940    *Kinishba: A Prehistoric Pueblo of the Great Pueblo Period.* Hohokam Museums Association and the University of Arizona, Tucson.

Dean, Jeffrey S.
1987    Thoughts on Hohokam Settlement Behavior: Comments on "The Hohokam Village." In *The Hohokam Village: Site Structure and Organization,* edited by D. E. Doyel, pp. 253–262. Southwestern and Rocky Mountain Division of the American Association for the Advancement of Science, Glenwood Springs, Colorado.

DiPeso, Charles C.
1956    *The Upper Pima of San Cayetano del Tumacacori: An Archaeo-historical Reconstruction of the Ootam of Pimería Alta.* Amerind Foundation Publications 7. Dragoon, Arizona.

Doyel, David E.
1984    From Foraging to Farming: An Overview of the Preclassic in the Tucson Basin. *The Kiva* 49(3–4):147–166.
1985    Current Directions in Hohokam Research. In *Proceedings of the 1983 Hohokam Symposium* Part 1, edited by A. E. Dittert and D. E. Dove, pp. 3–26. Arizona Archaeological Society Occasional Papers 2. Phoenix.
1987a   The Hohokam Village. In *The Hohokam Village: Site Structure and Organization,* edited by D. E. Doyel, pp. 1–20. Southwestern and Rocky Mountain Division of the American Association for the Advancement of Science, Glenwood Springs, Colorado.

Doyel, David E. (editor)
1987b   *The Hohokam Village: Site Structure and Organization.* Southwestern and Rocky Mountain Division of the American Association for the Advancement of Science, Glenwood Springs, Colorado.

Doyel, David, and Freg Plog (editors)
1980    *Current Issues in Hohokam Prehistory: Proceedings of a Symposium.* Arizona State University Anthropological Research Papers 23. Tempe.

Drennan, Robert D.
1983    Ritual and Ceremonial Development at the Early Village Level. In *The Cloud People: Divergent Evolution of the Zapotec and Mixtec Civilizations,* edited by K. V. Flannery and J. Marcus, pp. 46–50. Academic Press, New York.

Drennan, Robert D., and Carlos A. Uribe (editors)
1987    *Chiefdoms in the Americas.* University Press of America, Lanham, Maryland.

Earle, Timothy K.
1987    Chiefdoms in Archaeological and Ethnohistorical Perspective. *Annual Review of Anthropology* 16:279–308.

Ekholm, Gordon F.
1942    *Excavations at Guasave, Sinaloa, Mexico.* American Museum of Natural History Anthropological Papers 38(2). New York City.

Feinman, Gary, and Jill Neitzel
1984    Too Many Types: An Overview of Sedentary Prestate Societies in the Americas. In *Advances in Archaeological Method and Theory,* vol. 7, edited by M. B. Schiffer, pp. 39–102. Academic Press, New York.

Ferg, Alan, and Bruce B. Huckell
1985    The Tucson Basin Hohokam Occupation of the Rosemont Area, Northern Santa Rita Mountain. In *Proceedings of the 1983 Hohokam Symposium,* Part I, edited by A. E. Dittert, Jr. and D. E. Dove, pp. 199–222. Arizona Archaeological Society Occasional Papers 2. Phoenix.

Fewkes, Jesse W.
1912 Casa Grande, Arizona. *28th Annual Report of the Bureau of American Ethnology.* Washington, D.C.
1927 Archaeological Fieldwork in Arizona. In Explorations and Field-work of the Smithsonian Institution in 1926. *Smithsonian Miscellaneous Collections* 78:207–232. Washington, D.C.

Fish, Paul R.
1987 Comments on "the Hohokam Village." In *The Hohokam Village: Site Structure and Organization*, edited by D. E. Doyel, pp. 263–269. Southwestern and Rocky Mountain Division of the American Association for the Advancement of Science, Glenwood Springs, Colorado.

Fish, Paul R., Peter J. Pilles, Jr., and Suzanne K. Fish
1980 Colonies, Traders, and Traits: The Hohokam in the North. In *Current Issues in Hohokam Prehistory: Proceedings of a Symposium*, edited by D. E. Doyel and F. Plog, pp. 151–179. Arizona State University Anthropological Research Papers 23. Tempe.

Flannery, Kent V.
1972 The Origins of the Village as a Settlement Type in Mesoamerica and the Near East: A Comparative Study. In *Man, Settlement, and Urbanism*, edited by P. J. Ucko, R. Tringham, and G. W. Dimbleby, pp. 23–53. Gerald Duckworth and Co., London.

Flannery, Kent V. (editor)
1976 *The Early Mesoamerican Village.* Academic Press, New York.

Flannery, Kent V., and Joyce Marcus
1976 Formative Oaxaca and the Zapotec Cosmos. *American Scientist* 64(4):374–383.

Flannery, Kent V., and Joyce Marcus (editors)
1983 *The Cloud People: Divergent Evolution of the Zapotec and Mixtec Civilizations.* Academic Press, New York.

Ford, Richard I.
1974 Northeastern Archeology: Past and Future Directions. *Annual Review of Anthropology* 3:385–413.

Fulton, William S.
1941 *A Ceremonial Cave in the Winchester Mountains, Arizona.* Amerind Foundation Publications 2. Dragoon, Arizona.

Gladwin, Harold S., Emil W. Haury, E. B. Sayles, and Nora Gladwin
1937 *Excavations at Snaketown: Material Culture.* University of Arizona Press, Tucson.

Gregory, David A.
1987 The Morphology of Platform Mounds and the Structure of Classic Period Hohokam Sites. In *The Hohokam Village: Site Structure and Organization*, edited by D. E. Doyel, pp. 183–210. Southwestern and Rocky Mountain Division of the American Association for the Advancement of Science, Glenwood Springs, Colorado.

Gregory, David A., and Fred L. Nials
1985 Observations Concerning the Distribution of Classic Period Hohokam Platform Mounds. In *Proceedings of the 1983 Hohokam Symposium*, Part I, edited by A. E. Dittert, Jr. and D. E. Dove, pp. 373–388. Arizona Archaeological Society Occasional Research Papers 2. Phoenix.

Grove, David S.
1987 Torches, "Knuckledusters" and the Legitimization of Formative Period Rulership. *Mexicon* 9(3):60–65.

Gumerman, George J., and Emil W. Haury
  1979  Prehistory: Hohokam. In *Handbook of North American Indians*, vol. 9, Southwest, edited by A. Ortiz, pp. 75–90. Smithsonian Institution, Washington, D.C.
Hantman, Jeffrey L.
  1984  Regional Organization of the Northern Mogollon. *American Archeology* 4(3):171–180.
Haury, Emil W.
  1937  Bone. In *Excavations at Snaketown: Material Culture*, by H. S. Gladwin, E. W. Haury, E. B. Sayles, and N. Gladwin, pp. 154–155. University of Arizona Press, Tucson.
  1945  *The Excavation of Los Muertos and Neighboring Ruins in the Salt River Valley, Southern Arizona*. Peabody Museum of American Archaeology and Ethnology Papers 24(1). Cambridge.
  1950  *The Stratigraphy and Archaeology of Ventana Cave, Arizona*. University of New Mexico Press, Albuquerque.
  1962  The Greater American Southwest. In *Courses Toward Urban Life*, edited by R. J. Braidwood and G. R. Willey, pp. 106–131. Viking Fund Publications in Anthropology 32.
  1974  The Problem of Contacts Between the Southwestern United States and Mexico. In *The Mesoamerican Southwest*, edited by B. C. Hedrick, J. C. Kelley, and C. L. Riley, pp. 92–102. Southern Illinois University Press, Carbondale.
  1976  *The Hohokam: Desert Farmers and Craftsmen*. University of Arizona Press, Tucson.
  1980  Comments on the Hohokam Symposium. In *Current Issues in Hohokam Prehistory: Proceedings of a Symposium*, edited by D. E. Doyel and F. Plog, pp. 113–120. Arizona State University Anthropological Research Papers 23. Tempe.
Helms, Mary W.
  1979  *Ancient Panama: Chiefs in Search of Power*. University of Texas Press, Austin.
Howard, Jerry B.
  1987  The Lehi Canal System: Organization of a Classic Period Community. In *The Hohokam Village: Site Structure and Organization*, edited by D. E. Doyel, pp. 211–221. Southwestern and Rocky Mountain Division of the American Association for the Advancement of Science, Glenwood Springs, Colorado.
Irwin-Williams, Cynthia
  1979  Post-Pleistocene Archaeology, 7000–2000 B.C. In *Handbook of North American Indians*, vol. 9, Southwest, edited by A. Ortiz, pp. 31–42. Smithsonian Institution, Washington, D.C.
Irwin-Williams, Cynthia, and C. Vance Haynes, Jr.
  1970  Climatic Change and Early Population Dynamics in the Southwestern United States. *Quaternary Research* 1(1):59–71.
Johnson, Gregory A.
  1980  Rank-Size Convexity and System Integration: A View from Archaeology. *Economic Geography* 56:234–247.
  1982  Organizational Structure and Scalar Stress. In *Theory and Explanation in Archaeology*, edited by A. C. Renfrew, M. J. Rowlands, and B. A. Segraves, pp. 389–418. Academic Press, New York.
  1983  Decision-making Organization and Pastoral Nomad Camp Size. *Human Ecology* 11:175–199.

Joralemon, David
1974 Ritual Blood-Sacrifice Among the Ancient Maya: Part I. In *First Palenque Round Table 1973: Part 2*, edited by M. G. Robertson, pp. 59–75. Palenque Round Table Series II. Robert Louis Stevenson School, Pebble Beach.

Kelley, J. Charles
1966 Mesoamerica and the Southwestern United States. In *Handbook of Middle American Indians*, vol. 4, Archaeological Frontiers and External Connections, edited by G. F. Ekholm and G. R. Willey, pp. 95–110. University of Texas Press, Austin.

Kelly, Isabel T.
1978 *The Hodges Ruin: A Hohokam Community in the Tucson Basin.* University of Arizona Anthropological Papers 30. Tucson.

Kidder, Alfred V.
1932 *The Artifacts of Pecos.* Yale University Press, New Haven.

Kowalewski, Stephen A., Richard E. Blanton, Gary Feinman, and Laura Finsten
1983 Boundaries, Scale, and Internal Organization. *Journal of Anthropological Archaeology* 2:32–56.

LeBlanc, Steven A.
1982a The Advent of Pottery in the Southwest. In Southwestern Ceramics, a Comparative Review, edited by A. H. Schroeder. *The Arizona Archaeologist* 15:27–51. Phoenix.
1982b Temporal Change in Mogollon ceramics. In Southwestern Ceramics, a Comparative Review, edited by A. H. Schroeder. *The Arizona Archaeologist* 15:107–127. Phoenix.
1986 Aspects of Southwestern Prehistory: A.D. 900–1400. In *Ripples in the Chichimec Sea: New Considerations of Southwestern-Mesoamerican Interactions*, edited by F. J. Mathien and R. H. McGuire, pp. 105–134. Southern Illinois University Press, Carbondale.

Lightfoot, Kent G., and Gary M. Feinman
1982 Social Differentiation and Leadership Development in Early Pithouse Villages in the Mogollon Region of the American Southwest. *American Antiquity* 47:64–86.

MacNeish, Richard S.
1981 Tehuacan's Accomplishments. In *Supplement to the Handbook of Middle American Indians*, vol. 1, edited by J. A. Sabloff, pp. 31–47. University of Texas Press, Austin.
1986 The Preceramic of Middle America. *Advances in World Archaeology* 5:93–129.

Manrique C., Leonardo
1969 The Otomi. In *Handbook of Middle American Indians*, vol. 8, Ethnology, Part 2, edited by E. Z. Vogt, pp. 682–722. University of Texas Press, Austin.

Marcus, Joyce
1983 Zapotec Religion. In *The Cloud People: Divergent Evolution of the Zapotec and Mixtec Civilizations*, edited by K. V. Flannery and J. Marcus, pp. 345–351. Academic Press, New York.

Masse, W. Bruce
1982 Hohokam Ceramic Art. In Southwestern Ceramics: A Comparative Review, edited by A. H. Schroeder. *The Arizona Archaeologist* 15:71–105. Phoenix.

Mathien, Frances J., and Randall H. McGuire (editors)
1986 *Ripples in the Chichimec Sea: New Considerations of Southwestern-Mesoamerican Interactions.* Southern Illinois University Press, Carbondale.

McGuire, Randall H.
  1987   *Death, Society and Ideology in a Hohokam Community: Colonial and Sedentary Period Burials from La Ciudad.* Arizona State University, Office of Cultural Resource Management Report 68. Tempe.
McGuire, Randall H., and Ann Valdo Howard
  1987   The Structure and Organization of Hohokam Shell Exchange. *The Kiva* 52(2):113–146.
Meighan, Clement W. (editor)
  1976   The Archaeology of Amapa, Nayarit. *Monumenta Archaeologica* 2. Los Angeles.
Moore, James A.
  1983   The Trouble with Know-it-Alls: Information as a Social and Ecological Resource. In *Archaeological Hammers and Theories,* edited by J. A. Moore and A. S. Keene, pp. 173–191. Academic Press, New York.
Nelson, Richard S.
  1981   *The Role of a Pochteca System in Hohokam Exchange.* Ph.D. dissertation, Department of Anthropology, New York University. University Microfilms, Ann Arbor.
  1986   Pochtecas and Prestige: Mesoamerican Artifacts in Hohokam Sites. In *Ripples in the Chichimec Sea: New Considerations of Southwestern-Mesoamerican Interactions,* edited by F. J. Mathien and R. H. McGuire, pp. 154–182. Southern Illinois University Press, Carbondale.
Nicholas, Linda M., and Gary M. Feinman
  1989   A Regional Perspective on Hohokam Irrigation in the Lower Salt River Valley, Arizona. In *The Sociopolitical Structure of Prehistoric Southwestern Societies,* edited by S. Upham, K. G. Lightfoot, and R. A. Jewett, pp. 199–235. Westview Press, Boulder.
Nicholson, Henry B.
  1971   Religion in Prehispanic Central Mexico. In *Handbook of Middle American Indians,* vol. 10, Archaeology of Northern Mesoamerica, Part 1, edited by G. F. Ekholm and I. Bernal, pp. 395–446. University of Texas Press, Austin.
Olsen, Sandra L.
  1979   A Study of Bone Artifacts from Grasshopper Pueblo, AZ P:14:1. *The Kiva* 44:341–373.
  1980   Bone Artifacts from Kinishba Ruin: Their Manufacture and Use. *The Kiva* 46:39–67.
  1981   Bone Artifacts from Las Colinas. In *The 1968 Excavations at Mound 8, Las Colinas Ruins Group, Phoenix, Arizona,* edited by L. C. Hammack and A. P. Sullivan, pp. 291–295. Arizona State Museum Archaeological Series 154. Tucson.
Parsons, Elsie Clews
  1974   Some Aztec and Pueblo Parallels. In *The Mesoamerican Southwest,* edited by B. C. Hedrick, J. C. Kelley, and C. L. Riley, pp. 131–146. Southern Illinois University Press, Carbondale.
Plog, Stephen
  1984   Regional Perspectives on the Western Anasazi. American Archeology 4(3):162–170.
Renfrew, Colin
  1975   Trade as Action at a Distance: Questions of Integration and Communication. In *Ancient Civilization and Trade,* edited by J. Sabloff and C. C. Lamberg-Karlovsky, pp. 3–59, University of New Mexico Press, Albuquerque.

Reyman, Jonathan E.
1978    Pochteca Burials at Anasazi? In *Across the Chichimec Sea: Papers in Honor of J. Charles Kelley*, edited by C. L. Riley and B. C. Hedrick, pp. 242–262. Southern Illinois University Press, Carbondale.

Riley, Carroll L.
1963    Color-Direction Symbolism: An Example of Mexican-Southwestern Contacts. *América Indígena* 23(1):49–60.

Schele, Linda
1984    Human Sacrifice Among the Classic Maya. In *Ritual Human Sacrifice in Meso-america*, edited by E. H. Boone, pp. 7–48. Dumbarton Oaks, Washington, D.C.

Schele, Linda, and Mary Ellen Miller
1986    *The Blood of Kings: Dynasty and Ritual in Maya Art*. Kimbell Art Museum, Fort Worth.

Schroeder, Albert H.
1982    Historical Overview of Southwestern Ceramics. In Southwestern Ceramics: A Comparative Review, edited by A. H. Schroeder. *The Arizona Archaeologist* 15:1–26. Phoenix.

Seler, Eduard
1904    Venus Period in the Picture Writing of the Borgian Group. *Bureau of American Ethnology Bulletin* 28:355–391. Washington, D.C.

Seymour, Deni J.
1988    An Alternative View of Sedentary Period Hohokam Shell-Ornament Production. *American Antiquity* 53:812–829.

Sires, Earl W., Jr.
1987    Hohokam Architectural Variability and Site Structure During the Sedentary-Classic Transition. In *The Hohokam Village: Site Structure and Organization*, edited by D. E. Doyel, pp. 171–182. Southwestern and Rocky Mountain Division of the American Association for the Advancement of Science, Glenwood Springs, Colorado.

Smith, Bruce D.
1986    The Archaeology of the Southeastern United States: From Dalton to de Soto, 10,500–500 B.P. *Advances in World Archaeology* 5:1–92.

Speth, John D.
1988    Do We Need Concepts Like "Mogollon," "Anasazi," and "Hohokam" Today? A Cultural Anthropological Perspective. *The Kiva* 53:201–204.

Stone, Andrea
1985    The Moon Goddess at Naj Tunich. *Mexicon* 7(2):23–29.

Stuart, David
1984    Royal Auto-Sacrifice Among the Maya: A Study of Image and Meaning. *Res* 7/8:6–20.

Taylor, Walter W.
1966    Archaic Cultures Adjacent to the Northeastern Frontiers. In *Handbook of Middle American Indians*, vol. 4: Archaeological Frontiers and External Connections, edited by G. F. Ekholm and G. R. Willey, pp. 59–94. University of Texas Press, Austin.

Teague, Lynn S.
1984    The Hohokam Community. In *Hohokam Archaeology Along the Salt-Gila Aque-*

duct, *Central Arizona Project*, vol. 9, Synthesis and Conclusions, edited by L.
S. Teague and P. L. Crown, pp. 305–315. Arizona State Museum Archaeological Series 150. Tucson.

Tolstoy, Paul
1971    Utilitarian Artifacts of Central Mexico. In *Handbook of Middle American Indians*,
        vol. 10, Archaeology of Northern Mesoamerica, Part 1, edited by G. F. Ekholm
        and I. Bernal, pp. 270–296. University of Texas Press, Austin.

Tozzer, Alfred M.
1966    *Landa's Relación de las Cosas de Yucatan*. Kraus Reprint Corporation, New York.
        (orig. pub. in 1941 as Papers of the Peabody Museum of American Archae-
        ology and Ethnology 18. Cambridge.)

Trigger, Bruce G.
1984    Archaeology at the Crossroads: What's New? *Annual Review of Anthropology*
        13:275–300.

Trik, Aubrey S.
1963    The Splendid Tomb of Temple I at Tikal, Guatemala. *Expedition* 6(1):3–18.

Tuthill, Carr
1947    *The Tres Alamos Site on the San Pedro River, Southeastern Arizona*. Amerind
        Foundation Publications 4. Dragoon, Arizona.

Wilcox, David R.
1979    The Hohokam Regional System. In *An Archaeological Test of Sites in the Gila
        Butte–Santan Region, South-Central Arizona*, edited by G. E. Rice, pp. 77–126.
        Arizona State University Anthropological Research Papers 18. Tempe.
1980    The Current Status of the Hohokam Concept. In *Current Issues in Hohokam
        Prehistory: Proceedings of a Symposium*, edited by D. E. Doyel and F. Plog, pp.
        236–242. Arizona State University Anthropological Research Papers 23. Tempe.
1986a   The Tepiman Connection: A Model of Mesoamerican-Southwestern Inter-
        action. In *Ripples in the Chichimec Sea: New Considerations of Southwestern-Meso-
        american Interactions*, edited by F. J. Mathien and R. H. McGuire, pp. 135–
        154. Southern Illinois University Press, Carbondale.
1986b   A Historical Analysis of the Problem of Southwestern-Mesoamerican Con-
        nections. In *Ripples in the Chichimec Sea: New Considerations of Southwestern-
        Mesoamerican Interactions*, edited by F. J. Mathien and R. H. McGuire, pp. 9–
        44. Southern Illinois University Press, Carbondale.
1987a   The Evolution of Hohokam Ceremonial Systems. In *Astronomy and Ceremony
        in the Prehistoric Southwest*, edited by J. B. Carlson and W. J. Judge, pp. 149–
        168. Maxwell Museum of Anthropology Papers 2. Albuquerque.
1987b   New Models of Social Structure at the Palo Parado Site. In *The Hohokam Village:
        Site Structure and Organization*, edited by D. E. Doyel, pp. 223–248. South-
        western and Rocky Mountain Division of the American Association for the
        Advancement of Science, Glenwood Springs, Colorado.
1987c   *Frank Midvale's Investigation of the Site of La Ciudad*. Arizona State University
        Anthropological Field Studies 19. Tempe.
1988a   Rethinking the Mogollon Concept. *The Kiva* 53:205–209.
1988b   The Regional Context of the Brady Wash and Picacho Area Studies. In *Ho-
        hokam Settlement Along the Slopes of the Picacho Mountains*, vol. 6, Synthesis and
        Conclusions, edited by R. Ciolek-Torrello and D. R. Wilcox, pp. 244–267.
        Museum of Northern Arizona, Flagstaff.

n.d.    The Mesoamerican Ballgame in the American Southwest. In *The Mesoamerican Ballgame*, edited by V. L. Scarborough and D. R. Wilcox.

Wilcox, David R., and Charles Sternberg
  1983   *Hohokam Ballcourts and Their Interpretation*. Arizona State Museum Archaeological Series 160. Tucson.

Wobst, Martin H.
  1974   Boundary Conditions for Paleolithic Social Systems: A Simulation Approach. *American Antiquity* 39:147–179.
  1976   Locational Relationships in Paleolithic Society. *Journal of Human Evolution* 5:49–58.
  1977   Stylistic Behavior and Information Exchange. In *For the Director: Research Essays in Honor of James B. Griffin*, edited by C. E. Cleland, pp. 317–342. University of Michigan Museum of Anthropology Anthropological Papers 61. Ann Arbor.

Woodbury, Richard B.
  1961   A Reappraisal of Hohokam Irrigation. *American Anthropologist* 63:550–560.

Woodward, Arthur
  1930   Buried Treasure. In *Los Angeles County Employee*, June 1930. Los Angeles.

# CONTRIBUTORS

PATRICIA L. CROWN, Assistant Professor of Anthropology, Department of Anthropology, Arizona State University, Tempe, Arizona

JEFFREY S. DEAN, Professor of Dendrochronology, Laboratory of Tree-Ring Research, University of Arizona, Tucson, Arizona

WILLIAM H. DOELLE, Division Director, Center for Desert Archaeology, Tucson, Arizona

DAVID E. DOYEL, Adjunct Professor of Anthropology, Department of Anthropology, Arizona State University, Tempe, Arizona

GARY M. FEINMAN, Associate Professor of Anthropology, Department of Anthropology, University of Wisconsin, Madison, Wisconsin

PAUL R. FISH, Curator of Archaeology, Arizona State Museum; Research Professor, Department of Anthropology, University of Arizona, Tucson, Arizona

SUZANNE K. FISH, Research Archaeologist, Arizona State Museum, University of Arizona, Tucson, Arizona

ROBERT E. GASSER, Archaeologist and Compliance Coordinator, State Historic Preservation Office, Arizona State Parks, Phoenix, Arizona

GEORGE J. GUMERMAN, Director, Center for Archaeological Investigations; Professor of Anthropology, Department of Anthropology, Southern Illinois University, Carbondale, Illinois

SCOTT M. KWIATKOWSKI, Archaeobotanist, Soils System, Inc., Phoenix, Arizona

RANDALL H. McGUIRE, Associate Professor of Anthropology, Department of Anthropology, State University of New York, Binghamton, New York

GARY P. NABHAN, Associate Director, Phoenix Desert Botanical Garden, Phoenix, Arizona

JILL NEITZEL, Assistant Professor of Anthropology, Department of Anthropology, Connecticut College, New London, Connecticut

HENRY D. WALLACE, Research Archaeologist, Institute for American Research, Tucson, Arizona

# INDEX

▼▼▼▼▼▼▼▼▼▼▼▼▼

Pueblo III, 64, 65. *See also* Ceramic
types (Anasazi); Chaco interaction
sphere
Antelope Glyph site, 434
Antelope House, 442
Archaeomagnetic dating, 66, 71; date
list, 99–143
Archaic period, late, 92, 236; buried
sites, 241–42; exchange, 385–86;
figurines, 244; houses, 237; lithics,
237, 238; maize, 237, 295, 443; origin
of Hohokam, 235–36; Papagueria,
351; projectile points, 242; relation to
Cochise culture, 242; shell, 238, 244;
Tucson Basin, 295. *See also* Cochise
culture
Architecture. *See* Ballcourts;
Compounds; Courtyard group;
Houses; Platform mounds; Public
works
Arroyo cutting, 34, 292, 293
Artiodactyl use, 444–45
Avra Valley, 438
Axes, 187
Azatlan site, 259
AZSITE database, 283
Aztec: bloodletting, 465, 467

Bachi phase, 260, 263
Ballcourts: absent on smaller sites, 164;
astronomical alignment, 198; Cañada
del Oro phase, 291, 301; ceremonial
use, 213; construction over time, 200;
dating, Tucson Basin, 319, 321;
distribution, Tucson Basin, 304;
economic significance, 304–5; labor
requirements, 198–201, 212, 305;
integrative function, 162, 166, 252,
301, 302–3, 305, 394; nonresidential,
167; orientation, 198, 299; outside
Hohokam area, 252; replacement by
platform mound, 255; Rillito phase,
302; size, 201, 211, 218n7, 299, 302,
303, 305; Verde Valley, 354. *See also*
Ballcourt, sites with
Ballcourt site, 299
Ballcourt, sites with: exchange, 258,
303, 305; hierarchy, 249; Hohokam
regional system, 362, 401–2; not

central places, 393; spacing, 163, 251.
*See also* Ballcourts
Bandelier, Adolph, 1
Basin-and-Range Province, 31
BB:9:120: date, 141
BB:9:143, 441: date list, 134–35
BB:13:120, 294
BB:13:224, 441
BB:13:232, 299, 302
Beans: archaeobotanical evidence, 430–
31; origin, 244, 386; Tucson Basin,
430–31
Beeth-Ha-Ha-a site, 435
Black Mountain area, 292, 293;
ceramics, 308
Blackwater phase, 260, 263
Bloodletting, ceremonial, 467–69, 470
Bluff site, 65
Bone implements, 467–70
Bosque site, 299
Boundary Village, 299
Brady Wash sites: agave, 423, 441;
agriculture, 438; cotton, 429, 430;
date list, 107, 112, 113, 119, 122, 123,
124–25, 126, 127, 128, 129; little
barley grass, 435; maize, 423, 425;
plantain, 438; plant use, 440, 448
Bylas area, 64

Cacti, 432–33
Cahita warfare, 371–72
Calendrical scheduling of ceremonies,
213, 214, 255
Cañada del Oro phase: ballcourt sites,
291, 302; ceramics, 282; date list, 130–
31; dating, 74, 75, 76, 78, 87–88, 90,
93; overlap with Rillito phase, 88, 93;
settlement pattern, 291. *See also*
Colonial period
Canals. *See* Irrigation
Carpet site, 434
Carrying capacity and technological
change, 243
Casa Buena: agave, 423, 426, 441;
cotton, 428; late structures, 266; little
barley grass, 434, 442; maize, 423
Casa Grande, 2; bone implements, 468;
concentric plan, 255; cotton, 428;
date, 128; Great House, 202–3, 254,
255, 262; elites, 371; irrigation, 165;